More Other Homes and Garbage

Designs for Self-sufficient Living

Jim Leckie, Gil Masters, Harry Whitehouse

SIERRA CLUB BOOKS · SAN FRANCISCO

1981

The Sierra Club, founded in 1892 by John Muir, has devoted itself to the study and protection of the earth's scenic and ecological resources—mountains, wetlands, woodlands, wild shores and rivers, deserts and plains. The publishing program of the Sierra Club offers books to the public as a nonprofit educational service in the hope that they may enlarge the public's understanding of the Club's basic concerns. The point of view expressed in each book, however, does not necessarily represent that of the Club. The Sierra Club has some fifty chapters coast to coast, in Canada, Hawaii, and Alaska. For information about how you may participate in its programs to preserve wilderness and the quality of life, please address inquiries to Sierra Club, 530 Bush Street, San Francisco, CA 94108.

Library of Congress Cataloging in Publication Data

Main entry under title:

More other homes and garbage.

Edition of 1975 published under title: Other homes and garbage.

Includes bibliographies and index.
1. Dwellings—Environmental engineering.
    I. Leckie, Jim, 1939–

TH4812.078   1980   690′.8   79-22175
ISBN 0-87156-274-X

Cover design by Anita Walker Scott

Book design by Drake Jordan

Illustrations by Lynne Baxter, Bonnie Russell, and Irene Findikakis

Printed in the United States of America

10 9 8 7 6 5 4 3 2 1

Grateful acknowledgment is made to the following:

The American Society of Civil Engineers, for permission to reprint material from *Transactions of the American Society of Civil Engineers,* Volume 122, Paper No. 2849.

The American Society of Heating, Refrigerating and Air-conditioning Engineers, Inc., for permission to reprint material from *ASHRAE Guide and Data Book,* 1967; *ASHRAE Guide: Design and Evaluation Criteria for Energy Conservation in New Buildings (Proposed Standard 90-P),* 1974; *ASHRAE Transactions,* Vol. 80, Part II, 1974; *ASHRAE Guide: Systems,* 1970; *Handbook of Fundamentals,* 1967.

The Chemical Rubber Co., for permission to reprint material from *Standard Mathematical Tables,* Twenty-first edition. © 1973 The Chemical Rubber Co.

Dunham-Bush, Inc., West Hartford, Conn., for permission to reprint material from Dunham-Bush Form No. 6001-2.

Industrial Press, Inc., N.Y., for permission to reprint material from *Handbook of Air Conditioning, Heating and Ventilating* by Strock & Koral, 1965.

McGraw-Hill Book Co., for permission to reprint material from *Introduction* to the *Utilization of Solar Energy* by Zarem & Erway. © 1963 by McGraw-Hill Book Company.

The New Alchemy Institute and Richard Merrill and John Fry, for permission to reprint material from *Methane Digesters for Fuel Gas and Fertilizer* by Richard Merrill and John Fry. © Richard Merrill and John Fry.

Portola Institute, Menlo Park, Ca., and Kim Mitchell for permission to reprint material by Kim Mitchell from *The Energy Primer.* © 1974 by Portola Institute.

The Rodale Press, Emmaus, Pa., for permission to adapt and reprint material from *The Complete Book of Composting* by J. I. Rodale. © 1966 by J. I. Rodale; *The Encyclopedia of Organic Gardening* by J. I. Rodale. © 1973 by J. I. Rodale; *How to Grow Fruits and Vegetables by the Organic Method* by J. I. Rodale. © 1966 by J. I. Rodale; *Organic Gardening and Farming,* February 1972. © 1972 by the Rodale Press.

Slant/Fin Corporation, Greenville, N.Y., for permission to reprint material from a series of data sheets published by Slant/Fin Corporation. © 1966 by Slant/Fin Corporation.

Contents

1

2

3

Small-Scale Generation of Electricity From Renewable Energy Sources
by Gil Masters

4

Solar Thermal Applications
by Gil Masters with Harry Whitehouse

5

Acknowledgments:

Anyone who has ever embarked upon a writing expedition such as this is aware that the enterprise will almost certainly take longer than anticipated. In addition, it will accumulate a long list of debts of gratitude which the authors can easily acknowledge but cannot adequately repay. In neither of these respects is our effort an exception. We expected our revision project to take about six months. In a fruitless attempt to avoid becoming yet another case of tardy completion, we adopted a one-year horizon as a fail safe target. But fate is not easily trifled with, we are well into a one and one half years time as completion appears as a proverbial light at the end of the tunnel.

Over this period of time we were helped in many ways by many people. First, our editors at Sierra Club Books, Jon Beckmann and Jim Cohee, played a critical role by supplying generous support and seemingly unlimited patience to see us through our tasks.

In addition, we were dependent upon many colleagues and associates for factual materials and for the work of catching errors and omissions in what we had written. There were others whose work went well beyond that; they undertook responsibility for locating and obtaining materials and organizing information. For example, Bob Wenzlau was of enormous help in developing materials for the waste handling chapter. The contributions of Angelos Findikakis to the water power section of the electricity chapter are gratefully acknowledged. In the solar chapter the do-it-yourself collector design was developed by John Randolph and his students at The Evergreen State College in Washington. Special thanks to Lynne Baxter for her skill and imagination in visually bringing to life much of the book with her excellent illustrations and drawings. We also thank Irene Findikakis and Bonnie Russell for their contributions.

In addition we are deeply indebted to others for their assistance with our work: Al Umaña, Costa Halvadakis, Frank Zalatel, Frank Carroll, and Marty Jackson.

J. O. Leckie
G. Masters
L. Y. Young

Preface to the Revised Edition

Mankind's haphazard interventions in nature in the industrial-technological era have progressively undermined the stability of the natural systems on which our life and well-being depend. We can no longer take the abundance of natural resources, the stability of climate, or the purity of air and water for granted. Given the increase in our numbers and in the power of modern technology, the nature that once appeared so awesome is now known to be fragile and limited.

The crowding of our planet in the context of accelerating industrialization has caused a set of distinctive and uncertain hazards that are interlinked: population growth, limited resources, unstable ecosystems, political unrest, economic strains. Our failure to adjust our scale of human activity within these constraints has led to unnecessary suffering, ultimately deteriorates the life experience of individuals and groups, and worse, endangers life prospects for future generations.

Our initial efforts in writing the first edition of *Other Homes and Garbage* were stimulated by the enthusiasm and good spirit of many people who wished to alter their lifestyles but did not have access to much of the information that would allow them to choose intelligently from among the available options. Our first effort has met with wide acceptance, but the alternative lifestyle movement has not expanded as rapidly as our naive optimism led us to believe it would. Still, we avoid assuming what Kurt Vonnegut has described as the appropriate stance toward the future—"terminal pessimism."

We have also avoided the technophilic optimism of those who continue to regard technology as the ground from which ultimate solutions to our global problems will spring. That approach by itself is dangerously irresponsible. A more compelling optimism, which we have adopted, is associated with the repudiation of the high technology path. This optimism is expressed in many different forms, all essentially converging toward the need to revive the spiritual-philosophic center of human experience with emphasis on what E. F. Schumacher has called "voluntary simplicity." We believe that the alternative lifestyle movement remains underappreciated as a new force for change. Moreover, with our effort represented by this book, we again reaffirm our concurrence in Hermann Hesse's statement in *Steppenwolf*:

> *Every age, every culture, every custom and tradition has its own character, its own weakness and its own strength, its beauties and ugliness; accepts certain sufferings as matter of course, puts up patiently with certain evils. Human life is reduced to real suffering, to hell, only when two ages, two cultures and religions overlap. . . . Now there are times when a whole generation is caught in this way between two ages, two modes of life, with the consequence that it loses all power to understand itself and has no standard, no security, no simple acquiescence.*

It is now apparent for all to observe that there is a growing resistance to all aspects of the long-term modernization of industrialized society. The modernization trend has led to ever-increasing use and waste of precious resources and diminishing personal control over many aspects of our lives. A counterforce is visible in the environmental movement. The past trend has been toward high technology that is big, centralized, exploitive, intimidating, and that displaces people; the countertrend is intermediate or appropriate technology—a technology that is small-scale, decentralized, conserves resources, is environmentally benign, enhances individuals' lives, uses renewable resources, and places a larger share of our lives under our control.

Against this background, our overriding concern has been to bring together a large body of technical information and data in a format readable by the interested nontechnical layman—you.

We remain working optimists for the future of us all.

April, 1980

Mexico City, Mexico	JOL
Palo Alto, California	GM
New York, New York	LYY

So then always that knowledge is worthiest . . . which considereth the simple forms or differences of things, which are few in number, and the degrees and coordinations whereof make all this variety

Francis Bacon

INTRODUCTION

**Human needs and attitudes and
the earth's potential**

**Self-sufficiency and self-reliance:
changing current trends**

Creating your own living environment

**Designing to fit
your specific requirements**

**Fitting engineering to small-scale
individual needs**

WHERE WE ARE GOING

What This Book Is About

The book adventure on which you are about to embark owes its existence to a rather unusual set of circumstances. It may be of some interest (and perhaps provide some encouragement) for us to spend a few moments here describing the birth process. During the fall quarter, 1973, a group of us from the School of Engineering at Stanford began talking about organizing a small experimental workshop on self-sufficient living systems. We offered the course in the winter quarter through Stanford's Workshop on Political and Social Issues but, instead of the twenty or twenty-five students that we expected, over one hundred interested students and community people showed up on the first night. Consequently, we had to redesign our small workshop framework into sub-courses centered around the themes of the various chapters found in this book, with the general dissemination of information to occur through the format of a final consolidated report. It was on the basis of the initial rough sub-course reports that this book had its beginning. The original material has been reworked considerably, and a substantial amount of new material has been added by the coauthors. We want to acknowledge the student energy and enthusiasm which carried the original idea to fruition.

This book represents an attempt by engineers and other technically trained people to communicate practical, useful technical information in an interesting format and in terms that are comprehensible to nonspecialized people—you! We want to help you gain the ability to design—for and by yourself—technologies which will allow you to establish a lifestyle which is energetically and

materially more conservative than those most of us now lead. We hope to help people realize that such simplified lifestyles are possible without sacrificing the things that give quality to our lives.

If I am content with little, then enough is as good as a feast.—Dean Swift

It is inherent in human nature to want to be self-sufficient and self-reliant. Modern society has removed many of the opportunities for self-reliance by burying in technological jargon and terminology much of the information needed by nontechnical people for development of intelligent choices. We are here trying to remove many of the artificial barriers which can deter you from designing your own methane digester, solar heater, or whatever. What we *cannot* remove is your expense of time and energy to acquire the necessary information for alternative choices. It may be of some help if we develop some of our guiding philosophy to set the general context of our overall effort.

The distance is nothing; it is only the first step that is difficult.—Marquise du Deffaud

In modern times we have treated the earth as if its reserves of usable matter and energy were in never-ending supply, and as if time would quickly heal all wounds caused by our exploitation. As long as the human population was small and our activities constrained by limited access to energy, the damage we inflicted upon the environment was limited and usually correctable through the earth's natural cycles. Now, however, the demands made on the environment are often beyond nature's regenerative capacities. Humankind's narrow understanding of conservation and our shortsighted technological approach to satisfying only our immediately perceived needs have begun to seriously deplete stored reserves. Fossil fuels are being used at increasing rates, and the steady dwindling of accessible supplies is becoming apparent. Vast quantities of water are being used injudiciously and contaminated before their return to large water systems; pollution has nearly destroyed such rivers as the Hudson and such lakes as Erie. Even more far-reaching effects are being realized as the damage makes its way through food chains and into groundwaters. The Aswan Dam, built as a necessary instrument for Egypt's economic growth, prevents the Nile from depositing its rich silt on the surrounding agricultural valley during seasonal floods. As a result the Aswan reservoir is filling with sediment, human parasites are increasing in the stored water, crops downstream are suffering, and the Mediterranean Sea is lacking a major nutrient source. What is the real gain in situations like these?

To be self-sufficing is the greatest of all wealth.—
Porphyry

The earth's ecosystems are balanced and its resources are finite. With our present consumptive attitudes, fossil fuels *will* run out. Water systems *will* fail from pollution. Fertile soil *will* deteriorate and be eroded into sterile desert. These effects *will* alter catastrophically *every* dependent organic system, including our own.

It is true that more fossil fuels can form over the next few millions of years, and many damaged forests and lakes can heal in less than a thousand. But on a time-scale of human dimensions we must look toward shorter regeneration cycles to supply a larger part of our energy needs. All regenerative cycles, including those for water and fossil fuels, are dependent upon steady radiation from the sun. Each system thrives only when this energy is used efficiently. Specialization and bio-simplification—monoculturing, for example—decrease efficiency since a single species cannot utilize all available energy as effectively as a diversified community. So, while "excellent rangeland" in the United States may yield 5000 kilograms of cattle per square kilometer per year, an African savannah community may yield closer to 35,000 kilograms of large edible animals in the same area, and the American bison herds of two hundred years ago had an even larger yield. Yet the savannah and prairie communities, including the thriving indigenous flora, were self-sustaining and did not require extensive artificial energy investments to continue to be productive.

If there is sufficient energy for a large natural community to maintain a stable existence, then we also can

have enough energy if only we enter into a rational, ecological relationship with the earth. We must recognize the complexity of the natural world and acknowledge the limits of our understanding. The natural environment in its diversity can be viewed as a unique library of genetic information. From this library can be drawn new food crops, new drugs and vaccines, and new biological pest controls. The loss of a species is the loss forever of an opportunity to improve human welfare. The "public-service" possibilities of the global environment cannot be replaced by technology either now or in the foreseeable future, in some cases because the process by which the service is provided is not understood scientifically, in other cases because no technological equivalent for the natural process has yet been devised. In almost all cases there would be no need to create technological substitutes if only we would learn to live in harmony with our natural environment.

Nature . . . invites us to lay our eye level with her smallest leaf, and take an insect view of its plain.—
Thoreau

Choosing among a multiplicity of trivial options has been a constant burden to mankind. We can all generate a long list of choices which have caused us to waste much time and emotional energy. Modern technologies and distribution practices have increased the range of different deodorants, but have had little impact on the choices involving the real and unchangeable values of life—the attitudes, needs, and desires that determine happiness or suffering, hope or despair. We must all still struggle with the same appetites, passions, and hopes that motivated Homer's or Shakespeare's heroes. The genetic code acquired by the human species more than 50,000 years ago is so stable that it still determines the conditions necessary for human health, comfort, and happiness, regardless of ephemeral changes in technological and political systems. Even though modern technology provides us with synthetic fabrics and electrical heaters, we still try to achieve the same body temperature as the Eskimos with their fur parkas and igloos, and as Stone Age people sought to achieve with animal skins in their caves. Regardless of whether we live in isolated free-standing houses or on top of skyscrapers, we still seek to relate in a personal way to the number of people once present in primitive hunting tribes or neolithic villages. All the social and technological futures we invent turn out to be mere reformulations, in a contemporary context, of the ancient ways of life; when Old Stone Age people, in the semitropical savannah, had achieved fitness to their biological and social environment—the natural harmony with nature we have lost.

Beginning with the great migrations of the Stone Age from their semitropical Arcadia, human beings have suffered from various levels of Future Shock. In the half century between 1850 and 1900, we have seen the introduction of railroads, steamships, and electricity; of the telephone, telegraph, and photography; of antisepsis, vaccinations, anesthesia, radiography, and most of the innovations which have revolutionized the practices of public health and medicine. All of these advances have penetrated deeply and rapidly into the Western world. More recently we have seen the assimilation of aviation, television, the transistor radio, antibiotics, hormones, tranquilizers, contraceptive pills, and pesticides. It is not the development of these technologies which we regret but rather their misuse. We have allowed synthetic barriers to come between us and nature. Five thousand years ago, the Sumerians recorded on clay tablets their anguish about the generation gap, the breakdown of the social order, the corruption of public and domestic servants. They asked themselves a question that has been asked by every age: *Where are we going?* There seems to be a strong resistance to accepting the very simple answer implied in T.S. Eliot's words:

> The end of all our exploring
> Will be to arrive where we started
> And know the place for the first time.

To those of us involved in the effort represented by this book, Eliot's words mean that we shall continue to question our values, extend our knowledge, develop new technological forms, rediscover old technological answers, and experiment with new ways of life. Change there will be and change there must be, because this is an essential condition of life. But we are now discovering that spectacular innovations are not the best approach to the improvement of life and indeed commonly create more problems than they solve. We believe that the emphasis in the future will be less on the development of esoteric technologies than on the development of a conservatively decent world, designed to satisfy those needs of human nature that were woven into our genetic fabric during our evolutionary past. To state the obvious, in terms of humankind, evolution is not the solution to environmental disruption.

It is not pessimism to believe that there is no lasting security—it is simple realism. Fortunately, man has displayed a remarkable ability to change the course of social trends and start new ventures, often taking advantage of apparently hopeless situations to develop entirely new formats for living. Trends are not necessarily destiny. Whatever the circumstances, we must use our minds to select among the conditions and materials available in a given environment and organize them into new, humanized forms. With this in mind, we have brought together here some of the tools and information which will help individuals such as yourselves to begin the process of change.

> the brilliant young intellects of our age
> make their homes
> in geometrically decorated apartments
> and conduct their lives algebraically
> in aristotelian fashion
> they pursue their precise pleasures
> eating only
> in medically approved restaurants
> and in an objective scientific manner
> do everything to their lives
> except live them
>
> Roy Hamilton

Preparing for the Trip

> The journey of a thousand miles begins with one step.—Lao-Tsze

If you are a single man or woman with a demanding job in the city, you probably require living quarters quite different than those of a farmer in Colorado or a fisherman living in Maine. If you have a family of six children, each one demanding accommodation for his or her dog, cat, rabbit, or gerbil, you will want a place with amenities different from those you would find just right if you were a bachelor whose hobby is playing the piano. The ideal size, location, and design of a home are different in almost every case. Yet whoever you are and whatever your circumstances, you can be sure that if you have the understanding and willingness to take the time, you can design to fit your requirements.

Design is the making of plans which we know—or think we know—how to carry out. In this it differs from prophecy, speculation, and fantasy, though all of these may enter into design. Most often, we think of design as being concerned with physical objects, with a chair, a house, a city, or an energy system. But the broader the scope of our plans, the less feasible it is to separate the tangible object from the less tangible system of values or way of life which it is intended to support or complement. Politics and education enter into such broader plans not only as *means,* as part of the essential "how," but also as *ends,* as factors which modify the character of these plans. We do not, after all, make plans for the fun of it (at least most of us!). Fantasy is fun; design is hard work. We do it because we want to increase or encourage the things we like and remove or reduce the features of things—of our environment, of our lives—which we dislike. In this sense everyone is a designer, though only a few are professionals. We all seek not only to understand the world around us but to change it, to bring it nearer to an ideal and, in this way, create our own living environment. Design is thus always fundamentally both ethical and aesthetic.

Don't part with your illusions. When they are gone, you may still exist, but you have ceased to live.—Mark Twain

It may not be so obvious that the design process is also bound up with knowledge, and thus with science and engineering. Design is not fantasy alone; we must *know how* to achieve what we imagine and desire. Engineering and scientific information and tools are the means by which we change the situation we have to the one we would like to have. The history of science, technology, and design, at least in the sense we are discussing it, is a story of extraordinary success; to a great extent it is, in fact, the story of the human race. Yet this is not necessarily a fashionable view. It is more usual these days to say that science, technology, and design have failed. In part, this view stems from a weakness of the historical imagination; the full horror of the general condition of life, even but a hundred years ago, is simply not grasped by most of us who rail against the present. However, the criticism is also true—because design always fails to some degree.

From a philosophical point of view, it is not a paradox to say that design can succeed grandly and yet must fail. That is, the success of design does not relieve anxiety, because the satisfaction of a primary need nearly always allows secondary drives to come into play. So, relieved of the constant threat of starvation and other perils, we worry about economic crises or, more humanely, about the starvation and suffering of people remote from us. The relief of anxiety is accomplished not by the practical life, of which design is an important part, but by the contemplative life, which is often but quite mistakenly seen as opposed to design, whereas in fact it is design's necessary complement.

Thus happiness depends, as Nature shows,
Less on exterior things than most suppose.

Cowper

On a more immediate level, it is important to recognize that, even on its own terms, design is likely to fail. Designers are human, as are we all, and there are very severe limitations on our capacity to imagine many factors simultaneously. The "side effects" of a design—those unintentional results which follow upon the intended; the difficulty of imagining the needs and feelings of many different people; the effects of technical, social, and political change—these are common and indeed notorious causes of failure. Computers cannot solve these problems. Computers are marvelous tools, but, like other tools, they can magnify mistakes and errors of judgment just as much as they can assist well-conceived plans. And each of these potential pitfalls of design is enlarged and deepened as the scale on which we attempt to design is increased. An individual designing a solar unit for his or

her specific needs is more likely to succeed than the designer of an individual building; town planning runs more risks than planning an individual building. We want to encourage you to become your own designer. The basic purpose of this book is to place design tools and information in the hands of the nonspecialist. Only the individual can set the context and limits of his specific design project. Individual design is not only possible but usually successful, if only we choose our problems according to our capacities, abstain from putting all our eggs in one basket, and generally adopt the principle that engineering can be suited to small-scale individual needs, always keeping in mind the overall objective of compatibility with nature. Our designs and, ultimately, our living and working environments will approach a more harmonious level if we design within the framework of the principle of interdependency, remembering that everything we do affects something or someone else.

The information and design examples presented in this book should help you add a new dimension to your daily existence; to do intensive gardening in your urban backyard, to design and construct a solar preheater for your suburban hot-water system, or to design a totally independent electrical system for your country home. Whatever your living context and lifestyle, you will find ideas and information to allow you to gain a little more control over your own existence.

Out of the light that blinds my eyes
White as a laboratory coat,
I thank the test-tube gods so wise,
For now my psychic soul can't gloat.

In the fell clutch of modern hands
I have been twisted by the crowd.
Under environment's strong commands
My head is perfumed but not proud.

Beyond this place of gas and gears
Looms a horizon yet unknown,
And yet if war comes in my years
I'll find I'll not go there alone.

It matters not how others wait,
How charged with fees I get my bill,
I am your patient, Doctor Fate:
Let me tell you my troubles still.

Luis Miguel Valdez, "Victus: A Parody"

4

The Road Map

From the many types of low-impact technologies described in the following chapters, you must select the ones appropriate for your situation, for existing and/or proposed buildings or structures into which the alternative technology must be integrated in a compatible manner.

In Chapter 2 (Alternative Architecture), we have provided a technical and visual foundation for the incorporation of alternative technology within a single structure. However, we also feel that we should explore the sociological implications behind an alternative lifestyle movement. The origin of this movement, we believe, is the instinct to survive—survive the environmental and psychological degradations created by a technology of consumer convenience and infinite industrial growth. In the beginning, those making use of alternative technologies will be a small minority, the vanguard of a group which may lead us away from world destruction. In creating the forms to put alternative technology to use, we must allow for the variety of these people who are willing to change. We feel the idea of "optimum" solutions is too inflexible in the sense that a transitional movement is essentially experimental; and so we attempt where possible to provide criteria which will guide the user to his or her own best solution.

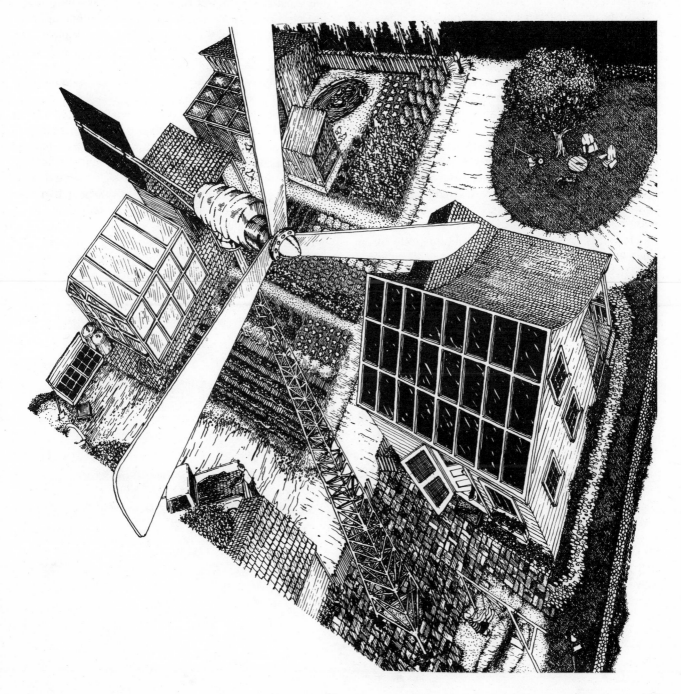

Low-impact technology must include ways and means by which natural, renewable energy sources may be used on a small scale to provide electricity for a single home or a small cluster of homes. In Chapter 3 we first discuss the fundamental concepts of electricity which are essential to the design of a home electrical system, including methods for estimating your own electrical energy demand. While there are presently only two economically realistic technologies using renewable sources of energy which can be used to meet that electrical demand—wind power and water power—it is quite likely that photovoltaics which convert sunlight directly into electricity will soon be useable. All three technologies are discussed in this chapter.

In the section on wind, techniques for measuring wind speeds and estimating the energy available are given. The functions of each piece of electrical equipment necessary in a complete wind-electric system are described, as well as techniques for calculating the necessary component specifications. Similar design calculations are then given for photovoltaics and water power systems. The intent is to lead you through sufficient amounts of material to allow you to design a generating system that is suited to the conditions of your own locale.

Providing for the thermal needs of a household is an especially important aspect of any dwelling design. Chapter 4 covers use of the sun for space heating. The chapter begins with the description of the solar resource which is simply the amount of sunlight that can be expected at any given location at any time of the year.

The ins and outs of capturing that sunlight with flat plate solar collectors is then described in considerable detail. You will be shown how to select the most suitable collector design for any given application in any given location and then how to predict the performance of that collector. Collector efficiency curves are important but potentially confusing so considerable attention is directed to their proper interpretation. This section concludes with collector installation details—how to attach collectors that will not be blown off in a high wind or cause roof leaks in a storm.

The most important use of flat plate collectors is for domestic water heating, so they are covered next. Comparisons are made between a number of system design options to help you select the proper one to meet your needs. Emphasis is given to collector freeze protection—the most crucial aspect of any hydronic system design. Flat plate collectors are also used for swimming pool and hot tub heating and these applications are explored.

When most people think of solar, they think of space heating and this important topic is covered at length. The mechanisms of heat loss are first described qualitatively but the real heart of the section is the review of techniques for quantitatively predicting the thermal requirements of a house. Many examples are provided, not only to illustrate the procedures but also to demonstrate the tremendous reductions in energy demands that can be realized in a thoroughly weatherized house.

Once space heating requirements have been reduced to their minimum we then show how to design solar systems to supply a good fraction if not all of the remaining demand. Simple but effective passive measures such as use of south-facing windows to let sunlight into the house, overhangs for shade control, and thermal mass for energy retention are discussed along with more exotic passive architectural ideas such as Trombe walls, attached green-

houses and underground housing. You will be shown how to design active solar space heating systems that use collectors, controls, pipes, ducts, pumps, blowers, thermal storage and so on. Finally we'll review the economics of solar energy systems. It's a long chapter but the explosion of new information in this field necessitates the extent of the coverage given. We hope this material will take you well beyond the basics and into the finer details of actual practical design.

Chapter 5 deals with methods and aspects of recycling organic waste. Since the average individual in the United States produces five pounds of solid municiple waste per day (agricultural wastes are still greater), there is considerable energy available here from conversion, in addition to the possible return of nutrients to the food cycle. Four conversion systems are described and analyzed: the methane digester, which produces bio-gas and high-nutrient sludge through anaerobic bacterial action; systems for recycling greywater; the Clivus Multrum and outhouse arrangements; anaerobic decomposition in septic tanks; and bacterial-algal symbiosis in oxidation ponds.

With the growing consumption of fresh water in the United States approaching 50 percent of the supply flowing in rivers daily, cleansing and recycling of water is necessary if severe depletion and pollution are to be avoided. In Chapter 6 several areas of the problem are studied for small-demand users: the sources (open-body, ground, recycled, and artificially collected) and transportation of water; impurity types and levels, disease sources, and available treatment options; and finally storage, in terms of water quality, intended usage, and the recharge rate of a given system. In each area the systems are considered for three- and fifteen-person units living an alternative lifestyle, but the methods and analyses are applicable to specific situations through extrapolation. Immediate expenditures in time and energy may be higher than for conventional systems, but the long-range cost should prove to be far less.

A self-sufficient living unit must be able to feed itself. In the chapter on agriculture and aquaculture (Chapter 7), we explain how this goal may be achieved, in some instances using waste material. Agricultural crops and techniques are covered in some detail, though not exhaustively. There are hundreds of other crops and techniques for their culture, but we have chosen to describe a few which we feel can be applied successfully to creating a self-sufficient home. We also consider whether aquaculture can be used to supply significant amounts of food. Aquaculture is aquatic agriculture, in which the crops are fish, shellfish, or algae. Aquaculture has existed for centuries and, although it is not practiced extensively in the United States, it should not be ignored because its food-producing potential is generally greater for a given area than that of agriculture. As in the other chapters, our study

has aimed toward supplying the needs of a single family or small cluster of families on limited acreage. Attempts have been made to allow for various climatic and soil conditions, and much of the information can be applied to both urban and suburban settings, as well as rural.

We wish you well on your journey through these pages and trust that you will enjoy learning and creating as much as we did in the preparation of the material. Remember: worthwhile things seldom come easy. We only hope that we have made the job somewhat easier and more enjoyable.

He who would arrive at the appointed end must follow a single road and not wander through many ways.—Seneca

ARCHITECTURE

**Changing energy practices:
the philosophy of transition**

**Land, wind, water, sun:
determining the best site**

Light, natural and man-made

Your house and what goes into it

**Homes of yesterday;
consciousness of tomorrow**

ALTERNATIVE ARCHITECTURE

Our Need For Change

American building technologies and practices have developed under a natural blessing: abundant land on which to scatter our homes; abundant materials with which to build and rebuild almost at will; abundant energy to process, transport, fabricate, and demolish these materials; and yet more energy to heat, cool, light, and power our buildings at heretofore unattainable levels of comfort and dependability. This abundance has shaped the whole of our culture. Furthermore, the notion that this abundance is unlimited has given legitimacy to the unrestrained depletion of our natural resources: we move to the suburbs rather than maintain or improve existing urban environments; we build houses to last twenty years instead of two hundred; to condition our structures, we adjust a thermostat rather than open a window or pull a drape. And so disappear the land, the materials, and the energy.

It is now possible to detect a growing disillusionment in the United States with the shortsighted, self-interested technology of the past. We have only begun to feel the effects of the depletion of once-abundant resources, and to see and smell the aftermath of their misuse, but it has been enough to raise to consciousness the desirability of changing our technologies and attendant lifestyles: from the *energy-intensive* practices which created modern society, to the *energy-conservative* technology which will be needed, not only to repair the damage (where possible), but merely to maintain our viability.

The goal of alternative architecture is an end to resource depletion. But its successful adoption involves far more than facts and figures. A new relationship to our world is called for, characterized by both respect and rev-erence for the place we inhabit. We cannot "rule the world" without paying a heavy price; far better to enter into a symbiotic relationship and preserve both the world and ourselves. An alternative lifestyle may well be the first step in an evolutionary process which might eventually bring about a more reasonable approach to the environment by society in general. Indeed, we now face an alternative technology which grows in a new context, stemming less from a concern with comfort and efficiency than from a need to reduce the undesirable impacts of our old technology. For the first time, our new tools did not develop in response to a lifestyle; rather, a new lifestyle evolved and is evolving as a response to old tools.

Architectural design is traditionally a response to a modeled use. Essential to the design of any living unit is a program, an orientation to the task, which supplies both objectives and constraints. For example, the five-day work week constrains all systems which require maintenance; no homeowner existing in that current lifestyle model will easily adapt to the increased investment of time called for by most aquaculture schemes. Certain constraints seem to be almost universal (dependence on a car, the work week, the need for sleep), while others are less easily generalized (the size and composition of the "family," the extent of personal flexibility, and so on). Given the difficulties regarding goals and constraints, it is not surprising to find differences of opinion among designers. Some, like Ken Kern, Art Boericke, and Barry Shapiro, are convinced that alternatives can only (or best) grow in the context of the forest and its lifestyles. Others, including Soleri and Kenzo Tange, interpret "alternative" as a lifestyle based on self-sufficiency in an urban context.

9

What seems clear is that, in an era of rapidly altering roles and models, alternative architecture must place a premium on design flexibility.

New technologies will demand some significant departures from accepted cultural norms. Some may require a degree of social reorganization. For example, to conserve the most energy, the heat source should be located in the center of a room. Americans, however, have traditionally relied upon perimeter heating, which keeps walls and corners warm. Consider the extent to which our room arrangements utilize the walls and corners. Unlike the Japanese, who focus their attention on the center of a room, Americans tend to line the walls of rooms with furniture and reserve the central areas as a circulation buffer. A single heat source placed at the center of a room or house will require that this longstanding, almost subconscious cultural norm be modified. Or if, for instance, the economics of heat loss demand a reduction of natural light in the house (fewer windows), we may see the rebirth, in appropriate climates, of the outdoor porch, with all its possibilities for more communication between neighbors.

To some degree our current atmosphere of experimentation calls for structural flexibility as well. Errors and failures sometimes demand a change in room organization or the capacity to install new or modify old mechanical systems. For this reason, designers should aim to develop a flexible arrangement which would allow some physical modification of the building, perhaps clustering the mechanical systems in a "core" area with easy access.

Generally we can view the philosophy of an alternative lifestyle as a philosophy of transition. When faced with a new technology, we must be capable of creatively adapting both the forms of our buildings and the forms of our lives. The kinds of architecture, the physical forms that will be generated in creating a resource-conservative relationship between the building and its environment, are still ill defined and experimental. But in other cultures and at previous times in our culture, architectures have existed and still exist which make both conservative use of consumable resources and maximum use of renewable resources.

As inspiration for an alternative architecture, we can look to what Bernard Rudofsky has termed "architecture without architects," the primitive architectures of the world that have, more often than not, developed in response to shortages of material and energy resources. In the absence of mechanical technologies, indigenous societies have depended on the ability of their building techniques to make the most effective use of landscape, climate, and architectural form, and the most permanent and economic use of materials in providing a habitable environment. We marvel at the ability of these builders who take a few materials—earth, stone, wood, grasses—to shape and assemble by hand, and yet who produce an architecture that adapts incredibly well to daily and seasonal climatic variations and that maintains a delicate balance of consumption and regeneration with its environment.

We cannot turn our backs on the fact that we live in a highly industrialized society. Where sophisticated technologies serve our goal and can be used effectively to reduce the depletion of resources, they should become a part of our alternative architecture. But we advocate an architecture that relates to its environment *in the same way* that primitive architecture does: symbiotically. To reduce energy and material waste, we must design simpler, smaller structures that use less highly processed building materials, that reuse discarded materials, and that make more permanent use of both. We must use fewer machines in the construction of our dwellings. We must learn to use fewer mechanical appliances to service our houses. And we must, above all, be willing to adjust our habits, physiology, and psychology, opening ourselves to the wonders and limits of the earth where we abide our little while.

Although our focus here is on the design of a new structure, much of the discussion and many of the ideas are directly applicable to the modification and improvement of existing structures, in both rural and urban settings. The scope of this chapter is limited to general relationships, concepts, and ideas; only occasionally do we touch on specific designs or solutions. The material is rather more integrative than differential—specific details on various technologies can be found in Chapters 3 through 7. Here we try to provide a general framework for the more detailed information to come.

Site Determinants In House Design

Elements of the natural environment were of vital concern in the design of early dwellings, placing major restrictions on the form of these structures. But upon the advent of cheap energy sources and high-density housing developments, the only environmental inputs attended to were maximum and minimum temperatures, for determination of the amount of insulation and the size of any necessary heating or cooling plants. It was difficult to design in harmony with nature simply because there was very little that was natural in the typical neighborhood.

That situation is changing. No longer is the abundance of concentrated energy resources so apparent, and there is a generally increasing awareness of ways in which the human sphere of activity interacts with the natural realm, as well as a growing desire for more direct interaction. In the field of domestic architecture, we are encouraged to take advantage of the topographical and climatic features of a given site to the fullest possible extent, minimizing the energy requirements of our houses and maximizing human comfort and pleasure within the home environment.

The site on which a house is located commits the house and its occupants to a physical and climatic environment. In the design of the alternative house, we are seeking two objectives in the relationship between the physical and climatic site characteristics and the house itself. The first, and by far the more important, is to use these characteristics to provide natural conditioning—non-resource depleting—cooling, heating, lighting, and powering. Also, if possible, we can try to use the site as a source of materials with which to build and maintain our structure.

Subsurface Characteristics

The composition of soils may influence the design of the house in several respects. Soil composition affects the design of building foundations. In general, this is an engineering question related to foundation size and reinforcing. But in some cases, adverse soil compositions, or water tables near the ground surface (as in marshy areas), may prohibit building or limit buildable area (Figure 2.1). Both conditions also determine the ease and practicality of subsurface excavation, either for the construction of buried or semi-buried structures, or for the benching of a sloped site to provide a flat building area. This is particularly important if hand excavation is anticipated. Excavation may also be limited or eliminated entirely because of the presence of subsurface rock, to the dismay of an ambitious planner. A high water table considerably complicates construction work and poses problems in waterproofing buried walls and in providing proper subsurface drainage around the building. And, if your soil happens to lend itself to adobe construction, this is a useful fact to note. For soil and water-table testing techniques, see *Site Planning* by Kevin Lynch.

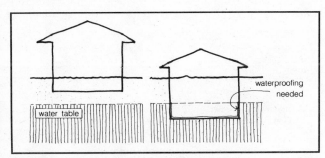

Figure 2.1 Construction below the water table.

As we will see in later chapters, soil composition and groundwater conditions may indirectly affect the location of a house on a site when the positioning of wells or on-site sewage systems is considered.

Topography

Landforms determine the natural water runoff patterns and, wherever possible, these drainage patterns should be avoided in siting the house, to reduce the need to divert water runoff around the building and to lower the risk of a flooded house in a particularly wet season. Extremely flat areas or slightly depressed areas, where ponding is likely to occur, should also be avoided. Ideally, building sites should have slopes from 2 to 4 percent; that is, enough slope to provide good drainage but not so steep that the building process is complicated.

The angle of the slope determines where building is or isn't practical. Building on steep slopes, above 10 percent, is considerably more difficult, consuming far more material, time, and money than building on flatter slopes. The inclination and orientation of the slope also affect both the amount of sunlight received and the resulting air temperature on the site. As you might suppose, southern slopes are generally warmer in winter.

Topography affects wind patterns by constricting the wind (Figure 2.2), increasing its velocities in certain areas, while sheltering others protectively. Slopes to the leeward side of winter winds are preferable for building sites (Figure 2.3). Hill crests, where wind velocities are increased, should be avoided in all but hot, humid climates. The bottoms of valleys and ravines, as well as topographic depressions, are likely to channel and trap cold air masses during the night and winter, and so should be avoided as building sites.

Figure 2.2 Wind channeled by hills.

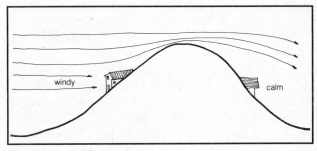

Figure 2.3 Building on slopes.

11

Surface Water

Because of their ability to absorb heat during warm periods and release it during cold periods, large water bodies such as lakes or the ocean exert a moderating influence on air temperatures, throughout the day as well as the year. Even small streams and ponds, in the process of evaporation, cool air temperatures in summer. In addition, there are usually breezes sweeping across the surface of a lake or down a river valley. Where possible, site water courses and water bodies, such as aquaculture ponds, should be used in conjunction with prevailing summer winds as conditioning elements for the house (Figure 2.4). A further effect from unshaded bodies of water is added heat from reflected light; thoughtful siting and use of strategic shading devices can offset this gain when it is undesirable. It is always best to build on high ground when close to large water sources, for both drainage purposes and protection against flooding.

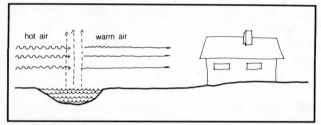

Figure 2.4   Cooling by a water-body.

Vegetation

Natural vegetation has numerous influences on the microclimate near the house (Figure 2.5). Healthy trees and shrubs provide shade, reduce glare, and in dense configurations are effective windbreaks. They also have a cooling effect in the summer, using heat for evapotranspirational processes in their foliage. They reduce the albedo (reflectivity) of the land surface, thereby reducing the possible heat gain of a house from outdoor reflection. Dense growths effectively absorb sound, enhance privacy, and are remarkably efficient air filters for dust and other particles. Vegetation generally looks nice and often smells better. It can support an animal population, which may or may not be desirable. However, in order to permit access to summer breezes, aid drainage, and reduce problems from pests, it is advisable to discourage forests or extensive vegetation too near the house.

One of the major contributions of trees on a site is the shade that they provide. Deciduous trees are ideal in this regard because shading is needed in summer, but is generally undesirable in winter when solar radiation is a benefit; and the leaf-bearing period of deciduous trees

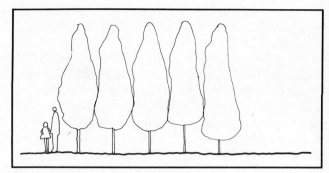

Figure 2.5a   Vegetation as fenestration.

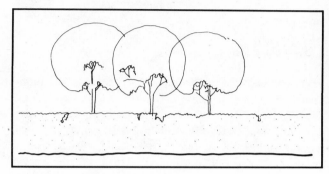

Figure 2.5b   Vegetation as fenestration.

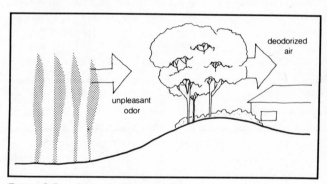

Figure 2.5c   Air purified by vegetation.

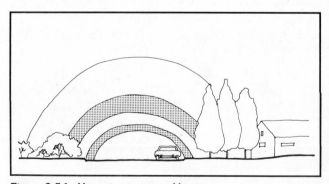

Figure 2.5d   Vegetation as a sound barrier.

native to any particular latitude spans exactly the period when shading is required for that latitude. These trees have the added advantage that, in an unusually cold spring or warm autumn, the leaves appear late and remain later, correspondingly, which is highly desirable. Trees are primarily effective at low sun angles, which makes them useful for intercepting early morning and late afternoon sun. Hence, for these purposes, their positioning on the east-southeast and west-southwest sides of the house is most efficient in northern latitudes. At higher sun angles, structural features of the house, such as louvers or screens, can provide needed shade.

The other classic function of vegetation is to provide a windbreak. In this respect, the ideal arrangement allows in summer breezes and blocks out cold winter winds. Obviously, this is not always possible. In many localities, however, the prevailing winds in summer and winter come from different directions, which makes the placement problem for hedges or rows of trees relatively simple. For this situation, evergreens are highly desirable, as they maintain dense growth in the winter. In other situations, it is possible to use deciduous hedges or deciduous trees with a low, open branch structure to direct summer air flow into your house, while these same plantings would present little obstruction to air flow in the winter.

In some cases, it is possible to place strategic plantings to combine shading and wind-directing benefits for optimum effect. In most cases, however, compromise is necessary. The full spectrum of plant use in house design is presented in *Plants, People, and Environmental Quality* by Gary Robinette. See also "Wind Protection" in this chapter for diagrams.

Man-made Characteristics

The man-made environment on and surrounding your site also influences the air temperature, sun, and wind. Air temperatures are raised by an abundance of hard, reflective surfaces like those of building or paving (Figure 2.6). Buildings, fences, and high walls also channel air movements and change wind patterns.

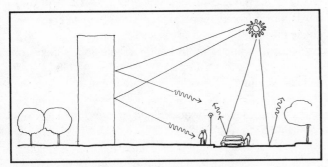

Figure 2.6 Temperature raised by reflective surfaces.

Climatic Factors In House Design

Climatic factors are obviously very important and, of these, temperature has the greatest impact. The extremes and averages of temperature as well as the duration of the various temperature ranges, in terms of both daily and yearly cycles, influence the size of the temperature-controlling facilities a house requires. They also dictate whether a house must be designed for optimum efficiency of cold exclusion or of heat dissipation, or whether some compromise of the two will prevail.

The other climatic factor which most affects human comfort is humidity. The amount of humidity has significance when it is tied to air temperature. Within the range of variation of these two factors, a human "comfort zone" can be described. Figure 2.7, a schematic diagram of Victor Olgyay's Bioclimatic Chart, depicts this zone and also shows corrective measures to be taken when conditions fall outside its limits. This diagram is naturally subject to variation on an individual basis, but gives workable guidelines. The shading line represents a limit above which shading is necessary and below which solar radiation becomes useful for heating.

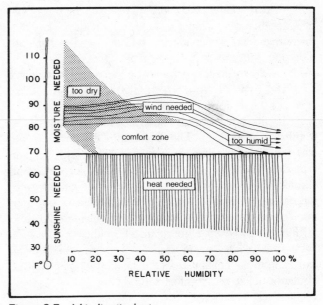

Figure 2.7 A bioclimatic chart.

The major effect contributed by solar radiation is heat, but light and consequent glare also have to be considered. Solar angles during different hours and seasons and the distribution of sunny and cloudy periods are important, particularly in terms of the feasibility of solar heating for the house. Wind is significant as a potential ventilation aid and cooling agent, as well as a potentially destructive force. Maximum velocities, average velocities, directions, and daily and yearly variations of all these factors are important, especially if you are considering a windmill as a power source. Finally, seasonal variations in rates of precipitation, total amounts, predominant direction (if any), and maximum snow loads (if any) influence the structural design.

In design, we encounter these climatic variables in three distinct relationships. The first is *general climate*, which determines the overall climatic character of a structure. While the differences in general climate are myriad, we usually refer to four distinct types in discussing specific design ideas: cold climates, in which our emphasis is principally on heat conservation, sun utilization, wind protection, and rain and snow protection; temperate climates, in which the emphasis is on striking a balance of all conditions; hot, arid climates, where our concern is with heat and sun control, wind utilization, rain utilization, and increased humidity; and lastly, hot, humid climates, where we try to promote heat, sun, and rain protection, wind utilization, and humidity reduction. Olgyay (*Design with Climate*) gives detailed methods for designing in response to climatic conditions, as well as specific design responses based on these four regional types.

The second relationship consists of the climatic variables as they interact with particular site characteristics to produce the *microclimate* of each individual site. It is these microclimatic conditions that are used in the conditioning of the resource-conservative house. The classic study of microclimate seems to be Geiger's *The Climate Near the Ground*, from which Olgyay and Lynch draw much of their information.

The third relationship consists of the microclimate as it affects our feelings of environmental comfort. We are reacting to this *bioclimate* when we feel hot and sticky on a summer day. (Additional discussion on bioclimate and climatology can be found in Chapter 4.) One purpose of design is to provide a comfortable bioclimate for our bodies, "comfortable" being somewhere between 70° and 80°F and 20 to 80 percent relative humidity (Figure 2.7). Where we refer to "warm" and "cool" periods of the year, we mean those times when climatic conditions fall either above or below this comfort zone.

Temperature and the Reduction of Heat Transfer

Temperature averages and extremes throughout the year dictate important design considerations of your house. Regional information is generally sufficient and can be found in the *Climatic Atlas of the United States,* as well as other sources. During at least a portion of each day, a difference in temperature will exist between the bioclimate you wish to maintain and the actual microclimate. This temperature differential encourages a process of heat transfer (convection) through the building materials of the house, heat traveling from higher to lower temperature

areas. Building materials and forms may be used to prevent unwanted heat transfer, since they have different transfer resistances. Where we wish to reduce heat transfer, those materials and techniques offering high resistance should be used. Resistances of various building materials and methods of calculating heat transfer are presented in Chapter 4. Climatic factors surrounding the house can also be controlled to reduce temperature differentials. Examples of no-cost/low-cost techniques for conserving energy in the typical home are given in *Technical Note 789,* issued by the National Bureau of Standards.

Insulation

Building insulation generally refers to materials of high resistance—glass fiber or mineral wool blankets and fill, polystyrene and polyurethane foam boards, vermiculite and perlite fill—that are effective because of small cellular voids in their structure. They are generally highly processed materials designed to be used with standard construction techniques, particularly to fill large structural cavities in stud-frame and concrete-block construction.

Good insulation conserves energy otherwise spent on heating and cooling, not only by reducing heat transfer, but by making available energy more useful. In winter, a person feels colder in an uninsulated house than in an insulated one, *even if* the internal air temperatures are the same. This is due to the cold-wall phenomenon. The cold interior surfaces of uninsulated walls absorb radiant heat rather than reflect it as the warm surfaces of insulated walls do, consequently causing a greater loss of body heat. Most people compensate for this chilling effect by raising the heat. This adjustment is unnecessary with good insulation. In summer, cold wall surfaces are desirable; insulating accomplishes this effect and also reduces, yearlong, drafts produced by temperature differences between walls and air. Finally, it reduces room-to-room and floor-to-ceiling temperature contrasts.

An insulating air space within a wall or roof is not as effective as that same space filled with an insulating material (Figure 2.8): temperature differences across the space cause the air to circulate and transfer heat. In standard wood-frame construction, the most common, cheapest manufactured insulation is mineral wool or fiberglass. It is furnished in widths suited to 16-inch and 24-inch stud and joist spacing, in blanket rolls 3 to 7 inches thick (available with reflective foil or vapor barrier on one side). Fiberglass has the advantage of being highly fire resistant and the disadvantage of being itchingly uncomfortable to work with.

Inch for inch, the best insulating material is polyurethane foam. One inch of urethane is equivalent to about two inches of fiberglass. An extremely versatile construction material, it is available in rigid sheets one-half to two inches thick or in liquid form with a catalyst for on-the-

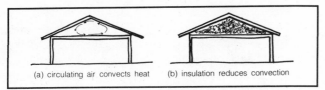

(a) circulating air convects heat   (b) insulation reduces convection

Figure 2.8 Heat convection in an attic.

job foaming. The liquid may be poured into forms or sprayed on with special equipment. In the hands of a skilled applicator, this material can be rendered into almost any sculptural form and will provide considerable structural support. In the hands of an unskilled applicator, it can easily turn into an utter mess and its high price makes experimentation a serious venture. If ignited, urethane burns explosively and emits noxious gases; it should be covered on the inside with a fireproof wall of plaster or sheet rock.

In house construction, a common type of rigid insulation is sheathing board made of processed wood or vegetable products, impregnated with an asphalt compound to provide water resistance. It is usually affixed to the exterior of a stud frame, often in addition to flexible insulation applied between the studs. Sheathing board also serves as a main structural component of the wall.

Loose-fill insulations like vermiculite, sawdust, shavings, shredded redwood bark, or blown-in fiberglass can be used in walls of existing houses that were not insulated during construction. They are also commonly added between ceiling joists in unheated attics. Vermiculite and perlite are often mixed with concrete aggregates to reduce heat loss.

Insulating was a common practice long before the advent of modern manufactured materials, and we might do well to consider the use of less energy-intensive materials than those commonly used in modern construction. Any shelter sunk into the earth is cheaply insulated. About thirty inches of packed dry earth is equivalent to one inch of urethane, but a lot cheaper. Although the earth may absorb a considerable amount of heat from the room during the day, this energy is not entirely lost, since the warmed earth will keep the room at a more uniform temperature throughout the cold night. Blocks of sod and moss are commonly used in northern countries where insulation is particularly important. Not to be overlooked for its insulation value is wood: as siding it is significantly better than plaster, and, as we mentioned earlier, sawdust is almost as good as fiberglass although it tends to settle in vertical wall cavities. Dried grass and straw matting work well as roof insulation when sandwiched between layers of plastic, although their fire hazard is great. Other useful examples are given in Kahn's *Shelter*.

The air inside a house normally contains much more water vapor than the outside air, due to cooking, laundering, bathing, and other domestic activities. In cold weather the vapor may pass through wall and ceiling materials and condense inside the wall or attic space, damaging finish or even causing decay of structural members. To prevent this penetration, a vapor barrier should be applied on the interior side of insulation, the most effective being asphalt-laminated paper, aluminum foil, and plastic film. Some building materials, such as fiberglass insulation and gypsum board, are available with vapor barriers factory affixed.

Surface Area

Heat transfer that occurs between the interior and exterior of your house is principally dependent on the surface area of materials separating inside from outside spaces. In extreme climates, we try to reduce these exposed surface areas. Simple, compact forms—domes, cubes, and other regular polygonal structures—offer less surface area for a given floor area than elongated or complex forms. Clustering of housing units, both horizontally and vertically, also reduces exposed surface areas of walls and roofs (Figure 2.9). In reasonably dry soils, buried, semi-buried, or excavated houses are feasible and have obvious insulation advantages.

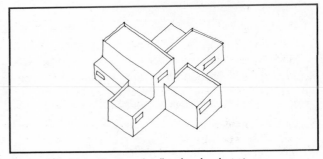

Figure 2.9 The reduction of wall surface by clustering.

Window Areas

Window glass has very little resistance to heat transfer; it transmits about twelve times as much heat per square foot as a fiberglass-insulated stud wall. When designing to prevent heat transfer, reduce window areas to the limit of your psychological need for visual contact with the outdoors. Minimum window-area standards (based on floor area) for dwellings are found in section 1405 of the Uniform Building Code. New recommendations which incorporate floor area and window types are described in *Technical Note 789*, issued by the National Bureau of Standards. Techniques for making the best use of a limited amount of window area, both for natural lighting and for visual contact, are presented later in this chapter.

When your psychological needs won't allow for a

great deal of reduction in window area, a half-inch air space between two sheets of glass can cut heat transfer in half. Also, two separate windows, one to four inches apart, produce the same reduction (Figure 2.10). When only a rough sense of visual contact is needed, glass blocks perform the identical service. But the most common and least expensive method is the use of curtains, blinds, or shutters on all window areas. Similar to double glazing, they reduce heat transfer by creating a dead air space between you and the outside environment. They are also useful for controlling light penetration into your house.

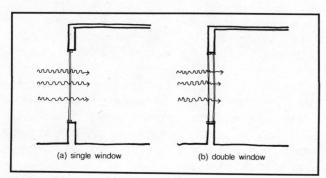

Figure 2.10 Heat transfer through windows.

Window frames are also points of heat transfer, through cracks between window and frame and, if metal frames are used, through the frame itself. Weatherstripping and wood frames should be used throughout.

Solar Protection

All sunlight, whether direct or reflected, whether striking directly the outer surfaces of your house or streaming through windows onto the floors or walls, is converted to heat. Light striking nearby ground surfaces and objects heats these materials, which also warms the air immediately surrounding the house. However, such heat loads can be minimized using several techniques.

House Orientation

The critical period for solar heat gain is usually a late summer afternoon when the sun is low. Orient the shorter side of your house toward the west (Figure 2.11), put rooms that require small windows on the western side, or locate here your storage, garage, and toilet facilities as thermal buffers (Figure 2.12).

In rooms with large windows, the windows should open to the south, where summer sun penetration can be controlled by overhangs or other shading devices; in climates where heat loss is not critical, they can open both to the north and south.

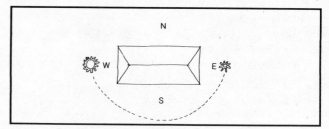

Figure 2.11 Orient the short side of the house toward the west.

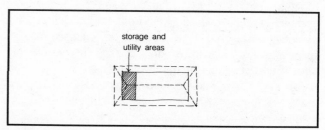

Figure 2.12 Locate nonhabitable space on the western side.

Shade

South walls can be shaded with roof overhangs but, due to early morning and late afternoon sun angles, overhangs are less effective on east and west walls (Figure 2.13). In hot climates, you can use porches, verandas, arcades, or double roofs to shade your walls and provide cooler outdoor spaces. However, their use in temperate and cool climates obstructs direct solar radiation, a point to consider in winter.

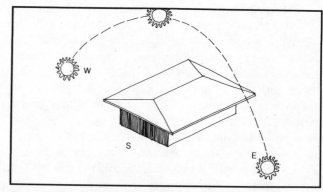

Figure 2.13 Overhangs are insufficient for east and west walls.

Deciduous trees and bushes provide shade in the summer and allow sun penetration in winter (Figure 2.14). Trees located to the southeast and southwest of the house will provide shade for both the roof and walls (Figure 2.15). East and west walls may be screened with low trees or bushes. A horizontal trellis with deciduous vines (such as grapes) can provide the same seasonal protective variability (Figure 2.16). Tree and bush sizes and shapes are shown in Ramsey's *Architectural Graphic Standards* and Lynch's *Site Planning*.

The heat gain from sunlight, like that caused by air temperature, is directly dependent upon the exposed surface area of your house; hence the same control techniques are applicable. In hot, arid climates, it is possible to cluster housing units (Figure 2.17) and to use minimum-surface structures. Buried or semi-buried (Figure 2.18) structures are also feasible.

Techniques for shading exterior surfaces are also obviously applicable for shading windows. In addition, specific window devices can be used. On a southern exposure, where incident sunlight is predominantly vertical, horizontal shading devices are most effective (Figure 2.19). On eastern and western exposures, vertical or parallel devices are required for the low sun angles. For maximum protection, use combinations of various devices. If these are a fixed part of your house, they should be sized to exclude sun only during the summer. Removable or retractable awnings, movable exterior louvers or shutters can be adjusted to the season. See *Design with*

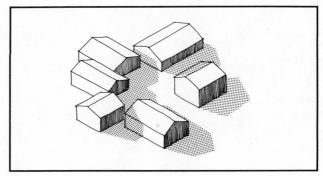
Figure 2.17 Cluster houses for shading.

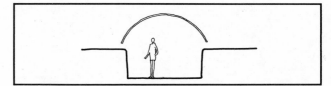
Figure 2.18 A semi-buried structure.

Climate (Olgyay), *Sun Protection* (Danz), and *Architectural Graphic Standards* (Ramsey) for detailed discussions and examples of technology.

Exterior shading devices are seldom completely effective; curtains, blinds, shades, and shutters are recommended. Curtains uniformly reduce sunlight while blinds allow both a reduction in intensity and a redistribution of light. Heat penetration may be reduced by up to 50 percent with either blinds or curtains, and by up to 75 percent with roller shades.

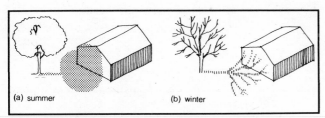
Figure 2.14 Shading by deciduous trees.

(a) summer (b) winter

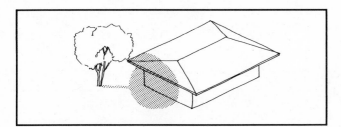
Figure 2.15 Shading SE or SW walls of the house.

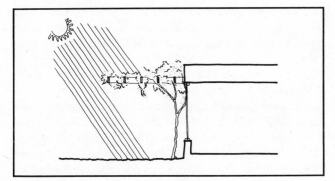
Figure 2.16 A deciduous vine arbor.

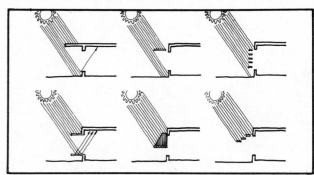
Figure 2.19 Horizontal shading devices.

The effective use of shading devices as a means of solar control will depend on the designer's ability to calculate the sun's position. Sun paths and altitudes for various latitudes in the United States can be determined by using the Sun Angle Calculator produced by Libby-Owens-Ford and provided with *Climate and House Design*, published by the United Nations. They may also be calculated by means shown in *Architectural Graphic Standards*.

Reflectivity

Glare from nearby water bodies or a sea of parked cars can be controlled both by proper siting of your house and by strategic use of bushes, berms, and fences (Figure 2.20). You can minimize excess glare from unshaded ground surfaces near the house by the use of ground cover (grass, ivy) that absorbs a fair amount of light. Reflectivities of various ground surfaces are shown in *Plants, People, and Environmental Quality* (Robinette).

Figure 2.20 Reducing glare from objects and water-bodies.

The more sunlight is reflected off the surface of your house, the less will be absorbed into building materials. In hot climates, use white or metallic surfaces; even in temperate areas, light colors should be used for protection during warm spells.

Solar Lighting

A well-integrated lighting system in any structure must make the best use of both natural and artificial light sources. To use daylight for inside lighting, the first obvious requirement is that the sky be bright enough to provide some lighting potential. Before going further, it would be wise to define the difference between sunlight and daylight. *Sunlight* comes in a straight line while *daylight* is reflected or refracted (also called *glare*). There are several factors that affect sky brightness for each particular location: latitude, altitude, time of year, time of day, amount of air pollution, and relative humidity. For any particular lot, the effect of the local terrain, landscaping, and nearby buildings must also be considered. It is handy to research the average number of clear days per year in your part of the country, or else the percentage of time that skies are clear during sunlight hours. Derek Phillips (*Lighting in Architectural Design*) devotes one chapter to daylighting, giving a method to calculate daylight levels in interior spaces and also general suggestions for the design and placement of windows.

Window Location

Because the reflectivity of the sky is generally much higher than that of the landscape, the quantity of light entering a window is directly related to the amount of sky visible through the window. Low windows transmit little light, and this light is at a poor angle for most activities (Figure 2.21). Raising most of your window area, but still keeping it low enough for a standing adult to see out, best compromises conflicting needs for visual contact and maximum light (Figure 2.22). Small, lower windows should then be provided only at specific sitting areas, such as in dining or living rooms.

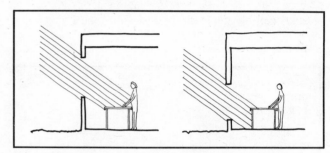

Figure 2.21 Light from high and low windows.

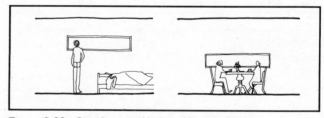

Figure 2.22 Specific uses of high and low windows.

Overhead skylights, clerestories, and monitors, which are less apt to be affected by obstructions surrounding the house, efficiently admit light into interior spaces. They can be used in such areas as bathrooms or bedrooms, where light is necessary but visual contact is not (Figure 2.23). Diffusing glass can be used to bathe the room with light and reduce over-contrast.

Kitchens, reading and writing areas, and work spaces all require intensive lighting and should be located near large windows. Areas requiring less intensive lighting—living or dining areas, toilets, bathrooms and bedrooms—should have correspondingly smaller windows (see also "Artificial Lighting" in this chapter).

Figure 2.23 A skylight.

Window Efficiency

There are three general classifications of glasses; each one has different advantages and disadvantages, but any choice must be made with heat-loss characteristics somewhere in mind. High-transmittance materials pass light easily and allow clear vision in either direction. Low-transmittance materials have brightness control, which increases as transmittance decreases. Finally, diffusing materials (suggested for skylight use) include opal and surface-coated or patterned glass and plastic. They are directionally nonselective: brightness is nearly constant from any viewing angle. This property is especially pronounced in highly diffused materials, but transmittance and brightness decrease as the level of diffusion increases. In other words, to get a uniform diffusion of light through a skylight with diffusion glass, you must sacrifice the level of brightness in the room and a sharp vision of the sky overhead.

The light transmission of windows is also impaired by external or internal shading devices. But compensations can be made. Permanent external shades should be sized to exclude sunlight only during warm periods. Even then, they can be designed to exclude direct sunlight, but to include some reflected and diffused light (Figure 2.24). Light reflected from the ground, from reflective window sills, and from adjustable or removable reflectors can also be used to increase diffused light entering interior spaces.

Contrast

Contrast between the outside environment viewed through a window and the darkness of an interior space

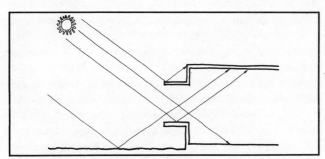

Figure 2.24 Sizing of a shading device to allow reflected light.

can cause the discomforts of glare and eye fatigue as your eyes constantly adjust from one lighting condition to another. This contrast can be reduced by using light-colored window frames, walls, ceilings, and floors throughout the interior of the house, because these reflective objects increase overall brightness in any space (see also "Interior Coloring" in this chapter).

Windows may be placed adjacent to perpendicular interior walls, so that the light reflected from those walls produces a contrast-reducing transition in light intensities (Figure 2.25) rather than a brilliant hole of light surrounded by an unlit wall. Where walls have considerable thickness, as in adobe construction, windows should be located on the wall's outer surface. The window opening should then be beveled, to form a transition surface between window and interior wall surface and also to allow more light penetration (Figure 2.26). This technique is also useful for skylights. Curtains and blinds, by reducing and redirecting sunlight, can also be used to reduce contrast and illuminate dark areas.

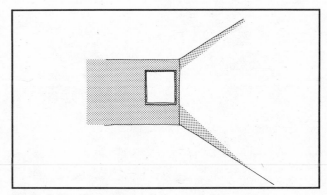

Figure 2.25 The transition of light provided by a wall.

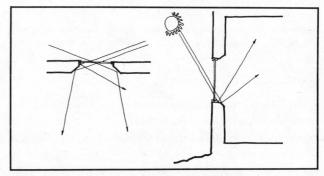

Figure 2.26 Reflected light from beveled openings.

Solar Heating

Around the country there are many homes and businesses that use solar power in some significant way, whether to heat a swimming pool or power an entire structure. As an abundant and nonpolluting source of energy, sunlight should be used as a principal method of heating

19

a resource-conservative house. Chapter 4 offers an extended discussion of this topic, but we mention here a few general points in passing.

Site Orientation

The slope of your site affects its solar potential at different times of the year. During the summer, total daily solar radiation will be approximately the same for northern, southern, eastern, or western grades of up to 10 percent. But in winter, southern slopes receive more sunlight because of low sun angle; this also raises microclimatic air temperatures. Southern slopes are preferred as building sites for regions with cold winters.

Solar Penetration

During cool periods, direct sunlight can be used as a method of heating. If fixed sunshades are used for protection during warm periods, they should be sized to allow partial light penetration during spring and fall and complete light penetration during winter (Figure 2.27).

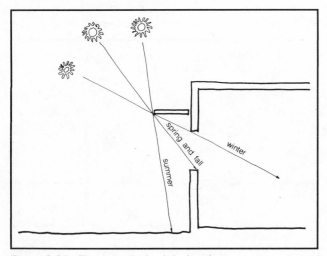

Figure 2.27 The sizing of a fixed shading device.

Heat Transfer

The capacity of certain materials to absorb heat has been used for centuries in certain climates to both heat and cool buildings. The method depends first on the use of such "massive" materials as earth, stone, brick, or concrete to enclose space; and second on a climate of predominantly warm or sunny days and cool nights. The massive material absorbs the heat of outside air temperature and incident sunlight during the day, stores the heat within its mass, and then reradiates the heat to the cool night air (Figure 2.28). As the quantity of a thermal mass surrounding any space is increased, and hence, as its ability to store heat is increased, the temperature variation within the enclosed space will diminish, coming closer to daily and seasonal temperature averages. For this reason,

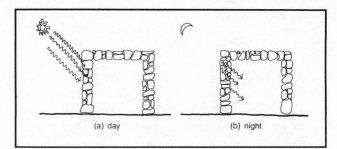

Figure 2.28 Heat transfer in massive construction materials.

caves and other underground dwellings maintain almost constant temperatures.

Sunny-day/cool-night climatic conditions are most prevalent in hot, arid regions where, unsurprisingly, we find, even today, extensive use of stone and earth as building materials and the indigenous use of underground housing. But, by incorporating thermal masses with other forms of heating and ventilating, and with the proper use of insulating materials, the range of climatic conditions in which they are applicable as space conditioners can be broadened. Chapter 4 presents several examples of contemporary houses that rely on this method of heat transfer for conditioning.

Solar Heaters

Ultimately, we seek a more predictable use of sunlight than primitive techniques may be able to supply. One solution was the development of a solar "heat-collection and storage" machine: a solar heater. The principle behind the heater is simple—a sheet of black, heat-absorbent material backed with heavy insulation to prevent thermal leakage is positioned to face the sun. Glass covers this collector to keep heat from reflecting back into space. Air or water pumped through the enclosed space is warmed and flows down into a well-insulated storage tank. The stored heat is then recirculated into interior spaces as needed.

Wind Protection

In contrast to the sun, wind should be utilized during warm periods and blocked during cool periods to aid in the natural conditioning of the house. In designing for wind protection and wind use, directions and velocities of the wind should be known in relation to cool and warm periods of the day and year. Of all climatic variables, wind is the most affected by your individual site conditions; general climatic data will probably be insufficient. Air movement along the outer surfaces of your house convects heat away from those surfaces and increases the heat transfer through building materials. Knowing the prevailing wind direction during the cool period, you can take steps to provide protection. Techniques for determining wind velocities and directions are discussed in Chapter 3.

Wind Paths

Both natural and man-made landforms and structures channel different climatic air movements into particular patterns. In all but hot, humid climates, these natural wind paths should be avoided when locating your house. On small sites there may not be much choice. If the site is hilly, the mid-portions of slopes are best, away from both high winds at the crests and cold air movements along the valley floors (Figure 2.29).

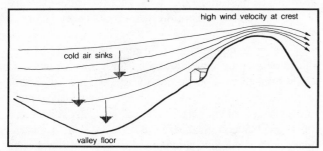

Figure 2.29   The location of a house on a hilly site.

House Orientation

In areas of cold or constant winds, the house should offer as little exposed surface area to the wind as possible. Designs should be compact and clustering of houses may be considered to reduce exposed wall area. In suitable soils, semi-buried structures are a possibility. Also, where cold winds are severe, your house plan should be organized so that it turns its back on the wind. The wall facing the wind should be windowless and well insulated. Closets, storage areas, toilets, laundry, and garage can also be used as buffers on the windward side. House entrances, large windows, and outdoor areas should then be located on the protected side.

Heat losses through building materials and through door and window cracks are directly dependent on exposure to and velocity of wind. As you can see, all the various techniques discussed under solar protection and heat transfer are appropriate for wind protection.

Tornadoes, hurricanes, and other destructive winds can demolish your house. In hurricane regions (generally the same hot, humid climatic regions that require light, open structures), enclosures can be designed that allow solar protection when open and wind protection when closed. In tornado and severe wind regions, use shutters to protect your glass.

Windbreaks

Fences, bushes, trees, and other site objects acting as wind barriers create areas of relative calm on their leeward side (Figure 2.30). Wind acting perpendicular to a more solid windbreak (a wall, earth berm, or building) is reduced in velocity from 100 percent at the break to about 50 percent at distances equivalent to about 10 or 15 heights from the break. Open windbreaks, such as trees and bushes, offer a maximum reduction in wind velocity of about 50 percent at a distance equivalent to about 5 heights. Evergreens, which retain their foliage throughout the year, are best for winter protection.

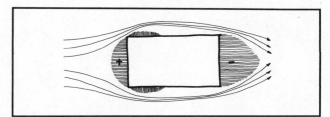

Figure 2.30   Air movement pattern around a house.

Windbreaks may also be an integral part of the house structure. Such protrusions as parapets or fin walls on the windward side of a house divert air movement away from other wall and roof surfaces (Figure 2.31).

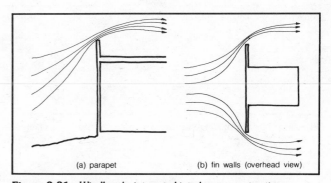

Figure 2.31   Windbreaks integrated into house construction.

Wind Use

Channeling Wind

Wind convects heat away from roof and wall surfaces. Consequently, windbreaks should be used to channel wind toward your house during warm periods (Figure 2.32). Where prevailing summer and winter winds come from the same direction, deciduous trees and bushes may be used to direct summer winds toward the house (when foliage acts as a barrier to wind movement); their winter bare branches allow cold winds to pass by, undeflected (Figure 2.33). Where summer and winter winds come from different directions, ventilation openings and windows should be placed in the direction of summer winds (Figure 2.34). If, however, such a window arrangement

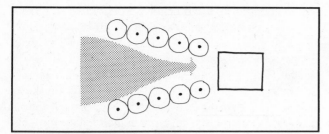

Figure 2.32 Channeling wind by trees.

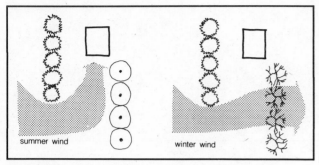

Figure 2.33 Channeling summer and winter winds from the same direction.

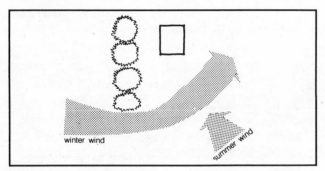

Figure 2.34 Channeling summer and winter winds from different directions.

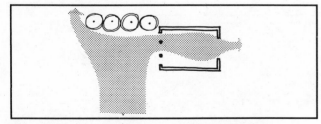

Figure 2.35 The deflection of summer winds into a house.

conflicts with proper solar protection, summer winds can be directed into the house by additional windbreaks (Figure 2.35).

In hot, humid climates, where maximum ventilation is required, the velocity of the wind, and hence its effectiveness as a cooling agent, can be increased by using windbreaks to constrict and accelerate wind flow in the vicinity of the house. Robert White shows many

configurations of trees and hedges and their use in modifying air movements into and around the house (see Bibliography).

Ventilation

The use of natural ventilation in cooling the alternative home is advisable because this is one of the few existing techniques which can replace the modern air conditioner. Air conditioning is not only expensive and a terrible energy drain, but can also damage your health since unnatural temperature differences are created. Proper ventilation both evacuates warm or stale air from your house and cools your body by encouraging evaporation of moisture from the skin. Two natural circulation techniques can be used: wind-induced *cross-ventilation* and *gravity ventilation*.

Two openings are necessary for proper cross-ventilation: one as an inlet, preferably on the windward side of the house where air pressures are high; and the other as an outlet on the leeward side where air pressures are low. Because of these pressure differences, rooms are most effectively ventilated by using a small inlet located near the bottom or middle of the windward wall and a large outlet in any position on the leeward wall (Figure 2.36).

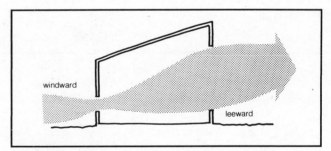

Figure 2.36 Effective ventilation.

The pattern and velocity of cross-ventilation within a room is modified by the location of vegetation, roof overhangs, and sunshades placed near the air inlets, and also by the type of inlets used. In general, use exterior elements to increase the wind pressure in the vicinity of your inlets. For example, proper location of trees near the house increases the velocity of air movement at ground level, and hence, air pressure. Roof overhangs and sun protectors tend to trap the wind, similarly creating higher air pressures. As shown in Figure 2.37, different types of window inlets can be used to direct air either into or above living areas. And if there are no winds to use, or if the house, even with large vents, still feels too stuffy, you can resort to the use of electric fans, to be mounted in either the exhaust vent or the ceiling.

Gravity ventilation of spaces is dependent on the fact that cool, dense air displaces warm, less dense air, forcing

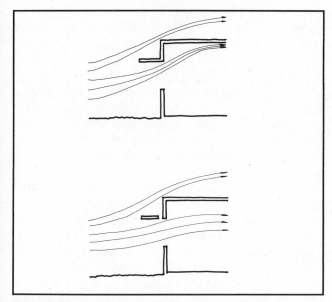

Figure 2.37 Air movement with different types of inlets.

the warm air to rise. By placing vents at different levels in interior spaces, cool air is drawn in through the lower inlet, while warm air is forced out through the higher outlet. The rate at which air circulates is directly dependent on the difference in air temperature, the height difference between the two vents, and the sizes of the two apertures. Air inlets should be as low as possible in areas likely to have the lowest air temperature, such as the north wall of the house. Keep these vents clear of shrubbery. Outlets should be located as high as possible and preferably in areas where wind movement can be used to create a suction or "stack" effect to aid in the ventilating process.

Gravity ventilation can be used for summer cooling, or in specific locations, such as bathrooms and kitchens, where air exchange rather than cooling is required. In all cases, the inlets and outlets should be closable to prevent heat transfer during cool periods.

We can also make direct use of the wind with airscoop ventilation. In this method, various types of scoops are placed on the roof or at the wind-blown sides of the house, with piping to circulate air into the home. Simple, low-power ventilating fans can successfully replace the use of such a system, usually eliminating the necessity for intricate piping arrangements. By using electric fans in conjunction with gravity air flow and intelligent shading and orientation techniques, the air temperature within a house can be significantly lowered.

The key to this claim lies in effective attic insulation and ventilation. During the course of the day the roof becomes very hot, radiating heat into the attic. An oven effect is created if this hot air is not allowed to escape; as night comes, it continues to radiate heat into the rooms below. This phenomenon is known as *heat lag*. With proper ventilation, the attic acts as an insulator by day

and heat lag is eliminated at night. Roofs with a high pitch (and so a tall attic) can be ventilated adequately by placing vents at the upper and lower extremes of the attic. This method of gravity ventilation is employed when the attic height exceeds 5 feet, since height differences are important in determining air flow rates; on flatter roofs electric fans must be used. Although electric fans can be mounted on the roof in the same manner as vents, to simply pump air out of the attic, in yet another installation air is pumped from the *interior* of the house into the attic, where the air escapes through vents. Thus the whole house is cooled. Here the fan should be centrally located in your attic so that uniform air circulation is promoted. It is also advisable that the underside of the roof be insulated, preferably by reflective insulation. A successful approach to roof ventilation without attics is the use of a double roof.

The fans mentioned earlier should be the slow type. These are quieter, more efficient, and well worth the extra price. Never use cheap fans, since they often need frequent repairs. Large attic fans should be wired to a thermostat, to prevent unnecessary operation. Do not forget that screens and louvers cut down on fan efficiency, so vent openings must be increased.

In warm climates it is imperative that the walls of the house remain cool, due to the fact that people cool themselves by radiating heat to the walls. When wall temperatures exceed 83°F (skin temperature), people become very uncomfortable even if breezes are introduced into the room. The most efficient means of cooling walls is to insulate them properly. A relatively new and untried way of cooling walls is to ventilate them through their core. Since hot air rises and the walls have considerable height, openings at the bottom and the top of the wall generate a strong air current. It is still important that these ventilated walls be heavily insulated, and all openings should be screened to prevent insects and small animals from entering. Ventilated walls should be used only in warm climates, since heat loss can be quite severe in cold weather.

Crawl space ventilation is of only minor importance. Minimum requirements are intended to drive off moisture accumulated under the house. During hot weather, the air in crawl spaces is generally cooler than the outdoor air, so thorough venting is actually undesirable.

In all climatic regions some ventilation is needed, but in cold, temperate and hot, arid climates this requirement should have little effect on the plan of your house. However, in hot, humid climates, plan your house around the need to maximize ventilation. Rooms should be open and elongated perpendicular to the wind. Areas that generate humidity, heat, and odors—kitchens and bathrooms—should be separated from other areas and also be well ventilated (Figure 2.38). Floors should be raised above the warm ground to allow circulation under the house (Figure 2.39).

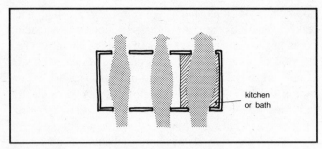

Figure 2.38   Ventilate odorous areas separately.

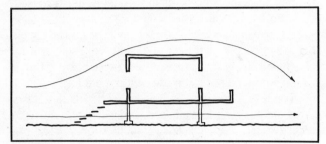

Figure 2.39   Air circulation with a raised floor.

Equipment

Artificial Lighting

The two most widely used artificial light sources today are incandescent and fluorescent lamps. In homes, incandescent lights are by far the more popular. The principle behind incandescent lighting is to heat metal to such a degree that it gives off white light, a wasteful process at best.

Fluorescent Light

Fluorescent lights work on a more complicated basis: light is produced by fluorescent powders which are excited by ultraviolet energy. But it is less important to understand how fluorescent lights work than it is to understand their efficiency, an efficiency on the order of 20 percent, compared to about 5 percent for incandescent lamps. Hence they use only a quarter the power for the same amount of light. Prove to yourself which source creates more waste heat by touching both types (be careful with the incandescent one).

In economic terms, the controlling factor in choosing a light source is not the initial cost or even the lifespan of the lamp, but rather the cost of operation. Since the initial cost and lifespans of incandescent and fluorescent lights are comparable, it is a wise choice to use fluorescent lights for general lighting needs. In the winter do not be fooled into thinking you can use the waste heat for warmth; solar power does the same job far more efficiently.

There are three general categories of hot cathode fluorescent lamps: preheat, instant-start, and rapid-start. In the preheat type, there is a short delay between the

time the circuit is turned on and the time the lamp produces light. The current is allowed through the cathodes to heat them; when this is accomplished the starter automatically opens the circuit so the light can start. In the instant-start variety, enough voltage is immediately supplied between the cathodes to operate the light as your fingers hit the switch. The rapid-start type, now the most common, uses low-resistance cathodes which are continually heated with but small energy losses. This variation requires lower starting voltages than instant-start lamps, and produces light in one to two seconds.

In a resource-conservative home, the sacrifice of one or two seconds certainly does not warrant the use of instant-start lamps. The rapid-start lamp appears to be your best choice of the three. Keep in mind that the frequency of starting a lamp is a major factor governing its lifespan. Lamp sizes range from 6 to 96 inches in length and from ⅝ to 2⅛ inches in diameter. By the way, if a windmill provides your energy, both incandescent and fluorescent lamps are available which run off direct current.

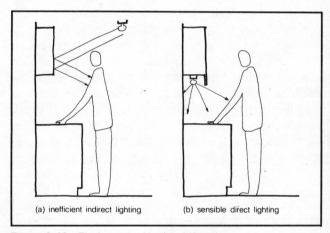

(a) inefficient indirect lighting   (b) sensible direct lighting

Figure 2.40   The location of kitchen lighting.

Lighting Techniques

In lighting your house, first consider the activities for which any space is used. Second, choose a means of lighting which is most practical. Direct lighting (or task lighting) should be used wherever possible. For example, one 60-watt bulb provides plenty of light to read by—even if the rest of the room is fairly dark. This procedure is far more sensible than putting lights all over the ceiling, lighting every corner of a room to the intensity necessary for reading in one specific spot. The same concept applies to living areas and bedrooms. There will be times, however, when small islands of light do not suffice; here indirect lighting can be used.

In kitchens, most activity is concentrated on the counter tops. Common sense suggests that lighting should be concentrated there, but kitchens traditionally

24

have been lit with one central light of staggering intensity. Instead, smaller fluorescent lights should be placed underneath the upper cabinets as shown in Figure 2.40, an arrangement less wasteful and which avoids any problems with shadows over your work area.

The rule for artificial lighting is *use direct light wherever possible,* especially in all stationary activities—reading, kitchen work, sewing, and so on. Another good idea is to place low-intensity light bulbs in closets to eliminate the need to turn on all the lights in your bedroom to choose a wardrobe. (It might also please any others who are trying to sleep at the time.)

For other activities where more general lighting is needed, our tendency has been to overlight. One of the most pleasant commodities we may discover in an alternative lifestyle is atmosphere. It takes only enough light to be able to read expressions to carry on a conversation. There are many satisfying ways to achieve indirect lighting, a few of which are shown in Figure 2.41. And, if we can enjoy any "inconveniences" which may occur as a result of using naturally supplied commodities, it will all be worthwhile. If the windmill should be calm for too long and there is no power for lighting, candles give ample light, burn cleanly, and provide wonderful atmosphere. Use common sense and take advantage of nature's surprises to produce a well-lit home.

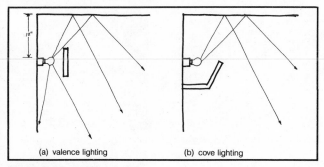

(a) valence lighting   (b) cove lighting

Figure 2.41 Lighting techniques.

Interior Coloring

The cheapest and most pleasant interior lighting during daytime hours is through natural sources. But in considering a self-sufficient system, we must also consider heat loss; windows, which account for approximately 15 percent of the overall heat loss, should be kept to a minimum. This is why interior coloring is so important. Light colors, because of their reflective capacities, spread the light around, giving you the best "mileage" from any particular light source (see Table 2.1). White, naturally, is the best color for this purpose, but other reflective colors can be used to relieve monotony.

Colors can also control your "psychological" room temperature to some extent. That is, colors with shorter wavelengths (green, blue, violet) create an impression of

Table 2.1 Reflectivity of Colors[a]

Color	Light Reflected
White	80–90%
Pale pastel (yellow, rose)	80%
Pale pastel (beige, lilac)	70%
Cool colors (blue, green pastels)	70–75%
Full yellow hue (mustard)	35%
Medium brown	35%
Blue and green	20–30%
Black	10%

Notes: a. From K. Kern.

being cold, while colors with longer wavelengths (yellow, orange, red) appear warm. Use warm colors on the north side of your house, or areas where there is minimal sunlight; on the south side, cool colors should be used.

Appearance is markedly affected by contrast. Thus a central chromatic area appears brighter if surrounded by a sufficiently large and relatively dark area, but dimmer if surrounded by a relatively light one. Interior glare content, for this reason, becomes an important category to be evaluated, since 1 percent contrast lost by glare requires a 15 percent increase in illumination. Comfortable reading on a glossy table requires considerably greater illumination than on a dull surface.

Lighting Standards

There has been a tendency over the years to continually raise the recommended light values for various tasks. Largely as a result of an intensive campaign financed and conducted by the electrical industry, these high recommendations have been followed closely. We can examine the standards in Table 2.2 as a representative example. Ken Kern, author of *The Owner Built Home,*

Table 2.2 Lighting Standards[a]

Task	Footcandles Required
Kitchen Activities:	
Sink	70
Working surfaces	50
Table games	30
Reading and writing:	
Books, magazines, newspapers	30
Handwriting, reproduction, poor copies	70
Desks (study purposes)	70
Music:	
Reading simple scores	30
Advanced scores	70
Grooming	30
General lighting:	
Passageways	10
Relaxation and recreation	10
Areas involving visual tasks	30

Notes: a. From I.E.S. *Standards for Various Home Activities.*

writes: "Illumination experts specify an artificial light intensity of from 50 to 100 footcandles for most visual tasks. But experts in the field of light and color conditioning warn against the use of more than 30 to 35 footcandles. . . . Further light intensity is apt to cause visual distraction."

So what exactly is the minimum amount of light a person needs to be comfortable? William Lam, a lighting consultant in Cambridge, Massachusetts, has a very simple definition: "Good lighting is lighting which creates a visual environment appropriate and comfortable for the purpose. This is a criterion that is measurable only by people using their own eyes and brains." He summarized his insights concerning lighting in six points:

First: we see well over a tremendous range of light levels.

Second: we see by the balance of light more than by the quantity.

Third: once 10–15 footcandles has been achieved, task visibility can be improved far more easily through quality changes rather than adding quantity.

Fourth: apparent brightness is determined by brightness relationships, not absolute values.

Fifth: we look at tasks only a small part of the time, but react to the environment all of the time.

Sixth: whether our response to the environment is to be favorable or unfavorable cannot be forecasted or explained by numbers—but by the exact design of everything in relation to what we want to see.

To set absolute personal lighting standards is impossible; therefore test for yourself the minimum amount of lighting you need for different activities.

Fireplace Design

Many of the changes made in creating the alternative home concern combining older, simpler, less energy-intensive designs with the technological advances of the present. A typical modern home makes scant use of its fireplace as a heat source, a waste implicit in the rather crude fireplaces now being installed. We are principally interested in heat-ventilating and free-standing fireplaces, both exceptional finds today. Few people are even familiar with some of the basic principles of fireplace operation.

Perhaps one of the most critical aspects of efficient use is the correct tending of the fire. A fire should always burn brightly and briskly. Whenever starting a fire, use a small amount of wood. Add more timber only after this initial wood is burning vigorously. Never force a fire to eat its way through a pile of wood. Obviously, other fuels should be burned with the same diligence and economy.

A healthy fire uses a tremendous amount of air both to burn its fuel and to dispose of waste gases and smoke. In order to accommodate this demand, the fire is raised above the hearth by means of a grate. Studies have shown that this step increases burning efficiency by 15 percent. Vents or windows must also bring air into the room from the outside; lacking air in a house weatherstripped and insulated properly, a fire does not burn well and smoke ebbs into the room.

Equally important is the exhaust of hot gases and smoke. Here we are concerned with the design of the chimney breast, throat, and flue. The required depth of the chimney throat for all fireplaces is between four and five inches. The small size of the throat, which can be adjusted by a damper, prevents drafts of cold air from blowing down your flue; yet it permits smoke and waste gases to rise (Figure 2.42). Because smoke spirals as it rises, round flues are more effective than square or cornered ones. The strength of the draft is also related to the temperature of the flue lining, so your flue should be well insulated. *Architectural Graphic Standards* (Ramsey and Sleeper) features data by which flue diameters can be calculated.

The only usable warmth escaping from the ordinary fireplace is radiant heat. Roughly three-quarters of the

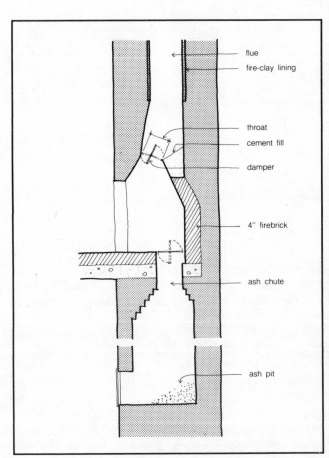

Figure 2.42   The construction of a typical fireplace.

heat produced by the fire is used to heat up exhaust gases, smoke, and the wall of the fireplace. In addition, a fire needs air to burn properly, so cold air is necessarily sucked into the room. Through the extensive use of ducting, heat-ventilating fireplaces (Figure 2.43) take advantage of this situation. They not only heat the fresh air entering the room, but also utilize 40 percent of the heat given off directly by the fire. The basic arrangement involves an intake vent connected to ducting which leads air across the back of the firebox. This hot air is then ducted to vents above the mantel. A natural air current is created by the hot air rising in the ducts as well as by suction created through the burning fire. A number of commercial models are available. They are provided with only a minimum of fireproof ducting, so if you wish to heat other rooms, cost for this rather expensive item must be considered. Fans can also be installed to accelerate the air flow.

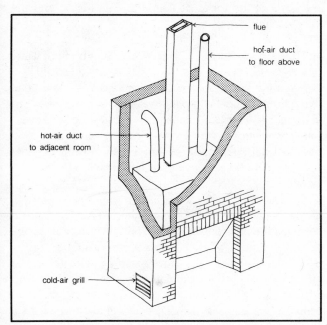

Figure 2.43a The construction of a heat-ventilating fireplace.

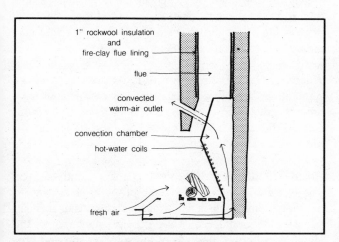

Figure 2.43b Air flows in a heat-ventilating fireplace.

Although the construction of fireplaces appears to be fairly rigid, fireplaces have been built chiefly out of salvaged materials, using, for example, a discarded water boiler as a fire box. For details see *The Owner Built Home* (Kern). Another effective heating device is the free-standing fireplace with a metal hood. Heat radiates in all directions from the fire, and once the hood is warm, it too gives off tremendous heat.

Materials

Due to our once-abundant supply of energy, there developed a tendency to use building materials—aluminum, steel, concrete, and plastics—which require intensive processing. Until this last century, the process of converting raw materials into building materials was accomplished principally by human labor. Because of this direct relationship between human effort and its product, the materials were used economically and constructed to last. We can still find wooden houses erected over two centuries ago, or stone houses dating back two millennia. Despite the fact that highly processed materials are inherently more durable, their high initial cost (attributable to expensive processing) requires that they be used in the smallest quantities possible. Today, most structures are designed and built under the guideline of *lowest initial cost;* consequently, they have a very short useful life.

Where building ordinances are not a problem, natural or alternative materials can be incorporated into design and used, with a little know-how, to produce sound construction. There are various sources for these low-cost and usually low-energy materials. Scrounge secondhand building materials—bricks, timber, steel, and glass—from demolition sites and dumps. One enterprising couple obtained enough timber to build their own home by offering to demolish dilapidated structures for other people, in exchange for the timber they could salvage. Or use processed materials that are considered waste products. Scrap bins in lumber yards are a good source. And bottles make excellent translucent bricks; you get not only a wall but light penetration as well. Tin cans have produced shelter. Sulphur, a waste product from oil and coal production, can be used for cement, and with sand aggregate, produces sulphur concrete (see Rybczynski's article, "From Pollution to Housing," listed in the Bibliography). One architecture student in London constructed a four-room dwelling from scrap materials and garbage collected within one mile of where the dwelling was built.

Natural materials that are readily available—stone, earth, driftwood, trees—require only manual energy. For centuries, people made stone cottages, log cabins, and adobe homes. These techniques, although a lost art among urban dwellers, can still provide structures that are

27

as sound as conventional homes and often have superior insulating properties. However, some knowledge of their limitations is necessary, and some skill is required if they are to be used effectively.

The energy required to produce and transport the materials of a typical house is equal to about ten years of household energy consumption. To reduce the need for transporting materials, wood should be the dominant building material in forested areas, earth in dry climates, stone where it is available, grasses where they grow rapidly and easily, and so forth. Where possible, materials from the building site itself should be incorporated. Useful information on design and construction techniques is contained in *The Owner Built Home* (Kern), and *Your Engineered House* (Robert). The National Bureau of Standards has also undertaken extensive experiments to establish the structure, sound reduction, heat transfer, water permeability, and other relevant properties of house construction for a wide range of materials. Their work is especially valuable because of an emphasis on materials for low-cost construction.

Primitive Architecture

There are four general traits which characterize primitive architecture: unsupplemented use of natural, locally available building materials and local construction skills; planning and massing as a result of specific functional requirements and site conditions, regardless of symmetry and generally accepted taste; an absence of ornamentation which is not part of the structure; and the identity of enclosing form and enclosed space. This architecture is a simple and original response, the most economic shaping of space and form for the maximum benefit of body and soul. Several interesting examples are found in *Native Genius in Anonymous Architecture* (Moholy-Nagy), *Shelter* (Kahn), *Architecture Without Architects* (Rudofsky), and in an article by Suzanne Stephens, "Before the Virgin

Met the Dynamo." We mention a few general types in the next section.

Types and Techniques

Troglodytic Shelters: In areas where soil and climate conditions are suitable, men have lived in caves throughout history. Simple caves can be enlarged and altered if the local rock or earth is sufficiently soft and porous. Because these shelters are below ground and thus insulated by the earth, they are usually cool in summer and warm in winter.

Nomadic Architecture: Nomadic structures must be readily portable as the lifestyle of the nomad is above all one of transience and motion, moving and changing with trade, livestock, and the seasons. Some examples include the tipi of the American Indian, the tents of the Bedouin, the yurts of the tribes of Asia and Asia Minor, and the igloo of the Eskimo.

Aquatic Architecture: The proximity of a body of water has always been an important consideration in siting a community. For thousands of years people have been living in houseboats, in pile dwellings, and in more conventional structures in canal cities linked by waterways rather than streets. An expanse of water serves as a cooling plant during the hot season; a bath or drink is never far away. On a houseboat your home is also your transportation.

Tree Houses: People of many cultures have lived in and amongst the tree tops in tropical and near-tropical zones. In cooler zones one is shaded from the summer sun by a leafy parasol while the bare branches of winter let the sun shine through. Air circulation is excellent.

Movable Houses: In some parts of the world, when a family or community moves, the house is either completely disassembled or picked up in large sections and then moved to a new location, provided the distance is not too far. These structures are usually lightweight and are often made from grasses or reed.

Towers: The usual function of towers has been either symbolic or defensive. They often express religious sentiments: grief, faith, hope, or prayer. In some agricultural cultures they are used for grain storage or as pigeon roosts.

Arcades and Covered Streets: Arcades and covered streets are an example of private property given over to an entire community. Their presence reminds us that city streets exist for people. They provide shelter from the elements, offering shade from the summer sun and protection from winter wind and rains.

little rainfall; wet climate may erode an adobe structure into a pile of mud. It is best used on a well-drained site. Walls are short and also thick for strength and insulation; doors and windows are placed away from corners and the roof is supported by rafters.

Rammed Earth: To make rammed-earth blocks, one uses a dampened mixture of humus-free soil and a stabilizing agent (usually portland cement) which is formed into blocks in a hand-operated press. (The Cinva-Ram press is commercially available.) Walls of rammed earth must be reinforced by a corner or pillar every ten feet. As with adobe, it is best to build on dry, flat, solid ground or rock as the compression of block upon block can cause sinking or settling.

Stone: There is little information available on laying up stone, partly because of the traditional secrecy of stone masons and partly because stone differs so much from area to area. Stonework is heavy and time-consuming but the materials are a gift of the earth and the structure often blends unobtrusively with the landscape. One can use mortar or simply pile stone upon stone as did the ancient Egyptians in their pyramids.

Building Materials

Materials and climate determine what is possible in terms of shelter within a particular context. The fact that over three hundred house forms have emerged from nine basic climate zones suggests that these specific forms derive more directly from socio-cultural factors than from restraints of either climate or materials. In spite of this diversity, almost all examples of vernacular architecture emphasize simple yet profound solutions to the problems of human comfort, using elementary building materials which require little or no basic transformation to be utilized.

The cost of a building material is roughly proportional to the ecological damage caused by its removal and refinement. In aesthetic terms, the less molecular rearrangement a material has undergone, the better it feels to be around and the more gracefully it will age. More often than not, natural, locally available building materials are the least refined and least polluting; they may also be self-regenerating.

Adobe: Adobe is the world's most abundant building material since its primary ingredient is earth. It is also the oldest and most popular form of earth construction. Ingredients vary but usually consist of clay soil mixed with sand, shredded grass, roots, straw, pottery shards, or gravel. These are formed into bricks and set out to bake in the sun. Adobe houses are most practical in areas with

Sod: Sod is a good building material for treeless grasslands. It is usually cut directly from the earth in long solid ribbons which are then sectioned into blocks measuring about 4-by-24-by-36 inches with a sharp spade. The sods are laid without mortar, grass down like huge bricks. Walls are two or three sods thick, with staggered joints. Every third or fourth layer is set crosswise to the vertical pilings for stability. The walls, which are excellent insulators, settle about six to eight inches in the first year. Sod roofs are also excellent insulators, but miserable water repellers; a wooden roof is best.

Snow: Although snow can be used only in the polar regions, there it has proved to be an instantly available building material with superior insulating qualities. After a bit of experience, one need only cut blocks of suitably dense snow and lay them in an upward spiraling fashion to form a dome. With a little body heat and a small heat source, the interior walls form an ice glaze which solidifies the structure. In subzero exterior conditions, Eskimos are often stripped to the waist in the warm interior of their igloo.

Wood: Wood is an ideal building material for many climates and cultures as it is relatively light, strong, durable, pleasant smelling, easy to work, readily available, and can be regenerated. Forms vary from simple twig and brush shelters and log cabins to the most elaborate, ornate structures conceivable. It is also a material which lends itself to recycling if one salvages from old buildings and other discards of the twentieth century.

Grasses: Various grasses have been employed as building materials throughout history. Reed has been used for frameworks, walls, and roofs; it insulates well and is light and easy to work with. Drawbacks include easy flammability and a relatively short life. Bamboo is flexible yet tough, light but very strong. This versatile plant splits easily in only one direction; it is pliant or rigid as the situation demands; it can be compressed sufficiently to remain sturdily in place in holes; after heating, it will bend and retain its new shape; one of the world's fastest growing plants, it also grows straight. As with reed, typical construction must include lashing of structural members.

In tropical climates woven grasses are often formed into houses. Here woven matting is supported by a simple

sapling superstructure to form walls and a roof. Thatch is perhaps the world's most commonly used roofing material. Although it is a time-consuming process to thatch a roof, the end product is a waterproof, insulated, biodegradable roof of reeds, straw, or fronds. Truly waterproof thatch requires a steep pitch and the overlap of all its elements.

Baled hay was used as a building material in arid grassland regions of the United States where the soil is too sandy for sod houses. Most of these structures now have concrete foundations or wooden floors. The best hay to use is harvested in the fall: it is tough and woody. The bales are two to four feet long and about two feet square. They are stacked like bricks, one bale deep with the joints staggered. Mortar can be used; man-high wooden poles are driven through the bales to hold them firmly together. The roof is usually a wooden frame with shingles. The insulating properties of baled hay are obvious. Equally obvious drawbacks include its fire hazard and the fact that hay is a choice breeding ground for many insects.

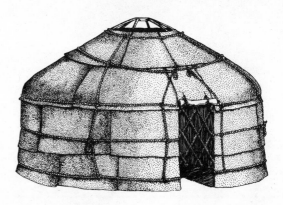

Skin and Fabric: Skins or woven fabrics stretched over a light portable framework have provided shelter for nomadic people throughout the ages. In the summer fabric tents are cooler than skin tents, although in the rainy season skin tents are far more waterproof. Typical materials include buffalo hide, woven sheep and goat hair, felt and canvas, and sheep and goat skin. Commonly available in the United States, canvas is easy to work with, cheap, covers space quickly, and lights with a translucent glow. It is relatively short-lived (five to ten years), biodegradable, and can be rendered water- and fire-resistant. Cool in the summer, canvas can also be adapted to winter conditions with proper insulation and a heat source.

Implications

The more we do for ourselves, the greater our individual freedom and independence. But rather than turn our backs completely on present-day technology, we should seek a responsible and sensitive balance between the skills and wisdom of the past and the sustainable products of the twentieth century. To strike this balance, we have much to learn from the past. These so-called "primitive" or "vernacular" structures, built by self-taught people on the basis of experience acquired through generations, were in one sense ideal: they usually fulfilled the needs and aspirations of a community in a design which was both serviceable and timelessly beautiful.

All architecture testifies to the essential nature of its creators, revealing through physical expression the private history of a culture, its ongoing struggle for material and spiritual survival. If the maintenance of human life is based on economy, the first premise of community life is the organization and upkeep of our resources, taking into account both human needs and environmental factors. Most vernacular architecture reflects an organic relationship to its setting; the buildings and inhabitants felt no need either to dominate or to submit to their surroundings. They achieved a sort of mutual coexistence in accord with the basic functions of both man and nature, a spontaneous and continuing experience of peoplehood within a community of experience quite a bit larger than merely human. We of the twentieth century have a long way to go in reordering our priorities. We have yet to learn that any significant departure from that greater community of experience is, in fact, pollution.

Bibliography

American Society of Heating, Refrigerating and Air-Conditioning Engineers. 1972. *Handbook of Fundamentals.* New York.

Anderson, L. O. 1971. *Wood Frame House Construction.* Los Angeles: Craftsman Book Company of America.

———. 1973. *How to Build a Wood Frame House.* New York: Dover Publications.

Aronin, J. 1953. *Climate and Architecture.* New York: Reinhold Publishing.

Banham, R. 1969. *The Architecture of the Well-Tempered Environment.* Chicago: University of Chicago Press.

Blackburn, G. 1974. *Illustrated House Building.* Woodstock, New York: Overlook Press.

Brand, S. 1974. *Whole Earth Epilog.* Baltimore: Penguin.

Caudill, W. W., Crites, S. E., and Smith, E. G. 1951. *Some General Considerations in the Natural Ventilation of Buildings.* Texas Engineering Experiment Station, Research Report no. 22.

Caudill, W. W., Lawyer, F. D., and Bullock, T. A. 1974. *A Bucket of Oil: The Humanistic Approach to Building Design for Energy Consideration.* Boston: Cahners Books.

Chermayeff, S., and Alexander, C. 1963. *Community and Privacy: Toward a New Architecture of Humanism.* Garden City, New York: Doubleday & Co.

Conklin, G. 1958. *The Weather Conditioned House.* New York: Reinhold Publishing.

Daniels, F. 1964. *Direct Use of the Sun's Energy.* New Haven, Connecticut: Yale University Press.

Danz, E. 1967. *Sun Protection: An International Architectural Survey (Architecture and the Sun).* New York: Praeger.

Dietz, A. G. H. 1971. *Dwelling House Construction.* Cambridge, Mass.: Massachusetts Institute of Technology Press.

Drew, J., and Fry, M. 1964. *Tropical Architecture in the Dry and Humid Zones.* New York: Reinhold Publishing.

Freestone Collective. 1974. *Dwelling.* Albion, Calif.: Freestone Publishing.

Fry, M., and Drew, J. 1956. *Tropical Architecture in the Humid Zone.* New York: Reinhold Publishing.

Geiger, R. 1957. *The Climate Near the Ground.* Cambridge, Mass.: Harvard University Press.

Gray, R. L. 1974. *The Impact of Solar Energy on Architecture.* Master's thesis. University of Oregon.

International Conference of Building Officials. 1973. *Uniform Building Code.* 1973 ed. Whittier, Calif.

Kahn, L., ed. 1974. *Shelter.* Bolinas, Calif.: Shelter Publications.

Kaufman, J. E. 1966. *IES Lighting Handbook.* 4th ed. New York: Illuminating Engineering Society.

Kern, K. 1972. *The Owner Built Home.* Homestead Press.

Libby-Owens-Ford. 1951. *Sun Angle Calculator.* Toledo, Ohio: Libby-Owens-Ford Glass Company.

Lowry, W. P. 1967. "The Climate of Cities." *Scientific American,* vol. 217, no. 2.

Lynch, K. 1971. *Site Planning.* 2nd ed. Cambridge, Mass.: Massachusetts Institute of Technology Press.

McHarg, I. 1969. *Design with Nature.* Garden City, New York: Doubleday & Co.

Moholy-Nagy, S. 1957. *Native Genius in Anonymous Architecture.* New York: Horizon Press.

Moorcraft, C. 1973. "Solar Energy in Housing." *Architectural Design* 43:656.

National Association of Home Builders Research Foundation. 1971. *Insulation Manual.*

National Bureau of Standards. 1973. *Technical Options for Energy Conservation in Buildings.* Technical Note no. 789. Washington, D.C.

National Oceanic and Atmospheric Administration. 1968. *Climatic Atlas of the United States.* Washington, D.C.: NOAA, U.S. Department of Commerce.

Olgyay, V. 1963. *Design with Climate: A Bioclimatic Approach to Architectural Regionalism.* Princeton, N.J.: Princeton University Press.

Pawley, M. 1973. "Garbage Housing." *Architectural Design* 43:764–76.

Phillips, D. 1964. *Lighting in Architectural Design.* New York: McGraw-Hill.

Portola Institute. 1971. *Whole Earth Catalog.* Menlo Park, Calif.: Portola Institute.

Ramsey, C. G., and Sleeper, H. R. 1972. *Architectural Graphic Standards.* New York: John Wiley & Sons.

Robert, R. 1964. *Your Engineered House.* New York: M. Evans and Co.

Robinette, G. O. 1972. *Plants, People, and Environmental Quality.* Washington, D.C.: National Park Service, U.S. Department of Interior.

Rubenstein, H. M. 1969. *A Guide to Site and Environmental Planning.* New York: John Wiley & Sons.

Rudofsky, B. 1965. *Architecture Without Architects.* New York: Museum of Modern Art.

Rybczynski, W. 1973: "From Pollution to Housing." *Architectural Design* 43:785–89.

——— . 1974. "People in Glass Houses. . . ." *On Site Magazine.*

Stein, R. G. 1973. "Architecture and Energy." *Architectural Forum* 139:38–58.

Stephens, S. 1974. "Before the Virgin Met the Dynamo." *Architectural Forum* 139:76–78.

"The Climate Controlled House": a series of monthly articles. *House Beautiful,* October 1949–January 1951.

United Nations. 1950. *Adobe and Rammed Earth.* New York: United Nations, Department of Economic and Social Affairs.

——— . 1971. *Climate and House Design.* New York: United Nations, Department of Economic and Social Affairs.

United States Geological Survey. 1970. *The National Atlas of the United States of America.* Washington, D.C.: U.S. Geological Survey, U.S. Department of Interior.

White, R. F. 1954. *Effects of Landscape Development on the Natural Ventilation of Buildings and Their Adjacent Areas.* Texas Engineering Experiment Station, Research Report no. 45.

Wolfskiill, L. A. (n.d.). *Handbook for Building Homes of Earth.* Washington, D.C.: Division of International Affairs, U.S. Department of Housing and Urban Development.

ELECTRICITY

Windmills, dams and solar cells

Demythologizing volts and watts

Figuring your electrical needs

Measuring wind and water:
what you need to know and how to know it

Choosing equipment:
what you need to get and where to get it

Getting ready for the day
when photovoltaics are cheap

SMALL-SCALE GENERATION OF ELECTRICITY FROM RENEWABLE ENERGY SOURCES

Generating Your Own Electricity

Most of us living in the United States have become so accustomed to cheap, abundant electrical power, available at the flick of a switch, that it is usually considered an absolute necessity. While it would probably be quite easy for some people to give up air conditioners, dishwashers, trash compactors, and that array of silly electric gadgets that are supposed to make our lives easier—electric toothbrushes, carving knives, can-openers, tie racks, and the like—it is more painful to contemplate doing without the hi-fi, electric lights, and refrigerator. People, of course, have done without all these things during most of our country's history, and indeed the majority of the world's people still does without them today. So they aren't necessary—but they are nice.

The question is, do we have to contribute to the long and growing list of environmental insults associated with the centralized production of electricity just to enjoy a few relatively simple pleasures? Isn't there some way to avoid not only the inflationary spiral in the price of energy but also help turn this country away from our dangerous dependence on imported and nuclear fuels?

This chapter explores in some detail three ways of doing just that. Small-scale generation of electricity from the wind or from a stream can be a realistic alternative right now, given the right geographic conditions, and electricity from the sun, generated with photovoltaics, is just around the corner.

At this point it is useful to point out that electricity is a very high-quality form of energy. By this we mean that it is extremely versatile; it can be used, for example, to power a motor, process information in a computer, heat and illuminate our rooms, electroplate the chrome onto our bumpers, and create sound and images in our entertainment equipment. Try to imagine doing all that with any other form of energy (low-temperature heat, for example) and you'll get an idea of what a marvelous tool electricity is.

In order to be as energy-efficient as possible, it is important to try to match the quality of an energy source to the particular task that we have at hand. It makes little sense to generate high-quality electricity in order to meet a low-quality energy demand such as heating water. For cooking and space heating, you should turn to alternatives such as solar power and methane, saving the electricity for tasks where its unique properties are required. In other words, plan on using as little electricity as possible.

Obviously, something as useful as electricity is not without its price, even if you generate it yourself. The price combines dollars with physical and mental effort, and the three can be traded off, one against the other. To produce it cheaply, you must become involved with your energy. Some of you will now be receiving your first exposure to electrical theory; it may not be the easiest of all exercises, but hang in there. The concepts are relatively simple and the calculations will be kept on a level that you should be able to handle with a minimum of pain.

Some Basic Electricity

The amount of theory required to design a home electrical system is fortunately small. One need only understand the relationships between five basic concepts: current, voltage, resistance, power, and energy.

Consider the very simple electrical circuit of Figure 3.1, which consists of a battery and a resistance load (e.g., a lightbulb) connected together by some wire conductors. The battery forces electrons to move through the circuit and, as the electrons move through the load, work is done (in this case the bulb emits heat and light). The number of electrons passing a given point in the circuit per unit time is called the *current*. Current is measured in amperes (amps, for short) where one amp corresponds to the flow of 6.24×10^{18} electrons per second.

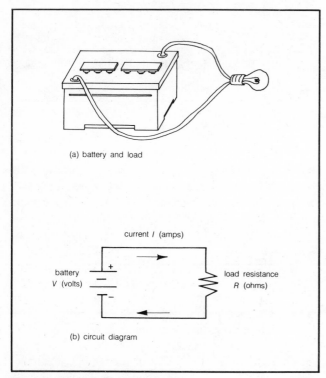

Figure 3.1 A simple electrical circuit.

In this battery-driven circuit, the electrons are always moving in the same direction down the wire; this is called *direct* current (dc). The current that you get out of the wall plug at home is *alternating* current (ac), in which the electrons head in one direction for a short time, then turn around and head back the other way for a while. This back-and-forth movement is characterized by its *frequency*, how many times it changes direction; in the United States that frequency is 60 cycles per second (now called 60 Hertz). Power companies prefer to work with ac because it is easier to generate and because it is easier to change the voltage from one level to another, which they must do to avoid heavy losses in their transmission lines.

Back to our circuit. The battery supplies a certain amount of *voltage*. Voltage is a measure of the "pressure" that is trying to force electrons down the wire. Increasing the voltage across a given load will increase the current through the load. Voltages are measured, handily enough, in volts and these may also be either ac or dc. A car battery typically puts out 12 volts dc and the wall socket voltage is somewhere between 110 and 120 volts ac.

The load in our circuit is characterized by its *resistance* to the flow of electrons. The amount of this resistance depends upon the material, its composition, thickness, density, temperature, etc. Insulators have very high resistances while conductors have very much lower resistances. The resistance is measured in ohms (and given the symbol Ω).

So now we have voltages, currents, and resistances. The equation relating the three is known as Ohm's law and states that

E.3.1 $$V = IR$$

V is voltage in volts, I is current in amps, and R is resistance in ohms. For example, a 12-volt battery will supply 6 amps to a 2-ohm load.

As electrons move through a load, they do work: lighting a lightbulb, turning a motor, heating a toaster, etc. The rate at which work is done is known as *power* and it is measured in watts or kilowatts (KW), where 1 KW equals 1000 watts (some useful conversions: 1 KW equals 1.34 horsepower equals 3412 Btu/hr). It is interesting to note that the power equivalent of consuming 3000 food calories per day is about 150 watts—so you might say the human body is roughly equivalent to a 150-watt machine.

The electrical power (P) consumed in a load is equal to the product of the current through the load multiplied by the voltage across the load:

E. 3.2 $$P = VI$$

Alternative forms, $P = I^2R$ and $P = V^2/R$, can be derived from Ohm's Law.

The final parameter of importance is electrical *energy*. Energy is simply the product of power and the length of time that the power is being consumed. Electrical energy is measured in watt-hours or kilowatt-hours (1000 watt-hours equals 1 kilowatt-hour equals 1 KWH). For example, a 100-watt bulb burning for 5 hours uses 500 watt-hours or 0.5 KWH of energy. A typical house in the United States consumes about 550 KWH per month; hopefully you will be designing your system to supply much less than this.

And that's about it! With this small amount of theory we can go a long way, so let's get started.

Resistance Losses in the Wire

Let us illustrate the relationships from the last section by considering an often overlooked, but important, aspect of electrical design—the losses in the wires which connect a power source (e.g., a battery) to the load. We will see the advantages of using high-voltage sources, heavy connecting wires, and short distances between source and load.

Example: Calculate the current in the circuit of Figure 3.1 when the battery voltage is 12 volts and the load is receiving 120 watts of power. Compare the current to that which would result if the same amount of power, 120 watts, is being delivered from a 120-volt battery.

Solution: For a 12-volt battery:

$$I = \frac{P}{V} = \frac{120 \; watts}{12 \; volts} = 10 \; amps$$

In the case of a 120-volt battery:

$$\frac{120 \; watts}{120 \; volts} = 1 \; amp$$

Now, compare the losses which would be encountered in the connecting wires in each of the two above cases. The wires have some resistance to them, call it R_w. Then the power lost in the wires, which is given by $P_w = I^2 R_w$, will be 100 times as much in a circuit with I equaling 10 amps as in one carrying only 1 amp! By raising the system voltage by a factor of 10, from 12 volts to 120 volts, losses in the connecting wires have been decreased by a factor of 100. In other words, the higher the system voltage, the lower the line losses. This is why electric companies, which must transmit power over hundreds or thousands of miles, raise their voltages on the transmission lines as high as they possibly can—some lines today carry 756,000 volts and lines are under development that will carry two million volts! And this is why, in your home electrical system, 120 volts is recommended over a 12-volt system, especially if you intend to supply a fair amount of power.

How much resistance is there in the connecting wire? That depends on the length of the wire, the diameter of the wire, and whether the wire is made of copper or aluminum. Wires are specified by their *gauge*—the smaller the gauge (or wire number), then the bigger its diameter and, consequently, the lower its resistance. House wiring is usually No. 12 or No. 14, about the same size as the lead in an ordinary pencil. To connect your windmill to your house, you may end up having to use very heavy, very expensive wire, such as No. 0 or No. 00 (sometimes written as 1/0 or 2/0), with a diameter of around one-third of an inch. Table 3.1 gives some values of wire resistance, in ohms per 100 feet, for various gauges of copper and aluminum. Copper is standard and preferred, though aluminum is sometimes substituted because it is cheaper. Also given is the maximum allowable current for

copper for the most common types of insulation, Types T, TW, RH, RHW, and THW. The most common wire in use is Type T, though Type RHW is often used for heavy currents. You must not use wire that is too small; it can overheat, damage its insulation, and perhaps even cause a fire. Moreover, wire that is too small will cause you to lose voltage in the wire so less power will be delivered to the load. To calculate the maximum voltage drop in the wire, you need to know the wire gauge, the length of the wire, and the maximum current that it will carry.

Table 3.1   Characterisitcs of Wire

Wire Gauge A.W.G.	Diameter (inches)	Resistance (ohms per 100 ft at 68°F) Copper	Resistance (ohms per 100 ft at 68°F) Aluminum	Max Current Types T,TW Copper (amps)	Max Current Types RH,RHW THW Copper (amps)
000	0.4096	0.0062	0.0101	195	200
00	0.3648	0.0078	0.0128	165	175
0	0.3249	0.0098	0.0161	125	150
2	0.2576	0.0156	0.0256	95	115
4	0.2043	0.0249	0.0408	70	85
6	0.1620	0.0395	0.0648	55	65
8	0.1285	0.0628	0.103	40	45
10	0.1019	0.0999	0.164	30	30
12	0.0808	0.1588	0.261	20	20
14	0.0641	0.2525	0.414	15	15

Example: Suppose our voltage source (battery or generator) is delivering 20 amps through No. 12 copper wire to a load 100 feet away. Calculate the voltage drop in the wire.

Solution: From Table 3.1, No. 12 copper wire has a resistance of 0.159 ohms per 100 feet. Since the load is 100 feet away from the source, there must be 200 feet of wire (to the load and back) with a total resistance of

$$R_w = 2 \times 0.159 = 0.32 \; ohms$$

The voltage drop in the wire is therefore

$$V_w = IR_w = 20 \; amps \times 0.32 \; ohms = 6.4 \; volts$$

If our voltage source in this example were 120 volts, then we would be losing about 5 percent of the voltage in the wires (leaving 113.6 volts for the load)—quite a bit of loss, but perhaps acceptable. If the source were only 12 volts, then more than half would be lost in the wires—clearly unacceptable!

As an aid to choosing the proper wire gauge, we have prepared Figure 3.2, based on allowing a 4 percent voltage drop in the connecting wires (electricians customarily shoot for a 2 percent drop, but we'll ease up a little here). A 4 percent voltage drop in a 120-volt system is about 5 volts; in the 12-volt system it is about half a volt. In either case, the load will receive about 8 percent less power than it would if it were located right next to the source. Figure 3.2 gives the maximum distance between source and load, for varying wire gauges, which keeps the wire voltage drop under 4 percent. The vertical axis on the left gives distances for a 120-volt system, and the axis on the right gives it for a 12-volt system. If you want to allow some other voltage drop you can still use this graph—for example, if you want only a 2 percent voltage drop, multiply the distances on the graph by 0.5; for a 6 percent drop, multiply distance by 1.5.

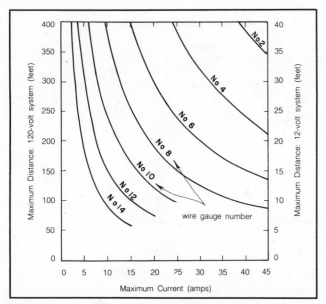

Figure 3.2 Maximum distance from voltage source to load for 4 percent voltage drop in connecting wires; for 12-volt and 120-volt systems using copper wire (see also Table 3.7).

Example: Choose the right wire to allow 20 amps to be delivered to a load 100 feet away from a 120-volt source, allowing a 4 percent voltage drop.

Solution: From Figure 3.2 at 20 amps, we see that No. 12 wire is good only to about 80 feet, but that No. 10 can go to 120 feet. So choose No. 10 wire.

Calculating Your Energy Requirements

The "design" of a small-scale electrical generation system is going to be a matter of matching your needs and your money supply to equipment (which you may be able to build, but which you are likely to have to buy). When you plugged into your giant utility company, you never had to worry about overloading their generators when you turned on an appliance. The home systems we are talking about here are different. If you want to spend lots of money, you can set yourself up with a system able to meet all conceivable demands. If you want to get by, spending as little as possible, you must have a clear idea just what your energy demands are likely to be, so that

you can pick the cheapest system to meet those needs adequately. It would be extravagant to install a system that can supply 600 KWH per month if you are only going to use 100 KWH. And it would be frustrating to spend a lot of money on a system that is too small, so that your ice cream keeps melting in the refrigerator.

This section, then, is on estimating how much electric energy you may need. We will then turn to choosing an appropriate wind, water, or photovoltaic system to meet those needs.

The place to start your demand estimate is with some old utility bills. They will tell you, month by month, how many kilowatt-hours you presently consume. Examine at least one full year's worth of bills since demands vary considerably with the seasons. Unless you have an air conditioner, summer demands are probably much lower than winter demands, as suggested in Figure 3.3. If your present lifestyle is comparable to that for which you are designing, then you have taken a big step towards a realistic estimate. If you don't have a year's worth of old bills lying around, phone your utility company and they will supply you with the required information from their records. But be prepared to cut a lot of waste out of your consumption. For example, on the first pass you may decide you want about 300 KWH per month to be supplied by a wind-powered system—but when you discover that wind systems cost about $3000 per 100 KWH, you may just back off a bit and start thinking small.

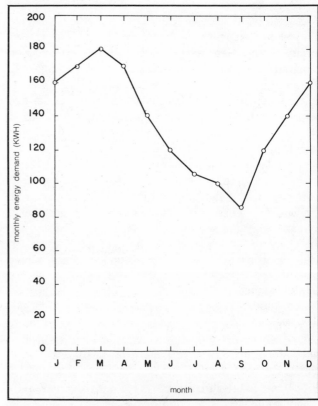

Figure 3.3 A sample of monthly electrical energy demands (summer demand is usually lower than winter).

The second approach to figuring your monthly energy demand is to calculate it from the energy demands of each appliance. Table 3.2 lists typical power requirements for a number of electrical appliances. To figure energy demand for an appliance, you must estimate the number of hours the appliance is used in a month and multiply that by the number of watts that the appliance

equals watt-hours. But there are some refinements which we can make to this procedure. First, the wattage figures given in Table 3.2 are averages; when at all possible, you should use the actual ratings that are given on your own appliances. There is usually a nameplate somewhere with the power consumption stamped right on it. Sometimes, instead of giving the watts required, the nameplate

Table 3.2 Approximate Monthly KWH Consumption of Household Appliances Under Normal Usage

Household Appliance	Rated Watts	Monthly KWH	Household Appliance	Rated Watts	Monthly KWH
Air conditioner (window)	1300	105	Oil burner or stoker	260	31
Blanket, electric	170	12	Radio	80	7
Broiler	1375	8	Radio-phonograph	105	9
Clock	2	1.5	Range	11,720	102
Clothes dryer	4800	80	Roaster	1345	17
Coffee maker	850	8	Refrigerator (12 ft^3)	235	58
Cooker (egg)	500	1	Refrigerator-freezer (15 ft^3)	330	70
Deep fat fryer	1380	6	Refrigerator-freezer (frostless, 15 ft^3)	425	135
Dehumidifier	240	32	Sewing machine	75	1
Dishwasher	1190	28	Shaver	15	0.1
Electrostatic cleaner	60	22	Sun lamp	290	1
Fan (attic)	375	26	Television (black and white, solid state)	75	9
Fan (circulating)	85	3	Television (color, solid state)	115	14
Fan (furnace)	270	30	Toaster	1100	3
Fan (roll-about)	205	9	Vacuum cleaner	540	3
Fan (window)	190	12	Waffle iron	1080	2
Floor polisher	315	1	Washing machine (automatic)	375	5.5
Food blender	290	1	Washing machine (nonautomatic)	280	4
Food freezer (18 ft^3)	300	130	Waterbed heater	300	100
Food mixer	125	1	Water heater (standard)	3000	450
Food waste disposer	420	2	Water heater (quick recovery)	4500	480
Fruit juicer	100	0.5	Water pump	335	17
Frying pan	1170	16			
Germicidal lamp	20	11	**In the Shop**	**Motor Size (horsepower)**	**Rated Watts**
Grill (sandwich)	1050	2.5			
Hair dryer	300	0.5	Bandsaw	0.50	660
Heat lamp (infrared)	250	1	Drill (portable, ⅜")	0.20	264
Heat pump	9600	—	(press)	0.50	660
Heater (radiant)	1300	13	Lathe (12-inch)	0.33	660
Heating pad	60	1	Router	0.75	720
Hot plate	1250	8	Sander (orbital)	0.20	300
Humidifier	70	12	(polisher)	1.50	1080
Incinerator	605	55	Saw (circular)	1.66	1080
Iron (hand)	1050	11	(saber)	0.25	288
Iron (mangle)	1525	13	(table)	1.60	950

draws during operation. For example, if you play a radio (80 watts) an average of 1 hour per day, then during a month's time (30 days) it would consume 30 times 80 watt-hours or about 2.4 KWH. If you do this calculation for each appliance and add up the results, you can come up with the needed figure.

As an example of how the procedure goes, consider Table 3.3, modeled for a quite modest home. Some of the big users of electricity—electric stove, water heater, or space heater—are not on this list since their energy should come from other sources (the sun or methane gas perhaps). The total of 142 KWH per month works out to about 5 KWH per day, which is about one-fourth of the American average.

So, this is the basic procedure—watts times hours

will give the current drawn; for example, "2A" would mean 2 amps. To get power, multiply that current by 115 volts (e.g., 2 amps × 115 volts = 230 watts). Another source of power ratings for appliances not in our list are department store catalogs such as the one Sears distributes.

You can also use your home's watt–hour meter to measure the actual power consumption of any given appliance. The horizontal disk in your meter rotates at a speed which is proportional to power consumption. If you look at the meter face (see Figure 3.4) you will see a calibration factor K_h that is equal to the watt–hours of energy consumed per revolution of the disk. So by timing the rate at which the disk turns and using the K_h factor you can determine the power consumption.

Table 3.3   Example of Monthly Energy Demand Calculation

Appliance	Power (watts)	Usage (hours/month)	Energy (KWH/month)
Clock	2	720	1.4
Refrigerator-Freezer	330	—	70
Sewing machine	75	15	1.1
Radio-phonograph	105	60	6.3
Television	115	90	10.4
Toaster	1100	5	5.5
Washing machine	375	2	0.8
Table saw	950	5	4.8
Lights (5 at 60-watt)	300	140	42.0

Total: 142 KWH/month

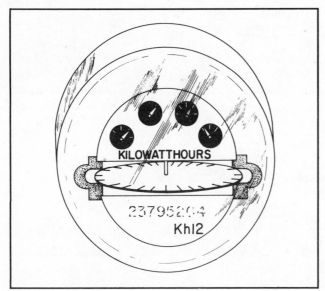

Figure 3.4   The Factor Kh on a watt-hour meter equals watt-hours per revolution of the disc.

Try it. Turn off all your lights and unplug all your appliances so that your meter completely stops. Then turn on several lights with known power demand, say four 100–watt light bulbs, and with a watch measure the number of revolutions per minute (*N*). See if it checks out with this formula:

E. 3.3

$$P(\text{watts}) = N\left(\frac{\text{rev}}{\text{min}}\right) \times K_h\left(\frac{\text{watt-hr}}{\text{rev}}\right) \times 60\left(\frac{\text{min}}{\text{hr}}\right)$$

With that reassurance you can go ahead and measure the power consumption of any other electrical device in your home. It is important to go through the extra step of comparing a fairly well known load like a lightbulb against the formula because for buildings with large power demands the meter sometimes records only a fixed fraction of the total power consumption. In those cases you need to multiply K_h by a "transformer factor" to get actual power consumed. This shouldn't be the case for a single-family residence, so for most of us Equation 3.3 is fine.

Example: With all other appliances off, and just a table saw running, we time the electric meter and find it takes 7½ seconds per revolution of the disk. The meter says K_h is 2. What power is being consumed?

Solution: Using Equation 3.3

$$P\text{ (watts)} = \frac{1}{7.5}\frac{\text{rev}}{\text{sec}} \times 60\frac{\text{sec}}{\text{min}} \times 2\frac{\text{watt-hr}}{\text{rev}} \times 60\frac{\text{min}}{\text{hr}}$$
$$= 960 \text{ watts}$$

Measuring watts and multiplying by our estimates of how many hours a month the appliance is used is fine for appliances that consume power when we turn them on and stop when we turn them off. Thermostatically controlled appliances, such as a refrigerator, are another matter. A refrigerator is turned on all the time but the compressor motor only runs some fraction of the time, so knowing its power rating alone does not let us calculate the energy consumed. As you can see from the sample calculation in Table 3.3, the refrigerator is liable to be the biggest single user of electricity in the house, which makes it particularly unfortunate to have to rely on a single "average" value given in a table. Energy consumption in refrigerators varies considerably, from brand to brand and model to model, and you may have a refrigerator that uses a lot more or a lot less than is given in the table. In 1961, the average refrigerator in the United States consumed about 70 KWH per month; but, by 1969, with increased size and such new gadgets as automatic temperature control, automatic ice-cube makers, and automatic defrosting, the average had increased more than 50 percent to about 110 KWH per month.

Most refrigerators today use quite a bit more than that—some use nearly 250 KWH per month—but the trend is reversing and there are now available a number of quite efficient 17-cubic-foot refrigerator-freezers that use less than 100 KWH per month.

A good source of energy consumption data for nearly 1000 different models of refrigerators and freezers is the annual "Directory of Certified Refrigerator/Freezers" of the Association of Home Appliance Manufacturers (AHAM), available for $1 from AHAM, 20 N. Wacker Dr., Chicago, Illinois 60606. And, at last, such energy data are finally being required on appliances as part of the Department of Commerce's Energy Labeling Program.

You can, of course, measure the energy consumption of your refrigerator by simply unplugging all of your home's appliances except for the refrigerator for say a 24-hour period and use the indicator dials on your electricity meter to measure the daily KWH used.

Since the refrigerator may dominate your electric energy consumption estimates, you may want to consider one powered by liquid propane (LP) gas instead. Such refrigerators have been used for years and are common now in the recreational vehicle industry. Not only can a gas refrigerator cut your electric *energy* demands but it can also save you money by reducing your peak *power* requirement. This is especially important if you are using an inverter to convert dc from a battery set to ac for the refrigerator. At $1 to $2 per watt of inverter capacity, the 2000 watts or so of start-up power that the refrigerator compressor motor demands may cost you several thousand extra dollars in electronic equipment.

We can further refine our demand calculations by estimating their variation from month to month, or at least from season to season. This will be necessary in order to see how well matched our monthly supply (wind, sun, stream flow) is to our load. If you're lucky, months with higher demands (winter, probably) will correspond to months with higher supplies (storm winds?).

Unless you are relying on the utility for backup power, you may need to separate your demands into "essential" and "convenience" categories. You may want to design your main electrical supply system to always meet the essential portion of demand and to meet the convenience portion whenever conditions are reasonably good. During those periods when the main system can't supply all of the convenience load, you can either do without or you can switch to a small auxiliary back-up unit to supply the power. Using this approach, you can get by with the smallest expenditure of money and still have a very reliable system. Later, when we work through some designs for a wind system, you'll see how to handle this calculation.

Finally—we'll mention it here and discuss it later when we look at inverters—you may have to identify separately those appliances which *can* run on dc or be modified to run on dc from those that *must* be supplied with ac. If your energy storage mechanism is batteries and batteries supply dc only, any appliance requiring ac will require a special piece of equipment called a dc-to-ac inverter. These inverters take power themselves, so we must raise our estimate of energy required by any ac appliances anywhere from 10 to 70 percent to include losses in the inverter. Consequently, to minimize energy requirements, you may want to run as much on dc as you can. But, don't worry about this factor yet; wait until we get to inverters.

That sums up the technique for calculating energy demand. You will probably run through the calculation several times as you balance apparent needs with what is available and what you can afford.

One final step remains: to estimate the maximum power to be drawn at any one time. We need this figure to pick our wire size and also as a check on the maximum current drain from the batteries. Furthermore, the same technique will be used for picking the proper inverter. It is simple—just look through your list of appliances and estimate the total number of gadgets liable to be turned on at the same time. For example, suppose that it is evening and the TV is on (115 watts); five 60-watt light bulbs are burning (300 watts); the refrigerator is on (330 watts); the blender is blending (290 watts); and someone starts using the table saw in the shop (950 watts). The total power demand will be

$$P_{max} = 115 + 300 + 330 + 290 + 950 = 1985 \ watts$$

If we have a 120-volt system, the maximum current will be

$$I_{max} = \frac{P_{max}}{V} = \frac{1985 \ watts}{120 \ volts} = 16.5 \ amps$$

From Table 3.1 we see that No. 14 wire carries a maximum current of 15 amps, but No. 12 will carry 20; choose No. 12 wire. Checking Figure 3.2, we see that No. 12 wire will allow the source and load to be about 80 feet apart and still lose less than 4 percent of the voltage in the wires.

Notice that a 12-volt system would be entirely impractical for this much power. The wire would have to carry 165 amps, so you'd probably need to use No. 3/0 wire, which is 0.4 inches in diameter—imagine wiring your house with that!

Electricity From the Wind

Humankind has been utilizing the energy in the winds for thousands of years, to propel sailboats, grind grain, and pump water; and, perhaps surprisingly, we have been using it intermittently for the generation of electricity for over seventy-five years. During the 1930s and 1940s, hundreds of thousands of small-capacity wind-electric systems were successfully used on farms and homesteads in the United States, before the spread of the rural electrification program in the early 1950s. In 1941 one of the largest wind-powered systems ever built went into operation at Grandpa's Knob in Vermont. Designed to produce 1250 kilowatts of electricity from a 175-foot-diameter, two-bladed prop, the unit had withstood winds as high as 115 miles an hour before it catastrophically failed in 1945 in a 25-mph wind (one of its 8-ton blades broke loose and was hurled 750 feet away).

The ease and cheapness with which electricity could be generated using fossil fuels caused interest in wind-electric systems to decline; it has only been in the last few years that interest has revived—for use in both small-scale home systems and large central utilities. When the first edition of this book was written only a few wind-electric systems were on the market, but by the beginning of 1980 there were at least two dozen manufacturers of small systems. In addition the government and utilities have become interested and machines with rotors as large as 300 feet in diameter, capable of generating as much as 3 megawatts each, are now operating. Wind farms consisting of hundreds of such units will soon be feeding the utility grids with electricity that will be as cheap as can presently be obtained from fossil and nuclear plants.

Our interest here, however, is in small systems capable of supplying a modest amount of electricity, to one house or maybe a small cluster of houses. Before we get into details, let us state some general conclusions. First, it is quite unlikely that you are going to be able to generate electricity at a cost that is competitive with the *current* price of utility-generated electricity. Even in areas with quite high windspeeds, even if you install the system yourself, and even if you include state and federal income tax credits, you will be lucky to generate electricity for less than about 10 to 15 cents per KWH. Compared to electricity which, across the United States, ranges from about 3 to 10 cents per KWH, on the surface it would appear that the economics are something less than spectacular.

If, however, you are willing to include in your calculation the likelihood of substantial increases in future electricity costs, a wind-electric system in many circumstances may represent a sound economic investment.

For example if you want to provide electricity to a rural site presently without it and your choice is between a wind-electric system, a fossil-fueled engine-generator set, or getting the power company to bring in several thousand feet of wire and poles (at roughly $5000 to $10,000 per mile), then the wind generator will not only be the most ecologically gentle system, but it will probably also be the most economical. As a rough rule of thumb, if wind speeds average at least 10 miles per hour, and power lines are at least a half mile away, then wind-electric systems are economically sensible alternatives.

What about homebuilt versus off-the-shelf component systems? Homebuilt systems are reasonably cheap and provide a great deal of invaluable practical experience. They teach you to appreciate the "features" in a commercial system, but they take a great deal of time to build, are not nearly as reliable, and won't last as long as commercial units. They also provide only a very limited amount of electricity per month. If you want to provide only enough energy to run a few lights and maybe a stereo or TV a few hours a day, a homemade system assembled out of quite readily available parts (automobile alternators, telephone pole towers, hand-crafted propellers, etc.) can be sufficient. You may be able to generate 20 to 30 KWH per month for a total system cost of under $1000.

To go into sufficient detail to enable you actually to build such a system takes more space than we have available here; such plans are quite readily available elsewhere (see Bibliography). We will, however, be sketching out most of the considerations that are involved in planning small homebuilt units.

If you add a refrigerator to your load, along with a few lights and some entertainment equipment, then you are out of the do-it-yourself category and into the commercial products market. We'll present later a summary of precisely what's available, along with approximate costs.

Finally, a note here about what to call these wind-electric systems. Strictly speaking, a "windmill" is a wind-powered mill used for grinding grain into flour; calling a machine which pumps water or generates electricity a "windmill" is somewhat of a misnomer. Instead, people are using more accurate, but generally clumsier, terminology: "wind-driven generator," "wind generator," "wind turbine," "wind turbine generator" (WTG), and so on, but it looks like "Wind Energy Conversion System" (WECS) is going to win out as the official term. A small system of the sort we're interested in here is then referred to as a SWECS.

Wind Energy Conversion Systems

Before we begin looking in detail at each of the components that make up a complete system capable of converting wind into electricity available at the wall outlet, let us briefly consider major system types as diagrammed in Figures 3.5 to 3.9.

Figure 3.5 illustrates a completely self-contained system for use in a remote site where utility power is not available. It includes battery storage and a standby generator to cover periods when the load demands more electricity than the wind is currently providing. The batteries provide direct current only and, while some loads can run directly on dc, many cannot and it is therefore necessary to include an *inverter*. An inverter converts dc to ac with the proper voltage and frequency to run such loads as tvs and ac motors. Since the inverter is costly and itself consumes energy, it is usually desirable to design the system to minimize the inverter size by running as many appliances as possible on dc. The house must then be wired with separate wall plugs for dc and ac.

The control box contains the necessary electronics to interface the generator with the battery bank as well as monitor the performance of the system. Included would be a *voltage regulator,* which adjusts the output of the generator so that it always supplies the proper voltage to the batteries. Without this regulation, the generator voltage would vary with the speed of the rotor and the batteries could be damaged.

Control boxes also often include provisions for dumping excess power into a resistance load (such as an electric water heater) once the batteries become fully charged so that the energy is not wasted. Finally, to prevent excessive discharge of the batteries, the control box

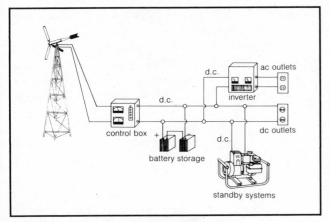

Figure 3.5 Self contained wind-electric system.

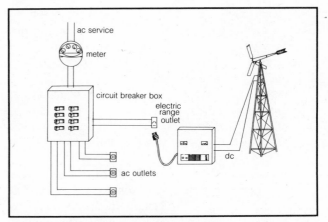

Figure 3.7 For single phase loads of less than 40 amps the Gemini synchronous inverter can simply be plugged into an electric range outlet.

should either disconnect the load or automatically start the auxiliary when battery voltage drops to a preset level.

Figure 3.6 illustrates a much simpler system which can be used when utility electricity is available to supplement the wind system. Notice that the batteries, standby system, and inverter are replaced by what is called a *synchronous inverter* and, moreover, that the need for separate ac and dc wiring systems within the house is eliminated (write to Windworks Inc., Rt. 3, Box 44A, Mukwonago, Wisconsin 53149 for further information). These are significant simplifications that greatly reduce the total cost of the system and make even city systems economically feasible. The synchronous inverter converts dc power from the WECS into ac and feeds as much power as is needed at that time to the load. Any excess power gets fed back into the utility grid giving you a KWH credit; any deficit power is made up by the utility. In essence you are using the grid for your energy storage and auxiliary backup.

the inverter automatically shuts down thereby ensuring that your WECS will not energize utility power lines during a power outage. While this feature is essential for safety when lines may be down or under repair, it also leaves you without any electricity during a utility outage.

With at least one synchronous inverter, the Sine-Sync (Real Gas and Electric, P.O. Box F, Santa Rosa, California 95402), it is possible to combine the features of battery storage and utility backup as shown in Figure 3.8. The advantage here is that during utility outages the synchronous inverter acts like a conventional inverter and generates ac power from the dc battery storage bank so you are not left without electricity. Finally, another advantage occurs if you are billed by the utility according to the time of day that you utilize their power. By locking out utility backup power during peak generating times you can avoid the high costs of peak power.

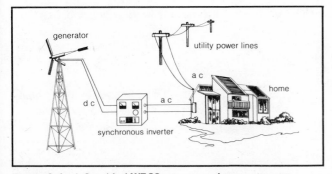

Figure 3.6 A Simplified WECS using a synchronous inverter.

The synchronous inverter can either be wired permanently to the circuit breaker box in the house or, for small systems, it can be plugged into a standard electrical range outlet as shown in Figure 3.7.

The synchronous inverter utilizes a control signal, taken from the utility lines, to establish the frequency and phase of the inverter output. Without this control input

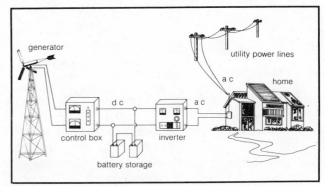

Figure 3.8 A WECS utilizing a synchronous inverter with battery storage.

Obviously any of these schemes for utilizing the utility for backup and storage requires their cooperation. They must buy your surplus electricity by law; however, they do have a right to require any safety features and power matching characteristics in the equipment that they deem necessary. A special electric rate schedule needs to

43

be applied; ratcheted watt-hour meters that separately measure energy sold to them and energy bought from them may be required. Well before you get heavily into the design of your system you should contact the utility and develop a cooperative relationship.

One way to reduce the possibility of utility interfacing difficulties is to use them only as a backup for your equipment and not as a means of energy storage. Rather than selling them excess energy you may choose to utilize it yourself in a lower priority load such as a water heater.

Figure 3.9 shows one way that this can be done. This system utilizes a modified synchronous inverter and a prioritized set of loads. The first priority load would typically consist of lights and appliances within the home. If at any time the WECS is not supplying enough power for this first priority load, then the synchronous inverter acts in its normal fashion to draw power from the utility to make up the deficit. If, however, the windplant is generating power in excess of this demand, then instead of sending it back onto the grid, the power gets dumped into a lower priority load such as a large hot-water storage tank used in the home's solar water or space heating system. Second priority loads differ from first priority loads in that they never call on the utility for backup.

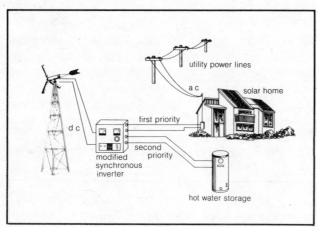

Figure 3.9 A synchronous inverter modified to send extra WECS energy to a second priority load rather than back to the utility.

Complementing an active solar water or space heating system with the excess WECS output can be an incredibly effective ploy. In clear weather the solar system heats the house, but during those stormy periods when the solar collectors are useless the wind system may be cranking out enough power to carry the house through.

This leads us to the question of just how much power is available from the wind. After we have answered that one we will be able to proceed with the process of matching components to the needs of your house.

Power in the Wind

Since it is a relatively straightforward calculation, let us sketch out the derivation of the formula for the power contained in the wind and the amount of that power that can be extracted by a WECS.

The kinetic energy (E) contained in a mass (m) of air moving at a particular velocity (v) is simply $E = \frac{1}{2}mv^2$. If we consider the mass of air passing through an area swept out by the windplant fan (A) in an amount of time (t), then $m = \rho A v t$, where ρ is the air-mass density. Since power is energy divided by time, the final expression for the power (P) contained in the wind is

$$\textbf{E. 3.4} \qquad P = \frac{\rho A v^3}{2}$$

Notice the power goes up as the *cube* of the wind speed, so that doubling the wind speed results in *eight* times the available power! Thus if some cross-sectional area of wind contains 10 watts at 5 mph, then it contains 80 watts at 10 mph; 640 watts at 20 mph; and 5120 watts at 40 mph. Or, another way to look at it is that one hour of wind at say 20 mph has the energy equivalent of 8 hours of wind at 10 mph or 64 hours of wind at 5 mph. A one-hour shot of 20 mph wind thus has more energy than over two-and-one-half days of 5 mph wind!

In order to evaluate this equation we'll need to know something about the density of air, ρ. At sea level and 60°F the density, call it ρ_o, is 0.00237 slugs per cubic foot (or 0.0763 pounds per cubic foot or 1.22 kilograms per cubic meter). Letting K_A represent an altitude correction, and K_T a temperature correction, we can write

$$\textbf{E. 3.5} \qquad \rho = \rho_o K_A K_T$$

Table 3.4 summarizes these factors. Notice the importance of the altitude correction factors. For example, the power in a given cross-sectional area of wind at 7500 feet is only about three-quarters the power at ground level, which will reduce the output from your wind machine considerably. On the other hand, the temperature corrections are more modest, affecting the answer by maybe 10 percent one way or another as we stray from the 60°F norm.

So far we have only dealt with the power in the wind. How much of that power can we actually convert to electricity? If we let e represent that conversion efficiency we can write the following equation for electrical power generated:

$$\textbf{E. 3.6} \qquad P_{gen} = \frac{1}{2}e\rho A v^3 = \frac{1}{2}e\rho_o K_A K_T A v^3$$

Plugging in a convenient but mixed set of units, if we let A be expressed in square feet, v in mph, and P_{gen} in watts, our equation reduces to

$$\textbf{E. 3.7} \qquad P_{gen} = 0.005 e K_A K_T A v^3$$

Or for a horizontal axis wind machine with prop diameter

Table 3.4 Air Density Correction Factors[a]

Altitude (ft)	0	2500	5000	7500	10,000
K_A	1	0.912	0.832	0.756	0.687

Temperature (°F)	0	20	40	60	80	100
K_T	1.130	1.083	1.040	1.00	0.963	0.929

Notes: a. After Park. Wind Power for Farms, Homes and Small Industry.

D, in feet, equation 3.8 becomes

E. 3.8 $P_{gen} = 0.004eK_AK_TD^2v^3$

Notice that power generated goes up as the square of the prop diameter, so doubling the diameter quadruples the output.

Example: For a wind machine with a 13.6-foot diameter prop and an overall efficiency of 25 percent, estimate the electrical power generated at 7500 feet and 20°F if the wind speed is 22 mph.

Solution: Using altitude and temperature correction factors from Table 3.4 in equation 3.8 results in

$P_{gen} = 0.004 \times 0.25 \times 0.756 \times 1.083 \times (13.6)^2 \times (22)^3$
$P_{gen} = 1612$ watts

It is possible to show that the maximum efficiency that any windmill can have is $e = 0.593$ or 59.3 percent, and that this occurs when the wind speed is slowed by two-thirds as it passes through the blades. Actual windmills, of course, have much lower efficiencies than this maximum. A well-designed rotor, for example, will extract about 70 percent of the theoretical maximum wind power. Furthermore, some power is lost in the gearing, which is about 90 percent efficient. And then the generator itself may be only 80 percent efficient (and that's a pretty good one). Since efficiencies are multiplicative, we can say as a reasonable estimate that wind generators are at best only about 30 percent efficient ($e = 0.593 \times 0.7 \times 0.9 \times 0.8 = 0.3$) in converting wind power to electrical power. Or, stated another way, windplants have efficiencies of about 50 percent of their theoretical maximum ($0.7 \times 0.9 \times 0.8 = 0.5$). Both of these ways of expressing efficiencies are commonly used, so it is important to know whether it is the percent of total wind power or of the theoretical maximum that is being referred to.

Making the assumption of a system efficiency, e, equal to 30 percent, we have plotted power generated for various rotor diameters in Figure 3.10. Notice the rapid increase in power output at the higher wind speeds and also note how little power is lost if a system simply "throws away" winds under about 8 mph (which most do).

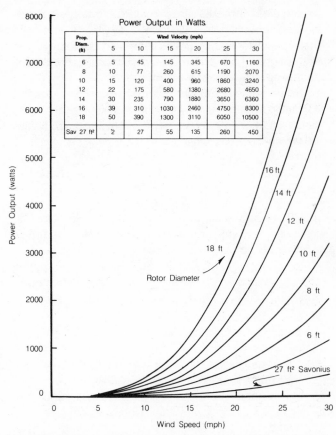

Power Output in Watts

Prop. Diam. (ft)	Wind Velocity (mph)					
	5	10	15	20	25	30
6	5	45	145	345	670	1160
8	10	77	260	615	1190	2070
10	15	120	400	960	1860	3240
12	22	175	580	1380	2680	4650
14	30	235	790	1880	3650	6360
16	39	310	1030	2460	4750	8300
18	50	390	1300	3110	6050	10500
Sav 27 ft²	2	27	55	135	260	450

Savonius based on efficiency of 20% of the theoretical maximum (overall efficiency 12%); prop based on efficiency of 50% theoretical max (overall 30%).

Figure 3.10 Power output for various wind speeds and motor diameters assuming efficiency of 50% of theoretical maximum. Also included is a 27-square-foot, 20% efficient Savonius rotor.

Example: The Whirlwind "Model-A" wind-driven generator has a 10-foot diameter prop and is rated at 2000 watts in a 25-mph wind at sea level and 60°F. What is the system efficiency, e, under those conditions? If e holds constant for other wind speeds, estimate the power this machine would produce in a 10-mph wind at 7500 feet with the temperature at 20°F.

Solution: Solving equation 3.8 for the efficiency, e, gives us

$$e = \frac{P_{gen}}{0.004K_AK_TD^2v^3}$$
$$e = \frac{2000}{0.004 \times 1 \times 1 \times 10^2 \times 25^3} = 0.32 = 32\%$$

Assuming this efficiency holds, we estimate the output under the new conditions to be

$P_{gen} = 0.004eK_AK_TD^2v^3$
$\quad\quad = 0.004 \times 0.32 \times 0.756 \times 1.083 \times 10^2 \times 10^3$
$\quad\quad = 105$ watts

Since wind generators are so responsive to higher

45

wind speeds, it makes sense to try to locate the plant in the best possible winds. One way is to place it on top of a tall tower, since wind speeds increase with altitude. The amount of increase is, of course, dependent on conditions at your own site; but to give you some idea of how much might be gained, *Standard Handbook for Mechanical Engineers* (Baumeister) gives the following relationship for the variation in wind velocity (v), with increasing height (H) on an unobstructed plain:

E. 3.9 $$\frac{v}{v_o} = \left(\frac{H}{H_o}\right)^n$$

v_o is the velocity at some reference height H_o, and n is an exponent that varies with wind speeds, but for our range of interest (5 to 35 mph) can be taken to be 0.2.

Since power varies as the cube of velocity, we can rewrite the above as a power ratio, where P is the power at height H and P_o is the power at height H_o:

E. 3.10 $$\frac{P}{P_o} = \left(\frac{H}{H_o}\right)^{3n}$$

Without a pocket calculator it is tricky to work with fractional exponents, so we have plotted this last equation in Figure 3.11, using a reference height of 5 feet. The figure indicates, for example, that there is about 3 times the wind power at 30 feet than there is at 5 feet, even though the wind speed is only about 1.4 times as great. Notice that we can use this graph to help estimate the marginal gain which might be obtained in going from one height to another.

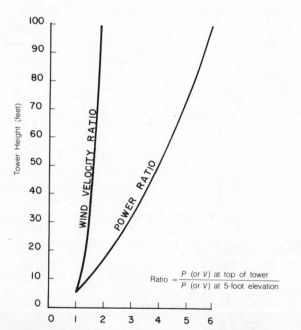

Figure 3.11 Increase in wind velocity and power with increasing height (unobstructed plain, referenced to 5-foot height).

46

Example: Use Figure 3.11 to estimate the increase in power which might be expected by increasing tower height from 30 feet to 80 feet.

Solution: At 80 feet there is about 5.3 times the power as at 5 feet; at 30 feet there is 3 times the power. Hence by going from 30 feet to 80 feet we gain by a factor of about $\frac{5.3}{3}$, or about 1.8.

Now for a warning and some trade-offs. The warning is that our formula is approximate and holds for an *unobstructed plain* only. Your site may be hilly and have bushes, trees, and buildings scattered around. So, before designing around this height bonus factor, you should make confirming wind-speed measurements at various heights on your own site.

The trade-offs are the increased cost of taller towers and increased losses in the connecting wires. The latter is less important and can be compensated for by using heavier (more expensive) wire. But towers are quite expensive, running somewhere around $20 per foot for a typical guyed tower in the 30- to 80-foot range (1980 prices).

Energy from the Wind

Now that we know how to estimate the *power* (watts) that a wind-driven generator will deliver at any given wind speed, we can move on to techniques for estimating the amount of *energy* (watt-hours) that a system will deliver each month. We have already learned how to calculate our monthly energy requirements, and now we'll learn how to use local wind information to match a wind-driven generator to those requirements. This section of the chapter presents the real heart of the wind-driven generator design procedure. We are going to take a bit of a zigzag route but, by the end of this section, we'll have a simple technique.

You're going to need to know *something* about the winds at your chosen site, but precisely what information do you need and how can it be obtained? Skipping over the last half of the question for the moment, let us look first at the kind of data that would be the most useful. What you would like to have is a month-by-month indication of how many hours the wind blows at each wind speed. If you had this data, you could calculate the power output (watts) at each wind speed, multiply this figure by the number of hours the wind blows at that speed, and then sum up the watt-hours from all the winds. This would give the monthly energy that could be supplied.

This kind of data is routinely accumulated at meteorological stations all across the country and is usually summarized in either table or graph form. An example is given in Figure 3.12, based on a 5-year average for Januaries in Minneapolis. The graph may be a bit tricky to interpret if you're not used to statistics; it says, for example, that the wind-speed equals or exceeds 15 mph about 20 percent of the time, 10.5 mph about 50 percent of the time, and so on.

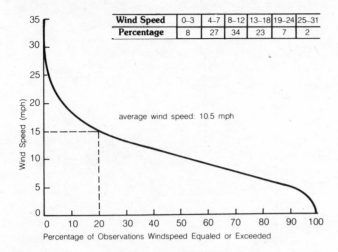

Wind Speed	0–3	4–7	8–12	13–18	19–24	25–31
Percentage	8	27	34	23	7	2

average wind speed: 10.5 mph

Figure 3.12 Wind velocity duration curve and wind-frequency table for Minneapolis in January (5-year average).

Let us calculate the amount of energy that we might get from this wind. The exercise may be a bit tedious for some, but don't worry; we are going to have a much simpler procedure a bit later on. For those that are still interested, there are some instructive points to be gained from this example.

We need to introduce two facts at this point. First, real wind-driven generators produce no output power until the wind reaches a certain minimum value called the *cut-in speed*. Below this speed the generator shaft isn't turning fast enough to produce a charging current. And second, real generators are not able to produce more power than their *rated* capacity without being damaged. The speed at which the generator produces *rated* power is called the *rated wind speed*, which we'll denote by v_R. For winds which exceed the rated speed, commercial systems are usually designed so that the rotor spills some of the wind; output power thus remains at roughly the rated capacity, preventing damage to the generator. When people talk about a 2000-watt generator, for example, they are referring to the power output at the rated wind speed (which is usually somewhere around 25 mph). Finally, for winds above the *furling wind speed*, the machine must be completely shut down to prevent damage. Figure 3.13 shows the comparison between the maximum power theoretically available and the actual power out of a typical wind system.

Example: Calculate the energy that a 6000-watt wind generator, having a cut-in speed of 8 mph and a rated speed of 25 mph, would produce in January in Minneapolis. The rotor is 18 feet in diameter.

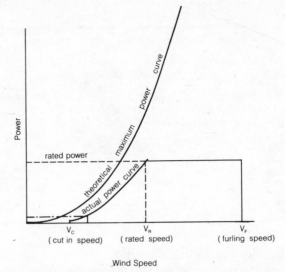

Figure 3.13 Theoretical power output from a WECS compared to actual output.

Solution: We first need to estimate the efficiency of this particular machine using Equation 3.8 at rated conditions:

$$e = \frac{6000}{0.004 \times 1 \times 1 \times (18)^2 \times (25)^3} = 0.296$$

We'll assume this efficiency holds so that we can calculate the power output at other wind speeds using Equation 3.8 (notice in this case the efficiency is close enough to the 30 percent assumed in Figure 3.10 that we could read power outputs directly from the graph).

For each of the wind speed intervals given in the table in Figure 3.12, estimate the following: (1) the number of hours the wind blows in that interval (percent observations × 720 hours per month, (2) the average wind speed in that interval, (3) the power delivered by the machine at that average speed (Equation 3.8), and finally (4) the KWH delivered from wind in that interval (power times hours). Sum the resulting KWH as has been done in Table 3.5. Notice that there is no output below cut-in and the output remains at 6 KW for winds higher than 25 mph.

So a little over 600 KWH could be expected. Not much energy has been lost by not picking up winds below 8 mph. The amount of this lost energy turns out to be only 12.8 KWH, very small in comparison to 607 KWH.

Now we could do this calculation month by month, but the drawbacks to this approach are fairly obvious: a lot of calculation is involved and everything depends on the required wind-distribution data. These data are often available from a nearby airport or weather bureau. Also, a number of years ago, the United States Department of Commerce published a series of reports called *Summary of Hourly Observations* for 112 cities across the country

47

Table 3.5 Minneapolis Wind Data (6-KW Plant)

Wind Range (mph)	% of Observations	Avg. Wind Speed (mph)	Hours per Month	Output KW (E. 3.8)	Energy (KWH)
0–3	8	1.5	57	0	0
4–7	27	5.5	195	0	0
8–12	34	10.0	245	0.4	98
13–18	23	15.5	165	1.4	230
19–24	7	21.5	50	3.9	195
25–31	2	28.0	14	6.0	84
32–38	0	35.0	0	6.0	0

Total: 607 KWH

(that's where our Minneapolis data came from), containing month-by-month wind summaries. That information may be helpful if you live near one of the chosen cities, but even then its usefulness is limited if you live on a site where wind conditions are considerably different. You might also try to get this wind data for your site by direct measurement, but it would take years to accumulate enough data to be statistically significant and the equipment required to do the job is quite expensive.

But let us regain some perspective. There is no way that we will ever be able to calculate *accurately* the amount of energy that the wind will provide. Wind is unpredictable. We're going to have to live with a great deal of uncertainty in our estimates, so it doesn't make much sense to calculate things out to the last decimal point. There is a simple way to estimate energy obtainable when only the *average* wind speed is known. It is based on the observation that wind-velocity duration curves such as the one in Figure 3.12 tend to have very similar shapes; by knowing only the *average* wind speed, the rest of the distribution is more or less predictable.

It is possible, then, to apply some fancy computerized mathematical techniques, based on wind distribution characteristics measured at many different locations, to correlate expected wind-generator energy outputs with average wind speeds.

Before we can apply this simple technique we need to introduce the notion of the windplant's *capacity factor* (*CF*). The capacity factor is the ratio of the energy delivered over a given period of time to the energy that would have been delivered if the generator were supplying rated power over the same time interval. To illustrate, our previous example predicted that a certain 6-KW machine would deliver 607 KWH over a 720-hour period in Minneapolis. Therefore its capacity factor would be

$$CF = \frac{607 \ KWH}{6KW \times 720 \ hr} = 0.14 = 14\%$$

If we had a way to predict capacity factors, energy delivered could be easily obtained with the following equation:

E. 3.11
$$energy \ delivered = \\ capacity \ factor \times rated \ power \times hours$$

Figure 3.14, based on correlations by Justus (see Bibliography) is just what we need to predict capacity factors and hence monthly energy delivered.

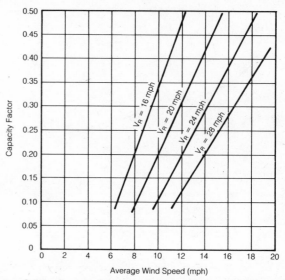

Figure 3.14 Capacity factor as a function of average windspeed for differing rated windspeeds. (Based on regression by Justus, 1978, with cut-in windspeed = 0.4 V_R).

In the figure, capacity factor is plotted against average wind speed with rated wind speed as a parameter. While the correlation assumes a cut-in wind speed of $0.4v_R$ (for example, an 8 mph cut-in for a machine rated at 20 mph), if your machine has a different cut-in speed it won't change the results significantly.

Example: Estimate the energy which a 6-KW generator, with rated wind speed of 25 mph, would supply in a month's time when the average wind speed is 10.5 mph. (This is our Minneapolis example again.)

Solution: Interpolating within Figure 3.14 for $v_R = 25$ mph, it looks like the capacity factor will be about 0.13. A 6-KW generator would therefore be expected to supply about

$$6 \ KW \times 0.13 \times 720 \ hr/mo = 562 \ KWH/mo$$

This estimate is about 11 percent lower than the 607 KWH per month calculated earlier. Such differences should further remind us that all predictions of windplant performance are going to be at best fairly crude.

Example: What size generator rated at 24 mph should be chosen to supply 200 KWH per month when average wind speeds are 12 mph? With a 30 percent efficient plant what prop diameter would be required?

Solution: From Figure 3.14, the capacity factor at 12 mph is 0.2, therefore

$$generator\ rating = \frac{200\ KWH/mo}{0.2 \times 720\ hr/mo} = 1.4\ KW$$

From Equation 3.8,

$$D = \left[\frac{1400}{0.004 \times 0.3 \times (24)^3}\right]^{\frac{1}{2}} = 9.2\ feet$$

Example: Which wind generator will deliver more energy in an area where winds average 12 mph: a 1-KW machine rated at 20 mph, or a 2.5-KW machine rated at 28 mph?

Solution: According to Figure 3.14, the 1-KW machine should deliver about

$$0.31 \times 1\ KW \times 720\ hr/mo = 223\ KWH/mo$$

while the 2.5-KW machine would deliver about

$$0.12 \times 2.5\ KW \times 720\ hr/mo = 216\ KWH/mo$$

The two machines put out approximately the same amount of energy in spite of the fact that one generator is much bigger than the other! *Don't be misled by considering only generator ratings—they must always be considered in conjunction with the rated wind speed of the whole plant in order to make any comparison valid.*

This last example points out the importance of the rated wind speed of a generator. The lower the rated wind speed, the greater will be the energy output per kilowatt of generator. So why don't manufacturers use much lower ratings? To lower the rated wind speed, a manufacturer must use a bigger (and hence more expensive) fan and must increase the gearing ratio (which also increases the cost). Also, if the average wind speed is fairly high, then a low rated speed means that much of the high-powered winds will be dumped and wasted because the generator is too small. There is, then, a problem in optimization when it comes to designing a windplant from scratch. One study indicates that, for sites with average winds around 10 mph, a low rated wind speed—around 15 to 20 mph—is best. For average wind speeds of 15 mph, it is best to use a 25-mph rating.

If you're not designing from scratch (very likely) and merely picking components, then you must simply compare windplant costs for equal monthly KWH delivered, following the technique outlined in the last example. To further assist you we have prepared Table 3.10, which lists a number of machines along with their likely KWH output for 12-mph average wind speeds.

Notice that you *cannot* estimate monthly energy merely by calculating the power out of the generator at the average wind speed and then multiplying this figure by 720 hours per month. The cubic relationship between power and wind speed makes speeds greater than the average have much more importance than speeds less than the average; such an estimating technique will give answers which are too low. There is a crude rule of thumb which suggests that energy per month is about two to two-and-one-half times the value which would be obtained by multiplying the power output at the average wind speed by the number of hours in the month.

Measuring the Wind

While month-by-month velocity duration curves for your site (averaged over several years) would provide the best information for determining what energy the wind could supply, such data are rather difficult to obtain. The required instrumentation is expensive and the time required to obtain statistically significant data is probably prohibitive. Moreover, the year-to-year variation in actual winds is enough to invalidate any precise calculations. So we may as well do something less precise, but easier.

We have seen that good energy estimates can be obtained from average wind speeds—data which are quite a bit easier to obtain. We recommend that you attempt to determine monthly average wind speeds over as many months as you can and then with the use of data from any nearby weather stations (such as airports, U.S. Weather Service stations, military installations, National Park Services, local air pollution agencies, and so on) estimate likely long-term averages for your site.

The procedure would be as follows. For each month that you measure an average wind speed find out whether the average wind speeds being recorded at the nearest official station are running above or below normal, and by how much. You adjust your measurements up or down accordingly under the assumption that if it was windier than normal at the local station it has probably been windier than normal at your site. This will enable you to crudely approximate many years' worth of measurements for a given month with only one month's worth of data.

If you can do this comparison for all 12 months of the year then you should have a reasonable data base from which to estimate likely windmill outputs. If you can only take a few months' worth of data then see if there is a correlation between your measurements and the local station's measurements. Both sets of data should be consistent with respect to each other. Maybe yours is always, say, 20 percent higher than theirs. Then you may take their long-term average wind data for the months you've missed and adjust it to your site (in this example, by raising it 20 percent). This way you get the benefit of many years' worth of measurements without having to accumulate them yourself.

By careful examination of Figure 3.14, we can see the importance of obtaining a fairly accurate estimate of average wind speeds. Very roughly, the amount of energy which can be supplied doubles for a 3-mph increase in average wind speed. The difference between a successful design and a disappointing one can therefore rest upon the difference of only a few miles per hour in our estimate.

There are several approaches to measuring wind speeds, varying from crude estimates based on the observation of physical phenomena to accurate and expensive measurement equipment. Table 3.6 gives some qualitative descriptions which may be helpful to get a feel for various wind speeds quickly.

Table 3.6 Qualitative Description of Wind Speed[a]

Wind Speed (mph)	Wind Effect
0–1	Calm; smoke rises vertically.
2–3	Direction of wind shown by smoke drift but not by wind vanes.
4–7	Wind felt on face; leaves rustle; ordinary vane moved by wind.
8–12	Leaves and twigs in constant motion; wind extends light flag.
13–18	Raises dust, loose paper; small branches are moved.
19–24	Small trees in leaf begin to sway; crested wavelets form on inland waters.
25–31	Large branches in motion; whistling heard in telegraph wires, umbrellas used with difficulty.
32–38	Whole trees in motion; inconvenience felt in walking against wind.

Notes: a. From *Standard Handbook for Mechanical Engineers* (Baumeister and Marks)

A better approach is to buy a simple hand-held wind gauge. Dwyer markets one for about $10 which is available from many boating, hobby, and scientific instrument supply houses as well as your local wind equipment distributor.

About the most you can hope to do with such simple techniques, though, is to try to train yourself to estimate wind speeds by their feel fairly accurately. Then you can call upon your previous experience at the site to help decide whether the winds are sufficiently strong to warrant further, more accurate measurements.

Fortunately, the accurate measurement of average wind speeds over a specified period of time not only yields one of the most useful pieces of information we could hope to get but it also happens to be one of the easiest measurements to make.

A rotating cup anemometer spins at a rate that is very nearly proportional to wind speed. This property not only means that we can determine instantaneous wind speeds by measuring the rpm of the cups, but more importantly the average wind speed over a given period—a month, for example—will be proportional to the total number of revolutions during that time period. So if we have a cup anemometer, attached to a counter that is calibrated to indicate miles of wind that have blown by, we merely divide the counter reading (in miles) by the number of

hours that have elapsed between readings to get the average mph over that time period. If the counter has sufficient capacity we may need to record data only once a month if monthly averages are all that is desired.

Such a device is sometimes referred to as a wind odometer or a wind data accumulator, and they are commercially available for anywhere from about $100 to $200. Several manufacturers (such as Sencenbaugh Wind Electric, P.O. Box 1174, Palo Alto, California 94306; and Natural Power, Inc., New Boston, New Hampshire 03070) will even rent you one for about $15 to $20 per month.

It is possible, however, to make one of your own with less than a day's worth of your time and a few dollars. Basically the idea is to connect the rotating cups to a counter. The counter can be a simple mechanical one capable of holding at least six digits and preferably seven, with the shaft of the rotor directly connected to the counter as shown in Figure 3.15. The disadvantage of this design is that with the anemometer mounted on a high pole it may be impossible to read the counter without taking the pole down each time.

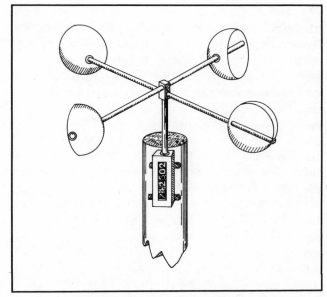

Figure 3.15 A rotating cup anemometer with mechanical counter.

It is highly desirable to be able to leave the anemometer at the proposed height of the windplant and still take data at ground level. The sketch given in Figure 3.16 will help you to build such an odometer using a cheap hand calculator modified both to count the revolutions and to display them.

The mechanical portion of the anemometer, up on the pole, is made with two foot-long $3/16$-inch-diameter brass tubes pushed through a $1\frac{1}{2}$-inch long, $7/16$-inch square brass tube, all of which is mounted on a shaft with some bearings. You can use a small model car motor, as

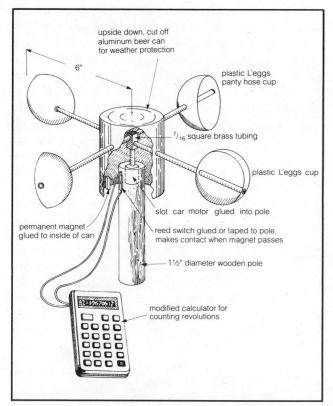

Figure 3.16 An anemometer with remote readout.

we have suggested in the figure. The motor is used only for its bearings, so find one that spins fairly easily. The tubes and motor can be obtained at most good hobby shops. The cups are readily available containers from L'eggs pantyhose. A weather-protecting shroud over the motor is made from an aluminum beer can, cut off and turned over. (Don't use a steel can or it will adversely affect the magnetic field which is used to sense rotations.)

To put this part of the anemometer together, first drill the holes in the square center tube and the aluminum can. Stagger the holes in the square tube so the cross arms pass one over the other. Push the cross arms through one side of the can, then through the square tube and out the other side of the can. Solder the tube joints and seal the can penetrations with glue. Drill holes in the cups, slide them over the arms, and glue them in place.

Turn the anemometer over and melt some solder into the square tube. Insert the shaft of the motor, being careful to obtain as accurate an alignment as possible. Stick the motor housing into a hole on the end of a 1½-inch diameter wood pole and glue it in place. The mechanical portion is now finished.

The electrical portion of the anemometer consists of a reed switch and magnet coupled to a modified hand calculator. The reed switch is glued or taped to the top of the pole within the rotating aluminum can. The magnet is glued to the inside of the can so that when it passes over the reed switch it pulls the contacts together, "mak-

ing" the circuit. With every rotation of the can the switch contacts make and break once, and what we need is a way to count these pulses.

There are electromechanical counters on the market for about $25 that could count these pulses, but such counters typically consume about 5 watts of power continuously. While that may not sound like much, it is enough to drain most car batteries in about a week's time, which would make it pretty difficult for us to make our system totally portable.

We could build up a low-power-consumption electronic circuit to count and display these pulses, but to do this, even with sophisticated integrated circuits and light-emitting diode (LED) displays, would be fairly time-consuming and expensive.

A really slick solution is to modify an inexpensive hand calculator to make it add up the counts and display the total. Some of these calculators go for only $5 to $10, which is a real bargain considering the sophisticated circuitry that you get. The modifications that you'll need to make to the calculator take only a few minutes and do not affect its continued use as a calculator. We will see that we can use the calculator not only to add the revolutions of the anemometer, but we can also automatically work in a calibration factor that lets the display read out in miles of wind directly if we want.

First, what kind of calculator can you use? You need one that has the right kind of logic. Try this on your calculator before you bust into it. Push the "1" key then the " + " key then a string of " = " signs. If every time you hit the " = " button the display adds one to the total then you've got the right kind of logic. What we're going to do is have the closing of the reed switch, in essence, push the " = " button each time the anemometer revolves.

The second factor to consider in choosing a calculator is how fast it drains its batteries. If the anemometer is to be located where you can simply plug the calculator into a socket then you needn't be concerned about battery life. In that case a calculator with either an LED display (red numbers) or a fluorescent display (green numbers) is best. These calculators can keep up with the anemometer at wind speeds of up to about 40 or 50 mph. They do draw about 0.2 to 0.3 watts, though, which means they'll run their own batteries down in only a day or so. You can buy a hefty rechargeable battery of the proper voltage and get about a month's use between charges, which is a satisfactory solution.

On the other hand a liquid-crystal display (LCD) calculator uses very little power, and its tiny batteries are usually good for anywhere from about one-and-one-half to three months' worth of constant use before needing to be replaced. For a totally portable anemometer an LCD calculator is probably the way to go. The problem with LCD calculators is that they begin to lose accuracy for wind speeds above about 25 mph. If you're in a very windy spot the anemometer will slightly underestimate the average wind speed as a result. If an LCD is your preference, be sure to get one that doesn't have an automatic power-off feature. Many do.

Having picked your calculator, you need to open it up (carefully) and peer inside. Your task is to figure out what happens in there when the equal key is pushed. If you are using an LED or fluorescent display calculator what you'll see is illustrated in Figure 3.17. The keyboard will be connected to the logic board with about 16 wires—all lined up next to each other. Set a multimeter to read ohms of resistance and with the two probes determine which pair of these 16 wires has high resistance with no keys pushed and zero resistance when the "=" key is pushed. With 16 wires there are potentially 120 pairs to test, and if it takes more than 5 minutes to find the right pair you're unlucky.

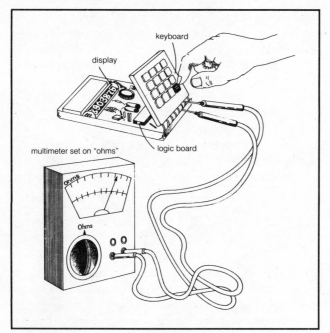

Figure 3.17 Determining which pair of wires corresponds to the "=" key.

circuit board to convenient nodes for making your solder connections. Solder your two wires, being careful to not overheat the board. Run the wires to the reed switch and you're done.

Calibration of your anemometer couldn't be easier. Put it on a pole so it extends at least three feet above your car, note the odometer reading in your car, and set the counter to zero. Now go for about a 10-mile drive varying your speed over the range of wind speeds you expect at your site. Do a lot of 10-mph driving mixed with some

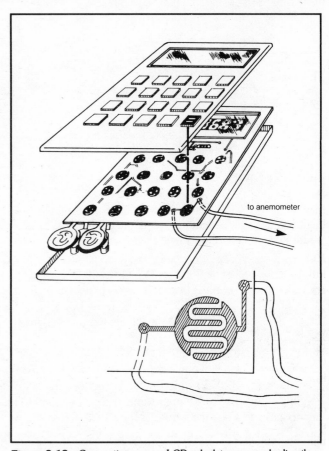

Figure 3.18 Connections on an LCD calculator are made directly to the printed circuit board.

When you think you've found the pair check it out by pushing the "1" followed by "+" and then short the pair of wires together several times to be sure it is counting. If it checks out, solder a pair of wires to the two you have found. Run the new leads out of the calculator and connect them to the reed switch. Spin the anemometer and check to see that the calculator properly totals the number of revolutions.

An LCD calculator looks a little bit different inside but is even easier to modify than the LED or fluorescent units. As shown in Figure 3.18, when a key is pushed it physically short circuits a pair of interlocking fingers on a printed circuit board. Find the interlocking fingers corresponding to the "=" key and trace their wiring on the printed

runs up to 30 or 40 mph. When you get back divide the counter reading by the miles driven, and you have your calibration factor in counts per mile.

There will be a wind speed above which your anemometer will lose accuracy due to the input-data frequency limitations associated with the calculator electronics. You could determine this upper limit by making higher and higher speed runs until the calibration factor starts to drop off.

Example: Suppose in calibrating your anemometer you record 10,000 revolutions in a 13-mile drive (these are realistic numbers by the way). What is the calibration factor? If the anemometer is set up at your site and records

100 revolutions per minute, what is the wind speed? If in a month's time it accumulates 5 million revolutions, what is the monthly average wind speed?

Solution: The calibration factor is

$$\frac{10{,}000 \; revolutions}{13 \; miles} = 770 \; revolutions/mile$$

At 100 rpm, the wind speed would be:

$$\frac{100 \; revolutions}{minute} \times \frac{mile}{770 \; revolutions} \times \frac{60 \; minutes}{hour}$$
$$= 7.8 \; mph$$

The monthly average wind speed would be:

$$\frac{5 \times 10^6 \; revolutions}{month} \times \frac{mile}{770 \; revolutions} \times \frac{month}{720 \; hours}$$
$$= 9.0 \; mph$$

If you want to be clever you can work the calibration factor directly into the calculator so that the output will be miles of wind that have past rather than a total which is just anemometer revolutions.

Example: For the above anemometer with 770 revolutions per mile calibration factor, how can we get the counter to indicate miles of wind directly?

Solution: One revolution corresponds to 0.0013 miles of wind ($1/770$). On the calculator enter 0.0013 followed by "+" followed by "–." Now each revolution will add 0.0013 to the display and the accumulated total will be in miles of wind passing the anemometer.

For most commercially available wind odometers, the counters are calibrated to indicate the number of $1/60$s of a mile that have passed. This makes it convenient to obtain current wind speed by merely measuring the number of counts per minute. For example if in one minute's time the counter adds 16 to the total then the wind speed was

$$\frac{16 \; counts}{minute} \times \frac{1 \; miles}{60 \; count} \times \frac{60 \; minutes}{hour} = 16 \; mph$$

That is, 16 counts per minute corresponds to a 16 mph wind, and so on.

Example: For our anemometer how can we get the counter to read with units of $1/60$ of a mile?

Solution: Using the calibration factor of 770 revolutions per mile we can write

$$\frac{60 \; (1/60 \; mile/mile)}{770 \; revolutions/mile} = 0.078 \left(\frac{1/60 \; mile}{revolution} \right)$$

If we enter "0.078" followed by "+" followed by "=" then every revolution will add 0.078 to the total, which is equivalent to the addition of $1/60$ of a mile of wind.

For example, if the counter total is increasing at say 12 counts per minute then the wind speed is 12 mph. If in a month's time the counter indicates say 390,000 more than it did at the beginning of the month, then the average wind speed for the month would have been

$$\frac{390{,}000 \; counts}{month} \times \frac{1 \; mile}{60 \; count} \times \frac{month}{720 \; hours} = 9.0 \; mph$$

Finally it should be mentioned that rather sophisticated commercially available wind-measurement equipment is becoming cheaper and more readily available. Natural Power, Inc. in New Hampshire, for example, markets wind-speed compilers for around $1000 that enable velocity duration curves to be prepared easily. They also manufacture a wind-energy monitor for under $500 that you program with the power versus wind speed characteristics of the wind generator you are going to use, and the output is in KWH that the windplant would have produced from your wind. Also, you can buy just the anemometer head itself from Maximum, Inc. (42 South Avenue, Natick, Mass. 01760).

When it comes time to set up the anemometer at your chosen site, we recommend using a telescoping TV mast with guy wires, turnbuckles, and ground anchors for support. Be sure to set the bottom of the mast on a flat, rigid surface with at least one square foot of area (like a board), or else the downward force of the mast will gradually push it into the earth. Figure 3.19 shows a typical installation.

Figure 3.19   Example of a mast installation.

Besides determining average wind speeds on a month-by-month basis, it is important to know something about the highest wind speeds you may encounter. Most windplants are designed to withstand winds as high as 80 mph and, if higher wind speeds are expected, there are extra-cost automatic controls which can be purchased.

Protection for winds of up to 140 mph can be provided with these devices.

Site Selection

Choosing the best site for the windplant involves a trade-off between conflicting demands: keeping it near enough to the house to minimize power loss in the connecting wires, yet placing it far enough away from such obstructions as buildings and trees to get it into the best winds. Obstructions which are higher than the windplant can disturb the wind for several hundred yards behind the obstacle and perhaps even 50 to 100 yards in front of the obstacle. The plant should therefore be located out of these disturbance zones. In hilly areas, the best spot is probably close to the top of a hill; but if this is impossible, it might be best to stay away from the hill altogether.

The plant should be located as high as possible and at least 15 to 20 feet higher than any nearby obstructions. It should not be placed on a roof; it could overstress the structure and probably will cause an unpleasant vibrational noise. Figure 3.11 indicated the advantages of tall towers; it is recommended that any tower be at least 40 feet high. At that height, winds may be 50 percent greater than at ground level and the power output may be several times as great.

These generalities cannot replace your own observations of the conditions that prevail on your land. Chances are either that your house is already built or that you will be picking your house site based on other criteria (solar exposure, privacy, etc.); if you keep the windplant within about 1000 feet of the house, then the number of good sites in that range is probably limited. You might hang ribbons or ping-pong balls on strings from poles erected at these considered sites and then watch their deflections with binoculars to see which site has the greatest winds. Since you are now only interested in relative conditions, you needn't worry about actual mile-per-hour comparisons.

The site should not be too far from the house, to avoid long line losses or the expense of very heavy wire. We have already seen how line losses can be computed once the current and wire gauge are known. Our earlier conclusion was that batteries and load should be kept as close together as possible to avoid losing too much battery voltage in the line. (In fact, the batteries should probably be located in or adjacent to the house.) We can perform the same calculations to estimate losses from the generator to the batteries. The maximum current to expect from your generator can be estimated by dividing the generator rated power by its voltage. It is then an easy matter to calculate line voltage drop (IR) and line power loss (I^2R) where R can be obtained from Table 3.1. To save you that trouble we have prepared Table 3.7, which gives line voltage and power losses for various values of current for both copper and aluminum wire. Also a *rough* estimate of wire costs has been included. Notice that aluminum wire of a given gauge number is approximately equivalent (in resistance) to copper wire two gauge numbers higher and costs roughly half as much (e.g., No. 4 aluminum costs half of what No. 6 copper costs and has the same amount of resistance). Therefore, when carrying large currents over long distances, you will probably want to use aluminum wire because it is cheaper. Let's do some examples to get a feel for these numbers.

Example: Estimate the line losses for a 6-KW generator in a 120-volt system if the generator is 1000 feet from the batteries and No. 0 copper wire is used.

Solution: Maximum current will be about

$$I_{max} = \frac{6000 \text{ watts}}{120 \text{ volts}} = 50 \text{ amps}$$

From Table 3.7 we see that, at 50 amps, line losses amount to about 10 volts (meaning the generator would have to produce 130 volts to supply 120-volt batteries) and about 500 watts (out of 6000 generated). And your wallet would lose something like $2200 just to pay for the wire! If instead we choose No. 3/0 aluminum wire, losses are the same but now the price is about $950. Spending nearly $1000 on wire and still losing nearly 10 percent of our power suggests that 1000 feet is probably about the maximum distance that you could afford to place this big machine from its load.

Table 3.7   Connecting Wire Voltage, Power Losses, and Rough Costs per 100-foot Separation between Generator and Batteries

Copper Wire No.	Copper 2-Wire $/100 ft	Aluminum Wire No.	Aluminum 2-Wire $/100 ft	Wire Voltage Drop (Volts/100 ft) I=10 amps	20A	30A	40A	50A	60A	70A	Wire Power Loss (Watts/100 ft) I=10A	20A	30A	40A	50A	60A	70A
000	360	—	—	0.12	0.24	0.38	0.5	0.62	0.74	0.86	1.2	5.0	11	20	32	44	60
00	300	0000	110	0.16	0.32	0.46	0.62	0.78	0.94	1.1	1.6	6.2	14	26	40	56	76
0	220	000	95	0.2	0.4	0.6	0.8	1.0	1.2	1.4	2.0	8.0	18	32	50	72	98
2	140	0	70	0.32	0.62	0.94	1.2	1.6	1.9	2.2	3.2	12.0	28	50	78	102	144
4	95	2	42	0.5	1.0	1.5	2.0	2.5	3.0	3.5	5.0	20.0	44	80	124	180	240
6	65	4	33	0.8	1.6	2.4	3.2	4.0	4.8	—	8.0	32.0	72	128	200	288	—
8	45	6	25	1.2	2.4	3.8	5.0	—	—	—	12.0	50.0	112	200	—	—	—
10	28	—	—	2.0	4.0	6.0	—	—	—	—	20.0	80.0	180	—	—	—	—

Example: Pick a wire size which would result in no more than a 2-volt drop from generator to battery in a 750-watt, 12-volt system. The tower is 50 feet high and is 100 feet from the batteries.

Solution: The total distance from generator to batteries is 150 feet so the drop is

$$\frac{2 \text{ volts}}{150 \text{ feet}} = 1.3 \text{ volts per 100 feet}$$

The generator voltage is 14 volts (12 + 2), so maximum current is about

$$I_{max} = \frac{750 \text{ watts}}{14 \text{ volts}} = 54 \text{ amps}$$

In the table we see that No. 0 copper wire or No. 3/0 aluminum wire has a loss of 1.2 volts per 100 feet at 60 amps; this will be satisfactory. Our example suggests that to keep a reasonable voltage drop in 12-volt systems, they need to be much closer to the load (probably not much more than 100 feet away).

Rotors

There are many kinds of rotors which can extract power from the wind. One way to classify them is whether they rotate about a vertical or horizontal axis. The two vertical-axis machines which are receiving the most attention these days—the Savonius rotor and the Darrieus rotor (Figure 3.20)—are actually rather old ideas, developed in the late 1920s. These rotors are interesting because they are always "headed into the wind"; there is no problem tracking gusty winds which constantly shift directions. Moreover, the heavy generator can be securely mounted on the ground and there is no need for slip rings to carry current from the generator to the wires connecting the load.

The Savonius, or S-rotor, rotates much slower than a modern two- or three-bladed propeller and is less than half as efficient in capturing the wind's energy. It must, therefore, be geared up considerably to match the speeds required by a generator and its cross-sectional area (to intercept the wind) must be quite large to make up for its inefficiency. The machines require a large surface area of material and so are heavy and hard to balance. Small do-it-yourself units can be made out of 55-gallon drums (see Hackleman's nice booklet in the Bibliography), but they deliver so little power that they hardly seem worthwhile. For example, a machine made from three 55-gallon drums stacked one on top of the other, having a cross-sectional area of about 27 square feet and an efficiency of about 20 percent of the theoretical maximum, produces about the same amount of power as a simple high-speed prop with a diameter of less than 4 feet. Hackleman's figures indicate that one such stack will probably yield less than 10 KWH per month in 10-mph average winds. Figure 3.10, in case you hadn't noticed, includes an approximate power-output curve for such a unit. S-rotors are not particularly appropriate for the generation of electricity, although their good-torque, slow-speed characteristics make them useful for such applications as pumping water.

The other vertical-axis machine, the Darrieus rotor, resembles a giant eggbeater. It has performance characteristics that approach a propeller-type rotor and there is reason to hope that present research efforts on these machines may soon result in a practical, economical design. However, they do have a problem with very low starting torque, so some sort of auxiliary starting system is required.

There are many different designs for horizontal-axis wind machines, but the one that probably springs to mind when you hear the word "windmill" is that romantic old, multibladed, slow-speed machine used all across the country for pumping water. Because these machines have many blades, they can develop a lot of torque (twist) in low-speed winds and are well-suited to their application. But they aren't designed to utilize high-speed winds efficiently, where the real power exists—to harness them you must have fewer blades. The fewer the blades, the faster the propeller rotates to be able to extract power from the passing wind. A high-speed prop having only two or three blades provides the best answer to the high rpm requirements of a generator; consequently, this is what most modern windplants have.

The efficiency of any rotor depends on the ratio of the speed of the tip of the rotor to the speed of the wind. This important quantity, called the *tip speed ratio*, is by definition

E. 3.12 $$tip \ speed \ ratio = \frac{2\pi r N}{v}$$

where *r* is the radius of the rotor, *N* is the rotational speed

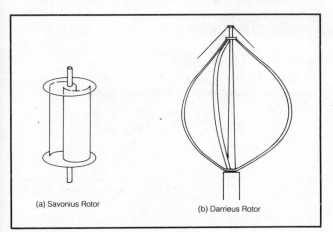

(a) Savonius Rotor

(b) Darrieus Rotor

Figure 3.20   Two vertical-axis wind machines.

(rpm), and v is the undisturbed wind speed ahead of the rotor. Figure 3.21 shows the power coefficients of various rotors as a function of their tip speed ratio, where the power coefficient is simply that fraction of the wind's power which the rotor actually extracts. While we indicated earlier that the maximum possible power coefficient is 0.593, Figure 3.21 shows that for lower tip speed ratios even this cannot be achieved. As you can see, the Savonius rotor and the American multiblade windplants produce maximum power at a tip speed ratio of about 1. The high speed two and three blade props in the figure reach their maximum output at a tip speed ratio of around 4 to 6 and their efficiency is more than double that of a Savonius rotor.

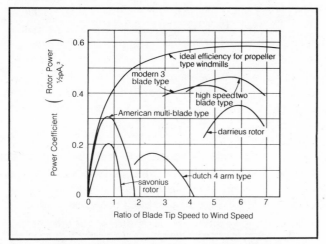

Figure 3.21 Typical power coefficients and tip speed ratios.

Knowing that a well-designed prop operates with a tip speed ratio of somewhere around 4 to 6 can give us some help in estimating the gearing that is required to match the prop to a generator.

Example: Calculate the rotational speed of a 10-foot propeller in 25-mph winds if the tip speed ratio is 4. What gear ratio should be used to match it to a generator which puts out its maximum power at 2500 rpm?

Solution: From the definition of tip speed ratio (rearranged), the speed of the rotor in 25-mph winds is

$$N = \frac{v \times tip\ speed\ ratio}{2\pi r}$$
$$= \frac{25\ miles/hr \times 5280\ ft/mile \times 4}{60\ min/hr \times 2\pi \times 5\ ft/rev}$$
$$= 280\ rpm$$

The gear ratio should be 2500:280, which is about 9:1.

This example gives some rough values for rotor speed, generator speed, and gear ratios that are fairly representative of homebuilt systems using car alternators.

Commercial systems are usually designed so that the generator turns much more slowly than the 2500 rpm in this example. This design feature greatly increases generator lifetime and reduces the gear ratio, but at the expense of increased generator size and cost. Dunlite, for example, uses a gear ratio of 5:1 to match a prop turning at 150 rpm to a generator which produces maximum power at 750 rpm. And Elektro, on all but its largest unit, avoids the problems of gearing altogether by running the propeller shaft directly into their very slow-speed generators.

Whatever kind of rotor you use, provision must be made to keep the machine from reaching dangerous speeds in high winds. Although there are many ways this can be accomplished, the techniques actually used for the most part are based either on the idea of swinging the whole machine more and more off the wind as wind speeds increase or on some sort of mechanism that changes the pitch of the blades.

Machines manufactured by Sencenbaugh Wind-Electric utilize a very simple but effective technique to swing them out of high-speed winds. The machine is mounted to the side of the main axis of the tower, and as winds increase the thrust acting along the axis of the propeller-generator assembly simply pushes the assembly around the tower and out of the wind. One of his machines under test at the Rocky Flats test center in 1977 survived winds in excess of 117 mph with no damage whatsoever.

Another way to have the machine swing off the wind is with an auxiliary pilot vane set parallel to the prop and perpendicular to the main vane. As the wind builds up, the force on this pilot vane eventually overcomes the guiding force of the main vane and the whole machine swings off wind.

Most bigger machines use the centrifugal force that is created at higher rpms to change the pitch of the blades automatically as the rated wind speed is neared, thereby spilling the excess wind. Dunlite (Quirk's), for example, uses spring-loaded weights attached to each prop shaft as shown in Figure 3.22. As the prop speed approaches the desired maximum, the centrifugal force on the weights overcomes the restraining effect of a magnetic latching system and the weights swing outward, thus moving the blades to a coarser pitch.

In addition to feathering or off-wind speed controls, some safety mechanism must be included so that you can halt the machine completely at any time. This can be accomplished with a folding tail vane which will place the propellers 90 degrees out of the wind.

Generators, Alternators, and Voltage Regulators

So the wind gets the rotor spinning and the rotor's shaft is coupled into the generator and the generator produces electricity. We know that a generator is characterized by

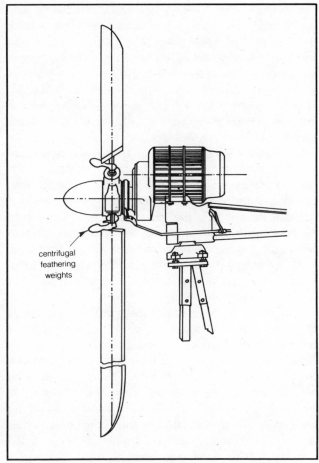

centrifugal
feathering
weights

Figure 3.22 Dunlite centrifugal-weight blade feathering system.

the number of watts that it produces at its rated wind speed, and we know how to choose the correct generator rating for our energy needs. We also know that two different generators can put out the same amount of power at a given wind speed, but one may be loafing along at a couple of hundred rpm and the other is zooming at several thousand rpm. The slower the speed of the generator, the longer it's going to last, the heavier it is, the less gearing it requires to match the rotor, and the more it costs. In other words, a generator specifically designed for a wind machine is going to look quite a bit different than the small high-speed jobs in your car.

We also know that an alternator is a special kind of generator; but to understand why alternators are recommended over other kinds of generators, we need to know something about how they work. Whenever a conductor (such as copper wire) passes through a magnetic field, the electrons in the conductor experience a force which tries to push them down the wire (creating a current). Any generator requires these three components: (1) some wire windings, called the *armature,* which carry the output current; (2) a source of a magnetic field, which in very small generators may be simply a permanent magnet, but in wind generators is always some *field* windings which must

be supplied with a small amount of control current (electrical currents create magnetic fields); and (3) a way to create relative motion between the armature and the field. That motion is created by spinning a shaft called the *rotor* within the stationary housing called the *stator.*

The big difference between an alternator and a dc generator (Figure 3.23) is in the location of the armature—whether it is spinning with the rotor (dc generator) or attached to the stationary stator (alternator). The armature, which carries maybe ten or twenty times as much current as the field, must somehow be connected to the stationary wires which carry the current to the batteries. In an alternator, the connection is direct since the armature is not rotating and this greatly simplifies the problem. In a dc generator, however, the connection must be made

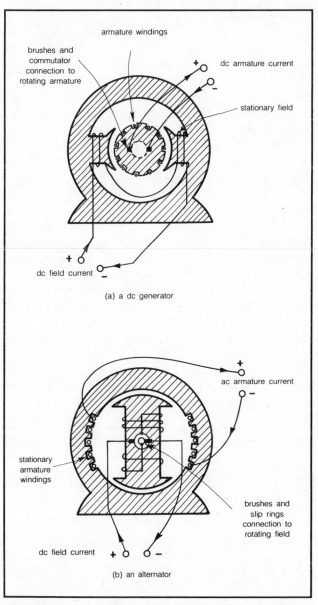

armature windings

brushes and
commutator
connection to
rotating armature

dc armature current

stationary field

dc field current

(a) a dc generator

ac armature current

stationary
armature
windings

brushes and
slip rings
connection to
rotating field

dc field current

(b) an alternator

Figure 3.23 A dc generator (a) has a stationary field and a rotating armature, and an alternator (b) has a rotating field and a stationary armature.

from the spinning rotor via commutator segments and brushes. The commutator and brushes take a lot of wear supplying the large currents from the armature; to give a reasonable lifetime between servicings, they must be well-designed—which means expensive. So for reasons of economy, lightness, and durability, alternators have the advantage. Moreover, for homebuilt systems, car alternators have further advantages: they are able to charge batteries at a lower rpm (typically 750–950 rpm, compared to over 1000 rpm for a car generator) and they also can supply more current (45–55 amps, compared to around 25–30 amps).

In an alternator, the current generated in the stationary armature is ac and its frequency varies as the rotor speed varies. Because it is variable frequency, we can't use it directly in appliances that require 60-cycle current; so we'll send it off to a battery instead. But if we sent ac directly to a battery, it would charge the battery half the time and discharge it the other half—no good. To avoid this problem, the current is *rectified* (converted to dc) by silicon diodes mounted in the housing itself so that what comes out of the alternator terminals is dc. (For you electrical engineers, Figure 3.24 is included, which shows how the 3-phase ac in the alternator is converted to dc.)

This takes care of the biggest part of the difficulty, namely picking off the large armature currents. But what about the small control current for the field which is spinning with the rotor? It can be supplied via slip rings and brushes and, since so little current is involved, this is not much of a problem; you must only check and replace the brushes periodically. Better still are the newer "brushless" alternators. (Current in stationary field windings creates a magnetic field which causes an ac current to flow in exciter windings on the rotor. This ac is rectified to dc by diodes mounted on the rotor and the dc creates the necessary magnetic field for the stationary armature.) They eliminate one of the few maintenance problems that wind generators have.

But where does the field current come from? A dc generator has enough residual magnetism in the field poles so that some current is generated even if there is no field current. This makes it possible to derive the field current right from the output of the generator itself (a shunt-connected generator). However, alternators and some dc generators get their field current from the battery; this presents a problem since, if the wind is not blowing, the batteries can simply discharge through the field windings. To prevent this discharge, expensive systems use a "reverse current relay," while in the homebuilt system some monitoring device, capable of sensing either propeller rpm or wind speed, is used to turn on the field.

The device that controls the operation of the generator and regulates transactions between generator and batteries is the *voltage regulator*. The voltage regulator regulates the output of the generator by rapidly switching the field current on and off. When the field is "on," the generator puts out as much current as it can; when it is "off," the output drops toward zero. The average output is determined by how much of the time the regulator allows the field to be on.

The regulator insures that the generator output will never be so great as to damage either the batteries or the generator itself. Batteries can be damaged and their useful lifetime shortened by charging them too rapidly or overcharging them. The rate at which batteries should be charged depends on the state of the charge already in them—they can take a lot without heating and gassing when they are discharged, but the charging rate must taper off as they approach full charge. This is handled automatically by the voltage regulator.

The other function of the regulator is to allow the generator output voltage to be adjusted to the proper level to compensate for the voltage drop in the lines connecting it to the batteries.

Energy Storage

Since we can't count on the wind to be blowing whenever we want to use electricity, and since the generator doesn't supply nice 60-cycle current at the proper voltage, a self-contained system must include some way to store energy. While a number of storage techniques are theoretically

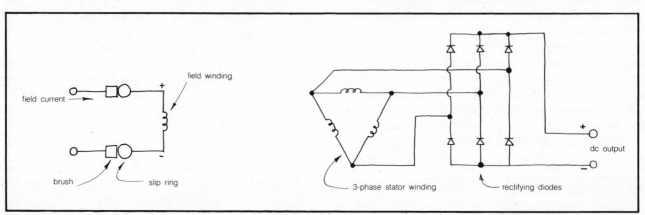

Figure 3.24 Circuit diagram for an alternator showing the rectification of the 3 phase armature current.

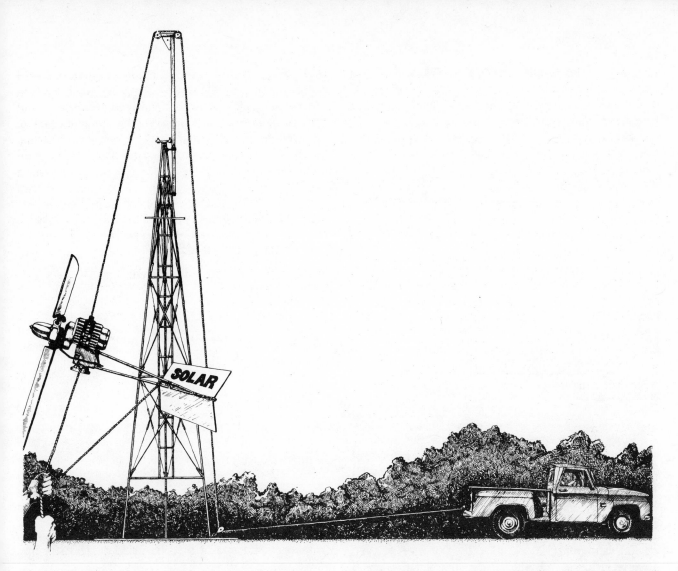

possible—flywheels, electrolysis of water to produce hydrogen, pumped storage, and compressed-air storage—it is the old standby, the battery, that presently offers the cheapest, most efficient, most convenient, and most readily available storage option for home usage. It is certainly to be hoped that some better storage mechanism will soon be available since batteries are a long way from being ideal; they're expensive, bulky, and require a fair amount of "tending to."

For the time being, then, we are stuck with batteries and our choice is primarily between lead-acid batteries similar to the ones used in automobiles and nickel-cadmium (Ni-Cad) batteries like those used in aircraft. While Ni-Cads have certain advantages—they are not damaged by moderate overcharging, are smaller, lighter and more rugged, and are not affected radically by cold weather—they are so expensive that lead-acid batteries are generally recommended.

While lead-acid *car* batteries could be used, these have been designed to provide short bursts of high current; subjected to the frequent deep discharging common in a wind system, their lifetime is seriously reduced. The most practical alternative is the long-life "stationary" or "home lighting" type of battery, designed for repeated cycling from fully charged to fully discharged states. These batteries will last for more than ten years under normal windplant use and some claim lifetimes of nearly twenty years under minimal discharge rates.

Batteries are rated according to their voltage and their storage capacity. Each cell of a lead-acid battery nominally produces close to 2 volts and, by arranging cells in series (connecting the terminals *plus* to *minus* to *plus* to *minus*, etc.), the cell voltages are additive so that any (even) voltage can be obtained. For example, a 12-volt car battery has 6 cells in series: to obtain 120 volts, we would need 60 cells in series or 10 12-volt batteries, or 20 6-volt batteries, and so on.

The most important characteristic of a battery is its storage capacity, and determining the proper amount of storage for a home system is one of the most important parts of the design. The storage capacity of a battery is measured in amp-hours at a given discharge rate. For example, a 240-amp-hour battery with an 8-hour discharge rate is capable of delivering 30 amps for 8 hours before its output voltage drops below a specified level; it would then have to be recharged. For discharge rates longer than the specified 8 hours, the storage capacity is increased (e.g., 20 amps could be drawn for longer than

12 hours); for faster discharges, the capacity is decreased (e.g., 40 amps could not be drawn for 6 hours). Figure 3.25 shows an example of how much the capacity of a battery can change for differing discharge rates. Batteries are usually specified for discharge rates of 8, 10, or 20 hours and it is, of course, important to know which you have.

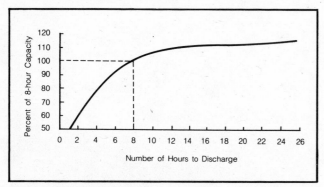

Figure 3.25 The variation in amp hour battery capacity for differing discharge rates with the 8-hour rate equaling 100%.

While it is the capacity in amp-hours that is usually given, we are really more interested in the amount of *energy* stored. Energy has units of watt-hours (or KWH) and, since watts are obtained by multiplying volts times amps, we can figure the energy stored in a battery by multiplying its amp-hour capacity by its rated voltage. For example a 120-volt, 240-amp-hour battery setup stores 28,800 watt-hours (120 × 240 = 28,800) or 28.8 KWH. If we were to use 7 KWH per day, the batteries would store a bit over 4 days' worth of electricity.

Example: Calculate the battery capacity required to provide 4 days of storage if we have calculated our monthly energy demand to be 150 KWH for a 120-volt system.

Solution: 150 KWH per month equals about 5 KWH per day so we want to provide

$$5 \ KWH/day \times 4 \ days = 20 \ KWH$$

which, at 120 volts, works out to be

$$\frac{20,000 \ watt\text{-}hours}{120 \ volts} = 167 \ amp\text{-}hours$$

So we need a 120-volt battery setup rated at 167 amp-hours. If we are using 6-volt batteries, then we will need 20 of them, each rated at 167 amp-hours.

There are several guidelines concerning how many days of storage you should attempt to provide; if too small a storage capacity is provided, the batteries will be charged and discharged at so rapid a rate that their lifetime will be reduced. As a rough rule of thumb, as long

as the prolonged charge or discharge current does not exceed 15 percent of the amp-hour rating, you'll get maximum battery life. So you can use the maximum current that the generator puts out to fix the minimum battery capacity. As the following example demonstrates, you simply multiply the maximum current by 7 to get minimum amp-hours.

Example: Suppose we have a 2-KW, 120-volt generator; what minimum storage capacity should be used? If our load is estimated at 150 KWH per month, how many days of storage does this correspond to?

Solution: The maximum current from the generator will be

$$\frac{2000 \ watts}{120 \ volts} = 16.7 \ amps$$

By the rule of thumb, batteries should have a capacity of at least

$$\frac{16.7}{0.15} = 16.7 \times 7 = 117 \ amp\text{-}hours$$

which, at 120 volts, is equivalent to

$$117 \ amp\text{-}hours \times 120 \ volts = 14,000 \ watt\text{-}hours = 14 \ KWH$$

At the demand rate of 5 KWH per day (150/30), this would supply

$$\frac{14 \ KWH}{5 \ KWH/day} \cong 2.8 \ days$$

This answer is fairly typical and indicates that you should probably figure on providing at least two or three days of storage. On the other hand, you should probably not figure on storing more than about four or five days' worth of energy for several reasons: (1) storage is expensive (somewhere around $80 per KWH); (2) if your winds are that bad, you should have a back-up system, a cheaper proposition than adding extra days of storage; and (3) if you have too much storage capacity, the batteries will be fully charged only infrequently and this will reduce their lifetime. They should be allowed to charge fully at least once every several weeks.

Finally, we should say something about location of the battery setup. We already know it should be as close to the load (house) as possible, to reduce line voltage losses. Moreover, batteries are sensitive to temperature—when cold, they cannot deliver as much of their rated capacity as when warm (you've experienced this on cold mornings in your car). For optimum performance they should be kept at around 75–80°F. Given line voltage losses and temperature considerations, batteries probably should be kept in the house or in a well-insulated shed adjacent to the house.

They should also be well ventilated since, during charging, batteries release hydrogen and oxygen (gassing) and hydrogen can be explosive. Finally, batteries should be kept clean and dry, off the floor, and only distilled water should be used to maintain the proper level of electrolyte.

DC-to-AC Power Inverters

Batteries supply only dc; if all of your appliances could operate with just dc, there would be no need for a dc-to-ac power inverter. And, in fact, a surprising number of typical home loads can run directly off of 110 to 120 volt dc: appliances which provide resistive heating (irons, toasters, electric blankets, coffee makers, fry pans, hot plates, waffle irons, and curling irons); incandescent lights; and small appliances with "universal" motors, having brushes and running on either ac or dc (vacuum cleaners, sewing machines, food mixers, shavers, and many portable hand tools). In addition, some loads can be modified to use dc: fluorescent lights (which, by the way, put out something like three times as much light per watt as incandescents) and motor-driven loads where the ac motor can be replaced with an equivalent dc motor.

There still remain some important appliances which need ac. Anything that uses a transformer (a hi-fi, TV, or those high-intensity lights) needs ac; synchronous motors (used in electric clocks and record players) and induction motors (split-phase motors, capacitor-start motors—used in heavier loads such as refrigerators and washing machines) must have ac. To handle such loads, an inverter is necessary.

There are two kinds of inverters: the older, less efficient, but decidedly cheaper rotary inverters which consist of a dc motor driving an ac alternator; and the newer solid-state electronic inverters. The biggest problem with rotary inverters is their low efficiency, which may be only about 60 percent even when they are putting out their rated power; their efficiency drops even further for smaller loads. If an appliance requires, say, 100 watts of ac power which it gets from a 60 percent efficient inverter, then the actual power drain from the battery is 167 watts (100/0.60 = 167). Thus our estimate of energy demand by appliances which require ac would have to be upped by almost 70 percent! Rotary inverters are a bit hard to find except at surplus electronic supply houses—the special Wind Power Access issues (such as Winter 1979) of *Wind Power Digest* list some.

Electronic inverters are quite a bit more efficient and require no maintenance, but they are fairly expensive—something like $200 for a fairly small 300-watt, 12-volt model to something like $5000 for a 3000-watt device. Prices of inverters of a given size can vary considerably,

depending on how "smooth" the output is. The output of less expensive units may more closely resemble a square wave than the true sinusoidal ac that some sensitive electronic loads may require. Electronic inverters have fairly high efficiencies, usually ranging from about 80 to 95 percent. At 80 percent efficiency, the energy estimate for ac appliances should be increased by 25 percent (1/0.8 = 1.25) to account for inverter losses. Electronic inverters are available for either 12-volt or 115-volt dc inputs.

Whether you choose a rotary or electronic inverter, there is a certain amount of standby power that is lost any time an inverter is turned on—even if there are no ac appliances drawing power. Hence it is desirable to include a switch (manual or automatic) which will turn the inverter on only when ac is needed.

Now, what size inverter should you buy and should you get more than one? There are enough trade-offs here between convenience, efficiency, and costs so that no absolute solutions exist—you'll have to weigh the factors and make your own decision. The least efficient but most convenient system would be an inverter large enough to supply your entire load with ac. Simply add up the maximum number of watts that are liable to be on at one time (hopefully not more than 2000 or 3000 watts), chunk out about $5000, and you can then wire your house entirely for ac. No messing around with modified appliances or separately wired sockets for dc.

A cheaper variation is to separate your loads into those that can run directly off battery-supplied dc and those that *must* use ac. Then figure the maximum ac power that will be on at any one time and pick an inverter which can supply that power. Obviously the inverter will be smaller and cheaper than it was in the first example, and less power will be wasted because most of the load operates from dc. But you must wire the house with separate outlets; also, you must be sure never to plug an ac appliance into a dc socket, a mistake which can destroy your appliance.

A third way to design a system is with separate small inverters for each ac load or outlet. This can be the most efficient choice, since inverter efficiency is highest when it is supplying maximum power. If you have one 1000-watt inverter and most of the time it is only putting out 100 watts for your hi-fi, then its efficiency will be poor (and will drain those precious KWH you worked so hard to accumulate). If instead you have two or three small inverters of a few hundred watts each, each turned on only as the demand arises, then efficiency is maximized. To know whether this latter approach is worth it, you'll need to determine—from manufacturers' spec sheets—the efficiency characteristics of inverters you are considering.

Besides such important specifications as power output, standby power drain, efficiency characteristics, voltage and frequency regulation, and wave shape, you need to determine the amount of *surge power* that the inverter can handle. Motors on such heavy-duty appliances as refrigerators and large shop tools have starting currents which may be many times greater than their normal operating currents (you've noticed your house lights dim as the refrigerator kicks on?); you must be sure your inverter can handle those transients (good ones can). Batteries, by the way, handle such surges with ease. Table 3.8 compares the surge power to running power for various sizes of induction motors and you can see the large increase during starting. Universal motors, we might note, require the same power to run as to start.

Table 3.8 Starting Power Compared to Running Power for Various Motors[a]

Motor Size (horsepower)	Watts Required to Start Motor			Running Watts
	Repulsion Induction	Capacitor	Split Phase	
1/6	600	850	2050	275
1/4	850	1050	2400	400
1/3	975	1350	2700	450
1/2	1300	1800	3600	600
3/4	1900	2600	—	850
1	2500	3300	—	1100

Notes: a. From *Electric Power From the Wind* by H. Clews.

Finally, in what is probably the most significant recent change in the viability of small WECS, if utility power is available then you now have the option to replace the batteries, separate ac and dc wiring systems, expensive power inverter, and auxiliary backup with a single, relatively inexpensive unit—the synchronous inverter (see Figure 3.6).

The concept is not new—elevators, for example, have long used similar devices for regenerative braking. During downward travel the kinetic energy of the elevator is used to turn a generator which returns power to the grid. Use in wind energy systems began with the introduction of the Gemini synchronous inverter manufactured by Windworks in Wisconsin. The Gemini is available in two sizes—a 4-KW unit and an 8-KW unit—at about one-sixth the per KW cost of conventional inverters. The capital cost of the entire WECS system is usually only a bit more than half that of a self-contained system with battery storage.

It should also be noted that synchronous inverters can be used with other nonconventional generating sources such as photovoltaics, and in fact this is likely to be their more important application.

While these cost reductions are truly significant, we must realize that these systems must compete with utility prices. A self-sufficient system, on the other hand, costs more but competes against higher cost diesel-generator sets, so the relative economics are not much different.

Auxiliary Power

For a completely reliable system in the absence of utility backup, you may need to include an auxiliary engine-generator to charge the batteries during prolonged periods of inadequate winds. Even if you are willing to do without electricity occasionally, this back-up unit may be necessary to return the batteries to their fully charged condition periodically; by this precaution, the batteries' useful lifetime is not decreased. Small auxiliary power-plants usually burn gasoline, but some are available which run on LP-gas, diesel, or natural gas, and it should be relatively easy to get one to run on methane from a digester.

Answering the questions of whether or not to include a back-up power generator, and if you do, how big it

Table 3.9 Monthly Energy Supplies from 2-KW Wind Generator in San Francisco and Minneapolis

Month	Energy Demand (KWH)	San Francisco				Minneapolis		
		Wind Speed (mph)	Supply from 2-KW Gen. (KWH)	Supply Minus Demand (KWH)		Wind Speed (mph)	Supply from 2-KW Gen. (KWH)	Supply Minus Demand (KWH)
Jan	160	8.2	100	−60		10.5	160	0
Feb	170	8.8	110	−60		11.0	180	+10
Mar	180	11.2	190	+10		12.1	240	+60
April	170	12.6	260	+90		12.8	270	+100
May	140	14.0	350	+210		12.5	250	+110
June	120	15.0	440	+320		11.7	220	+100
July	110	14.2	360	+250		9.8	140	+30
Aug	100	13.2	300	+200		9.5	130	+30
Sept	90	12.5	260	+170		10.6	170	+80
Oct	120	10.0	150	+30		11.0	180	+60
Nov	140	7.6	80	−60		12.0	230	+90
Dec	160	8.4	100	−60		11.1	190	+30
Monthly Average	138	11.3	225	—		11.3	197	—

should be will in part depend on your analysis of month-by-month wind speeds and load requirements. For example, if your monthly winds and power demands are relatively in balance, then a small backup unit would be all that you would need. If, however, there is a big mismatch and some months the windplant is just not going to be enough, then a larger backup would be required.

To illustrate this point, consider the problem of meeting the month-by-month demands given in Figure 3.3 in both San Francisco and Minneapolis (both cities have the same average wind speed). Table 3.9 gives monthly demand and monthly winds for each of the two cities and the corresponding KWH outputs of a 2-KW wind generator, and lists the differences between supply and demand.

As you can see from the table, the 2-KW generator would be sufficient in every month in Minneapolis and, in most months, there is a good deal of extra power available. This "extra power" could help take the system through months when the winds are less than average. (Remember, when you see a long-term "average" wind speed for some location for some month, approximately half the time the real monthly average will be less than the long-term average—so overdesign is essential if you want to minimize the use of standby power.) Our conclusion is that, in Minneapolis, the 2-KW generator would almost always handle the entire load and an auxiliary power source, if you had one at all, could be small. A standby source of 1000 watts (about as small as they come) would boost the supply by 30 KWH per month, running only one hour per day, and that boost would probably be sufficient.

On the other hand, in San Francisco the load and supply are terribly mismatched. Winds are high in the summer, when demand is low. In the winter, demand is high and winds are low; there are four months for which the generator alone is insufficient. You could increase the size of the wind generator to meet winter demands but the 2-KW unit is already capable of supplying two to three times the summer demand. (With so much extra capacity during the summer, you might consider using some of it to heat water for your solar home. Each 100 KWH of extra capacity per month is enough to raise the temperature of 20 gallons of water by about 70°F every day—easily one person's hot-water needs.) It would be cheaper to include a fair-sized auxiliary power unit and then figure on running it an hour or so per day during the winter. You should probably not choose a standby unit with greater capacity than the wind generator: you may charge the batteries at too fast a rate. In our example, a 2-KW standby unit running one hour per day would give an extra 60 KWH per month, enough to carry us through the winter.

Gasoline-powered standby powerplants of appropriate size (1000 to 6000 watts) cost on the order of $200 to $400 per 1000 watts. Prices vary, depending on such quality factors as whether the model runs at 1800 rpm or

3600 rpm (the 1800-rpm units last longer and are more expensive) or whether it has manual or electric starting. All of these units are generally unpleasant (they are noisy, require maintenance, produce pollution, have relatively short lifespans, and consume fossil fuels) and it would seem advisable to plan your system so that the standby is needed as little as possible.

These units produce good 60-cycle, 115-volt ac power, but if you want to connect one directly to your load, remember that it must have enough capacity to handle the maximum power drawn at any one time, including the large surge currents required by some motors to start (Table 3.8). Frequently the standby will be too small to be used in this way and instead will see service recharging your battery setup. In this case, you'll need to include a full-wave bridge rectifier using silicon diodes to convert the auxiliary ac to the dc required by batteries.

What is Available?

Since the "design" of most wind-electric systems consists of matching component specifications to perceived requirements, it is important to know what's available. As was mentioned earlier, the number of small-WECS manufacturers has increased at a fairly rapid rate over the last few years, so any listing that we can provide here will undoubtedly become outdated in the next few years. The magazine *Wind Power Digest* periodically publishes special *Wind Access Catalog* issues and that is your best source of current information. At any rate, Table 3.10 will give you an idea of the equipment available in 1980 as well as the addresses that you can write to for detailed information.

Economic Evaluation

OK, you've decided you have consistently strong winds close enough to your homesite to deliver enough energy to meet your spartan needs. The key question remaining then, is how much do these systems cost and do they represent a reasonable investment for your money compared to other alternatives?

Obviously, with inflation running along at its recent high clip, any cost estimates that we publish here will need to be increased considerably in a few years. At the same time, however, the value of the energy your WECS will produce will correspondingly look better and better as inflation continues, more than cancelling out the rising equipment costs.

At the risk of these figures looking ridiculously low in the near future, given inflation, let us at least lay out the bare bones 1980 cost of components for a modest system in both remote and utility-backup settings. This will give us a chance to demonstrate some economic analysis techniques; techniques which you can duplicate with more recent costs.

Table 3.10 Summary of Available Wind Machines

Manufacturer	Model	Rated Power (watts)	Rated Wind Speed (mph)	Rotor Diameter (ft)	Nominal Voltage (volts)	Approximate KWH/mo in 12-mph average winds
Aero Power Systems 2398 Fourth Street Berkeley, California 97410	SL 1500	1430	25	10	14/28	185
Altos P.O. Box 905 Boulder, Colorado 80302	BWP-8B BWP-12A BWP-12B	1500 2200 2000	28 28 28	7.6 11.5 11.5	24 115/200 24	130 190 170
American Wind Turbine 1016 E. Airport Rd. Stillwater, Oklahoma 74074	12-ft 16-ft	1000 2000	20 20	11.5 15.3	— —	220 445
Dakota Sun & Wind P.O. Box 178 Aberdeen, South Dakota 57401	BC4	4000	27	14	110	400
Dunlite c/o Enertech Corp. P.O. Box 420 Norwich, Vermont 05055	81 002550	2000	25	13.5	12/24/32 48/110	260
Dynergy Corp. P.O. Box 428 1269 Union Ave. Laconia, New Hampshire 03246	5-meter Darrieus	3300	24	15	—	475
Energy Development Co. 179 E. R.D. 2 Hamburg, Pennsylvania 19526	440 445	20,000 45,000	25 25	38 40	240 —	2600 5800
Enertech Corp. P.O. Box 420 Norwich, Vermont 05055	1500	1500	22	13.2	115	270
Kedco Inc. 9016 Aviation Blvd. Inglewood, California 90301	1200 1600 1620	1200 1900 3000	22 20 25	12 16 16	14/28 14 0-180	215 425 390
Millville Wind & Solar 10335 Old Drive Millville, California 96062	10-3-Ind	10,000	25	25	220	1300
North Wind Power Co. P.O. Box 315 Warren, Vermont 05674	2KW Eagle 3KW	2000 3000	22 27	13.6 13.6	32/110 32/110	360 305
Pinson Energy Corp. P.O. Box 7 Marston Mills, Massachusetts 02648	C2E (Vertical)	2000	24	12	120/240	290
Sencenbaugh Wind Electric P.O. Box 1174 Palo Alto, California 94306	400-14HDS 500 1000	400 500 1000	20 24 23	7 6 12	14 14/28 14/28	90 75 160
Independent Energy Systems Inc 6043 Sterrettania Road Fairview, Pennsylvania 16415	Skyhawk	4000	23	15	—	635
Whirlwind Power Co. Box 18530 Denver, Colorado 80218	Model A	2000	25	10	12/24 32/48 120/240	260
Winco-Wincharger 7850 Metro Parkway Minneapolis, Minnesota 55420	1222H	200	23	6	12	32
Wind Power Systems, Inc. P.O. Box 17323 San Diego, California 92117	Storm-Master 10	6000	18	32.8	—	1650

System A:	2KW, 22 mph, Remote System
Rotor, generator, controls	$3500
15 KWH battery bank	1200
40-ft guyed tower	700
1500-watt inverter	3500
Miscellaneous, wiring, etc.	1000
	$9900

System B	2KW, 22mph, Utility Backup
Rotor, generator, controls	$3500
4KW synchronous inverter	1000
40-ft guyed tower	700
Miscellaneous, wiring, etc.	1000
	$6200

These figures should be adjusted upward if you do not plan to do the design and installation yourself, and they should be adjusted downward to account for various state and federal tax credits. The current version of the federal tax credit lets you subtract from your federal income tax 40 percent of the first $10,000 of cost, for a maximum credit of $4000.

System A would have an after-federal-tax cost then of $9900 − (0.4 × 9900) = $5940. System B would have an after-tax cost of $3720. In addition, a number of states have tax credits as well. California's credit, for example, would bring the final cost of system A down to $4455 and system B down to $2790. Since the tax credits vary from state to state, you should check with your local agencies to determine their current status.

How can we decide whether or not these costs represent a reasonable investment? There are many ways to try to compare an initial outlay of money to savings that will accrue over the lifetime of the equipment, including use of life-cycle costs, payback periods, and annual costing. We'll discuss the first two approaches later, in the chapter on solar energy. For now we will illustrate the annual costs technique, which is based on the premise that you borrow the money for the system at some interest rate, i, over some number of years, n. The annual payments on the loan plus any money spent on maintenance becomes your annual cost, which can then be divided by the annual KWH delivered to give a cost per KWH that can be compared to other alternatives.

All we need for this approach is a way to calculate annual payments A required to pay off a loan P given interest i and term n. Equation 3.13 gives us the required relationship, and Table 3.11 summarizes some typical values of A/P (the capital recovery factor).

E. 3.13
$$A = P\left[\frac{i(1+i)^n}{(1+i)^n - 1}\right]$$
$$= P \times (capital\ recovery\ factor)$$
$$= P \times CRF$$

Example: Suppose a 20-year, 12 percent loan is used to pay off system A in a region where winds average 11 mph. Include existing federal tax credits. Calculate the average cost per KWH.

Solution: Figure 3.14 indicates a capacity factor for this 2-KW, 22-mph system of about 0.2. In a year's time then (8760 hours) we would expect about

$$0.2 \times 2\ KW \times 8760\ hr/yr = 3500\ KWH/yr$$

Table 3.11 indicates a capital recovery factor of 0.1339, so the annual payments on this $5940 remote system would be:

$$0.1339 \times \$5940 = \$795/yr$$

Neglecting any added costs due to maintenance, insurance, and so forth, the cost of electricity over the next 20 years would be

$$\frac{\$795/yr}{3500\ KWH/yr} = 0.23 = 23¢/KWH$$

Table 3.11 Capital Recovery Factor, A/P

n	8%	9%	10%	11%	12%	13%	14%	15%
1	1.0800	1.0900	1.1000	1.1100	1.1200	1.1300	1.1400	1.1500
2	0.5608	0.5685	0.5762	0.5839	0.5917	0.5995	0.6073	0.6151
3	0.3880	0.3951	0.4021	0.4092	0.4164	0.4235	0.4307	0.4380
4	0.3019	0.3087	0.3155	0.3223	0.3292	0.3362	0.3432	0.3503
5	0.2505	0.2571	0.2638	0.2706	0.2774	0.2843	0.2913	0.2983
6	0.2163	0.2229	0.2296	0.2364	0.2432	0.2502	0.2572	0.2642
7	0.1921	0.1987	0.2054	0.2122	0.2191	0.2261	0.2332	0.2404
8	0.1740	0.1807	0.1874	0.1943	0.2013	0.2084	0.2156	0.2229
9	0.1601	0.1668	0.1736	0.1806	0.1877	0.1949	0.2022	0.2096
10	0.1490	0.1559	0.1628	0.1698	0.1770	0.1843	0.1917	0.1993
15	0.1168	0.1241	0.1315	0.1391	0.1468	0.1547	0.1628	0.1710
20	0.1019	0.1095	0.1175	0.1256	0.1339	0.1424	0.1510	0.1598
25	0.0937	0.1018	0.1102	0.1187	0.1275	0.1364	0.1455	0.1547
30	0.0888	0.0973	0.1061	0.1150	0.1241	0.1334	0.1428	0.1523

This is quite a bit more than any of us is paying for utility electricity now, but is considerably less than it would cost you if you used a gasoline-driven generator. And remember, this example is for a remote system where cheap utility power is not available.

We should also note that it has been more or less assumed that the components would all have the same lifetime as the loan period (20 years). If the system outlasts the loan then it delivers free energy in those final years. If it doesn't last as long then we need to modify our calculation.

Example: Assume the batteries in system A only last 10 years but the rest of the system lasts 20. If a new battery set is purchased for $2500, 10 years from now, on a 10-year, 14 percent loan, compute the annual costs.

Solution: Our initial 20-year loan costs us $795 per year, so for the first 10 years our electricity costs 23 cents per KWH as above. The second loan, whose payments will be (Table 3.11)

$$A = \$2500 \times 0.1917 = \$479/year$$

makes the annual cost during the last 10 years be

$$\frac{\$795 + \$479}{3500\ KWH/yr} = 0.36 = 36¢/KWH$$

which is about what a gasoline-powered generator costs to operate today.

Example: For what cost does system B deliver electricity under the same conditions as in the previous example?

Solution: Borrowing the $3720 after-tax-credit cost on a 12 percent 20-year loan means our annual payments would be (Table 3.11):

$$\$3720 \times 0.1339 = \$498/yr$$

In 11-mph average winds, the system delivers 3500 KWH per year so the cost per KWH is

$$\frac{\$498}{3500\ KWH/yr} = 0.14 = 14¢/KWH$$

It should be pointed out that this last figure of 14 cents per KWH assumes the utility buys back power at the same price that it sells it to you for. If they don't pay that much then you will not get the full dollar savings anticipated above. On the other hand, given a very significant new piece of legislation called the Public Utilities Regulatory Policy Act (PURPA), it may very well be that utilities will pay you *more* for your electricity than you pay them when you buy it back. The dust hasn't settled on this issue yet, but it looks like utilities will have to pay you the avoided cost of new energy while they only charge you a rolled-in average cost of new and old sources, which is considerably less. Your equivalent cost of electricity generated by your WECS will therefore potentially be a bit cheaper than this calculation would indicate.

The cost of WECS electricity seems high only until you compare it to the rapidly rising cost of utility electricity. If utility prices increase at only 15 percent per year then they double every 5 years. At these rates electricity that now costs 6 cents per KWH would cost 12 cents in 5 years, 24 cents in 10 years, 48 cents in 15 years, and 96 cents in 20. Over the life of the WECS it will easily pay for itself and in those later years will seem an incredible bargain.

Design Summary

1. Locate your best site, set up an anemometer, and with the acquired data, attempt to determine a month-by-month estimate of average wind speed.

2. Estimate your energy requirements using old bills or the "watts times hours" approach. Do it for at least each season and, better still, for each month. You may want to divide the demand into "essential" and "convenience" components and design the wind system to always supply at least the essential portion.

   If yours is a remote site then for ac appliances you'll need to increase the demand according to the efficiency of the inverter. It is also recommended that all estimates be increased by about 30 percent to allow for battery inefficiencies, line losses, and less-than-average winds.

3. Using Figure 3.14 and the section "What is Available," pick a generator that will meet your needs. If you have a relatively good match between monthly winds and monthly demands, the generator can be picked to meet at least the essential portion and perhaps most of the convenience demand. There are certain trade-offs involving auxiliary power sources and flexibility in your requirements, so hard and fast rules cannot be given here. If it seems that in some months there will be a fair amount of surplus power generated, you may want to use that surplus to augment a solar water-heating system.

4. If you are going to use a synchronous inverter, you must check with your utility to establish the costs and conditions of service. Pick an inverter with a rating at least as high as that of your generator and one capable of meeting your peak demands.

5. If you are going to have an auxiliary power source, you can pick its size based on estimates of the shortfall between wind-generator output and demand. The standby should probably be smaller in watts generated than the wind generator, but large enough so that you won't have to run it more than an hour or so a day during months with light winds.

6. If batteries are to be used, pick an amp-hour storage capacity at least 7 times the maximum current the generator will supply. You may want to increase that storage figure if it doesn't give sufficient days of capacity during any given month.

7. Pick the power rating of the inverter(s) to be able to handle all the ac loads.

You will undoubtedly work through several designs as you evaluate the trade-offs between costs, convenience, and reliability; but no matter what design you settle on, there are a few things to keep in mind. Always.

First, stay conservative—always overestimate the load and underestimate the supply. It is better to be surprised at how little you need to use that auxiliary power unit than to be disappointed at how often it is running. Second, when you advance to the assembly and operating stages, you must constantly be concerned with safety. The mechanical forces that build up when one of these units starts operating in high winds are very dangerous and the amounts of electrical power generated can be lethal.

I hope this presentation has given you enough information to get your design well under way. Additional information can be obtained from the manufacturers listed in Table 3.10 or from the list of useful references at the end of the chapter. Final details can be checked out with the distributor from whom you purchase your components. The energy is there—it's not exactly free, but it will never run out and it's clean. Let's use it.

Electricity From Photovoltaics

If only they were cheap. Photovoltaic cells, or "solar cells," at a low enough cost, could revolutionize energy production and consumption patterns around the world. No moving parts, quiet, safe, reliable, long-lasting, modular in nature so they can be used for the smallest as well as the largest applications, easy to handle and install, pollution-free in operation, and running on the free energy from the sun, these cells are ideally suited for onsite applications.

Photovoltaic cells are semiconductor devices that convert sunlight directly into electricity. While the first practical cells were manufactured back in the 1950s, their high cost has limited their usefulness to the space program and certain remote applications where only small amounts of power are required. That seems about to change.

The price of photovoltaics is most often expressed in dollars per watt of electricity that would be generated when the cells are exposed to full sunlight—full sunlight being defined as 1000 watts per square meter, or 100 milliwatts per square centimeter (which is roughly 317 Btu/hr per square foot or 93 watts per square foot). Government purchases of photovoltaic arrays, fully encapsulated to protect them from the weather, ran around $100 per peak watt in 1970; they are now (1980) running about $8 per watt, and the Department of Energy's goals indicate $1- to $2-per-watt arrays by the end of 1982 and 50-cents-per-watt arrays by 1986 (all in 1975 dollars).

To translate these prices into more meaningful terms, an array that costs 50-cents-per-watt that produces the equivalent of full output for 6 hours per day all year round, and is financed with a 20-year, 11 percent loan would produce electricity costing less than 2.9 cents per KWH. Even adding the costs of power conditioning, storage, and mounting hardware, this suggests that the falling price of photovoltaics will cross the rising cost of utility-generated electricity by the mid-1980s.

Brief Theory of Operation

When a photon of light collides with an atom in a semiconductor, it can transfer that energy to one of the atom's electrons. If the photon's energy is sufficient (greater than the "band gap" of the material), then the negatively charged electron can be freed of its attachment to any particular atom and is able to move randomly through the semiconductor.

Meanwhile, the atom left behind has a vacancy or "hole" where the electron used to be, and since it lacks one of its electrons the atom is left with a net positive charge. A neighboring electron can leave its atom to fill the hole, but that has the effect of merely moving the hole to the next atom. Holes, then, can be treated as positive charges which are free to move around in much the same way as their partners, the freed electrons.

An electrical current can be created if these hole-electron pairs can be separated from each other before they have a chance to recombine. This separation is accomplished by a small electric field, or force, created within the semiconductor at the junction between dissimilar sections of the material.

Almost all of the solar cells now in use start with a single crystal of highly purified silicon to which carefully controlled amounts of impurities (or dopants) are added. Referring to Figure 3.26, the rear of the cell is doped with an impurity such as boron that contributes a few extra holes of its own (holes are positive and this side is referred to as being made of p–type material); the front is doped with arsenic or phosphorus, which contributes free electrons, and this side is then n–type (negative) material. Within the immediate vicinity of the p–n junction thus formed there exists a permanent electric field created by the initial migration of the holes and electrons contributed by the dopants.

When light strikes the cell, hole-electron pairs are formed in both the p and n regions. Holes which migrate into the electric field at the junction are pushed into the

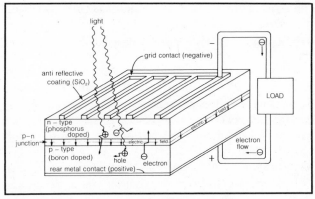

Figure 3.26 Example of a silicon photovoltaic cell.

p–side and similarly electrons are pushed into the n–side. If an electric load is connected between the metal contacts on the two surfaces, an amount of current will flow that is directly proportional to the intensity of the sunlight.

Historically, the manufacture of silicon photovoltaics has involved a number of expensive processes. First a 2- to 3-inch-diameter cylinder of pure single-crystal silicon is grown by slowly pulling a seed crystal out of a crucible filled with molten silicon. The cylinder is then sawn into thin wafers, with about half of the cylinder being lost as sawdust. Polishing the wafer, creating the junction, adding the metal contacts, and applying an antireflective coating require many hours of hand labor. These processes will obviously have to be streamlined and automated if the Department of Energy's cost goals are to be achieved with silicon cells.

While most solar cells are made this way, a good deal of attention is being directed toward "heterojunction" photovoltaics made by joining two dissimilar semiconductors, such as cadmium sulfide (CdS) and copper sulfide (Cu_2S). Due to their much better light absorption properties, such cells can be made much thinner than their silicon counterparts—so thin that it is likely they will be produced with relatively simple spray or vapor deposition processes. These thin-film cells, while potentially much cheaper than silicon cells, have been less attractive in the past due to their lower efficiencies and shorter lifetimes, but rapid progress is being made to combat both of these shortcomings.

Progress is also being made with cells made of polycrystalline silicon, and even amorphous silicon, as well as gallium arsenide cells that are particularly effective when solar concentration is utilized.

Voltage-Current Characteristics

Before we can design photovoltaic power systems we must know something about the electrical characteristics of individual cells. Then we can start stacking the cells up in arrays to meet any voltage, current, power, or energy requirements desired.

Figure 3.27 shows the relationship between voltage produced and current generated for a typical silicon solar cell—this one being a 3-inch-diameter disk exposed to full sun. There are several important quantities that need to be defined.

One is the *open-circuit voltage, V_{oc},* that corresponds to the voltage produced when no current is allowed to flow. For silicon cells V_{oc} is about 0.56 volts in full sun at 25°C. Another is the *short-circuit current, I_{sc},* which is the current that flows from the cell if the leads are shorted together so that the voltage across the cell is zero. In full sun at a temperature of 25°C, I_{sc} is typically about 0.2 amps per square inch or 0.03 amps per square centimeter (30 milliamps per square centimeter). This 3-inch-diameter cell has an I_{sc} of 1.4 amps.

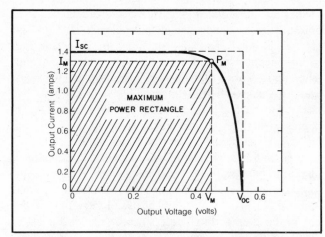

Figure 3.27 Characteristic curve of a typical cell showing location of maximum power point (Motorola, 3″ diameter, case temperature 25°C).

We can operate the cell anywhere along this V versus I characteristic curve. Which combination of V and I would result in the maximum power output, P_M, from the solar cell? Since power is the product of V and I we certainly don't want to operate with $V = V_{oc}$ or $I = I_{sc}$, since the power delivered at either point would be zero. Geometrically, power can be thought of as the area of the rectangle formed under the characteristic curve with voltage as one side and current the other, with the operating point locating the upper right corner. Maximum power then corresponds to the biggest rectangle we can fit under the curve.

The solar cell may be forced to operate at this maximum power point either by connecting the leads directly to a voltage V_M (such as a battery that we may want to charge) or by connecting the cell to a load with resistance $R = V_M/I_M$ ohms.

Another term of interest is the *fill factor,* which in Figure 3.27 is the ratio of the area of the crosshatched maximum power rectangle to the area of the larger rectangle formed with V_{oc} and I_{sc} as sides. Knowing that silicon cells typically have fill factors of 70 to 80 percent means we can estimate a given array's power output by merely measuring its V_{oc} and I_{sc}—two very simple measurements—and multiplying their product by about 75 percent.

Example: For the 3-inch diameter silicon cell in Figure 3.27, what is the cell efficiency at the maximum power output and what is the fill factor?

Solution: From the figure, $V_M = 0.45$ volts (about 80 percent of V_{oc}) and $I_M = 1.3$ amps. The cell area is 45 square centimeters so

$$efficiency = \frac{cell\ power}{solar\ power}$$

68

$$= \frac{(0.45 \ volts \times 1.3 \ amps)}{0.1 \ watt/cm^2 \times 45 \ cm^2}$$

$$= 13\%$$

which is typical for a silicon photovoltaic, though some are as high as 15 percent. The fill factor is

$$fill \ factor = \frac{max \ power \ out}{V_{oc}I_{sc}} = \frac{0.45 \times 1.3}{0.56 \times 1.4} = 75\%$$

which is fairly common, though some cells exceed 80 percent.

So far we've only shown performance at full sun and nominal solar cell temperature. Figure 3.28 shows the effect of variations in solar intensity with the axes normalized to the conditions of full sunlight. Notice the short-circuit current varies linearly with changes in intensity but V_{oc} shifts only modestly. In fact, if the cell is operated with its voltage fixed at about 80 percent of V_{oc} (or about 0.45 volts per cell), the power output will be nearly optimum for quite a range of solar intensities.

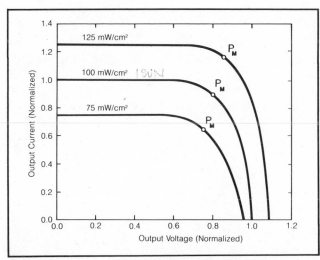

Figure 3.28 Showing variation in silicon photovoltaic output characteristics as solar intensity changes.

The variation in cell characteristics with changes in temperature is very important. As shown in Figure 3.29, I_{sc} barely changes as the cell heats up but V_{oc} changes considerably. For example, suppose we had been operating at the maximum power point at 25°C (77°F) with V_M = 0.8 on the normalized scale; should the cell heat up to 60°C (140°F), the output current and power would drop nearly 50 percent!

To help maintain performance, then, the array should be kept cool. One way to help do this is to mount it on an aluminum heat sink to help dissipate the incoming energy that is not being converted to electricity. Another is to cool it with flowing air or water, in which case we can

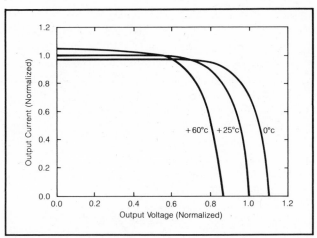

Figure 3.29 Silicon cell performance decreases as temperature increases.

not only generate electricity but can also pick up some "waste" thermal energy which could be used elsewhere. This "cogeneration" increases the overall efficiency of converting sunlight into useful energy and could help bring economic viability just that much sooner.

One way to avoid decreases in current delivered as temperatures rise is to operate the cell at roughly 60 percent of the open circuit voltage instead of 80 percent. This lets us design with an assured current delivery rate without regard to temperature, but obviously it results in lower cell efficiencies when temperatures are low. This conservative design philosophy is frequently used for remote battery charging operations, as we'll see later.

Photovoltaic Arrays

When photovoltaics are wired in series, as shown in Figure 3.30(a), the voltages add and current through each cell is the same; when they are wired in parallel [Figure 3.30(b)] the voltage stays the same as for an individual cell but the currents add. Sizing arrays thus involves determining the number of cells in series, forming a module, to give proper voltage, and determining the number of modules in parallel to give proper current or power [Figure 3.30(c)].

To avoid diurnal variations in power to the load, such arrays are usually used as battery chargers and the batteries then provide nighttime power. To prevent the batteries from discharging back through the photovoltaic array at night, it is necessary to use a one-way current valve, called a diode, placed in the circuit as shown in Figure 3.31. If this is a silicon diode (typically), then while it is conducting current it has a voltage drop of about 0.6 volts which must be accounted for when the photovoltaic array is being sized. Many manufacturers are including Schottky diodes in their arrays because such diodes lose only about half the voltage drop of their silicon counterparts.

The characteristics of the batteries to be charged also

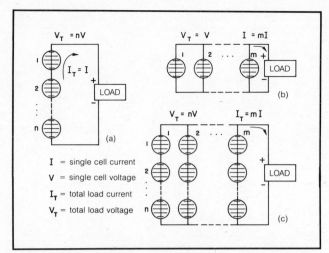

I = single cell current

V = single cell voltage

I_T = total load current

V_T = total load voltage

Figure 3.30 Photovoltaic arrays: (a) cells in series, voltage adds, (b) cells in parallel, currents add, (c) series-parallel, voltage and current add.

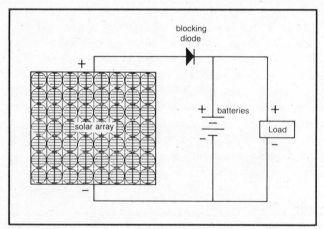

Figure 3.31 A photovoltaic battery charger requires a blocking diode.

need to be included in the sizing of our array. The two most likely candidates for charging are lead-acid batteries and nickel-cadmium (Ni-Cad) batteries.

Lead-acid batteries consist of a number of cells arranged in series with each cell having a nominal discharge voltage of about 2.1 volts. We must therefore apply more than 2.1 volts per cell from the array in order for the current to run into the battery to give it its recharge. Lead-acid batteries are generally charged with a constant-voltage source that supplies a float charge of about 2.3 volts per cell (at 25°C). As the battery comes up to full charge, its voltage rises and the charging current correspondingly decreases to a low enough level that overcharging does not occur.

When solar cells are used to charge lead-acid batteries, they can usually be connected directly to the batteries with just the blocking diode between them as long as the maximum current (in amps) delivered by the array in full sunlight is less than about 15 percent of the amp-hour rating of the batteries. In some circumstances a voltage

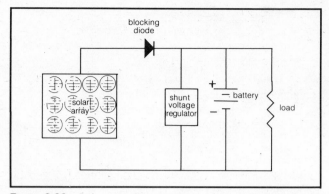

Figure 3.32 A shunt regulator protects the batteries from being overcharged.

regulator may be called for to protect the batteries from overcharging, as is suggested in Figure 3.32.

Ni-Cad batteries have a nominal discharge voltage of 1.25 volts per cell and a typical charging voltage (at 25°C) of about 1.45 volts per cell, so our photovoltaic array will have a different number of solar cells in series when charging Ni-Cads than when charging lead-acids.

Example: Design a silicon photovoltaic array to deliver 10 amps peak to a 12-volt lead-acid battery at 25°C. Assume 3-inch silicon cells with the characteristics given in Figure 3.27.

Solution: The 12-volt lead-acid battery has six cells, which means the charging voltage should be about

$$6 \times 2.3 = 13.8 \; volts$$

The solar cells should supply this much voltage plus an extra 0.6 volts to cover the drop in the blocking diode. A module must have then, in series,

$$\frac{(13.8 + 0.6) volts}{0.45 \; volts/cell} = 32 \; cells$$

The maximum-power-point current in full sunlight is 1.3 amps per cell, so to deliver 10 amps we'll need 8 modules in parallel (10 ÷ 1.3 = 7.7). The full array then would have a total of 256 cells arranged with 32 cells per module in series, with 8 parallel modules.

The above array was designed for cell temperatures of only 25°C (77°F). If we were to use it to charge batteries the year round, then during the summer months, unless special cooling measures were taken, the cells would undoubtedly reach higher temperatures. As solar cell temperatures increase, their characteristic curve shifts to the left by about 2.2 millivolts per Centigrade degree, as was shown in Figure 3.29. If a battery is holding the photovoltaic voltage constant and if we have designed the array to operate at the 25°C maximum power point, then as temperatures increase cell output current may have to drop.

Fortunately lead-acid batteries also exhibit a voltage drop as temperatures increase, though not as much as the solar cells do (about 30 millivolts per Centigrade degree for a 12-volt battery), so to a modest degree the two offset each other.

Many photovoltaic manufacturers design their 12-volt modules with more cells in series than the 32 we just calculated, so that each cell can operate at a lower voltage and hence be less subject to current changes as temperatures increase.

A frequently used ambient design temperature is 40°C (104°F). At this elevated temperature the recommended charging voltage for a 12-volt lead-acid battery drops to about 13.3 volts and the design voltage for the photovoltaics drops to around 0.38 volts per cell, which results in arrays having 36 or 37 cells in series.

Annual Performance

The previous examples have shown how we can design an array to deliver, under peak sunlight conditions, any amount of voltage, current, and power that we want. If such an array is put out in the sun all year round, a key question to ask is, what total amount of energy could be delivered? The answer to the question depends not only on the individual cell characteristics but the tilt angle of the array and local insolation (sunshine) conditions as they vary from hour to hour and month to month.

To calculate monthly or yearly performance of a solar cell array it is useful to reintroduce the notion of a capacity factor (CF). The capacity factor over a given period of time is the ratio of the amount of energy actually delivered to the amount that would have been delivered if the system were putting out full power the whole time. Moving terms around, we can say that

E. 3.14 energy delivered = capacity factor × rated power × total hours

Since photovoltaics deliver an amount of current that varies linearly with incident sunlight and since their operating voltage is relatively constant, the capacity factor can be approximated merely by taking the ratio of sunshine striking the array (the insolation) to the amount of sun that would be available if we had full sunlight (100 milliwatts per square centimeter) 24 hours a day. Typical annual capacity factors in the United States range from about 20 to 25 percent.

Once the capacity factor for a given month, or year, is known solar panel energy output is easily calculable from Equation 3.14.

Example: Calculate the monthly and annual energy delivered by a solar cell array rated at 18 watts peak if the panel is located in Santa Maria, California, faces south, and has a 60° tilt angle. Solar radiation is given in Table 3.12.

Table 3.12 Solar Radiation on a 60° Surface in Santa Maria

Insolation (10^3 Btu/ft²-month)

Jan	Feb	Mar	Apr	May	June	July	Aug	Sept	Oct	Nov	Dec
47	46	54	50	46	43	46	50	50	52	46	47

Solution: Let's work out the numbers for January. Insolation on the panel is given as 47,000 Btu per square foot. Earlier we stated that full sun was defined as 100 milliwatts per square centimeter or 317 Btu/hr per square foot, so the January capacity factor works out to be

$$CF = \frac{actual\ insolation}{full\ sun\ insolation}$$
$$= \frac{47{,}000\ Btu/ft^2\text{-}mo}{317\ Btu/hr\text{-}ft^2 \times 24hr/day \times 31\ day/mo}$$
$$= 0.20$$

Since the array delivers 18 watts in full sun, then by Equation 3.14 the January energy delivered would be:

$$energy = 0.20 \times 18\ watts \times 24\ hr/day \times 31\ day/mo$$
$$= 2680\ \ \ watt\text{-}hours/mo\ \ \ = 2.68\ KWH/mo$$

The calculations for the rest of the months are presented in Table 3.13.

The annual capacity factor of 0.209 means that on the average the cells receive the equivalent of about 5 hours per day of full sunlight. Notice that by having picked such a steep tilt angle for the array we have minimized the month-to-month variation in energy delivered. If this array were to be powering a remote site with a constant demand for power we would have to even up

Table 3.13 Capacity Factor and Energy Delivered by an 18-watt Array in Santa Maria

Month	Jan	Feb	Mar	Apr	May	Jun	July	Aug	Sept	Oct	Nov	Dec	Annual
CF	0.20	0.22	0.23	0.22	0.20	0.19	0.20	0.21	0.22	0.22	0.20	0.20	0.209
Energy Delivered KWH/mo	2.68	2.66	2.78	2.85	2.68	2.46	2.68	2.81	2.85	2.95	2.59	2.68	32.7

those output fluctuations with a battery storage bank capable of carrying excess energy from the good months on into the poorer months. The steep tilt angle therefore helps keep the necessary battery storage capacity to a minimum.

Photovoltaics with Synchronous Inverter

If utility power is available, the most exciting prospect for a home electric system is to combine a solar-cell array with a synchronous inverter as shown in Figure 3.33. Recall from the wind-electric system discussion that synchronous inverters convert dc power to ac with the proper voltage, frequency, and phase to match the electricity coming from the utility. If more power is being generated by your solar cells than is needed by the load, the excess is fed back to the utility (in essence running your electric meter backwards giving you the equivalent KWH credit). If insufficient power is being generated, the utility makes up the deficit. Thus your home always has the electricity it needs without the need for any separate battery storage.

For many utilities, the peak demand for power comes during the summer on hot, sunny days when everyone turns on their air conditioners. This is just when your photovoltaic array will be putting out its maximum amount of power and hence you may actually help the utilities shave their peak demand and reduce their need for new generating capacity.

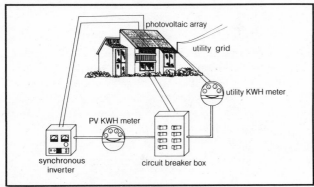

Figure 3.33 Residential photovoltaics array with synchronous inverter.

Example: Size a photovoltaic system which will generate an average of 500 KWH per month (typical for a single family residence) in an area with an annual capacity factor of 0.2, using 12 percent efficient silicon cells.

At $1 per watt for the cells, $2 per square foot of cells for the mounting hardware, $0.25 per watt for the synchronous inverter, and $500 for miscellaneous wiring, estimate the cost of the system. If the system is financed with a 20-year, 12 percent loan, what would be the cost per KWH?

Solution: Rearranging Equation 3.14 to solve for the peak power of the array gives

$$peak\ power = \frac{500\ KWH/mo \times 12\ mo/yr}{0.2 \times 8760\ hr/yr} = 3.4\ KW$$

At 12 percent efficiency and 93 watts/ft² (full sun) the area of cells would be:

$$\frac{3400\ watts}{0.12 \times 93\ watts/ft^2} = 305\ ft^2$$

The total system cost would then be

Solar cells, 3400 watt @ $1/watt	$3400
Mounting Hardware, 305ft² @ $2/ft²	610
Synchronous inverter, 3400 watt @$0.25/watt	850
Miscellaneous wiring	500
Total	$5360

From Table 3.11 the capital recovery factor for a 12 percent, 20-year loan is 0.1339 so the annual payments would be

$$A = P \times CRF = 5360 \times 0.1339 = \$717/yr$$

Over a year's period this system would sell the utility as much electricity during the days as it buys back during the nights, for a net exchange of zero. If the utility would buy back electricity at the same price that they sell it, our cost per KWH would be

$$\frac{\$717/yr}{500KWH/mo \times 12\ mo/yr} = 11.9¢/KWH$$

As an average cost of electricity for the next 20 years, this is not bad. With the various state and federal tax credits applicable now, that cost would be reduced to a level that is comparable to the price utilities charge today.

Sizing Battery Storage

In sizing battery storage we must distinguish between applications where an auxiliary electric energy source is available to supplement the photovoltaic array (such as a diesel-generator set) and truly remote applications where the photovoltaics must reliably supply 100 percent of the year-in year-out demand (such as a lighted buoy floating in the ocean somewhere).

There is no "right" way to size storage when auxiliary energy is available, though there are some guidelines that should be adhered to. For example, the full-sunlight charging current from the photovoltaic array should not exceed the recommended charging rate for the batteries. This constraint should cause no difficulty since you'll want to have enough battery capacity to hold at least one long sunny day's worth of energy anyway. That means you won't be charging the batteries at anything much faster than an 8-hour rate, which is sufficiently slow to avoid overheating of the batteries.

Another factor to remember is that batteries should not be discharged below about 40 percent of their rated capacity if battery lifetime is to be maximized. Also note that, especially in the winter, the solar cell array may not be able to fully charge a large battery bank and the auxiliary may periodically have to be used to bring them up to a full charge condition.

The more difficult design job involves sizing battery storage when no auxiliary power is available. The following example illustrates a straightforward design approach that gives reasonable results. We'll follow it with a more elegant procedure if you want to get fancy.

Example: Size an array and determine the storage requirements for a remote system capable of delivering 0.25 watts continuously into a 9-volt load in Santa Maria, California. This could be the power supply for the hand calculator used with the anemometer we designed in the wind measurement section of this chapter. Size the storage so that fully charged batteries would be no more than 60 percent discharged after five days with no solar input.

Solution: Let's use a 60° tilt angle for the array so that we can use the capacity factors from the previous example. The worst month is June, with a capacity factor of 0.19. Using Equation 3.14, our array must have a peak power rating of

$$\frac{0.25 \; watts \; \times \; 720 \; hours/mo}{0.19 \; \times \; 720 \; hours/mo} = 1.3 \; watts$$

Let's add a safety factor of 30 percent, giving us an array capable of delivering $1.3 \times 1.3 = 1.7$ peak watts.

To charge a 9-volt battery we'll need to supply roughly 10 volts peak (allowing for the diode drop, and so on), which, at 0.45 volts per cell (silicon), would require

$$\frac{10 \; volts}{0.45 \; volts/cell} = 22 \; cells \; in \; series$$

In addition we'll need enough cells in parallel to supply 1.7 watts/10 volts = 0.17 amps. Individual cells about one square inch each can do that. The maximum battery discharge will be

$$5 \; days \; \times \; 24 \; hr/day \; \times \; 0.25 \; watts = 30 \; watt\text{-}hours$$

To be no more than 60 percent discharged, the batteries must be rated at 30 watt-hours/0.6 = 50 watt-hours, or (at 9 volts) 5.5 amp-hours.

The above example used capacity factors to determine the worst month, and the array sizing was based on meeting that worst-case condition. You can sometimes do

a better job of sizing by trading off battery storage capacity for photovoltaic area. That is, by including more storage capacity, energy from the good months may be carried over into the poorer months, making it possible to use a somewhat smaller solar cell array. The following procedure can be used for such longer-storage designs.

1. Using Equation 3.14, calculate the peak power rating of the solar cell array that would deliver the annual energy required by the load. It is best to do this calculation for a steep tilt angle, say the latitude plus 20° as a starting point.

2. Set up a table with month-to-month insolations, resulting capacity factors, solar cell array energy outputs, and energy demands.

3. For each month calculate the excess (or deficit) energy generated by the photovoltaics sized in step 1.

4. To start the storage requirement calculation, assume the batteries are fully charged at the beginning of the year. Then keep a running total, month by month, of the state of discharge of the batteries. In months where there is more energy delivered from the array than the batteries need to be brought to full charge, the accumulated discharge doesn't go positive but is fixed at zero. Continue this running total through the year and into the next year until the pattern of monthly discharges begins to repeat itself (this puts us into a steady state solution that is independent of our initial assumption of fully charged batteries on January 1).

5. Find the month with the greatest level of battery discharge, given as so many KWH. This capacity should be augmented by an amount of storage that corresponds to a string of no-sun days that might happen to occur at the end of the worst month found above.

6. For maximum lifetime, the batteries must be big enough so that they never drop below a 40 percent charge. Therefore dividing the maximum KWH of discharge found in step 5 by 0.6 will tell us the battery capacity needed to cover the monthly variation in solar flux plus a string of rainy days and still have a tolerable level of charge in the batteries. The capacity can also be expressed in the more usual amp-hours of storage by dividing the watt-hours by the system voltage.

7. To account for the variation in insolation from year to year and the losses in charging and discharging the battery bank, the solar cell array should be increased beyond the size calculated in step 1 by about 30 percent.

8. Repeat the procedure for a larger solar cell array and compare total costs.

Notice this procedure starts by finding the smallest

solar cell array to cover the annual load and then the resulting battery capacity to carry us from month-to-month. If we increase the array size we can decrease the storage capacity required. If we reduce the tilt angle we can probably use a smaller array but more storage would be required. To find the economically optimum solution would require several iterations of this procedure and hence could require a computer. Suffice it to say that as long as solar-cell prices are high, an array slightly larger than the minimum will usually work out quite well.

Example: Size a solar-cell array and battery storage bank to reliably deliver 3 KWH per day to a load in Santa Maria, California (this could be a small house, for example). Allow storage for five continuous days of no sun.

Solution: Let us use a 60° tilt for the array since we already have the monthly capacity factors worked out from a previous example.

First we must size the array in terms of its rated (peak) power:

$$rated\ power = \frac{annual\ energy\ delivered}{annual\ CF \times 8760\ hr/yr}$$
$$= \frac{3000\ watt\text{-}hr/day \times 365\ day/yr}{0.209 \times 8760\ hr/yr}$$
$$= 598\ peak\ watts$$

The succeeding steps require month-by-month calculations. Let's work them out for January and just present the results for the other months in a table.

$$January\ output = rated\ power \times CF \times$$
$$24\ hr/day \times 31\ days/mo$$
$$= 598 \times 0.20 \times 24 \times 31$$
$$= 88,900\ watt\text{-}hours$$
$$= 88.9\ KWH$$
$$January\ demand = 31\ days/mo \times 3\ KWH/day$$
$$= 93\ KWH$$

$$January\ excess\ generated = 88.9 - 93$$
$$= -4.1\ KWH\ (deficit)$$

Filling in the table for the other months follows this same procedure (Table 3.14). Notice how the accumulated deficit adds up. If the batteries are fully charged on January 1, then at the end of January they have been discharged by 4.1 KWH. In February 4.4 KWH can be added to the charge, which means they regain full charge (no deficit) at the end of February. By the end of the first year the accumulated discharge is 14.3 KWH. Thus the end of January in the second year leaves the batteries discharged by 18.4 KWH. By the end of April, however, they are fully charged again and the steady state monthly discharge pattern begins to repeat itself.

The maximum discharge is 18.4 KWH due to monthly variations in sunshine; we must then add 5 days × 3 KWH/day or 15 KWH of storage to allow for a string of rainy weather at the end of January when the batteries are at their lowest charge. The maximum total discharge then becomes 18.4 + 15 = 33.4 KWH. For this to be 60 percent of the total storage capacity (leaving a 40 percent charge) we divide by 0.6 to get 33.4/0.6 = 55 KWH total capacity. For a 120-volt system this can be translated to

$$\frac{55,000\ watt\text{-}hours}{120\ volts} = 458\ amp\text{-}hours$$

Finally, step 7 recommends a safety factor of 30 percent for the photovoltaic array, which makes its final power rating 777 peak watts (1.3 × 598). At 1979 prices of $8 per watt for photovoltaics and $60 per KWH for batteries, the total system would cost $6200 for cells and $3300 for batteries for a total of about $9500. That's pretty steep for roughly 90 KWH per month!

It is a good idea to repeat the procedure with a larger array size to reduce the amount of storage required.

Table 3.14   Calculating the Accumulated Deficit for Battery Storage Sizing, Santa Maria Example

Month	Days/mo	CF	Energy Delivered (KWH/mo)	Energy Demand (KWH/mo)	Excess Generated (KWH/mo)	Accumulated Deficit First Year (KWH)	Accumulated Deficit Second Year (KWH)
Jan	31	0.20	88.9	93	−4.1	−4.1	−18.4
Feb	28	0.22	88.4	84	4.4	0	−14.0
Mar	31	0.23	102.3	93	9.3	0	−4.7
Apr	30	0.22	94.7	90	4.7	0	0
May	31	0.20	88.9	93	−4.1	−4.1	−4.1
June	30	0.19	81.8	90	−8.2	−12.3	−12.3
July	31	0.20	88.9	93	−4.1	−16.4	−16.4
Aug	31	0.21	93.4	93	0.4	−16.0	−16.0
Sept	30	0.22	94.8	90	4.8	−11.2	−11.2
Oct	31	0.22	97.9	93	4.9	−6.3	−6.3
Nov	30	0.20	86.1	90	−3.9	−10.2	−10.2
Dec	31	0.20	88.9	93	−4.1	−14.3	−14.3
Annual	365	0.209	1095	1095	0		

Example: Redo the previous example with a 10 percent larger solar cell array and compare the total costs.

Solution: Instead of using 598 watts peak output for the basic array size, let's try 660 watts. The presentation of the calculation in Table 3.15 shows that the array always meets the required demand. Batteries are required only for a five-day string of bad weather, that is, 15 KWH. For battery lifetime, dividing by 0.6 gives the total storage requirement as 25 KWH or 2080 amp-hours at 12 volts.

Table 3.15   Reworking the Santa Maria Example with a Larger Array

Month	CF	Energy Delivered (KWH/mo)	Energy Demand (KWH/mo)	Excess Generated (KWH/mo)	Accumulated Deficit, KWH
Jan	.20	98	93	5	0
Feb	.22	97	84	7	0
Mar	.23	113	93	10	0
Apr	.22	104	90	14	0
May	.20	98	93	5	0
June	.19	90	90	0	0
July	.20	98	93	5	0
Aug	.21	103	93	10	0
Sept	.22	104	90	14	0
Oct	.22	108	93	15	0
Nov	.20	95	90	5	0
Dec	.20	98	93	5	0

Increasing the array size by 30 percent as a safety factor gives an 858-watt array. At $8 per watt and $60 per KWH this system costs $6864 for cells and $1500 for batteries for a total of $8364, a considerable savings over the initial design.

The Future

Once cells drop below about $1 per watt the cost of remote systems will no longer be critically dependent on cell prices but rather will be dominated by batteries, support racks, design and installation costs, inverters, and miscellaneous electronic equipment. For many installations, especially those in areas where utility electricity is available, many of these fixed costs can be eliminated. Home generated electricity can be fed back into the grid with a synchronous inverter, eliminating battery costs; conventional electric-driven air conditioning equipment could be run directly off the photovoltaics—here demand and supply are roughly coincident and storage requirements are minimal or eliminated entirely; electric cars could get their energy from photovoltaics, shifting the battery costs to the vehicle itself rather than the photovoltaic system.

Imagine driving your pollution-free electric car to work and plugging into the solar cell array mounted on the parking structure, while you go about your business in a building whose air conditioning system runs directly off the cells on the roof, then returning to your home, which of course already heats and cools itself with the sun but now even provides for its own electrical needs.

Electricity From A Stream

If you are fortunate enough to have a small stream flowing through your property, you may be able to use it to generate electricity for your home. If your needs are modest, you will probably be amazed at how small a flow is required. A meandering stream, rolling along at only a couple of miles per hour and having a cross section of only a few square feet, gives up more energy in falling several feet than you are likely to need to power *all* your electrical appliances. In this section you will learn how to estimate the energy that your stream can supply and some methods by which that energy can be captured, stored, and converted into electricity.

Power and Energy from Water

A stream contains two kinds of energy: by virtue of its velocity, it has *kinetic* energy; and by virtue of its elevation it contains *potential* energy. The kinetic energy in most streams is not great enough to be useful; it is the potential energy between two sites of differing elevations that we try to exploit. Very simply, the idea is to divert some of the water from a site upstream, transport it along an elevated conduit, and then let it fall through a waterwheel or hydraulic turbine located at a lower elevation downstream. The turbine (or waterwheel) turns a generator which produces electricity. The water then returns to the stream.

The amount of power obtainable from a stream is proportional to the rate at which the water flows and the vertical distance which the water drops (called the *head*). The basic formula is

$$\text{E. 3.15} \qquad P = \frac{QHe}{11.8} = \frac{AvHe}{11.8}$$

where P is the power obtained from the stream in kilowatts; Q is the flow of water in cubic feet per second (cfs); A is the average cross-sectional area of the stream in square feet; v is the average velocity of the stream in feet per second; H is the height the water falls (head) in feet; 11.8 is a constant which accounts for the density of water and the conversion from ft-lb/sec to KW; and e is the overall conversion efficiency.

The above relationship tells us how much power a stream has to offer. To account for the various losses which occur during the conversion to electricity, we have included in the above estimate an efficiency factor, e, which includes the conversion efficiency of the turbine or water wheel, as well as losses associated with the generator and any gearing. Table 3.16 gives some representative values for conversion efficiencies of various types of prime mover (to be described later); these efficiencies should be multiplied by about 0.75 to account for generator and gearing losses. As can be seen waterwheels are considerably less efficient than turbines with overall efficiencies, *e*, of probably around 0.4 at best, while turbines may achieve an *e* of something closer to 0.6.

Table 3.16 Representative Efficiencies for Various Types of Waterwheels and Turbines[a]

Prime Mover		Efficiency Range
Waterwheels:	Undershot	25–45%
	Breast	35–65%
	Poncelot	40–60%
	Overshot	60–75%
Turbines:	Reaction	80%
	Impulse	80–85%
	Crossflow	60–80%

Notes: a. From *Micro-Hydro Power: Reviewing An Old Concept*, by R. Alward et al.

In order to use Equation 3.15, the stream flow rate (*Q*), or the velocity (*v*) and cross-sectional area (*A*), must be determined. In a later section we indicate how to measure these important quantities, but for now let's look at some example calculations.

Example: At 50 percent conversion efficiency, how much power could be obtained from a flow of water having a cross-sectional area of 1 square foot, a velocity of 1 foot per second, and a fall of 10 feet?

Solution: We use our formula and find that

$$P = \frac{AvHe}{11.8} = \frac{1 \times 1 \times 10 \times 0.5}{11.8}$$

$$= 0.42 \; KW = 420 \; watts$$

Now 420 watts may not seem like much until you realize that if this power can be obtained 24 hours a day, in a month's time we could accumulate about

$$0.42 \; KW \times 24 \; hr/day \times 30 \; days/month$$
$$= 300 \; KWH/month$$

This is enough electrical energy to run lights, refrigerator, freezer, power tools, pumps, hi-fi, and so on; probably all you would need unless you used an electric water heater or electric space heating. (See "Calculating Your Energy Requirements" in this chapter.)

This example points out how little the *average* flow can be and yet be sufficient to meet our monthly *average* electrical-energy demand. You will recall, however, that we must be concerned not only with average electrical demand, but also with *peak* power demand. While our sample stream can deliver 420 watts continuously, what happens when we flip on a few appliances and demand jumps to several thousand watts? Either we must always have sufficient flow in the stream to provide that peak power demand or we need a way to store up energy when it is not needed to provide for these peaks. With a wind system it was recommended that such storage be provided by batteries or, if possible, the utility grid. For a water system we have the additional alternative of storing potential energy in a reservoir of water behind a dam and drawing the reservoir down as necessary to meet peak demands.

System Considerations

There are some fundamental differences between one water-power system and another. The key determinants include the physical characteristics of your site (do you have large flows and a small head or vice versa or something in between?); for what purpose are you generating the power (to run some low-speed mechanical loads or to generate electricity); and whether it is a truly remote site or is utility backup power close at hand.

If your requirement is to generate power for low-speed, high-torque, mechanical loads such as for milling and grinding operations or heavy shop machinery like saws, lathes, and drill presses, then in some circumstances a big, slow-turning waterwheel may be appropriate. Later we will describe various types of waterwheels.

For electrical loads, a highly geared-up waterwheel may work fine, but in most circumstances, a high-speed, hydraulic turbine such as the one shown in Figure 3.34 makes much more sense.

For such electrical applications, the type of turbine to use is highly dependent on the combination of head and flow available. Obviously, the higher the head available the lower the flow required to produce a given amount of power, and this consideration will dictate the size and type of turbine to use. Later we will describe the various turbines available and the proper circumstances for their use.

"High head" installations, by definition, are typically considered to be those with at least 50 feet of available head, while "low head" installations have less—some as little as 5 to 10 feet. One advantage of high head installations is that less water needs to be moved around, which means smaller diameter piping can be used and the physical size of the turbine is reduced; both factors helping to

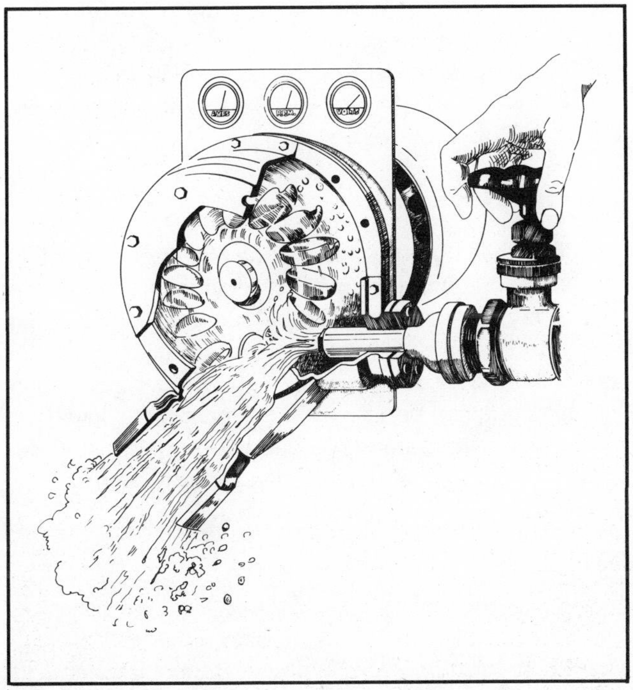

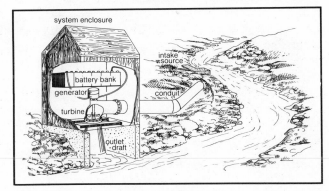

Figure 3.35 Typical low head installation.

Figure 3.34 A hydraulic turbine connected to an electrical generator.

Figure 3.36 Typical high head installation.

reduce installed costs. For example, one turbine, the Hydromite described later, is so small it weighs only 6.5 pounds and could fit into a shoe box, yet it can deliver enough energy to meet the electrical appliance demands of most households.

Figure 3.35 illustrates a typical low head installation with a relatively short large-diameter closed conduit (called a penstock), while Figure 3.36 illustrates the high head counterpart. In both cases the intake is shown coming directly from the stream, though a dam could be used to increase available head. The intake should be protected with a trash rack of spaced iron bars to screen incoming debris, and it is also a good idea to build a small holding chamber to allow silt to settle out.

The final key consideration in the initial planning of a microhydro installation is whether or not you will need some means of storage, and, if so, what type.

Systems With No Storage

If flows are sufficient, it may be desirable to design the system with no storage—everything gets sized to meet peak power demands and the excess power potential at any given time is simply not utilized. A dam may be incorporated, but its purpose is merely to increase head; the pond does not get drained down to meet peak demands.

Example: What flow rate, Q, is required to meet a peak power demand of 6 KW from a 50 percent efficient system with 10 feet of available head?

Solution: Rearranging Equation 3.15 gives us

$$Q = \frac{11.8\,P}{He} = \frac{11.8 \times 6}{10 \times 0.5} = 14.2\ cfs$$

If this much flow is available then we could generate as much as

$$6\,KW \times 720\ hr/mo = 4320\ KWH/mo$$

but this probably greatly exceeds our electric energy requirements (unless the house uses electric space heating). Some means must be provided then to track the demand for power so that our turbine-generator delivers only what is needed. This is accomplished with a governor.

Governors can be mechanical or electrical. The mechanical ones control power either by diverting flow on and off of the turbine blades or by regulating the amount of flow through the turbine. The speed of the turbine shaft may thereby be controlled, making possible the use of a synchronous generator which puts out 60-cycle ac ready for home use. An example of this type of setup is the Hoppes Hydroelectric Unit manufactured by James Leffel and Company, which is shown in Figure 3.37.

Electronic governors regulate output by controlling

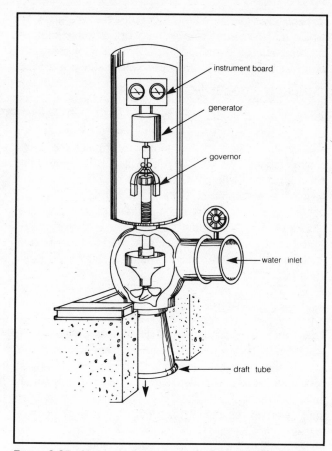

Figure 3.37 Hoppes hydroelectric unit with mechanical governor.

the generator rather than the turbine. The generator governor can either act simply as a voltage regulator, varying the field current (see "Wind Energy Conversion Systems" in this chapter) according to load, or can be even nicer and divert excess power to secondary loads such as your solar hot-water storage tank (we did this in the wind section as well, if you recall).

Systems With Storage

For most small hydro systems some form of energy storage will be required to meet peak demands, and the choices are three: a dam can be built and the resulting pond can be drawn down as needed; a battery storage bank with inverter can be used; and finally, if it is available, the utility grid can be used with a synchronous inverter.

Traditionally, storage has been accomplished with a pond. The energy that can be delivered from such storage is given by the following expression:

E. 3.16 $$E = \frac{VHe}{42,500}$$

where E is given in KWH; V equals the pond volume in cubic feet; e is the conversion efficiency; and H is the average head, in feet, over the period of generation.

Example: What volume of water would be necessary to provide 10 KWH of storage (about one day's worth of energy for a small household) if the average head available is 12 feet and the overall efficiency is 50 percent?

Solution: Rearranging Equation 3.16 gives

$$V = \frac{42,500 \times 10}{12 \times 0.5} = 70,830 \ ft^3$$

A pond 120 feet by 120 feet and 5 feet deep would have this volume, so you can see this is a fairly large body of water.

There are a number of reasons why drawing down a reservoir to meet peak demands is less than ideal. It would make downstream flow sporadic, which could upset the local ecology, your downstream neighbors, and could even be a violation of local water laws. The pond, too, would be constantly filling and emptying, which from the point of view of aesthetics and recreational benefits is less than desirable. And you have to build a dam, which can be an extensive undertaking that will change the character of your stream. Finally, the penstock, turbine, and generator all have to be sized for peak flows, which makes them bigger and hence more expensive than if they're designed for average flows.

A better alternative is to use a system designed for average power demands and use batteries for storage. Such a system, as shown in Figure 3.36, is entirely analogous to the self-sufficient wind system of Figure 3.5. A dc generator charges batteries which supply dc to some loads and, by means of an inverter, ac to others. The major difference has to do with sizing the battery storage; while wind systems may have to rely on the batteries for days on end with no charging current, hydro systems are always delivering some current to the batteries. This not only means increased battery lifetime, but it also means much less battery storage capacity needs to be provided.

The amount of battery storage required depends on the usage pattern throughout the day. Clearly if the daily load curve is flat, meaning the power demand is constant and equal to the power being generated, there is no need for any storage. It is when there are large peaks separated by periods of low demand that the most storage is required. In most household circumstances if the batteries are sized to store somewhere between one-half of a day's average energy demand and a full day's demand, then they will easily cover any peak power periods without excessive discharge.

Example: What flow rate would be required to supply 400 KWH per month from a 60 percent efficient system with a 50-foot head? What size generator should be used and what battery storage capacity would give a half day's worth of storage in a 32-volt system?

Solution: The average power demand would be

$$\frac{400 \ KWH/mo}{720 \ hr/mo} = 0.55 \ KW$$

so our generator needs to have at least this capacity. The flow rate, from equation 3.15, is

$$Q = \frac{11.8P}{He} = \frac{11.8 \times 0.55}{50 \times 0.6} = 0.22 \ cfs$$

or about 100 gallons per minute.

One-half day's energy demand is

$$\frac{1}{2} \times \frac{400 \ KWH/mo}{30 \ days/mo} = 6.7 \ KWH/day$$

so a 32-volt battery bank would be rated at

$$\frac{6700 \ watt\text{-}hour}{32 \ volt} = 209 \ amp\text{-}hour$$

Figure 3.38 shows the state of battery charge through a sample day with a rather peaked demand curve as

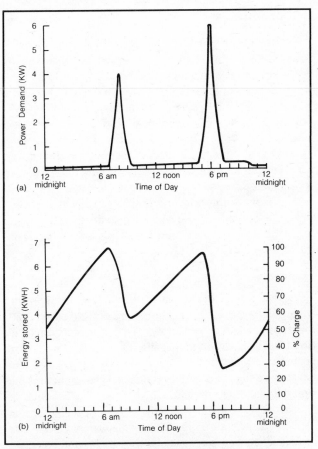

Figure 3.38 This rather extreme demand curve (a) causes batteries sized at ½ days storage to be excessively discharged in the evenings (b).

79

shown. In this fairly extreme case, the batteries sized at a half day's storage drop to a low of 30 percent of full charge at 7 P.M. It would be better if the state of charge could be held to at least 40 or 50 percent, so a slightly larger capacity should be specified.

Finally, as was true with wind systems, if utility power is available, and if the utility will go along with it, then you can eliminate the battery storage entirely by coupling your system through a synchronous inverter as is shown in Figure 3.39. This is the cheapest system of all since penstock, turbine, and generator are sized for average power demands rather than peak and no expensive battery and inverter system is required.

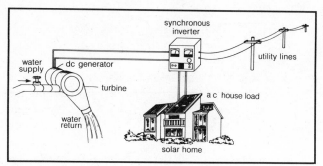

Figure 3.39 A hydro system coupled to the utility grid.

Estimating Water Flows

It is quite important to know not only average stream flows, but also minimum and maximums to be expected. You'll need to estimate minimum flows in order to be sure you'll always have enough power; you'll need maximum flows to be able to design your structures so that they will not create a danger during peak flooding. If you have lived on the property for a long time, you may be able to recall past conditions; or you may have to gather this sort of information from neighbors who are more familiar with the area.

Looking at the flow is one thing, but actually measuring it is something else. We will now describe two ways to go about measuring stream flows: the float method and the weir method.

Float Method

As we saw in our equation, the flow Q through the stream equals the cross-sectional area of the stream (A) measured at any site multiplied by the average velocity (v) of the water through that site ($Q = Av$). To apply the float method, first pick a section of stream about 100 feet long where the cross section is relatively constant and the stream is relatively straight.

To estimate the cross-sectional area of the stream at a given site, measure the depth of the water at a number of equally spaced points across the stream and calculate their average. The number of points needed depends on

the irregularity of the cross section, but five or ten should do. The cross-sectional area is then determined by multiplying the width of the stream times the average depth. Do this at several "typical" points and average your results to obtain a more accurate answer.

To estimate the velocity, first measure the distance between two fixed points along the length of the stream where the cross-sectional area measurements were made. Then toss something that will float—a piece of wood or a small bottle—into the center of the stream and measure the length of time required for it to travel between the two fixed markers. Dividing the distance by the time gives you the average velocity of the float. But since the stream itself encounters drag along its sides and bottom, the float will travel a bit faster than the average velocity of the stream. By multiplying the float velocity by a correctional factor of about 0.8, an estimate of average stream velocity is obtained.

Example: Estimate the flow rate Q for the stream whose cross section is shown in Figure 3.40. The width is 6 feet and the five depth measurements are (in feet) 0.3, 0.5, 1.0, 1.2, and 0.5. A float traveled a distance of 100 feet along the stream in 50 seconds.

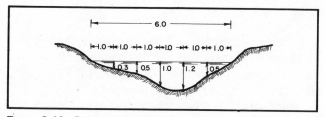

Figure 3.40 Determining a stream's cross-sectional area.

Solution: The average depth is

$$d = \frac{0.3 + 0.5 + 1.0 + 1.2 + 0.5}{5} = 0.7 \ ft$$

The cross-sectional area is therefore

$$A = 6 \times 0.7 = 4.2 \ ft^2$$

The stream velocity, including the correctional factor of 0.8, is

$$v = \frac{100 \ ft}{50 \ sec} \times 0.8 = 1.6 \ ft/sec$$

The flow rate is thus

$$Q = Av = 4.2 \times 1.6 = 6.7 \ cfs$$

Weir Method

This method gives more accurate results than the float method, but it requires a bit more work in that a weir must be constructed. Figure 3.41 shows the basic arrangement.

80

A water-tight, rectangular-notched dam is constructed and provision is made for measuring the height of the water surface above the notch. The weir should be located in the center of the stream, its crest should be sharp (as shown in the figure), and the streambed in front of the weir must be as flat as possible. The head H is measured several feet upstream from the weir, as shown. The dimensions of the weir and the head are all that are needed to obtain accurate flow measurements, using the following hydraulic relation:

E. 3.17 $Q = CLH^{3/2}$

where Q equals the flow in cfs; L equals the width of the weir opening in feet; C equals a discharge coefficient; and H equals the head above the weir in feet.

The discharge coefficient (C) can be determined from Figure 3.42, given the head (H) and the dimensions of the weir (P is the height from the streambed to the weir opening; b is the width of the stream).

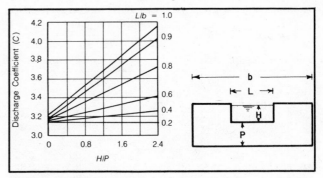

Figure 3.42 Discharge coefficient for a notched, sharp-crested weir (after King and Brater, 1963).

From Figure 3.42, the coefficient is determined to be $C = 3.3$. So the flow is

$$Q = 3.3 \times 2.4 \times (0.6)^{3/2} = 3.7 \text{ cfs}$$

If you install the weir permanently and put a scale on the measuring stick for the head, you can easily prepare a discharge chart. Then, any time you want to measure flow, you just read your stick and find the flow on your chart.

Conduits

To take advantage of the upstream head, the water must be transported to the powerhouse in some sort of conduit. The conduit can be an open channel, as is usually the case when a waterwheel is used, or a full-pressure conduit (pipe), which is usually required for turbines. Sometimes both are used.

Water is conveyed through conduits at the expense of part of its energy, which is lost mostly because of the friction between the water and the walls of the conduit. These losses are reduced as conduit size increases, but costs increase correspondingly. Also, in open channels, reducing the slope decreases the water's velocity, thereby reducing head losses; but again, this requires larger channels to provide the same total flow rate. There are trade-offs involved in any design. In most circumstances you'll be using a turbine which requires water to be delivered under pressure and the best conduit choice is PVC pipe, which has less head loss and is cheaper than its steel or concrete counterparts.

To help you size the conduit, Table 3.17 gives flow capacity and friction loss for straight Schedule 40 PVC thermoplastic pipe. Steel pipe in fair condition will have about double the head loss shown.

To determine the head loss associated with valves and elbows in the pipe, you can use Table 3.18. The values given are the length of straight pipe which would have the same head loss as the valve or fitting. So you just add these equivalent lengths to the actual length of straight pipe to get total head loss.

As a general design guideline you should try to keep

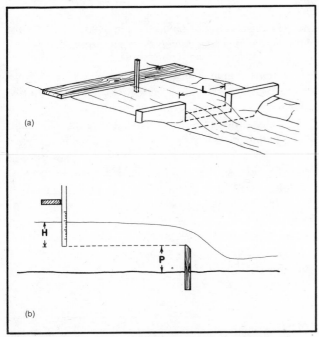

Figure 3.41 Weir and measurements to determine stream flow.

Example: A rectangular-notched, sharp-crested weir having a crest 0.5 feet above the streambed and a width of 2.4 feet sits in a channel 4 feet wide. The head is determined to be 0.6 feet. Calculate the flow.

Solution: To get the coefficient C from Figure 3.42, we need the following ratios:

$$\frac{L}{b} = \frac{2.4}{4.0} = 0.6 \qquad \frac{H}{P} = \frac{0.6}{0.5} = 1.2$$

Table 3.17 Head Loss per 100 Feet of Schedule 40 PVC Pipe

Pipe Size	Flow Rate (gpm)												
	50	100	150	200	250	300	400	500	750	1000	2000	3000	4000
2"	5.79	20.9											
2½"	2.42	8.72	18.5										
3"	0.81	2.93	6.20	10.6									
4"	0.21	0.76	1.61	2.75	4.16	5.83	9.93						
5"	0.07	0.24	0.52	0.88	1.34	1.87	3.19	4.82					
6"	0.03	0.10	0.22	0.37	0.56	0.78	1.33	2.00	4.25	7.23			
8"	0	0	0.05	0.09	0.14	0.20	0.34	0.51	1.08	1.84			
10"	0	0	0	0.04	0.05	0.07	0.11	0.17	0.36	0.61	2.19		
12"	0	0	0	0	0	0	0.05	0.07	0.15	0.26	0.94	1.99	3.41

flow speeds in pipe to something less than about 5 feet per second and your overall head loss in the pipe to less than 10 percent of the available head.

Example: Determine the head loss with 0.22 cubic feet per second of flow through 400 feet of 4-inch PVC pipe containing four 45° elbows and one gate valve, three-quarters open.

Solution: Each elbow is equivalent to 5.4 feet of pipe and the gate valve adds another 11.7 feet, so the total equivalent length of pipe is $4 \times 5.4 + 11.7 + 400 = 433$ feet. Our flow rate is

$$0.22 \; ft^3/sec \times 7.5 \; gal/ft^3 \times 60 \; sec/min = 100 \; gpm$$

so from Table 3.17 the head loss is 0.76 feet per 100 feet of pipe. Our total loss is then

$$\frac{0.76}{100} \times 433 = 3.3 \; feet$$

It is important to remember to use the net head (available vertical head minus pipe friction head loss) for H in Equation 3.15.

Example: With a vertical head of 50 feet and the 4-inch PVC pipe of the last example carrying 0.22 cfs, what power would be generated by a 60 percent efficient system?

Solution: The net head is $50 - 3.3 = 46.7$ feet, so, using Equation 3.15, the power generated would be

$$P = \frac{QHe}{11.8} = \frac{0.22 \times 46.7 \times 0.6}{11.8} = 0.52 \; KW$$

The loss of head in the pipe has cost us about 7 percent of the available power, which seems acceptable.

If your channel is an open one, then we need to be able to pick its size and slope to deliver the amount of water required with a tolerable head loss.

If the channel is simply a ditch in the ground, its slope will be largely determined by the terrain. But if you have a choice, a slope of about 0.1 to 0.3 percent (corresponding to a head loss of 1 to 3 feet per 1000 feet of conduit) is to be recommended. As a rough guideline, channels should be designed to produce flow velocities on the order of 3 to 6 feet per second (less if there may be an erosion problem in the channel).

The design of a conduit consists of picking the dimensions of both the conduit cross section and the conduit's slope so that it transports a given flow of water with

Table 3.18 Equivalent Lengths of Fittings, in Feet of Pipe.

Fitting	Pipe Diameter							
	2"	2½"	3"	4"	6"	8"	10"	12"
Globe Valve, Conventional fully open	58.6	70.0	86.9	114.1	171.8	226.1	283.9	338.2
Angle Valve, fully open	25.0	29.8	37.1	48.6	73.3	96.4	121.1	144.3
Gate Valve, fully open	2.2	2.7	3.3	4.4	6.6	8.6	10.9	12.9
three-quarters open	6.0	7.2	8.9	11.7	17.7	23.3	29.2	34.8
half open	27.6	32.9	40.9	53.7	80.9	106.4	133.6	159.2
quarter open	155.0	185.2	320.1	302.0	454.9	598.6	751.5	895.4
90° Standard Elbow	5.5	6.2	7.7	10.1	15.2	20.0	25.1	29.8
45° Standard Elbow	2.8	3.3	4.1	5.4	8.1	10.6	13.4	15.9
90° Long Radius Elbow	4.3	5.1	6.3	8.3	12.5	16.5	20.7	24.7

minimal head loss. The head loss in an open channel is equal to the slope; while in a pressure conduit, the head loss depends only on the velocity of the water and the diameter and material of the pipe. The nomograph of Figure 3.43, which applies to both the channel and the pipe cases, enables us to work out graphically the required calculations.

Example: Find the slope needed to convey 7 cfs in the trapezoidal rock channel whose base has a width (*D*) of 2 feet, whose sides are inclined at 1:1.5, with water flowing at a depth (*d*) of 1 foot (Figure 3.43).

Solution: The solution is worked out on the nomograph as follows: on the right-hand graph, locate the point corresponding to (*d/D*) = 0.5 for the cross section with z = 1.5, and project it horizontally to the left edge of the graph. From there, the line is drawn down through the point corresponding to *D* = 2 on the width line to the Center Reference Line. From the Center Reference Line, project up through the Discharge point *Q* = 7 cfs to the Friction Loss scale, where we read off a value of about 4 feet of head for *every* 1000 feet of channel. So the slope is 0.4 percent.

This example indicates how to calculate the amount of head lost in conveying water from the dam site to a distant powerhouse. You will need to do this sort of calculation in order to decide whether it makes sense to locate the powerhouse near the dam or whether sufficient extra head can be gained to locate it elsewhere.

Turbines

The most logical way to generate electricity from water is with a turbine; their efficiency is typically in the 80 percent range and their high rotational speed provides a good match to the needs of an electrical generator. Fortunately in the last few years a number of new small turbines have been introduced to the marketplace and, coupled with sophisticated electronic controls and storage schemes, it is now possible to utilize microhydro power with little change in your stream and quite reasonable economics.

Turbines are classified as either impulse or reaction types. *Impulse* turbines use the kinetic energy of water squirting out of a nozzle at high speed to turn the turbine wheel (called the *runner*). It is usually turbines of the impulse type that are utilized in high head situations. The Pelton wheel, the Turgo wheel, and the cross-flow turbine are all examples of impulse turbines.

In *reaction* turbines, part of the available head is converted to kinetic energy and the rest remains as pressure head. The flow takes place under pressure, which means the whole unit is enclosed in a case as opposed to the open housing of an impulse turbine. Reaction turbines are classified as of the Francis design or propeller design and are useful in low to medium head installations.

Pelton Wheel

The Pelton wheel, which was first developed in America and patented back in 1880, is the most common impulse turbine. The turbine in Figure 3.34 is a Pelton wheel, and as can be seen, a nozzle shoots a high-speed stream of water against a series of curved paddles or buckets attached to a small wheel.

These turbines are used only in high head situations (above 50 feet) where their efficiencies, while typically closer to 80 percent, can in some cases be in the low 90s. As high head devices they can be physically quite small, which means they rotate at high speed and are thus well matched to the demands of an electric generator.

Independent Power Developers, Inc. (Rt. 3, Box 174-1, Sandpoint, Idaho 83864) manufacture a tiny 4-inch Pelton wheel. The turbine is directly coupled to a 32-volt dc generator which can produce up to 2000 watts or about 1400 KWH per month. The turbine-generator set sells for around $1000, while a complete installation with turbine, generator, batteries, inverter, and pipe probably runs closer to $5000. Table 3.19 gives some representative monthly energy productions from this unit.

Table 3.19 Energy Output (KWH/mo) from Independent Power Developers' 4-Inch Pelton Wheel/Generator

Head (ft)	Flow Rate (gpm)			
	15	20	25	30
50	80	110	—	—
100	160	215	270	325
150	240	325	400	480
200	320	430	540	645
250	400	540	670	800

Another manufacturer of Pelton wheels is Small Hydroelectric Systems & Equipment (15220 S.R. 530, Arlington, Washington 98223). They have been producing 4.5-, 9-, and 18-inch wheels designed for outputs from a few hundred watts to 50,000 watts. Systems with outputs exceeding 2000 watts can be purchased with Woodward governors and synchronous generators for direct conversion to 60-cycle ac. Their turbines have been designed to accommodate as many as four jets, so that a given turbine can be used in a variety of head and flow combinations. For example, supplying 20 gpm onto their 4½-inch wheel with a 50-foot head delivers 100, 200, 300, or 400 watts, depending on how many jets are utilized.

Table 3.20 gives some idea of the many combinations that these systems allow; notice when four jets are used on the 9- and 18-inch wheels, two wheels are stacked together. The cost of the turbines alone runs somewhere around $700 for the 4½-inch wheel to $1500 for a pair of 9-inch wheels; a complete 15 KW system with alternator and governor starts at about $6000. They are now

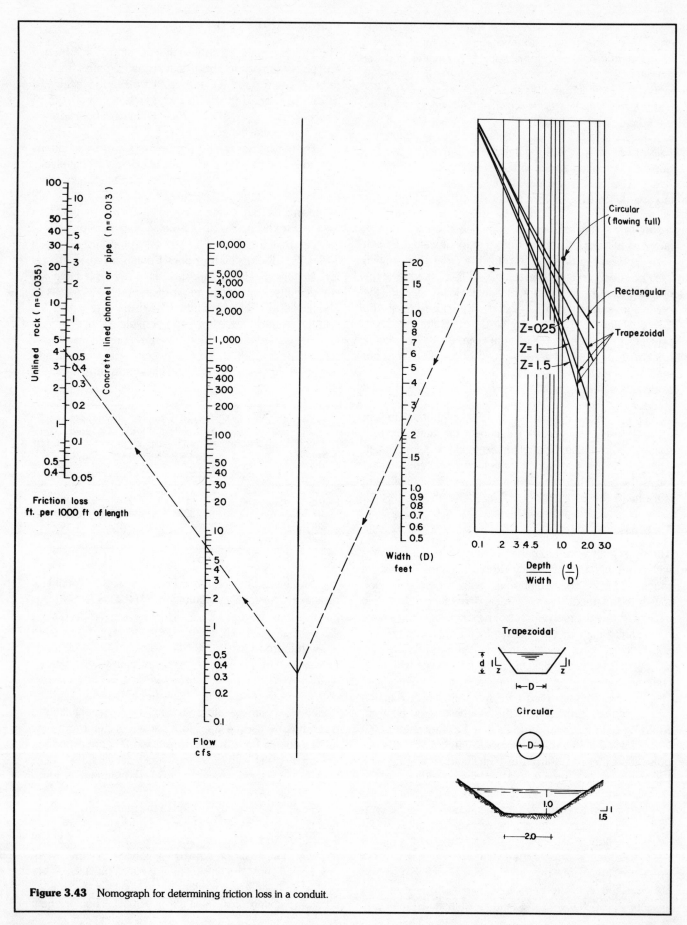

Figure 3.43 Nomograph for determining friction loss in a conduit.

Table 3.20 Example of Power Outputs from Three Pelton Turbines from Small Hydroelectric Systems & Equipment[a]

Head (ft)	gpm/jet	4½inch 1 jet (watts)	4 jet (watts)	9-inch gpm/jet	1 Wheel 1 jet (watts)	2 Wheel 4 jet (watts)	18-inch gpm/jet	1 Wheel 1 jet (watts)	2 Wheel 4 jet (watts)
25	14	25	100	40	125	500	125	250	1000
50	20	100	400	54	275	1100	180	800	3200
75	24	180	720	67	550	2200	216	1750	7000
100	28	280	1120	77	800	3200	252	2500	10,000
150	34	500	2000	95	1450	5800	306	5000	20,000
200	39	800	3200	108	2200	8800	356	7500	30,000

Notes: a. Assumes generator conversion factor of 1 KW/hp.

introducing a new line of wheels with improved characteristics. Write them for their newest catalog.

Other sources of Pelton wheels include Alaska Wind & Water Power (P.O. Box G, Chugiak, Alaska 99567); Pumps, Pipe and Power (Kingston Village, Austin, Nevada 89310); and Elektro GmbH (St. Gallerstrasse 27, Winterthur, Switzerland).

There is another impulse turbine called a Turgo wheel that is similar to a Pelton, but the runner has a different shape and the jet comes in from the side rather than dead center. The Turgo spins faster than a Pelton and has a smaller size for the same output, which potentially means the product could cost less and be better matched to the requirements of a high-speed generator. It is available from one manufacturer, Gilbert Gilkes and Gordon, Ltd. (Kendal, Westmorland, England).

Banki/Michell (Cross-Flow) Turbine

The Banki/Michell turbine was first invented by the Australian engineer A. Michell in the beginning of this century. Later, the Hungarian professor D. Banki improved and patented it. Today it is most widely known by his name, although sometimes it is called a Michell or cross-flow turbine. Banki turbines have been built for heads from 3 to 660 feet, with rotational speeds of between 50 and 2000 rpm; they are especially recommended in medium head situations (about 15 to 50 feet).

The main parts of a Banki turbine are the runner and the nozzle (Figure 3.44). A jet discharged from the rectangular nozzle strikes the blades on the rim of the runner, flows over the blade, passes through the inner space of the runner, and then strikes the blades for a second time. Efficiencies of manufactured units are on the order of 80 to 88 percent and, unlike reaction types, these turbines are efficient over a wide range of flows.

Banki turbines can be built at home by a fairly skilled person. Students at Oregon State University nearly thirty years ago built such a turbine, which turned out to have an efficiency of 68 percent. And H. W. Hamm describes how to build a 12-inch Banki turbine (see Bibliography).

The Ossberger-Turbinenfabrik (D-8832 Weissenburg 1. Bay, Postfach 425, West Germany), which has installed thousands of these turbines, is now joined in the marketplace by an American company, Bell Hydroelectric (3 Leatherstocking St., Cooperstown, New York 13326).

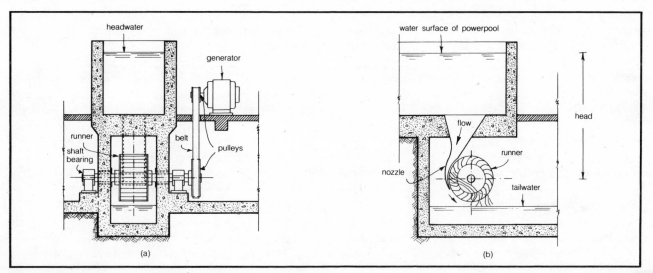

Figure 3.44 Two views of a Banki/Michell turbine (after Hamm).

Reaction Turbines

For low head installations reaction turbines are the ones most commonly used. Rather than having the runner be shot at by a stream of water as is the case with impulse turbines, reaction turbine runners are completely immersed in water and derive their power from the water's mass rather than its velocity (see Figure 3.45).

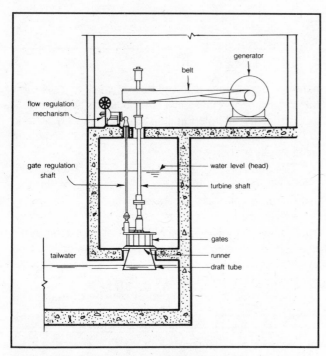

Figure 3.45 Example of a small hydroelectric facility using a Sampson turbine from James Leffel and Co.

A commonly used reaction turbine design has a runner that looks like an outboard motor propeller. Many large (megawatt) installations use a propeller type runner with variable-pitch blades which can be adjusted according to flow (Kaplan turbine), but on small installations this degree of sophistication would be too expensive.

Independent Power Developers, Inc. of Idaho manufactures a fixed-pitch propeller turbine designed for heads of from 5 to 50 feet. Their basic 3 KW system including batteries and inverter costs something like $4000.

James Leffel and Company (Springfield, Ohio 45501) has been manufacturing reaction turbines since 1862. Their Hoppes Hydroelectric system (Figure 3.37) is well suited to the low-power applications being considered here. It is a very compact unit with a generator mounted on the same shaft as the turbine. It comes with a governor for regulation of the rotational speed and is available with either ac or dc generators. Standard sizes deliver from 0.5 KW to 10 KW with heads of from 8 to 25 feet at a cost

of from about $7000 to $13,000. Table 3.21 gives several available sizes.

There is a new miniturbine available now from Canyon Industries (5346 Mosquito Lake Road, Deming, Wyoming 98244). Called the Hydromite, it will produce 150 to 700 watts with flows of 30 to 40 cfm on quite modest heads of 15 to 34 feet. The turbine itself costs less than $500.

Table 3.21 Sample Hoppes Hydroelectric Units[a]

Capacity (KW)	Range of Heads (ft)	Range of Flows (cfs)
0.5	8–12	1.7–1.1
1.0	8–25	3.2–1.1
2.0	8–25	5.5–1.8
3.0	8–25	7.8–2.6
5.0	8–25	12.7–4.3
7.5	11–25	13.3–6.3
10.0	12–25	16.3–8.0

Notes: a. Available from James Leffel and Company.

Other sources of reaction turbines include: G & A Associates (233 Katonah Ave, Katonah, New York 10536); Barber Hydraulic Turbines Ltd. (Barber Point, P.O. Box 340, Port Colborne, Ontario, Canada, L3K5W1); Elektro GmbH (St. Gallerstrasse 27, Winterthur, Switzerland); Jyoti Ltd. (R. C. Dutt Rd, Baroda — 390 005, India); and Land and Leisure Services, Inc. (Priory Lane, St. Thomas, Launceston, Cornwall, England).

Waterwheels

Waterwheels are turned both by the weight of water in their buckets and by impulse. Their efficiency, which may be anywhere from 35 to 85 percent, is little affected by varying flow rates and they are not damaged by sand and silt in the stream. Waterwheels are categorized according to the location at which the water strikes the wheel. An *overshot* wheel (Figure 3.46) accepts water at the top of its rotation; its downward-moving side is overbalanced by the water and this overbalance keeps it in slow rotation. The *breast* wheel receives water halfway up its height (Figure 3.47) and turns in the opposite direction as an overshot type. Breast wheels are not recommended because they are relatively inefficient and are harder to build and maintain than overshot wheels. Lastly, the *undershot* wheel (Figure 3.48a) is powered by water as it passes under the wheel. One version of the undershot wheel is the *Poncelet* wheel of Figure 3.48b. By curving the vanes to reduce the shock and turbulence as the water strikes the blades, a Poncelet wheel is able to achieve much higher efficiencies than an ordinary undershot.

Waterwheels are a rather "low" technology; they can be built without much in the way of special skills, materials, or tools. The shaft of a waterwheel can be coupled

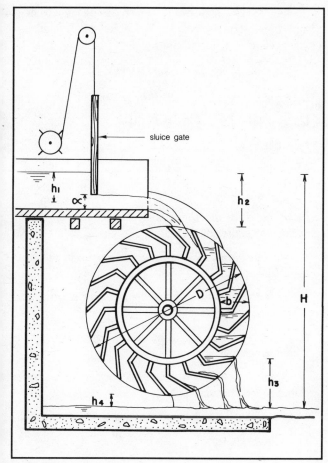

Figure 3.46 An overshot wheel.

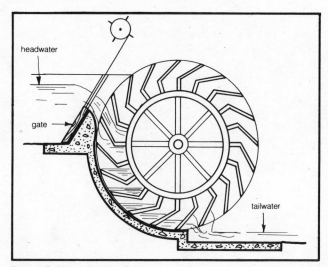

Figure 3.47 A breast wheel.

by means of belts and pulleys directly into such low-speed mechanical loads as saws, lathes, water pumps, and mills; but their low turning speed makes it difficult to couple them into electrical generators. A typical waterwheel turns at something like 5 to 15 rpm and, since an automobile generator needs 2000 to 3000 rpm to put out much current, a gear ratio of about 300:1 would be required. Such high gear ratios are quite difficult to attain, which severely limits the usefulness of the waterwheel–automobile-generator combination. There are generators, used in commercial wind-electric plants, which put out significant power at lower rpms; however they are considerably more expensive.

To speed up the rotation of a shaft, pulleys and belts

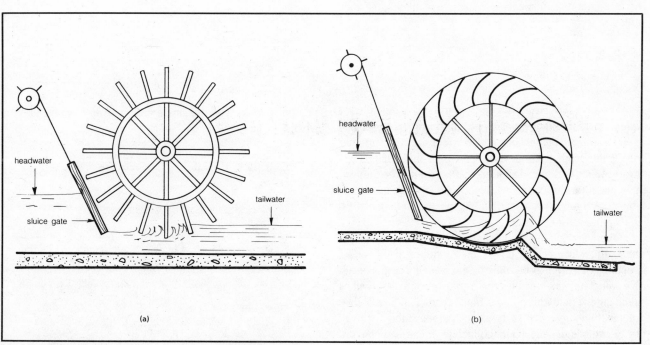

Figure 3.48 A simple undershot wheel (a) and a Poncelet wheel (b).

can be used, as shown in Figure 3.49. The ratio of the speeds of the shafts is equal to the ratio of the diameters of the pulleys:

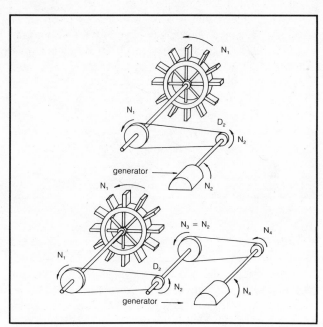

Figure 3.49 Slow turning water wheels need to be geared up.

E. 3.18
$$\frac{N_2}{N_1} = \frac{D_1}{D_2}$$

To obtain a speed increase of, say, 20 to 1, the diameter of one pulley would have to be 20 times the diameter of the other. For large speed increases, the step-up should be done in stages, as shown in Figure 3.49. In this case, the total increase in speed is equal to the product of each pulley ratio:

E. 3.19
$$\frac{N_4}{N_1} = \frac{D_1}{D_2} \times \frac{D_3}{D_4}$$

Overshot Wheels

The overshot wheel was one of the most widely used waterwheels in olden times. It has a number of sheet iron or wooden buckets around its periphery and is supplied with water from a flume over its top. If the buckets are smoothly curved and designed so that the water remains in them until the lowest possible point in the wheel's rotation, then relatively high efficiencies on the order of 60 to 75 percent are possible.

Overshot wheels can be used when the available head ranges from 5 to 30 feet; the diameter of the wheel is usually selected to be about three-fourths of the available fall. The flow through the flume is controlled with a sluice gate. The width of the wheel is usually 4 to 8 inches greater than the width of the sluice gate and the depth of the buckets is usually 10 to 16 inches. It is more efficient to have the buckets only about one-half to two-thirds full, to minimize water spillage.

There are several formulas which can be used to help design an overshot wheel. The variables are defined below, as well as in Figure 3.46:

D = diameter of the waterwheel (ft)

w_b = width of the buckets (ft)

w_s = width of the sluice gate (ft)

b = depth of the buckets (ft)

N = wheel rotational speed (rpm)

α = height of sluice gate opening (ft)

h_1 = head on the sluice gate, measured from water surface to center of opening (ft)

h_2 = vertical distance from water surface in flume to top of wheel (ft)

h_3 = vertical distance between tailwater surface and point where buckets start to empty (ft)

h_4 = vertical distance from bottom of wheel to tailwater surface (ft)

H = total available head, from surface of water in flume to tailwater surface (ft)

H_w = effective head for generating power (ft)

Q = flow rate (cfs)

The rotational speed of the wheel is given by

E. 3.20
$$N = \frac{70\sqrt{(h_2)}}{D}$$

The width of the buckets, assuming they are about two-thirds full, is given by

E. 3.21
$$w_b = \frac{30Q}{(D-b)bN}$$

The dimensions of the sluice gate opening, α and w_s, are related by

E. 3.22
$$w_s = \frac{Q}{6\alpha\sqrt{(h_1)}}$$

The effective head that the wheel sees is

E. 3.23
$$H_w = H - \frac{(h_3 + h_4)}{2}$$

and the power generated in kilowatts is given by

E. 3.24
$$P = \frac{QH_we}{11.8}$$

where the efficiency e is roughly 0.65 to 0.75.

Example: Design an overshot wheel for a site where the available head H is 16 feet and the flow is 8 cfs.

Solution: The wheel diameter should be about three-quarters of the fall so

$$D = 0.75 \times 16 = 12 \text{ feet}$$

Allowing a half-foot clearance between the wheel and the tailwater means h_4 equals 0.5. From the geometry

$$h_2 = H - (D + h_4) = 16 - (12 + 0.5) = 3.5 \text{ feet}$$

the rotational speed will be

$$N = \frac{70\sqrt{(h_2)}}{D} = \frac{70\sqrt{(3.5)}}{12} = 10.8 \text{ rpm}$$

Selecting the bucket depth to be 1.2 feet makes its width

$$w_b = \frac{30Q}{(D-b)bN} = \frac{30 \times 8}{(12-1.2) \times 1.2 \times 10.8} = 1.7 \text{ feet}$$

If a half-foot clearance is allowed between the top of the wheel and the bottom of the sluice gate, then the depth of water in the flume will be 3 feet. We will want the sluice gate to be narrower than the width of the buckets and we must try to find a value for α that will make this work out. Assume we open the gate 20 percent so α is 0.6 feet. Then by the geometry

$$h_1 = 3 - (0.6/2) = 2.7 \text{ feet}$$

we find that

$$w_s = \frac{Q}{6\alpha\sqrt{(b_1)}} = \frac{8}{6 \times 0.6 \times \sqrt{(2.7)}} = 1.35 \text{ feet}$$

That's good: it allows for some dispersion of the water as it is discharged from the gate. Finally, if we assume the buckets are shaped so that they don't start to release their water until they reach a point 2.5 feet from the tailwater, then h_3 equals 2.5 feet. The effective head is therefore

$$H_w = H - \frac{h_3 + h_4}{2} = 16 - \frac{2.5 + 0.5}{2} = 14.5 \text{ feet}$$

Assuming the efficiency of the wheel to be 65 percent, we find the power generated to be

$$P = \frac{QH_w e}{11.8} = \frac{(8 \times 14.5 \times 0.65)}{11.8} = 6.4 \text{ KW}$$

Undershot Wheels

A regular undershot waterwheel has radial paddles which are turned by the force of the water flowing beneath the wheel. The paddle design is quite inefficient and wheel efficiencies of only 25 to 45 percent are typical. They are used with heads of about 6 to 15 feet and have diameters which are typically 10 to 15 feet.

The Poncelet wheel is an improved version of an undershot wheel. By curving the vanes to create smoother interaction with water released from the sluice gate, efficiencies of 40 to 60 percent are possible. These wheels can be used with quite low heads (about 3 to 10 feet). The wheel diameter is usually taken to be about double the head, plus 4 to 8 feet; a 14-foot diameter is usually as small as they come. The vanes are placed 10 to 14 inches apart along the periphery if they are made of metal, and 14 to 18 inches if they are wooden.

Breast Wheels

Breast wheels take their name from the arc of masonry or wood sheathing that encloses the wheel from the point where the water enters the wheel to the point it is discharged. Water is thus confined between the wheel and the breast and this close spacing can cause problems if sticks or rocks get jammed inside. The buckets of breast wheels are specially formed to allow air to escape as water flows in, which complicates construction. Because efficiencies are generally less than the overshot or Poncelet wheel and construction is also more difficult, breast wheels are not generally recommended.

Dams

While the availability of batteries and synchronous inverters for storage reduces the need for them, dams can still be important as a way to increase the available head. The reservoir created can also be useful for livestock watering, fire protection, and general recreation. The first step in building a dam is to select a suitable site. You should find a spot where the stream is narrow and the banks are high. Keep in mind the need to develop as much head as possible; a place where the stream is relatively steep is best. Bear in mind, too, the high cost of transmitting electrical currents at low voltages over long distances (see "Site Selection" in this chapter); you will want the site to be not much more than 1000 feet from the house.

The height of the dam will depend on the amount of water to be stored, the head needed, the topography of the site, the available materials, and your expertise. The cost, work, and materials associated with building a dam increase rapidly with dam height. If you want a dam higher than about 5 feet, you will need the advice of a qualified engineer; indeed, many states require an engineer by law.

The best season to build a dam is late summer, when stream flows are lowest. You will probably need a diversion channel to allow the stream to bypass the dam during construction. Also, it is wise to set up a time schedule for your work to be sure that you can finish the job before fall rains start.

The dam must be designed properly to enable it to withstand safely the forces acting upon it: the hydrostatic pressure of water trying to overturn the dam or slide it downstream; the uplift caused by water which finds its way between the dam and its foundation; and while concrete dams can handle overflows, earthfill dams may be washed away if they are overtopped.

Water seeping through the foundation can undermine a dam and cause its failure. If you are lucky enough to have a streambed of solid rock, you don't have to worry; but most beds consist of permeable sand or gravel. One way to prevent seepage in such beds is to use sheet piles, set one right next to another to form an impermeable wall. The depth to which the piles must be driven depends on the kind of soil, the thickness of the permeable layer, and the depth of the water in the pond. If the pervious soil in the bed is not very deep, the sheet piles can be driven down to the solid rock below, as shown in Figure 3.50a. If the pervious layer is deep, then it is recommended that the foundation be sealed by covering the streambed upstream of the center of the dam with a blanket of impervious material such as clay (Figure 3.50b).

The dam itself may be any of a number of types. The most common low dams are earthfill, rockfill, crib, framed, and gravity dams.

Earthfill dams, such as those in Figure 3.50, may be constructed from clay, sand, gravel, or a combination of these elements, depending on what's available. To be on the safe side, the slope of the downstream side should be 1:2 and on the upstream side it should be about 1:2.5 or 1:3. To prevent seepage through the dam, clay is the best construction material. If you don't have enough clay for the whole dam, then a core of clay in the center (Figure 3.50) is satisfactory. The slopes on the clay core can be about 5:1. Along the sides of the core, you must have a transition zone of material of grain size intermediate between clay and the material used to construct the main body of the dam. If you don't have any clay at all, the dam can be sealed by putting a plywood or masonry wall in the core.

Since earthfill dams can be washed away if they are overtopped by water, a well-designed and well-constructed bypass spillway must be provided. Even with a good spillway, the dam should be built high enough to provide a substantial safety factor to prevent overflow during the maximum expected flood. The less information on floods that you have, the higher this safety margin should be; a washout could result in considerable destruction for which you can be (legally) liable.

Rockfill dams are similar to earthfill dams, except that the rock construction allows steeper slopes on the dam faces as shown in Figure 3.51. A slope of 1:1.3 is typical. One common way to prevent seepage through this type of dam is to cover the upstream face with concrete or asphalt.

Crib dams are probably the closest to a beaver's dam. They are made of logs or timber stacked as shown in Figure 3.52. The logs are spaced 2 or 3 feet apart, with stones or gravel to fill the openings. To prevent leakage through the dam, cover the upstream face with planks. If excess water is to be allowed to spill over the dam, then the downstream face also should be covered. Crib dams are built only to very low heights.

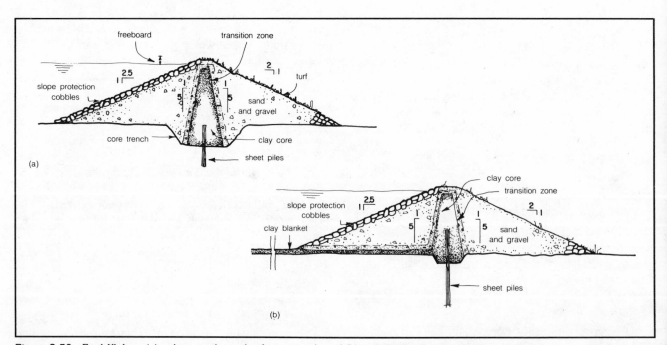

Figure 3.50 Earthfill dams (a) with center sheet piles driven to rock, and (b) sealed with an underlying layer of clay.

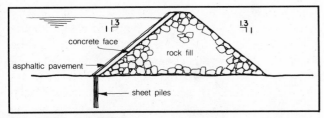

Figure 3.51 A rockfill dam.

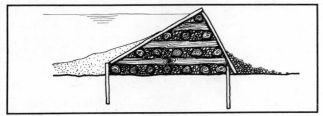

Figure 3.52 A crib dam.

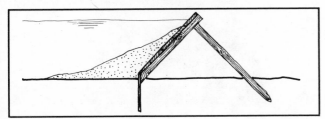

Figure 3.53 A framed dam.

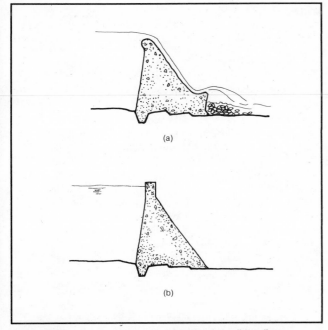

Figure 3.54 Gravity dams, with (a) and without (b) spillway.

Framed dams are also made of wood (Figure 3.53). The sheeting which faces the water must be well supported, calked, and preserved with some water sealant. The spacing of the frame depends on the thickness of the timber and the water pressure acting on it (i.e., the height of the water in the pond).

Finally, gravity dams are made of masonry or concrete and, as shown in Figure 3.54, the spillway can be part of the dam. Discharged water from the spillway may eventually erode the streambed and start to undermine the dam foundation unless a concrete stilling basin or some rocks are used to dissipate the energy of the falling water.

Before filling the pond for the first time, some preparatory measures are recommended. It is good practice to clear the reservoir of all trees and bushes and clear a marginal strip around the water's edge. This will help prevent undesirable tastes and odors caused by decaying plants in the bottom of the pond, and enhance its usefulness for agriculture, drinking water, and safe swimming.

Final Thoughts

As we have seen in this section, a great deal of power can be obtained from quite small stream flows, with heads that are not too difficult to obtain. Even so, not many people are likely to have the optimum set of conditions required for a hydroelectric station. For those that do, there are a number of important things to consider before attacking that nice creek that flows through the corner of your property.

You must thoroughly check out the water-rights laws which apply to your area before doing anything to alter "your" stream—and this applies to uses other than power, such as irrigation or water supply. Unfortunately, these laws vary so much from area to area that there are few generalizations that can be made. You should realize, however, that just because you own the land does not necessarily mean you own the water that passes over it.

The likelihood of your being able to secure the necessary water use permits easily will be greatly increased if your disruption of the stream is kept to a minimum. Run-of-the-river installations are obviously preferable to ones requiring construction of a dam. If a dam is necessary, you may need a permit from the Corps of Engineers and certain mitigating measures may be required, such as construction of a fish ladder. A short introduction to the regulatory conflicts you are likely to encounter can be found in *Micro-Hydro Power: Reviewing an Old Concept* (see Bibliography).

While government interest in your project may seem an intrusion at the permit stage, you may appreciate it in the long run. The Department of Energy is actively encouraging small hydro projects with a small grants program, and there are various state and federal tax credits for renewable energy that may apply.

In the right circumstances a small hydro project can be your most cost-effective way to meet your electrical needs with minimal environmental effect. You may even be able to swim around in your own energy "bank."

Bibliography

Wind-Electric Sources

Baumeister, T., and Marks, L. S. 1974. *Standard Handbook for Mechanical Engineers*. New York: McGraw Hill. This book has a short (but good) chapter on wind by E. N. Fales.

Cheremisinoff, N. P. 1978. *Fundamentals of Wind Energy*. Ann Arbor, Michigan: U. of Michigan Press.

Eldridge, F. R. 1975. *Wind Machines*. Washington, D.C.: The National Science Foundation. A well presented overview of wind power basics.

Energy Task Force. 1977. *Windmill Power for City People*. A step-by-step documentation of an urban system actually tied into the grid with a synchronous inverter. Available from the Energy Task Force, 156 Fifth Avenue, New York, New York 10010.

Golding, E. W. 1955. *The Generation of Electricity by Wind Power*. New York: Philosophical Library. The standard, but old, textbook.

Hackelman, M. A. 1974. *Wind and Windspinners*. Focus is on Savonius rotors, but packed with practical advice for any homebuilt system. Available from Earthmind, 4844 Hirsh Road, Mariposa, California 95338.

———— 1980. *At Home With Alternate Energy: A Comprehensive Guide to Creating your own Systems*. Culver City, California: Peace Press. Covers wind especially but also includes material on other energy sources.

Inglis, D. R. 1978. *Wind Power and Other Energy Options*. Ann Arbor, Michigan: University of Michigan Press.

Justus, C. G. 1978. *Winds and Wind System Performance*. Philadelphia: Franklin Institute Press. Theoretical wind analysis that provided basis for correlation used in our Figure 3.14.

Park, J. and Schwind, D. 1978. *Wind Power for Farms, Homes, and Small Industry*. Washington, D.C.: U.S. Department of Energy. Just about the best thing written on all aspects of small WECS. Available from NTIS, U.S. Department of Commerce, Springfield, Virginia 22161.

Sencenbaugh, J. 1978. *Sencenbaugh Wind Electric Catalog*. While this is really a manufacturer's catalog, it contains a wealth of practical information applicable to any wind installation. Available from Sencenbaugh Wind Electric, P.O. Box 11174, Palo Alto, California 94306 for $2.

Syverson, C. D. and Symons, J. G. 1974. *Wind Power*. Mankato, Minnesota: Wind Power. Many good design guidelines and details. Available from Wind Power, P.O. Box 233, Mankato, Minnesota 56001.

Wind Power Digest, Bristol, Indiana. A quarterly publication that is essential for keeping up with the field. Check back issues for systems you can build (e.g. Spring 1976, Summer 1979). Their special "Wind Access Catalog" editions are great updates. Subscriptions cost $8 per year. Write to 54468CR31, Bristol, Indiana 46507.

Photovoltaic Sources

Moll, E. M. 1975. *Wind/Solar Energy*. New York: Howard W. Sams & Co. A practical little book on solar and wind applications.

Pierson, R. E. 1978. *Technicians and Experimenters Guide to Using Sun, Wind, and Water Power*. New York: Parker Publications. Useful if you want to buy a few cells and try them out.

Pulfrey, D. L. 1978. *Photovoltaic Power Generation*. New York: Van Nostrand Reinhold. Fairly technical; light on practical applications.

Solarex Corporation. 1979. *The Solarex Guide to Solar Electricity*. Washington, D.C.: Solarex Corporation. Just about the only simple and useful book around, from one of the manufacturers.

Water-Power Sources

Alward, R., Eisenbart, S., and Volkman, J. 1979. *Micro-Hydro Power: Reviewing an Old Concept*. Butte, Montana: The National Center for Appropriate Technology. This is a very good update of hydro information. Available for $5.25 from NTIS, 5285 Port Royal Road, Springfield, Virginia 22161.

Hamm, H. W. (n.d.) *Low-Cost Development of Small Water-Power Sites*. Mt. Rainier, Maryland: Volunteers in Technical Assistance. An interesting book containing, among other things, practical instructions on how to build your own Banki/Michell turbine. Available from: VITA, 3706 Rhode Island Avenue, Mt. Rainier, Maryland 20822.

"Hydroelectric Power from a Hoppes Hydroelectric Unit," Bulletin H-49, and "Improved Vertical Samson Turbines," Bulletin 38. Springfield, Ohio: James Leffel and Co. The two above bulletins give information on small turbines manufactured and available from James Leffel and Co., Springfield, Ohio 45501.

King, H. W. and Brater, E. F. 1963. *Handbook of Hydraulics*. 5th ed. New York: McGraw Hill.

Lindsley, E. F. 1977. "Water Power for Your Home." *Popular Science*, May 1977. A really outstanding article.

McGuigan, D. 1978. *Harnessing Water Power for Home Energy*. Charlotte, Vermont: Garden Way Publishers. The best book around; features details on many actual installations and sources of further information.

Mockmore, C. A., and Merryfield, F. 1949. *The Banki Water Turbine*. Bulletin Series no. 25. Corvallis, Oregon: Oregon State College. This book describes a Banki turbine made by students of the university and analyzes the results of experiments performed with that turbine.

Mother Earth News. 1974. *Mother Earth News: A Handbook of Homemade Power*. New York: Bantam Books. A good handbook with information on homemade waterwheels and turbines.

SOLAR THERMAL APPLICATIONS

**Thermal comfort: what it is
and how your body maintains it**

**Energy from the sun: how to
collect, store, and distribute it**

**How much heat
your house will require**

**Heating hot water, pools
and hot tubs**

**Passive and active
space heating analysis**

SOLAR THERMAL APPLICATIONS

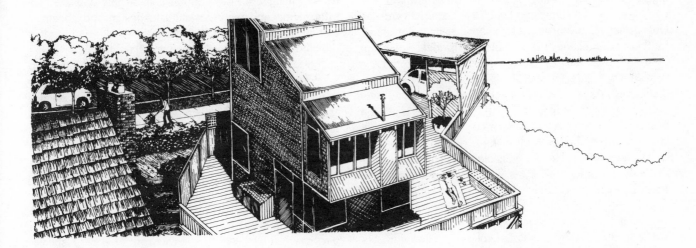

Introduction

The era of cheap fossil fuels, upon which our industrial society has been built, is nearing its end. U.S. production of oil and gas peaked nearly a decade ago and has been declining ever since; world production of these fuels will peak by the end of the 1990s.

Coal supplies will last longer, but the environmental price we'll pay for increased reliance on this inherently dirty fuel will be high. It would also appear likely that the CO_2 released during combustion would change the world's climate, with potentially devastating effects on agriculture, long before the world's relatively abundant reserves are consumed.

Nuclear fission, even if the problems of safety, waste storage, and plutonium diversions can be adequately addressed, will do little to reduce our dependence on petroleum, and fusion remains a dream.

That pretty much leaves solar energy in its many forms combined with an all-out effort to improve the efficiency with which we use energy as the most viable option in the coming years. Solar energy can be used to heat water, buildings, and industrial processes; it can be captured and stored during photosynthesis and the resulting biomass used directly as firewood or converted into portable liquid or gaseous fuels such as alcohol or methane; it can be converted into electricity in hydroelectric facilities, or by wind turbines, or by photovoltaic cells. The proper solar conversion technology is very closely coupled to the end use for that energy.

In this chapter, we address that one quarter of U.S. energy consumption that goes to heating and cooling of buildings and heating of service hot water. While many of the techniques for applying solar energy to these end uses have been around for centuries, it has only been in the last few years that they have become widely accepted. Indeed, with rapidly escalating costs of conventional fuels a virtual certainty through the coming decades, it can legitimately be said that any house built from now on that doesn't utilize solar to the maximum extent feasible is obsolete the day it is completed.

This is a fairly long chapter so before we get wrapped up in detail let us take a brief overall look at what is to follow. The chapter is divided into a number of major sections covering climatology, collectors, domestic hot-water and pool systems, thermal comfort, building heat loss and analysis, passive solar heating, active solar systems, and finally solar economics.

The solar resource section introduces you to the sources and interpretation of sunshine data that are essential to the design of any solar system. Techniques for determining the sun's position at any time are given along with data and procedures for evaluating its intensity on any surface under clear sky or cloudy conditions. Finally, methods for evaluating any potential shading problems that a site might have are presented.

Many systems use flat-plate collectors to convert sunlight into useful heat, and these important system components are described in the next section. You will be shown how to evaluate the individual parts of a collector and how to interpret manufacturer's efficiency curves to predict collector performance.

The next two sections introduce you to the most important applications of flat-plate collectors—the heating of domestic hot water and swimming pools. Many possible system diagrams are discussed with the goal of helping you choose the simplest, most efficient system for your own particular climate and needs.

The remainder of the chapter covers solar space heating. The thermal comfort section is concerned with the conditions contributing to a livable indoor environment. Unfortunately, this turns out to be an elusive undertaking, for there are presently no physiological models which can accurately describe integrated human response to climatic surroundings in terms specific enough to provide design guidelines. As a result, subjective personal sensitivity (what indoor conditions make you comfortable) is still the best guide to planning for indoor comfort. We hope that this section will help establish these personal guidelines by alerting you to certain physiological ramifications to, say, indoor temperature levels. The temperature level you select has a marked effect on the energy needed to heat your home. Heating requirements, typically, drop by 25 percent if you are willing to live at 65°F rather than 75°F. This adjustment implies smaller solar collection surfaces and less initial cost. But what of the effects on comfort?

The heat loss section introduces you to the theory of heat transfer and explains techniques for minimizing heat losses from buildings. The methodology for calculating heat loss is explained in detail, with sample calculations included to help you through the process. Means to compute seasonal heating requirements, which aid in determining the economic implications of a particular heating design, are also discussed.

Knowing how much energy needs to be supplied, we can then move on to techniques for meeting those needs. In the section on passive solar heating we examine a range of simple, inexpensive, but extremely effective ways to let the sun heat a house without the use of collectors and mechanical pumps or blowers. The use of windows, Trombe walls, greenhouses, and thermal mass will be illustrated and their effectiveness quantitatively predicted.

The section on active space heating systems covers methods of capturing energy by collectors, delivering it to a thermal storage unit, and distributing it throughout the house as needed. Such systems, while more complicated and hence more expensive than passive systems, offer a degree of energy control that is hard to obtain with passive systems.

Readers familiar with the first edition of this book will notice a significant departure from the design philosophy formerly expressed in this chapter. Our emphasis in the first edition was on designs for self-sufficient, 100 percent solar-heated houses. By backing off from that goal to one of a perhaps 60 to 75 percent solar contribution, the size and cost of the solar heating system can be cut in half. This more cost-effective philosophy is typical within the industry today.

The final section on economics will introduce you to the many ways that solar systems can be compared to their conventionally fueled counterparts.

We might mention that Chapter 2 presented a number of architectural features and siting considerations that are preliminary to the design of any solar house and that Chapter 3 covers the use of solar energy to generate electricity. Our goal in this chapter is to supply you with the information and technical skills to design and construct workable solar heating systems for a small building. It is directed at the person with very little technical background. You should do quite well if you have the spirit to read passages two or three times for full comprehension, the initiative to pursue the references for further details, and the confidence to handle simple, but sometimes tedious, algebraic computations. We assume some rudimentary knowledge of construction techniques, or else a knowledgeable friend. Finally, we suggest a willingness to experiment: learn from both your successes *and* your failures.

A word about units is in order. When dealing with energy or energy rates, we will use units of *Btu* and *Btu per hour* (Btu/hr). A Btu is a measure of energy, specifically, the amount of energy necessary to raise the temperature of 1 pound of water by 1 Fahrenheit degree (1F°). The seleccction of the Btu as a standard energy unit was made reluctantly. The United States is the last remaining adherent to this (and other) English units. The rest of the world has adapted to the metric (Systeme International, or SI) unitary standard, and the United States will undoubtedly follow suit in the next decade. In the meantime, most of the tabular and graphic information we have is in the English system of units—hence the decision. Should the need to convert units arise, Table 4.1 should be of some help.

The Solar Resource

Before any solar energy system can be designed, the local climate must be thoroughly investigated. Information on the amount of sunshine striking our collection surface for any time of the year must be coupled with data on temperature, wind speeds, and humidity before the proper type of solar system can be picked and components sized.

Where Is the Sun?

The availability of solar energy depends upon latitude, season, and weather patterns. Dependency upon the first two variables becomes obvious when one understands the trajectory of the earth around the sun. Figure 4.1 depicts a highly simplified model of this relationship.

The path of the earth around the sun is not a circle but an ellipse (though not a very pronounced ellipse). Since the sun is at one focus of the ellipse, the distance between the sun and the earth varies throughout the orbit. The earth is closest to the sun in December (89.8 million miles) and farthest in June (95.9 million miles).

Table 4.1 Useful Conversion Factors

Length
    1 ft = 0.3048 m
    1 in = 2.54 cm
Area
    1 ft² = 0.0929 m²
    1 in² = 6.452 × 10⁻⁴ m²
Volume
    1 ft³ = 1728 in³ = 0.0283 m³
    1 ft³ = 7.48 gallons
Mass and Density
    1 lbmᵃ = 0.453 kilograms
    1 lbm/ft³ = 16.018 kg/m³
Energy
    1 Btu = 778 ft-lbf = 252 calories = 1055.1 joule
    1 therm = 100,000 Btu
    1 KWH = 3413 Btu
Energy Flux
    1 langley = 1 cal/cm² = 3.69 Btu/ft² = 41840 joule/m²
Power
    1 KW = 3413 Btu/hr
    1 hp = 2545 Btu/hr = 550 ft-lbf/sec = 745.7 watts
Thermal Conductivities
    1 Btu/hr-°F-ft = 1.731 watt/°C-m
    1 Btu-in/hr-ft²-°F = 0.14423 watt/°C-m
Overall Heat-Transfer Coefficient
    1 Btu/hr-ft²-°F = 5.6783 watt/°C-m²
Heat Flow
    1 Btu/hr-ft² = 3.155 watts/m²
Pressure
    1 lbf/in² = 1 psi = 27.8 in-H₂O = 2.31 ft-H₂O = 6895 Pascal

Notes: a. The notation "lbm" refers to a unit of *mass*, as distinguished from "lbf," which denotes a *force*. The metric system avoids the ambiguity, mass is expressed in grams or kilograms, and force in dynes or newtons.

This relatively small variation makes an appreciable difference in the radiation intensity, since the intercepted radiation decreases with the square of the distance. Those of us in the northern hemisphere may thus ask, "Why isn't it warmer in January?" This is related to the earth's tilt, which is also depicted in Figure 4.1. The tilt, combined with orbital factors, gives rise to our seasons.

Figure 4.2 looks at the earth's tilt in a slightly different (and ancient!) perspective. Here we consider the earth fixed, spinning around its north-south axis, and the sun sitting somewhere out in space, slowly moving up and down as the seasons progress. On June 22 (the summer solstice)

the sun reaches its highest point, and a ray drawn to the center of the earth at that time makes an angle of 23.45° with the earth's equator. At the vernal (March 21) and autumnal (September 23) equinoxes the sun is directly over the equator; on December 22 (the winter solstice) the sun is 23.45° below the equator.

That angle formed between the plane of the equator and a line drawn from the center of the earth to the center of the sun is called the solar declination. The solar declination, δ, which varies between ±23.45°, can be found for any day of the year from the following relationship:

E. 4.1 $\delta = 23.45 \sin [360 \times (284 + N)/365]$

where N is the day number in the year ($N = 1$ is January 1, $N = 365$ is December 31). This expression will be useful later when we calculate shadow patterns.

Also shown in Figure 4.2 is a south-facing collector situated at latitude L on the earth's surface and tipped up relative to its local horizon at an angle equal to L. As can be seen, with this tilt angle the collector is parallel to the axis of the earth and at noon, during the equinoxes, the sun's rays are striking the collector at their best possible angle, that is perpendicularly. In fact, this figure readily leads to the conclusion that a good rule of thumb for year-round collection of solar energy would be to face your collector south and tip it up at an angle equal to your latitude.

If you want to emphasize winter collection for space heating, a collector tilt angle equal to your latitude plus 10° or 15° will give you the best performance. If you use a tilt angle of 10° or 15° less than your latitude you can maximize summer performance for a pool system. These rules of thumb should be used only as preliminary guidelines; as we will see later rather large deviations can be tolerated before system performance will be significantly reduced.

In many situations, knowledge of the sun's position in the sky at any given time of day is important. We all know that the sun rises in the east and sets in the west and reaches its high point sometime around noon. We can pinpoint the sun's location at any given time by means

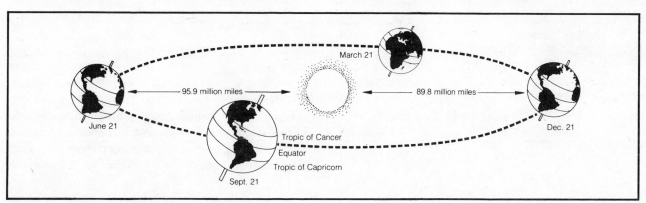

Figure 4.1 The motion of the earth around the sun.

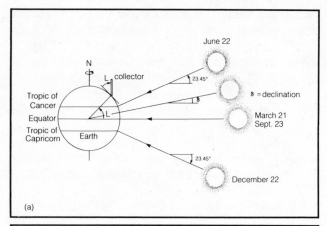

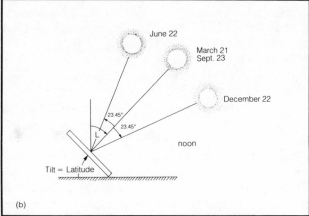

Figure 4.2 A collector tilted to the south at an angle equal to its latitude is perpendicular to the sun's rays at noon on the two equinoxes.

of an altitude angle, α, and an azimuth angle, a_s, as shown in Figure 4.3. The altitude angle at noon α_N is easily obtained from Figure 4.2 and is given by

E. 4.2 $\alpha_N = 90° - L + \delta$

Knowing your latitude, it is easy to obtain the highest and lowest noon angle from Equation 4.2. For example, if

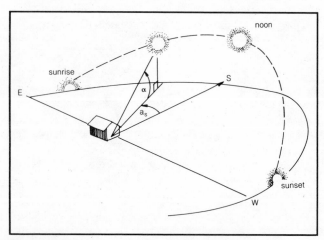

Figure 4.3 Identifying the altitude and azimuth angle of the sun.

your latitude is 40° north then the highest the sun ever reaches in the sky is $90 - 40 + 23.45 = 73.45°$ and the lowest noon angle is $90 - 40 - 23.45 = 26.55°$.

For any other time of day, the sun's altitude can be found from the relationship:

E. 4.3 $sin\ \alpha = cos\ L\ cos\ \delta\ cos\ h + sin\ L\ sin\ \delta$

where h is called the hour angle and is equal to 15° for each hour away from solar noon. That is to say, when the sun is due south it is solar noon and $h = 0$; two hours before solar noon it is 10:00 A.M. by sun time and $h = 30°$; and so on.

Finally, we can obtain the azimuth angle from the relationship:

E. 4.4 $sin\ a_s = \dfrac{cos\ \delta\ sin\ h}{cos\ \alpha}$

But relax, these important angles are tabulated for various latitudes in Appendix 4C along with the sun's clear sky intensity. We include them here in equation form in case your latitude is not close to one of those listed and you want very precise results.

If you're mathematically inclined, you might like to see these equations in action so let's do an example.

Example: Where is the sun at 9:00 o'clock in the morning (sun time) on February 21 at a latitude of 40°?

Solution: We first need to find the solar declination from Equation 4.1. February 21 is the 52nd day of the year so

$$\delta = 23.45\ sin\ [360(284 + 52)/365] = -11.2°$$

At 9:00, h is $3 \times 15° = 45°$, so now we can find the altitude angle from Equation 4.3:

$$sin\ \alpha = cos\ 40°\ cos\ (-11.2°)\ cos\ (45°) + sin\ 40°$$
$$\times\ sin\ (-11.2°)$$
$$\alpha = 24°$$

The azimuth angle can be found from Equation 4.4:

$$sin\ a_s = \frac{cos\ (-11.2°)\ sin\ 45°}{cos\ 24°}$$
$$a_s = 50°$$

So the sun is 50° east of south and up at an angle of 24°. (Bless those little hand calculators.)

If you do much solar design in a particular area you may find it convenient to graph the altitude angle a and azimuth angle a_s once and for all and keep the result handy. Such a graph, drawn for a 37½° north latitude, is

---

*Equation 4.4 works fine for azimuth angles less than 90°. For larger angles, subtracting a_s from 180° gives the correct result.

presented in Figure 4.4. The crossing lines indicate the hourly position of the sun. Later we'll see an important application of this graph as an aid to predicting times of the year when our collection surface is shaded by southerly obstructions.

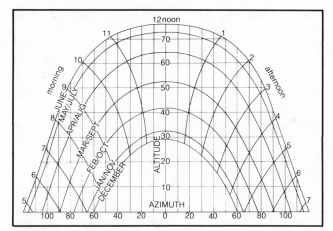

Figure 4.4 Solar altitude and azimuth for 37½° north latitude.

In looking at Figure 4.4 did you happen to notice that morning sun will strike the north side of your house during the summer? The June 21 azimuth angle at sunrise in this example is about 120° east of south, which puts it all the way around to the northeast quadrant.

Finally, for the sake of completeness, let us introduce one more equation. For most solar work, it is fine to deal exclusively in solar time (ST), where solar noon is the time at which the sun is due south, but you may have occasion to want to use local standard (clock) time (LT) instead. The following relationship connects these two time systems:

E. 4.5 $ST = LT + 4 (LT_{meridian} - longitude) + E$

where $LT_{meridian}$ is the local time meridian, which is given for the various time zones in the United States in Table 4.2; and where E is a factor called the equation of time, which corrects for various earth-orbit phenomena. Figure 4.5 gives E.

Example: What is the local standard time at solar noon in Washington, D.C. (longitude 77° west) on April 1st?

Solution: Washington is on eastern time so the LT-meridian is 75°. On April 1 E is about −5 minutes, and at solar noon ST is 12:00. Solving for local time from Equation 4.5

$$LT = 12:00 - 4(75 - 77) - (-5)$$
$$= 12:00 + 8 + 5 = 12:13$$

One little reminder: during the summer you may be

Table 4.2   The Local Time Meridians for U.S. Standard Time Zones

Time Zone	LT-meridian
Eastern	75°
Central	90°
Mountain	105°
Pacific	120°
Yukon	135°
Alaska-Hawaii	150°

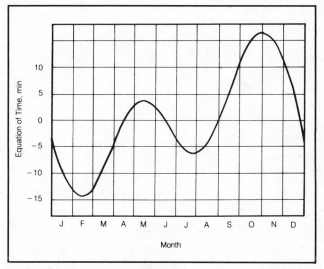

Figure 4.5   Equation of time (E).

on daylight savings time, and the local time solved for using Equation 4.5 must be *increased* by one hour to give clock time.

Solar Insolation

The thermal exchange between the sun and earth is a superb example of radiation heat transfer. The sun radiates inconceivable amounts of energy derived from continuous nuclear fusion reactions. Due to the tremendous distances involved, only a small portion of this energy is intercepted by the earth. Even then, only about 80 percent of this energy reaches the earth's surface. The short, or ultraviolet, wave lengths are largely absorbed in the upper atmosphere, while other wave lengths are attenuated to a lesser extent. Most of the radiation that reaches us, eight minutes after leaving the sun, is either visible or else of infrared (long) wave length. The attenuating effects of the atmosphere can be seen in Figure 4.6.

Even with attenuation, the amount of energy reaching the earth's surface is staggering. The solar energy falling on the continental United States in a year is about a thousand times that of our annual energy consumption! The problem, of course, is harnessing this widely dispersed and intermittent energy resource.

99

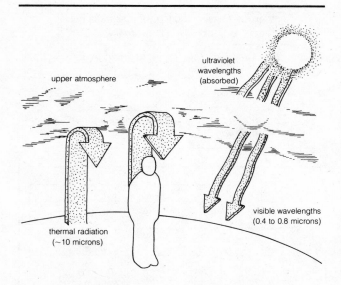

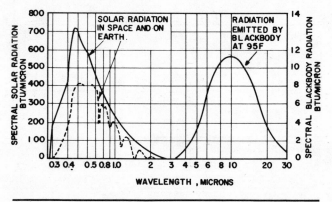

Figure 4.6 Spectral characteristics of solar and infrared radiant energy (1 micron = 0.0001 centimeter).

The rate at which solar energy strikes a surface of unit area is called the *solar insolation* (not to be confused with the insulation in your attic). Originally the term was reserved for energy striking a horizontal surface, but it has become an accepted practice to let the term apply to surfaces with any orientation. The units that we will use for insolation are Btu/hr-ft², though the SI units of watts/m² are increasingly being advocated (1 Btu/hr-ft² = 3.155 watts/m²).

It is possible to calculate theoretical "clear sky" values for solar insolation striking a surface with any orientation at any time of the day, any day of the year. The American Society of Heating, Refrigerating, and Air Conditioning Engineers (ASHRAE), for example, publishes these values for a variety of latitudes and tilt angles, and we have included their data for south-facing surfaces in Appendix 4C. A sample of this most useful information is given in Table 4.3. Notice that hourly values of the sun's altitude and azimuth angles are given along with the clear sky insolation.

The values of daily total clear sky insolation for one particular latitude have been plotted in Figure 4.7. One interesting thing to note from the figure is the rather good performance that a vertical surface (a south-facing window, perhaps) will be able to deliver in a space-heating application. Vertical surfaces can be seen to receive on the order of 80 to 90 percent as much energy in the middle of winter as a collector tilted at the optimum angle equal to the latitude plus 10° or 15°. Moreover, very little energy strikes a vertical surface in the summer, when it is not wanted, and even that amount is easily reduced with properly sized overhangs.

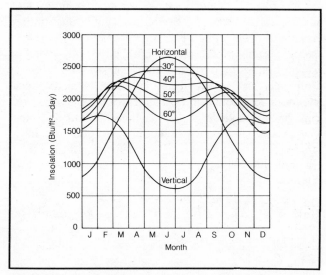

Figure 4.7 Total daily clear sky insolation on south facing surface at different tilt angles, 40° north latitude.

Table 4.3 Sample Clear Sky Insolation[a]

	Solar Time		Solar Position		Btu/hr-ft² Total Insolation on Surfaces						
							South Facing Surface Angle with Horiz.				
Date	AM	PM	Alt	Azm	Normal	Horiz.	30	40	50	60	90
Jan 21	8	4	8.1	55.3	142	28	65	74	81	85	84
	9	3	16.8	44.0	239	83	155	171	182	187	171
	10	2	23.8	30.9	274	127	218	237	249	254	223
	11	1	28.4	16.0	289	154	257	277	290	293	253
		12	30.0	0.0	294	164	270	291	303	306	263
Surface Daily Totals					2182	948	1660	1810	1906	1944	1726

Notes: a. From ASHRAE *Handbook of Fundamentals* for January at 40° latitude. See Appendix 4C for complete set of ASHRAE tables.

This wonderfully convenient phenomenon is at the heart of most passive solar energy designs where vertical south-facing glass is used as the collecting surface.

If cloud cover and other meteorological wonders were never present the clear sky ASHRAE information would be a sufficient (and welcome) indicator of solar availability for any locale. Unfortunately, things are a bit more complicated.

In the real world, fog, clouds, and even air pollution can appreciably reduce the incoming solar radiation, so the ASHRAE tables are of limited help. To compound the problem, very few places in the country have been measuring sunshine for a long enough time to build up a statistically significant data base.

For those stations that have been collecting solar data the results are usually presented in one of two ways. Either the results are given as a "percent sunshine"—that is, the average percentage of daylight hours in a given month that the sun is capable of casting a shadow—or as measured horizontal insolation.

Percent sunshine data are the more readily available, though less useful, form of information. Most weather stations have been collecting it, and examples for major cities are given in Table 4.4. As we'll see later, one way to predict solar system performance is to do all your calculations with ASHRAE clear sky insolations then multiply your values of monthly energy collected by the corresponding monthly percent sunshine. The obvious assumption then is that the system delivers nothing useful under cloudy skies. In some circumstances (such as with an active solar heating system) that assumption is quite true, though with others (such as a passive solar system) it is overly pessimistic and the system will actually deliver a fair amount of useful energy on even the cloudiest of days.

Table 4.4 Percent of Possible Sunshine in Major Cities

STATE AND STATION		Length of record (yr.)	Jan.	Feb.	Mar.	Apr.	May	June	July	Aug.	Sept.	Oct.	Nov.	Dec.	Annual
Ala	Montgomery	25	47	53	58	64	66	65	63	65	63	66	57	50	59
Alaska	Juneau	30	33	32	37	38	38	34	30	30	25	19	23	20	31
Ariz	Phoenix	80	78	80	83	89	93	94	85	85	89	88	83	77	86
Ark	Little Rock	32	46	54	57	61	68	73	71	73	68	69	56	48	63
Calif	Los Angeles	32	69	72	73	70	66	65	82	83	79	73	74	71	73
	Sacramento	27	45	61	70	80	86	92	97	96	94	84	64	46	79
	San Francisco	38	56	62	69	73	72	73	66	65	72	70	62	53	67
Colo	Denver	26	72	71	69	66	64	70	70	72	75	73	65	68	70
Conn	Hartford	21	58	57	56	57	58	58	61	63	59	58	46	48	57
Del	Wilmington [1]	25	50	54	57	57	59	64	63	61	60	60	54	51	53
D.C	Washington	27	48	51	55	56	58	64	62	62	62	60	53	47	57
Fla	Jacksonville	25	57	61	66	71	69	61	59	58	53	56	61	56	61
	Key West	17	72	76	81	84	80	71	75	76	69	68	72	74	75
Ga	Atlanta	41	47	52	57	65	69	67	61	65	63	67	60	50	61
Hawaii	Honolulu	23	63	65	69	67	70	71	74	75	75	67	60	59	68
Idaho	Boise	35	41	52	63	68	71	75	89	85	82	67	45	39	67
Ill	Chicago	33	44	47	51	53	61	67	70	68	63	62	41	38	57
	Peoria	32	45	50	52	55	59	66	68	67	64	63	44	39	57
Ind	Indianapolis	32	41	51	51	55	61	68	70	71	66	64	42	39	58
Iowa	Des Moines	25	51	54	54	55	60	67	71	70	64	64	49	45	59
Kans	Wichita	22	59	59	60	62	64	69	74	73	65	66	59	56	65
Ky	Louisville	28	41	47	50	55	62	67	66	68	65	63	47	39	57
La	Shreveport	23	49	54	56	55	64	71	74	72	68	71	62	53	64
Maine	Portland	35	55	59	56	56	56	60	64	65	61	58	47	53	58
Md	Baltimore	25	51	55	55	55	57	62	65	62	60	59	51	48	57
Mass	Boston	40	54	56	57	56	58	63	66	67	63	61	51	52	59
Mich	Detroit	32	32	43	49	52	59	65	70	65	61	56	35	32	54
	Sault Ste. Marie	34	34	46	55	55	56	57	63	58	46	41	23	28	48
Minn	Duluth	25	49	54	56	54	55	58	67	61	52	48	34	39	54
	Minneapolis-St. Paul	37	51	57	54	55	58	63	70	67	61	57	39	40	58
Miss	Jackson	11	48	55	61	60	63	67	61	62	58	65	54	45	59
Mo	Kansas City	3	64	54	61	65	67	72	84	69	51	62	46	54	64
	St. Louis	16	52	51	54	56	62	69	71	66	63	62	49	41	58
Mont	Great Falls	33	49	57	67	62	64	65	81	78	68	61	46	46	64
Nebr	Omaha	40	55	55	55	59	62	68	76	72	67	67	52	48	62

[1] Data not available; figures are for a nearby station.

Continued on page 102

Table 4.4 *continued*

State	City		Jan	Feb	Mar	Apr	May	June	July	Aug	Sept	Oct	Nov	Dec	Ann
Nev.	Reno	33	66	68	74	80	81	85	92	93	92	83	70	63	80
N.H.	Concord	34	52	54	52	53	54	57	62	60	54	54	42	47	54
N.J.	Atlantic City	15	49	48	51	53	54	58	60	62	59	57	50	42	54
N. Mex.	Albuquerque	36	73	73	74	77	80	83	76	76	80	79	78	72	77
N.Y.	Albany	37	46	51	52	53	55	59	64	61	56	53	36	38	53
	Buffalo	32	34	40	46	52	58	66	69	66	60	53	29	27	53
	New York[2]	99	50	55	56	59	61	64	65	64	63	61	52	49	59
N.C.	Charlotte	25	55	59	63	70	69	71	68	70	68	69	63	58	66
	Raleigh	21	55	58	63	64	60	61	61	61	60	63	63	56	60
N. Dak.	Bismarck	36	54	56	60	58	63	64	76	73	65	59	44	47	62
Ohio	Cincinnati	60	41	45	51	55	61	67	68	67	66	59	44	38	57
	Cleveland	34	32	37	44	53	59	65	68	64	60	55	31	26	52
	Columbus	24	37	41	44	52	58	62	64	63	62	58	38	30	53
Okla.	Oklahoma City	23	59	61	63	63	65	73	75	77	69	68	60	59	67
Oreg.	Portland	26	24	35	42	48	54	51	69	64	60	40	27	20	47
Pa.	Philadelphia	33	50	53	56	56	57	63	63	63	60	60	53	49	58
	Pittsburgh	23	36	38	45	48	53	60	62	60	60	56	40	30	50
R.I.	Providence	22	57	56	55	55	57	57	59	59	58	60	49	51	56
S.C.	Columbia	22	56	59	64	67	66	65	64	65	65	66	64	60	63
S. Dak.	Rapid City	33	54	59	61	59	57	60	71	73	67	65	56	54	62
Tenn.	Memphis	25	48	54	57	63	69	73	72	75	69	71	58	49	64
	Nashville	33	40	47	52	59	62	67	64	66	63	64	50	40	57
Tex.	Amarillo	34	69	68	71	73	73	77	77	78	74	75	73	67	73
	El Paso	33	78	82	85	87	89	89	79	80	82	84	83	78	83
	Houston	6	41	54	48	51	57	63	68	61	57	61	58	69	56
Utah	Salt Lake City	38	47	55	64	66	73	78	84	83	84	73	54	44	70
Vt.	Burlington	32	42	48	52	50	56	60	65	62	55	50	30	33	51
Va.	Norfolk	19	57	58	63	66	67	68	65	65	64	60	60	57	63
	Richmond	25	51	54	59	62	64	67	65	64	63	59	56	51	60
Wash.	Seattle-Tacoma	10	21	42	49	51	58	54	67	65	61	42	27	17	49
	Spokane	27	26	41	53	60	63	65	81	78	71	51	28	20	57
W. Va.	Parkersburg	78	32	36	43	49	56	59	62	60	59	54	37	29	48
Wis.	Milwaukee	35	44	47	51	54	59	63	70	67	60	57	41	38	56
Wyo.	Cheyenne	40	61	65	64	61	59	65	68	68	69	68	60	59	64
P.R.	San Juan	20	65	69	74	69	61	57	64	65	59	59	57	56	63

[2] City office data.

Source: U.S. National Oceanic and Atmospheric Administration, *Comparative Climatic Data*.

The most meaningful sunshine data available are measured values of *average horizontal insolation,* though even these need to be massaged somewhat to make them useful. Figure 4.8 shows some plots of average horizontal insolation across the United States, and Table 4.5 lists values of average daily horizontal insolation, $\overline{H}$, on a month-by-month basis, for Grand Lake, Colorado. Similar data for nearly all the measurement stations in the United States are given in Appendix 4F.

In addition to horizontal insolation, Table 4.5 and Appendix 4F give two other useful bits of information. The average monthly daytime ambient temperature, here called t_o, is given along with a factor K_t that we might refer to as a cloudiness index. This latter factor, K_t, is the key to converting average horizontal insolation into insolation striking a collector surface at some other tilt angle—which is, after all, the kind of information we are really after.

Rather complex procedures have been developed by

Table 4.5   Sample Insolation Data for Grand Lake, Colorado[a] (Latitude 40°15′N)

	Jan	Feb	Mar	Apr	May	June	July	Aug	Sept	Oct	Nov	Dec
$\overline{H}$	735	1135.4	1579.3	1876.7	1974.9	2369.7	2103.3	1708.5	1715.8	1212.2	775.6	660.5
K_t	0.541	0.615	0.637	0.597	0.553	0.63	0.572	0.516	0.626	0.583	0.494	0.542
t_o	18.5	23.1	28.5	39.1	48.7	56.6	62.8	61.5	55.5	45.2	30.3	22.6

Notes: a. See Appendix 4F for a more extensive listing.
 b. $\overline{H}$ is average daily horizontal insolation, Btu/ft²-day.
 K_t is a cloudiness index.
 t_o is average daytime temperature, °F.
 From Liu and Jordan, 1963. "A Rational Procedure for Predicting the Long-Term Performance of Flat-Plate Solar Energy Collectors." *Solar Energy.* Vol 7, No 2, pp. 71–74.

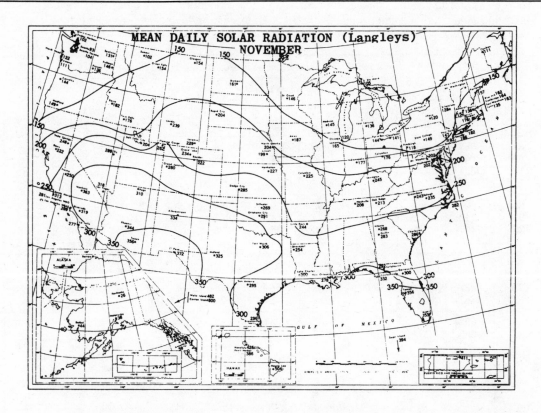

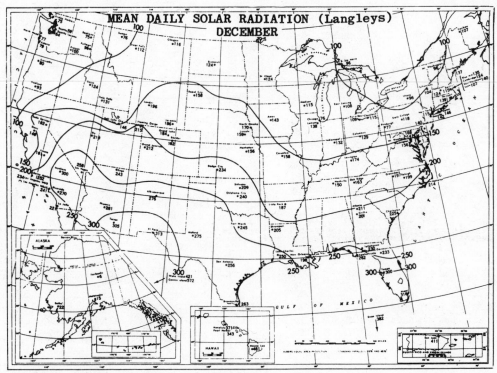

Figure 4.8 Mean daily solar radiation in November and December in langleys/day (one langley equals 3.69 Btu/ft²).

B. Y. H. Liu and R. C. Jordan at the University of Minnesota for converting measured average horizontal insolation values to insolation expected on a tilted surface. Their procedures have been simplified at Colorado State University and we have simplified them a step further in Table 4.6.

Table 4.6 Average Daily Insolations on South-Facing Tilted Surfaces[a]

30° North Latitude

Tilt Angle	K_t	Jan.	Feb.	Mar.	Apr.	May	June	July	Aug.	Sept.	Oct.	Nov.	Dec.
15°	0.3	633	767	880	991	1045	1054	1048	1011	913	798	656	604
	0.4	874	1049	1185	1322	1394	1405	1397	1349	1229	1083	905	833
	0.5	1120	1334	1508	1668	1725	1738	1729	1686	1551	1377	1161	1076
	0.6	1379	1630	1828	2004	2072	2088	2077	2025	1880	1684	1418	1324
30°	0.3	683	800	888	962	982	989	984	962	905	819	702	656
	0.4	963	1113	1215	1283	1312	1305	1298	1383	1229	1208	984	930
	0.5	1259	1447	1549	1620	1620	1595	1605	1602	1565	1462	1278	1215
	0.6	1568	1793	1894	1946	1925	1894	1907	1926	1898	1814	1606	1532
45°	0.3	700	800	856	895	888	882	879	883	861	812	714	682
	0.4	1008	1130	1173	1193	1171	1147	1157	1177	1171	1141	1015	979
	0.5	1326	1482	1509	1493	1448	1399	1413	1472	1494	1475	1338	1303
	0.6	1680	1847	1861	1811	1716	1658	1674	1747	1828	1842	1688	1647
90°	0.3	561	597	559	510	460	441	445	485	530	575	556	557
	0.4	822	850	768	642	557	516	536	608	707	815	812	819
	0.5	1103	1132	975	787	645	574	600	711	899	1068	1084	1112
	0.6	1413	1426	1202	906	690	624	636	814	1079	1338	1383	1439

35° North Latitude

Tilt Angle	K_t	Jan.	Feb.	Mar.	Apr.	May	June	July	Aug.	Sept.	Oct.	Nov.	Dec.
20°	0.3	587	725	848	975	1034	1054	1043	996	886	654	611	555
	0.4	821	999	1152	1313	1378	1405	1391	1328	1203	1040	723	782
	0.5	1066	1290	1466	1641	1723	1756	1739	1679	1518	1333	1194	1014
	0.6	1107	1598	1807	1990	2070	2088	2088	2014	1857	1641	1378	1271
35°	0.3	635	762	848	938	982	978	979	948	878	780	658	608
	0.4	910	1073	1172	1263	1294	1289	1291	1276	1203	1093	931	876
	0.5	1201	1402	1517	1594	1619	1612	1597	1595	1532	1421	1232	1161
	0.6	1520	1757	1869	1934	1923	1914	1918	1916	1874	1772	1551	1474
50°	0.3	654	762	818	872	877	869	873	870	828	774	668	630
	0.4	948	1089	1142	1175	1156	1144	1149	1159	1137	1093	965	923
	0.5	1266	1444	1480	1486	1429	1396	1403	1450	1465	1433	1284	1243
	0.6	1625	1818	1822	1784	1714	1653	1662	1740	1791	1798	1633	1589
90°	0.3	544	597	571	534	491	478	479	518	547	384	545	538
	0.4	814	869	792	700	613	579	582	651	751	830	809	811
	0.5	1107	1169	1030	860	714	652	675	782	953	1105	1089	1110
	0.6	1434		1266	1014	794	718	746	919	1160	1404	1408	1447

40° North Latitude

Tilt Angle	K_t	Jan.	Feb.	Mar.	Apr.	May	June	July	Aug.	Sept.	Oct.	Nov.	Dec.
25°	0.3	536	687	814	951	1026	1058	1043	974	851	717	566	504
	0.4	763	966	1114	1281	1369	1412	1388	1312	1165	995	800	725
	0.5	1007	1252	1429	1631	1728	1765	1738	1656	1483	1293	1051	960
	0.6	1273	1569	1759	1977	2076	2098	2087	2008	1828	1613	1323	1211
40°	0.3	584	730	814	915	964	982	968	927	843	741	609	554
	0.4	853	1038	1134	1245	1285	1296	1291	1248	1165	1050	881	816
	0.5	1139	1369	1476	1571	1606	1601	1596	1576	1496	1382	1173	1098
	0.6	1463	1730	1831	1923	1930	1923	1917	1913	1843	1730	1495	1413
55°	0.3	600	735	779	844	860	873	862	850	796	735	617	580
	0.4	890	1059	1095	1148	1147	1135	1135	1134	1103	1050	909	863
	0.5	1203	1415	1430	1451	1418	1402	1403	1437	1432	1393	1232	1177
	0.6	1560	1805	1787	1778	1702	1661	1662	1722	1766	1765	1582	1528
90°	0.3	524	606	578	562	578	513	521	535	562	582	530	518
	0.4	800	894	819	737	664	640	653	701	780	847	800	792
	0.5	1100	1209	1072	922	796	747	763	861	1003	1138	1088	1099
	0.6	1440	1558	1344	1107	913	830	852	1013	1234	1448	1417	1441

Table 4.6 *continued*

45° North Latitude

Tilt Angle	K_t	Jan.	Feb.	Mar.	Apr.	May	June	July	Aug.	Sept.	Oct.	Nov.	Dec.
30°	0.3	485	604	769	929	1023	1058	1037	956	821	676	515	470
	0.4	710	860	1078	1262	1364	1412	1383	1299	1139	957	743	684
	0.5	951	1129	1391	1606	1722	1764	1728	1639	1454	1247	993	927
	0.6	1218	1421	1723	1947	2069	2120	2097	1987	1790	1571	1263	1192
45°	0.3	532	636	776	886	952	971	963	909	807	702	557	525
	0.4	794	915	1095	1215	1269	1295	1255	1224	1124	1018	822	790
	0.5	1083	1221	1434	1548	1586	1601	1587	1462	1454	1342	1110	1076
	0.6	1402	1560	1788	1895	1926	1923	1907	1895	1819	1705	1424	1399
60°	0.3	551	631	743	816	849	851	825	826	763	697	571	556
	0.4	837	928	1060	1111	1132	1121	1129	1113	1066	1012	855	846
	0.5	1152	1246	1392	1420	1417	1384	1395	1409	1395	1352	1170	1166
	0.6	1504	1597	1749	1756	1701	1639	1652	1709	1732	1736	1524	1527
90°	0.3	504	539	581	573	563	546	550	557	574	583	511	523
	0.4	778	799	834	776	723	699	705	742	804	860	780	809
	0.5	1084	1092	1099	985	888	819	847	929	1043	1163	1070	1128
	0.6	1434	1412	1396	1199	1024	939	974	1114	1310	1499	1419	1488

Notes: a. Adapted from *Solar Heating and Cooling of Residential Buildings* (Colorado State University); units are Btu/ft²-day.

Table 4.6 gives average insolations on tilted surfaces as a function of latitude, month, tilt angle, and K_t. You will find this table to be one of your most important solar design aids.

Example: Find the average daily insolation striking a vertical south-facing window in Grand Lake, Colorado in January.

Solution: From Table 4.5 or Appendix 4F, we see that the latitude of Grand Lake is very close to 40° and the value of K_t in January is 0.541. In Table 4.6 we see that for $K_t = 0.5$ the insolation on a vertical surface is 1100 Btu/ft²-day and at 0.6 it is 1440 Btu/ft²-day. Interpolating between them gives an estimate of

$$\overline{H}_{90°} = 1100 + 0.41(1440 - 1100) = 1239 \ Btu/ft^2\text{-}day$$

Suppose we are not so lucky as to be near one of the stations for which we have listed values of K_t? If measured average horizontal insolations are available then we can find K_t from the following relationship:

E. 4.6
$$K_t = \frac{\overline{H}}{\overline{H}_o}$$

where $\overline{H}$ is the average daily horizontal insolation on the ground and $\overline{H}_o$ is the average radiation on a surface parallel to the ground but located just outside of the atmosphere (the extraterrestrial daily insolation).

Values of $\overline{H}_o$ are given in Table 4.7 for each month of the year and a number of latitudes.

Example: Suppose the average horizontal insolation in January is 600 Btu/ft²-day at a location with latitude of 30° north. Estimate the insolation on a south-facing surface tilted at 45° in January.

Solution: From Table 4.7, $\overline{H}_o$ is 1854 Btu/ft²-day so $K_t = 600/1854 = 0.324$. From Table 4.6 we find the insolation on a 45° surface when $K_t = 0.3$ is 700 Btu per square foot and at $K_t = 0.4$, it is 1008 Btu per square foot. Interpolating gives

$$H_{45°} = 700 + 0.24(1008 - 700) = 774 \ Btu/ft^2\text{-}day$$

Table 4.7 Values of $\overline{H}_o$, the Extraterrestrial Daily Insolation[a]

Latitude	Jan	Feb	Mar	Apr	May	June	July	Aug	Sept	Oct	Nov	Dec
25°N	2107	2478	2896	3271	3496	3530	3491	3335	3018	2593	2196	1998
30°N	1854	2264	2745	3212	3488	3588	3532	3307	2902	2399	1953	1738
35°N	1593	2034	2574	3129	3489	3625	3551	3759	2763	2188	1701	1471
40°N	1326	1791	2384	3024	3460	3643	3551	3188	2604	1962	1441	1201
45°N	1058	1538	2175	2897	3415	3643	3531	3096	2425	1723	1176	933
50°N	792	1277	1951	2751	3352	3627	3495	2984	2229	1472	912	670

Notes: a. Units are Btu/ft²-day.

Fortunately, some states are beginning to take the drudgery out of these insolation calculations by presenting precomputed values for all their measurement stations. An excellent example of this service to solar designers is the *California Solar Data Manual* published by that state's Energy Commission. An example of their data presentation is given as Table 4.8.

There are several important things to notice in Table 4.8. One is that total annual insolation varies by only a few percentage points as tilt angles range from about 15° to 45°—so the total is rather insensitive to tilt angle. The other is that collecting surfaces facing southeast or southwest have annual total insolations that are again only a few percentage points lower than for surfaces facing due south. Quite a range of collector orientations are tolerable with minimal loss in insolation.

As you may have noticed, the list of cities for which good insolation data are available is appallingly short. With the surge of interest in solar design has come some real motivation to expand the data base. One promising new technique for doing so involves the analysis of cloud cover patterns as photographed by orbiting weather satellites. Though it will take a number of years to establish a significant history of insolation measurements made this way, once it is done the data will cover every square mile of surveyed territory and solar design will become just that much easier and more accurate.

Determining Shade Patterns at a Particular Site

So far we have learned how to determine where the sun is at any time of the day, how intense it is on clear days, and how to obtain average daily insolation values given the mixture of cloudy and sunny days that occur in any area. But all of these answers assume that your collection surface, be it passive or active, has a direct shot at the sun and is not hidden in the shade behind the neighboring apartment house.

It is, of course, crucial for you to be able to evaluate any potential shading problems that your candidate site has before going on to the design and installation of your solar system. While we could use Equations 4.3 and 4.4 along with some fancy trigonometry to evaluate shading, in actual practice it makes much more sense just to go out to the site and make a few simple measurements.

There are a number of ways to make shading measurements, varying from relatively awkward but cheap to extremely simple but more expensive. You can do a perfectly fine job with just a pocket compass, plastic protractor, plumb bob, and a graph of solar azimuth versus altitude for your latitude. The graph can be made up from the ASHRAE tables of Appendix 4C or from Equations 4.3 and 4.4 and will look similar to the one in Figure 4.4.

The approach is simple. You will situate yourself at

Table 4.8   Precomputed Insolation Data for San Jose, California, Showing Total Expected Radiation on a Tilted Surface[a]

Surface Orienta-tion	Angle of Tilt (Degrees from Horizontal)	Direct Beam + Diffuse (Ground Reflection Excluded)												
		Jan	Feb	Mar	Apr	May	June	July	Aug	Sept	Oct	Nov	Dec	Annual
South	15	30	34	51	64	69	71	74	68	59	46	31	26	624
South	30	35	38	54	63	65	66	68	66	60	50	36	31	633
South	45	38	40	53	59	58	56	59	60	58	51	38	34	605
South	60	39	39	50	51	47	44	47	50	53	49	38	34	542
South	75	37	36	43	40	34	31	33	38	44	44	36	33	450
South	90	33	30	34	28	20	17	19	24	33	37	32	30	336
SE,SW	15	28	32	49	63	69	71	74	67	57	44	29	24	608
SE,SW	30	31	35	51	62	66	67	69	65	57	46	32	27	606
SE,SW	45	32	35	49	58	59	59	62	60	55	46	33	28	575
SE,SW	60	32	33	45	51	51	50	52	52	50	43	32	28	518
SE,SW	75	29	30	39	42	40	39	41	42	42	38	29	26	437
SE,SW	90	25	25	31	32	29	27	29	31	33	31	25	23	342
E,W	15	23	28	45	60	68	71	73	65	53	38	24	20	566
E,W	30	22	27	42	56	64	67	68	61	50	36	23	19	535
E,W	45	21	25	39	51	58	60	62	55	46	34	22	18	488
E,W	60	19	22	35	45	50	52	53	48	40	30	19	16	430
E,W	75	16	19	29	38	42	43	44	40	34	26	17	14	362
E,W	90	13	15	24	30	33	34	34	32	27	21	14	11	287
Ground Reflection for Reflectivity = 0.2 (Multiply by RHO/0.2 for Reflectivity = RHO)														
Any	15	0	0	0	0	0	0	0	0	0	0	0	0	2
Any	30	0	0	1	1	1	1	1	1	1	1	0	0	8
Any	45	1	1	1	2	2	2	2	2	2	1	1	1	17
Any	60	1	1	2	3	3	4	4	3	3	2	1	1	29
Any	75	2	2	3	5	5	5	6	5	4	3	2	1	43
Any	90	2	3	5	6	7	7	7	7	5	4	2	2	58

Notes: a. From *California Solar Data Manual*, California Energy Commission, 1978; units are kBtu/ft²-mo.

the proposed site of the solar collectors and scan the southern horizon looking for potential obstructions that may cast shadows onto your spot. With a compass you'll measure azimuth angles of the obstructions and with the protractor and plumb bob you'll measure their altitude angles.

First you'll need to learn how to use a compass. Get one that lets you sight onto an object to read its azimuth. Remember a compass points to magnetic north rather than true north and that deviation must be corrected for. Figure 4.9 shows lines of equal magnetic deviation drawn onto a map of the United States. The deviation in San Francisco can be seen to be about 17°E; along the east coast of Florida it is essentially zero; and up in New Hampshire it is about 16°W. A deviation of 17°E, for example, means that the compass points 17 degrees east of true north. To get the correct azimuth angle you must add the magnetic deviation to the compass reading if the deviation is east and you must subtract it if it is a west deviation. That is,

E. 4.7

$$\begin{aligned} true \\ azimuth \end{aligned} = \begin{aligned} compass \\ azimuth \end{aligned} \begin{cases} + \; magnetic \; deviation \; (east) \\ - \; magnetic \; deviation \; (west) \end{cases}$$

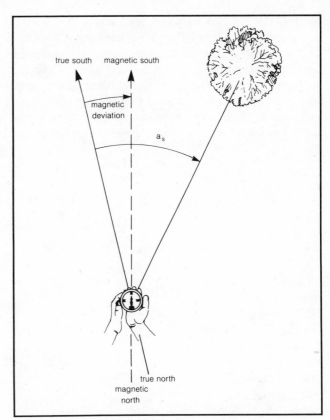

Figure 4.10 Correcting for an east magnetic deviation when measuring azimuth a_s.

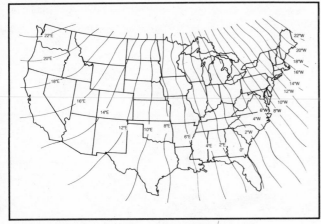

Figure 4.9 Lines of equal magnetic deviation.

Figure 4.10 shows this correction for a site with a magnetic deviation that is east.

Now that you can read your compass correctly, continue with the scan of your southern horizon. Face due east and note the obstructions in that direction, if any. Measure the altitude angle of the obstruction using the protractor and plumb bob as shown in Figure 4.11. Plot that data point—90° east of south and whatever altitude angle α that you just measured—onto the graph of solar altitude and azimuth. Repeat this procedure, scanning the entire southern horizon in azimuthal steps of approximately 20°.

As you go along measuring azimuths and elevations, plot the data onto your graph paper and you will obtain a profile of all of the southern obstructions. The resulting

cross plot immediately reveals at what time of day and what months of the year shading will be a problem at your candidate site. If, for any given month and hour, the obstruction profile is above the sun position, then the sun will be behind the obstruction and your site will be shaded. Conversely, whenever the solar position is above the obstruction profile the site will receive direct sunlight.

Figure 4.12 illustrates the concept where the proposed solar house has a couple of trees to the southeast and a small building to the southwest. In this example, the site receives full sun all day long from March through September but in February and October we lose about an hour at around 4:00 P.M. From November through January the site is shaded from 8:30 A.M. to 10:00 A.M.

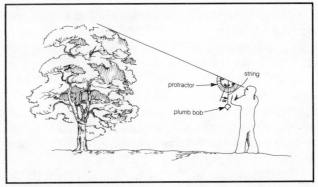

Figure 4.11 Measuring the altitude angle, α, of an obstruction with a protractor and plumb bob.

107

but receives full sun after that until about 2:30 in the afternoon. This site would be ideal for a summer pool-heating system and would be quite good for a year-round application such as domestic hot water. It would, however, be rather marginal for space heating, since in the deep winter it receives only a bit over four hours of good sun each day. By trimming that left tree a little, though, the site would be improved enough to make it quite reasonable.

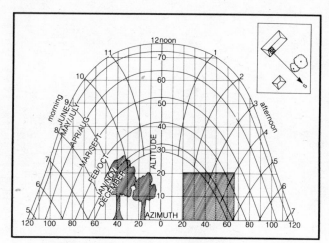

Figure 4.12 Example of a shading profile.

If there is any flexibility about where your collection surface can be located, this technique should be repeated at the various candidate sites. Having the hard copies of your obstruction drawings in front of you and the ASHRAE tables of hourly insolation next to you, you can easily select the location with the most daily sunshine.

There are several site assessment packages on the market and if you think you are going to repeatedly make such measurements, the extra money spent for a professional setup may well be worth it for the added convenience. One, marketed under the name Sunbloc (Pacific Sun, Inc., 439 Tasso Street, Palo Alto, California 94301), uses the same technique just outlined except that the compass and protractor are replaced by a hand-held surveyor's transit (see Figure 4.13) and the kit comes with a pad of sheets similar to that shown in Figure 4.4.

Another site assessment product is called a Solar Site Selector (Department SA-10, 105 Rockwood Dr., Grass Valley, California 95945). Here the designer views the southern horizon through a little peephole and sees the obstructions superimposed onto a diagram which is printed on a transparent plastic sheet (Figure 4.14). The shading pattern can be assessed at a glance. The only drawback is that it is not as easy to compare different sites since no hard copy of the individual obstruction patterns is obtained.

Solar Pathways, Inc. (Valley Commercial Plaza, 3710 Highway 82, Glenwood Springs, Colorado 81601) offers

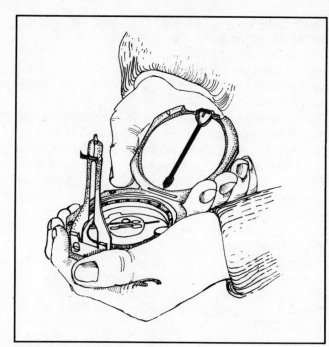

Figure 4.13 A hand held surveyor's transit for measuring azimuth and altitude angles.

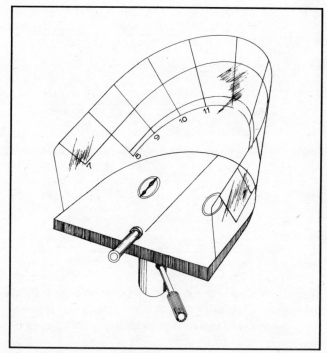

Figure 4.14 Solar site selector.

still another approach with their Solar Pathfinder. As shown in Figure 4.15, a clear plastic hemispherical dome is positioned on a carefully leveled surface. The user looks straight down into the center of the device and sees reflections of surrounding obstacles on the transparent dome. The images are seen superimposed onto a sun path grid, and again any potential obstructions are obvious at a glance. Hard copies of the assessment can be obtained by tracing the images onto the transparent paper provided, and a quantitative evaluation can be obtained directly from the sun path grid provided.

To conclude, the value of a shading assessment made in the field cannot be overestimated. Not only is it surprisingly easy to draw erroneous conclusions by just eyeballing the situation, but solar access laws are being enacted in many areas now that will guarantee that no one comes in at a later time with a tree or building that shades

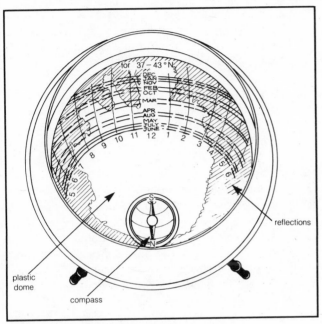

Figure 4.15 The solar pathfinder for site assessment.

your solar surface. Your hard copy assessment of the obstructions at the time of installation may be your best documentation in the event of a dispute.

Solar Collectors

In many solar applications, especially domestic water heating and active pool heating, the heart of the system is the flat-plate collector. While flat-plate collectors are inherently very simple devices, there are a great many variations possible for different applications and differing climatic conditions. This section describes the principal features of these collectors and how the various options affect the performance and utility of the unit. Since the principal use for collectors is water and pool heating, the discussion will focus on liquid-based (hydronic) collectors, although most of the comments are equally applicable to air collectors.

The general configuration of a medium-temperature, hydronic, flat-plate collector is shown in Figure 4.16. An absorber plate is encased in a weatherproof housing and insulated from below. A liquid, usually water or a water

and antifreeze solution, is circulated through an array of flow passages that are somehow affixed to the plate. Glazing, usually single- or double-paned tempered glass, reduces convective and radiative losses from the absorber plate, which increases the collector's performance at higher temperatures. For pool applications where collector temperatures may not be much above ambient, the glazing is frequently omitted.

Figure 4.17 shows a quite different approach to a

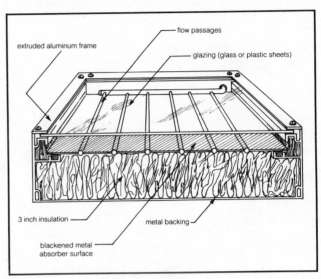

Figure 4.16 A typical hydronic flat plate collector.

hydronic collector. In this trickle-type or Thomason Open-Flow panel, the fluid is pumped to a header at the top of the collector where it squirts out and dribbles down the troughs of a sheet of corrugated metal. The metal is painted black, and the water gets heated by the sun as it trickles down; it is collected in a gutter at the bottom of the panels. This is a very simple and inexpensive design that is apparently quite effective for warming water, though the efficiency is less than a tube-and-plate collector at the temperatures usually required for water and space heating.

While almost all water- and pool-heating systems use hydronic collectors, when it comes to active space heating air collectors are becoming equally popular. Many variations are possible in the design of an air collector, but most look something like Figure 4.18a. Air is forced under the absorber plate rather than between the glazing and plate. This leaves a dead air space above the absorber, which acts as a good thermal insulator and also keeps the underside of the glass from getting mucked up by dirty air.

Absorber Plate

The heart of any collector is the absorber plate. Collectors which heat liquids for water and space heating invariably utilize metal as the absorber material due to its excellent

109

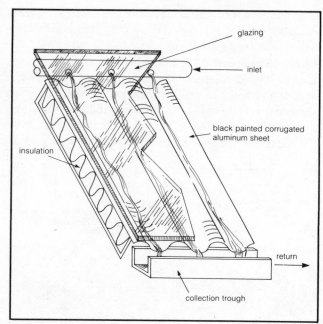

Figure 4.17 Trickle type collector.

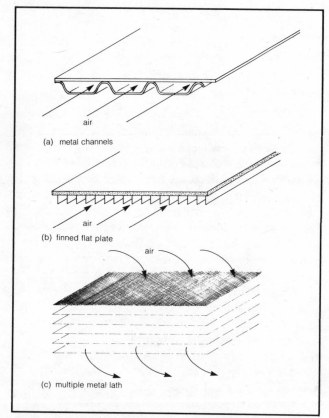

Figure 4.18 Air collector absorber plate variations.

We should make clear the distinction between the flow tubes and the plate that the tubes are attached to. The tubes and plate (or fins) *together* make up the absorber. While some hydronic panels use flow passages made of aluminum or steel, both are subject to rapid and debilitating corrosion unless carefully protected. Neither steel nor aluminum should be used with ordinary water, and copper flow passages are essential in any situation involving potable water in the collector.

While most liquid systems use copper flow tubes for their superior corrosion resistance, there is less unanimity when it comes to the fin material. Many manufacturers produce a composite absorber plate consisting of copper tubes mechanically attached to another metal, usually aluminum. This approach offers a modest cost advantage over an all-copper absorber and it does use less of that potentially scarce resource. The difficulty lies in obtaining a good thermal bond between the two dissimilar metals that will provide good performance over the life of the collector. With the collector cycling daily through a temperature range of typically 100°F and occasionally 200°F or more, the stresses created in a rigid bond, due to differential expansion, can be considerable. So, most such absorbers use a pressed, snap-fit connection between the materials that can provide a certain amount of give (see Figure 4.19). While there has been concern raised about the potential for galvanic corrosion between the two dissimilar metals, the lack of a liquid connecting path between the copper and aluminum makes the possibility quite unlikely. And, fortunately, even if such a problem should ever arise, it would result in the degradation of the aluminum fin rather than the copper tube, so at least it would not cause the system to spring a leak.

If an all-copper absorber is used, the bonding problem is simplified considerably. The tubes can simply be soldered to the plate and the resulting bond has good mechanical and thermal characteristics. Two manufacturers, notably Revere Copper and Brass and Olin Corporation, offer all-copper absorber plates with integral flow passages. Here, the fins and flow passages are intimately connected in a continuous metal juncture—no soldered or mechanical bonds are used.

The Olin Solarbond absorber plate is comprised of two distinct sheets of metal bonded together using a high-pressure rolling procedure. Before the bonding operation, the desired flow pattern is silk-screened on one of the sheets. The silk-screening material is actually a release agent or "stopweld" which permits the inflation of flow passages with a high-pressure air probe after the bonding process. The net result is an integral fin/tube plate with excellent heat-transfer properties.

Revere's process, patented in the 1950s, starts with a foundry core box into which three parallel graphite rods are positioned. Molten copper is poured into the core box to form a solid ingot of copper around the rods. The ingot

thermal conductivity and ability to withstand high temperatures. Depending on the manufacturer, copper, a combination of copper and aluminum, or steel is used. For pool applications metal may be used but plastic absorbers are more common.

110

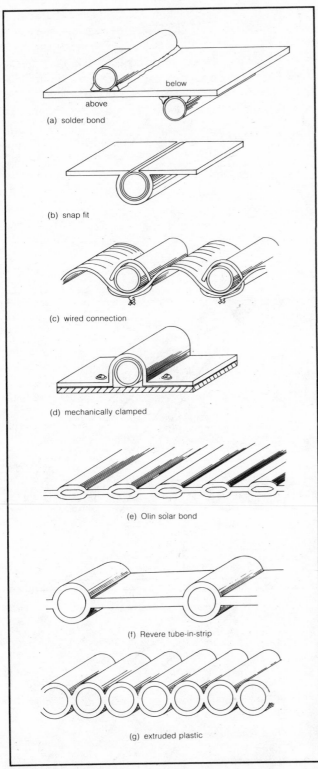

Figure 4.19 Various methods of bonding flow tubes to the absorber plate in hydronic collectors.

(a) solder bond

above / below

(b) snap fit

(c) wired connection

(d) mechanically clamped

(e) Olin solar bond

(f) Revere tube-in-strip

(g) extruded plastic

is then rolled on a conventional mill roll until a sheet 0.032 inches thick is produced. In the rolling process, the graphite rods are crushed.

The resulting tube-in-strip material (see Figure 4.19)

is cut to length and the flow passages (defined by the crushed graphite) are inflated with 750-psi air. Thus, the Olin and Revere plates are totally integrated and exhibit an exceedingly high heat-transfer fin efficiency.

Another consideration in the design of an absorber plate is the choice of flow pattern—whether to make it parallel or sinusoidal, as shown in Figure 4.20. In the parallel configuration the pressure drop through the panel is lessened, which makes it easier for a small pump to maintain the good flow rates required for maximum collector efficiency. On the other hand the added complexity of a parallel pattern—all those joints to solder—increases the cost and the probability of leaks.

Notice in Figure 4.20a, that the parallel pattern has

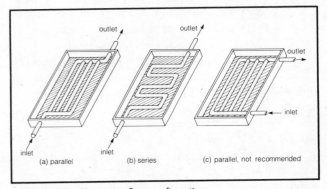

outlet   outlet   outlet

inlet   inlet   inlet

(a) parallel   (b) series   (c) parallel, not recommended

Figure 4.20 Alternative flow configurations.

been established with the inlet at one corner and the outlet at the diagonally opposite corner. This helps assure even flow through each riser tube. In Figure 4.20c, however, the flow through the right hand riser tubes will be greater than that through those tubes way over on the left, so this pattern is not recommended.

Appendix 4G gives a detailed step by step procedure for building your own flat plate collector using readily available materials and simple skills.

Absorber Plate Efficiency Factor

Realizing that the absorber may have any tube spacing desired and the plate may be made of copper, aluminum, or steel with a variety of thicknesses, how can we compare the effectiveness of various combinations of these design parameters?

There is a quantity called the collector efficiency factor, or sometimes called the plate efficiency, designated in the literature by F', that in essence compares the relative effectiveness of different absorber plates. A value of F' equal to 1 would be a thermodynamically perfect absorber, and the temperature of the plate would be the same as the temperature of the fluid flowing through the tubes. Note that F' is *not* the overall efficiency of the collector. The overall efficiency is a measure of the fraction of the

111

sun's energy striking the collector that is captured and taken off to be used somewhere.

The collector efficiency factor depends not only on the characteristics of the absorber but also on the number of sheets of glazing used in the collector. Figure 4.21 shows F' for absorbers with flat black paint used in collectors with two, one, or no sheets of glazing as a function of the center-to-center spacing of the flow tubes (assumed to be ½ inch in diameter). Steel, aluminum, and copper with various thicknesses are shown as the parameter. Negligible thermal resistance is assumed between the tube and fins.

Notice that with any of the materials shown, it is easy to obtain as high a plate efficiency as desired merely by bringing the tubes closer and closer together. Of course as you decrease tube spacing you increase the number of tubes, and if each one has to be physically attached to the plate the costs can quickly get out of hand.

If the manufacturing process is one that creates the tubes and plate at the same time, as in the case of the Olin solar bond absorber or the extruded plastic pool collector shown in Figure 4.19g, then costs may not be related to the number of tubes and they can be quite closely spaced or even butted together.

In most circumstances, however, a trade-off must be made between tube spacing, fin material, fin thickness, costs, and absorber efficiency, and that's where Figure 4.21 comes in.

Suppose, for example, a tube spacing of 5 inches on centers is selected for a collector with a single sheet of glazing. If we were to use a steel fin with a 0.010-inch thickness, the efficiency factor would be only about 72 percent. By increasing the fin thickness to 0.040 inch that efficiency jumps to about 87 percent. By switching to aluminum, a much better conductor, we can get about a 90 percent efficiency factor with a much thinner fin of only 0.010 inch. Using copper, which is about twice as good a conductor as aluminum, we can get even higher efficiencies; a 5-inch tube spacing with 0.040-inch copper, for example, has an efficiency that is 98 percent of that of a perfect plate.

Notice too how the tube spacing becomes even less critical as the number of sheets of glazing increases. The collector becomes more forgiving of a poor absorber design when the glazing is there to help suppress thermal losses.

Later we'll see how this efficiency factor, F', affects the overall efficiency of the collector; but first we must discuss the rest of the collector.

Absorber Surface Coatings

The absorber must have some sort of darkened surface to help it collect the incoming energy. An obvious coating to consider is ordinary black paint, provided it can withstand moderately high temperatures.

112

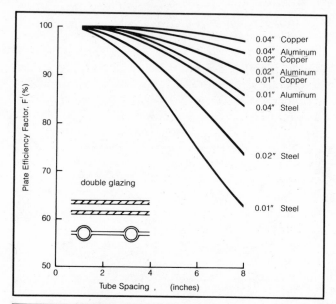

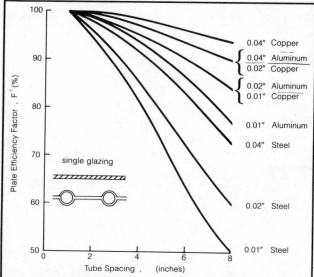

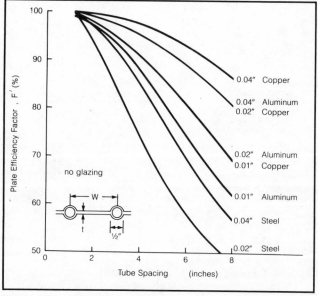

Figure 4.21 Plate efficiency factors.

Probably the most popular paint used by collector manufacturers is a black enamel marketed under the name Nextel® by 3M. Though it is quite expensive (over $50 a gallon), it does have one of the highest absorptances of any surface available. Good preparation of the absorber surface is required to get the optimum result; if you intend to do it yourself, write 3M and ask for publications 50-1 and 52-2 for their application instructions.

Other recommended paints that exhibit good absorptance characteristics and that can handle high temperatures include Kalwall's Black Absorber Paint (P.O. Box 237, Manchester, New Hampshire 03105) and Martin's Flat Black Latex or Latextra Acrylic Latex. Rustoleum also manufactures a Flat Black and a Midnight Black that are easily applied, adhere very well, and easily withstand large variations in temperature and humidity, but they are not quite as good at absorbing sunlight as the previously mentioned paints.

While black paints can be excellent absorbers, more sophisticated coatings strive not only for high absorptance, α (the fraction of the incoming radiation absorbed), but for low emittance, ε, as well. All objects radiate energy to their cooler surroundings, and the emittance of the object refers to how well it radiates that energy compared to a perfect emitter (formally, a blackbody). We don't want our absorber to be throwing energy away by radiation, so a low emittance is a highly desirable property.

Now, it turns out that for any given wave length the absorptance of an object is the same as its emittance, so how can it be possible to create a surface with high absorptance and low emittance at the same time? The trick is to realize that incoming solar radiation has very short wave lengths of about 0.2 to 2 microns (millionths of a meter), but the radiation emitted by a body at the temperature of our absorber plate has entirely different wave lengths, typically from about 3 to 50 microns (infrared). If you'll go back to Figure 4.6 you'll see these relationships.

So we can, theoretically, create a surface that has high absorptance (or emittance) in the short solar wave lengths, but low emittance (absorptance) in the longer infrared wave lengths. In essence, we can have our cake and eat it too. Such a coating is referred to as a selective surface.

Unfortunately, most common coatings which have high absorptance to the incoming short wave length solar energy also exhibit high emittances to the longer wave length energy being radiated away. That Nextel paint, for example, has a (short wave length) absorptance of about 0.96, which is excellent, but its (long wave length) emittance is close to 0.90, which isn't so good.

There are two popular selective surfaces commonly used today. One is a copper-oxide coating that is reasonably selective, having an absorptance of about 0.89 and an emittance that typically ranges somewhere between 0.1 to 0.3. Notice that some sacrifice in absorptance has

been made to get the lower emittance.

The other selective surface most commonly used is an electrodeposited black chrome. Provided coating parameters are controlled within reasonable tolerances, excellent absorptance and emittance characteristics are obtained. Based on considerable field experience outside the solar industry, properly applied black chrome surfaces can have lifetimes in excess of 20 years when exposed to temperatures of less than 500°F (as is the case in all flat-plate collector configurations). When applied to copper surfaces, a nickel flash substrate is required for stability and humidity resistance. One disadvantage to black chrome is that the resulting surface doesn't look as good as a flat black paint. They tend to reflect a rainbowlike hue (Newton's rings) that some people find unattractive.

Table 4.9 lists the key properties of these popular surfaces, and Figure 4.22 illustrates the selective nature of a black chrome surface. Notice how nicely the absorptance drops (and hence emittance) as the wave lengths exceed about 3 microns.

Selective surfaces are generally cost-effective when operating temperatures in excess of 140°F are required and/or space limitations exist for the collector array. Thus, for pool-heating applications in the vicinity of 85°F, a selective surface would be a very poor investment. For domestic water and space heating in the vicinity of 140°F,

Table 4.9 Absorber Coating Properties

Coating	Typical Supplier	Absorptance	Emittance	Cost/ft²
Black Paint	3M, Nextel	0.96	0.90	$0.30/ft²
Copper Oxide	Enthone	0.89	0.10–0.30	$0.50/ft²
Black Chrome	Olympic Plating	0.95	0.07	$1.25/ft²

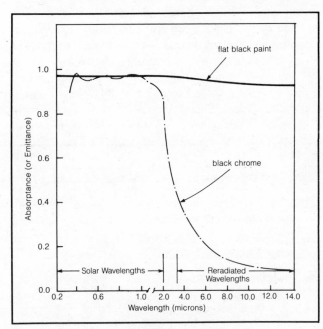

Figure 4.22 Spectral properties of absorber coatings.

113

the choice is less clear. Collectors equipped with a selective surface for these uses will collect more energy per square foot than a painted surface, but cost a comparable amount more. For absorption cooling, which requires temperatures in excess of 180°F, a selective surface should be considered mandatory if a flat-plate collector is used.

Glazing Options

While some flat-plate collectors consist of just an absorber plate alone, if the difference between the collector temperature and ambient temperature is more than about 20°F then some form of glazing must be used to control losses.

Obviously any glazing considered must be relatively transparent to incoming solar radiation, but cost, appearance, resistance to degradation from the weather, impact resistance, and low transmittance to the long wave length energy radiated from the plate are also important characteristics. In addition, if you are building your own collector, the ease with which you can cut, drill, and handle the material may dominate your decision.

We can categorize glazings as being either glass or plastic, but within those designations there are a variety of options.

Glass is the most commonly used glazing in professionally built collectors. It is the least subject to degradation from light, heat, and weather and is unquestionably the most attractive. Unsupported spans up to 8 feet are common as compared to 2- to 3-foot spans allowable with plastic. Tempered glass, which is the only kind that should be used, is also quite tough; it takes a rather strong blow from a sharp object to cause it to shatter. It can break, however, and if potential vandalism is considered a problem then you may be better off with plastic glazing. In addition glass weighs more and costs more than plastic and once it is tempered you can't alter its size, so it is less convenient to use in a do-it-yourself collector. Table 4.10 presents a compilation of properties for various grades of tempered glass, classified according to both thickness and iron-oxide content. Examining, for example, the ³⁄₁₆-inch thicknesses, it can be seen that the solar energy transmis-

sion—that is, the solar energy which successfully makes its way through the glass—increases from 81 percent for ordinary float glass to 90.5 percent for water-white crystal.

The increased transmission is directly attributable to the reduction of the iron-oxide content in the glass. Iron oxide is the material which lends a greenish tint to ordinary window glass. Water-white crystal is a tempered glass with very low iron-oxide content, giving rise to a clear white appearance when the glass is viewed from the edge.

The transmission losses, which range from 9.5 to 19 percent in the example cited above, arise from two effects. The first, surface reflection, is independent of the iron-oxide content. The second, absorption, is dramatically affected by the iron level. Table 4.10 lists the reflective and absorptive properties of the various glass grades.

It should be noted that these values of reflectance are for sunlight striking the glass at a perpendicular angle. As the incidence angle (the angle between the sun's rays and a line drawn perpendicular to the glazing) increases, so will the reflectance. Not only does reflection off the glass increase, but at the same time the absorptance of the painted absorber surface below decreases, compounding the losses.

Figure 4.23 shows the drop-off in the product of glass transmittance (τ) and plate absorptance (α) as the incidence angle increases for a painted surface with no glazing, single glazing, and double glazing. The assumed normal incidence angle value of τ is 0.88, and the normal α is assumed to be 0.96. As can be seen the effects of off-axis incidence are fairly modest for angles less than about 45°, but beyond that they quickly become devastating.

Water-white glass, while advantageous from the transmission standpoint alone, has an additional benefit. Because of manufacturers' custom, water-white glass is supplied with a fine pattern on one surface. The effect is not unlike shower glass, although the overall impact of the patterning is much less pronounced. The resulting collector appearance is visually much "softer," and specular reflection is considerably reduced. As a result, your collector is much less likely to reflect sunlight onto your neighbor's window or into the eyes of a passing motorist.

Among the many plastic glazings available, the ones most suitable for solar collectors are made of fiberglass-

Table 4.10 Properties of Glass

Glazing Media	Solar Energy Transmission (per sheet)	Losses per Sheet (Reflections plus Absorption)a	Nominal Maximum Sizes (Recommended)	Weight (lb/ft²)
Ordinary Clear Lime Glass (Float) (Iron-Oxide Content 0.10% to 0.13%)	1/8"—85%	8.2%R + 6.8%A	34" × 76"	1.63
	3/16"—81%	8.0%R + 11.0%A	36" × 96"	2.51
Sheet Lime Glass (Low Iron-Oxide Content—0.05% to 0.06%)	1/8"—87%	8.1%R + 4.9%A	34" × 76"	1.63
	3/16"—85%	8.0%R + 7.0%A	36" × 96"	2.51
Water-White Crystal Glass (0.01% Iron Oxide)	5/32"—91%	8.0%R + 1.0%A	34" × 76"	2.03
	3/16"—90.5%	8.0%R + 1.5%A	36" × 96"	2.51

Notes: a. R stands for reflection, A for absorption.

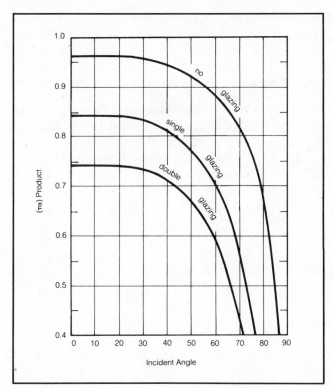

Figure 4.23 Effect of incident angle on transmittance-absorbtance product (⅛ inch glass with 88 percent normal transmittance, flat black paint with normal 96 percent absorbtance). After ASHRAE 1978 Applications.

reinforced polyester. Kalwall's Sun-Lite and Vistron's Filon are both excellent examples of this type of material.

Sun-Lite panels come in 4- or 5-foot widths in thicknesses of 0.025-, 0.040-, and 0.060-inch with transmission factors in the 85 to 90 percent range. Even though they transmit as much radiant energy as does a good quality glass, they diffuse the light somewhat, giving the material a murky appearance. In addition, the thinness of the glazing coupled with its relatively large coefficient of thermal expansion makes it difficult to get a perfectly flat surface, which also detracts from its appearance.

Filon panels are manufactured with fiberglass-reinforced, acrylic-fortified polyester resin with a Tedlar surface for additional ultraviolet (UV) protection. By blocking the UV, a modest loss in solar transmittance results and the overall transmission of sunlight is about 86 percent. Filon panels, like Sun-Lite panels, are light and easy to work with, but both are subject to thermal degradation if subjected to prolonged exposure at temperatures in the 200°F range. Since these temperatures can be reached quite easily in a collector left stagnant during the summer, some means of automatically venting the panel should be incorporated in the design. Kalwall does offer a simple bimetallic Temp-Valve for this purpose.

Another plastic option is the use of very thin (0.001- to 0.004-inch) films. DuPont's Tedlar and Teflon are examples, as is 3M's Flexiguard 7410. While these films offer the twin advantages of very high transmittance (around

93 to 96 percent) and quite low cost, they don't have much structural integrity and tend to wrinkle and sag. If used as an outer glazing their lifetime is considered to be on the order of five years. As an inner glazing some of these materials are subject to embrittlement within an even shorter period of time.

Another major disadvantage of any of these plastic films is their inability to suppress the energy that is being lost from the absorber plate by reradiation. The most desirable combination of properties for a glazing material would be for it to have a high transmittance factor for the incoming short wave length solar energy but a low transmittance for the long wave length radiation trying to escape from the plate. Glass and fiberglass-reinforced polyesters have nearly ideal properties in this regard but, as can be seen in Figure 4.24, Tedlar does not.

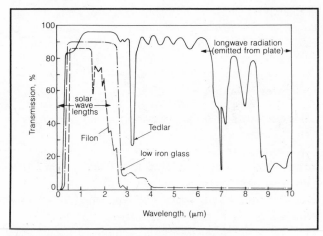

Figure 4.24 Transmission through various glazings.

Finally, there are some rigid plastic glazings that are being used to some extent, though with limited success. Acrylics have good solar transmission factors comparable to water-white glass, and they withstand UV and weathering well. However they soften at about 180°F and if the resulting sag lets them touch your stagnant absorber panel they are liable to melt. Polycarbonates are better able to withstand high temperatures, but they have lower transmittances and degrade more quickly under prolonged UV exposure.

Insulation

Medium-temperature collectors require insulation on the back and sides of the absorber plate. Considering that the largest heat-loss factor is the front glazing system, cost-effective insulation levels are limited to the equivalent of 3 inches of fiberglass at the rear and approximately 1 inch on the sides.

Popular insulations include fiberglass batting, expanded foams, and combinations thereof. Fiberglass batting is more bulky and must be carefully selected to have

115

a low binder content. The binder is a gluelike material which gives fiberglass shape but is prone to outgassing when the fiberglass is exposed to elevated temperatures. The outgassed materials appear as a cloudy coating on the inside surface of the glazing. Experienced manufacturers utilize the low-binder fiberglass to preclude this event.

Expanded foam insulations have the advantage of high insulating values per inch of thickness. A major drawback, however, is their upper temperature limit. Many foamed insulations (such as polystyrene) actually melt at temperatures around 200°F! Outgassing begins at even lower temperatures. These temperature levels can appear in even the simplest, single-glazed collectors during stagnation.

The only foamed insulation with high temperature performance abilities is trademarked Isocyanurate. This insulation is rated for 400°F operation and, while suitable for painted absorbers, should not be used in direct contact with selectively coated absorber plates. The best material for selective surface collectors remains fiberglass.

Collector Housing

The basic function of the collector housing is to provide a dead air space for the absorber plate and general protection from the elements. Most commercial collectors utilize either aluminum or steel cases though some use weather-resistant woods such as redwood. The case also serves the important function of supporting the glazing system.

A properly designed case will feature a watertight gasketing system and provisions for field replacement of glazing in the event of breakage or damage. The back of the collector should also be comprised of a water-resistant material and be capable of withstanding long periods of dampness, mold, and mildew. Materials such as pressboard or masonite are not recommended for this service. The exterior surface of the collector frame is usually painted or anodized for weather protection.

The overall size and weight of the collector is variable, but some industry standards are emerging. Due to a finite number of stock glass sizes, collectors are generally built on 34-inch widths and lengths of 77, 84, and 93 inches. On special order, certain manufacturers offer ganged arrays for large projects. For instance, Revere Copper offers collector modules with net areas in excess of 150 square feet, factory preplumbed with a single inlet and outlet connection. Lifted into place by crane, these oversized collectors can reduce site labor costs dramatically.

The weight of a collector will be in the vicinity of 4 to 6 pounds per square foot, depending primarily on the type of glazing and whether single or double glazing is specified. Thus, roof-loading considerations are modest. However, it should be noted that a 20-square-foot collector (about 110 to 120 pounds) is about the maximum size

conveniently handled by two people on a roof. Larger collectors should be specified only when lifting apparatus is available.

Overall Collector Performance

Having described the individual parts of a collector—the absorber, coating, glazing, and insulation—we come to the bottom line, which is how effectively the collector as a whole converts sunlight into useful thermal energy. This will lead to the notion of collector efficiency and the interpretation of manufacturer's efficiency curves.

What we are trying to do is transfer useful heat from the absorber plate to our collector fluid. That rate of heat transfer, q_u, is simply the difference between the energy absorbed by the plate, q_{abs}, and the energy lost from the plate to the ambient environment, q_{loss}. That is,

E. 4.8 $\qquad q_u = q_{abs} - q_{loss}$

as shown in Figure 4.25.

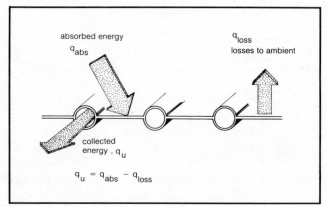

Figure 4.25 Energy balance on the absorber plate.

Now, the energy absorbed is simply the product of the insolation striking the collector and the fraction that makes it through the glass that gets absorbed by the plate.

E. 4.9 $\qquad q_{abs} = IA\tau\alpha$

where I is the insolation* on the tilted collector surface (Btu/hr-ft²), A is the collector aperture area (ft^2), τ is the overall transmission factor for the glazing, and α is the absorptance of the surface.

We can also model the thermal losses to the ambient by the following:

E. 4.10 $\qquad q_{loss} = U_L A(T_p - T_a)$

where U_L is an overall collector heat-loss coefficient (Btu/hr-ft²-°F) that depends on the number of sheets of glazing,

---

*A word about notation. We will be using the symbol I for instantaneous insolation rates and H for daily or monthly total amounts of insolation.

the emissivity of the surface, and the amount of insulation on the back; T_p is the average plate temperature (°F); and T_a is the ambient temperature (°F).

Combining equations 4.9 and 4.10 lets us write

E. 4.11 $q_u = IA\tau\alpha - U_L A(T_p - T_a)$

Finally, let us define the overall collector efficiency, η, to be the ratio of the energy collected to the energy striking the collector:

E. 4.12 $\eta = \dfrac{energy\ collected}{energy\ incident} = \dfrac{q_u}{IA}$

$$= \tau\alpha - \dfrac{U_L}{I}(T_p - T_a)$$

Example: Consider a typical single-glazed, nonselective surface collector with a heat loss coefficient, U_L, of 1.5 Btu/hr-ft²-°F. The transmittance of the glass is 0.87 and the absorptance of the surface is 0.95. How much energy would be collected by 20 square feet of collector exposed to 300 Btu/ft²-hr of sunlight, if the average plate temperature is 120°F and it is 35°F outside? What would be the collector's efficiency?

Solution: Using Equation 4.11 we have

$q_u = 300 \times 20 \times 0.87 \times 0.95 - 1.5 \times 20$
$\qquad \times (120 - 35)$
$q_u = 4960 - 2550 = 2410\ Btu/hr$

Since the panel is exposed to $20 \times 300 = 6000$ Btu/hr, its efficiency will be

$$\eta = \dfrac{2410\ Btu/hr}{6000\ Btu/hr} = 0.40 = 40\%$$

In most circumstances a system designer will be working from manufacturers' efficiency curves rather than directly from parameters such as τ, α, and U_L. So we need to become acquainted with the various ways that efficiency can be presented.

We could, for example, plot Equation 4.12. To simplify matters, let us begin by fixing the insolation, I, at a nice bright 300 Btu/hr-ft² and the ambient temperature at a balmy 70°F; then we can display efficiency curves in the manner of Figure 4.26. Here we are plotting typical collector efficiency versus average absorber temperature for a number of glazing and coating options. (Actually, the upper horizontal axis lets us read efficiency versus temperature difference between absorber and ambient, eliminating the 70° air temperature assumption.)

Several important features in these curves should be noted. One is that we cannot make any blanket statements such as "two sheets of glazing are better than one" or "glazed collectors are more efficient than unglazed collectors." Consider two sheets of glazing versus one sheet, for example. For collector temperatures less than about 125°F (under the ambient conditions stated) it would appear that single glazing is *more* effective than double! How can this be so?

The reason is that while double glazing does reduce the heat losses from the absorber to the ambient air (reduces U_L), it also reduces the amount of insolation making it to the absorber in the first place (lowers τ). For relatively small temperature differences between the plate and ambient, it is more important to improve the amount of energy reaching the plate than it is to reduce the thermal losses from the plate. For very small temperature differences it may even be better to have no glazing at all!

Another important thing to notice in Figure 4.26 is that *all* of the collector types become less efficient as their operating temperatures increase. This seems pretty reasonable, since the greater the difference in temperature

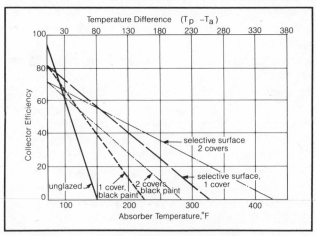

Figure 4.26 Typical efficiencies under fixed ambient conditions of 300 Btu/ft²-hr insolation and 70° F air temperature.

between the absorber and ambient the greater will be the heat lost to the ambient, and more losses means less energy can be collected. Turning that around, if we want to maximize efficiency and thereby collect the most energy, we should operate the collector at as low a temperature as possible.

For example, suppose we want to deliver some heat to a swimming pool by pumping some of the 80°F pool water through a collector array and then returning it to the pool. Would it be better to pump the water slowly through the collectors, giving it plenty of time to absorb the sun's energy so that it returns to the pool at say 140°F, or should we speed it through the panels so that it returns to the pool at a mere 85°F?

Heating the water to 140°F will certainly be more impressive in terms of hot pipes and steaming water, but by examining Figure 4.26 we see that the higher temperature will result in lower efficiency. Hence we will collect more energy and do a better job of heating the pool if we deliver water at 85°. This conclusion runs counter to many people's intuition and it is important to get it right in your mind.

Knowing that it is more efficient to operate a pool collector at around 85°F, how many sheets of glazing should be used? Looking at the efficiency curves under these fairly ideal conditions of temperature and sunlight, it appears that an unglazed collector has greater efficiency than one with single glazing, which in turn is more efficient than the collector with double glazing. Moreover, the unglazed collector is by far the cheapest. This is why, for most pool applications where the collectors are used in fairly mild summer conditions, an unglazed collector usually represents the most cost-effective choice. Glazed collectors are usually considered only for windy sites or for facilities where year-round pool heating is desired.

In contrast to pool heating, service water-heating and space-heating applications require temperatures in the 120° to 160°F range. At those temperatures an unglazed collector is clearly unacceptable; the thermal losses are nearly as great as the solar gains and very little net energy would be collected.

As the average plate-to-ambient temperature difference increases from say 10 to 20°F for a pool to say 50°F for a domestic hot-water system, we would select a single glazed collector rather than an unglazed one; as we get into higher temperature differences of say 80°F or so, then a double-glazed collector or a single-glazed collector with selective surface would probably be specified.

For even higher temperature differences, such as might be required for absorption cycle cooling, selective surfaces are a must. It is in these specialized applications, where the collector is required to deliver energy at a temperature of 180°F or so, that focusing collectors also become cost-effective.

NBS and ASHRAE Efficiency Curves

While Figure 4.26 was useful for gaining familiarity with the general appearance of efficiency curves, it is not the way the data are usually presented. There are two reasons for a slightly more complicated figure being called for. One is that we fixed the insolation at a certain value in order to draw Figure 4.26, and of course that is an unrealistic assumption. The second is that we used average absorber plate temperature as our indication of collector temperature. What we really want is some measure of the temperature of the fluid going through the collector. Not only would that be easier to use but it would be much easier to measure in the first place.

There are two commonly used techniques for measuring and presenting collector efficiencies and, though they are similar, there are some very important but subtle differences that we should understand.

One test procedure, developed by the National Bureau of Standards (NBS), is based on the *average* temperature of the fluid in the collector, $\overline{T}_f$, where

E. 4.13 $$\overline{T}_f = \frac{T_i + T_o}{2}$$

and T_i is the inlet temperature of the fluid and T_o is the outlet temperature. A modification to Equation 4.11 lets us write the useful energy collected in terms of $\overline{T}_f$ as follows

E. 4.14 $$q_u = F'[I\,A\tau\alpha - U_L A\,(\overline{T}_f - T_a)]$$

where F' is that collector plate efficiency factor that we plotted back in Figure 4.21.

Things are beginning to come together now with the reintroduction of F', which you'll recall is the factor that accounts for tube spacing, fin thickness, and absorber material. In a perfect absorber plate, F' is 1 and the plate temperature is the same as the fluid temperature. For less than perfect plates, the average fluid temperature is less than the plate temperature and the resulting decrease in collector performance shows up in equation 4.14 as F'.

Equation 4.14 can be used to solve for collector efficiency as follows:

E. 4.15 $$\eta = \frac{q_u}{IA} = F'[\tau\alpha - \frac{U_L}{I}\,(\overline{T}_f - T_a)]$$

The term $(\overline{T}_f - T_a)/I$ is referred to as the collector fluid parameter, and the NBS method of presentation plots collector efficiency versus this parameter; the result is a straight line. Figure 4.27 shows such a plot for three different collectors manufactured by Revere.

It takes a while to get used to this presentation, so let's try a quick example. Suppose the fluid in a collector is entering at 120°F and leaving at 130°F while exposed to 250 Btu/hr-ft² insolation and the ambient temperature is 40°F. The fluid parameter would be [(120 + 130)/2 − 40°]/250 = 0.34. The three glazed collectors in Figure 4.27 would have efficiencies of 26, 39, and 48 percent.

The other method of presenting collector efficiencies is based on a test procedure developed by the American Society of Heating, Refrigerating, and Air Conditioning Engineers (ASHRAE). The ASHRAE tests differ from the NBS tests in two important ways: ASHRAE uses the fluid inlet temperature T_i in its fluid parameter rather than $\overline{T}_f$, and the ASHRAE efficiency is based on the *gross* area of the collector, which is determined by the outer dimensions of the whole collector, frame and all, while the NBS efficiency is based on the *effective* area of the absorber plate alone. These differences are summarized in Table 4.11, while examples of the ASHRAE presentation are given in Figure 4.28.

Most of the technical literature in the solar field today is written with the ASHRAE approach to collector performance. We introduce it here so you can become fa-

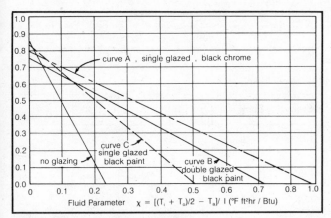

Figure 4.27 Typical NBS test results.

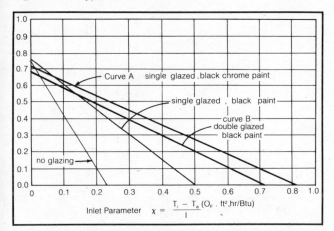

Figure 4.28 Typical ASHRAE test results.

Table 4.11 Key Differences in the NBS and ASHRAE Efficiency Curves

	ASHRAE 93-77	NBS 74-635
Fluid Parameter	$(T_i - T_a)/I$	$(\overline{T}_f - T_a)/I$
Efficiency	q_u/IA_{gross}	q_u/IA_{eff}

miliar with the jargon; later, when we describe the computer simulation of systems, we'll use this material again.

In a manner analogous to Equations 4.11 and 4.14 let us write the useful energy collection rate, q_u, in terms of the collector inlet temperature, T_i, as

E. 4.16 $q_u = F_R[IA\,\tau\alpha - U_L A\,(T_i - T_a)]$

The new factor introduced here, F_R, is called the collector heat removal factor. It can be thought of as the ratio of the energy actually removed to the energy that would have been removed if the whole absorber plate stayed at the nice cool inlet temperature, T_i. The actual value of F_R depends on F' and the fluid flow rate, but it is typically in the range of 0.85 to 0.95 for hydronic collectors and something closer to 0.67 for some air collectors.

To get instantaneous collector efficiency, we divide through by the insolation striking the panel giving

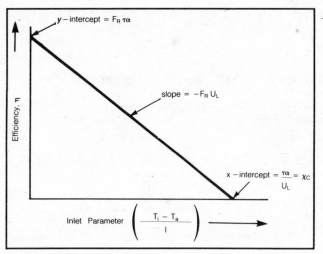

Figure 4.29 Identifying the key collector parameters from an ASHRAE efficiency plot.

E. 4.17 $\eta = \dfrac{q_u}{IA} = F_R[\tau\alpha - \dfrac{U_L}{I}(T_i - T_a)]$

When η is plotted versus the fluid parameter, $(T_i - T_a)/I$, a straight line results. The intercept on the vertical axis is $F_R\tau\alpha$, the intercept on the horizontal axis is $\tau\alpha/U_L$, and the slope of the line is $-F_R U_L$. These relationships are shown in Figure 4.29.

A word of warning with regard to efficiency curves is in order. Measurements of collector efficiency are extremely difficult to perform precisely. Thus, when comparing efficiency curves it is important that they have been provided by reputable, independent testing agencies. Tests performed by the manufacturer should be treated with a jaundiced eye.

Average Collector Efficiencies

So far we have only dealt with the *instantaneous* efficiency of a collector under a given set of operating conditions. It is more useful, for design, to be able to find daily or monthly *average* efficiencies. Fortunately, to some extent, we can use average operating parameters with either the NBS or ASHRAE curves to find an average efficiency.

Example: Collector B in Figure 4.27 is turned on at 7:30 A.M. and turned off at 4:00 P.M., during which time it is exposed to a total insolation of 2058 Btu/ft². At 7:30 A.M. the circulating fluid in the collector is about 60°F, and by the time the collector turns off at 4:00 P.M. the collector fluid is 140°F. During this period of time the ambient temperature has averaged 45°F. How much energy has been collected?

Solution: We can find the average fluid parameter from

119

$$\overline{T}_f = \frac{140 + 60}{2} = 100°F$$

$$\overline{T}_a = 45°F$$

$$\overline{I} = \frac{2058\ Btu/ft^2}{8\frac{1}{2}\ hr} = 242\ Btu/hr\text{-}ft^2 \qquad so$$

$$\frac{\overline{T}_f - \overline{T}_a}{\overline{I}} = \frac{100 - 45}{242} = 0.23°F\text{-}ft^2\text{-}hr/Btu$$

which, from Figure 4.27, yields an average efficiency of 50 percent. The energy collected then is

$$\eta \cdot H = 0.50 \times 2058 = 1029\ Btu/ft^2$$

We might carry this example a bit further and ask what collector area would be required to heat 80 gallons of water per day under the above conditions? We can write the energy required for this task

$$Qreq = \frac{80\ gal}{day} \times 8.34\ \frac{lbm}{gal} \times (140 - 60)°F \times 1\ \frac{Btu}{lbm\text{-}°F}$$

$$= 53,400\ Btu/day$$

If one square foot of collector supplies 1029 Btu per day, then we need

$$A = \frac{53,400\ Btu/day}{1029\ Btu/ft^2\text{-}day} = 52ft^2$$

It turns out that 80 gallons per day is a reasonable estimate of the hot water demands for a family of four and the 2058 Btu/ft²-day insolation is typical for a clear winter's day. In other words, just over 50 square feet of panel could supply the domestic hot water requirement for a typical family on a good day.

Just to get you in the right ballpark when looking at collector efficiency curves, Table 4.12 gives some typical average operating conditions and the resulting average fluid parameters (NBS) for what might loosely be called reasonably good solar days.

A bit earlier we said average conditions "to some extent" could be used for determining average performance. Let's define that a little more carefully. Averaging is a legitimate technique to use during any period of time that the collector is actually operating. You cannot, however, simply use total daily insolation divided by the total hours of daylight to get the average insolation for your fluid parameter. That is because the collector does not run from sunup to sundown; if it did, there would be periods of time in the morning and late afternoon, and any time the sun goes behind a black cloud, when the collector losses would exceed the gains. When losses exceed gains, the fluid should not be circulated or else it will be cooled as it passes through the collector.

The amount of insolation that just makes the energy absorbed equal the energy lost is called the *critical inso-*

Table 4.12 Typical Range of Average Fluid Parameter During Clear Days

Application	$\overline{T}_f$	$\overline{T}_a$	$\overline{I}$	$\dfrac{\overline{T}_f - \overline{T}_a}{\overline{I}}$
Swimming Pools	85°F	70° / 60°	275 / 250	0.05 / 0.10
Domestic Hot Water	100°F	60° / 40°	250 / 200	0.16 / 0.30
Space Heating	120°F	50° / 25°	250 / 225	0.32 / 0.42
Absorption Air Conditioning	180°F	90° / 70°	275 / 250	0.33 / 0.45

lation, I_c. The collector fluid should only be circulated when the actual insolation *exceeds* the critical insolation, that is, between times t_1 and t_2 in Figure 4.30.

The critical insolation can be determined easily from either the NBS or ASHRAE efficiency curves by picking off the value of the fluid parameter that makes the efficiency of the collector equal to zero. Call that value X_c, then

E. 4.18
$$I_c = \frac{T_f - T_a}{X_c}$$

For example, the efficiency of collector B in Figure 4.27 goes to zero at a fluid parameter equal to 0.7. Suppose it is morning, the ambient temperature is 35°F, and we want to start heating our domestic hot water, which is currently sitting at 60°F. Suppose the controller waits until the collector is 15°F above the tank temperature before starting the system. The morning insolation required before the system would turn on would be

$$I_{c_{A.M.}} = \frac{60 + 15 - 35}{0.7} = 57\ Btu/hr\text{-}ft^2$$

But by late afternoon conditions have changed. Our stor-

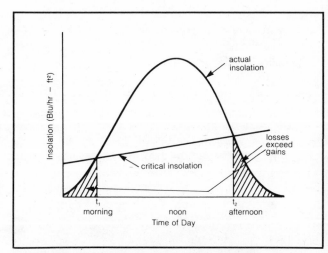

Figure 4.30 The collector fluid should be circulated only during the period when actual insolation exceeds critical insolation.

age tank is up at about 140°F and it's now 55°F outside. To continue to run the system the insolation needs to exceed

$$I_{c_{P.M.}} = \frac{140 - 55}{0.7} = 121 \; Btu/hr\text{-}ft^2$$

We could look in Appendix 4C, where hour-by-hour clear sky insolations are given, to determine at roughly what time in the morning the critical insolation is reached and the system turns on, and at what time it would later turn off. The insolation between those hours could be averaged and an average efficiency determined. For example, let's continue with collector B, which is turned on in the morning when the insolation exceeds 57 Btu/hr-ft² and is turned off in the afternoon when the insolation falls below 121 Btu/hr-ft². Let's locate the collector at 40° north latitude with a tilt angle of 40°, and figure its daily output in February. Appendix 4C gives us the hourly insolation values listed in Table 4.13, from which we can estimate the start-up time to be roughly 7:30 A.M., the shut-off time to be 4:00 P.M., and the insolation during those 8½ hours to be 2058 Btu/ft². We should not try to be too precise in these estimates of start-up and shut-off times, since we are going to be ignoring the additional reflective losses of the glazing when the sun is way off the axis of the collector.

Table 4.13 Insolation Between Start-Up and Shut-Off

Time	Insolation	
7 A.M.	21 Btu/hr-ft²	
8	122	◆ Start-up 7:30
9	205	
10	267	
11	306	Total insolation between 7:30 A.M. and
12	319	4:00 P.M. = 122 + 205 + 267 +
1 P.M.	306	306 + 319 + 306 + 267 + 205 +
2	267	122/2 = 2058 Btu/ft²
3	205	
4	122	◆ Shut-off 4:00
5	21	
Daily total =	2162 Btu/ft²	

Notice that we shall assume that the value of insolation given by ASHRAE for any particular time of the day applies for the half-hour before that time as well as the half-hour after that time. So for example at 4:00 P.M. the insolation is given as 122 Btu/hr-ft², which we will assume applies from 3:30 to 4:30 P.M. Since our collector shuts off at 4:00 P.M. it picks up 122/2 = 61 Btu/hr-ft² between 3:30 and 4:00 P.M.

Now we can find the average fluid parameter. The collector raises water from 60 to 140°F so $\overline{T}_f = 100°F$. The morning temperature was 35°F and the afternoon was 55°F, so we'll assume $\overline{T}_a = 45°F$. The average hourly insolation is 2058/8½ = 242 Btu/ft²-hr. The average fluid parameter (NBS), then, is

$$\frac{\overline{T}_f - \overline{T}_a}{\overline{I}} = \frac{100 - 45}{242} = 0.23$$

From Figure 4.27 the average efficiency is 50 percent. The daily energy collected is thus 0.5 × 2058 = 1029 Btu/ft². The overall daily efficiency (percent of the whole day's insolation collected) is thus 1029/2162 = 47 percent.

This procedure is fairly tedious and the results are only applicable to clear sky conditions. When clouds, rain, snow, and clear skies are all mixed together into monthly average insolations we are stuck with either approximating some sort of average efficiency or we need to revert to some of the more sophisticated techniques based on computer simulations. We'll deal with such complications later when we describe specific system applications.

Hydronic Collector Plumbing

Many manufacturers offer hydronic collectors with the option of having either internal or external manifolds. Collectors set up for external manifolding have one inlet and one outlet tube, usually extending out of the top and bottom of the panel as shown in Figure 4.31(a). With external manifolding the collectors can be mounted side by side, directly against each other, and the connections between them are made outside of the modules. All external piping must be insulated and weatherproofed.

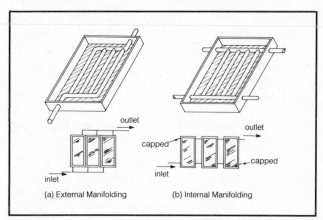

Figure 4.31 Internal and external manifolding in hydronic collectors.

With internal manifolds, each collector has two side penetrations near the bottom of the panel and two near the top as shown in Figure 4.31(b). Usually the interconnections between the panels require that they be separated by a couple of inches (though some have interlocking O-ring assemblies that let the panels be pushed directly together).

The advantage of internal manifolds is that almost all of the manifold is inside of the collector frame and therefore need not be insulated and protected from the weather. In fact the manifold becomes an absorber surface itself. The end result can be a neater array that's also easier to assemble. One potential drawback to internal manifolding is that the number of panels that can be arranged in a parallel row is limited by the maximum flow rate that the manifold itself can handle.

To prevent erosion-corrosion of copper it is necessary to restrict the flow velocity of the fluid in the tubing to something less than 5 feet per second; but to keep pressure drops to a reasonable level and hence minimize pumping power, it is a good idea to keep it closer to half that speed. Table 4.14 gives the flow rates for various sizes of type L copper tube that result in flow speeds of 5 feet per second and the corresponding pressure drops.

With either form of manifolding, it is also important to design the plumbing to assure equal flow through each collector. To achieve flow balance among collectors, the reverse-return piping arrangements shown in Figure 4.32(a) are recommended. Using this configuration (which can be expanded to almost any size array in a building-block fashion), the flow tends to balance naturally since the pressure drop through each flow path is nearly identical. On the other hand, the parallel piping configuration, shown in Figure 4.32(b), tends to exhibit uneven flow between collector modules. The fluid has a tendency to short-circuit through the first collector and starve the last. This effect can be counteracted by strategically located balancing valves or hydronic circuit setters, but can be avoided altogether by employing a reverse-return configuration. In general, a parallel arrangement is recommended for three or four collectors at most, and then with reservation.

Figure 4.32(c) indicates that collectors may be plumbed in series, provided the overall array has provisions for flow balancing. Generally, a maximum of three collectors are so plumbed. If a greater number are connected in series, the flow rate necessary to service the branch reaches the erosion limit for the individual modules and pressure drops become substantial.

Figure 4.33 shows a typical relation between the collector flow rate and its measured pressure drop. This information is for pump sizing and should be available from the collector manufacturer upon request. The particular model cited is an 18-square-foot glazed model used in

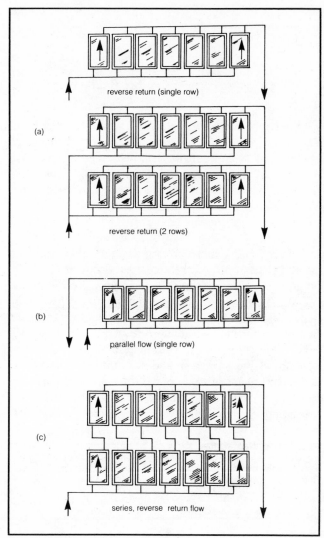

Figure 4.32 Collector arrays should be plumbed with reverse return manifolding.

water- and space-heating applications. Generally, these applications would require flow rates in the vicinity of 0.02 to 0.03 gpm per square foot of surface, or 0.36 to 0.54 gpm total. Note that the expected pressure drop is substantially less than 0.5 feet of water, which is quite typical. Thus, in most plumbing systems, the collector pressure drop is not a dominant factor in the overall hydraulics.

It is recommended that all joints in copper tubing in and near the collector be soldered using 95/5 tin-antimony solder, which has a high enough melting point not to be affected by collector stagnation temperatures. Regular 50/50 tin-lead solder is adequate further from the collector.

All piping to and from the array should be insulated to reduce heat loss. The most common insulation uses closed cell foams called elastomers (such as Armaflex® or Rubatex®). Elastomeric insulation will rapidly deteriorate under exposure to the elements unless jacketed or painted with a manufacturer-approved coating. Repainting

Table 4.14 Flow Rates and Corresponding Pressure Drops That Produce Maximum Recommended Flow Speeds of 5 Feet per Second in Type L Copper Tubing

Nominal Size	Flow rate (gpm)	Pressure drop (ft/100 ft)
½″	3.6	27
¾″	7.5	16
1″	13	11
1½″	28	7.2
2″	48	4.8
3″	106	2.9

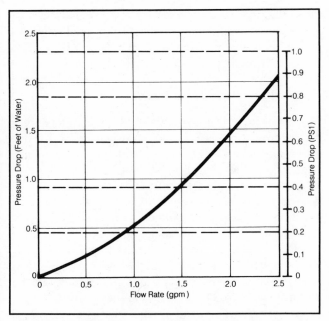

Figure 4.33 Pressure drop information for standard length modular solar-energy collector.

may be required every five years or so. Fiberglass, rigid urethane, or isocyanurate foams are also popular.

Underground piping should be insulated, wrapped in roofing paper, sealed with hot pitch, and buried below the frost line. Some codes will not allow any buried joints, so soft copper tubing should be used if turns or long runs are required.

Collector Installation Tips

The most critical step in any active system installation is the attachment of collectors to the roof. The collectors must be attached securely enough to withstand wind and snow loads (100 mph winds on a sloped surface will increase the loading by as much as 25 pounds per square foot) as well as to accommodate continued expansion and contraction of the array as it heats and cools each day. Penetrations must be made to accommodate mounting bolts, plumbing runs, and control wiring. Through all this the roof must remain absolutely watertight, year in and year out.

For roofs that are likely to need repair or replacement during the lifetime of the collector array, special attention needs to be paid to the problems that the array will be likely to cause. Easily removable collectors, or collectors that are flashed right into the roof itself, or arrays that are set high enough above the roof to allow access underneath them will greatly simplify future reroofing.

Roofing problems can, of course, be avoided altogether by locating the collectors elsewhere, such as on a ground-mounted rack which is securely attached to concrete footings. Mount the collectors so their bottom edge is at least a foot or two above the ground to avoid problems of mud splashing and snow accumulation. Remem-

ber, too, that if the collectors are allowed to stagnate in the summer, they will become hot enough to cause burns so that children, especially, should be made aware of the potential danger.

In general, collectors mounted on sloped roofs should either be elevated at least 1½ inches above the roof surface (shakes, shingles, and so on) or flashed directly into the roof in such a way as to form a watertight covering. Collectors which are laid directly onto shingles can cause deterioration of the roof as accumulating moisture under the panel leads to growth of mildew, fungus, and mold. In addition, in cold climates, ice dams can form drawing water under shingles by capillary action.

Figure 4.34 suggests one way to make attachments to shingled, sloped roofs. Mounting blocks of redwood, cedar, or even metal channel are laid on the roof sheathing with a liberal layer of silicone sealant or fibrous roofing cement between them. Metal flashing covering the blocks that slides under the upper shingles and over the lower shingles helps insure the roof's integrity. A mounting angle made of a metal compatible with the collector frame is used to connect the panels or collector rack to the mounting blocks.

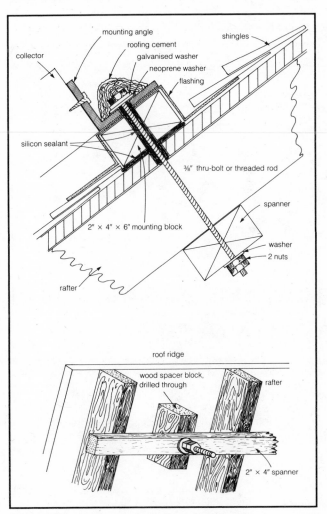

Figure 4.34 Attachment of collectors to sloped roofs.

The angle and blocks are secured to the roof with thru-bolts or threaded rods that connect to 2-by-4-inch spanners laid under the rafters. It is also a good practice to use snug-fitting, predrilled wood spacers to keep the spanner from sagging as the nuts are tightened up. Be sure to apply generous quantities of sealant to holes, mounting blocks, and over the nuts and washers on the mounting angle.

It is possible to screw lag bolts directly into the rafters, but this practice is to be discouraged. Not only is it hard to hit the rafters dead center, but the bolts can loosen in time. Sometimes, such as when the attic is completely unaccessible, it may be necessary to use lag bolts. When predrilling through the roof into the rafter, make the hole several sizes smaller than the lag bolt and be sure the bolt goes at least two inches into the rafter. Goosh it up with plenty of sealant.

On flat roofs, provision must be made for connecting the collector rack to the horizontal surface. In Figure 4.35(a) a pitch pan with rack attachment mount is bolted to the roof using either the spanner or lag bolt method. The pitch pan is flashed and filled with pitch or roofing cement. Pitch pots are not permanently waterproof and may require periodic replacement of the roofing cement.

In Figure 4.35(b) a curb mount is shown flashed into

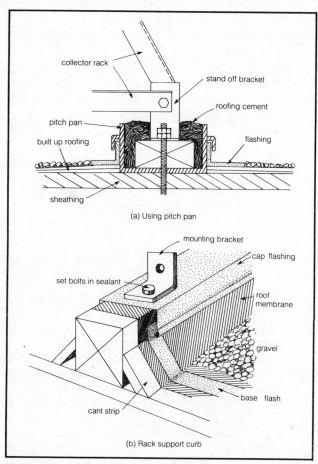

(a) Using pitch pan

(b) Rack support curb

Figure 4.35 Two methods for securing collector racks to flat built up roofs.

the roof surface. This approach is frequently used on large arrays where distribution of the load is important. An added bonus is that the rack needn't be disturbed when reroofing is required.

Higher-Performance Collectors

At present there is not really any strong competition to the flat-plate collector for the water-heating and active space-heating market. At the moderate temperatures required for these applications (less than 150°F), the flat-plate collector has advantages of less cost, greater simplicity, and at least equal, if not greater, efficiency when compared to the variety of concentrators and evacuated-tube collectors now being introduced.

There are applications such as absorption air conditioning and industrial process heating where higher temperatures are required, and it is for these markets that the advanced collector designs begin to make sense.

One way to boost the performance of a collector is to put the absorber in a vacuum, thereby reducing the heat lost by convection between plate and glazing. There are a number of approaches possible, two of which are shown in Figure 4.36. Figure 4.36(a) shows the Corning Cortec evacuated-tube collector, which features a U-shaped copper tube affixed to the underside of a selectively coated copper absorber plate. Figure 4.36(b) shows the Owens-Illinois Sunpak™, which consists of concentric glass tubes that the circulating fluid passes through. These tubes are inside of a third, outer, glass tube and a vacuum is drawn between them.

The second way to boost performance of a collector is by some form of concentration of the incoming sunlight before it strikes the absorber. The simplest thing to do is to couple a conventional flat-plate collector with a fixed flat reflector. Winter performance of a steeply tilted collector can be quite easily enhanced by an additional 50 percent or so with a horizontal reflecting surface as suggested in Figure 4.37(a). Summer performance, for air conditioning, can be enhanced with a flat reflector tipped up toward the north as shown in Figure 4.37(b).

Collectors with curved reflecting surfaces are what usually come to mind when we think of concentrators. By reflecting sunlight onto a point or a line, a concentrator can have a large aperture area to collect the incident energy, while maintaining a relatively small absorber area. Since thermal losses from the absorber are proportional to its area and temperature, a small absorber area means that relatively high temperatures can be maintained without excessive losses. It also means modest temperatures can be achieved with lower insolation than a flat plate requires.

Although the ideal focuser would have a parabolic cross section, either as a parabolic dish or a parabolic trough (Figure 4.38), collectors with hemispherical or cylindrical shapes are easier to produce and can be almost

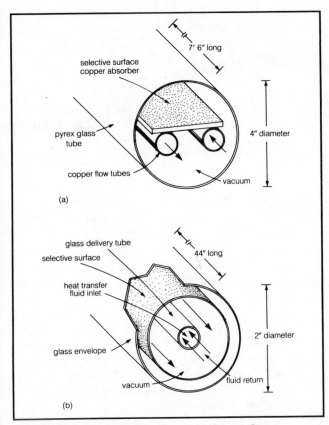

Figure 4.36 Evacuated-tube collectors (a) Corning Cortec (b) Owens-Illinois

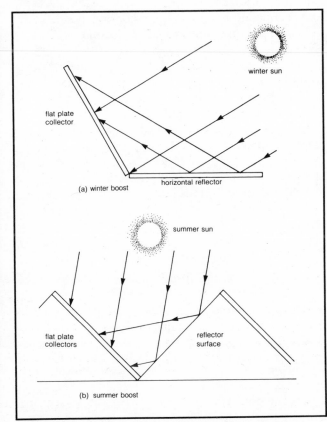

Figure 4.37 Enhancement of collector performance with flat reflectors.

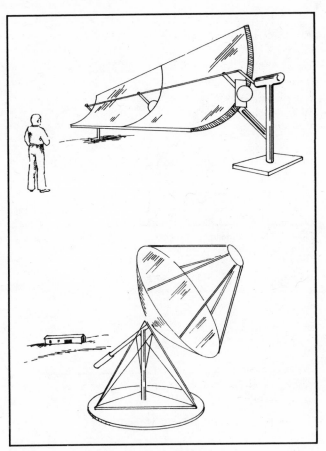

Figure 4.38 Designs for focusing collectors.

as efficient. The reflector can be made of almost any material and covered with thin aluminized mylar, or it may be made by simply flexing shiny sheet metal.

Most concentrators require some sort of tracking mechanism, which adds to their complexity, cost, and maintainability, and is the principal disadvantage of this approach. Another drawback is that the reflector will only be able to concentrate the direct portion of the sun's rays, while the diffuse portion is largely lost.

Figure 4.39 shows the usual presentation of a concentrating collector's efficiency curve in comparison with that of a single glazed, selective surface flat-plate collector. While at first glance the concentrator looks so much better, note the very high values of fluid parameter that are displayed. If you recall Table 4.12, we indicated that the fluid parameter for domestic water heating was usually in the range of 0.16 to 0.30 and space heating from about 0.32 to 0.42. For water heating there would appear to be no advantage to this concentrator and for space heating the advantage is modest.

There are some reflector shapes that can be used to achieve good concentration with only periodic adjustments. The compound parabolic concentrator (CPC) or Winston collector has the distinction of being capable of achieving the theoretical maximum concentration possible for a given acceptance angle. In the original CPC

125

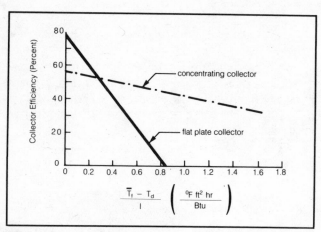

Figure 4.39 Comparing efficiency of a concentrating collector to a single glazed, selective surface flat plate collector.

concept, as shown in Figure 4.40, each side of the trough is a section of a parabola with its focus at the bottom of the opposite side. Many variations of this design are being experimented with and it is likely to be a shape that we'll see in advanced designs in the future.

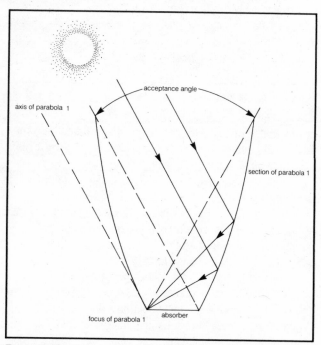

Figure 4.40 A cross section of a compound parabolic concentrator.

Solar Domestic Water Heating

The simple heating of water in residences and commercial facilities for washing clothes, bodies, and dishes consumes as much energy as the Alaskan pipeline delivers. Moreover most new water heaters installed today heat with electricity, which is not only the least efficient way to convert a fossil fuel into heat but also the most expensive.

Water heating is a nearly ideal application of solar technology. It is a year-round consumer of energy, so money spent on solar equipment derives some payback every month of the year. In addition the temperature requirements are modest; heating water from say 50°F to 130°F or 140°F means the average temperature is only 90 to 100°F, so the collectors will operate with relatively high efficiencies. And finally, the systems are physically small enough to be easily accommodated in almost any residence and inexpensive enough for most people to afford.

It is interesting to note that the solar water-heating industry was well underway during the first years of this century, though it declined substantially with the arrival of cheap natural gas. That era has about ended now, and the solar domestic water heater is becoming an ever more common sight in the United States today.

There are many solar hot-water system designs to choose from, and the main purpose of this section will be to help you decide which one most closely meets your needs. The key features that distinguish one system from another are:

1. Whether the heat-absorbing fluid is circulated from collector to storage, or whether the collector and storage are the same unit.

2. Whether the circulating fluid is pumped from one place to another, or whether it circulates by natural convection.

3. Whether the system uses one tank for hot-water storage and another for auxiliary backup heating, or whether both functions are accomplished in one tank.

4. (And the most important) what method of freeze pro-

126

tection is used: drain down, recirculation, or use of antifreeze.

Breadbox Water Heater

The breadbox water heater system has to be the easiest, simplest, cheapest, and most foolproof way to preheat water for domestic use. As suggested in Figure 4.41, the system is simply a water-heater tank that has been stripped of its insulation, painted black, and put inside of an insulated glazed "breadbox."

Hinged, insulated doors with a shiny reflective surface are a desirable option, especially in areas where the nights are cold. In areas with mild winters, or in almost any area during the summer, the system will perform well enough to supply preheated water for early evening uses even without a night cover. Figure 4.42 shows two examples of how easily such a unit can be either retrofitted onto the side of a house or designed into the building roof structure.

The tank is plumbed in series with the home's existing hot-water heater. No circulation between the tanks needs to be provided. As the user draws water out of the regular water heater it is replaced by preheated water from the breadbox. The regular water heater tops up the temperature as required, ensuring a continuous supply of hot water to the home regardless of weather conditions.

The set of three valves shown in the figure are there to allow isolation of the breadbox system from the regular water heater. Should it ever be required to repair or replace the breadbox system, the two normally open valves (n.o.) can be closed and the normally closed one (n.c.) opened, and the household will run on its regular water heater alone. We'll see this three-valve combination in other two-tank system diagrams.

As hot water is drawn from the tap the cold city water that would normally enter the home's regular water heater now goes into the breadbox heater. It is highly desirable to have that cold water inlet to the breadbox enter near the bottom of the breadbox tank so that it doesn't mix with the warmer water above it. In other words, if the tank is horizontal be sure to arrange it so the cold water inlet is toward the ground.

Better still, the breadbox tank should be mounted vertically. The cold water enters near the bottom of the tank through a long plastic dip tube. The warmer solar heated water is less dense than the cold entering water, so it floats on top without much mixing. This stratification is highly desirable.

The breadbox tank should be sized to hold at least one day's worth of hot-water use. As a rule of thumb an individual uses about 20 gallons of hot water per day, so that would suggest 80 gallons worth of preheat storage for a family of four. Rather than have one 80-gallon tank,

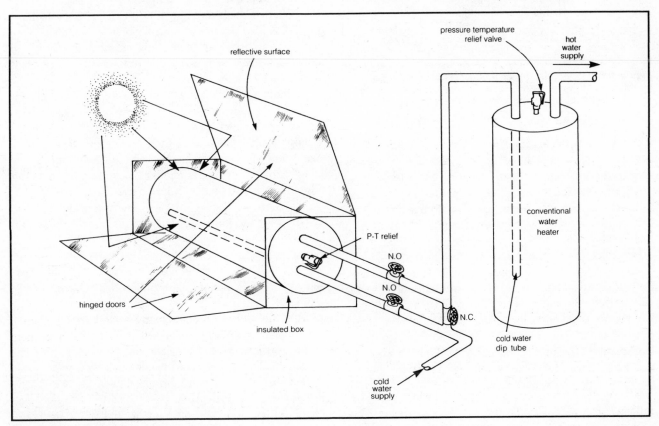

Figure 4.41 Bread box water heater system.

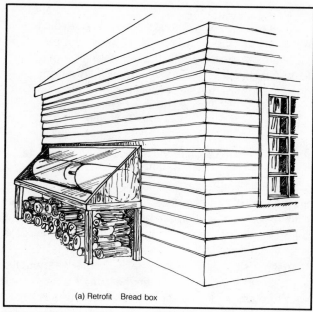

(a) Retrofit   Bread box

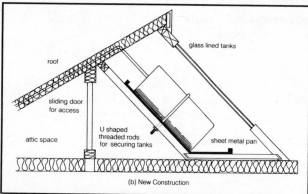

(b) New Construction

Figure 4.42 In mild climate, the need for reflectors and night insulation is reduced and bread box water heaters can be easily retrofitted or designed into new construction.

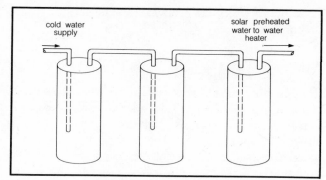

Figure 4.43 Multiple tanks should be plumbed in series.

it would be better to have two 40s or even three 30s. Several smaller tanks have more cross-sectional area to absorb the sun's energy than does one larger tank.

If no reflectors are used, it is desirable to have more than one day's energy use in collector/storage tanks. This is because even on a good day you may only be able to raise an individual tank's temperature by something like 30°F. If you have, say, twice the daily use in collector/storage tanks, then the average residence time in the tank for our preheat water is two days and (without losses) it can be raised by more like 60°F before being used.

Figure 4.43 shows the proper way to plumb a series of small tanks. They should be arranged in series rather than parallel. This helps stratification so the incoming cold won't cool down the hottest water which is ready to enter the home's regular water heater.

Thermosiphon Systems

While combining the storage and collector in one unit (the

breadbox system) is simple and cheap, it is not as efficient or convenient for the user as a system that separates those two functions.

The simplest circulating hot-water system is one that uses thermosiphoning to transfer energy from the flat-plate collectors to the storage tank. When water in a collector is heated, its density decreases and the water becomes more buoyant. If there is cooler, heavier water above it the fluids will want to exchange places and a natural convective circulation loop can be established.

Figure 4.44 shows a schematic diagram for a typical thermosiphoning system. Notice the top of the collectors need to be at least two feet below the bottom of the storage tank to prevent the system from reverse siphoning as the collector cools at night. If you can't arrange to have the full 2-foot clearance, then a check valve (a one-way valve) should be put in the line connecting storage to collectors to assure that the system doesn't run backwards at night and dissipate all your hard-won gains.

Thermosiphoning is a fairly delicate process and care should be taken to avoid high spots in the lines where pockets of air can form which would stop the flow. All piping should be at least ¾-inch diameter to decrease the likelihood of steam bubbles lodging in the tubing.

A tank with side penetrations as shown (such as the Rheem Solar-Aid tank) should be specified, as extra penetrations are extremely helpful in thermosiphon systems. Other things to notice about the diagram include that same combination of three valves for isolating the solar portion of the system from the regular water heater should it ever be necessary. Note that this is also a two-tank system, with one solar preheat tank and a separate auxiliary tank.

On the output of the auxiliary water heater is shown a mixing (or tempering) valve. A sketch of one is given in Figure 4.45(a). This is basically an anti-scalding device for safety. The solar-heated water can sometimes reach temperatures well beyond the usual 140° that a conventional water heater would deliver, and the mixing valve bleeds in just the right amount of cold water so that a preset temperature is never exceeded. While the mixing valve could be placed between the two tanks and accom-

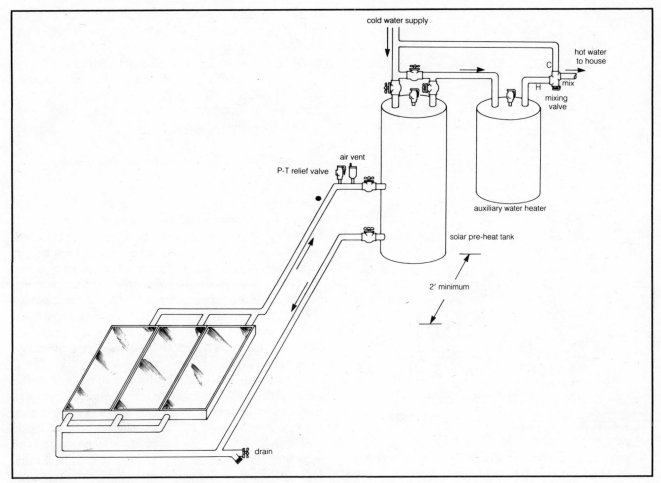

Figure 4.44 Thermosiphoning domestic water heating system.

plish the same function, it is better to put it on the output of the second tank. That lets both tanks store potentially very hot water, increasing your carryover and decreasing the likelihood that the auxiliary will need to turn on.

Finally, note that valves between tank and collector are suggested with an air vent, hose bib, and pressure-temperature relief valve on the collector side of the valves. The valves are there to allow you access to the collector loop without having to drain the solar tank. The hose bib lets you drain the collectors, which you might need to do on freezing nights, for example.

The air vent shown in Figure 4.45(d) serves two purposes. One is to help get rid of air in the lines when the collector is being filled, and the other is to let air into the system when you want to drain the water out of the panels. Air vents can be used this way, as vacuum breakers, if you don't anticipate the need to dump the collectors very often. They admit air rather slowly, however, and in many circumstances it is better to install a special vacuum breaker as shown in Figure 4.45(c).

Every tank in a pressurized system should have a temperature-pressure relief valve [shown in Figure 4.45(b)] for safety, but notice that we have also included one above the collectors. If the collector valves should be shut off for

one reason or another, the collector fluid could be isolated with no room for expansion should the temperature change in the collectors, so the relief valve will prevent excessive pressures.

The advantages of a thermosiphon system, compared to one where the fluid must be pumped around the loop, are significant. Eliminating the pump eliminates the cost of buying the pump, the cost of the controller that tells the pump when to turn on and off, and the cost of wiring the controller.

There are serious disadvantages, however. An obvious one is the physical constraint imposed by requiring storage to be above the collectors. If the collectors are on the roof then the solar tank may have to be perched up in the rafters in the attic somehow. The solar tank would typically be a 65- or 80-gallon water-heater tank, which is a fairly bulky and heavy item to be jockeying around in an attic. Once filled with water, the unit weighs six or seven hundred pounds. And woe be the day that the tank springs a leak if you haven't set it in a catch-pan with a drain.

Probably a more serious constraint on the widespread use of thermosiphon water heaters is the problem of freeze protection. Virtually every metal hydronic solar

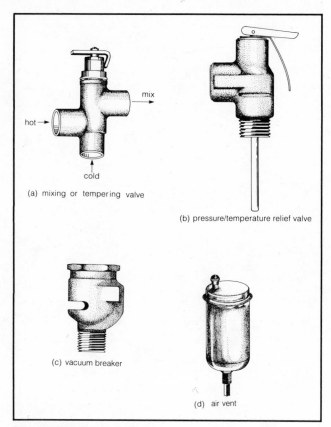

Figure 4.45 Plumbing fittings.

collector used anywhere in the United States outside of Hawaii needs to be protected against freezing. It even freezes once in a while in Florida and Southern California, and it only takes once to burst your collector flow tubes and potentially cause serious property damage. It should be noted, by the way, that collectors can freeze even if the ambient air temperature doesn't reach 32°F. Radiation losses from the plate can depress the plate's temperature by several degrees below ambient.

The system as shown could be used in an area with a very mild climate if the collectors are simply manually drained on those few occasions when a frost is imminent. Another simple approach for such areas is to install the collectors either inside the house itself behind a window or inside an attached solar greenhouse. In either case the moderating effect of the warmer temperatures around the collector may be sufficient to prevent freezing.

Some people have attached electric resistance heat tape to the absorber which is automatically turned on as the collectors approach freezing, but that seems a bit wasteful in any but very mild climate areas. And some success has been achieved with a temperature-sensitive valve which, on a cold night, automatically opens slightly, allowing water to dribble from the tank through the collectors and down a drain.

None of these approaches can be used with assurance in an area with severe winters. It might be possible to use automatic motorized valves to dump the water out of the collectors at night, but this approach is subject to malfunction if conventional automatic valves are used. And finally, it should be possible to use antifreeze in the collector loop with a heat exchanger in the storage tank to isolate the antifreeze from the potable water supply, but the heat exchanger needs to be carefully designed to avoid high spots where air can accumulate, which would prevent the thermosiphoning action.

Pumped System With Recirculation Freeze Protection

The physical constraints imposed by a thermosiphoning system can be eliminated if a small circulation pump is included. The pump allows the collectors to be put in their most convenient place, usually the roof, and the tank in its most convenient place, the basement or utility room.

Figure 4.46 shows a typical system schematic, most of which we are already familiar with. The three-valve isolation is there, the solar preheat and conventional water heaters are there, the tempering valve and air vent are there. We do have a pump, controller, sensors, and check valve to explain.

The pump for a water-heater system of this sort can (and should) be very small, typically about $1/20$ of a horsepower, drawing something like 80 watts of electrical power while operating. Notice that since the collector loop is always filled with water the pump does not have to be large enough to raise water, against the force of gravity, to the roof. The water coming down from the collectors sucks the collector supply water up, so all the pump has to do is overcome the friction losses in the pipes.

Later we'll see how to properly size pumps, but for now suffice it to say that an oversized pump can significantly reduce the economic benefits that the solar system should deliver. While your collectors are busily collecting energy you don't want your pump to be throwing it away in parasitic losses.

Notice that the pump has isolation valves placed on each side of it. They are there to allow the pump to be easily removed from the loop to allow for servicing or replacement. In addition a strainer is located before the pump to help collect any sediment. It is a good idea, by the way, not to place the pump at the lowest point in a system, since that is where sediment is most likely to settle.

The collector loop has a check valve in it to prevent back circulation at night. When the water in the collectors is colder than the water in the solar tank, reverse thermosiphoning would occur without it, dissipating most of the energy gained during the day.

While the check valve could be placed anywhere in the collector loop and still prevent back circulation, it is best to locate it in the collector supply line. If it is located in the collector return leg, it makes it difficult to fill the system since there would be a tendency to get an air lock

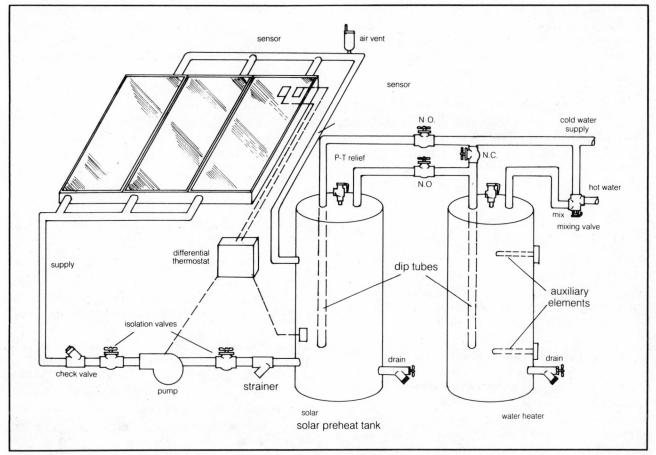

Figure 4.46 A two-tank, direct, solar water heater with recirculation freeze protection.

between the air vent and check valve.

The differential thermostat controls the pump, telling it when to turn on and turn off. There are temperature sensors, usually thermistors, mounted near the collector output and near the bottom of the solar tank, which connect to the controller. When the collector sensors indicate that the collector is warmer than the tank by a certain amount (usually 10 to 15°F), the controller turns the pump on. When the collector temperature drops to within a few degrees of the tank temperature, the controller turns the pump off.

This simple controller logic applies to all of the solar hot water systems that we will examine. In this particular system, however, we have indicated an extra freeze sensor on the collectors. When the freeze sensor drops to somewhere around 37°F, the controller turns the pump on. This sends a shot of warm water up to the collectors to prevent them from freezing. Once the sensor sees that the panels are warmed up, the controller turns the pump off. On a chilly night the pump will cycle—on for about a minute, then off for maybe 30 minutes, then back on again.

This method of freeze protection, though quite popular in areas with infrequent freezing, has some serious drawbacks that should be recognized. First of all, it is

wasteful of energy. On a chilly night you can easily throw away half of the energy gained during the day. On a clear night the air temperature around the collectors is usually about 5°F warmer than the absorber plate, so that a sensor set at 37°F will activate the pump whenever the ambient drops below about 42°F. Obviously this method of freeze protection should only be used in areas with very mild winters.

More serious, though, is the possibility of the system not working properly on that cold night so the collectors freeze and possibly burst. If there is a coincident power failure and freeze night, or if the controller or pump malfunctions on a freeze night, then you may lose the system.

An even more subtle problem arises if the check valve doesn't seat tightly, perhaps due to some corrosion or dirt that may take several years to accumulate. Without the check valve, back circulation will start when the collectors cool down. That warms the collector sensor, momentarily turning the pump on, which stops the reverse siphon. The collector sensor cools, the pump goes off, and reverse siphoning begins again. This oscillation has the effect of keeping the freeze sensor warm while allowing the bottom of the panels to cool down, and freezing can result.

If you understand that argument, you might be tempted to put the freeze sensor at the bottom, or inlet, side, of the collectors. Don't do that or you'll freeze the collectors for sure! The normal cold night recirculation process will send warm water to the collectors, but as soon as the warm water enters the panels the sensor will shut the pump off. Thus the top of the panels will never be warmed up and they'll freeze.

Obviously if you live in an area where freezing is a serious concern then this method of protection is totally inadequate. Fortunately, there are a number of other options to turn to, but first let's consider the possibility of combining the functions of solar storage and auxiliary backup into one tank.

One-Tank Systems

If an electric water heater is used rather than one fueled with oil or natural gas, it is possible to use a single tank to act as solar preheat storage and auxiliary backup. For the moment, we needn't be concerned with freeze protection; the one-tank versus two-tank arguments are the same for any method of freeze protection.

Figure 4.47 shows an electric water-heater tank with two heating elements used in a one-tank solar system. Only the upper heating element should be connected. The idea is to have the upper electric element heat the top one-third of the tank without heating the bottom two-thirds. In an undisturbed tank this is possible since the hot water will float on top of the colder bottom water.

This thermal stratification is amazingly stable and if left on its own there would be very little mixing between the two temperature regimes. Thus it would be possible to heat the top of the tank electrically while independently providing solar heat to the bottom of the tank.

The advantages of a one-tank system are fairly obvious. Not having to buy the second tank reduces the cost of the system; plumbing only one tank means less labor cost; it is easier to retrofit the system since you don't need to find extra floor space near the existing water heater; and finally, thermal losses are reduced since only one tank is losing heat rather than two.

There are some disadvantages, though, mostly related to the loss in collector efficiency due to the imperfect stratification in the tank. With the pump running, there is enough turbulence created in the tank to mix some of the upper water with the rest of the tank. That means the electric element has a tendency to do some of the heating that we would like our collectors to be doing. Instead of the collectors providing efficient preheating of incoming cold tap water with the electric element topping it off, to some extent the reverse is true. With the electric element doing some of the preheating, the efficiency of the collectors drops. Thus a given collector area will provide fewer Btu when operating into a one-tank system.

Another disadvantage becomes evident during a string of rainy days when the solar system is inoperative. The household is left with the equivalent of a single-

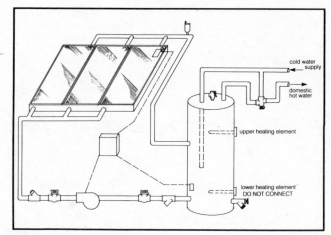

Figure 4.47 A one tank system.

element electric hot-water heater with storage roughly equivalent to one-third of the tank volume. With an 80-gallon tank and a 4500-watt heating element that means you'll have about 28 gallons of effective storage with a recovery rate of around 25 gallons per hour. A single, long hot shower can "empty" the tank and the next person will have to wait an hour before there will be enough hot water for a second shower.

There are two ways to reduce this inconvenience. One is to size the tank a bit larger to give more reserve volume. Thus instead of it being the usual 65- or 80-gallon tank of a two-tank system, you might size a 100- or 120-gallon tank. The second option is to provide for manual operation of the lower heating element (through its thermostat, of course). During inclement weather, the flip of a switch will provide you with full reserve volume and double-element recovery.

It is important to note that you should not use a fuel-fired water heater in this one-tank configuration. With the burner located at the bottom of the tank there can be no stratification to separate the "solar storage." The burner will always keep all of the tank up to whatever temperature the thermostat is set at. The solar system can only top up that temperature inefficiently.

Finally, with natural gas in some areas being so much cheaper than electricity, it makes little sense to replace a gas-fired water heater with an electric one just to have a one-tank solar hot water system. The cost of the auxiliary electricity may exceed the value of the natural gas displaced by the solar system, and the users will end up paying more for their hot water with the solar system than without it.

Freeze Protection With Antifreeze

The domestic hot-water systems discussed so far have been examples of what are referred to as *direct* heating systems. In an *indirect* system the fluid in the collectors is not the same water that flows out the household's hot-water taps.

A closed-loop, indirect heating system is shown in Figure 4.48. By separating the collector loop from the potable water supply it is possible to use something other than water as the heat-transfer fluid; something that won't freeze. Water/glycol antifreeze mixtures are the most common, though various oils and silicone fluids are sometimes used.

For simplicity the system is shown in a one-tank configuration, though obviously the two-tank arrangement is an easy extension. We have chosen to illustrate a heat exchanger internal to the tank. Tanks are also available with heat exchangers that wrap around the outside of the tank, and some systems use a completely separate external heat exchanger with two pumps to circulate collector fluid and tank fluid.

Since the heat-transfer fluid is constrained, provision must be made to allow for its expansion and contraction as the collectors go through their daily temperature cycles. That is the function of the expansion tank, which is basically a chamber with a diaphragm to separate the heat-transfer fluid from a cushion of pressurized air. The expansion tank screws into an air purger, which is a simple

wide spot in the pipe with a scoop to help any air trapped in the lines make its way out the air vent.

While both propylene glycol and ethylene glycol have been used as the heat-transfer fluid, propylene glycol is much to be preferred. Ethylene glycol is toxic, and if it is used then a double-walled heat exchanger is absolutely necessary. (In a double-walled heat exchanger, the heat-transfer fluid must leak through two separate barriers before it can contaminate the potable water.) Propylene glycol has nearly the same thermal properties as its ethylene counterpart, but it is relatively nontoxic (in fact it's a rather common food additive—check the label on that can of Mountain Dew you're drinking) and many jurisdictions will allow single-walled heat exchangers.

Water/glycol antifreeze mixtures for solar use should contain an added inhibitor to help maintain the proper pH (acid-base) stability of the fluid. One of the disadvantages of water/glycol solutions is that when they are exposed to high temperatures, on the order of 250 to 300°F, they break down into organic acids which can attack the plumbing (though the freeze protection remains). Thus the pH of the antifreeze solution should be tested period-

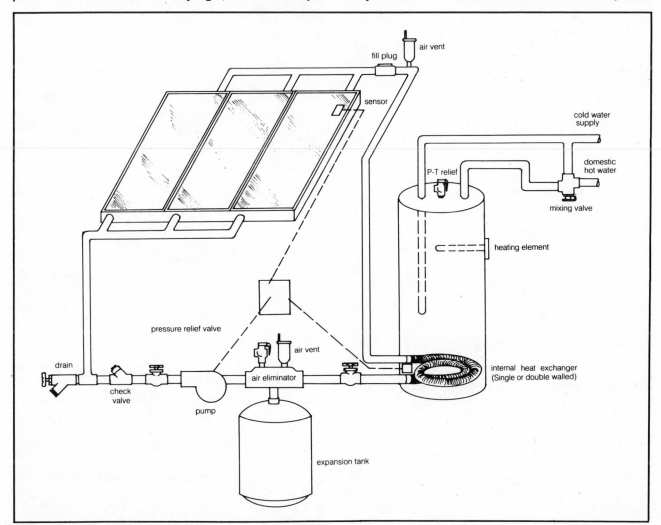

Figure 4.48 A one tank indirect system with antifreeze protection.

ically, especially if the collectors have been subjected to prolonged stagnation. The pH can easily be checked with litmus paper, and the solution should be replaced when it turns acidic. Until more is known about the durability of glycol in collector systems, testing should take place at least once a year.

The degree of freeze protection for various mixture strengths of antifreeze to water are given in Table 4.15. A 50/50 solution of propylene glycol and water is good down to about −25°F, for example. It should be pointed out that glycol solutions should not be used with galvanized plumbing, since the inhibitors react with the zinc. Also, glycol solutions can leak through joints where water will not, so an especially good job of plumbing must be done.

Table 4.15 Freeze Point, Specific Heat, and Viscosity for Various Heat-Transfer Fluids[a]

	Freeze Point (°F)	Specific Heat (Btu/lbm-°F)	Viscosity (centipoise)
Water	32	1.00	0.5–0.9
Ethylene Glycol			
20%	15	0.93	- - -
30%	4	0.87	- - -
40%	−12	0.81	- - -
50%	−32	0.76	1.2–4.4
Propylene Glycol			
20%	18	0.96	- - -
30%	8	0.94	- - -
40%	−7	0.89	- - -
50%	−25	0.85	1.4–7.0
Paraffinic Oils	15	0.51	12–30
Aromatic Oils	−100	0.45	0.6–0.8
Silicone Oils	−120	0.38	10–20

Notes: a. Since viscosity is sensitive to temperature the values are given for a range of roughly 80° to 140°F. From U.S. H.U.D. *Installation Guidelines*, 1979 and CRC *Handbook of Applied Engineering Science.*

To avoid the problems of high-temperature breakdown of glycol solutions, the use of other heat-transfer fluids such as oils or silicones has been suggested. Some of these are tricky to handle—silicones leak readily through piping flaws, for example, and aromatic oils will dissolve roofing tar if spilled.

All of these alternatives have the disadvantage of lower specific heats and higher viscosities than water/glycol mixtures. The specific heat of a fluid is the number of Btu required to raise one pound of it by one degree Fahrenheit. To carry energy off at a given rate, a circulating fluid with low specific heat must either be pumped faster or else be allowed to rise higher in temperature in the panel than one with a high specific heat, such as water. If the temperature rise is higher then the collector efficiency drops. If the fluid must be pumped faster then the parasitic pumping power will be greater. In either case, losses go up.

Compounding the problem of low specific heat is the higher viscosity of most of these fluids. The higher the viscosity, the more the liquid is like syrup, which raises pumping power even more.

To summarize, the key advantage that a closed-loop antifreeze system has is positive freeze protection. The systems are not dependent on the reliability of any mechanical devices, which is what makes them the most popular in harsh climates.

On the negative side, the extra components and more complicated storage tank add several hundred dollars to the cost of the system. And the overall system efficiency is a few percentage points less than a direct system, since the collectors must run hotter to encourage heat transfer through the heat exchanger.

Drainback Systems

Systems can be designed so that the pump is the only thing that gets water up to the collectors and hence when the pump turns off the water drains back into the storage tank. An example of such a *drainback* system is shown in Figure 4.49. Notice that the tank requires a heat exchanger with large surface area to be placed near the top of the tank rather than the bottom. The pressurized city water stays within the heat exchanger coils so that the storage tank itself can be unpressurized, allowing the water to fall back into it. Unpressurized atmospheric fiberglass storage tanks are ideal for this application providing they have a gel that is designed to withstand water at 212°F.

Since the collectors drain every time the pump is turned off there is no fluid in the collectors to freeze, which means ordinary tap water can be used in the tank. While these systems are simple and inexpensive their efficiency is less than a direct system. And since the pump must overcome gravity to fill the collector loop it must be sized larger than would be required in a pressurized system.

State Water Heater Company markets a variation on this drainback concept. Their specially designed storage tank contains several unpressurized pods filled with water within a pressurized tank. The pump circulates the unpressurized water to the collectors, as called for, allowing the water to drain by gravity when the pump shuts off.

Draindown Systems

As with drainback systems, *draindown* systems also provide freeze protection by dumping the water from the collectors on cold nights. The difference is that no heat exchangers are used and the collectors fill each day under the pressure of the city water supply.

One way to provide draindown is with three automatic solenoid valves as shown in Figure 4.50. The solenoid valves are arranged so that in the event of a power failure they shift to the positions that drain the system. This means that under normal solar collecting conditions they are constantly drawing electrical power, typically

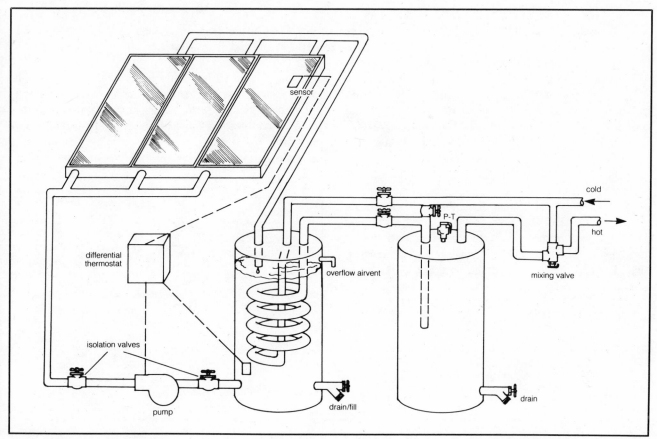

Figure 4.49 A drainback system.

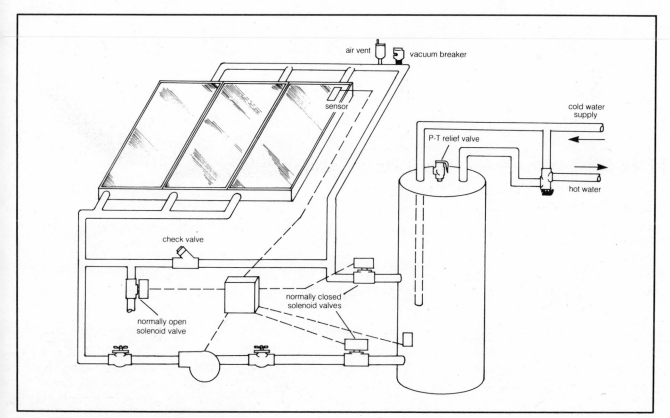

Figure 4.50 Draindown system with soleroid valves.

around 7 watts each, to stay in the circulation configuration. This may not sound like much but it actually slices a significant portion of your solar energy savings. In practice, the use of solenoids has not worked out well; they stick in one position or the other all too frequently.

Several manufacturers have recently introduced draindown valves which combine the functions of the three solenoids in one package. The Sunspool valve (439 Tasso Street, Palo Alto, California 94301), as illustrated in Figure 4.51, consumes only 2 watts and drains automatically during a power failure. It is shown in a draindown system in Figure 4.52.

Draindown systems have the advantage of directly heating the potable water without the need for a heat exchanger, which improves system efficiency and keeps costs down. They do involve moving parts, however, which are exposed to new water every day. If the water source is extremely hard, and corrosion is known to be a problem, then another freeze-protection scheme may be called for.

Sizing Considerations

Once the system configuration is established it is necessary to size the collector area, storage volume, pump size, and piping diameter. In turn, the sizing depends on expected hot-water demands, the percentage of that demand to be met with solar, and the temperature of the incoming cold water that has to be heated.

With regard to hot-water demand, a good estimate for residential users is 20 gallons of hot water at 140°F per person per day. We might fine-tune that estimate some and reduce the figure by about 4 gallons per person per day if the household has no washing machine and raise it by about 15 gallons per family per day if a dishwasher is used. These refinements should be kept in per-

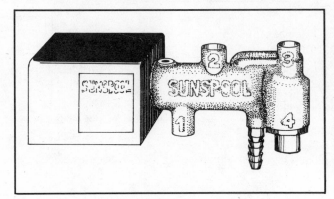

Figure 4.51 Sunspool draindown valve.

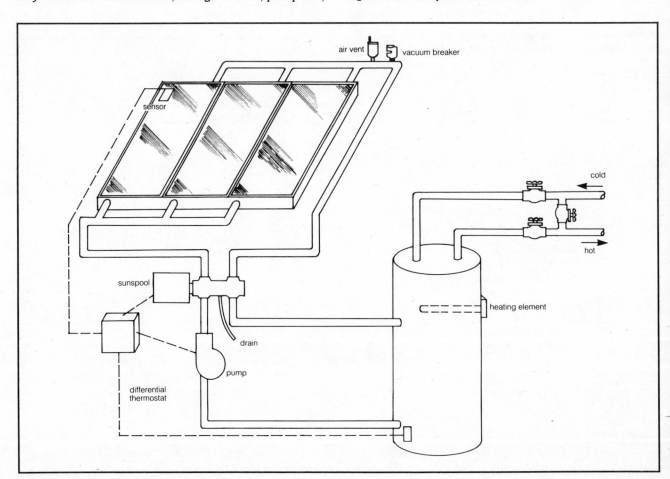

Figure 4.52 Draindown with a sunspool valve.

spective, however, since the hot-water demands of a family are much more sensitive to lifestyle considerations than they are to the particular mix of appliances.

Since it takes 1 Btu to raise one pound of water by 1°F and there are 8.34 pounds of water in a gallon, we can determine the energy required to raise G gallons per day by ΔT degrees with the following equation:

$$L\left(\frac{Btu}{day}\right) = G(gal/day) \times 8.34 \, (lbm/gal)$$
$$\times \Delta T(°F) \times 1 \left(\frac{Btu}{lbm°F}\right)$$

For example, a family of four needing 80 gallons of 140°F water per day with a cold-water source temperature of 50°F requires

$$L = 80 \times 8.34 \times (140° - 50°) = 60,048 \, Btu/day$$

to heat their water.

On a clear day at latitudes typical of the United States a collector tilted at an angle roughly equal to its latitude will be exposed to about 2000 Btu/ft²-day. It is not unreasonable to expect an average collector efficiency of 40 to 50 percent during the mild months of the year, which means that the collector area required for a hot-water system could be estimated to be about

$$A = \frac{L}{\eta H} = \frac{60,048 \, Btu/day}{0.45 \times 2000 \, Btu/ft^2\text{-}day} = 67 \, ft^2$$

What percentage of the annual hot-water load might this be expected to supply? As a quick estimate we might say that it will supply all the hot-water needs on a clear day, which leads us to ask what percentage of the days in a year are clear? That of course varies from place to place but for most it will be somewhere between 50 and 75 percent, so we would expect 67 square feet of collector to provide something like two-thirds of the annual needs of a typical home in a favorable climate area.

We could refine the procedure considerably. For example, the temperature of the cold-water source was assumed to be a constant 50°F, while in reality, depending on your water source, that temperature may vary considerably from season to season. It is not unusual to have water from a river or reservoir in the 30s during the winter and in the 70s during the summer. That means much more energy would be needed to heat a gallon of water to 140°F in the winter than the summer. Well water, of course, is much less variable in temperature.

Month-by-month calculations could be made to account for variations in insolation, ambient temperatures, resulting collector efficiencies, cold-water temperatures, and so on. Such procedures can easily become tedious and so are frequently performed on a computer.

One simulation done for 11 cities across the United States resulted in the graph shown in Figure 4.53. In it, the annual fraction of the hot-water load carried by solar is plotted versus the ratio $H_J A/L$, where H_J is the average solar radiation on a horizontal surface in January (Btu/ft²-day); A is the collector area (ft²); and L is the January hot-water load (Btu/day). The collector is assumed to have a tilt angle equal to its latitude.

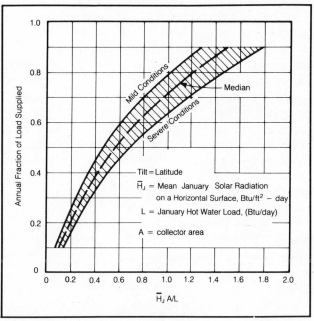

Figure 4.53 Fraction of annual load supplied by solar as a function of January conditions (U.S. Department of Commerce, *Design of Systems*, 1977).

Example: Estimate the collector area required to supply 70 percent of the annual hot-water demand in Fort Worth for a family using 80 gallons per day. The January cold-water temperature is 46°F.

Solution: The January load is

$$L = 80 \times 8.34 \times (140 - 46) \times 1 = 62,717 \, Btu/day$$

From Appendix 4F the horizontal insolation in January is 936.2 Btu/ft²-day. Using the median value from Figure 4.53, at a 70 percent annual fraction, means $H_J A/L$ is about 0.95, so

$$A = \frac{0.95 \, L}{H_J} = \frac{0.95 \times 62,717}{936.2} = 64 \, ft^2$$

Obviously even Figure 4.53 gives a pretty crude estimate, and the results should not be expected to be much closer than 10 percent to the actual value. Since a range of values of $H_J A/L$ are given for any particular percentage of annual load, you might use this spread to account for

137

such factors as collector efficiency, ambient temperatures, and insolation and cold-water variations with season.

For example, if your collector has double glazing, you are in a fairly warm climate, and the cold-water source warms up considerably during the year, you might use the lower extreme for $H_J A/L$ (meaning less collector area is required for a given hot-water fraction) and vice versa.

Later, in the section on f-chart, we will describe a much more accurate procedure for estimating monthly and annual solar hot water performance. It is, however, a much more tedious procedure and for most Figure 4.53 will give sufficiently accurate estimates.

A word of caution should be inserted here. While it would be possible to achieve a very high annual performance factor in almost any climate by simply providing a very large collector area, this may not be desirable. A large collector area can deliver too much heat during the summer and boiling may even result. It may also be economically unreasonable, since the cost of adding collectors may exceed the marginal value of the increased useful energy delivered. Fifty to seventy-five square feet of collectors seems to be the norm across the United States.

With the collector area established, the other components are usually sized to match the array size. The solar preheat storage tank can be sized at about 1.5 gallons of storage per square foot of collector area. This is based on the rule of thumb that on a warm, clear day one square foot of collector will heat as much as 1.5 gallons of water from tap temperatures to 140°F. So hot-water storage tanks typically tend to hold 80 or 100 gallons.

The fluid flow rate through the collectors is not critical; 0.02 to 0.03 gallons of flow per minute (gpm) per square foot of collector is recommended. This will cause the circulating fluid to be heated by about 10 to 15°F on each pass through the collector during the middle of the day. The following equation presents the relationship between temperature increase and flow rate:

E. 4.19 $\quad q_u = \dot{m}C_P\Delta T = \eta AI$

where q_u is useful energy collected (Btu/hr); $\dot{m}$ is the fluid flow rate (lbm/hr); C_P is the specific heat (Btu/lbm-°F); ΔT is the temperature increase through the collector (°F); η is collector efficiency; A is collector area (ft²); and I is insolation on the panels (Btu/ft²-hr).

For example, on a clear warm day with $\eta = 50$ percent, $I = 300$ Btu/ft²-hr, $A = 50$ ft², and water circulating at 0.03 gpm/ft², we have

$$\dot{m} = 0.03 \ gal/min\text{-}ft^2 \times 50 \ ft^2 \times 8.34 \ lbm/gal \\ \times 60 \ min/hr = 750 \ lbm/hr$$

and

$$\Delta T = \frac{\eta AI}{\dot{m}C_P} = \frac{0.50 \times 50 \times 300}{750 \times 1} = 10°F$$

Since we are suggesting collector areas on the order of 50 to 75 square feet, flow rates of between 1 gpm and 2 gpm are about right.

As to pipe sizes, for residential hot-water systems the choice is between ½- and ¾-inch diameter. While there are trade-offs between pump sizes and tubing diameters, suffice it to say that ½-inch-diameter copper pipe should be used on collector arrays smaller than about 60 square feet. Three-quarter-inch tubing will suffice for arrays from 60 to well beyond 100 square feet.

Later when we describe heat distribution systems we'll learn how to size pumps. For hot-water systems very small ⅟₃₅ horsepower or ⅟₂₀ horsepower pumps (for example the Grundfos UM 25-18 or UP 25-42) are all that are usually required. In open systems where fresh water is in contact with the pump, a bronze or stainless steel pump should be specified. For systems circulating antifreeze in a closed loop, less expensive cast-iron pumps can be used.

Solar Hot Tub/Domestic Water System

With the increasing popularity of hot tubs, it is of interest to consider the use of solar collectors to deliver the necessary Btu. While many designs are possible, the following approach (Figure 4.54) lets the same collector array heat both hot tub and domestic water.

Heat transfer to the tub is accomplished by laying in several turns of soft copper tubing under the seats. There should be no solder connections in these turns to minimize the potential for leaks which could contaminate the potable water supply. You should check local building codes to be sure a single-wall heat exchanger is acceptable. If it is not you will have to go to an external heat exchanger with an added pump.

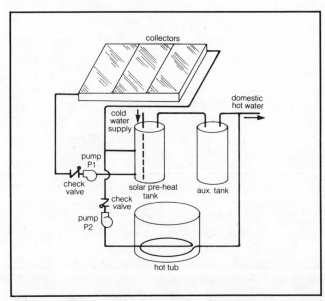

Figure 4.54 Solar hot tub/domestic hot water system (controls and freeze protection not shown).

Pump P_1 is controlled with the usual differential thermostat. Control of P_2 can also be accomplished with a differential thermostat that turns the pump on when the top of the preheat tank is warmer than the top of the auxiliary tank. The pump should also have a manual override, perhaps with a timer, so you can heat the hot tub with the auxiliary water heater when the solar system isn't up to temperature. And the hot-tub thermostat should be used as a high temperature shut-off.

The necessary filtering and, oh yes, the stimulating bubbly action is provided with conventional hot-tub equipment not shown in the figure.

One way to estimate the extra collector area required for the hot tub is to measure its temperature drop over a day's time with no auxiliary heating after running it up to about 105°F. Then, size the collector array to deliver that extra heating.

For example, suppose a 600-gallon hot tub is heated to 105°F, the auxiliary is then shut off, and we begin our soak. Dragging our totally relaxed body out of the tub, we put the cover on, come back a day later and measure the temperature to be 95°F. The heat loss is therefore

$$600 \; gal \times 8.34 \; \frac{lbm}{gal} \times \frac{1Btu}{lb°F} \times 10°F$$

$$= 50{,}000 \; Btu/day$$

The collectors run quite efficiently at this low temperature and we might estimate that 1000 Btu/ft²-day can be collected on a good day. That suggests about 50 extra square feet of collector, which means we should probably double the array size of a typical domestic water-heating system.

Swimming Pool Systems

Another popular application of flat-plate collectors is to the heating of swimming pools. The economics are generally excellent, in part due to the fact that there is no need for a separate storage tank or collector pump (the pool and its circulator satisfy those functions) and in part due to the modest temperature requirements, which usually means inexpensive, unglazed, uninsulated collectors are quite sufficient.

A typical solar pool-heating system is shown in Figure 4.55. When the collector sensor indicates useful energy can be gained, the control valve is closed and flow is diverted through the array. When energy can no longer be collected, the valve opens and the array drains. The check valve is there to prevent backwashing the filter during draindown.

Before we can size the collector array we need to acquire some feeling for the thermal requirements of a swimming pool. In order to hold a pool at a given temperature, the thermal losses due to conduction, convection, radiation, and evaporation must be offset by the

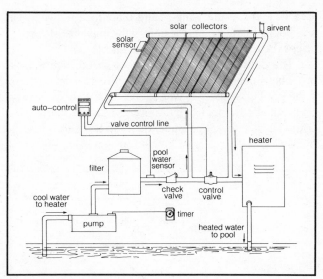

Figure 4.55 Solar pool heating system.

combination of direct solar gains, collector gains, and/or pool heater inputs.

Unfortunately, as we shall see, estimating these gains and losses with any degree of certainty is a dubious exercise. Losses are not only dependent on pool and air temperatures, which can be reasonably estimated, but also upon wind speeds, humidity, and cloud cover—conditions which are not generally known with any degree of accuracy. Direct solar gains by the pool depend on available insolation, shading conditions, and estimates of reflection and absorption. Undaunted by these concerns for accuracy, let us proceed. Using reasonable judgement our answers should be in the right ballpark anyway.

Letting q_c, q_{cv}, q_r, and q_e be the rates at which energy is lost due to conduction, convection, radiation, and evaporation, respectively, and letting q_{sg} be the rate at which the pool collects solar energy, we can write the following equation for the supplemental heating, q_{in}, required to hold the pool at any given temperature:

E. 4.20 $\qquad q_{in} = q_c + q_{cv} + q_r + q_e - q_{sg}$

Let's deal with the losses first. There are *conductive* losses from the pool to the ground, q_c, but once the surrounding dirt has been heated up a bit, these become negligible. In fact, if the pool cools down, some of that energy is returned.

Convective losses are not negligible. Air that comes in contact with the surface of the pool is warmed and moves on. The rate of this convective heat transfer is proportional to the temperature difference between the air and water and the constant of proportionality is very much dependent on the wind speed. Putting this into equation form, we have

E. 4.21 $\qquad q_{vc} = h_{cv} \, A \, \Delta T$

where q_{cv} is convective loss (Btu/hr), A is pool surface area (ft²), ΔT is the temperature difference between air and pool (°F), and h_{cv} is the convective heat transfer coefficient (Btu/hr-ft²-°F) given in Figure 4.56.

The dependence of h_{cv} on wind speed means we'll probably have to make our first approximation (guess). If the pool is reasonably well sheltered, we suggest using an h_{cv} of about 1 to 1.5. If the pool is in a windy site then your first investment probably ought to be in some windbreaks rather than a solar heating system.

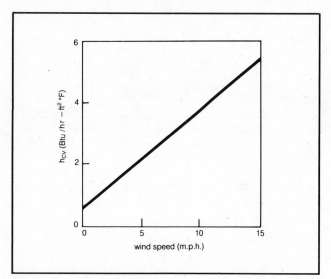

Figure 4.56 Variation in convection coefficient with windspeed (Based on Root, *Solar Energy*, 1959).

Radiation losses from the pool could theoretically be estimated with an equation that involves pool temperatures and "sky" temperatures each raised to the fourth power. A difficulty arises in that the "sky" temperature is a poorly defined quantity related to, but not equal to, the air temperature. Researchers who have looked at this question suggest that at typical pool temperatures and atmospheric moisture contents, it is possible to estimate radiation losses with the simple relationship

E. 4.22 $q_r = (20 + \Delta T)A$

where q_r is in Btu/hr, when $(20 + \Delta T)$ is in °F and A is in ft². If you want the units to come out, imagine the right side of the equation to be multiplied by a radiation heat-transfer coefficient of 1.0 Btu/hr-ft²-°F.

Finally, there is energy lost from the pool by *evaporation*. At the interface between the air and pool surface, water molecules are heading in both directions—into the pool from the humid air, and out of the pool as some of the liquid water gathers enough energy to transcend to the vapor state.

We shouldn't be surprised then to see that the rate of evaporation will depend on the difference between the "vapor pressure" of the air that is in intimate contact with

the pool and the ambient water vapor pressure some distance away. It will also depend on how quickly the newly vaporized water moves away, that is, on the wind speed. Finally, as water evaporates, it takes energy with it (about 1047 Btu/lbm for water at typical pool temperatures) so the remaining pool water is cooled.

Combining these factors, we can write for evaporation losses

E. 4.23 $q_e = 200\, h_{cv}\, (P_w - P_a)A$

where q_e is in Btu/hr; h_{cv} is the same coefficient found in Figure 4.56; P_w is the water vapor pressure of the air immediately above the pool (psi); P_a is the water vapor pressure in the surrounding air (psi); and the factor 200 is there to clean up the units and account for the energy required to vaporize water.

The water vapor pressure in equilibrium with the pool, P_w, can be obtained directly from Figure 4.57 at the temperature of the pool. The ambient water vapor pressure, P_a, can also be obtained from Figure 4.57 if the value obtained there, at the temperature of the air, is multiplied by the prevailing relative humidity, a factor that fluctuates considerably throughout the day and night. More uncertainty.

In estimating average humidity, it is sometimes helpful to note that it usually reaches its maximum just before dawn and drops to its minimum in the early afternoon. Weather stations usually measure it at 4:00 A.M., 10:00 A.M., 4:00 P.M., and 10:00 P.M., so for many locations there is a good data base.

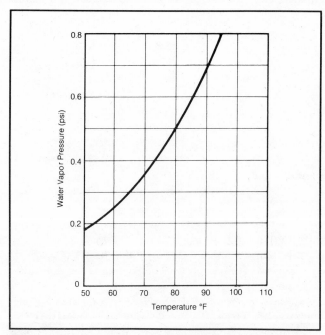

Figure 4.57 Water vapor pressure for use in calculating evaporative losses.

There is another approach for estimating evaporation losses, based on the rate at which the level of the pool drops due to evaporation. Letting D be the rate at which the level drops (inches per week), and remembering that about 1047 Btu are required to evaporate one pound of water, we can write

E 4.24
$$q_e\left(\frac{Btu}{hr}\right) = \frac{D\ in.}{week} \times \frac{1\ ft}{12\ in.} \times A\ ft^2 \times$$
$$62.4\ \frac{lbm}{ft^3} \times 1047\ \frac{Btu}{lbm} \times \frac{1\ week}{168\ hr}$$

$$q_e = 32.4DA$$

As we shall see later when we do an example, evaporation quite frequently dominates the total pool heat loss. This is why a pool cover that may do nothing more than prevent evaporation can be so incredibly effective.

Finally, let's consider the "free" solar gains of the pool itself, q_{sg}. Typically something like 80 percent of the incident solar energy is absorbed by the pool water. The remainder is either reflected off the surface or bounced off the white pool walls or bottom. Black-bottom pools will, of course, reflect less and hence pick up a few extra percentage points.

Example: Suppose we want to estimate the energy required to keep a 600-square-foot pool at 80°F during late spring when the air temperature averages 60°F and horizontal insolation averages 2400 Btu/ft²-day.

Solution: The pool is in a nice sheltered location, so we will estimate the convective coefficient to be about 1.0 Btu/hr-ft²-°F. The local weather station tells us humidity values at 4:00 A.M. average 85 percent, while the 4:00 P.M. values are more like 65 percent. So let's estimate the average relative humidity to be about 75 percent. From Figure 4.57, at the 80°F pool temperature we read off P_w to be 0.51. At the ambient temperature of 60°F, Figure 4.57 gives a water vapor pressure of 0.26, which we must multiply by the relative humidity of 0.75 to get P_a. Using Equations 4.21 through 4.23 and multiplying by 24 hours per day gives us the loss terms:

$q_{cv} = 1.0 \times 600 \times (80 - 60) \times 24 = 288,000$ Btu/day

$q_r = (20 + 80 - 60) \times 600 \times 24 = 576,000$ Btu/day

$q_e = 200 \times 1.0(0.51 - 0.75 \times 0.26) \times 600 \times 24$
$= 907,000$ Btu/day

Notice how dominant the evaporative losses are! Adding the losses up, we get a total of about 1.77 million Btu/day.

The solar gains will be about 80 percent of the horizontal insolation (assuming the pool is never shaded), so

$$q_{sg} = 0.8 \times 600 \times 2400 = 1.15 \times 10^6\ Btu/day$$

The total supplementary energy that needs to be supplied to keep the pool at 80°F is

$$q_{in} = (1.77 - 1.15) \times 10^6 = 0.62 \times 10^6\ Btu/day$$

Notice that if we could cut our evaporative losses by about two-thirds we could keep the pool at 80°F with no auxiliary energy input at all! A simple sheet of clear plastic that you remove when you want to swim could easily do that.

Pool covers are absolutely the cheapest way to heat a pool. They will very often pay for themselves in fuel savings in less than one swimming season. Not only do pool covers significantly reduce heat losses caused by evaporation, but they correspondingly reduce the water and chemical losses. The pool that we just calculated, for example, would lose over 3000 gallons of water per month without the cover.

Another important point that this example illustrates is the importance of solar gains. Without them, the input required from the active collector array and/or pool heater would be nearly tripled. That suggests that an opaque, insulating pool cover left on the pool during the day will not save as much energy as one that lets the sun shine through. It also emphasizes the importance of locating the pool in a sunny spot. An unheated, fully shaded pool can easily be 10°F colder than one located in the sun.

Figure 4.58 shows the result of this sort of calculation

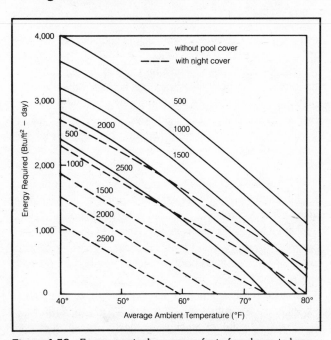

Figure 4.58 Energy required per square foot of pool area to keep pool at 80° F for various average ambient temperatures and horizontal insolation. Pool is sheltered ($h_{cv} = 1$), relative humidity is 60 percent and the cover is assumed to reduce daily evaporative losses by two thirds.

141

for pools held at 80°F under varying ambient conditions with and without a night pool cover. The only effect assumed for the pool cover is that it reduces evaporation by two-thirds, roughly corresponding to the cover being removed during the day for swimming.

Suppose we were to heat this pool with unglazed collectors having the efficiency curve shown in Figure 4.28. The collector inlet temperature T_i is the pool temperature, or about 80°F. Ambient during the day will be somewhat above the 24-hour average temperature of 60°F, say $T_a = 65°F$.

We'll assume the collectors are at the recommended tilt angle of roughly latitude minus 15°. A quick check into Appendix 4C indicates that insolation during late spring and summer months on such a surface is about the same as for a horizontal surface. Over roughly a 10-hour day that averages out to about 240 Btu/ft² per hour, giving us an average (inlet) fluid parameter of about

$$\frac{\overline{T}_i - \overline{T}_a}{\overline{I}} = \frac{80 - 65}{240} = 0.063$$

From Figure 4.28, the collector efficiency is thus about 59 percent (notice the single-glazed collector efficiency is not much higher, about 63 percent). If we let A_c be the collector area in square feet, then to collect the necessary 620,000 Btu we need

$$A_c\ (ft^2) \times 0.59 \times 2400\ (Btu/ft^2\text{-}day) = 620,000\ Btu/day$$
$$A_c = 435\ ft^2$$

That's equal to about two-thirds of the surface area of the pool, a not unusual sizing ratio.

Perhaps surprisingly, one-half to two-thirds of the surface area of the pool in collectors is a rule of thumb used fairly commonly throughout the United States. That is because collectors are usually sized to extend the swimming season through a critical month or so under climatic conditions that are not dissimilar from one place to another.

By the way, if you are interested in building your own pool collector there is an excellent publication available called *How to Design and Build a Solar Swimming Pool Heater* (Copper Development Association, 405 Lexington Avenue, New York 10017; free). This report also covers the analysis of pool losses and sizing of collector arrays.

Figure 4.59 shows how the energy required to keep a pool at 80°F varies through the year for a location having relatively mild weather (average temperature in the low 50s in the winter, high 60s in the summer). Also shown is the energy that would be delivered by an unglazed collector array sized at half the surface area of the pool with a tilt angle of 30°.

Even in this area with mild winter temperatures, it

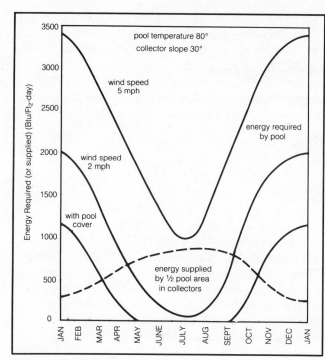

Figure 4.59 Example of energy required to heat a pool in a mild climate, and energy supplied by half the pool area in unglazed collectors. Pool cover is assumed to reduce evaporative losses by two thirds.

would take an outrageously large collector array to heat the pool in the middle of winter. Thermal losses are way up, while solar gains are way down. Moreover, use of a pool cover gives nearly the same swim season as does a collector array and does so at a much lower initial cost—but pool covers are less convenient and do not last nearly as long as collectors. Needless to say, both are popular and easily pay for themselves in fuel savings many times over during their lifetimes.

Thermal Comfort

While many contemporary homes cater to some of the more frivolous human desires, the basic function of the home remains the same—to maintain a comfortable thermal environment. But just what *is* a comfortable thermal environment? More specifically, what environmental parameters are involved, and what ranges can be tolerated to maintain a feeling of thermal comfort?

The answers to these questions are crucial, since they affect the energy consumed for space heating in a big way. Unfortunately, they can't be answered definitively. Thermal comfort is a very subjective feeling and has successfully resisted scientists' efforts to quantify it. However, certain guidelines have been established; and understanding both the basic biological aspects of thermal comfort and the environmental indices related to comfort and

142

health can only help us to design homes that respond to the particular people who live in them.

Biology and Comfort

Human beings are mammals and, as mammals, we possess certain unique thermal systems. The body is its own source of thermal energy and can adapt to a wide range of environmental conditions. The adaption process depends upon some incredibly sensitive control mechanisms in your body. Let's look at them briefly.

To start with, you have two sets of heat-sensing organs in your skin. One set senses the outflow of heat from your body to surroundings at lower temperatures. The other set senses the inward flow of heat from objects or surroundings of higher temperatures. The outflow sensors lie very close to the skin's surface, and most of these are congregated in the fingertips, nose, and the bends of the elbow. About two-thirds of their number are proximate to the openings of sweat glands.

The inflow sensors lie deeper in the skin and are concentrated in the upper lip, nose, chin, chest, forehead, and fingers. Both sets of sensors trigger reflexes which control blood circulation through the skin. These reflexes play an essential role in heat balance, which we will talk about shortly.

The most important temperature-sensing system is located in the hypothalamus, a gland at the base of the brain, right above the pituitary. It works like a thermostat, monitoring changes in blood temperature caused by thermal events inside the body and also by temperature gradients across the skin. Like other mechanical thermostats, the one in your hypothalamus has a set point, usually close to 98.6°F. If the sensory input to your thermostat registers the body temperature at less than the set point, it will initiate physiological responses to increase the body temperature. The reverse occurs if the body temperature is too high. In this way, your body constantly strives to maintain a thermal equilibrium or heat balance, and you usually feel comfortable when this balance is achieved with the minimum amount of thermoregulation. This, then, is a simplified version of the biological basis of comfort.

Factors Involved in Thermal Equilibrium

Thermal equilibrium and the resulting sense of comfort are achieved by physiological and behavioral responses that control the amount of heat produced in the body and the amount of heat lost from the body. We will talk about the physiological responses which control thermoequilibrium in a later section. But, first, we should define the standard methods of heat transfer that result from these physiological responses, and discuss their relationship to thermoequilibrium in your body. The factors important to thermoregulation are: (1) metabolic rate (M); (2) conductive and convective exchange (C); (3) radiative exchange (R); and (4) evaporative exchange (E). A brief definition of each of these factors is helpful.

Metabolic Rate

Right now, the sandwich you ate for lunch is being turned into energy for the growth, regeneration, and operation of your body. This is an example of metabolic activity. Such metabolic processes are about 20 percent efficient; the other 80 percent of the energy generated is rejected as heat. The rate of metabolism is primarily controlled by the level of bodily activity. For example, if you're playing football, your metabolic rate will increase in order to supply your body with the extra energy needed to play the sport. Consequently, your metabolic energy production will increase greatly. To make things a little more complicated, your metabolic rate can differ slightly with weight, sex, age, and state of health.

Conductive and Convective Heat Exchange

Energy is lost by heat conduction through direct physical contact with objects of lower temperatures. Heat is gained by direct contact with objects of higher temperatures. When you heat up a chair by sitting in it, you are losing heat by conduction. When a heating pad warms up your aching back, you are gaining energy by conduction.

Convection has much the same physical basis as conduction, except that an additional mechanism of energy transfer is present: one of the heat-transfer agents is a fluid (air, in many cases). The air molecules exchange energy with an adjacent object, in what is initially a conductive heat-transfer process. However, in the case of convection, the air molecules are moving and thus can carry, or convect, significant amounts of energy. In this way the normal conduction process is enhanced.

There are two types of convection: natural and forced. In forced convection, the air has some significant velocity relative to the object it encounters; when you stand in a stiff breeze, run on a windless day, or sit in front of a fan, you experience forced convection. Natural convection arises due to the heating or cooling of air when it contacts an object. As the air changes temperature, it changes density and rises or falls. This "self-generated" free convection is quite common in indoor environments.

Radiant Heat Exchange

Heat transfer can also arise from the exchange of electromagnetic waves. Your body will lose or gain energy depending on the temperature, texture, and geometric arrangement of the objects around you. This is probably the most complicated mechanism of heat transfer, and is quite important in establishing thermal comfort. To exchange energy by radiant means, the objects need not be in contact. Rather, they simply must be in "sight" of one another.

Light is a form of electromagnetic energy in wave lengths which are detectable by our eyes. Our interest in radiant heat transfer centers around wave lengths we find invisible—those in the infrared portion of the spectrum. You continually experience invisible radiant heat transfer. A warm electric stove element can be felt many inches away. A crackling fire produces a warm, tingly sensation in your hands and cheeks. These sensations are the result of radiant heat transfer via infrared electromagnetic waves (although the fire also produces radiant energy in the visible wave lengths).

These waves, like light, travel through the air with little or no degradation and permit your body to interact thermally with walls, windows, and other objects which make up your total environment. Direct contact with the radiating source is not necessary, which makes radiation effects particularly subtle and often mysterious. A classic example is that of a room with a large window area. On a cold day, occupants can feel distinctly uncomfortable even though the air temperature in the room is 75 or 80°F. The discomfort arises from radiant heat losses to the cold window surfaces. Similarly, people can feel inexplicably hot if their environment contains a large number of hot surfaces—even if the air temperature is held at 65°F.

Evaporative Heat Loss

Respiratory passages and lungs are sites of continuous evaporative heat loss. In moderate to high temperatures, sweating of the skin is a major source of evaporative heat loss. Heat is lost in evaporation because it takes energy to turn liquid water into water vapor.

Figure 4.60 summarizes the various modes of heat

transfer available to your body. These modes, along with metabolic energy production, are used to maintain thermal equilibrium. A simple relation describes the interaction between these mechanisms:

E. 4.25 $\quad Q = M \pm R \pm C - E$

Here Q is the change in the thermal energy content of your body, zero in an equilibrium condition. This condition is achieved by physiological reactions which appropriately alter M, R, C, and E. (Don't confuse the "R" here—radiant heat exchange—with an "R" to come later—resistance.)

Figure 4.61 shows the interplay of these mechanisms at various room temperatures, assuming a constant relative humidity (RH) of 45 percent. The metabolic rate is nearly constant over the range from 60 to 100°F, but the evaporative heat loss rises rapidly to dominate at high temperatures. At lower temperatures, convection and radiation play the dominant roles. Pure conduction usually has little effect on bodily heat loss.

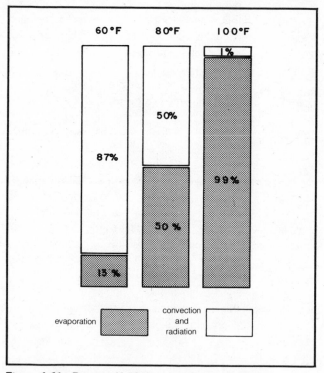

Figure 4.61 Percent of body heat loss due to evaporation, convection, and radiation (relative humidity fixed at 45%).

Describing the Indoor Environment

Air temperature is a well-known environmental index. When combined with three other indices, relative humidity, mean radiant temperature (MRT), and air velocity, a fairly complete description of the indoor environment results.

As shown in Figure 4.61, *air temperature* affects two methods of heat exchange which are essential to the en-

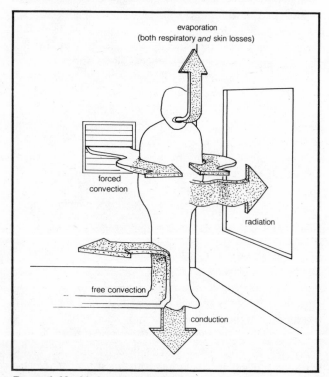

Figure 4.60 Modes of body heat loss.

ergy balance of your body—convection and evaporation. In fact, it is the principal parameter that can affect your state of comfort when your body is close to its optimal comfort zone. Most heating systems are designed with this fact in mind and concentrate single-mindedly on air-temperature control. *Relative humidity* is an oft-neglected, but important, index of environmental comfort. Simply stated, it is a measure of the quantity of water vapor in the air. It is typically reported in percent, with the percentage referenced to a "saturated" state in which the air holds all the vapor it can without some condensation occurring. The relative humidity is closely tied to air temperature, since warmer air can retain more moisture. Thus, if air with a fixed quantity of water vapor is heated, the relative humidity drops.

Relative humidity can be measured with a wet bulb/dry bulb thermometer combination. The dry bulb thermometer has an everyday mercury or alcohol design which measures the air temperature. The wet bulb thermometer is identical in construction, except that a water-soaked wick is placed around the bulb. The wick promotes evaporation of the water surrounding the bulb, thereby depressing the thermometer reading. The lower the relative humidity, the higher the evaporation rate, and the greater the temperature depression. The difference in readings between the wet and dry bulb thermometers thus can be directly correlated with relative humidity and both specifications are used interchangeably.

High relative humidity results in a muggy atmosphere and stifles the evaporative cooling mechanism. Low-humidity conditions tend to make people very uncomfortable; dry skin, dry mucous membranes, and contact lens discomfort are common symptoms. Excessive drying can also weaken wooden structural members and furniture. While high-humidity conditions are often difficult to rectify, low-humidity situations are easily handled with indoor plants or inexpensive humidifiers.

The *mean radiant temperature (MRT)* is a measure of radiative effects arising in a room. We mentioned in the preceding section that walls and windows which communicate with the outdoors can have inside surface temperatures well below the room air temperature. The cold surfaces can cause significant discomfort, and later sections describe insulating techniques to alleviate this problem.

Air velocity refers to the speed of the air moving through the room. High velocities tend to increase convective heat losses; we say it feels "drafty." Very low velocities or stagnant conditions are undesirable in that odors, moisture, and indoor pollutants can rapidly accumulate. Indeed, these problems arise long before any significant oxygen depletion occurs. The odor problem is tied to both health considerations and aesthetics. Excessive moisture can be downright destructive to furniture and the interior portions of walls, ceilings, and floors. Unless suitable vapor barriers are incorporated into a structure, walls literally can rot from moisture.

The problem of accumulating indoor air pollutants is a newly recognized one that has serious implications for designers and residents of very well insulated buildings. We'll take a further look when we assess the heat loss in a building due to ventilation.

Optimal Settings for Indoor Environments

Now that we have looked at the factors which affect thermal comfort, we ask the question, "Are there really optimal settings for these factors that will produce the most desirable indoor climate?" Researchers have conducted many studies on optimum comfort conditions, and have come up with general comfort indices like "operative temperature," "resultant temperature," "effective warmth," "effective temperature," "revised effective temperature," and so on.

The most widely used comfort criteria are set by the American Society of Heating, Refrigerating, and Air-Conditioning Engineers (ASHRAE). ASHRAE standards serve as a guide for architects and engineers in the space-conditioning trade. The latest comfort standards are given in Table 4.16 and are formally referred to as Standard 55-74. These criteria are referenced to persons performing light office work and wearing appropriate clothing.

Table 4.16 Thermal Comfort Conditions (ASHRAE Standard 5/5-74)

Air Temperatures	73–77°F
Relative Humidity	20% to 60%
Mean Radiant Temperature	Equal to air temperature[a]
Air Velocity	10–45 ft/min

Notes: a. For every degree the *MRT* is below 70°F, increase the air temperature by 1°F.

By way of comparison, Figure 4.62 presents some experimental results compiled by R. G. Nevins of the Institute for Environmental Research. A large sample of sedentary people was exposed to varying air temperature and humidity and questioned as to their personal comfort. If we consider "slightly warm" and "slightly cool" as acceptable states, we have extended that comfort range significantly.

It is interesting to note that recent comfort criteria established in the United States differ from those reported in the 1920s. These, in turn, differ substantially from those obtained in England. Why is this? A host of factors could account for the differences, including physical ability to acclimatize to lower temperatures, physical activity, psychological state, and type of clothing worn.

The first factor—the body's ability to acclimatize—is dependent upon general physical health. If you move from one set of environmental extremes to another, your body will undergo pronounced physiological changes. Blood volume and viscosity alter, heart rate varies, and

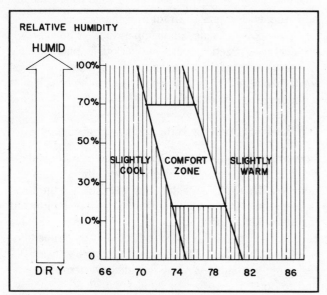

Figure 4.62 A baseline comfort chart (after R. G. Nevins, Institute for Environmental Research, Kansas State University).

blood circulation undergoes appropriate changes. Frequent exposure to various environments strengthens the body's ability to acclimatize quickly and effectively.

Physical activity will also affect the temperature at which a person feels comfortable. Metabolic rate (probably the most important parameter in coping with temperature extremes) can range widely: 220 Btu/hr while sleeping; 325 Btu/hr while reading or resting; 550 Btu/hr when sweeping the floor; and even higher rates for intense physical exercise. The temperature of our environment must be adjusted according to the state of physical activity: a person skiing in 40°F temperatures might be perfectly comfortable, while a person trying to read or write at similar temperatures would find it intolerable. Consequently, the average American today—bound to either office, auto, or home (all heated or cooled to maintain a very limited temperature range) and getting precious little outdoor physical exercise—might well require higher temperatures to be comfortable than an American of the 1920s, who lived in a house subject to much greater temperature variation and engaged in more physical work, without benefit of a car or various other labor-saving machines.

Of course, psychological conditioning is another real consideration. If you're not used to (or can't produce) a high indoor temperature, you don't expect it. In such places as England, where central heating is not as common as in the United States, people normally become acclimatized to lower indoor temperatures. The same is undoubtedly true with air conditioning; the more it is available, the more people demand its use in summer months.

Psychological conditioning also greatly influences what people perceive as their alternatives to discomfort.

The fourth factor, the type of clothing worn indoors, is an obvious example. It is always possible to put on warmer clothes or additional layers of clothing when we feel chilly. But for most people with access to a thermostat, such an alternative is not always considered.

Perhaps it is time to re-evaluate our indoor dress habits and to start weaving garments that insulate our bodies instead of merely decorating them. Maybe it is time for people to toughen up a little, to get our bodies in shape, to quit pampering ourselves psychologically, and to put on warmer clothes when relaxing around the house instead of cranking up the thermostat. But it's not necessarily that simple. Important health and efficiency considerations *do* remain as we decide what indoor conditions to design for in a structure using solar heating: these are the considerations that determine our needs for heat storage and auxiliary heating should our solar system break down or an extended cloud cover cause us to use up all our stored solar energy.

First, consider your likely indoor activities. It's all well and good to say we should always be physically active; but if you're a guitarist, or an avid reader, or a writer, chances are you're going to need warmth available on a fairly constant basis to keep the fingers movable. Second, determine the low extreme of outdoor temperatures in the area you plan to build. You may be able to withstand temporary 30°F temperatures quite well when you're healthy, active, and warmly dressed; but it could have severe consequences for any sudden sickness or other emergency, particularly if accompanying weather conditions make medical assistance difficult to acquire.

Remember, too, that individuals have susceptibilities to cold temperatures and humidity which no comfort index can pinpoint. When your fingers are turning blue, an expert's statement that your environment is at a comfortable temperature is going to be no comfort at all. Your best guide is your own body. Practice being aware of various indoor climatic conditions and how they make you feel—when you're healthy or sick, active or just hanging out. Ultimately, this self-study will be your best guide.

Climate Data

Before *any* heating system can be designed, the local climate must be thoroughly investigated. Climatological data are primarily needed to estimate the most severe heating load, although related data can be used to predict the monthly or annual energy expenditures for space heating. Specific climatological factors affecting heating requirements include the temperature difference between the inside and outside of the dwelling, the wind conditions, and shading. The temperature difference is most important, since the rate of heat loss is directly related to this quantity. The overall effect of temperature difference

146

is gauged in two ways: using minimum design temperatures and heating degree-day tabulations.

The most rapid *rate* of heat loss experienced by your building will occur, as you might imagine, when the outside temperature is lowest. This maximum rate may only occur for several hours a year; nonetheless, your heating system must be designed to cope with this situation. The problem is analogous to buying an automobile with a 200-horsepower engine. Driving normally, you seldom use more than 30 or 40 horsepower—the rest of the engine capacity is held in reserve.

Minimum outside design temperatures have been recommended by ASHRAE, and are tabulated for major cities and towns across the country. Table 4.17 is an abbreviated version for Alabama. Note that three temperatures are listed for each locale. The median of annual extremes is computed from thirty or forty years of temperature data, using the coldest temperature recorded each year. The values in columns labeled *99* or *97.5* percent are temperatures which are *exceeded* for that percentage of the time during the three months of December, January, and February. For example, in Auburn, Alabama, the 99 percent design temperature is 21°F, which means that it was colder than 21°F for 1 percent of the time covered in the three-month period. Design temperatures for your particular city or region can be found in Appendix 4A, or in a copy of the ASHRAE *Handbook of Fundamentals* (found in any library). Local chapters of ASHRAE publish even more complete design tables for areas in their jurisdiction. Another way to estimate the outside minimum design temperature is to contact a local office of the National Weather Service. They can supply you with average minimum temperatures and the record low temperature measured in your area.

Notice that in Table 4.17 (and Appendix 4A) an indication of relative wind velocities is given along with the design temperatures. The wind entries are a very rough indication of average wind speeds during winter months: VL signifies very light; L, light; M, medium; and H, high. The data are of limited use since wind conditions are so closely tied to the topographic conditions within the immediate vicinity of your residence. But they do serve to remind us that heat losses can be significantly affected by increasing wind speeds, so proper selection of your building site and use of windbreaks is important.

While the *minimum* design temperature aids in determining the maximum *rate* of heat loss, in solar design we are usually more interested in longer term, *average* energy requirements. The key to calculating such monthly and annual heating demands is the concept of degree-days. *Degree-days* accumulate for every day that the average ambient temperature is less than 65°F. If for each such day the average ambient temperature is subtracted from 65°F and these differences are summed over a month's time, the total would be monthly degree-days. Over a

Table 4.17 Winter Weather Data and Design Conditions for Major Cities in Alabama[a]

Col. 1 State and Station	Col. 2 Latitude ° '		Col. 3 Elev, Ft	Winter			Col. 5 Coincident Wind Velocity[e]
				Col. 4			
				Median of Annual Extremes	99%	97½%	
ALABAMA							
Alexander City..	33	0	660	12	16	20	L
Anniston AP....	33	4	599	12	17	19	L
Auburn.........	32	4	730	17	21	25	L
Birmingham AP.	33	3	610	14	19	22	L
Decatur........	34	4	580	10	15	19	L
Dothan AP.....	31	2	321	19	23	27	L
Florence AP....	34	5	528	8	13	17	L
Gadsden........	34	0	570	11	16	20	L
Huntsville AP...	34	4	619	8	13	17	L
Mobile AP......	30	4	211	21	26	29	M
Mobile CO......	30	4	119	24	28	32	M
Montgomery AP.	32	2	195	18	22	26	L
Selma-Craig AFB	32	2	207	18	23	27	L
Talladega.......	33	3	565	11	15	19	L
Tuscaloosa AP..	33	1	170r	14	19	23	L

Notes: a. See Appendix 4A for complete listings.

year's time, it would be yearly degree-days. For example, on a day when the average ambient temperature (actually the average of the day's minimum and maximum) is 40°F, we would add (65° − 40°) or 25 degree-days into our total. On a day with average temperature equal to 67°F we would add in zero degree-days (days with average temperature above 65°F are not counted). If the average temperature were to be 40° every day in the month, we would accumulate a total of 30 × 25 = 750 degree-days for that month.

The nice thing about degree-days is that they are directly proportional to the amount of heat required for a house. For example, a house in Duluth, Minnesota (10,000 degree-days per year) would require twice the heat in a year's time as the very same house located in Pittsburgh (5,053 degree-days) and three times as much as if located in Rome, Georgia (3,326 degree-days).

Why the 65°F base temperature? Measurements made nearly 50 years ago indicated that residences kept at 70°F did not require supplemental heating until the ambient dropped to about 65°F. The heat generated in-inside the house by people, appliances, and typical solar gains through windows was found to be sufficient to maintain the temperature inside about 5°F above ambient. With today's better-insulated buildings and our lower interior thermostat settings, it would seem reasonable to lower the base temperature. In fact, we will do that later in the chapter when we actually start to use degree-days.

Degree-day data are quite readily available on a monthly and annual basis (both of which are important to our design procedures). Table 4.18 gives an excerpt from the ASHRAE *Guide and Data Book* to show you the format, while Appendix 4B gives you their complete listing. More extensive listings for your state can be obtained for 25 cents from the National Climatic Center (Federal Building, Asheville, North Carolina 28801). Ask for your state's "Monthly Normals of Temperature, Precipitation, and Heating and Cooling Degree-Days." (Cooling degree-days, by the way, are used in calculating air conditioning loads and are based on subtracting 65°F from daily average temperatures.)

Heat Loss in Dwellings

A dwelling is designed to create an artificial environment—a living space climatically detached from the outdoors. The heat loss experienced by a building reflects the degree of separation. Our goal is to minimize heat losses in order to reduce the energy requirements for heating. The more successful we are, the more attractive solar heating becomes. We begin with a more detailed discussion of the heat-transfer modes introduced earlier, when we considered the thermal aspects of physical comfort.

Basically, heat is thermal energy which is transferred between two objects because of a temperature difference between them. The direction of energy transfer is from the higher to the lower temperature. No net heat transfer occurs between two objects at the same temperature. Obviously, all our basic heat-loss problems arise when outside temperature is lower than the inside temperature of our home. Furthermore, the amount of heat transferred in a given time interval (the rate of heat transfer) is generally proportional to the difference in temperature between the two bodies in question: the greater the tem-

perature difference, the greater the rate of heat transfer.

What we want to do is calculate both the maximum rate at which our building is going to lose heat, and the total heat lost over a given period of time, such as a month or a winter. These calculations are absolutely essential if we want to size a passive or active solar heating system properly, (or, for that matter, the furnace in a conventional house).

Mechanisms of Heat Loss

Given the concepts of heat and temperature difference, we can begin to quantify the aspects of heat transfer and other mechanisms of energy loss. As we mentioned in the section on thermal comfort, there are three classic mechanisms of heat transfer: conduction, convection, and radiation. An additional energy loss will occur when the living space exchanges air with the environment. This air exchange is called either ventilation or infiltration, depending on whether it is intentional or not. We introduced most of these terms when we calculated heat losses from swimming pools. But we need to look at them more carefully now.

Conduction

Conduction is the transfer of energy through a medium by direct molecular interaction. Excited (hot) molecules transfer some of their vibrational energy to their cooler neighbors. This energy transfer on the molecular level results in a large-scale flow of energy from higher to lower temperature regions. Cooking with a frying pan is a good introduction to conduction heat transfer. The energy from the pan is conducted along the handle and eventually reaches your hand. This effect is accentuated if the handle is short and/or made of metal.

Table 4.18   Average Monthly and Yearly Degree-Day Totals for Major Cities in California[a]

Station	Avg. Winter Temp	July	Aug.	Sept.	Oct.	Nov.	Dec.	Jan.	Feb.	Mar.	Apr.	May	June	Yearly Total
Bakersfield.............A	55.4	0	0	0	37	282	502	546	364	267	105	19	0	2122
Bishop................A	46.0	0	0	48	260	576	797	874	680	555	306	143	36	4275
Blue Canyon...........A	42.2	28	37	108	347	594	781	896	795	806	597	412	195	5596
Burbank...............A	58.6	0	0	6	43	177	301	366	277	239	138	81	18	1646
Eureka................C	49.9	270	257	258	329	414	499	546	470	505	438	372	285	4643
Fresno................A	53.3	0	0	0	84	354	577	605	426	335	162	62	6	2611
Long Beach...........A	57.8	0	0	9	47	171	316	397	311	264	171	93	24	1803
Los Angeles...........A	57.4	28	28	42	78	180	291	372	302	288	219	158	81	2061
Los Angeles...........C	60.3	0	0	6	31	132	229	310	230	202	123	68	18	1349
Mt. Shasta............C	41.2	25	34	123	406	696	902	983	784	738	525	347	159	5722
Oakland...............A	53.5	53	50	45	127	309	481	527	400	353	255	180	90	2870
Red Bluff.............A	53.8	0	0	0	53	318	555	605	428	341	168	47	0	2515
Sacramento...........A	53.9	0	0	0	56	321	546	583	414	332	178	72	0	2502
Sacramento...........C	54.4	0	0	0	62	312	533	561	392	310	173	76	0	2419
Sandberg.............C	46.8	0	0	30	202	480	691	778	661	620	426	264	57	4209
San Diego............A	59.5	9	0	21	43	135	236	298	235	214	135	90	42	1458
San Francisco.........A	53.4	81	78	60	143	306	462	508	395	363	279	214	126	3015
San Francisco.........C	55.1	192	174	102	118	231	388	443	336	319	279	239	180	3001
Santa Maria..........A	54.3	99	93	96	146	270	391	459	370	363	282	233	165	2967

Notes: a. See Appendix 4B for complete listings.

A poor conductor is one which retards heat transfer; it is known as an insulator. The most important measure of an insulator is its thermal conductivity (k). Thermal insulators are materials which have low values of k; porcelain, glass, wood, and dry soil are good examples. By comparison, metals (such as copper and aluminum) have high thermal conductivity and so are poor thermal insulators. This is one reason why, in cooking, metal handles get very hot while wooden handles don't. To insulate your home, we seek a material which is economical, practical, and has a low k-value.

Table 4.19 lists the thermal conductivities of common substances. Scan it for familiar materials, recalling that low conductivities imply good insulators. Note that the units are rather awkward: k is given in Btu-in/hr-ft²-°F.

This is no cause for concern; we will explain how to deal with these units in due time.

Two other quantities enter into conduction heat transfer: the area and thickness of the insulating materials. The rate of heat flow (Btu/hr) is directly proportional to the area through which the heat energy can move. For instance, if 100 Btu/hr is transferred through 1 square foot of a given insulation, then we know that 200 Btu/hr will be transferred through 2 square feet of the same insulation. This concept becomes clear if we think of water flowing through a hole—the bigger the hole, the greater the amount of water flowing through it (other things being equal). More to the point, the larger the surface area of your house, the greater the heat-loss problem. The rate of heat flow is inversely proportional to the thickness of

Table 4.19   Thermal Conductivity (k) of Miscellaneous Substances at Room Temperature

Material	Density at 68°F (lbm per cu ft)	Conductivity k (Btu-in/hr-ft²-°F)	Material	Density at 68°F (lbm/per cu ft)	Conductivity k (Btu-in/hr-ft²-°F)
Air, still	—	0.169–0.215	Mineral wool		
Aluminum	168.0	1404–1439	Board	15.0	0.33
Asbestos board with cement	123	2.7	Fill-type	9.4	0.27
Asbestos, wool	25.0	0.62	Nickel	537.0	406.5
Brass, red	536.0	715.0	Paper	58.0	0.9
Brick			Paraffin	55.6	1.68
Common	112.0	5.0	Plaster		
Face	125.0	9.2	Cement	73.8	8.0
Fire	115.0	6.96	Gypsum	46.2	3.3
Bronze	509.0	522.0	Redwood bark	5.0	0.26
Cellulose, dry	94.0	1.66	Rock wool	10.0	0.27
Cinders	40-45	1.1	Rubber, hard	74.3	11.0
Clay			Sand, dry	94.6	2.28
Dry	63.0	3.5-4.0	Sandstone	143.0	12.6
Wet	110.0	4.5-9.5	Silver	656.0	2905.0
Concrete			Soil		
Cinder	97.0	4.9	Crushed quartz		
Stone	140.0	12.0	(4% moisture)	100.0	11.5
Corkboard	8.3	0.28	Fairbanks sand		
Cornstalk, insulating board	15.0	0.33	(4% moisture)	100.0	8.5
Cotton	5.06	0.39	(10% moisture)	110.0	15.0
Foamglas	10.5	0.40	Dakota sandy loam		
Glass wool	1.5	0.27	(4% moisture)	110.0	6.5
Glass			(10% moisture)	110.0	13.0
Common thermometer	164.0	5.5	Healy clay		
Flint	247.0	5.1	(10% moisture)	90.0	5.5
Pyrex	140.0	7.56	(20% moisture)	100.0	10.0
Gold	1205.0	2028.0	Steel		
Granite	159.0	15.4	1% C	487.0	310.0
Gypsum, solid	78.0	3.0	Stainless	515.0	200.0
Hair felt	13.0	0.26	Tar, bituminous	75.0	—
Ice	57.5[a]	15.6	Water, fresh	62.4	4.1
Iron, cast	442.0	326.0	Wood		
Lead	710.0	240.0	Fir	34.0	0.8
Leather, sole	54.0	1.1	Maple	40.0	1.2
Lime			Red oak	48.0	1.1
Mortar	106.0	2.42	White pine	31.2	0.78
Slaked	81–87	—	Wood fiber board	16.9	0.34
Limestone	132.0	10.8	Wool	4.99	0.264
Marble	162.0	20.6			

Notes: a. At 32°F.

the insulating material, which is just a way of saying that thicker insulation reduces heat loss. If we insulate with 6 inches of fiberglass instead of 3 inches, then we will reduce the wall's heat-loss rate by about 50 percent.

In summary, four factors affect the rate at which heat energy conducts through a substance: the temperature differential, the thermal conductivity of the substance, the heat-transfer area, and the thickness of the substance. This information is related by a simple conduction equation:

E. 4.26 $$q_c = A\frac{k}{t}(T_1 - T_2) = A\frac{k}{t}\Delta T$$

where q_c equals the rate of heat transfer by conduction (Btu/hr); A equals the area (ft²); k equals the thermal conductivity (Btu-in/hr-ft²-°F); t equals the thickness (in); and T_1, T_2 equal the inside and outside surface temperatures (°F). Note that the equation reaffirms our discussion: q_c increases if A, k, or $(T_1 - T_2)$ increases. The inverse relationship between q_c and t is also verified: as t increases, q_c will decrease. Let's perform a simple calculation to get a feel for the numbers and units involved.

Example: Suppose we had a wall of dry clay 4 inches thick, with a surface area of 50 square feet. If one face is held at 75°F and the other at 35°F, let's find the rate of heat transfer.

Solution: Using Table 4.19, we find a thermal conductivity of 3.5 to 4.0 Btu-in/hr-ft²-°F. We'll choose the higher value and estimate the maximum heat-transfer rate. Using Equation 4.26, we find

$$q_c = (50 \text{ ft}^2)\left(\frac{4.0 \text{ Btu-in/hr-ft}^2\text{-}°F}{4 \text{ in}}\right)(75 - 35)°F$$
$$= 2000 \text{ Btu/hr}$$

Convection

Convection is the transfer of heat by fluids and gases in contact with solid surfaces. In the context of a building it is the transfer of heat between air and an element of the building structure such as a wall, window, or ceiling. When warm air inside our house comes in contact with the colder inside surface of, say, a wall, it transfers some heat to that wall. As it does so, it cools, becomes more dense, and falls, to be replaced by more warm air.

Outside, the opposite is happening. The outer surface of our wall is warmer than the cold surrounding air and it transfers heat to that air. Moreover, the air outside is likely to be moving rapidly past the wall, increasing the ease with which the heat can be transferred.

In either case, we can describe the rate of heat transfer as being directly proportional to the difference in temperature between the surface of the wall and the surrounding air. The constant of proportionality is the con-

vective heat-transfer coefficient. And, of course, the larger the surface area in contact with the air, the greater will be the heat transfer rate. Putting these together we have

E. 4.27 $$q_{cv} = A\, h_{cv}(T_a - T_s)$$

where q_{cv} equals the rate of heat transfer due to convection (Btu/hr); A is the surface area (ft²); h_{cv} is the convective coefficient (Btu/hr-ft²-°F); and T_a and T_s are the temperatures of air and surface. The direction of heat transfer is, of course, determined by which is the larger, T_a or T_s.

Just as was the case for swimming pools, the convective coefficient depends on how fast the air is moving past the surface. For instance, h_{cv} is roughly 1 Btu/hr-ft²-°F for the "free" convection taking place inside the house, but it may very well be as much as 10 Btu/hr-ft²-°F on the outside if it is very windy.

Example: Compute the convective heat loss from a 100-square-foot wall whose outside surface temperature is 50° while exposed to moving air at 10°F. Assume a convective coefficient of 5 Btu/hr-ft²-°F.

Solution: Using Equation 4.27, we have

$$q_{cv} = 100 \text{ ft}^2 \times \frac{5 \text{ Btu}}{hr\text{-}ft^2\text{-}°F} \times (50 - 10)°F$$
$$= 20,000 \text{ Btu/hr}$$

Radiation

Radiation is the transfer of heat by electromagnetic waves. Solar energy was already given as an example of radiant energy in transit; hence, we see that radiant energy does not need a medium through which to move. If we have two bodies at different temperatures in a closed, evacuated system (that is, a vacuum, which eliminates the other transfer modes of conduction and convection), their temperatures will eventually equalize by the exchange of radiant energy.

Sitting in a room, our bodies radiate energy to our surroundings and they, in turn, radiate energy back to us. While a quantitative analysis of this phenomenon is very complicated, there are some useful qualitative concepts that we can easily understand.

One is that we will lose energy at a much faster rate to a cold window surface than to the same area of a warmer wall right next to it. In fact, it is possible to feel quite chilly in a room with a lot of glass even though the air may be at a supposedly comfortable temperature. It will be important for us to remember this later when we explore the usefulness of large expanses of south-facing glass as passive solar collectors. If we can keep that inside surface of the window from getting too cold, we will be more comfortable. One way to do that is by using double or triple glazing. Another is to locate heat delivery registers right under the windows (this also reduces the draft caused by the downward flowing air coming in contact with the window).

Another factor of importance as we sit in this room, radiating away, has to do with the emittance of the surface that we are radiating to. Surfaces with low emittance reflect radiant energy rather than absorbing it (for opaque surfaces, reflectance is one minus emittance; low emittance means high reflectance).

Most common building materials, such as wood, glass, masonry, and nonmetallic paints, have a relatively high value of emittance, usually somewhere between 0.8 and 0.9, and hence they easily absorb radiant energy. Shiny metals, on the other hand, have low emittance, and hence reflect a good portion of the radiant energy striking them. Aluminum foil has an emittance of only about 0.05 (meaning 95 percent of the radiant energy striking it is reflected), which is why it is used on one or both sides of many insulating materials. The foil, then, helps keep radiant energy in the room, reducing the overall rate of heat loss.

At the risk of adding confusion, we should also note that radiation heat-transfer effects depend not only on temperatures, but also on wave lengths. For example, white paint has a high reflectance, hence a low emittance, in the short visible wave lengths (around 1 micron; see Figure 4.6), so we might think it would be useful as a thermal reflector, just as the aluminum foil was. The thermal energy that we are trying to contain is, however, at much longer wave lengths (closer to 10 microns), and at these wave lengths white paint becomes a good absorber, so it would be a poor substitute for the foil.

If you are getting the feeling that radiant heat transfer can get complicated, you are right. You'll notice we haven't written any equations yet. It is very difficult to handle radiation heat-exchange rates quantitatively, but that does not mean they will be omitted from our calculations. The usual way to handle radiation losses from a house is to smuggle a radiation heat-transfer coefficient into the convective coefficient, call it a surface conductance, or a film coefficient, and go about your business.

Air Exchange

There is another way a house can lose energy. Whenever air leaves a heated space, it takes thermal energy with it. The warm air is replaced by cold air which must be heated in order to maintain a comfortable temperature. This air exchange can take place in two ways—by infiltration and by ventilation. Infiltration is unintentional air exchange which occurs because of various leaks in the house; the shabbier the construction, the greater the infiltration. Large amounts of infiltration take place around the edges and through the joints of windows and doors. Wall-floor joints and corner joints are also potential leakage areas.

Ventilation is the intentional exchange of air to avoid stuffiness, odors, and pollutants. Ventilation requires that our structure "exhale" warm air, and so a loss of energy necessarily results. During the heating season, we seldom worry about ventilation in small buildings because normal infiltration rates have a sufficient ventilating effect. Natural ventilation is deliberately encouraged through open doors or windows during the summer.

Later in this section, we will see that heat losses due to air exchange can be a sizable fraction of the total building losses, especially if ample amounts of insulation are used throughout. To reduce infiltration, special attention should be paid to caulking and weatherstripping, especially during construction. Air-lock entries on exterior doors also help by preventing blasts of cold air from getting into the house each time the door is opened.

Not only does air leak in and out through cracks around windows and doors, but some also passes through walls and ceilings. To prevent this, many superinsulated houses are being built today which seal off the house with 6-mil-thick polyethylene sheets fastened to the inside of the framing during construction. Not only does the polyethylene keep heat losses to a minimum, it also acts as a vapor barrier. Without a vapor barrier, water vapor in the air can condense into the insulation as it cools on its way through the wall, greatly reducing the effectiveness of the insulation.

While reduction of unwanted infiltration is important, it is also important to realize that we need a certain amount of ventilation to flush out indoor air pollutants—the nitrogen oxides and carbon monoxide from our gas appliances, and morpholine from our furniture polish, the hydrated aluminum from our deodorants, the vinyl acetate copolymer resins from our hair sprays, the fumes from cleaning fluids, the formaldehyde that escapes from wallboard and carpet adhesives and from solidifying urea-formaldehyde insulating foams, the radioactive gas radon that is given off by some building materials, to say nothing of the carcinogens given off in cigarette smoke.

The usual leaky house probably experiences at least one complete air change per hour. That is, an amount of air equivalent to the volume of the house leaks out and is replaced by cold incoming air, once per hour. That is enough to keep the air inside fresh. Some extremely tight houses being built today reduce the infiltration rate to one-tenth of that value. So how can these especially tight houses be kept comfortable and, for that matter, safe for human occupancy? The answer is that ventilation must be provided to flush out pollutants and keep the air fresh. But wouldn't we be just as well off with a leaky house then?

Remember that infiltration is unwanted air exchange while ventilation is under control of the user. The trick to ventilating a tight house without a lot of heat loss is to use an air-to-air heat exchanger, or heat recuperator, at the single point where the warm, stale inside air is allowed to exit and the cold, fresh outside air is allowed to enter. Such a device is shown in Figure 4.63. It is claimed that 70 to 80 percent of the heat can be squeezed out of the exhaust air. Outside air at 0°F, for example, might be pre-warmed up to 50 or 60°F before entering the house, so ventilation with minimal heat loss is possible.

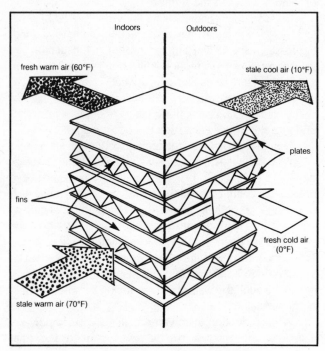

Figure 4.63 This Mitsubishi air-to-air heat exchanger warms incoming cold fresh air with the warm but stale air being exhausted from the house.

Later we'll see how to quantify infiltration losses. For now, simply note that infiltration rates should be reduced as low as possible through careful attention to detail during construction. At worst, you may have to open a window once in a while.

Thermal Resistance and Coefficient of Transmission

Let us return to the mechanisms of heat transfer that do not involve the exchange of air, that is, conduction, convection, and radiation. All three are involved in the usual heat-transfer problem that we must solve. Obviously, it would greatly simplify things if we could somehow combine all of them into one overall relationship. That is accomplished by introducing the notion of thermal conductance, U, or its reciprocal, thermal resistance, R.

Consider Figure 4.64, which illustrates the mechanisms involved in transferring heat from the interior space at temperature T_i to the ambient at temperature T_o. It should be obvious by now that the overall rate of heat transfer will probably be proportional to the temperature difference $(T_i - T_o)$ and the area of the surface that the

heat is passing through. So, let us write such an equation:

E. 4.28 $$q = UA(T_i - T_o)$$

where q is the rate of heat loss (Btu/hr); A is the surface area (ft²); T_i and T_o are the inside and outside temperatures (°F); and the new factor, U, is the overall coefficient of heat transmission, or *thermal transmittance*, measured in Btu/hr-ft²-°F.

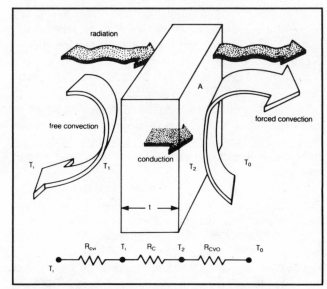

Figure 4.64 Heat transfer mechanism for a simple wall.

Another way to express the same notion is with a *thermal resistance, R*, as follows:

E. 4.29 $$q = \frac{A}{R}(T_i - T_o)$$

where $R = 1/U$ and has units of hr-ft²-°F/Btu.

If we can somehow determine these U-values or R-values for the various components of a building such as the windows, walls, floor, ceiling, and doors then the calculation for the rate at which the whole building loses heat becomes a reasonably straightforward exercise. If we know the U-value for the walls, for example, we just multiply it by the area of walls and the temperature difference across them and we'll have the total loss through the walls. We do the same for the windows, the ceiling, the doors, and floors. Add them up, throw in a calculation for infiltration, and we're done. Obviously there are complications that we'll introduce later, but conceptually this is where we are headed.

Let's get back to Figure 4.64 and the problem of finding the overall thermal resistance of the basic wall represented. It will be useful for us to note the electrical analog to the heat-transfer problem that we are trying to solve. If we consider heat loss per unit of area, call it q', we can rewrite Equation 4.29 as

152

E. 4.30 $\qquad q' = \dfrac{(T_i - T_o)}{R} = \dfrac{\Delta T}{R}$

If you will, heat flow is being pushed by the temperature differential and resisted by the thermal resistance.

Equation 4.30 is exactly analogous to Ohm's law for electrical circuits $I = V/R$, wherein current I (the thing that flows) equals voltage V (the thing that pushes the flow) divided by R (the electrical resistance to that flow). It should not surprise us then to learn that we can deal with thermal resistances in much the same way that electrical engineers use electrical resistances. Figure 4.64, in fact, shows us the thermal circuit for this wall consisting of a convective resistance in series with a conductive resistance and another convective resistor.

Now, for our wall, the rate of heat transfer by radiation and convection from the inside air to the inside surface of the wall will be

E. 4.31 $\qquad q_{cvi} = A \, h_i (T_i - T_1)$

where h_i is the inside film coefficient (which, you will recall, includes the effects of radiation and convection; its units are Btu/ft²-hr-°F) and T_i and T_1 are the temperatures of the inside air and inside wall surface.

Comparing this equation with Equation 4.29 suggests the convective resistance to heat flow would be

E. 4.32 $\qquad R_{cvi} = 1/h_i$

Moving on, if we consider this wall to be a simple homogeneous barrier with thickness t and conductivity k, we can write the conductive heat transfer through the wall as

E. 4.33 $\qquad q_c = A \dfrac{k}{t}(T_1 - T_2)$

where T_1 and T_2 are the temperatures of the surfaces of the wall on the inside and outside of the building.

Again, by comparison with Equation 4.29, the thermal resistance due to conduction will be

E. 4.34 $\qquad R_c = \dfrac{t}{k}$

This makes good sense, doesn't it? The greater the thickness of the wall, the more it will resist heat flow. And the lower the conductivity of the materials within the wall, the more it will resist losing heat.

Finally, the outside wall surface will deliver heat to the ambient at a rate equal to

E. 4.35 $\qquad q_{cvo} = A \, h_o (T_2 - T_o)$

where h_o is the outside film coefficient. It is common prac-

tice to assume that the wind is blowing at 15 mph when calculating h_o so it will not have the same value as the free convective coefficient inside, h_i.

Again, by comparison with Equation 4.29, we can write the outside convective resistance as

E. 4.36 $\qquad R_{cvo} = 1/h_o$

Each one of these thermal resistors, R_{cvi}, R_c, and R_{cvo}, are acting to impede the loss of heat from the interior to the ambient. Their combined effect is the sum of their individual efforts and we can write the total thermal resistance as

E. 4.37 $\qquad R = R_{cvi} + R_c + R_{cvo}$

E. 4.38 $\qquad R = 1/h_i + t/k + 1/h_o$

This is what we have been trying to get. The only thing we need now are values for the film coefficients, and those are supplied by ASHRAE, reproduced here in Table 4.20. Notice how surface emittance has crept into the coefficients. Unless the surface in question is highly reflective, you should use the "nonreflective" values corresponding to an emittance equal to 0.9.

If you are the average nontechnical person, you may be somewhat confused at this point. That's fine—this is the most difficult section in the chapter. Take a look at this next example, then go back and read the section again. See if it doesn't make more sense the second time around.

Example: How can we figure the heat loss across a window?

Table 4.20 Film Coefficients (h) and Resistances (R)

Position of Surface	Direction of Heat Flow	Surface Emittance					
		Non-reflective $\varepsilon = 0.90$		Reflective $\varepsilon = 0.20$		Reflective $\varepsilon = 0.05$	
		h_i	R	h_i	R	h_i	R
STILL AIR							
Horizontal	Upward	1.63	*0.61*	0.91	*1.10*	0.76	*1.32*
Sloping—45 deg	Upward	1.60	*0.62*	0.88	*1.14*	0.73	*1.37*
Vertical........	Horizontal	1.46	*0.68*	0.74	*1.35*	0.59	*1.70*
Sloping—45 deg	Downward	1.32	*0.76*	0.60	*1.67*	0.45	*2.22*
Horizontal	Downward	1.08	*0.92*	0.37	*2.70*	0.22	*4.55*
MOVING AIR (Any Position)		h_o	R	h_o	R	h_o	R
15-mph Wind (for winter)	Any	6.00	0.17				
7.5-mph Wind (for summer)	Any	4.00	0.25				

Notes: From ASHRAE 1977 *Fundamentals* Units for R-values are hr-ft²-°F/Btu

Solution: Figure 4.65 shows the window, which we'll assume is ¼-inch-thick glass. From Table 4.20, for a non-reflective vertical surface we read h_i to be 1.46 (or R_{cvi} = 0.68) for still inside air, and an h_o of 6.0 (or R_{cvo} = 0.17) for the assumed 15-mph winter conditions. Referring to Table 4.19, the thermal conductivity of glass is about 5 Btu-in/hr-°F-ft². The overall resistance is the sum of the three individual resistances (from Equation 4.38):

$$R = R_{cvi} + R_c + R_{cvo}$$
$$R = \frac{1}{1.46} + \frac{0.25}{5} + \frac{1}{6.0}$$
$$= 0.68 + 0.05 + 0.17 = 0.90 \frac{hr\text{-}ft^2\text{-}°F}{Btu}$$

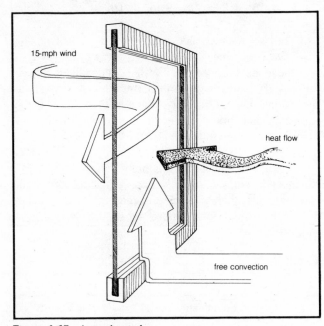

Figure 4.65 A simple window.

The overall coefficient of transmission is simply the reciprocal of this value, or

$$U = \frac{1}{R} = \frac{1}{0.9} = 1.1 \frac{Btu}{hr\text{-}ft^2\text{-}°F}$$

Notice how little effect the glass itself has on the calculation (only about 5 percent of the R-value is due to the glass, the rest is film resistance). Also note that our result is independent of specific outside or inside temperatures. Also, our calculations are very general in that they are based on one square foot of window pane.

Example: Now let's treat a more specific problem. What would be the total heat transfer for 25 square feet of window surface subjected to a 70°F indoor air temperature and a 30°F outdoor air temperature?

Solution: Using our results in Equation 4.28 we find

$$q = UA(\Delta T)$$
$$= \left(\frac{1.1\ Btu}{hr\text{-}ft^2\text{-}°F}\right)(25\ ft^2)(70 - 30)°F$$
$$= 1100\ Btu/hr$$

Heat Transfer Through a Composite Wall

Next consider the composite wall shown as a cutaway in Figure 4.66. We will assume that the inside air temperature is 70°F and the outside air temperature is 30°F. Our job is to estimate the rate of heat transfer through the wall.

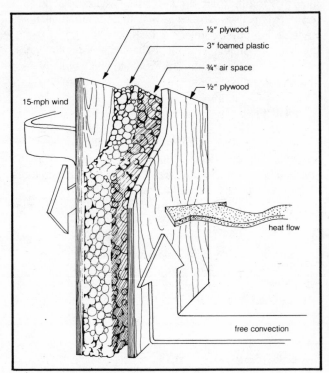

Figure 4.66 A simple composite wall.

Since heat must flow through each element in turn (including the convective resistances), the system can again be represented by a series circuit. Let's start from the inside and move outward. The first resistive element is the convective (or film) resistance. We would expect free convection on this inside wall so from Table 4.20 we find

$$R_{cvi} = 0.68 \frac{hr\text{-}ft^2\text{-}°F}{Btu}$$

The ½-inch plywood sheet represents a conductive resistance, and the thermal conductivity of plywood can be found in a number of references. Table 4.19 lists values for wood, but information more pertinent to the construction trade is listed in Appendix 4D. This appendix makes our job particularly easy in that it already includes the thermal resistance as well as the thermal conductance (C). The thermal conductance is related to the thermal resistance in the following way:

E. 4.39
$$C = \frac{1}{R}$$

For ½-inch plywood we find (under the section of Appendix 4D labeled "Building Board")

$$R_1 = \frac{1}{C} = 0.62 \; \frac{hr\text{-}ft^2\text{-}°F}{Btu}$$

Next, we encounter an enclosed air space. In reality, the air space involves two additional convective (or film) resistances and a single term to account for conduction across the air gap. The combined effect of these resistances is tabulated in Table 4.21. For a ¾-inch vertical air space with no reflective foil, we find the resistance to be

$$R_2 = 0.96 \; \frac{hr\text{-}ft^2\text{-}°F}{Btu}$$

Table 4.21   Air-Space Resistances (R) for 50°F Mean Temperature[a]

Position of Air Space	Direction of Heat Flow	Air Space Bounded by Ordinary Materials		Air Space Bounded by Aluminum Foil	
		0.75-inch R	4-inch R	0.75-inch R	4-inch R
Horizontal	Upward	0.78	0.85	1.67	2.06
Horizontal	Downward	1.02	1.23	3.55	8.94
Vertical	Horizontal	0.96	0.94	2.80	2.62

Notes: a. From ASHRAE *Handbook of Fundamentals*; units of hr-ft²-°F/Btu.

Incidentally, did you notice that a foil-lined air space has nearly three times the resistance of an ordinary air space?

The 3-inch foam plastic represents another conductive resistance and the values in Appendix 4D are applicable ("Board and Slabs"). We have a number of plastics to choose from. The entries differ in density or manufacturing technique; some are expanded using freon gas, R-11 or R-12, while others simply use air. For our example, let's choose "polyurethane, R-11 exp." so k equals 0.16 Btu-in/hr-ft²-°F. Using Equation 4.34, we compute the resistance for the 3-inch thickness:

$$R_3 = \frac{t}{k} = \frac{3 \; in}{0.16 \; Btu\text{-}in/hr\text{-}ft^2\text{-}°F}$$
$$= 18.75 \; \frac{hr\text{-}ft^2\text{-}°F}{Btu}$$

Note the relatively large size of this thermal resistance; foamed plastic is an excellent insulating material!

The remaining sheet of plywood can be handled in the usual way ($R_4 = R_1 = 0.62$). The outside convective coefficient is obtained assuming a 15-mph wind (Ta-

ble 4.20) and R_{cvo} comes to 0.17. Total resistance is simply the sum of the individual elements.

$$R_{total} = 0.68 + 0.62 + 0.96 + 18.75$$
$$+ 0.62 + 0.17$$
$$= 21.8 \; \frac{hr\text{-}ft^2\text{-}°F}{Btu}$$

The heat transfer per square foot of wall area is given by Equation 4.30.

$$q' = \Delta T/R = (70-30)°F/21.8 \; \frac{hr\text{-}ft^2\text{-}°F}{Btu}$$
$$= 1.83 \; Btu/hr\text{-}ft^2$$

To obtain the total heat transfer in, say, a 200-square-foot wall, we simply multiply our result by 200:

$$q = 1.83 \; Btu/hr\text{-}ft^2 \times 200 \; ft^2 = 366 \; Btu/hr$$

Simplified Heat-Transfer Calculations

The previous examples illustrate a step-by-step method to compute the total thermal resistance of a wall. The details will be particularly useful to those who are experimenting with new building techniques and materials. In many situations, however, wall construction follows a set pattern, and thermal resistance calculations for these "standard" walls have been computed. The results are reported in terms of the coefficient of transmission (U).

U-values are given for several window configurations in Table 4.22. Note that a single pane with an outdoor (exterior) exposure has a coefficient of 1.10, in agreement with the calculated value in the last section. Also note that double-pane windows (that is, modular windows with two sheets of glass separated by an air space) have a significantly lower U-value. Essentially, the thermal resistance of the double-pane window is twice that of a single pane.

Analogous values for solid wooden doors are given in Table 4.23. You can see that the addition of a storm door lowers the overall conductance significantly. Doors of nonstandard construction can be handled with the basic thermal resistance techniques discussed earlier. For instance, a hollow door is treated as a sort of composite wall.

Overall conductances and resistances for typical walls, ceilings, and elevated floors have been computed by ASHRAE and are given in Appendix 4E, a sample of which is given here as Table 4.24. Our job is getting easier and easier; all we have to do is look up the proper values.

Consider the frame wall construction illustrated in Table 4.24. The first column of numbers shows how the R-value for an uninsulated wall is derived, component by component, for a section of wall between the 2- by 4-inch

Table 4.22 U-values of Windows and Skylights

PART A—VERTICAL PANELS (EXTERIOR WINDOWS, SLIDING PATIO DOORS, AND PARTITIONS)—FLAT GLASS, GLASS BLOCK, AND PLASTIC SHEET

Description		Exterior		Interior
		Winter	Summer	
Flat Glass				
single glass		1.10	1.04	0.73
insulating glass—double				
0.1875-in. air space		0.62	0.65	0.51
0.25-in. air space		0.58	0.61	0.49
0.5-in. air space		0.49	0.56	0.46
0.5-in. air space, low				
emittance coating				
e = 0.20		0.32	0.38	0.32
e = 0.40		0.38	0.45	0.38
e = 0.60		0.43	0.51	0.42
insulating glass—triple				
0.25-in. air spaces		0.39	0.44	0.38
0.5-in. air spaces		0.31	0.39	0.30
storm windows				
1-in. to 4-in. air space		0.50	0.50	0.44

PART B—HORIZONTAL PANELS (SKYLIGHTS)—FLAT GLASS, GLASS BLOCK, AND PLASTIC DOMES

Description		Exterior		Interior
		Winter[i]	Summer	
Flat Glass				
single glass		1.23	0.83	0.96
insulating glass—double				
0.1875-in. air space		0.70	0.57	0.62
0.25-in. air space		0.65	0.54	0.59
0.5-in. air space		0.59	0.49	0.56
0.5-in. air space, low				
emittance coating				
e = 0.20		0.48	0.36	0.39
e = 0.40		0.52	0.42	0.45
e = 0.60		0.56	0.46	0.50
Glass Block				
11 × 11 × 3 in. thick with				
cavity divider		0.53	0.35	0.44
12 × 12 × 4 in. thick with				
cavity divider		0.51	0.34	0.42
Plastic Domes				
single-walled		1.15	0.80	—
double-walled		0.70	0.46	—

PART C—ADJUSTMENT FACTORS FOR VARIOUS WINDOW AND SLIDING PATIO DOOR TYPES (MULTIPLY U VALUES IN PARTS A AND B BY THESE FACTORS)

Description	Single Glass	Double or Triple Glass	Storm Windows
Windows			
All Glass	1.00	1.00	1.00
Wood Sash—80% Glass	0.90	0.95	0.90
Wood Sash—60% Glass	0.80	0.85	0.80
Metal Sash—80% Glass	1.00	1.20	1.20
Sliding Patio Doors			
Wood Frame	0.95	1.00	—
Metal Frame	1.00	1.10	—

Notes: from ASHRAE 1977 Fundamentals; units are Btu/hr-ft²-°F

Table 4.23 U-Values of Solid Wood Doors[a]

Thickness[b]	No Storm Door	Winter Storm Door[c]		Summer No Storm Door
		Wood	Metal	
1 in	0.64	0.30	0.39	0.61
1¼ in	0.55	0.28	0.34	0.53
1½ in	0.49	0.27	0.33	0.47
2 in	0.43	0.24	0.29	0.42

Notes: a. From ASHRAE *Handbook of Fundamentals*; units are Btu/hr-ft²-°F.
  b. Nominal thickness.
  c. Values for wood storm doors are for approximately 50 percent glass; for metal storm doors values apply for any percent of glass.

framing members. The total R-value is 4.44 hr-ft²-°F/Btu.

The second column shows the same calculation, but this time it has been done through a section of wall that includes the 2- by 4-inch studs. the thermal resistance through the studs is higher, 7.81 hr-ft²-°F/Btu.

There are, then, two parallel heat conduction paths, one through the framing and one between framing. To find a composite average conductance for the whole wall, we must weigh the U-values of each by their respective areas, which we can do with the following equation:

E. 4.40 $\quad U_{av} = SU_s + (1 - S)U_i$

where U_{av} is the average U-value for the building section, U_s is the U-value for area backed by the framing, U_i is the U-value between framing members, and S is the fraction of the wall area backed by the framing members.

A typical 2-by-4-inch stud wall on 16-inch centers has about 20 percent of its area backed by framing (including multiple studs, plates, headers, sills, band joists, and so on). The total U-value for the uninsulated stud wall in Table 4.24 would be

$$U_{av} = 0.2\left(\frac{1}{7.81}\right) + 0.8\left(\frac{1}{4.44}\right) = 0.206 \ Btu/hr\text{-}ft^2\text{-}°F$$

Notice even this has been worked out for us by ASHRAE and presented at the bottom of the tables.

The second set of two columns in Table 4.24 shows the same calculations repeated with 3.5-inch R-11 fiberglass insulation in the wall cavity. Between the studs the R-value is 14.43 hr-ft²-°F/Btu, but by the time you take into account the framing, the overall R-value is back down to 1/0.081 or R-12.3. The overall thermal resistance of the wall is therefore not much different from the R-value of the insulation alone. It is quite common to talk of an R-11 wall, or an R-19 ceiling, when really that is the value of the insulation alone.

Not too long ago, new houses usually had no insulation at all in their walls. Since then, building codes have changed and at least R-11 insulation is required almost everywhere. Why R-11? That happens to be the thermal resistance of fiberglass batts that just fit in the 3½-inch

Table 4.24 Coefficients of Transmission *(U)* of Frame Walls[a]

These coefficients are expressed in Btu per (hour) (square foot) (degree Fahrenheit) difference in temperature between the air on the two sides), and are based on an outside wind velocity of 15 mph

Replace Air Space with 3.5-in. R-11 Blanket Insulation (New Item 4)

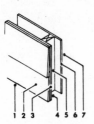

Construction	1 Resistance (R)		2 Resistance (R)	
	Between Framing	At Framing	Between Framing	At Framing
1. Outside surface (15 mph wind)	0.17	0.17	0.17	0.17
2. Siding, wood, 0.5 in.× 8 in. lapped (average)	0.81	0.81	0.81	0.81
3. Sheathing, 0.5-in. asphalt impregnated	1.32	1.32	1.32	1.32
4. Nonreflective air space, 3.5 in. (50 Fmean; 10 deg F temperature difference)	1.01	—	11.00	—
5. Nominal 2-in. × 4-in. wood stud	—	4.38	—	4.38
6. Gypsum wallboard, 0.5 in.	0.45	0.45	0.45	0.45
7. Inside surface (still air)	0.68	0.68	0.68	0.68
Total Thermal Resistance (R)	R_i=4.44	R_s=7.81	R_i=14.43	R_s=7.81

Construction No. 1: $U_i = 1/4.44 = 0.225$; $U_s = 1/7.81 = 0.128$. With 20% framing (typical of 2-in. × 4-in. studs @ 16-in. o.c.), $U_{av} = 0.8 (0.225) + 0.2 (0.128) = 0.206$ (See Eq 9)

Construction No. 2: $U_i = 1/14.43 = 0.069$; $U_s = 0.128$. With framing unchanged, $U_{av} = 0.8(0.069) + 0.2(0.128) = 0.081$

Notes: a. From ASHRAE 1977 Fundamentals

cavity of a 2-by-4-inch wall. Increasing the wall's resistance usually requires a change in the way the wall is constructed.

One way to do that is make the wall out of 2-by-6-inch studs on 24-inch centers rather than 2-by-4s on 16-inch centers, which lets you insert (nominally) 6-inch thick R-19 fiberglass batts. R-19 can also be obtained by framing the wall with 2-by-4s, laying in 3½ inches of fiberglass, then nailing an inch of styrofoam on the outside of the studs.

Even heavier insulation can be obtained by building a double wall. A conventionally framed house with R-11 insulation between 2-by-4s can have interior walls built immediately adjacent to the exterior walls. By staggering the studs of the two walls the thermal short-circuiting effect of framing can be reduced and walls with total *R*-values of R-25 to R-40 can be obtained.

Such unconventional building practices would have been thought outrageous a few years ago, but now we know that what is really outrageous is the way houses used to be built.

Heat Loss to Adjacent Unheated Spaces

We now have the tools to analyze the rate of heat loss through a wall or whatever based on the *U*- or *R*-value of the construction element, its area, and the temperature difference across the element. It is this last aspect that we want to consider now. For the most part, the temperature difference across the building element in question is simply the difference between the temperature inside the house and the ambient temperature outside. But what about a floor over an unheated basement or a wall that separates a heated room from an adjoining unheated workshop? The temperatures in these adjacent unheated spaces are probably quite different from the ambient and

we must take this into account.

Figure 4.67 illustrates the problem. The heated space can be considered to be the volume contained inside of the insulating envelope of the building. Interior walls within the heated space need not be considered in a heat-loss calculation since it is assumed the temperature is the same on both sides of such walls.

Many homes have insulation in the ceiling rather than the roof itself with the resulting attic space being fairly well ventilated to preclude attic condensation. The temperature in the attic will be somewhere between the interior temperature, T_i, and ambient, T_o. If the ceiling is well insulated, it is common practice to assume the attic is at the ambient temperature T_o. The heat loss is then calculated using ceiling areas rather than roof areas, and the temperature differential is the full difference between inside and ambient.

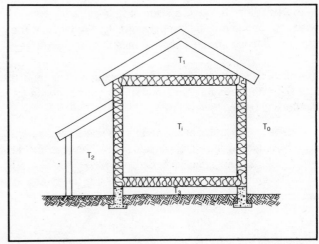

Figure 4.67 Defining the building envelope and temperatures of adjacent unheated spaces.

157

For elevated floors over ventilated crawl spaces, the temperature in the crawl space will vary widely depending on the number and size of vents, amount of warm piping present, ground temperature, and degree of floor insulation. A designer needs to exercise a certain amount of judgment here, but our recommendation is to consider the crawl space to be halfway between the inside temperature and ambient.

When doing the heat-loss calculation for an entire house, it is often useful to evaluate all surfaces as if they had T_i on one side of them and T_o on the other. We can do this if we "adjust" the surface area involved.

To illustrate, consider our floor over a crawl space. We can write

E. 4.41 $\qquad q_f = U_f A_f (T_i - T_{cs})$

where the subscript f refers to the fact that we are dealing with a floor. T_i is the inside temperature and T_{cs} is the crawl space temperature.

If we assume the crawl space temperature is midway between the inside and the ambient temperature we can write

$$T_{cs} = \frac{T_i + T_o}{2}$$

which when substituted into E. 4.41 gives

E. 4.42
$$q_f = U_f A_f[T_i - \frac{(T_i + T_o)}{2}] = U_f\left(\frac{A_f}{2}\right)(T_i - T_o)$$

E. 4.43 $\qquad q_f = U_f A_{eff}(T_i - T_o)$

where

E. 4.44 $\qquad A_{eff} = A_f/2$

That is, the actual heat loss through the floor is the same as the heat loss through a floor of half the area but exposed to the full outside temperature, T_o. We will find the use of "effective" areas to be a convenient shortcut.

Example: Calculate the heat loss through a 40-by-50-foot floor over a ventilated crawl space if the U-value for the floor is 0.05.

Solution: No ambient temperature is specified, so we'll do it per degree temperature difference between inside and ambient. The effective floor area is $\frac{1}{2} \times 40 \times 50 = 1000$ square feet. From Equation 4.43, the heat loss will be

$$q_f = 0.05 \frac{Btu}{hr\text{-}ft^2\text{-}°F} \times 1000 \; ft^2 = 50 \frac{Btu}{hr\text{-}°F}$$

With the answer specified this way, we can quickly determine floor losses under any variations in outside temperature.

Example: Find the rate of heat loss through the floor in the previous example given an inside temperature of 70°F and an ambient temperature of 20°F. What would be the total energy lost in a month's time if the average ambient temperature is 30°F?

Solution: The rate of loss when it is 20°F outside is

$$q_f = 50 \frac{Btu}{hr\text{-}°F} \times (70 - 20)°F = 2500 \; Btu/hr$$

In a 30-day month with average outside temperature of 30°F, the floor will lose

$$50 \frac{Btu}{hr\text{-}°F} \times (70 - 30) \; °F \times 720 \frac{hr}{mo}$$
$$= 1.44 \times 10^6 \; Btu$$

What about heat loss through a floor over an unheated basement? The temperature in the basement will be somewhere between the temperature of the rooms above and the ground temperature. If there is a furnace located in the basement, it can be assumed that heat given off will warm the air near the basement ceiling enough to allow us to neglect any heat loss through the floor.

Finally, how should we treat a closed, attached garage or unheated workshop? Again, no hard and fast rules can substitute for real judgment, but for our purposes, we can assume such unheated spaces are halfway between indoor and outdoor temperatures. We could, then, calculate the loss through the adjoining wall based on an effective wall area of half the real wall, but exposed to full ambient cold.

Heat Loss from Ground Floors and Underground Walls

Heat loss from basement floors and subterranean walls can be treated with a modified form of the heat-loss equation:

E. 4.45 $\qquad q = U^*A$

Values of U^* are given for various groundwater temperatures (T_{gw}) in Table 4.25. The inclusion of the water temperature eliminates the need for a temperature-difference term in Equation 4.45. As a result, the units of U^* are different from the other U-values in the preceding sections. In most localities, the groundwater temperature remains around 50°F, independent of season. More accurate data can be obtained from your local water utility.

A popular method to compute heat loss from concrete floors at grade (ground) level utilizes the perimeter

Table 4.25 *U*-Values for Ground-Water Temperatures*

T_{gw}	Basement Floor U^*	Subterranean Walls U^*
40°F	3.0	6.0
50°F	2.0	4.0
60°F	1.0	2.0

Notes: a. From ASHRAE *Handbook of Fundamentals*; units are Btu/hr-ft².

of the floor as an indicator of the potential heat loss. The reasoning here is that horizontal conduction losses from the inner area of the floor to the outer perimeter can be significantly higher than the losses "straight down" if the edges of the concrete slab are "exposed." (The method *does*, however, include a factor for losses "straight down.") The governing equation is given by

E. 4.46 $q_{floor} = F_2 P_e (T_i - T_o)$

where P_e is the exposed perimeter of the floor (in feet). A special heat-loss factor is denoted by F_2 and has units of Btu/hr-ft-°F. For this equation to apply, two conditions must be satisfied. First, the floor slab must be properly insulated and waterproofed. Figure 4.68 shows some recommended techniques and materials. Zonolite polystyrene foam is a popular slab insulating material (Grace/Zonolite, 62 Whittemore Avenue, Cambridge, Massachusetts 02140). It should cover the vertical edges of the floor and extend several feet under the edge. The vapor barrier or waterproofing can be either sheets of thin plastic film or a coating which is applied on-site. The UniRoyal Corporation (Mishawaka, Indiana 46544) markets such a coating "system" which combines special sealants and thin plastic membranes. Many other coatings are available, and we suggest you contact a building supply house for details.

By the way, it is conventional practice to refer to the total distance that the edge insulation goes down the footing and under the slab as the "width" of the insulation—not to be confused with its thickness.

As a second condition, the ratio of the slab area to the exposed slab perimeter must be *less* than 12 to 1. The edge of the slab is considered to be *exposed* if it faces the outside air. Values of F_2 are given in the figure.

Example: Compute the heat loss experienced by a 16-by-20-foot concrete slab edged with 1.5 feet of insulation. The conductance of the insulation is 0.35 Btu/hr-ft²-°F and the temperature differential is 50°F.

Solution: Equation 4.46 and the F_2 data in Figure 4.68 are valid if the ratio of the slab area divided by the slab perimeter (A/P_e) is less than 12.

$$P_e = 16 + 16 + 20 + 20 = 72 \ ft$$

and

$$A = 16 \ ft \times 20 \ ft = 320 \ ft^2$$

so that the ratio is

$$\frac{A}{P_e} = \frac{320}{72} = 4.4$$

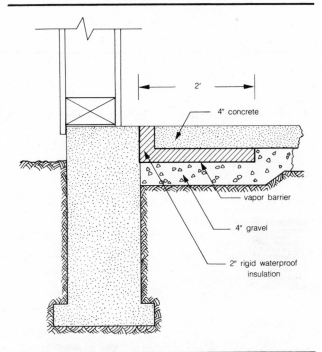

Conductance of Insulation[a]	Total Horizontal and/or Vertical Width of Insulation		
	Values of F_2[b]		
	1 foot	1.5 feet	2 feet
Unheated Slabs[c]			
0.15	0.29	0.26	0.25
0.20	0.38	0.35	0.33
0.25	0.49	0.44	0.42
0.30	0.58	0.52	0.50
0.35	0.67	0.61	0.59
0.40	0.77	0.70	0.67
Heated Slabs[c]			
0.15	0.32	0.28	0.27
0.20	0.43	0.39	0.37
0.25	0.57	0.58	0.48
0.30	0.70	0.62	0.59
0.35	0.83	0.75	0.71
0.40	1.00	0.88	0.83

Notes: a. In Btu/hr-ft²-°F.
b. In Btu/hr-ft-°F.
c. In the case of unheated slabs, temperature difference is design indoor minus design outdoor temperature. In the case of heated slabs, temperature difference is the temperature of the heating medium on the slab minus the outside design temperature. For unheated slabs, use $F_2 = 1.11$.

Figure 4.68 Typical floor construction and values of F_2 for use in Equation 4.46.

159

which is less than 12. Thus, from Figure 4.68 we can take the value

$$F_2 = 0.61 \frac{Btu}{hr\text{-}ft\text{-}°F}$$

and consequently Equation 4.46 gives us the heat loss from the floor:

$$
\begin{aligned}
q &= F_2 P_e (T_i - T_o) \\
&= \left(\frac{0.61\ Btu}{hr\text{-}ft\text{-}°F}\right)(72\ ft)(50°F) \\
&= 2196\ Btu/hr
\end{aligned}
$$

Heat Loss Due to Infiltration

There are two ways to calculate infiltration losses: the air-exchange and the crack-estimation methods. The *air-exchange equation* is based on the number of total air changes per hour for a dwelling of a given volume. This equation is written as

E. 4.47 $q = 0.018(T_i - T_o)nV$

where q equals the heat loss in Btu/hr, n equals the num-ber of air changes per hour, V equals the volume of the dwelling (ft³), T_i equals the inside temperature (°F), T_o equals the outside temperature (°F), and 0.018 is the number of Btus required to raise 1 cubic foot of air by 1°F. It is the product of the density of air (0.075 lbm/ft³) and its specific heat (0.24 Btu/lbm°F).

The number of air changes per hour, n, for most residences is probably about 1 to 1½. When more attention is paid to caulking, weatherstripping, and fewer openings and closings of exterior doors, n can be more like ½ to ⅔. Once an estimate is made of the air exchange rate, the calculation for q is simple. We just need to estimate the volume of the house and plug into Equation 4.47.

If the building is so tight that infiltration is reduced to below about ½ an air change per hour, then ventilation should be introduced to keep the air fresh as was discussed earlier. In such circumstances, an air-to-air heat exchanger such as the one shown in Figure 4.63 should be considered. We could then modify our heat-loss analysis depending on the manufacturer's estimates of the performance of the heat exchanger.

The *crack-method* is based on estimates of the rate at which air leaks through cracks around windows and doors. Table 4.26 gives these infiltration rates expressed

---

Table 4.26   Infiltration (I) through Cracks of Windows and Doors[a]

Type of Window	Remarks	Wind Velocity, Miles per Hour					
		5	10	15	20	25	30
Double-Hung Wood Sash Windows (Unlocked)	Around frame in masonry wall—not calked	3	8	14	20	27	35
	Around frame in masonry wall—calked	1	2	3	4	5	6
	Around frame in wood frame construction	2	6	11	17	23	30
	Total for average window, non-weatherstripped, $\frac{1}{16}$-in. crack and $\frac{3}{64}$-in. clearance. Includes wood frame leakage	7	21	39	59	80	104
	Ditto, weatherstripped	4	13	24	36	49	63
	Total for poorly fitted window, non-weatherstripped, $\frac{3}{32}$-in. crack and $\frac{3}{32}$-in. clearance. Includes wood frame leakage	27	69	111	154	199	249
	Ditto, weatherstripped	6	19	34	51	71	92
Double-Hung Metal Windows	Non-weatherstripped, locked	20	45	70	96	125	154
	Non-weatherstripped, unlocked	20	47	74	104	137	170
	Weatherstripped, unlocked	6	19	32	46	60	76
Rolled Section Steel Sash Windows	Industrial pivoted, $\frac{1}{16}$-in. crack	52	108	176	244	304	372
	Architectural projected, $\frac{1}{32}$-in. crack	15	36	62	86	112	139
	Architectural projected, $\frac{3}{64}$-in. crack	20	52	88	116	152	182
	Residential casement, $\frac{1}{64}$-in. crack	6	18	33	47	60	74
	Residential casement, $\frac{1}{32}$-in. crack	14	32	52	76	100	128
	Heavy casement section, projected, $\frac{1}{64}$-in. crack	3	10	18	26	36	48
	Heavy casement section, projected, $\frac{1}{32}$-in. crack	8	24	38	54	72	92
Hollow Metal, Vertically Pivoted Window		30	88	145	186	221	242
Doors	Well fitted	27	69	110	154	199	—
	Poorly fitted	54	138	220	308	398	—

Notes: a. Units are ft³/hr-ft; from ASHRAE *Handbook of Fundamentals*.

as cubic feet of air per hour that leak through each foot of crack for various wind speeds and construction techniques.

In calculating the air exchange rate by the crack-estimation method, we don't simply multiply the infiltration values from Table 4.26 by feet of crack because some cracks are letting air in and others are letting it out. It is only the air coming in that needs to be heated, so it is more reasonable to use something less than the full crack lengths. If the cracks are distributed fairly equally on all four sides of the building, it is common practice to use half the crack lengths in the calculations. We can then write the following equations:

E. 4.48 $\ infiltration\ rate = \left(\dfrac{L\,I}{2}\right)_{windows} + \left(\dfrac{L\,I}{2}\right)_{doors}$

where L is feet of crack, I is infiltration from Table 4.26 (ft³/hr-ft), and infiltration rate is (ft³/hr).

Finally, heat loss due to infiltration is simply

E. 4.49 $\ q = 0.018\,(T_i - T_o) \times infiltration\ rate$

Example: Suppose a building has two 3-by-5-foot weatherstripped, double-hung, wood-sash windows of average construction, and three 2-by-4-foot nonweatherstripped windows of the same construction. The dwelling also has two well-fitted 3-by-7-foot doors on opposite sides of the building. The windows are reasonably (if not evenly) distributed around the house so we can use half of the total crack length. The wind is at 10 mph; the temperature is 70°F inside and 25°F outside. Assuming there are no windbreaks around the building, let's estimate the heat loss by infiltration.

Solution: First, we find the total crack length, or perimeter of the three types of openings, and the appropriate values of I to use in Equation 4.48. Adding up the total window and door perimeters, we find the results listed below:

	Feet of Crack L	I (ft³/hr-ft)
Weatherstripped windows	32	13
Nonweatherstripped windows	36	21
Doors	40	69

The values of I are taken directly from Table 4.26. Note the difference that weatherstripping makes on the windows! We can now compute the infiltration rate to be

$$\frac{32}{2} \times 13 + \frac{36}{2} \times 21 + \frac{40}{2} \times 69 = 1966\ ft^3/hr$$

The heat loss per degree temperature difference would be

$$0.018\,\frac{Btu}{ft^3\text{-}°F} \times 1966\ ft^3/hr = 35.4\ Btu/hr\text{-}°F$$

and under the stated conditions, the loss would be

$$35.4\,\frac{Btu}{hr\text{-}°F} \times (70 - 25)\ °F = 1593\ Btu/hr$$

When calculating infiltration heat loss by the crack method, it is a good idea to check your answer to see whether it is sufficient to cover ventilation needs of the residents. One yardstick to apply is a recommended ventilation requirement of about one-half air change per hour.

Heat Load Calculations

Thus far we have been concerned with heat loss for specific parts of a dwelling—walls, windows, doors, and so on. Now we can reconstruct the house and determine the *overall heat losses* or *heat load*.

Traditionally, these calculations have been used for sizing furnaces to meet the worst-case heating loads, those associated with the most adverse probable climatological conditions of temperature and wind. Hence the first step was to specify the *design conditions*, which usually means the temperature which is exceeded 99 percent of the time in the winter months (see Appendix 4A). From that, and the U-value techniques we have described, a worst-case heat load was determined.

In solar work we are more interested in averages—how much energy is required in a month's time? What percentage of a year's heating can be met with solar? And so on. We will, of course, be concerned with worst-case conditions if we need to size the backup furnace, but this is of secondary importance.

We will find it more useful to calculate building heat-loss factors that are independent of the outside temperature. Factors that tell us how many Btu per hour are required per degree temperature difference between the inside and the outside, or better still, how many Btu are required per day per degree temperature difference—that is, Btu/degree-day.

For any given element in a building, we are now used to calculating its UA product in Btu/hr-°F. Even the heat loss from the edge of slabs and by infiltration can be thought of as a UA product, since they can be written as so many Btu lost per hour per degree temperature difference. We will define the sum of the individual UA products for the building elements to be the total *heat-loss coefficient* for the building:

E. 4.50 $\ UA = (UA)_{walls} + (UA)_{ceiling} + (UA)_{floor}$
$\qquad\qquad + (UA)_{doors} + (UA)_{windows} + (UA)_{inf}$

Our procedure will involve setting up a table with

161

areas, U-values, and UA products for all of the building surfaces. The total UA-value will tell us the number of BTU per hour required to keep the house warm per degree of temperature difference from the inside to the outside. One result is that we can easily size an auxiliary furnace by simply multiplying the UA-value by the maximum $(T_i - T_o)$ that is to be expected.

A Conventional Dwelling

As an example, consider the simple 1500 square-foot single-story house illustrated in Figure 4.69. It rests on an unheated concrete slab with 160 feet of perimeter, which we'll edge with two feet of rigid foam insulation of conductance 0.15. The walls are of standard 2-by-4-inch construction filled with R-11 fiberglass batts. There are 300 square feet of double-pane windows and two 2-inch-thick solid wood doors. There is a ventilated attic and the ceiling has R-19 insulation in it.

Let's find the total heat-loss coefficient for the building, and while we're at it we will size a furnace. For now, let's not assume any solar heating system, though later we'll add one.

Let's start at the top and work down. Even though there is a peaked roof, the area of the ceiling is what is important, and this is 1500 square feet. To find an appropriate U-value, we look in Appendix 4E and there in Table VII we find U-values for frame construction ceilings under an unheated attic space. With R-19 insulation, read off an R-value of 20.69 between the joists and an R-value of 10.75 through the joists. We could combine these using Equation 4.40, but that is already done for us in the table. The combined result is a U-value of 0.053. For the ceiling then:

$$(UA)_{ceiling} = 0.053 \frac{Btu}{hr\text{-}ft^2\text{-}°F} \times 1500 \ ft^2 = 80 \ Btu/hr°F$$

For the walls, we go back to Table 4.24 and find an average U-value of 0.081 for 2-by-4-inch walls with R-11 insulation. We need the wall area. We'll assume standard 8-foot walls (we don't need to include the triangular gables because they are not part of the insulated building envelope). The perimeter is 160 feet so the gross wall area is $8 \times 160 = 1280$ square feet. But we must subtract the 300 square feet of windows and another 42 square feet for the two doors (we'll assume a door is roughly 3 by 7 feet). So our net wall area is 938 square feet and the UA product becomes

$$(UA)_{walls} = 0.081 \frac{Btu}{hr\text{-}ft^2\text{-}°F} \times 938 \ ft^2$$
$$= 76 \ Btu/hr\text{-}°F$$

The windows are double-pane and we'll assume a half-inch air space. Table 4.22 gives us a U-value of 0.49. So the UA product is

$$(UA)_{windows} = 0.49 \frac{Btu}{hr\text{-}ft^2\text{-}°F} \times 300 \ ft^2 = 147 \ Btu/hr°F$$

The two doors have a total area of 42 square feet and Table 4.23 indicates a U-value of 0.43 with no storm door. The UA product is then $0.43 \times 42 = 18 \ Btu/hr\text{-}°F$.

The floor is a slab with a perimeter of 160 feet. The ratio of floor area to perimeter is $1500/160 = 9.3$, which is less than 12 so we can use Equation 4.46. The perimeter has been well insulated with two feet of foam with conductance of 0.15, and Figure 4.68 gives us an F_2 factor of 0.25 Btu/hr-ft. The UA product for the floor is then

$$(UA)_{floor} = 0.25 \frac{Btu}{hr\text{-}ft} \times 160 \ ft = 40 \frac{Btu}{hr\text{-}°F}$$

Finally, we need to calculate infiltration. Let's take the

Figure 4.69 Single story house for heat loss calculation.

easy way out and use the air-change method. If this were a poorly constructed house, we might use 1 air change per hour. If it has been constructed with special care and attention to detail, we might use about ½ air change per hour. Since the designer hasn't gone all out to make this an energy-conserving house (having used only R-11 in the walls and R-19 in the ceilings), we'll assume the builders are only caulking and weatherstripping in the obvious places with a resulting infiltration rate of ⅔ of an air change per hour. The volume of the house (remember those 8-foot ceilings) is

$$1500 \ ft^2 \times 8 \ ft = 12,000 \ ft^3$$

So, using Equation 4.47 (without the ΔT) gives

$$(UA)_{inf} = 0.018 \ \frac{Btu}{ft^3 \text{-}°F} \times \frac{2}{3} \ \frac{air \ change}{hr}$$

$$\times \ 12,000 \ \frac{ft^3}{air \ change} = 144 \ Btu/hr\text{-}°F$$

We are ready now to assemble the results into a table and find the overall building heat-loss coefficient. Table 4.27 summarizes the results for this building and indicates a total heat-loss factor of 505 Btu/hr°F. Notice that in this insulated house, the windows and infiltration dominate the heat loss, each accounting for 29 percent of the total. Added wall and ceiling insulation would help but the major gains could be accomplished by tightening up the building, perhaps adding a heat recuperator on the exhausted air, and either reducing the window area or using triple glazing. In a bit, we'll see that we can get those windows working for us by having them let solar energy into the house, so let's not advocate reduced window area yet.

It is a simple step now to size an auxiliary furnace for this house for any location we choose. Suppose we want to locate it in Salt Lake City. Checking Appendix 4A, we see that the 99 percent temperature is 5°F. That is, during the winter months of December, January, and February 99 percent of the total hours are above 5°F, so let's use that as our design temperature. If we want to be able to maintain a 70°F inside temperature while it is 5°F outside, our design load, q_{design} is

Table 4.27 Heat Loss Summary for Conventional House

	Area (ft²)	U-value (Btu/hr-ft²-°F)	UA (Btu/hr-°F)	% Total
Ceiling	1500	0.053	80	16
Walls	938	0.081	76	15
Windows	300	0.49	147	29
Doors	42	0.43	18	3
Floor	(160 × 0.25)		40	8
Infiltration (0.018 × ⅔ × 12,000)			144	29
Total (UA)			505 Btu/hr-°F	

E. 4.51
$$q_{design} = UA(T_i - T_{design})$$
$$= 505 \ \frac{Btu}{hr\text{-}°F} \times (70 - 5)°F$$
$$= 32,825 \ Btu/hr$$

Given the many assumptions made in calculating this design load, it is wise to specify a furnace with somewhat greater capacity. But how much greater? A larger furnace capacity doesn't add much to the cost of the heating system, so designers used to play it safe by oversizing by typically 50 to 100 percent. While such large furnaces do assure the user that the house need never be cold, and they do allow quick warm-up of the house if necessary, they are fuel-inefficient. It is much more efficient for a smaller furnace to run somewhat continuously than for a larger one to cycle on and off repeatedly. Some building codes now restrict furnace oversizing to 30 percent, so let's use that amount.

Our furnace, then, should be specified to have an output of

E. 4.52
$$q_{furnace} = 1.3 \times q_{design}$$
$$q_{furnace} = 1.3 \times 32,825 \ Btu/hr$$
$$= 42,700 \ Btu/hr \ or$$
$$\qquad thereabouts.$$

A Superinsulated House

Suppose we rework our 1500-square-foot conventional dwelling. As designed, the conventional dwelling, with its R-11 wall insulation, R-19 ceiling insulation, double glazing, insulated slab, and relatively low air-exchange rate, would probably be considered a model of energy efficiency in most areas of the country. Let's take this insulated house and rebuild it from the top down with maximum reasonable energy efficiency in mind. We will call the result a superinsulated house after the term coined by William Shurcliff.

Starting with the ceiling, we can easily put in another layer of R-19 insulation. The original ceiling had an R-value of just about 19, so the new ceiling will be about an R-38 ($U = \frac{1}{38} = 0.026$).

The walls could be filled with R-19 insulation, if we chose to build them with 2-by-6-inch studs. Let's go a step beyond that and make an 8-inch-thick double wall with two rows of 2-by-4-inch studs separated by a 1-inch air space (Figure 4.70). Each layer of wall will be filled with R-11 insulation. To a close approximation, the thermal resistance of the wall will be that of the original wall (about R-12) plus the new R-11 added for a total R-value of about 23 ($U = \frac{1}{23} = 0.043$). We could calculate this more carefully, but given the degree of uncertainty involved in some of the other calculations (infiltration in particular), it doesn't warrant the effort.

For the windows, let's use triple glazing with ½-inch air spaces. From Table 4.22 we find the U-value to be

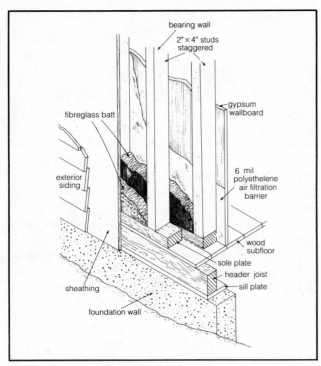

Figure 4.70 Double wall construction details.

0.31 Btu/hr-ft²-°F. We should also consider reducing the window area. The original building had 300 square feet of windows, which is equivalent to 20 percent of the floor space in glass, which is as much as many building codes allow. Whether we should reduce the window area is largely dependent on the location of the windows. South-facing windows generally let more solar energy in than they let heat out, so they should be kept. Windows on the east, west, and north sides should be reduced. Let's suppose we can eliminate 50 square feet of east, west, and north windows so that we are left with 250 square feet of glass. (The wall area will, of course, be increased by 50 square feet.)

For our doors, we will provide vestibules (small entrance halls). This way there are really two doors separating the interior heated space from the cold environment. Not only will infiltration losses be greatly controlled, but so will losses through the door itself. How shall we estimate the U-value for the resulting combination? One way would be to say it is like putting on a storm door. Looking in Table 4.23, we see storm doors reduce the U-value by nearly half. Another way to think of it is that the vestibule is an unheated adjacent space with temperature somewhere between inside and outside. Again, it seems reasonable to figure that the heat loss factor is about half the 0.43 that it would have been for a single door. Let's use a U-value of about 0.22. We'll handle the reduced infiltration around the door separately.

What about the floor slab? We are already using the maximum insulation shown in Figure 4.68. Perhaps we should abandon the slab and try another type of floor.

Unheated floor slabs, even though they are insulated, are not usually comfortable in very cold climates anyway. So let's use an elevated wood floor.

Turning to Appendix 4E, Table VII, we find "Coefficients of Transmission (U) of Frame Construction Ceilings and Floors." But since this one table covers both floors and ceilings (often one person's floor is another's ceiling), we will have to be careful in using it. For example, it says "Heat Flow Up," which is fine if it is a ceiling, but not so fine if it is a floor. Our heat flow is going down. How can we correct for this difference?

Notice the convective resistances for the top and bottom surfaces (still air) are given as 0.61. Back in Table 4.20 we see that for horizontal surfaces with heat flow down, the correct values are 0.92; so we need to pull out the two 0.61 resistances and replace them with two 0.92 resistances.

The floor/ceiling in the table has lath and plaster on its bottom surface, which is a bit silly when used as a floor. So we'll substitute something worthwhile—an inch of expanded polyurethane foam board. Appendix 4D gives a thermal conductivity of 0.16 for the polyurethane, so it has a conductive resistance of

$$R_c = \frac{1 \ inch}{0.16 \ Btu\text{-}in/ft^2\text{-}°F\text{-}hr} = 6.25 \ \frac{hr\text{-}ft^2\text{-}°F}{Btu}$$

For good measure let's put 6 inches of R-19 fiberglass batts between the joists, held up by the polyurethane. The batts don't quite fill the space, so about 1½ inches of horizontal air space remains. Table 4.21 indicates a ¾-inch air gap (downward flow) has about an R-1.02 and a 4-inch gap has R-1.23. Let's use R = 1.05 for our 1½-inch air space.

Our floor now looks like that in Figure 4.71. Using the format of Table VII in Appendix 4E, as well as many of the values there, let's tabulate the resistances both between the joists and through the joists (Table 4.28). The total thermal resistance between the joists is 29.92 and through the joists it is 18.93. With 10 percent framing, the overall U-value of the floor assembly becomes (using Equation 4.40)

$$U_{floor} = 0.1 \left(\frac{1}{18.93} \right) + 0.9 \left(\frac{1}{29.92} \right)$$
$$= 0.035 \ \frac{Btu}{hr\text{-}ft^2\text{-}°F}$$

That was a fair amount of work to go through, but it gave us a chance to exercise some of our skills as well as clarify the use of Appendix 4E, so hopefully it seemed worth it. If this floor is over a crawl space whose temperature is assumed to be midway between that of the inside and ambient, we will use an effective floor area of half the actual area. The UA product is thus

$$(UA)_{floor} = 0.035 \ \frac{Btu}{hr\text{-}ft^2\text{-}°F} \times \frac{1500 \ ft^2}{2} = 26 \ \frac{Btu}{hr\text{-}°F}$$

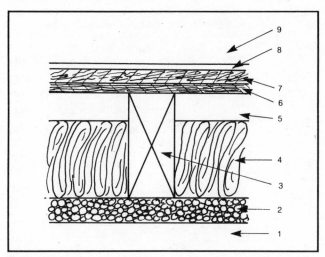

Figure 4.71 The well insulated floor for the superinsulated house (see table 4.28).

Table 4.28 Determining the Overall *U*-value for the Floor of Figure 4.71

| | Resistance | |
Construction	Between Joists	Through Joists
1. Bottom surface (still air)	0.92	0.92
2. Polyurethane (R-11 exp)	6.25	6.25
3. 2-by-8 in floor joist	—	9.06
4. R-19 insulation	19.00	—
5. Airspace, 1.5 in	1.05	—
6. Wood subfloor, 0.75 in	0.94	0.94
7. Plywood, 0.675 in	0.78	0.78
8. Resiliant tile	0.05	0.05
9. Top surface (still air)	0.92	0.92
Total thermal resistance (R)	29.92	18.93

Well, we did save some over the slab, which had a loss of 40 Btu/hr-°F.

What about infiltration losses? In the conventional dwelling, we took the short-cut approach and merely estimated the air changes per hour. Let's use this chance to redo the calculation using the crack-method.

We got the window area down to 250 square feet, but we haven't said anything about what type of windows or what sizes are involved. For purposes of analysis let us assume 10 windows, 25 square feet each, 5 feet on a side, which gives us a total perimeter of 200 feet (10 windows × 4 sides × 5 feet per side). Checking Table 4.26, at a design wind speed of 15 mph, there is quite a range of infiltration rates per foot of crack, depending on window type chosen. The best seems to be heavy casement, $1/64$-inch crack, with a loss of 18 ft³/hr-ft. Since this is to be a tight building, we'll use that.

We also have two doors, 3 by 7 feet each, with a total perimeter of 40 feet. Table 4.26 has a value of 110 ft³/hr-ft for a well-fitted door in 15 mph winds. This house, however, has vestibules which will reduce the apparent wind speed on the inner door to certainly no more than the 5-mph value given in the table. So we'll use that: 27

ft³/hr-ft. From Equation 4.48, the infiltration rate from the windows and doors (using half their crack lengths) will be

$$infiltration \ rate = \frac{200}{2} \times 18 + \frac{40}{2} \times 27$$
$$= 2340 \ ft^3/hr$$

By using polyethylene vapor and infiltration barriers in the walls we can assume the wall infiltration rate is nil and the total from the cracks around windows and doors is all that needs to be computed for the house.

The original dwelling was assumed to have $2/3$ of an air change per hour or 8000 cubic feet per hour ($2/3 \times 8$ ft × 1500 ft²). So we are considerably below that estimate. We are so low that we should check to see if this infiltration rate is sufficient to cover all the ventilation requirements. The 2340 cubic feet per hour is the same as 39 cubic feet per minute (cfm). At a recommended 25 cfm per person this is not nearly adequate for a family. In terms of air changes per hour we have

$$\frac{2340 \ ft^3/hr}{8 \ ft \times 1500 \ ft^2/air \ change} = 0.19 \frac{air \ change}{hour}$$

Both of these indicators suggest ventilation beyond the unavoidable infiltration is required. To bring us up to a recommended ½ air change per hour would require that we bring in

$$ventilation = 0.5 \frac{air \ change}{hour} \times 12,000 \frac{ft^3}{air \ change}$$
$$- 2340 \ ft^3/hr \ (inf)$$
$$= 3660 \ ft^3/hr$$

With such a tight house we can funnel the ventilation air through an air-to-air heat exchanger (Figure 4.63) to pick up some of the heat from the warm, but stale, air that is being exhausted. Let's assume a 70 percent efficiency for this heat-transfer process, so the ventilation losses become

$$(UA)_{vent} = 0.018 \frac{Btu}{ft^3 \text{-} °F} \times 3660 \frac{ft^3}{hr} \times 0.3 = 20 \frac{Btu}{hr \text{-} °F}$$

We can now assemble these totals into Table 4.29, where they are compared to the conventionally insulated house that we calculated previously.

We have been able to reduce the heating demands of what was already a quite well-insulated house in half! Houses that are built this way needn't cost a whole lot more than their conventional counterparts. Back in 1980 some builders were estimating the costs for a 1500-square-foot superinsulated dwelling at about $500 for the extra 2-by-4s for the double wall, $600 for the extra wall insulation, $600 for the added floor and ceiling insulation, $400 for the triple glazing, and $400 for the heat recu-

Table 4.29 Summary of Heat-Loss Factors for a Conventionally Insulated and Superinsulated 1500-Square-Foot-House

| | Area (ft²) | Superinsulated | | | Conventional |
		U-value	UA	% Total	UA
Ceiling	1500	0.026	39	15	80
Walls	988	0.043	42	17	76
Windows	250	0.31	77	30	147
Doors	42	0.22	9	4	18
Floor	1500/2	0.035	26	10	40
Infiltration	(0.018 × 2340)		42	16	144
Ventilation	(0.018 × 3660 × 0.3)		20	8	—
Total Heat-Loss Coefficient			255 Btu/hr-°F		505 Btu/hr-°F

perator. A total of about $2,500. Even if it is double that, it represents an addition of only a few percent to the cost of a new house.

Superinsulating a house can not only slash heating and cooling bills, but makes it all that much easier for a solar system (passive or active) to provide the other half of the heating. Some superinsulated houses already built use no auxiliary heating system at all. The solar gains from the windows plus the internal loads of people and appliances are sufficient to keep the interior cozy, even in the coldest parts of the country. The savings on a heating system can offset a good fraction of the added costs of superinsulation.

Energy Efficiency Figure of Merit

Having laboriously computed the heat-loss coefficients for modest-sized insulated and well-insulated homes, we can use the results to help us describe one measure of the relative energy efficiency of any dwelling. Let us introduce another U-factor, call it U_o, which is the overall heat-loss factor, UA(Btu/hr-°F), divided by the square feet of floor space in the house, A_{fs}.

E. 4.53 $$U_o = \frac{UA}{A_{fs}}$$

A_{fs} is not necessarily the same as the area of floor losing heat to the environment, which we called A_f. A two-story home with 1000 square feet on each floor would have 1000 square feet of floor losing heat, but 2000 square feet of living space—so A_{fs} would be 2000.

If U_o is multiplied by 24 hours per day, the result is a commonly used figure of merit for the energy efficiency of a house. It is the Btu required per square foot of floor space per degree-day.

E. 4.54 $$\text{figure of merit} = 24\frac{hr}{day} \times U_o \frac{Btu}{hr\text{-}°F\text{-}ft^2}$$
$$= 24\, U_o \frac{Btu}{ft^2\text{-}degree\text{-}day}$$

Our conventional dwelling would have a loss factor of

$$U_o = \frac{505\ Btu/hr°F}{1500\ ft^2} = 0.337 \frac{Btu}{hr\text{-}°F\text{-}ft^2}$$

and

$$24U_o = 24\frac{hr}{day} \times 0.337\frac{Btu}{hr\text{-}°F\text{-}ft^2}$$
$$= 8.1 \frac{Btu}{ft^2\text{-}degree\text{-}day}$$

The superinsulated house would have a loss factor of

$$24U_o = \frac{24\dfrac{hr}{day} \times 255\dfrac{Btu}{hr°F}}{1500\ ft^2} = 4.1 \frac{Btu}{ft^2\text{-}degree\text{-}day}$$

As these examples indicate, only modest attention to conservation can easily result in homes with losses on the order of 8 Btu/ft²-degree-day. Extremely energy-efficient homes can have losses that are half that value, while uninsulated, poorly constructed ones can easily lose twice that much.

Seasonal Heating Requirements

We have seen how easy it is to calculate the design load and furnace size for a dwelling once the overall heat loss coefficient, UA, is found. It is also very easy to calculate the monthly and annual energy demands using this same factor.

If we multiply UA (Btu/hr-°F) by 24 hours per day, the result will be the number of Btu required per day to keep the house warm for each degree of temperature difference between the inside temperature and average outside temperature. That is, $24UA$ is the number of Btu required per degree-day. Multiplying $24UA$ by monthly degree-days gives energy required per month. That is,

E. 4.55 $$Q = 24UA(DD)$$

where Q is the monthly heat required (Btu/mo); 24 is hours per day; UA is the loss coefficient (Btu/hr-°F); and (DD) is the degree-days per month (°F-days/mo).

We can do the same for annual heating requirements:

E. 4.56 $$Q_A = 24\ UA\ (DD)_A$$

where Q_A is the annual heating required (Btu/year), and $(DD)_A$ is degree-days per year (°F-days/yr).

Example: Estimate the amount of heat required in January for the 1500-square-foot conventional house designed previously. How much energy would be required annually?

Solution: We located this house in Salt Lake City, if you recall, and calculated its *UA* product to be 505 Btu/hr-°F. In Appendix 4B, we find there are 1172 degree-days in January and 6052 annually. So for January

$$Q_{Jan.} = 24\ UA(DD)_{Jan.} = 24\ \frac{hr}{day} \times 505\ \frac{Btu}{hr\text{-}°F}$$
$$\times 1172\ \frac{°F\text{-}day}{mo}$$
$$= 14.2 \times 10^6\ Btu$$

On an annual basis, the energy required is

$$Q_A = 24\ UA(DD)_A = 24 \times 505 \times 6052$$
$$= 73.4 \times 10^6\ Btu/yr$$

As it turns out, the use of degree-days with a base of 65°F in the above calculations tends to overestimate the actual heating requirements. To understand why, we should remind ourselves of the derivation of degree-days. For each day that the average ambient temperature is less than 65°F, the number of degree-days that accrue is equal to the difference between 65°F and the average outside temperature. The 65° base was chosen because it was determined that if the furnace could bring a poorly insulated house up to 65°, then the internal loads would bring the house on up to about 70°F. With even modest insulation, internal heat sources can raise the temperature to closer to 75°F as the following example illustrates.

Example: Suppose the furnace brings the 1500-square-foot conventional dwelling up to 65°F. How much warmer would the interior be if there are four people (at 250 Btu/hr each) in the house, along with a dog (at about 200 Btu/hr), and 1100 watts worth of electrical appliances operating (a single toaster uses that much!)?

Solution: First we need to add up the number of Btu of internal gain. The conversion factor for electrical loads is 3413 Btu/KWH.

$$internal\ gain = 4 \times 250\ \frac{Btu}{hr} + 200\ \frac{Btu}{hr}$$
$$+ 1100\ watts \times 3.413\ \frac{Btu}{watt\text{-}hr}$$
$$= 4950\ Btu/hr$$

Going back to our original formula (Equation 4.28),

$$q = UA\Delta T$$

$$\Delta T = \frac{q}{UA} = \frac{4950\ Btu/hr}{505\ Btu/hr\text{-}°F} = 9.8°F$$

So the loads will raise the temperature by 9.8°F above what the furnace is providing. That is, if the furnace brings the house up to 65°F, the internal loads take it on up to 74.8°F.

Since a 65°F base for degree-days tends to put an insulated house at about 75°F, we should modify our procedure for the lower thermostat settings that are advocated today. We can do that by changing the degree-day base with the aid of Figure 4.72. A 60°F base should result in an insulated house with 70°F inside temperatures; a 55°F base should yield 65°F; and so on. To use Figure 4.72, go in on the *x*-axis with the number of degree-days (base 65°F) as determined from local sources or from Appendix 4B. Find the desired interior temperature (or its corresponding degree-day base) and read off modified degree-days. The modified degree-days can then be used in Equation 4.55 to determine monthly heating requirements.

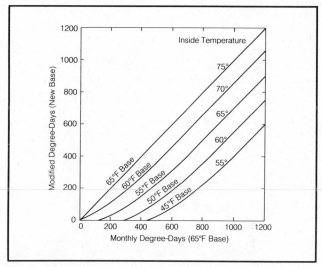

Figure 4.72 Modified degree days for differing base temperatures or thermostat settings.

Example: For our 1500-square-foot conventional dwelling with 505 Btu/hr-°F heat-loss coefficient and internal loads sufficient to keep the house 10°F above ambient, determine the additional heat required from the furnace in a January with 1172 degree-days if the thermostat is kept at 68°F.

Solution: Interpolating within Figure 4.72 at the January value of 1172 degree-days and a 68°F inside temperature we find about 960 modified degree-days. The January heating requirement would be (using Equation 4.55)

$$Q_{Jan.} = 24\ UA(DD)_{Jan.} = 24 \times 505 \times 960$$
$$= 11.6 \times 10^6\ Btu/mo$$

which is a reduction of about 19 percent compared to the 65°F-base, 75°F-interior example. Using this technique

167

on a month-by-month basis for Salt Lake City yields a total of about 4400 modified degree-days (see Table 4.30) and an annual consumption of 53.3 × 10⁶ Btu. This represents a whopping 27 percent reduction over the 75°F thermostat setting!

With our superinsulated house, the internal gains can easily keep the building 20°F above ambient and a degree-day base of something more like 48°F would be reasonable. The degree-days in Salt Lake City at this 48°F base, listed in Table 4.30, total only 2380.

Table 4.30 Modified Degree-Days for Salt Lake City

Month	Degree-Days (65°F Base)	Modified Degree-Days (58°F Base)	Modified Degree-Days (48°F Base)
Sept	81	30	0
Oct	419	240	40
Nov	849	640	370
Dec	1082	870	570
Jan	1172	960	660
Feb	910	710	410
March	763	550	270
April	459	270	60
May	233	100	0
June	84	30	0
TOTAL	6052	4400	2380

The heating requirements of the superinsulated house in Salt Lake City with the furnace bringing the house up to 48°F and the internal gains bringing it the rest of the way would require only

$$Q_A = 24\ UA(DD)_A = 24 \frac{hr}{day} \times 255 \frac{Btu}{hr\text{-}°F}$$
$$\times\ 2380\ °F\text{-}day$$
$$= 14.6 \times 10^6\ Btu/yr$$

Notice that reducing the heat-loss factor roughly in half with the extra insulation reduces the annual heating required by about a factor of four. The energy saved by reducing the heat-loss factor is compounded by the reduction in the degree-day base. This Salt Lake City example is summarized in Table 4.31.

Cost of Heating

Since we can now compute annual heating energy demand, we should be able to find the cost of that energy. Table 4.32 lists the energy content of typical heating fuels with some estimate of the efficiency with which they can be converted into Btu delivered. At the rate that energy costs are escalating, it would be silly to put any dollar costs into this table. Check with your local supplier or utility to get current prices.

Example: The 1980 cost of fuel oil is about $1.00 per gallon. Estimate the cost of keeping our conventional

Table 4.31 Space Heating Comparison for Example Houses[a]

	Heat Loss Coefficient (Btu/hr-°F)	Degree-Day Base (°F)	Modified Degree-Day (°F-day/yr)	Annual Heating (Btu/yr)
Conventional Insulation	505	58	4400	53.3 × 10⁶
Superinsulation	255	48	2380	14.6 × 10⁶

Notes: a. 5000 Btu/hr internal gains, 68° thermostat, Salt Lake City degree-days.

Table 4.32 Energy Value of Various Fuels

Fuel	Energy Content (typical units)	Representative Conversion Efficiency	Delivered Btu
Natural gas	100,000 Btu/therm	70	70,000 Btu/therm
No. 2 Fuel Oil	141,000 Btu/gal	70	98,700 Btu/gal
Propane	92,000 Btu/gal	70	64,000 Btu/gal
Coal	13,000 Btu/lb	60	7,800 Btu/lb
Electricity	3,413 Btu/kwh	100	3,413 Btu/kwh
Wood	30 × 10⁶ Btu/cord[a]	50[b]	15 × 10⁶ Btu/cord

Notes: a. Oak.
b. Air-tight wood stove.

home at 68°F through one heating season in Salt Lake City.

Solution: It was determined that this house needed 53.3 × 10⁶ Btu per heating season. At 98,700 Btu/gal delivered energy and $1.00 per gallon the annual cost would be

$$53.3 \times 10^6\ \frac{Btu}{yr} \times \frac{1\ gal}{98,700\ Btu} \times \frac{\$1.00}{gal} = \$540/yr$$

The fuel for the superinsulated house (assuming no solar gains) would cost

$$14.6 \times 10^6\ \frac{Btu}{yr} \times \frac{1\ gal}{98,700\ Btu} \times \frac{\$1.00}{gal} = \frac{\$148}{yr}$$

The extra insulation, which might cost $3,000, would be saving $392 per year at 1980 fuel prices. An extra $3,000 on a 30-year, 12 percent mortgage would add $372 per year to the mortgage payments—less than the fuel savings in the first year.

Insulate, insulate, insulate and then insulate some more!

Some Concluding Thoughts

By now you should have a good feel for heat-loss calculations. Your expertise can be used to size *any* heating system, not only solar systems. With regard to minimizing heat loss, let common sense be your guide. We would, however, like to make a few closing comments.

As you know, a poorly insulated house will require large amounts of energy to maintain a given environment. Many builders choose this option to save a few dollars on insulation; the owner is then saddled with horrendous fuel bills for the life of the home. Aside from fuel costs, these poorly insulated homes can be very uncomfortable. One subtle effect is related to the mean radiant temperature of the room. As you recall, your body can transfer significant amounts of energy by radiation. A poorly insulated house has cold interior walls and your body continually loses energy to these surfaces. To compensate, the room air temperature must be raised significantly. We've often seen temperatures close to 80°F required before the occupants felt comfortable. The higher air temperature results in more heat loss and even higher fuel bills! Even then, conditions are far from satisfactory; the air is drier and one often feels stifled. Remember: insulate to save energy *and* be comfortable.

Even in a home with good wall insulation, windows pose a problem for much the same reasons outlined above. They not only permit the escape of great amounts of energy, but they create low mean radiant temperatures. Architects usually compensate by keeping furniture away from the windows or placing a heating unit just below the window surface. The heater blankets the window with warm air, increasing the temperature of the inside surface. Of course, this compensation costs a lot in the way of energy.

Double-pane windows alleviate this situation significantly, since they have twice the thermal resistance of single-pane windows. Unfortunately, the cost is also about double that of single-pane glass—which is expensive if you've priced glass lately. Nonetheless, in virtually any climate, they will pay for themselves many times over during the life of the building. Even triple-glazed windows should be given serious consideration. Complete listings of multipane window manufacturers can be found in Sweet's *Architectural Catalog*. (This multi-volume set can be found in any major library; it contains *every* conceivable component used in building construction. We *highly* recommend this reference.)

We might say a few words about *quality* construction. Insulation will be purposeless if your house is carelessly constructed. Resulting infiltration losses can ruin the best-laid plans; window and door frames are classic culprits. If you are not absolutely certain of construction techniques, you might pick up a copy of *The Home Building Book* (D. Brown) or *Your Engineered House* (R. Roberts). Both cover all the technical details of house construction.

If you should run into a special heat-loss problem not covered here, we recommend the ASHRAE *Handbook of Fundamentals* or any of the heating and ventilating texts listed in the Bibliography. You now should have sufficient background to understand and apply anything they present.

Summary of Methodology:

Calculating Heat Loss

1. From floor plans and elevations determine the areas of walls, windows, doors, ceilings, and floors.

2. Decide upon values of insulation to use and calculate resulting *U*-values and *UA*-values for each building element.

3. Calculate infiltration losses by either the air-exchange method or the crack-method. If the crack-method is used, check whether or not excess ventilation air is liable to be required.

4. Size the auxiliary furnace by multiplying the sum of the *UA*-values by the design temperature difference. Use either the 97½ percent or 99 percent design temperatures from Appendix 4A. Add an oversizing factor of about 30 percent.

5. Calculate monthly energy requirements using monthly degree-days (Appendix 4B) modified for your desired thermostat setting (Figure 4.72). Sum them for annual heating demand. Determine the cost of heating the dwelling using current fuel cost figures.

Constructional Considerations

1. Don't skimp on insulation—fill all appropriate constructional voids.

2. Seal around windows and doors—try to use weatherstripped units. Seal walls where necessary. Draperies help reduce window losses.

3. Minimize non-south-facing window area and the number of doors in the house.

4. Double-paned windows cut heat losses in half. Storm doors can also cut heat losses. Both are good investments in colder climates.

5. By fitting south-facing windows with overhangs, we can trap solar energy during the winter, when the sun is low in the sky, and also keep out the high, hot summer sun.

6. Underground or subsurface construction has a heat-loss advantage, because ground temperatures below the freeze line are higher than ambient air temperatures. Disadvantages are higher cost, more construction labor, and the necessity of a stronger constructional design.

7. It is nearly impossible to *over*-insulate, because excess insulation costs (relatively) so little money.

8. Avoid large metal fasteners which extend completely through a wall. Because of their low *k*-value, they are heat-transfer "freeways."

9. Externally exposed flooring edges can be sources of substantial heat loss, so insulate the flooring perimeter.

10. Don't neglect ceiling (or roof) insulation; warm air rises, and the temperature differential will be greater near the ceiling, which means more potential heat loss.

11. Many insulations should not be packed, because packing destroys dead air space. Follow directions when you install insulation.

Solar Space Heating

There has evolved a hierarchy of strategies for dealing with the maintenance of a comfortable thermal environment within a building. The first priority is *energy conservation*. Until the heating requirement for a residence is reduced to its lowest practical value, it makes little sense to attempt to derive a significant fraction of that demand with solar techniques. It is generally easier and cheaper to control heat losses than to supply solar gains. The same is true on the cooling side. The best single element in a cooling strategy is simply not to let the sun and heat into the building in the first place.

The next level of energy management is on the supply side. Proper placement of windows, use of overhangs for shading, heat absorbing mass, roof ponds, thermal walls, building orientation, and so on all contribute to the collection and control of solar energy for heating. These same elements combined with operable vents and movable insulation reduce the need for cooling as well. Such techniques which do not involve pumps or blowers moving energy from a collector array to storage and from there to the house are referred to as *passive solar systems*. The house itself becomes one big combined collector and storage unit that you just happen to live in.

Active solar systems are what most people think of when they hear about solar space-heating systems. Large arrays of flat-plate collectors on the roof and a box of rocks or tank of hot water in the basement along with an assemblage of pumps, valves, blowers, and controls make up the image. The cost and complexity of active systems suggest that they be considered after conservation and passive techniques have been used to their fullest. On the other hand, the precise control of internal temperatures that active systems allow and the somewhat lesser demands placed on the design of the house itself are reasons for their being given serious consideration.

Passive Systems

The beauty of passive systems is their subtle simplicity. A properly placed tree, an overhang of just the right length,

a masonry wall here and there instead of wood-framed construction, a clerestory window bringing light and heat to a north room, a roof vent, and a damper that you open at night can all contribute greatly to the ability of a house to heat and cool itself.

To maximize the potential to utilize such passive ideas requires careful planning at the very earliest stages of design. Chapter 2 of this book highlighted such important considerations as topography, shading, prevailing wind patterns, and use of vegetation that can influence the choice of building site and you might want to go back over that material at the outset of your design.

For many of us, there may be little choice as to location of the house, but we do usually have control over its general shape and orientation. In the northern hemisphere the winter sun rises in the southeast, stays low in the sky, and sets in the southwest, exposing the south side of a building to more sun than any other wall orientation. Maximizing passive gains, then, suggests that the building have lots of south-facing surfaces with large windows. In the summer, when we don't want to heat the building, the sun is high in the sky when it is to the south, making it easy to shade those windows with simple overhangs or vine-covered trellises.

On the other hand, the morning and late-afternoon sun in the summer is low in the sky and directed against the east and west walls of the building. Moreover, since the sun is low at those times, overhangs on the east and west sides provide little shading protection (Figure 4.73). That suggests reducing the areas of these walls and minimizing the area of windows in them to help reduce the cooling load. Figure 4.73 also shows one way to use vegetation to screen east and west windows in the summer

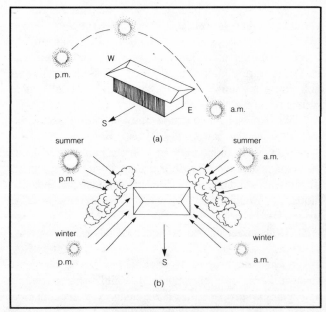

Figure 4.73 Summer shading: (a) overhangs don't work well on east and west sides; (b) proper use of vegetation can provide summer shade without blocking winter sun.

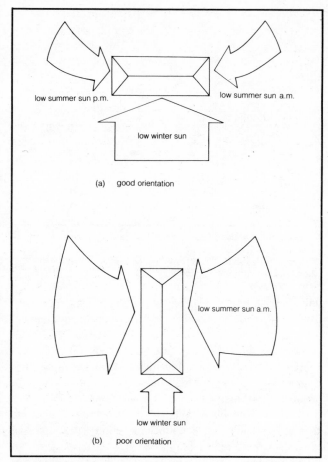

low summer sun p.m.   low summer sun a.m.

low winter sun

(a)   good orientation

low summer sun a.m.

low winter sun

(b)   poor orientation

Figure 4.74 A building with its long axis in the east west direction is easier to heat and cool.

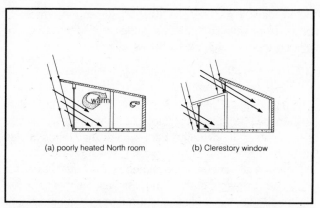

(a) poorly heated North room   (b) Clerestory window

Figure 4.75 Heating of isolated north rooms can be simplified with clerestory windows. These are examples of direct gain systems.

without reducing their winter gains. As suggested in Figure 4.74, then, a building with its long axis running east and west has a distinct advantage in both heating and cooling seasons as compared to the same building rotated so its axis runs north and south.

There is another reason for preferring an east-west building orientation, which has to do with distribution of passive gains throughout the living space. Since the sunshine is being collected on the south side it is much easier for that heat to migrate naturally to the north side of the house if the distance it has to travel is small. If the house is fairly deep, it may be necessary to force warm air into the northern rooms with a small blower. A simple approach is to use clerestory windows, which let light and heat directly into the back of the house as suggested in Figure 4.75.

Having decided on the orientation of the building, there are some guidelines that should be considered for room placement. Since the sun is going to be providing its best heating and lighting on the south side of the building, that's where the living spaces that are occupied for the greatest amount of time should be located. The north side of the house is better suited for closets, storage areas, hallways, and utility rooms. Kitchens and bathrooms can

provide some of their own heating demands during cooking and bathing times, so their location is quite flexible.

Placement of the most often used rooms can be guided somewhat by the location of the sun at different times of the day. In the morning, in the winter, you will probably want quick warm-up of your bedroom and breakfast areas, which suggests their placement on the east end of the house. During the day you will want the sun in the main living areas of the house, so they are best located on the south. In the late afternoon you may want to warm up the family room or a study, so perhaps a west-end location should be considered.

Attached garages are best located either on the north as a buffer to the cold north wind or on the west as a buffer to the late-afternoon hot summer sun (Figure 4.76).

Obviously, there is no best floor plan. We each have our own tastes and needs, but with these simple guidelines in mind, your chances of ending up with a successful design should be increased. We can now move on to the

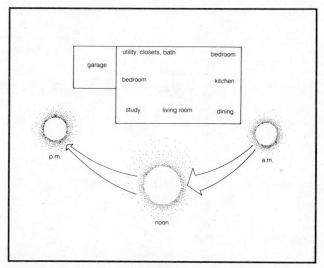

garage	utility, closets, bath	bedroom
	bedroom	kitchen
	study living room	dining

p.m.

a.m.

noon

Figure 4.76 Room placement should be influenced by the sun's trajectory.

actual design of the solar heating systems themselves. Since all passive systems take advantage of the ability of glazing to let energy into a building, let's start there.

Windows

The ability of an ordinary window to let more solar energy in than the thermal energy it loses is the essence of passive solar heating. In virtually every area of the United States outside of Alaska, a double-glazed, south-facing window will allow more energy to be gained by the house, through the heating season, than will be lost back out that window. If, in addition, movable insulation covers the windows at night, then the energy gained on even the worst days of the year will usually be more than the total day and night losses. That makes a south-facing window better than the best insulated wall.

Let's consider this phenomenon in more detail. Sunlight striking a sheet of glass is partially reflected, partially absorbed, and partially transmitted. The amount of reflection is about 8 percent for incident angles up to about 30°, rises to 15 percent at a 60° incident angle, and of course at a 90° incident angle the incoming sunlight is parallel to the glass and reflection can be considered equal to 100 percent.

The absorptance also varies with incident angle, the thickness of the glass, and its iron-oxide content. Ordinary window glass is typically ¼-inch thick, clear float, with an absorptance, at modest incident angles, of about 14 percent. That leaves about 78 percent of the incoming sunlight able to be transmitted directly through the glass.

But what happens to the energy absorbed by the glass? As Figure 4.77b suggests, some of it is radiated and convected into the house, and some goes back outside. With 15-mph winds, about 20 percent of the heat absorbed by the glass ends up in the house and 80 percent returns to the ambient. With still air inside and out, that would rise to 50 percent.

It would seem then, that a calculation for total energy

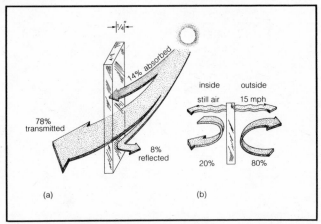

Figure 4.77 Ordinary ¼ inch clear float glaze, near normal incident angle. (a) About 78% of incoming sunlight is transmitted; (b) of the 14% absorbed, about 20% is convected and radiated into the interior when outside winds are 15 mph.

gained by a window could be quite complex, involving quality and thickness of glass, variations in incident angle, ground reflectance, and so on. Fortunately, ASHRAE publishes tables of clear sky Solar Heat Gain Factors (*SHGFs*) for vertical windows with various compass orientations for a range of latitudes. They are based on a ground reflectance of 0.2 and a single pane of ⅛-inch-thick clear float glass. When multiplied by a Shading Coefficient (*SC*) that accounts for other thicknesses of glass and numbers of panes, an overall solar gain can be found. We can write an equation for clear sky solar gains as

E. 4.57 $Q_{sg} = A \times SHGF \times SC$

where Q_{sg} is the solar energy gained by a vertical window (Btu/day), *SHGF* is the solar heat gain factor (Btu/ft²-day; see Table 4.33), *A* is the window area, (ft²); and *SC* is a dimensionless Shading Coefficient given in Table 4.34.

We know how to calculate losses from a window. On a daily basis, we can write

Latitude	24°N		32°N		40°N		48°N	
Orientation	**S**	**SE,SW**	**S**	**SE,SW**	**S**	**SE,SW**	**S**	**SE,SW**
Jan	1680	1317	1706	1279	1626	1177	1402	988
Feb	1398	1272	1560	1308	1642	1299	1626	1229
March	916	1139	1178	1234	1388	1307	1534	1344
April	488	936	720	1066	976	1193	1210	1309
May	374	788	500	930	716	1081	966	1232
June	374	724	450	867	630	1022	872	1183
July	382	773	496	913	704	1062	948	1212
Aug	486	911	704	1038	948	1161	1174	1271
Sept	902	1101	1148	1190	1344	1255	1474	1283
Oct	1350	1232	1506	1264	1582	1253	1558	1181
Nov	1650	1295	1676	1257	1596	1156	1372	968
Dec	1736	1311	1704	1240	1550	1098	1232	857

Table 4.33   Solar Heat Gain Factors (*SHGFs*) for ⅛-inch Clear Float on 21st Day of Month[a]

Notes: a. Units are Btu/ft²-day. From ASHRAE, *1977 Fundamentals*.

Table 4.34 Shading Coefficients (SC)[a]

Glazing	Shading Coefficient
⅛-in single	1.00
¼-in single	0.94
⅛-in double	0.88
¼-in double	0.81

Notes: a. From ASHRAE, 1977 *Fundamentals*

E. 4.58 $Q_L = 24\,U_w A\,(\overline{T}_i - \overline{T}_o)$

where Q_L is the loss (Btu/day); U_w is the window transmittance (Btu/hr-ft²-°F), which can be obtained from Table 4.22; 24 is hours per day; and $\overline{T}_i$ and $\overline{T}_o$ are the average inside and outside temperature over a day's time (°F).

Combining Equations 4.57 and 4.58 gives us the net solar gain for a clear day:

E. 4.59

$$Q_{net} = A\,[(SHGF)(SC) - 24\,U_w\,(\overline{T}_i - \overline{T}_o)]$$

Example: What is the net solar gain through a double-glazed, ¼-inch, south-facing window on a clear day in January when the inside temperature is held at 70° F while the ambient averages 10°F? The latitude is 48° (corresponding roughly to the U.S./Canadian border).

Solution: From Table 4.33, the Solar Heat Gain Factor is 1402 Btu/ft²-day. From Table 4.34, the Shading Coefficient for ¼-inch double glazing is 0.81. In Table 4.22 we find a U-value for the glass of 0.49 Btu/hr-ft²-°F. No window area is specified so we will do it on a square-foot basis:

$$Q_{net} = 1402\,\frac{Btu}{ft^2\text{-}day} \times 0.81 - 24\,\frac{hr}{day}$$
$$\times 0.49\,\frac{Btu}{hr\text{-}ft^2\text{-}°F} \times (70 - 10)°F$$
$$= 430\ Btu/ft^2\text{-}day$$

Thus, even under these fairly extreme conditions each square foot of window acts like a furnace delivering a net 430 Btu on a clear day in the middle of January. The temperature would have to drop to −26°F and stay there for 24 hours before the window would simply break even, with clear sky gains equalling day and night losses!

Even on cloudy days, the window can be a net gainer of energy if it is insulated at night. If an inch of urethane foam is put up over the windows at night, the energy gained on a completely overcast day is usually enough to offset day and night losses even with the ambient temperature as low as 10 or 15°F. While such temperatures are not that unusual on clear days in many of the colder parts of the country, they are not that common on cloudy days. Overcast days are usually warmer than clear ones

due to the absorption of the earth's long wave radiation by the clouds, which reduces the ease with which the earth cools. So on the coldest days it is frequently clear and the windows work very well; on the cloudy days it is frequently warmer and the windows with night insulation at least break even.

The simplest form of movable insulation is heavy drapery that fits tightly over the windows when drawn. Better still is a special insulating curtain called Window Quilt (Appropriate Technology Corporation, P.O. Box 975, Brattleboro, Vermont 05301) that reduces the U-value of double glazing to about 0.19 Btu/hr-ft²-°F when closed (Figure 4.78).

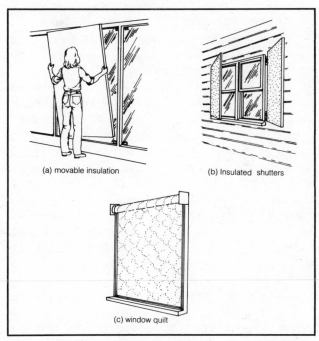

Figure 4.78 Night insulation.

There are any number of other schemes for movable insulation, ranging from simple outside shutters that are manually opened and closed to Zomeworks' Beadwall (P.O. Box 712, Albuquerque, New Mexico 87103). Beadwall consists of two sheets of glass with a 3-inch air space that can be filled with thousands of styrofoam beads at the flick of a switch. When filled, the U-value is down around 0.1. At the other end of the complexity scale, Zomeworks also sells magnetic clips that you can attach to lightweight sheets of rigid insulation. By sticking thin steel strips onto the interior side of the windows themselves, the insulation is magnetically held in place. And it is easily removed (but not so easily stored). For a whole book of insulation ideas see W. A. Shurcliff's *Thermal Shutters and Shades,* 1980.

About an inch of urethane foam can bring the overall U-value of a double-glazed window from its usual 0.49 down to about 0.11 (R-9). As a first approximation, if such insulation is left up 16 hours per day, the 24-hour

173

average U-value for the window will be about

E. 4.60 $\quad U_w = \dfrac{0.49 \times 8 + 0.11 \times 16}{24}$

$\qquad\qquad = 0.24 \ Btu/hr\text{-}ft^2\text{-}°F$

This value can be used for calculating average losses from night-insulated windows when doing the overall heat loss analysis for the house.

Direct Gain Systems

The simplest solar heating system is just an array of south windows that let the sun directly into the living space as was diagramed in Figure 4.75. In addition to the windows, a protective overhang and some heat-absorbing mass may be called for, and the resulting combination is referred to as a *direct gain system*.

Direct gain systems are popular because of their simplicity and low cost, but they are the most difficult to control of all the solar heating techniques. Consider the task of letting enough sunlight in during the day to cover the building losses at night; during the daytime collection hours, the rate of gain must be three or four times the rate at which the building is losing heat. To soak up that excess heat and thus prevent the building from being too hot during the day, the interior of the building must have a lot of mass and as much of that mass as possible needs to be directly exposed to the incoming sunlight. In the evening the warm mass cools down giving back some of its heat and thus keeping the building warm.

This process of absorption and release is a slow one and can result in fairly large temperature swings within the residence. Late afternoon temperatures 15°F warmer than early morning temperatures are probably to be expected. The greater the amount of mass included, the better the control becomes. Our job as designers will be to analyze these factors so that we get the proper balance of window area, quantity of mass, and overhang size.

Preliminary Glazing Area

Given the problems of temperature control, a very reasonable design philosophy is to put in no more window area than is required to heat the house through a 24-hour period on a clear day in the middle of winter. Since January usually has the most severe combination of temperature and solar radiation, it is usually used as the design month.

With what we already know we can write fairly easily the equations for window area that will result in clear sky gains equalling average 24-hour building losses. For the clear day gains in Btu/day (from Equation 4.57)

$$Q_{sg} = A_{dg} \times SHGF \times SC$$

For the losses we can write

E. 4.61 $\quad Q_L = 24 \ UA \ (\overline{T}_i - \overline{T}_o)$

$\qquad\qquad = 24 \ U_o A_{fs} \ (\overline{T}_i - \overline{T}_o)$

where UA is the building loss coefficient (Btu/hr-°F), $24U_o$ is the loss measured in Btu/ft²-degree-day, A_{dg} is the direct gain area (ft²), A_{fs} is the floor space area (ft²), $\overline{T}_i$ is the average interior temperature and $\overline{T}_o$ is the 24-hour average ambient temperature.

Let's solve for the ratio of window area to floor space area by setting Equation 4.57 equal to Equation 4.61:

E. 4.62 $\quad \dfrac{A_{dg}}{A_{fs}} = \dfrac{24U_o(\overline{T}_i - \overline{T}_o)}{SHGF \times SC}$

A conventionally insulated house typically has a heat-loss factor, $24U_o$, of something like 8 Btu per square foot of floor space per degree day. Using that factor the ratio of direct gain area to floor space area in Equation 4.62 has been plotted in Figure 4.79 as a function of the average 24-hour January temperature for houses at several latitudes.

A direct gain surface sized using Equation 4.62 or Figure 4.79 can be expected to capture enough energy on a clear day to maintain an average inside temperature of 65°F through a 24-hour period with no internal gains from people and appliances. Such internal loads will raise the temperature into the low 70s. Notice this is an average temperature; the amplitude of the variation above and below this average will depend on the amount of thermal mass.

Since the glazing area chosen in Figure 4.79 is

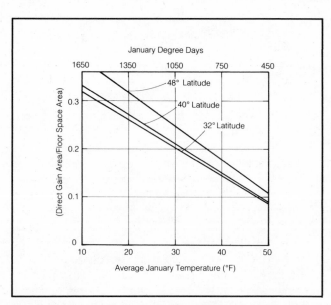

Figure 4.79 Ratio of direct gain area to floor space area required to heat a residence on a clear day in January (8 Btu/ft²-degree day house).

enough to carry the house on a clear day, we can use the percentage of sunshine in January to estimate conservatively the fraction of the January house-heating demand carried by solar.

Example: Make a preliminary sizing estimate for the recommended direct gain area for a conventional 1500-square-foot house in Salt Lake City (40° north latitude).

Solution: In Appendix 4B we find Salt Lake City has about 1172 degree-days in January. Figure 4.79 shows a ratio of gain to floor area of about 0.23. The glazing area would be 23 percent of 1500 square feet, or about 350 square feet of glass. The percent of sunshine in Salt Lake City in January is given back in Table 4.4 as 47 percent, so we would expect this much glass to carry about half the January load. That is quite a decent percentage. Usually if a solar system can provide half the January load, it will provide something like two-thirds to three-fourths of the annual heating demand.

The Solar Load Ratio Method

While Figure 4.79 is useful for a first-cut sizing of a direct gain system, it does not tell us how well the system will perform month by month. To this end, a relatively simple procedure has been devised at the Los Alamos Scientific Laboratory in New Mexico by Wray, Balcomb, and McFarland (see Bibliography) that is referred to as the Solar Load Ratio method.

The Monthly Solar Load Ratio (*SLR*) is a dimensionless parameter defined as

$$\text{E. 4.63} \quad SLR = \frac{monthly\ transmitted\ solar\ radiation}{monthly\ thermal\ load}$$

The numerator is the estimated solar radiation that passes through the glazing into the house (Btu/mo); the denominator is the thermal energy required to heat the house during that same month. The procedure involves calculating *SLR* on a month-by-month basis. Then, using a correlation based on a computer model, the monthly solar heating fraction and the auxiliary energy required are determined. The results can be summed across the full heating season to determine the annual fraction of the heating load met by the solar system.

The monthly transmitted solar radiation is potentially a difficult calculation. Clear sky values from the ASHRAE tables should not be used directly because they do not account for the average mix of clear and cloudy weather. We could take average measured horizontal insolation, use Table 4.6 to estimate insolation on a vertical surface, and then multiply the result by the average transmittance of the glass. But that is a time-consuming task. Realizing these complexities, the Los Alamos team has devised a simpler procedure.

If we let Q_T be the solar energy transmitted through the south glass per unit area (Btu/ft²-mo) and A_{dg} be the direct gain area (ft²), then for any given month we can write

E. 4.64 *Monthly Transmitted Solar Radiation*

$$= Q_T A_{dg} = \left(\frac{Q_T}{Q_H}\right) \cdot Q_H \cdot A_{dg}$$

where Q_H is average measured horizontal insolation (Btu/ft²-mo) and the horizontal-to-vertical factor (Q_T/Q_H) can be found from Figure 4.80. Notice that (Q_T/Q_H) already includes the transmittance of the (assumed) double glazing. It also accounts for ground reflectance (a value of 0.3 is assumed). Equation 4.64 lets us calculate the numerator of the solar load ratio knowing only the window area and average horizontal insolation. The denominator, which is monthly building load, can be obtained from the building load factor times the degree days:

E. 4.65 *monthly thermal load = 24UA(DD)*

The load ratio method was derived with the usual 65°F base for degree days, which means internal loads will probably take the average temperature into the 70s. You may fine tune the procedure by using degree days modified to a lower base (as we described in an earlier section), or you can subtract internal loads from the thermal load before putting it into the *SLR* equation. Such modifications complicate matters a bit and are probably not worth doing, given the crudeness of the whole pro-

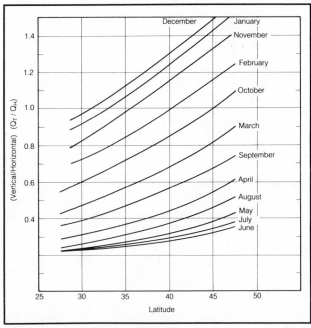

Figure 4.80 The ratio of transmitted energy to horizontal radiation, (Q_T/Q_H). Derived from Balcomb, et. al., 2nd Passive Solar Conference, 1978.

cedure. The results should be conservative if internal loads are omitted.

Having defined everything well enough to calculate the Solar Load Ratio, we can go to the real quantities of interest: the fraction of the month's energy that is met by solar, called the Solar Heating Fraction (*SHF*); and the remaining energy to be supplied by the auxiliary.

The Solar Heating Fraction is obtained from Figure 4.81. Two curves are drawn, one corresponding to a direct gain situation with no night insulation, and the other for double glazing covered with R-9 insulation from 5:00 P.M. to 8:00 A.M. (If night insulation is used, a day-and-night averaged *U*-value of 0.24 Btu/hr-ft²-°F should be used in the heat-loss calculation.)

Example: Let's take a 1500-square-foot house in Salt Lake City with 350 square feet of direct gain glazing and a heat-loss factor of 530 Btu/hr-°F. Calculate the January Solar Heating Fraction.

Solution: From Appendix 4F we find the average horizontal insolation in January to be 622.1 Btu/ft²-day (which is 19,285 Btu/ft²-mo), and in Appendix 4B we find there are 1172 degree-days.

The latitude of Salt Lake City is about 40°46′ north, so from Figure 4.80 we find

$$\frac{Q_T}{Q_H} = 1.25$$

Plugging our values into Equations 4.63, 4.64, and 4.65 gives

$$
\begin{aligned}
SLR &= \frac{\left(\dfrac{Q_T}{Q_H}\right) Q_H A_{dg}}{24\,UA(DD)} \\[2mm]
&= \frac{1.25 \times 19{,}285\ \text{Btu/ft}^2\text{-mo} \times 350\ ft^2}{24\ hr/day \times 530\ \dfrac{Btu}{hr\text{-}°F} \times 1172\ \dfrac{°F\text{-}day}{mo}} \\[2mm]
&= \frac{8.4 \times 10^6}{14.9 \times 10^6} \\[2mm]
&= 0.57
\end{aligned}
$$

Nothing was said about night insulation, so we will assume none is used. From Figure 4.81 we read off a Solar Heating Fraction of about 47 percent. (That is just what we had estimated from the preliminary sizing analysis, by the way.)

We can now find the auxiliary energy (*AUX*) required in January from

E. 4.66
$$
\begin{aligned}
AUX &= (1\text{-}SHF) \times monthly\ load \\
&= (1 - 0.47) \times 24 \times 530 \times 1172 \\
&= 7.9 \times 10^6\ Btu
\end{aligned}
$$

The analysis of this house for a complete year is

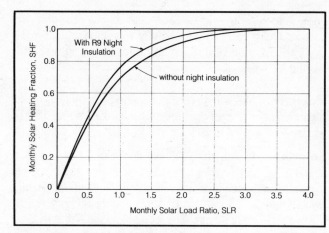

Figure 4.81 Solar heating fraction for direct gain system. (After Wray, 3rd Passive Solar Conference, 1979)

shown in Table 4.35. As can be seen, the total auxiliary requirement is 27.7×10^6 Btu per year.

The annual solar heating fraction is the fraction of the total annual load (76.9×10^6 Btu) met by the solar system.

$$
\begin{aligned}
SHF &= 1 - \left(\frac{AUX}{annual\ load}\right) \\[2mm]
&= 1 - \frac{27.7}{76.9} = 0.64
\end{aligned}
$$

In this cold area, night insulation would certainly seem called for. Let's see how much better we could do.

Example: Suppose the 350 square feet of direct gain area is insulated at night. Find the January Solar Heating Fraction and auxiliary energy requirement.

Solution: The building heat-loss coefficient of 530 Btu/hr-°F includes 350 square feet of $U = 0.49$ Btu/hr-ft²-°F double glazing. The new *U*-value for that glazing is about 0.24 Btu/hr-ft²-°F (Equation 4.60) when night insulated, which changes the building *UA* value to

$$
\begin{aligned}
UA &= 530\frac{Btu}{hr\text{-}°F} - \left(350\ ft^2 \times 0.49\frac{Btu}{hr\text{-}ft^2\text{-}°F}\right) \\[2mm]
&\quad + \left(350\ ft^2 \times 0.24\ \frac{Btu}{hr\text{-}ft^2\text{-}°F}\right) = 442\ Btu/hr\text{-}°F
\end{aligned}
$$

The new January load is thus

$$
\begin{aligned}
Q_{Jan.} &= \frac{442\ Btu}{hr\text{-}°F} \times \frac{24\ hr}{day} \times 1172\ °F\text{-}day \\[2mm]
&= 12.4 \times 10^6\ Btu
\end{aligned}
$$

The Solar Load Ratio becomes

$$SLR = \frac{8.4 \times 10^6\ Btu/mo}{12.4 \times 10^6\ Btu/mo} = 0.68$$

176

Month	Degree Days	Monthly Load (10⁶Btu)	Horizontal Insolation Q_H (10³Btu)	$\dfrac{Q_T}{Q_H}$	Monthly Transmitted (10⁶Btu)	SLR	SHF	AUX (10⁶Btu)
Sept	81	1.0	50.7	0.58	10.3	10.3	1.00	0.0
Oct	419	5.3	38.7	0.87	11.8	2.2	0.94	0.3
Nov	849	10.8	23.6	1.17	9.7	0.9	0.65	3.8
Dec	1082	13.8	17.1	1.32	7.9	0.6	0.48	7.2
Jan	1172	14.9	19.3	1.25	8.4	0.6	0.47	7.9
Feb	910	11.6	27.6	1.00	9.7	0.8	0.60	4.6
March	763	9.7	40.3	0.70	9.8	1.0	0.70	2.9
April	459	5.8	54.4	0.45	8.6	1.5	0.84	0.9
May	233	3.0	70.8	0.32	7.9	2.6	0.98	0.1
June	84	1.0	76.8	0.30	8.1	8.1	1.00	0.0
Totals	6052	76.9						27.7

and from Figure 4.81 we find

$$SHF = 0.58$$

so the January auxiliary is

$$AUX = (1 - 0.58) \times 12.4 \times 10^6 = 5.2 \times 10^6 \; Btu$$

which cuts our January fuel bill by $(7.9 - 5.2) \times 10^6$ $= 2.7 \times 10^6$ Btu, as well as leading to greater comfort within the house since the radiation cooling to the cold glass will be greatly reduced.

The Solar Heating Fraction correlations were derived for a reference design that assumes double glazing with normal transmittance of 0.747; thermal mass equivalent to a 6-inch-thick layer of concrete distributed among floor and walls so that surface area of the mass equals three times the glazing area; an air-temperature range in the building of 65 to 75°F; and no overhang was assumed so that the glazing is always fully exposed to the sun.

Let's examine some of these factors further.

Thermal Mass

The energy gains during the day in excess of the thermal demands during the day need to be stored, both to prevent daytime overheating and to provide carryover heating through the night. That energy is stored in thermal mass, usually by changing the temperature of that mass.

The amount of energy ΔQ (Btu) that a volume of mass V (ft³) soaks up as it goes through a temperature change ΔT_m (°F) is given by

E. 4.67 $\Delta Q = \rho C_p \, V \Delta T_m$

where ρ is the density of the material (lbm/ft³) and C_p is its specific heat (Btu/lbm-°F). The product of specific heat and density has units of (Btu/ft³-°F), which means it tells us the number of Btu that can be stored in one cubic foot of material as it goes through a temperature change of

1°F. The higher this number the better, if we want to keep the storage volume down.

The three most commonly used storage materials are water, concrete, and rocks, and the best way to compare these is in terms of their ρC_p product. Table 4.36 gives the appropriate values along with those for several other common building materials. In terms of energy storage per unit of volume, nothing beats water. For a given temperature increase, it is twice as good as concrete, three times as good as a rock pile, and six times as good as wood.

We said that the purpose of the mass is to soak up the excess energy gained during the daylight hours. We can write an equation for the desired amount of energy storage as

energy storage = daytime solar gains − daytime building losses

Table 4.36   Storage Properties of Thermal Mass

Material	Density, ρ (lbm/ft³)	Specific Heat, C_p (Btu/lbm°F)	ρC_p (Btu/ft³°F)
Water	62.4	1.0	62.4
Concrete (sand and gravel or stone aggregate)	140	0.22	30.8
Basalt Rock	184	0.2	36.8
Rock Pile (40% voids)	110	0.2	22.0
Gypsum Board	50	0.26	13.0
Plywood	34	0.29	9.9
Brick	120	0.19	22.8
Adobe	106	0.24	25.4

We should calculate the storage requirements based on a clear day, since that is when the maximum difference between daytime collection and loss occurs. That means we can use the clear sky Solar Heat Gain Factors and Shading Coefficients. Our losses can be determined using the heat-loss coefficient of the building, UA, and the average daytime inside and ambient temperatures T_{id} and T_{ad}. The energy to be stored, ΔQ, is the difference between gains and losses, so

177

E. 4.68 $\Delta Q = \rho C_p V \Delta T_m$

$$= A_{dg} \times SHGF \times SC - UA(\overline{T}_{id} - \overline{T}_{ad})t_d$$

where t_d is the number of hours during a clear day that the window is transmitting energy and V is the volume of mass that increases in temperature ΔT_m.

What values shall we use for all of the variables in Equation 4.68? First we should pick a design month, and January is a logical choice. Given the combination of gains, losses, and likely overhang shading, the maximum ΔQ is likely to occur then. $SHGF$ and SC can be determined from Tables 4.33 and 4.34, A_{dg} is just the direct gain area, ρC_p will depend on the storage medium, and UA is found from a heat-loss calculation. All those factors are straightforward. For the rest, we need to exercise some amount of judgment that ranges from quite straightforward estimates to seat-of-the-pants guesswork.

An estimate for the average daytime interior air temperature, $\overline{T}_{id}$, is easy enough to make. Suppose we are hoping to have the house swing through only a 10°F temperature range, that is from say 75°F during the day to 65°F at night. We could then estimate the daytime temperature inside to be about 75°F.

To estimate the average daytime ambient temperature, $\overline{T}_{ad}$, we can use the values given in Appendix 4F or, if your city is not listed, we can use monthly degree–days to find a reasonable value. The 24-hour average ambient temperature in January can be found using

E. 4.69 *24-hour average* $\overline{T}_a = 65 - \dfrac{(DD)_{Jan}}{31}$

The daytime average temperature can be estimated by adding 5 to 10°F to the 24-hour average.

The only remaining factors are storage volume required, $V(ft^3)$, its temperature swing, ΔT_m, and the day length, t_d. For day length, about 7 hours seems reasonable. The volume is what we are looking for so that is OK. The real guesstimate comes in picking a value for ΔT_m. See if this seems reasonable. The sun that shines *directly* onto mass is going to cause that mass to increase by some amount, ΔT_{md}. That mass will heat the air and cause it to increase by a lesser amount, call it ΔT_{air}. That air will move around distributing its heat to *indirectly* exposed mass by convection. That indirectly exposed mass will increase in temperature by some lesser amount still, call it ΔT_{mi}. That is,

$$\Delta T_{md} > \Delta T_{air} > \Delta T_{mi}$$

which is illustrated in Figure 4.82. Let us guess that a 20°F swing in the temperature of directly exposed mass will cause the desired 10°F swing in air temperature, which will cause a 5°F swing in the temperature of mass not directly exposed to the air. That makes directly exposed

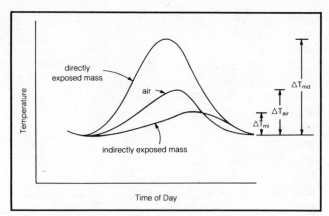

Figure 4.82 Assumed variations in air and mass temperature.

mass store four times the energy per unit volume as indirectly exposed mass, so it is four times as useful to us.

Example: For a 530 Btu/hr-°F house in Salt Lake City with 350 square feet of direct gain area, estimate the amount of directly exposed concrete that should be used for thermal storage.

Solution: Let's do it step by step, though we could just plug into Equation 4.68. The daytime gains on a clear January day will be

$$Q_{sg} = A_{dg} \times SHGF \times SC$$
$$= 350 \ ft^2 \times 1626 \ \frac{Btu}{ft^2\text{-}day} \times 0.81$$
$$= 460{,}970 \ Btu/day$$

The daytime loss will be

$$Q_L = UA(\overline{T}_{id} - \overline{T}_{ad})t_d$$
$$= 530 \ \frac{Btu}{hr\text{-}°F} \times (75 - 29.4)°F \times 7 \ hr$$
$$= 169{,}200 \ Btu/day$$

The energy to be stored is

$$\Delta Q = 460{,}970 - 169{,}200 = 291{,}770 \ Btu/day$$

If the concrete swings 20°F, then from Equation 4.67

$$V = \frac{\Delta Q}{\rho C_p \Delta T_m} = \frac{291{,}770 \ Btu/day}{\dfrac{140 \ lbm}{ft^3} \times \dfrac{0.22 \ Btu}{lbm°F} \times 20°F}$$

$$= 473 \ ft^3$$

This suggests that we need about 473 ft³/350 ft² or 1.4 cubic feet of directly exposed concrete per square foot of glass. Since only the outer few inches or so of concrete will really fluctuate through such large temperature swings, we should probably figure on at least 3 square feet of concrete surface for each cubic foot of volume calculated. That works out to be about a minimum of *four or five square feet of concrete surface for each square foot of direct gain glazing.* More would be even better.

It turns out that any house designed with the criteria for direct gain sizing used in our example will require about the same amount of mass per square foot of glazing. This is, if your glazing area was chosen to provide enough gain on a clear January day to cover a full 24 hours worth of losses, then the amount of mass required is about 1½ cubic feet of concrete per square foot of glazing. Moreover, that concrete needs to have a surface area that is exposed to the sun at some time in the day of at least four or five square feet per square foot of glazing. Four cubic feet of indirectly exposed mass can displace the need for one cubic foot of directly exposed. Concrete that is more than about four inches below the surface of a slab can count as indirectly exposed mass.

Directly exposed mass should not be covered with carpet; ceramic tile, however, works very well as a surface. You cannot oversize the mass, and the greater the surface area of mass per unit volume the more effective it will be.

If water is used as the storage medium, then only half the volume of storage is required, which works out to about *5 or 6 gallons of storage per square foot of direct gain glazing.* Since energy distributes itself very rapidly by convection within a volume of water, there is not the same concern for maximizing the surface area exposed to the sun as there is for concrete.

While these rules of thumb are probably quite reasonable (they are not dissimilar to those advocated by others, and at least the assumptions are spelled out here in case you want to deviate), remember that they apply to direct gain structures designed to completely carry a clear winter's day with the windows. If less window area is used, significantly less mass may be required. At some point, for example, there will be no need for any mass at all!

Unless the direct gain surface is large enough to cause overheating during the day, the mass is unnecessary. So, if in your present house, for example, you are tempted to put some water barrels behind a few south windows in the winter, they are probably unnecessary and you may as well let the sun come straight into the house.

Thermal mass plays an important role in any passive cooling strategy that may be as important as its role in the winter heating season. During the day in the summer, the mass absorbs heat from the interior, helping to keep the structure cool. At night the house is opened up to allow the relatively cool night air to take the heat out of the mass and carry it back outside. The natural flushing of the house can be increased with vents located at high points in the interior on the leeward side of the house and low dampers on the windward side, as suggested in Figure 4.83.

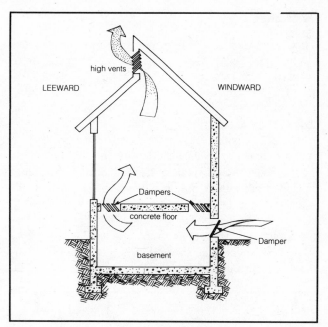

Figure 4.83 Summer night ventilation cools the mass.

An intriguing variation on the cooling of thermal mass at night has been devised by Living Systems in Winters, California (Figure 4.84). Designed for the hot Central Valley of California, the system features a rooftop evaporative "cool pool" connected to columns of water inside the house. In summer the connecting valves are opened, allowing the water to thermosiphon between the interior columns and the exterior pond. The heat absorbed by the columns during the day convects up to the roof at night, where it is cooled by evaporation.

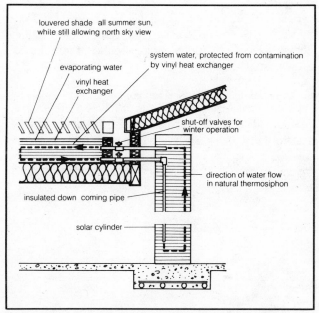

Figure 4.84 The cool pool design of Living Systems features evaporative cooling of water mass. The valves are closed in the winter (*Solar Gain*, California Office of Appropriate Technology, 1980).

Overhangs

Large expanses of windows need protection from the summer sun. South windows are well suited to the use of overhangs since the sun is so high in the sky in the summer. The trick, of course, is to design an overhang so that it keeps the sun off the windows in the summer while allowing winter sun in.

One thought would be to choose the overhang so that the windows are just shaded when the sun is at its highest on June 21st, as suggested in Figure 4.85a. If that date is chosen then the south wall will receive a fair amount of sun later in the summer when it is probably even hotter. In fact, a sliding glass door with a shade line just reaching its base at noon in June will be more than 50 percent covered by sunlight in August at noon at latitudes as far north as 40°.

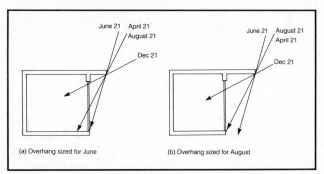

Figure 4.85 An overhang sized to shade the window in June may allow too much gain in August.

A more reasonable design would be one that shades the windows in the hot month of August, as suggested in Figure 4.85b. Picking the overhang distance, Z, that causes a shade line at noon to fall a distance of y down the south side of the building (see Figure 4.86) requires that we solve a little trigonometry problem. From the figure we can write

E. 4.70 $\qquad y = Z \tan \alpha_N$

where α_N is the altitude angle of the sun at noon, obtainable from Equations 4.1 and 4.2 or from Table 4.37.

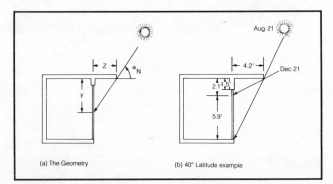

Figure 4.86 Calculating an overhang for a 6½ foot glass door in August at 40° north latitude.

Table 4.37 Sun Altitude Angle at Noon on the 21st Day of Each Month[a]

Month	α_N	Month	α_N
January	$70-L$	July	$110.6-L$
February	$80-L$	August	$102.3-L$
March	$90-L$	September	$90-L$
April	$101.6-L$	October	$79.5-L$
May	$110-L$	November	$70.2-L$
June	$113.5-L$	December	$66.5-L$

Notes: a. L stands for latitude.

To save you the trouble of solving these equations we have prepared Figure 4.87, which shows the distance y that the shade line will reach at noon for various overhang lengths on both August 21 and December 21.

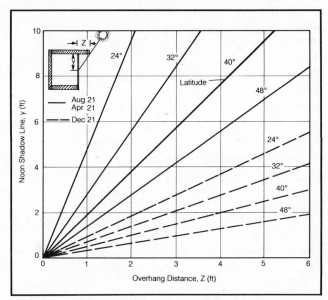

Figure 4.87 Dependence of noon shadowline on overhang distance, for various latitudes and design months.

Example: Suppose we have 6½-foot-high glass patio doors being used as direct gain surfaces on the south side of an 8-foot wall at 40° north latitude. What overhang size would result in the shade line just reaching the bottom of the doors at noon on August 21?

Solution: We can read off a distance $Z = 4.2$ feet from Figure 4.87. To see where the December shade line reaches, we use the same figure at an overhang distance of 4.2 feet and read off the shade line as $y = 2.1$ feet. So the glass will have its bottom 5.9 feet exposed at noon in December (see Figure 4.86b).

Fixed overhangs typically involve compromises. In the above example, we could shorten the overhang to let in all of the December sun, but that lets in more August sun. We are already letting in some morning and afternoon sun anyway, so reducing the overhang would not be such a good idea if summers are particularly hot.

180

Of probably more importance, by shading the glass from the August sun we are also shading it from the April sun. In many areas of the country it is still chilly in April and those direct gains would feel really good. Depending on climate, then, you might want to consider movable shading that you can adjust as the seasons progress. Better still, a trellis with leafy deciduous vines for shading (Figure 2.16) can track the seasons naturally.

Once an overhang has been designed, it may be necessary to go back over the month-by-month Solar Load Ratio calculations to reduce the Solar Radiation Transmitted calculations by the fraction of the window area that is shaded each month.

Thermal Storage Walls

Rather than distributing thermal mass among the walls and floors as is done in a direct gain system, there are some advantages to putting the mass directly behind the window, with only a few inches separating the two, as suggested in Figure 4.88. Such systems are referred to as *indirect gain* systems. If the mass is concrete or adobe, it is usually referred to as a *Trombe wall,* after its French inventor Felix Trombe. Sometimes the mass is water contained in barrels, in steel culverts set on end, or in fiberglass tubes stacked vertically one against the other, in which case the result is called a *water wall.*

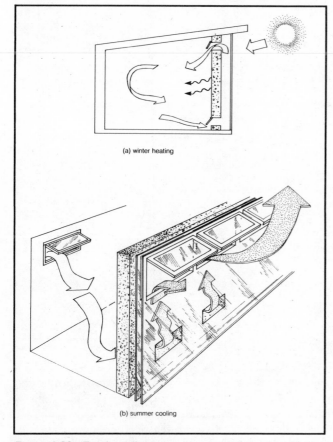

(a) winter heating

(b) summer cooling

Figure 4.88 Trombe wall system.

Thermal mass wall systems add a degree of comfort control that is hard to obtain in a direct gain system. The wall reduces daytime overheating, glare, and potential fading of fabrics by immediately capturing the incoming sunlight. In a well-designed Trombe wall, the energy captured during the day slowly works its way through the concrete by conduction and begins to emerge on the interior face in the early evening just as it is beginning to be needed the most.

Trombe walls can be designed with or without interior vents. Interior vents allow the adjacent room to be heated during the day by convection. As the air between the wall and glazing heats up during the day, it rises and passes into the room, to be replaced by cooler air taken off the floor. The vent area should be distributed evenly between upper and lower vents with their total combined area equal to about 2 percent of the wall area. It also helps to space them so that the lower vents are not directly under the upper vents. This helps distribute the air flow across the wall more evenly.

It is advantageous to design the vents so that they can be adjusted to provide anything from fully closed to fully open operation. At night they must be closed to prevent the nighttime cooling of the wall from causing reverse convective air currents. In fact, it may be that you will find the vents should always be kept closed. The vents may allow something like 30 percent of the incoming energy to be transferred directly to the interior during the day by convection. If the outside temperatures during the day are mild, or, more likely, if you can heat the house with direct gain windows during the day, you would be better off storing as much of the Trombe wall gains as possible for use at night, which means keeping the vents closed or just not putting them in in the first place. The added degree of control that the vents allow would suggest that they be put in even if you end up never opening them.

If vents are provided in the top of the glazing (Figure 4.88b) then the Trombe wall can be opened up during the summer to increase convective cooling. By closing the upper interior vents and opening the lower ones, the rising warm air in the Trombe wall air space helps to draw in cooler air from the north side of the house.

The thickness of a wall and its composition will greatly influence its performance characteristics. Masonry walls don't store as much heat per unit of volume as their water counterparts do and they don't absorb it as quickly. When the outer surface of a water wall gets warmed by the sun, convection currents quickly carry the heat away, keeping that surface cooler and reducing the losses. On the other hand, the lack of convection in a concrete wall can prove advantageous by providing a time delay of about three-quarters of an hour per inch of concrete before the inner surface reaches its peak.

If a masonry wall is too thin, there is not much storage and the resulting higher temperatures increase both the losses to the outside and interior temperature fluctuations.

And the time delays may be too short. It is recommended that concrete walls be in the range of 12 to 18 inches thick, while adobe, because of its lower conductivity, can be more like 8 to 12 inches.

Double glazing should be used for mass walls, though it does not necessarily have to be glass. Kalwall Corporation (P.O. Box 237, Manchester, New Hampshire 03105), for example, markets insulated fiberglass sheets that are much easier for the do-it-yourselfer to work than glass and cost less. Since you are not going to be looking through it anyway, the diffusion of light that it causes is of no concern. Kalwall also sells fiberglass storage tubes 12 inches or 18 inches in diameter that can be used as the water wall behind the glazing. If the tubes are filled with plain water they are somewhat translucent and the result is a very effective mass wall that also lets natural daylighting into the room.

Other manufacturers are beginning to introduce tubes containing hydrated salts, which undergo reversible chemical reactions as they absorb energy and then release it. These hydration reactions are physically similar to the phase change that occurs as a substance freezes or melts and so the salts involved are usually referred to as phase change materials (PCMs). Solids, such as ice, absorb energy when they melt and give it back when they freeze, and they do so without any temperature change. The energy stored without a change in temperature is referred to as latent heat, as opposed to the sensible heating we have dealt with so far. Some of these salts being introduced commercially can store quite a bit of energy as they pass through their melting temperature and that can be taken advantage of in a water wall. Hydrated calcium chloride ($CaCl_2 \cdot 6H_2O$), for example, melts at 81°F and, in so doing, absorbs 82 Btu per pound of material which it gives back when it freezes. One cubic foot of this material heated from 75 to 100°F stores the same amount of energy as 4.4 cubic feet of water or about 9 cubic feet of concrete heated through the same temperature range. So these salts would appear capable of storing much more energy per unit of volume than normal substances, making them an attractive option.

Mass Wall Performance

A simple model of a Trombe wall was analyzed on a computer for the first edition of this book and though the results are not transferrable for design purposes, they do give a feel for the mechanisms involved. In this model, each square foot of a 12-inch-thick concrete wall was "exposed" to 1350 Btu of solar energy per day. The solar intensity varied with time to simulate the traverse of the sun during the day. The outside temperature varied from a maximum of 70°F at 2:00 P.M. to a minimum of 30°F at 2:00 A.M. The simulated design included a ¼-inch cover glass and a 6-inch air gap. A polystyrene cover was placed over the outer glass surface at "night."

The results of the analysis are shown in Figures 4.89 and 4.90. Figure 4.89 depicts the temperature distribution in the wall at various times over a 24-hour period. The solutions reflect the conditions of the wall after five days of operation with full sun and the specified outside temperature conditions. Note that the average wall temperature is on the order of 110°F.

Figure 4.90 plots the energy flow into the room and also the energy lost from the outer wall face, both as functions of time. The units are Btu per hour per square foot of wall surface. Note that the maximum energy transfer into the room occurs around midnight and is on the order of 18 Btu/ft²-hr. The energy lost from the front face is substantial during the daylight hours, but is dramatically reduced at night with the addition of the polystyrene insulator. Much of this energy could be directed into the dwelling with an appropriate natural- or forced-convection system, as in the Trombe design. Figure 4.90 also indicates the amount of thermal energy stored as a function of time, referenced to 70°F. For instance, a 400-square-foot wall, a foot thick, would contain nearly 400,000 Btu of thermal energy at 4:00 P.M.—a substantial cushion for inclement weather.

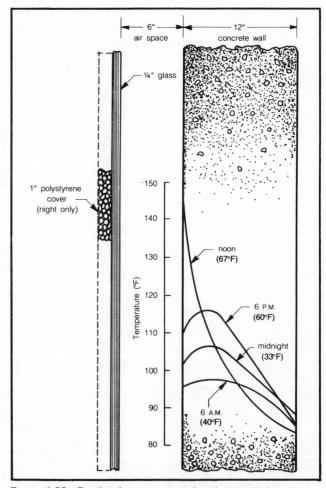

Figure 4.89 Results of a computer analysis for a south-facing concrete wall: temperature distribution as a function of time.

182

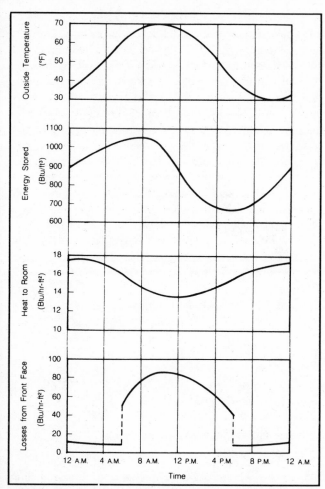

Figure 4.90 Results of a computer analysis of a south facing concrete wall: energy flows and storage capacity.

Fortunately, it is no longer necessary to have the benefits of a computer around to predict the performance of Trombe walls and water walls. The Solar Load Ratio methods developed at the Los Alamos Scientific Lab have also been applied to mass walls. The procedure is virtually the same as for direct gain *SLR* and *SHF* calculations. Let's review the steps.

1. Calculate the monthly radiation transmitted using Figure 4.80 to convert average horizontal insolation to radiation that passes into the house.

2. Calculate the monthly building load, which is the product of the building heat-loss factor in Btu/degree-day and the monthly degree-days. Internal loads may be subtracted if desired. To calculate the building heat-loss factor you will need a *U*-value for the Trombe or water wall. Appropriate values are given in Table 4.38 for walls with and without night insulation.

3. Find the Solar Load Ratio

$$SLR = \frac{monthly\ radiation\ transmitted}{monthly\ building\ load}$$

Table 4.38 *U*-Values for Direct Gain, Trombe Wall, and Water Wall Surfaces With and Without R-9 Night Insulation.[a]

	Plain Double Glazed	Night Insulation
Water Wall	0.33	0.18
18″ Trombe Wall	0.22	0.12
Direct Gain	0.49	0.24

Notes: a. After Balcomb, 2nd Passive Solar Conference 1978; units are Btu/hr-ft²-°F.

4. Using Figure 4.91 for Trombe walls or Figure 4.92 for water walls, find the monthly solar heating fractions.

5. Calculate the auxiliary energy requirements from *AUX = (1 − SHF)* × monthly load. Sum the auxiliary consumption and find the annual Solar Heating Fraction.

Example: Suppose we take our 1500-square-foot house, which has a heat-loss factor of 530 Btu/hr-°F including 350 square feet of direct gain surface, and replace the glass with a 350-square-foot Trombe wall. Find the January Solar Heating Fraction in Salt Lake City.

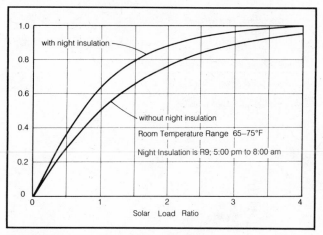

Figure 4.91 Solar heating fraction for vented, double glazed, 18-inch thick Trombe wall with backdraft dampers.

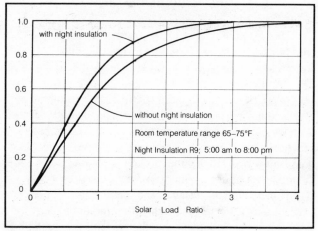

Figure 4.92 Solar heating fraction for double glazed water wall with ¾ ft³ water per square foot of glazing (Balcomb, 2nd Passive Solar Conference, 1978).

183

Solution: Getting rid of 350 square feet of direct gain surface reduces the heat-loss coefficient by

$$350 \; ft^2 \times \frac{0.49 \; Btu}{hr\text{-}ft^2\text{-}°F} = \frac{171 \; Btu}{hr\text{-}°F}$$

Replacing it with 350 square feet of Trombe wall with a U-value of 0.22 adds back in

$$350 \; ft^2 \times 0.22 \; Btu/hr\text{-}ft^2\text{-}°F = 77 \; Btu/hr\text{-}°F$$

The new heat-loss factor is therefore

$$530 - 171 + 77 = 436 \; Btu/hr\text{-}°F$$

January has 1172 degree-days (Appendix 4B) and an average horizontal insolation of 622.1 Btu/ft²-day (Appendix 4F). The horizontal-to-vertical factor, Q_T/Q_H, is 1.25 (from Figure 4.80). The Solar Load Ratio is therefore

$$
\begin{aligned}
SLR &= \frac{radiation\ transmitted}{monthly\ load} \\
&= \frac{622.1 \; Btu/ft^2\text{-}day \times 31 \; day/mo \times 1.25 \times 350 \; ft^2}{436 \; Btu/hr\text{-}°F \times 24 \; hr/day \times 1172 \; °F\text{-}day/mo} \\
&= \frac{8.44 \times 10^6 \; Btu}{12.26 \times 10^6 \; Btu} \\
&= 0.69
\end{aligned}
$$

The Solar Heating Fraction (Figure 4.91—no night insulation) is

$$SHF = 0.38$$

The auxiliary energy required is

$$
\begin{aligned}
AUX &= (1 - SHF) \times load \\
&= (1 - 0.38) \times 12.26 \times 10^6 \; Btu \\
&= 7.6 \times 10^6 \; Btu/January
\end{aligned}
$$

These answers should be compared very carefully with our earlier example, where this same house had 350 square feet of direct gain surface instead of Trombe wall. The direct gain house had a January Solar Heating Fraction of 47 percent compared to the Trombe wall house's 38 percent. That makes the direct gain house better, right? Wrong! What is really important is not the Solar Heating Fraction, but the auxiliary energy required. The direct gain house needed 7.9 million Btu in January, while the Trombe wall house needs only 7.6 million!

The difference relates to the fact that the direct gain house has a much larger heating requirement to start with since it loses so much out the glazing. This is a subtle but important point akin to watching the donut rather than the hole.

Rather than having your whole south wall in either Trombe wall, with its lack of light and view, or direct gain area, with its uncontrollability and lack of privacy, it would seem that some of each would be the best alternative. Windows in the Trombe wall, for example, can act as a direct gain area, as operable vents, and can let you reach in and do a certain amount of inside-the-glass window washing. Or the windows can be completely separated from the Trombe wall.

The Solar Load Ratio method can be applied to such mixed systems with a slight modification. First, find the overall building heat-loss factor including the mixed south wall. With that and the total gain area, a single Solar Load Ratio can be obtained. At that value of SLR find the Solar Heating Fraction that you would have gotten if the whole system were direct gain; call it SHF_{dg}. Then find the Solar Heating Fraction at that same SLR corresponding to a Trombe wall system; call it SHF_{tw}. The real Solar Heating Fraction is just a weighted estimate of the two:

E. 4.71 $\quad SHF = \dfrac{A_{dg}}{A_t} SHF_{dg} + \dfrac{A_{tw}}{A_t} SHF_{tw}$

where A_{dg} is the direct gain area, A_{tw} is the Trombe wall area, and A_t is the total gain area equal to $A_{dg} + A_{tw}$.

Other Passive Systems

There have been many other innovative approaches to the passive capture of the sun's energy for home heating and cooling that represent more radical departures from conventional architecture than the simple direct gain and mass wall systems already described.

Greenhouses

The use of an *attached greenhouse* on the south side of a house (Figure 4.93) can provide a portion of a home's heating as well as creating an environment that allows the year-round growth of plants. During the day, the excess heat generated in the greenhouse can be transferred into adjacent rooms of the house either by natural convection through operable windows or vents, or by small thermostatically activated fans. At night the greenhouse is closed off so that it does not draw heat from the main building.

Usually, the wall separating the greenhouse is a thermal storage wall that absorbs heat during the day and releases it at night into both the house and the greenhouse. Alternatively, the separating wall can be an insulated stud wall in which case the thermal mass necessary to keep the greenhouse from freezing can be provided with containers of water. Usually, 55-gallon drums are the most convenient, due to their availability and large volume of storage per container. A larger number of small containers such as 5-gallon square cans can also be used

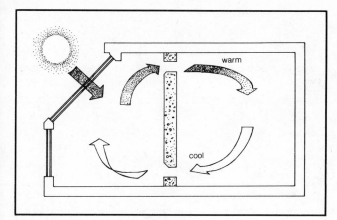

Figure 4.93 An attached greenhouse.

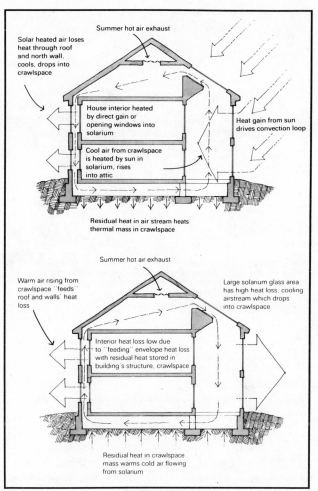

Figure 4.94 Convective loop house operation. From *The Integral Urban House,* © 1980 by the Farallones Institute.

and, in fact, are sometimes recommended over 55-gallon drums.

During the summer, the greenhouse needs to be well ventilated and must be capable of being completely isolated from the adjacent living space.

Double-Envelope Houses

Lee Porter Butler (573 Mission St., San Francisco, California 94105) has devised a rather striking variation on the use of an attached greenhouse that he calls an Ekose'a house. Others call it a convective loop house or double-envelope house because in cross section there would appear to be one house inside of another (Figure 4.94) with a convective loop between them.

As suggested in Figure 4.94, during a winter day, the warmed air in the greenhouse space rises over the roof of the inner house, and as it cools on the northern side of the loop, it falls. To complete the circuit, the air passes under the house, transferring some of its remaining heat to the "earth store." At night the process may reverse to liberate the heat from storage and thereby continue to surround the inner house with tempered air.

Another novel innovation involves the use of a "cool tube" consisting of several parallel runs of perhaps 18-inch diameter pipe laid underground. During the summer, outside air is drawn into the tube as the warm air at the peak of the house is vented. The air traveling through the tube is cooled as it passes underground and to some extent is dehumidified as the moisture condenses out.

Earth-Sheltered Housing

We all know that the temperature of the ground several feet below the surface does not change much in comparison to the daily and annual variations in the air above it. By putting the major portion of a house underground while leaving its south face open to the southern sun, we can combine the advantages of natural lighting and solar heating with the climate-moderating effects of earth mass

(Figure 4.95). The earth protects the house from both the summer heat and the winter cold, making this a particularly effective strategy in areas of the country where climate extremes are severe. An earth-sheltered house is also better protected from heat-robbing wind, so infiltration losses are cut drastically.

The temperature underground at the depths we're talking about here is certainly not constant. While it doesn't vary on a daily basis, over the course of a year it can exhibit sizable fluctuations depending on how far below the surface you go. At a depth of 4 inches, the variation in temperature about the annual mean air temperature ranges from about ± 18 to 25°F, depending on where you are in the country. Depending on soil conditions, the temperature fluctuations 10 feet below the surface may still be anywhere from plus or minus a few degrees to maybe ± 10°F about the mean. The walls of a house situated between those depths could easily be exposed to average temperatures that range between about 45°F and 65°F. Those are, however, certainly easier conditions to deal with than air temperatures that may soar over 100°F in the summer and below 0°F in the winter.

185

Figure 4.95 An underground house.

Besides damping the temperature fluctuations from winter to summer, the earth also provides a desirable flywheel effect—a time lag that can shift the peak ground temperature to early fall and the minimum ground temperature to early spring. Figure 4.96 illustrates this added bonus. As a rule of thumb, for soils with average thermal properties, this time lag amounts to about one week per foot of depth below the surface. So the underground portions of the house see their most severe environment not in January or July when air temperatures are at their extreme, but rather in March and September when the air is more comfortable.

The use of earth offers great promise as a thermal buffer, but it does require careful planning and design. The following general guidelines have been offered in a National Solar Heating and Cooling Information Center publication, *Passive Design Ideas for the Energy Conscious Builder:*

Gentle south slopes are ideal for underground structures. You can build into the hill and still have the benefits of southern exposures.

Avoid low-lying depressions. Heavy, cold air will settle in them, and there is increased danger from frost and dampness.

Make sure that surrounding construction such as parking lots and septic systems don't drain or leak into your site area.

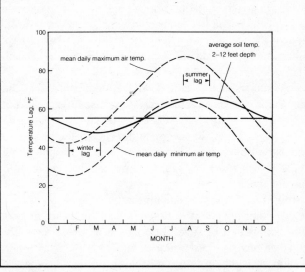

Figure 4.96 Not only does the earth provide a buffer against air temperature extremes, but it also provides a thermal lag. (After K. Labs, "Underground Building Climate," *Solar Age*, 1979).

Identify ground water levels, and seasonal variations in level, before you decide on building location and excavation depth.

Assure adequate soil percolation for sunken courtyards and atrium areas. Consider installing overflow drains if you foresee problems in this area.

Any structural system can be used—providing it is de-

signed for proper loads. A general rule is 150 pounds per square foot (PSF) for grass-covered roofs and 400 PSF where small trees are to be supported. Don't forget to add snow and pedestrian loads.

Wall design is generally the same as any below-grade construction. Insulation, however, must be placed between the earth and the exterior wall of the structure; this allows the structure to store heat, avoiding continuous loss of heat to the earth. The best currently available material is styrofoam with its closed cell construction, and the insulation can be reduced in thickness as the depth below grade increases.

When berming earth against existing walls, it's advisable to add cement plaster on metal lath between the earth and the insulation—this to prevent roots, insects and rodents from getting to the existing walls.

Butyl sheeting is a good material for waterproofing, and it also serves as a vapor barrier.

To control dampness inside, use dehumidification or circulating air.

Earth pipes (ducts buried in the earth) may be used for cooling or for prewarming outside cold air for winter fresh air supply.

Examine all local building codes, especially in relation to fire exits and ventilation. Increased air circulation may affect energy usage.

Study the lighting carefully. It is important to determine how it affects interior comfort and energy use for an underground structure.

Active Solar Heating

As was stated earlier, every new residence should be designed with energy conservation as a first priority. Beyond that, if at all possible, the building should be shaped and oriented so that it has a major axis running in the east-west direction, with its window areas concentrated on the south side. Further energy savings can be realized by applying the passive techniques of the previous section or by augmenting a conventional heating system with an active solar system.

Active systems, as we mentioned earlier, use large arrays of flat-plate collectors with pumps or blowers that force a heat-transfer fluid from collectors to storage and from storage through the home heat distribution system. They are obviously more complex than passive systems, and hence more costly and more likely to require periodic maintenance. In some circumstances, however, active systems have advantages over passive systems that justify the attention that they continue to receive.

For example, active systems with roof-mounted collectors are less likely to be plagued by shading problems. A neighbor's house or a row of trees very often can completely shade the south side of a house while leaving the roof line totally exposed to the sun. In fact, even if the entire house is shaded, active systems offer the flexibility that allows collectors to be mounted on the garage or some other adjacent building or even on a rack in the yard.

When high solar heating fractions are desired, active systems can be more akin to a conventional lifestyle than most passive systems. Especially in cold climates, most passive systems require movable insulation to be put up at night and taken down in the morning, and larger than normal inside temperature fluctuations must be expected since thermal mass serves no function unless its temperature changes.

In terms of the design of a house, active systems with their need for steeply tilted collector arrays may constrain the roof design, but passive systems with their need for large southern exposures and limited ability to distribute heat can constrain the interior design. Another hurdle with passive designs, which hopefully will be eliminated in the near future, is the difficulty associated with predicting their performance under widely varying climatic conditions and interior design constraints. Suppose the glazing is not really facing south; suppose a new owner wants carpeting over the thermal mass floor; suppose the Trombe wall overheats the adjacent space, but a back room ends up being too cold; suppose the view is to the north? As more experience with passive systems is obtained and the results more widely disseminated among designers, most of these uncertainties will be eliminated.

As a prospective user of solar energy, an understanding of both system types is important since your final decision is usually not whether to apply one or the other, but whether to use an active system to supplement whatever passive gains you have already realized.

General Systems Considerations

In the next few sections, we are concerned with the transfer of energy between the components of a heating system. Referring to Figure 4.97, you can see that there are basically two energy transfer (or circulation) loops—one between the collectors and the storage unit, and another connecting the storage system and the living space. Often (but not always) these loops are physically separated, since different collection media may be used in the respective loops.

The *collector-to-storage* or *first loop* simply transfers energy from the collector to the storage device. Of course, there *are* some subtleties involved. We must take steps to prevent freezing and minimize corrosion, and define operating strategies to optimize energy collection. The major function of the *storage-to-interior* (*second loop*) is the ef-

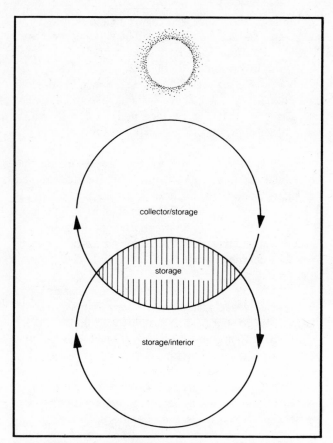

Figure 4.97 The two circulation loops of a solar heating system.

fective distribution of stored thermal energy throughout the interior environment. In many ways, this loop is more complex than the collector/storage loop. The design of a balanced and responsive distribution system requires considerable expertise. Fortunately, there is a good deal of prior art in the field of heating and ventilating, so that we can use standardized design techniques. But before discussing either loop in detail, we need to address some more general considerations.

The principal difference between one active solar heating system and another is the fluid used in the collector/storage loop. Both air and water (or water/antifreeze solutions) have been successfully used in every climatic area of the country. Cost and performance of the two system types has not differed markedly for comparably sized collector arrays. Neither has a corner on the market, which suggests that there are trade-offs involved in deciding between the two system types.

Air systems have the potential to be the more trouble-free of the two. There will never be a problem with freezing, boiling, or corrosion, and leaks are not catastrophic. That combination is enough to make them the system of choice for many users.

On the other hand, *liquid systems* use much less pumping power; the piping takes less space and is easier to route, since 1-inch water tubing, for example, can be used instead of 14-inch ducts running from collector to

storage; water storage takes about one-third the volume of an air system's rock storage bin; summer collection of energy for domestic water is more efficient with a liquid system; and finally, the liquid system interfaces with almost any heat distribution system while an air system is compatible only with forced-air distribution. These factors, which are inherent to the two system types, coupled with the wider availability of liquid system components, tend to compensate for the extra care that must be given to liquid system design. So both system types are used and recommendable.

Liquid Systems

In earlier sections of this chapter, we dealt with the design of hydronic collectors and their application to the heating of domestic water. Conceptually, the collector loop in a liquid-based space heating system is much like a large version of a solar water-heating system. There is a collector array, pump, controller, storage tank, assorted valves, and connecting piping, and there is the same concern for freeze protection.

Once energy has been collected and tucked away in the storage tank, some of it must be distributed around the house as needed and some must be used to preheat domestic water. While a great number of system variations are possible to accomplish these tasks of collection, storage, and distribution, those of Figures 4.98 and 4.99 are among the simplest and most efficient. Let's look at the way these systems work.

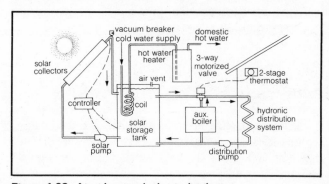

Figure 4.98 Liquid system hydronic distribution.

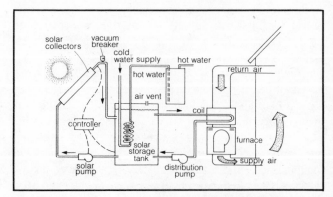

Figure 4.99 Liquid system with forced air distribution.

The collector loop in each of these system diagrams is the same. The solar pump turns on when the differential controller indicates that energy can be collected. Water is circulated through the panels and back to the storage tank. While that looks very similar to a regular domestic water-heating system, there is an important difference— a difference that goes beyond the fact that the collectors and storage are larger.

While nearly all domestic water-heater systems use pressurized tanks, the storage tanks used in solar space-heating systems are almost always unpressurized and vented to the atmosphere. Pressurized tanks in the size range we are talking about here (say 500 to 1000 gallons) are just too expensive, so systems are designed to use lighter, cheaper "atmospheric" tanks. Use of unpressurized tanks means we can protect against freezing by simply letting the system drain whenever the pump turns off, and that is what is done in Figures 4.98 and 4.99. The advantage of this method of freeze protection is simplicity and higher system efficiency. The disadvantage is that the solar pump must be big enough to raise water against the pull of gravity up and over the highest point in the collector array. A bigger pump means we'll spend a bit more on electricity to run the pump, which will reduce the overall system savings. In almost all circumstances, however, this parasitic loss is modest (especially compared to using a blower in an air system), but it does require careful selection of the pump to be used.

By putting a heat exchanger between collectors and storage, the pumping power can be reduced. In Figure 4.100(b) the heat exchanger is just a coil of copper tubing inside the storage tank; in Figure 4.100(c) it is a more efficient external heat exchanger requiring two pumps. For freeze protection, the collector loop must contain an antifreeze solution, and of course provision must be made for expansion and contraction of the collector fluid.

On particularly cloudy days, there is another bonus to using a heat exchanger in the collector loop rather than using a drainback system. A drainback system may be constantly draining and filling as clouds drift by, which is not only hard on the pump, but can also cause a fair amount of gurgling in the pipes that may be annoying. The added complexity and cost of a heat exchanger in the collector loop and the resulting decrease in performance

that the heat exchanger causes are disadvantages that need to be weighed.

Just as there are a number of variations in the way collector loops can be designed, so there are different ways that domestic water can be heated from the solar storage tank. The water in the storage tank is not only unpressurized, but is also of dubious quality, which requires, then, a heat exchanger. The heat exchanger allows full city water pressure and also protects the potable water from contamination.

The systems diagramed in Figures 4.98 and 4.99 use a one-pass heat exchanger for hot water, which is just a coil of maybe 60 to 100 feet of ¾-inch copper tubing immersed in the top of the storage tank. This approach is the ultimate in simplicity and really works quite well. A fair amount of complexity needs to be added to get only slightly better domestic water preheating. Figure 4.101 shows several recirculation schemes which are sometimes used. They involve at least one extra pump, a controller for that pump, and potentially an extra domestic water preheat tank.

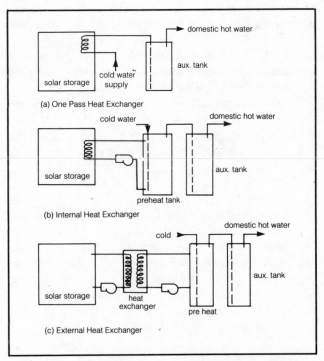

Figure 4.101 Alternative ways to preheat water for domestic use.

For space heating, the heat from solar storage must somehow be distributed around the house. In Figure 4.98, a hydronic distribution scheme is diagramed which might use baseboard heaters of the sort shown in Figure 4.102 or may involve running hot-water pipes in the floor or ceiling for radiant heating. As shown in the figure, an auxiliary boiler is located in parallel with the solar storage tank. If the solar-heated water is incapable of keeping the house warm, the three-way motorized valve closes off the

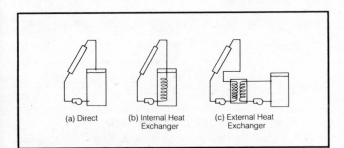

Figure 4.100 Various collector loop options (not all essential plumbing is shown).

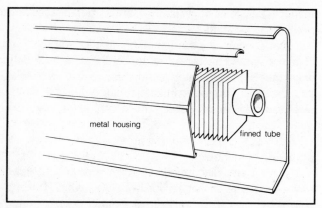

Figure 4.102 A typical baseboard unit.

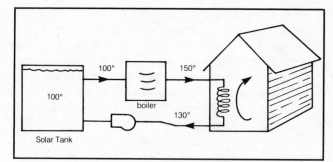

Figure 4.103 Putting the boiler in series with the tank and load is not recommended, since it may heat the solar tank.

solar loop, forcing the water to circulate through the auxiliary boiler, which then heats the interior.

Control of a hydronic baseboard distribution loop is best accomplished with what is called a two-stage thermostat. Like any thermostat, a two-stage stat lets you dial in whatever room temperature you want. Whenever the room temperature drops below that set point the first stage of the thermostat turns on the pump, which circulates water from the solar storage tank through the baseboard loop. If the room temperature drops another degree or two, the second stage of the thermostat energizes the motor-valve, which diverts the baseboard flow through the auxiliary boiler, which then heats the house.

This is a very effective control strategy that maximizes the utilization of the solar heat. Less effective control schemes usually make the decision to fall back on the boiler based on some arbitrarily fixed minimum storage temperature even though under mild heating loads a lower water temperature might still do an adequate job.

You might wonder, why not put the boiler in series with the solar storage tank instead of in parallel? If you did, you could avoid the use of the three-way valve and the more expensive two-stage thermostat; the boiler would always insure that plenty of hot water would run through the distribution loop. The problem is that the boiler can end up heating the solar tank as well as the house, as the example in Figure 4.103 indicates. Let's say the water in storage is 100°F and the boiler boosts it to 150°F. As it passes through the distribution loop, it drops typically 20° in the process of heating the house, which means 130°F-water is being returned to storage while only 100°F-water is being taken from storage. The solar storage tank will then be heated to 130° by the boiler. That reduces the collector efficiency the next day, since the collectors are always starting with a very high source temperature. The parallel boiler scheme is much more efficient, automatically squeezing the most Btu possible out of the solar system.

The forced-air auxiliary system is similar in strategy to the hydronic loop just described. The solar-heated water runs through a water-to-air heat exchanger, called a hot-water coil (Figure 4.104), on the inlet or "return" side of a conventional furnace. The solar-heated water preheats the air before it passes through the furnace. Control is again best accomplished with a two-stage thermostat that turns on the circulating pump and furnace blower with the first stage and the auxiliary with the second.

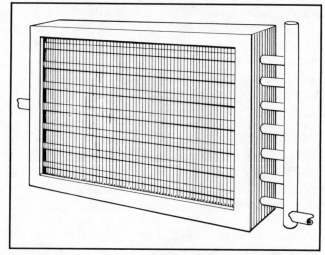

Figure 4.104 Typical water/air heat exchanger or hot-water heating coil (after Wave-Fin coils manufactured by Dunham-Bush, Inc.).

Once the system schematic is decided upon, you can move on to sizing the individual components, the most important of which are the collector array and storage tank, so let's start there.

Collector Sizing

There are a number of analytical techniques that can be used to evaluate the performance of a collector array, ranging from intelligent guessing to quite sophisticated and involved modeling. The more factors you try to include the more involved the calculations become. What we do in this section should be viewed as reasonable but not something to bet your last dollar on.

Perhaps the place to begin is by asking the question, just what fraction of your heating demands do you want to supply with solar equipment? Very small collector areas result in low equipment costs but high auxiliary fuel bills. Large collector arrays cost a lot of money but result in low auxiliary fuel costs. With appropriate estimates of equipment costs and future costs of auxiliary heating fuel we can imagine that there might be an optimum collector area that would result in the lowest combined cost of fuel and equipment. These relationships are illustrated in Figure 4.105. The location of the optimum is very closely tied to your estimate of the future costs of fuel to run your auxiliary equipment. If conventional fuels only go up modestly in cost, then a low solar heating fraction would be optimum; if they go out of sight, then a high percentage solar is best. Most now consider the optimum collector area to be one that supplies about two-thirds to three-fourths of the annual space-heating demand. Roughly translated, that means that if you can supply something like 40 or 50 percent of the January load, then the annual coverage will typically be in the two-thirds to three-fourths optimum range.

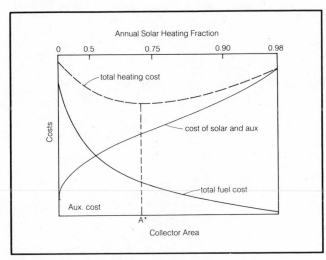

Figure 4.105 Solar system economics.

Let's work out a simple procedure that can be used to estimate the collector area required to supply a given fraction of the January load. Once that area has been found we will use a procedure known as *f*-chart to estimate the monthly and annual solar heating fractions.

Our simple procedure involves estimating the average collector efficiency on a clear day, multiplying that by the insolation on a clear day, then multiplying that by the days per month and the monthly percentage sunshine. The result is an estimate of the average energy collected in a month's time per square foot of panel, which can be used to choose a collector area.

The key assumption here is that the panels collect no energy when it is cloudy. That turns out to be a pretty good estimation, since the critical insolation required to raise water above the storage tank temperature in the winter is usually more than is coming through the clouds. Notice that this assumption would not be true for a simple

solar water heater, which can do some useful heating in cloudy weather since it gets to start with cold tap water at something like 50°F. The space heater storage tank will seldom be below about 90° to 100°F and that is too high for most collectors to reach in cold, cloudy weather.

So we need to estimate a clear sky daily collector efficiency. We can do this very carefully or we can use the broad brush approach. Let's relax and do it fairly casually. We of course need a collector efficiency curve to work with, obtainable from the collector manufacturer. Most likely you'll be using either a panel with a flat black absorber coating and double glazing or one with a selective surface and single or double glazing. For purposes of illustration, let's use the collector efficiency curve of Figure 4.106. This is an ASHRAE curve, which means the fluid parameter is in terms of collector *inlet* temperature rather than *average* fluid temperature. The curve corresponds roughly to a single-glazed, selective surface panel.

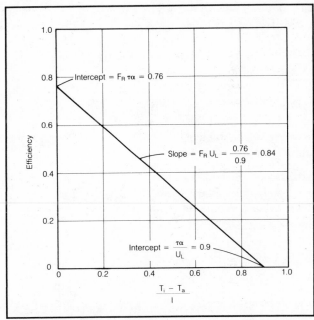

Figure 4.106 Example ASHRAE collector efficiency curve showing derivation of $F_R \tau\alpha$ and $F_R U_L$. Collector is a single glazed selective surface.

We need average values for collector inlet temperature, daytime ambient temperature, and insolation on the panel. From those we can find an average efficiency.

The inlet temperature to the panels is the temperature of the water being taken from storage, so we need an average storage temperature during the day. With storage sized the usual way at about two gallons of water per square foot of collector, a storage tank will swing in temperature by about 40°F per day. That means the average storage temperature will be about 20°F above its morning low. How low you can let the tank fall before it isn't useful for space heating depends on the characteristics of the heat distribution system. Reasonable values are 90°F for a radiant system, 100°F for a forced-air system, and 120°F for a baseboard system. So we shall assume an average inlet temperature to the panels of 110°F for a radiant slab; 120°F for a forced-air system; and 140° for a baseboard loop.

To estimate average daytime ambient temperatures you can use the values given in Appendix 4F if your city is listed; otherwise, estimate it from degree-days, by adding say 5°F to the 24-hour temperature. That is, use

E. 4.72 $$\overline{T}_{ad} = 70 - \frac{(DD)}{d}$$

where $\overline{T}_{ad}$ is the average daytime temperature, (DD) is degree–days for the month, and d is the number of days in the month.

The last factor to estimate is average hourly insolation on the panels on a clear day. Appendix 4C lists hour-by-hour values of insolation along with daily totals for various latitudes and tilt angles. It's a little sloppy, but reasonable values for average insolation can be obtained by dividing the clear day total insolation by the number of hours that the insolation is above about 80 Btu/hr-ft². That number of hours is easy to estimate from the tables.

Example: Estimate the energy collected on a clear January day in Reno (39½° north latitude) by a panel with efficiency given in Figure 4.106, tilted at a 50° angle. Assume a forced-air heating system.

Solution: Since it's a forced-air system, we'll assume an average inlet temperature, T_i, of 120°F. Let's use the degree-day approach to estimating the average daytime ambient temperature.

$$\overline{T}_{ad} = 70 - \frac{DD}{d} = 70 - \frac{1073}{31} = 35°$$

(The 1073 degree-days came from Appendix 4B.) Checking Appendix 4C at 40° north latitude and 50° tilt, we see that there are 1906 Btu/ft² on a clear day and that insolation exceeds 80 Btu/hr-ft² from 8:00 A.M. to 4:00 P.M. Our estimate for average insolation is thus

$$\overline{I} = \frac{1906 \text{ Btu/ft}^2\text{-day}}{8 \text{ hr/day}} = 238 \frac{Btu}{ft^2\text{-}hr}$$

giving us an average fluid parameter of

$$\overline{X} = \frac{\overline{T}_i - \overline{T}_{ad}}{\overline{I}} = \frac{120 - 35}{238} = 0.36 \frac{°F\text{-}hr\text{-}ft^2}{Btu}$$

From Figure 4.106 we estimate the daylong efficiency at 44 percent and the energy collected, Q_c, to be

$$Q_c = 0.44 \times 1906 = 838 \text{ Btu/ft}^2\text{-day}.$$

If 838 Btu/ft² are collected on a clear day, we can get a rough estimate of monthly energy collected by multiplying that value by the days per month and the monthly percent sunshine. Thus for Reno, with 66 percent sunshine in January (Table 4.4), we would estimate that 1 square foot would collect

$$Q_c = 838 \frac{Btu}{ft^2\text{-}day} \times 31 \frac{days}{mo} \times 0.66$$

$$= 17{,}150 \text{ Btu/ft}^2\text{-}mo$$

We are about ready to tie this all together. We can estimate monthly solar energy required by adding the hot-water load to the space-heating load. From these we can estimate collector area required.

Example: Estimate the collector area required to deliver 50 percent of the energy required in Janaury by a house in Reno with a heat load factor of 505 Btu/hr-°F and a hot-water load of 80 gallons per day brought from 60° up to 140°F. Assume a forced-air system.

Solution: First determine the loads:

$$hot\ water = 80 \frac{gal}{day} \times 8.34 \frac{lbm}{gal} \times \frac{1\ Btu}{lbm\ °F}$$

$$\times (140 - 60)°F \times 31 \frac{days}{mo}$$

$$= 1.6 \times 10^6 \text{ Btu/mo}$$

$$space\ heat = 505 \frac{Btu}{hr°F} \times 24 \frac{hr}{day} \times 1073 \frac{°F\text{-}day}{mo}$$

$$= 13.0 \times 10^6 \frac{Btu}{mo}$$

Letting L be the total load, we have

$$L = (1.6 + 13.0) \times 10^6 = 14.6 \times 10^6 \text{ Btu/mo}$$

The collector area, A_c, to deliver half that energy with a panel that delivers 17,150 Btu/ft²-mo would be

$$A_c = \frac{0.5\,L}{Q_c} = \frac{0.5 \times 14.6 \times 10^6 \text{ Btu/mo}}{17{,}150 \text{ Btu/ft}^2\text{-}mo} = 425 \text{ ft}^2$$

So we have an estimate for the collector area required to deliver half of January's hot-water and space-heating load (and therefore probably three fourths of our annual load). The procedure was simple enough to tempt us to use it month-by-month to evaluate the annual solar heating fraction. To do so would invite more error than we should feel comfortable with. As monthly solar heating fractions approach 100 percent the accuracy of this procedure drops off. Doubling the above collector area, for example, will not yield 100 percent solar heating in January, but something more like 80 percent, (the old law of diminishing returns), so we need to be careful.

The most popular method used today to estimate monthly solar heating fractions was developed at the University of Wisconsin by Beckman, Klein, and Duffie (for a complete description of the procedure see their book, *Solar Heating Design By the f-Chart Method*). Called the *f*-chart procedure, it is the result of many hundreds of computer simulations performed for both liquid and air systems. The procedure requires calculation of two dimensionless parameters, *X* and *Y*, which integrate basic information on the collector design, the building load, and local environmental conditions. These parameters are then used in Figure 4.107 (for liquid systems) or Figure 4.119 (for air systems) to find the monthly fraction, *f*.

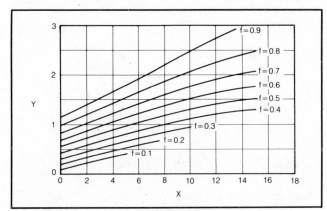

Figure 4.107 f-chart for liquid system (from *Solar Heating Design by the f-chart Method*).

The two parameters are defined as

E. 4.73 $$X = \frac{F_R'U_LA_c(T_r - \overline{T}_a)\Delta t}{L}$$

and

E. 4.74 $$Y = \frac{F_R'(\overline{\tau a})A_cH_T}{L}$$

Most of the factors in *X* and *Y* are quite straightforward:

A_c = gross collector area (ft²)
H_T = monthly average insolation on the collector surface (Btu/ft²-mo)
L = combined hot-water and space-heating load · (Btu/mo)
T_r = reference temperature = 212°F
$\overline{T}_a$ = monthly average 24-hour temperature (°F)
Δt = total number of hours in the month

There are a pair of terms that need a few words of explanation, $F_R'U_L$ and $F_R'(\overline{\tau a})$. They almost look like F_RU_L

and $F_R\tau a$, factors which can be read off of the collector efficiency curve (see Figure 4.106 or 4.29):

$F_R\tau a$ = *the vertical axis intercept of ASHRAE efficiency curve*
F_RU_L = *the slope of the ASHRAE efficiency curve*

The transmittance-absorptance product, τa, obtained from a collector efficiency curve really applies to sunlight coming in at a nearly perpendicular angle to the collector plate. The value $(\overline{\tau a})$ is a monthly average transmittance-absorptance product that has been adjusted to account for the times that incidence is not near normal. Klein recommends an approximation:

E. 4.75 $$(\overline{\tau a}) = 0.93\ \tau a$$

The other unusual term is F_R', which is the collector heat-removal factor, F_R, multiplied by a penalty factor if there is a heat exchanger in the collector loop. Analysis of the heat exchanger penalty is beyond our means here, but if there is a fairly well-designed heat exchanger in the collector loop, we can use a penalty factor of about 0.95. No heat exchanger, no penalty factor and $F_R' = F_R$.

Thus, for our purposes we have the adjustments shown in Table 4.39. Let's use the *f*-chart to work out the performance of the collector array that we sized awhile ago.

Table 4.39 Adjustments to Efficiency Curve Parameters for Use in f-Chart

	No Collector Loop Heat Exchanger	*With Collector Loop Heat Exchanger*
$F_R'\ (\overline{\tau a})$	$0.93F_R\tau a$	$0.88F_R\tau a$
$F_R'U_L$	F_RU_L	$0.95F_RU_L$

Example: Estimate the January solar heating fraction for a house in Reno with a load of 14.6 × 10⁶ Btu using 425 square feet of collector with efficiency given in Figure 4.106. Assume no heat exchanger in the collector loop. Average monthly insolation on the collector is 41,000 Btu/ft²-mo; January has 1073 degree-days.

Solution: The parameters we need for *X* and *Y* are

A_c = 425 ft²
H_T = 41,000 Btu/ft²-mo
L = 14.6 × 10⁶ Btu/mo
T_r = 212°F
$\overline{T}_a$ = $65 - \dfrac{1073}{31} = 31°F$
Δt = 31 × 24 = 744 hr

$F_R'\ (\overline{\tau a})$ = $0.93\ F_R\tau a = 0.93 \times 0.76 = 0.70$
$F_R'U_L = F_RU_L = 0.84$

193

Plugging in,

$$X = \frac{0.84 \times 425(212 - 31)744}{14.6 \times 10^6} = 3.3$$

$$Y = \frac{0.70 \times 425 \times 41,000}{14.6 \times 10^6} = 0.83$$

From Figure 4.107 at these coordinates, we find $f = 0.5$; that is, a 50 percent solar heating fraction. We certainly would have hoped for it to be about 50 percent, since that was how we found the collector area in the first place using the percent sunshine method. In Table 4.40 the rest of the months are calculated using the f-chart, and the final annual fraction works out to be

$$SHF = \left(1 - \frac{24.5}{95.9}\right) = 74.4\%$$

So it is as we suggested: sizing for 50 percent of the January load resulted in very nearly 75 percent of the annual load.

The f-chart in Figure 4.107 has been developed for a nominal value of collector flow rate equal to 0.02 gpm per square foot of collector, and a storage volume equivalent to 2 gallons of water per square foot of collector. Account is also taken of the effectiveness of the heat exchanger that heats the house. Variations in these parameters about these nominal values must be fairly large before the annual solar heating factor changes significantly. Interested readers are referred to *Solar Heating Design By the f-Chart Method.*

The f-chart can also be used to predict monthly solar fractions for a solar domestic water heater with collector loop heat exchanger as a separate system without the space-heating function. The value of Y to use is the same

as is given in Equation 4.74, but a new definition for X is used:

E. 4.76

$$X = \frac{F_R'U_L A_c (11.6 + 1.18T_w + 3.86T_m - 2.32\bar{T}_a)\Delta t}{L}$$

where

T_w = hot water temperature (e.g., 140°F)
T_m = temperature of the cold water mains (e.g., 60°F)
L = monthly hot water load (Btu/mo)

So if we were ambitious enough, we could do a month-by-month calculation that would result in an annual solar fraction that should bear greater resemblance to reality than the crude approach suggested way back in Figure 4.53.

Storage Considerations

Liquid systems invariably use a tank of water for solar energy storage. By elevating the temperature of storage, T_s, above its minimum useful temperature, T_{min}, we will store an amount of energy Q_s equal to

E. 4.77 $\quad Q_s = \rho C_p V (T_s - T_{min})$

where ρC_p is the product (62.4 lbm/ft^3 × 1 btu/lbm°F = 62.4 Btu/ft^3-°F) and V is the storage volume in cubic feet. Since ρC_p is fixed by the characteristics of water and T_{min} is essentially determined by the characteristics of the storage-to-load distribution system, the amount of energy stored depends entirely on the volume of storage and how hot we make it.

Month	Degree Days (°F-day)	Space[a] Heat Load (10⁶Btu)	Hot-[b] Water Load (10⁶Btu)	Monthly Load L (10⁶Btu)	H$_T$[c] (10³Btu)	T̄^{a} (°F)	X	Y	Solar[d] Fraction f	AUX (10⁶Btu)
Jan	1073	13.0	1.6	14.6	41	31	3.3	0.83	0.5	7.3
Feb	823	9.9	1.6	11.5	44	37	3.6	1.14	0.7	3.5
Mar	729	8.8	1.6	10.4	56	40	4.4	1.60	0.85	1.6
Apr	510	6.2	1.6	7.8	60	46	5.5	2.29	1.0	0
May	357	4.3	1.6	5.9	61	54	7.1	3.08	1.0	0
June	189	2.3	1.6	3.9	55	61	9.9	4.20	1.0	0
July	43	0.5	1.6	2.1	61	69	18.1	8.64	1.0	0
Aug	87	1.0	1.6	2.6	61	67	14.8	6.98	1.0	0
Sept	204	2.5	1.6	4.1	60	60	9.5	4.35	1.0	0
Oct	490	5.9	1.6	7.5	55	50	5.7	2.18	0.95	0.4
Nov	801	9.7	1.6	11.3	39	40	3.9	1.03	0.62	4.3
Dec	1026	12.4	1.6	14.0	37	33	3.4	0.78	0.47	7.4
TOTALS	6332	76.7	19.2	95.9	631	49				24.5

Table 4.40   An *f*-chart Example for Reno

Notes: a. Heat-loss factor = 12,100 Btu/degree-day.
   b. 80 gal/day from 60° to 140°F.
   c. From the *California Solar Data Manual*, 40° tilt.
   d. Values of $X > 18$ or $Y > 3$ imply $f = 1.0$.

These two factors, storage volume and temperature swing, can be traded off against each other. We can have a small tank that gets very hot or a large tank that is hardly elevated above its minimum useful temperature, and both can be storing the same amount of energy. Which is better? In terms of system performance, the big tank is better, since a lower storage temperature means lower inlet temperature to the collectors, which increases their efficiency. Studies of the improvement in system performance as storage volume increases indicate that there should not be less than 1 gallon of storage per square foot of collector, and moreover that not much will be gained by increasing storage beyond about 2 gallons of water per square foot of collector. The recommended amount of storage is 2 gallons per square foot.

If you recall, f-chart was derived with an assumed storage volume of 2 gallons per square foot. For other storage volumes, the correction factor of Figure 4.108 is multiplied times the X parameter to get a new value, which can be used in the chart.

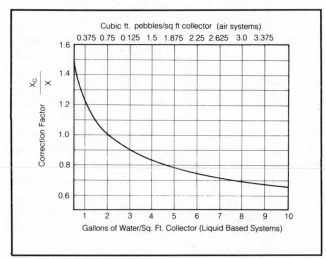

Figure 4.108 Corrections to the X-factor for different storage volumes. (from *Solar Heating Design by the f-chart Method*).

Example: Recalculate the January solar fraction for the previous example assuming 1 gallon of storage and 4 gallons of storage per square foot of collector.

Solution: The Y value stays the same, namely $Y = 0.83$. The correction factor for X at 1 gallon per foot (Figure 4.108) is 1.22, so the appropriate value to use is $X = 1.22 \times 3.3 = 4.0$. The results for all three storage volumes are assembled in Table 4.41. As can be seen, the performance changes are modest enough that we can generally skip this refinement.

Storage tanks sized at 2 gallons per square foot of collector have enough capacity to carry the house through about one day's heating demand. If you want to size the tank to give you several days' carryover, then the array must be large enough to capture more energy on a clear

Table 4.41 The Reno Example Reworked for Three Different Storage Volumes (January)

	Y	X Correction	X	f_{Jan}
1 gal/ft²	0.83	1.22	4.0	0.47
2 gal/ft²	0.83	1.0	3.3	0.50
4 gal/ft²	0.83	0.83	2.7	0.54

day than is required to heat the house for the day. That way, as you pass through a string of clear days the excess can be accumulating in storage, waiting for the cloudy period that will follow.

Another reason for deviating from the rule of thumb in storage sizing would be if your design strategy is to heat the house passively in clear weather but to heat from accumulated storage in cloudy weather. A relatively small active array with a large storage volume could be putting away Btu on clear days, to be withdrawn only during cloudy weather.

Distribution Loop Considerations

As was mentioned before, liquid systems are compatible with most heat distribution systems. While the detailed design of such distribution systems is beyond the scope of this chapter, there are some basic considerations that we can explore. Fortunately, there is considerable literature on heating-system design and a great deal of accumulated knowledge among heating contractors and mechanical engineers to refer to for a more careful exposition.

Consider first the use of baseboard heaters of the sort shown in Figure 4.102. Many people rank baseboards as one of the quietest, most comfortable heat distribution systems. They are, however, usually sized for 180°F circulating water, which we certainly aren't going to try to achieve with a solar system. If we expect to use them with solar water down around 120°F or so, we must expect to put in a considerably longer distribution loop. Usually manufacturers list performance of their baseboard units down to 150°F, but we would like to know what they'll put out at even lower temperatures. One major manufacturer (Slant/Fin Corporation, 100 Forest Dr., Greenvale, New York 11548) has tested their units at temperatures down to 90°F and published de-rating factors that we have reproduced in Table 4.42. By multiplying the rated output at 150°F by the de-rating factor at the temperature of concern, we can determine the output at the lower temperature.

For example, the Slant/Fin model 83A has a rated output at 150° of 490 Btu/hr-ft. With 120°F water running through it, the output would be reduced to 0.55 × 490 = 270 Btu/hr-ft. At this low temperature, depending on design loads, it may or may not be possible to heat the house without an unacceptably long length of baseboard. That doesn't rule out their use, however, since the auxil-

Table 4.42 De-Rating Factor for Copper-Aluminum Fin-Tube Baseboard

Water Temp. (°F)	Multiplier Times 150°F Rating	Outputs at 1 gpm (Btu/hr-ft) Model Number[a]			
		30–75	30–50	83A	81A
150	1.0	380	420	490	520
140	0.84	319	352	411	437
130	0.69	262	290	338	359
120	0.55	209	231	270	286
110	0.41	155	172	201	213
100	0.28	106	118	137	146
90	0.17	65	71	83	88

Notes: a. Slant/Fin products. Outputs at 65°F entering air.

iary boiler can always be set at a high enough temperature to assure adequate heating under the worst conditions of low solar temperature and high heating demand.

Example: Suppose a house with heat-loss factor of 505 Btu/hr-°F is located in an area with a design temperature of 10°F. What length of 83A baseboard would be required if the average loop temperature is 120°F?

Solution: The design load is

$$q = UA\Delta T = \frac{505 \; Btu}{hr\text{-}°F} \times (70 - 10)°F = 30,300 \; \frac{Btu}{hr}$$

The required baseboard length would be

$$\frac{30,300 \; Btu/hr}{270 \; Btu/ft\text{-}hr} = 112 \; ft$$

If only 90 feet could be conveniently located around the house, what temperature water would be required to heat the house under the worst conditions? The baseboard would need to put out

$$\frac{30,300 \; Btu/hr}{90 \; ft} = 336 \; Btu/hr\text{-}ft$$

Table 4.42 indicates that Model 83A can put out that much if its temperature is 130°F. The parallel auxiliary boiler should therefore be set at 130°F so it will handle the load if the solar water can't. With this shorter baseboard sometimes the solar water could handle the design load and sometimes not, and the beauty of the two-stage thermostat control described earlier is that the switching back and forth is done automatically in such a way as to maximize the use of the solar-heated water. If it is 50°F outside and it only takes 100°F water to heat the house, and if that's available in the tank, that is what will be used. The auxiliary only comes on when the combination of solar temperature, outdoor temperature, and baseboard length are insufficient to do the job.

A typical hydronic distribution system for a small

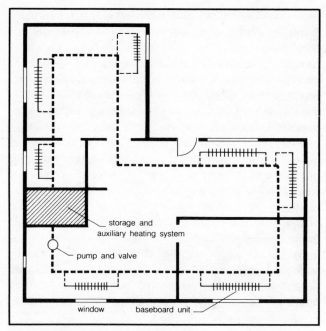

Figure 4.109 A one-pipe hydronics loop for a small building.

dwelling is sketched in Figure 4.109. This configuration is known as the "one-pipe" scheme, probably the most popular for small systems. Hot water leaves the storage tank and traverses the circulation loop, returning anywhere from 10 to 30°F cooler than when it left. Each room in the house has one or more baseboard registers which perform the actual transfer of heat into the room air. An uninsulated length of pipe would do the job, but finned pipe is much more efficient.

Figure 4.110 illustrates some of the piping details

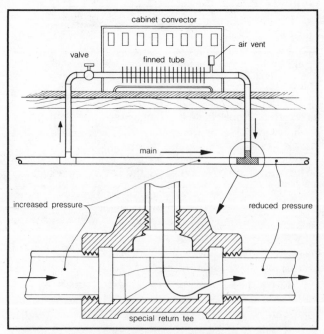

Figure 4.110 Details of plumbing to and from a baseboard convector.

used with this type of baseboard heater. The valve shown is used to control the heat flow into the room. Alternatively, many units have a louvered control which restricts natural convection around the fins, thus reducing heat transfer. The pipe tee returning from the heater is of a special "venturi" design to encourage circulation through the unit. Finally, a small air vent is provided to remove trapped air whenever necessary.

Placement of the heating units is based on the requirements in specified parts of the dwelling. They are usually located along outside walls, often directly under windows to compensate for the higher local losses. The number and/or length of the baseboard convector units in any given room depends on the design heat loss from that room. Earlier, we computed the total design heat loss from an entire building. This figure can be subdivided into individual components reflecting different rooms or sections of the house and the total feet of baseboard distributed accordingly.

Baseboard convectors aren't the only way to distribute heat throughout the dwelling. Especially in colder climates where the length of baseboard might be prohibitive and in areas where air conditioning is also required, forced-air systems make an attractive alternative.

The key design problem in such a system is the choice of the hot-water coil. You would like to choose one that allows adequate heating with the lowest possible solar storage temperature. That usually requires a pretty hefty coil with a larger than normal air-circulation rate.

You will need to look at manufacturers' specs to pick the coil. Specifications for some of the units by Magic Aire (P.O. Box 5148, Wichita Falls, Texas 76307) are presented in Table 4.43 to give you an idea of what is available.

For example, our house with a design load of 30,300 Btu/hr could be heated with only 100°F water from storage if model HW-3 is chosen. Let's see if we can't check some of the numbers given in the table for this model. If the water flow rate is the specified 7.2 gpm and if it enters at 100°F and leaves at 91.1°F, then we would expect the unit to have extracted

$$7.2 \frac{gal}{min} \times 8.34 \frac{lbm}{gal} \times 1 \frac{Btu}{lbm°F} \times (100 - 91.1)°F$$

$$\times 60 \frac{min}{hr} = 32,065 \frac{Btu}{hr}$$

That's pretty close to their rating of 32,112 Btu/hr. On the airflow side, we can also estimate the Btu delivered:

$$0.018 \frac{Btu}{ft^3\text{-}°F} \times 1200 \frac{ft^3}{min} \times 60 \frac{min}{hr} (84.6 - 60)°F$$

$$= 31,881 \frac{Btu}{hr}$$

Again, the numbers are reassuringly close to values we would have expected. That should give us some confidence in predicting the performance of the unit at other conditions.

There is a measure of heat exchanger performance that we can introduce at this point, called the *effectiveness*, ε. The heat exchanger effectiveness is simply the ratio of the actual amount of heat transferred to the air stream to the amount that would have been transferred if the air had been heated all the way up to the temperature of the entering water. It is a very intuitive notion that plays a central role in heat exchanger analysis. Since the energy transferred to the air stream is proportional to its temperature change, the effectiveness boils down to a simple ratio of temperatures:

E. 4.78 $$\varepsilon = \frac{LAT - EAT}{EWT - EAT}$$

where *LAT* is leaving air temperature, *EWT* is entering water temperature, and *EAT* is entering air temperature. For heat exchanger HW-3 at an entering water temperature of 100°F, the effectiveness would be

$$\varepsilon = \frac{84.6 - 60}{100 - 60} = 0.62$$

Table 4.43   Characteristics of Some Horizontal Solar Hot-Water Coils by Magic Aire

Model Number	Rated cfm	GPM	P.D.[a] (ft)	Entering Water 100°F			Entering Water 140°F		
				Heating Capacity (Btu/hr)	LAT[b] (°F)	LWT[c] (°F)	Heating Capacity (Btu/hr)	LAT (°F)	LWT (°F)
HW-2	800	4.8	3.48	20,926	84.0	91.3	41,665	107.8	122.6
HW-3	1200	7.2	7.65	32,112	84.6	91.1	59,051	105.1	123.6
HW-4	1600	9.6	2.89	41,637	83.9	91.3	80,131	105.9	123.3
HW-5	2000	12.0	3.98	51,808	83.9	91.4	99,642	105.7	123.4
HW-7½	3000	18.0	5.01	92,243	88.2	89.8	184,101	116.3	119.5

Notes: a. P.D. is pressure drop at design water flow rate.
   b. LAT is leaving air temperature assuming 60° entering air.
   c. LWT is leaving water temperature.

There is another unit on the market that combines the convenience of a baseboard convector with the greater heat-transfer rates that are possible when air is blown across the heat exchanger. Called a Chill Chaser (Turbonics, Inc., 11200 Madison Avenue, Cleveland, Ohio 44102), the device is a one-room heater designed to run off any source of hot water (Figure 4.111). It contains its own three-speed pump, fan, and heat exchanger designed to interface with a hot-water heater, boiler, or solar storage tank. It is especially useful when used with a slightly oversized solar hot-water system as a heater for a back room or some area of the house not adequately warmed by the central heating system. Table 4.44 gives some of the specifications.

Table 4.44	Output of a Turbonics Chill Chaser[a]				
		Entering Water Temperature			
Speed	*gpm*	*120°F*	*140°F*	*160°F*	*180°F*
Med	0.8	3600	5200	6700	8200
Med	1.0	4000	5600	7200	8700
Med	1.2	4300	5900	7400	9000
High	1.5	5150	7250	9350	11,250
High	2.0	6000	8500	11,000	13,000

Notes: a. Units are Btu/hr.

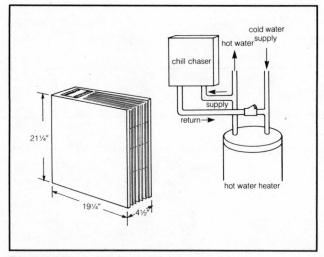

Figure 4.111 A Chill Chaser™ hot water room heater.

Pump Sizing

Collector-to-storage and storage-to-load loops require pumps to force the liquid from one place to another through combinations of pipes, valves, elbows, storage tanks, collectors, heat exchangers, and so on. An important aspect of every liquid system design is the choice of pump and pipe diameter to insure that the flow rate is sufficient to meet the design goals. A pump that is too small won't do the job and one that is too big will waste electricity unnecessarily.

The problem is to match the characteristic curve of

a pump to the characteristic curve of the system that the fluid is circulating through. The characteristics of both pump and system are expressed in terms of pressures and flow rates. The greater the flow rate desired, the more pressure the pump has to exert against the retarding friction (pressure "drops") of the fluid passages. Flow rates are usually expressed in gallons per minute (gpm), while pressures are measured either in pounds per square inch (psi) or in "feet of water." The conversion factor between feet of water and psi is easy enough to remember if you just picture a cube of water one foot high exerting its weight of 62.4 pounds onto its base of 144 square inches. One foot of water exerts a pressure of 62.4 lbm/144 square inches or 0.433 psi. So one foot of water pressure equals 0.433 psi and 1 psi equals about 2.3 feet of water.

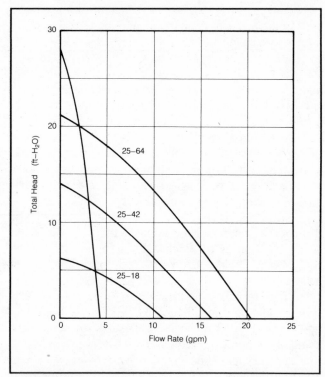

Figure 4.112 Example pump curves (25-64, 25-42, and 25-18 are Grundfos; 898 is a Richdel pump).

Figure 4.112 gives performance curves for several small pumps frequently used in solar work. The pump labeled 25-18, for example, is a Grundfos stainless steel ⅟₃₅ horsepower, 75-watt pump that is very often used in solar water heater systems. As the curve indicates, at no flow conditions this pump would be able to raise water only about 6 feet against gravity; at the other extreme, if there were no resistance to flow, this pump would deliver water at about 11 gpm. In actual operation in a closed loop it will operate somewhere between these extremes. Just where is what we need to find out.

The resistance of water pipe depends on water flow rate and pipe diameter; representative values are given in

Table 4.45. The units are feet of head per 100 feet of pipe. For example, at 2 gpm, ½-inch pipe loses 6.4 feet of head for each 100 feet of pipe, so that 50 feet of such pipe would drop the pressure by 3.2 feet of head at 2 gpm. It may sound a bit confusing to talk in terms of feet of head and feet of pipe, so we must keep them straight.

Table 4.45 Pressure Loss Due to Friction in Type M Copper Tube[a]

Flow	Nominal diameter			
gpm	½"	¾"	1"	1½"
1	1.8	0.5	—	—
2	6.4	1.2	0.5	—
3	13.1	2.3	0.7	—
4	21.6	4.1	1.2	—
5	31.7	6.0	1.6	0.2
10		19.8	5.8	0.9
15		40.5	11.5	2.1

Notes: a. Copper Development Association; units are ft-H_2O per 100 feet of tube.

Table 4.46 gives the pressure drop of various plumbing fittings expressed as equivalent lengths of pipe. For example, each ½-inch 90° Ell in a plumbing run adds to the pressure drop the same amount as would one foot of straight pipe. So we can add up all the bends and valves in a pipe run and find what equivalent length of straight pipe would have the same drop.

Table 4.46 Friction Loss in Valves and Fittings Expressed as Equivalent Length of Tube[a]

			90° Tee			
Fitting Size (in.)	Standard Ells		Side Branch	Straight Run	Gate Valve	Globe Valve
	90°	45°				
½	1.0	0.6	1.5	0.3	0.2	7.5
¾	1.25	0.75	2	0.4	0.25	10
1	1.5	1.0	2.5	0.45	0.3	12.5
1½	2.5	1.5	3.5	0.8	0.5	23

Notes: a. Copper Development Association; units are feet.

Example: Calculate the pressure drop in a plumbing run that includes 150 feet of ½-inch copper pipe, 30 90-degree elbows, and 5 open gate valves for flow rates of 1 gpm, 2 gpm, and 3 gpm.

Solution: Adding up the equivalent length of tube using Table 4.46:

150 feet of ½-inch tube	150 feet
30 ½-inch Ells @ 1.0	30 feet
5 ½-inch gate valves @ 0.2	1 foot
Total equivalent length	181 feet of pipe

Using Table 4.45 we can now figure the total pressure drop for this plumbing run at the given flow rates:

$$1\ gpm:\quad 1.8\frac{ft\text{-}H_2O}{100\ ft} \times 181\ ft = 3.3\ ft\text{-}H_2O$$

$$2\ gpm:\quad 6.4\frac{ft\text{-}H_2O}{100\ ft} \times 181\ ft = 11.5\ ft\text{-}H_2O$$

$$3\ gpm:\quad 13.1\frac{ft\text{-}H_2O}{100\ ft} \times 181\ ft = 23.7\ ft\text{-}H_2O$$

A plot of these values of flow rate and pressure drops is called the characteristic curve of the plumbing system, or just the system curve. If we plot the system curve on the same set of axes as the pump curves, the intersection points tell us the flow rates that each pump would produce. We have done this in Figure 4.113 and can now read off the answers:

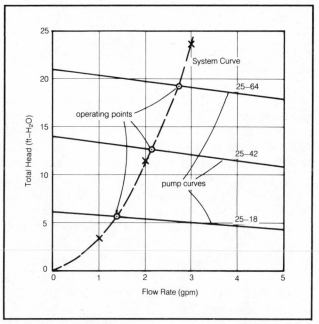

Figure 4.113 The intersection of a pump curve with the system curve shows resulting fluid flow rate.

pump 25-18	flow rate = 1.4 gpm
pump 25-42	flow rate = 2.1 gpm
pump 25-64	flow rate = 2.7 gpm

Let's make this into a little more realistic exercise by sizing a pump for a closed loop domestic water-heating system with three collector panels and a hot-water tank with internal heat exchanger. Figure 4.114 gives the manufacturer-supplied curves for the heat exchanger and a single collector, along with a sketch of the system. We will assume we have the same plumbing run as in the previous example—that is, the equivalent of 181 feet of ½-inch copper tubing.

We need to derive a new system characteristic curve to include the storage tank and collector panels. We can once again pick several flow rates and calculate resulting total loop pressure drops. We have already done it for the

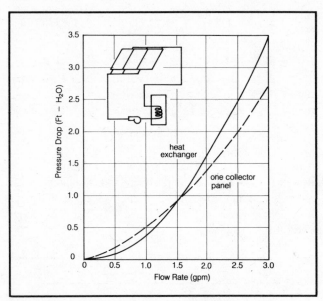

Figure 4.114 Pressure drop for internal heat exchanger storage tank and typical hydronic collector.

plumbing run at 1, 2, and 3 gpm so let's use those values and add in the effects of panels and tank. The heat exchanger is straightforward. For each flow rate, just read off the pressure drop from Figure 4.114: 1 gpm, 0.4 ft-H_2O; 2 gpm, 1.6 ft-H_2O; 3 gpm, 3.5 ft-H_2O.

What about the collectors? If the flows are balanced (and we did plumb them in reverse return fashion to help balance them), then the flow through each panel is only one-third of the total loop flow. Since the collectors are all in parallel they have the same pressure drop across each of them. We can read the collector array pressure drop then by reading the values off Figure 4.114 at values of flow equal to one-third the loop flow:

loop = 1 gpm, collector @ ⅓ gpm, drop = 0.1 ft-H_2O
loop = 2 gpm, collector @ ⅔ gpm, drop = 0.3 ft-H_2O
loop = 3 gpm, collector @ 1 gpm, drop = 0.5 ft-H_2O

These results are summarized in Table 4.47. As can be seen, the collector pressure drop is negligible in relation to the plumbing and heat exchanger. Now we can plot these points on the pump curves and find the pump that gives us whatever flow rate we desire. But what about the pumping power required to get the water all the way up

Table 4.47 Pressure Drops for a Three-Collector Array and Internal Heat Exchanger Example[a]

Loop (gpm)	Plumbing	Heat Exchanger	Three Collectors	Total
1	3.3	0.4	0.1	3.8
2	11.5	1.6	0.3	13.4
3	23.7	3.5	0.5	27.7

Notes: a. Units are ft-H_2O.

to the roof? Don't we have to add the feet of head corresponding to the feet up to the top of the collectors?

The answer is no. As long as the collector loop is completely filled with water, the energy required to lift the fluid on the supply side will be returned when it falls down the return side. It is a siphon. All the pump has to do is overcome the friction in the loop, which will let us get away with a very small pump.

Getting back to our example, what flow rate would we like? It is usual to recommend flow rates of from about 0.02 to 0.03 gpm per square foot of collector. At such rates the water will be heated by about 10 to 15°F on each pass through the collectors. Since this is a three-panel system, it probably is roughly 50 to 60 square feet in area, which means we should shoot for anywhere from about 1.0 to 1.8 gpm.

Plotting the system curve from the values in Table 4.47 onto the pump curves results in Figure 4.115. The 25-18 pump will produce about 1.3 gpm of flow while the 25-42 will yield about 1.9 gpm. Either would be fine for this application so we might as well pick the one with the lower power consumption, the 25-18.

While the example just worked was specific to a domestic water loop, the procedure is applicable to any of the hydronic loops in a liquid system. You must obtain the pressure drop curves for each of the various components of the loop and from them calculate total pressure drops in the loop for various flow rates. When these are plotted, the intersection of the resulting system curve with

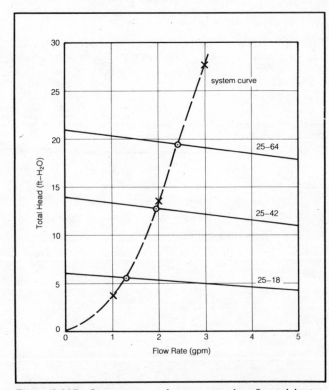

Figure 4.115 System curve and pump curves for a 3-panel, heat exchanger domestic water loop.

the pump curve gives the flow rate that would result.

Often if a single pump cannot be found which produces just the right flow rate, then a combination of pumps in series or in parallel may be used. Two equal pumps in series produce double the head for any given flow rate, and two equal pumps in parallel produce double the flow for any given head.

Solar-Assisted Heat Pumps

Since it is unlikely that your design will result in 100 percent solar heating, you will need to pick an auxiliary unit to supplement your solar gains. We have indicated rather conventional approaches in Figures 4.98 and 4.99, but there is an alternative that is especially attractive if you need summer cooling as well. The alternative is a solar-assisted water-source heat pump.

Heat pumps are not new, but they are enjoying a renewed interest in the marketplace. A heat pump can extract heat from a cold place and put it into a warmer place, which may sound a little strange until you realize that all refrigeration devices do the same thing. Your refrigerator, for example, takes heat out of the cool six-pack that you just brought home from the market, and rejects that heat out the condenser coils on the back of the refrigerator, heating the kitchen.

Imagine, if you will, removing the door of your refrigerator and moving the box to an open window. You would extract heat from the cold outdoors and pump it into the room. You could even reverse the process in the summer, turn the refrigrator around, and take heat out of the kitchen, rejecting it to the warmer outdoors. (Unfortunately, home refrigerators are not designed to handle the high heat loads of a house so our scheme is impractical.) This is just what a heat pump does, though, with an internal reversing valve arrangement, so the same unit heats in the winter and cools in the summer.

Now a heat pump doesn't do all this for free, of course; energy has a tendency to resist moving from a cold place to a warmer one so it must be forced. In a heat pump that forcing is accomplished with a motor-driven compressor. In the winter the key question, then, is how much heating we get compared to the energy required to run the compressor. The ratio of the rate at which heat is delivered to the energy required to power the system (in the same units) is called the coefficient of performance (*COP*):

$$\text{E. 4.79} \quad COP = \frac{\textit{heat to living space}}{\textit{energy input to heat pump}}$$

In other words, the *COP* is the ratio of what you get out to what you put in. The *COP* is closely tied to the temperature of the heat source: the warmer it is, the better the *COP*. The *COP* with a source temperature down around 0°F may be about 1.5, but with a source at 40 or 50°F it may be up around 2 or 3.

Heat pumps that extract energy from outside air and deliver it to the house as hot air are known as air-to-air heat pumps. Some heat pumps extract energy from a water source and are known as water-to-air heat pumps. Either can be used as a simple backup heater for a solar system, acting independently without being physically tied into the solar tank. Of the two, water-source heat pumps (for example, Vanguard Heat Pump, 9133 Chesapeake Dr., San Diego, California 92123) are perhaps the more interesting since they can extract heat from such relatively warm places as a nearby lake, or groundwater pumped from a well, or even from the ground itself if a heat exchanger is buried in the soil. And of course, if coupled with a solar system, the heat source could be a tank of solar-heated water as suggested in Figure 4.116.

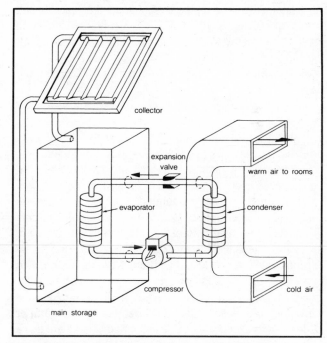

Figure 4.116 A heat pump used in conjunction with a low-temperature thermal-storage device.

In milder climates, for those fortunate enough to have a swimming pool, a solar-assisted water-source heat pump would seem to have great potential (Figure 4.117). In the winter, your unglazed collector array along with a solar pool cover may not be able to get the pool to swimmable temperatures, but it can probably hold it at a much warmer temperature than ambient. Even with the heat pump drawing energy out of the pool, the solar system may be able to hold the temperature well above the night air temperature, which means the heat pump *COP* can remain fairly high. In the summer, the heat pump uses the pool as a heat sink, supplementing the solar heating system.

While systems of this sort are in operation now, they need to be quite carefully designed, meaning you would be well advised to seek the assistance of a qualified professional before proceeding.

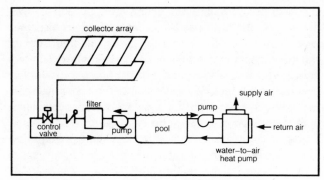

Figure 4.117 A solar-assisted water-source heat pump with swimming pool.

Air Systems

Air systems are conceptually similar to the water-based systems already described. There is a collector-to-storage loop and a storage-to-load distribution loop, but in addition, there is almost always a mode that allows direct heating of the house from the collector array during sunny days.

As is the case with water-based systems, there are a number of ways to accomplish the same goals of collecting, storing, and distributing heat. Figure 4.118 shows one such system. The principal components include the collector array; a heat storage unit; an air handler containing a blower, a hot-water coil, and two motorized dampers; two manually operated dampers that are set twice a year; a couple of automatic back-draft dampers that insure one way flow of air; and finally, an auxiliary furnace perhaps with an air-conditioning coil. All of these components are connected with ducts and are controlled by various thermostats and temperature-sensing devices.

To describe the system's operation, let us begin in the winter heating season. Manually operated bypass damper D-2 is closed and damper D-1 is opened. There are three modes of operation possible: direct heating of space from the collector array during the day when the house calls for heat; storage of heat in the rock bin during the day when the house thermostat is satisfied; and space heating from storage while the collectors are not operating.

To heat directly from the collectors, both the furnace fan and the air handler fan are turned on and motorized dampers MD-1 and MD-2 are opened. Return air from the house passes through the collectors, the air handler, and the furnace and emerges back in the house. If air from the collectors is not hot enough to maintain the desired interior temperature, the second stage of the house thermostat kicks in the auxiliary heating unit in the furnace.

If the thermostat is satisfied and sensors indicate a warmer temperature at the collector outlet than the bottom of the rock storage bin, the system switches to its collector-to-storage mode. The air handler is turned on and motorized damper MD-1 is opened and MD-2 is

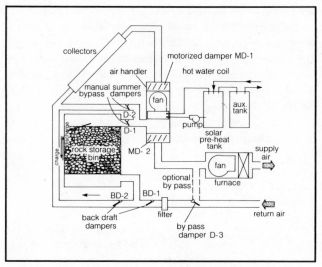

Figure 4.118 An air collection and distribution system with rock storage.

closed. The warm air from the collector is forced through the rock bin from top to bottom. As the air passes through the bin, the rocks near the top receive the greatest amount of heating and rocks progressively deeper in the pile receive less and less. If the bin is well designed (which means deep enough), the air emerging from the bottom of the rock pile will have lost all its heat and be back at room temperature. The air returning to the collectors, then, is almost always relatively cool, roughly 70°F. With such low inlet temperatures, air collectors can perform with equal or better efficiency than their water counterparts, which usually must operate with much higher inlet temperatures.

The third mode of operation corresponds to the house calling for heat when the collectors can't provide any. Heating is from storage, drawn by the furnace fan with MD-1 closed and MD-2 open. Notice that the air movement during discharge of storage is from the bottom up. Cool room return air gets warmer and warmer as it passes through the bin, emerging at its hottest possible temperature, usually within a few degrees of the hottest rocks. One of the distinct advantages of rock storage is its inherent ability to maintain thermal stratification, keeping the hottest temperatures at the top of the bin for maximum heating of the room space and the coolest temperatures at the bottom, which assures coolest collector inlet temperatures and hence maximum array efficiency. This highly desirable thermal stratification is not nearly as effective in a water-storage tank due to the convective currents, which distribute the heat rather easily.

Service hot-water heating is accomplished with a hot-water coil in the air handler or somewhere in the duct on the outlet side of the collectors. A small pump circulates water through the coil and back to a solar preheat storage tank. In the winter it is common for about half of the hot-water demands to be met with this arrangement.

As the heating season comes to an end, it may no

longer be desirable to heat the rock storage bin, since its losses may add unwanted heat to the house. At this same time, however, there is still a requirement for domestic hot water. This is the time to go down to the basement and close bypass damper D-1 and open D-2. Now with the motorized damper MD-1 open and MD-2 closed, the air handler will short-circuit the house and rock storage, circulating air from collectors through the hot-water coil and back to the collectors. While the hot-water demands can usually nearly all be met in this mode, the large amount of power drawn by the blower is a distinct disadvantage. A ¾-horsepower blower drawing 850 watts for eight hours a day will eat up enough electricity to heat nearly half the water usually required by a family of four.

The final aspect to this particular air system is the optional bypass duct indicated by broken lines in Figure 4.118. It serves two functions. One is to allow the user to include air conditioning in the auxiliary unit. With bypass damper D-3 down, the air conditioner can draw return air directly from the house, cool it, and supply it back to the living space without interference from the solar system. The bypass duct can also serve a function in the winter heating season by allowing a different air flow rate through the collectors than goes through the heat-distribution system. The ideal air flow rate through the panels is about 2 cubic feet of air per minute (cfm) per square foot of collector, which means, for example, that a 400-square-foot array would require about 800 cfm. If the auxiliary furnace/air conditioner has been designed to require 1200 cfm, then the additional 400 cfm would flow through the bypass duct.

Sizing Considerations

The f-chart procedure that we described in the section on liquid systems can also be applied to air systems with only minor modifications. The f-chart for air systems is given in Figure 4.119. The variables X and Y are defined as before:

$$X = \frac{F_R U_L A_c (T_r - \overline{T}_a)\Delta t}{L}$$

$$Y = \frac{F_R(\overline{\tau\alpha})A_c H_T}{L}$$

where A_c is collector area (ft²), T_r is a reference temperature (212°F), $\overline{T}_a$ is the 24-hour average ambient temperature (°F), H_T is average insolation on the panels (Btu/ft²-mo), Δt is the hours per month, L is the combined water and space heating load (Btu/mo), $F_R U_L$ is the slope of the ASHRAE collector efficiency curve, and $F_R(\overline{\tau\alpha})$ can be taken as 0.93 times the Y-axis intercept of the collector efficiency curve. Notice that the collector heat removal factor F_R doesn't have a prime on it for air systems. That's because there is no heat exchanger in the collector loop.

The f-chart for air systems has been derived with an

assumed rock storage bin sized at the recommended value of ¾-cubic foot of rock per square foot of collector area. For other storage volumes, the X factor can be multiplied by the correction factor given back in Figure 4.108. The standard flow rate used in the derivation was 2 cfm per square foot of collector. Different flow rates can be corrected by using Figure 4.120. Neither of these correction factors will affect estimates of annual solar heating fraction by much until your design is considerably different from the recommended nominal values.

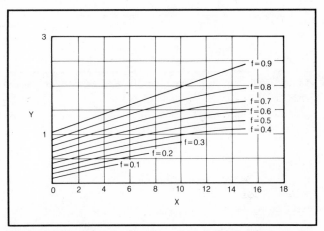

Figure 4.119 f-chart for air systems (from *Solar Heating Design by the f-chart Method*).

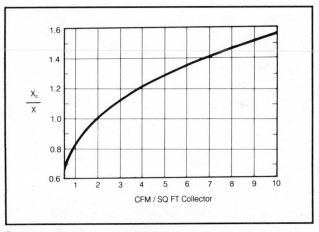

Figure 4.120 Collector air flow rate correction factor.

Let's work the same example that we did back in the liquid system section, but this time we'll use air collectors for comparison. We need a typical air-collector efficiency curve, and one is given in Figure 4.121.

Example: Find the January Solar Heating Fraction for a house in Reno with a load of 14.6×10^6 Btu using 425 square feet of air collector with efficiency given in Figure 4.121.

Solution: From the last time we did this problem we know

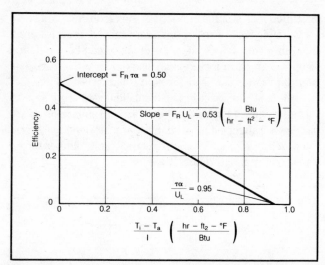

Figure 4.121 Typical efficiency curve for double-glazed flat back air collector.

$$\overline{H_T} = 41{,}000 \; Btu/ft^2\text{-}mo$$
$$\overline{T_a} = 31°F$$
$$\Delta t = 744 \; hr$$

and from the efficiency curve

$$F_R(\overline{\tau\alpha}) = 0.93 F_R(\tau\alpha) = 0.93 \times 0.5 = 0.47$$
$$F_R U_L = 0.53 \; Btu/hr\text{-}ft^2\text{-}°F$$

Plugging in:

$$X = \frac{F_R U_L A_c (T_r - \overline{T_a}) \Delta t}{L}$$
$$= \frac{0.53 \times 425 \, (212 - 31) 744}{14.6 \times 10^6} = 2.1$$

$$Y = \frac{F_R(\overline{\tau\alpha}) A_c H_T}{L}$$
$$= \frac{0.47 \times 425 \times 41{,}000}{14.6 \times 10^6} = 0.57$$

From Figure 4.119, the value of f can be found to be 0.45, which is slightly less than the water collector delivered.

With the f-chart technique to help size the collector array, we can move on to some of the other system components. The air-flow rate should be designed for 2 cfm per square foot of collector. At this flow rate the air will be heated from 70°F to roughly 140° on one pass through the collectors during the best parts of the day. With the flow rate determined, the ducts to and from the collectors can be sized using Figure 4.122. In the figure flow rates in cfm are plotted along the y-axis with friction losses in the duct in inches of water per 100 feet of duct along the x-axis. Notice the pressure drops in ducts are expressed in similar units to the ones used for the water pipe. To minimize fan power requirements and duct noise, it is

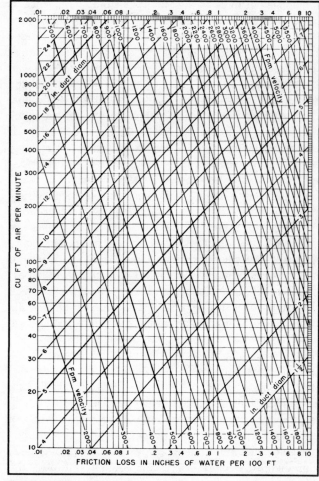

Figure 4.122 Friction of air in straight ducts for volumes of 10 to 2000 cfm.

Based on Standard air of 0.075 lb/ft³ density flowing through average, clean, galvanized metal ducts having approximately 40 joints per 100 ft. Caution: Do not extrapolate below chart.

recommended that the ducts be designed with pressure drops of 0.08 inches of water per 100 feet. That puts us into the graph at a given point and the duct size can be read directly.

For instance, suppose we wanted to size the ducts for that 425-square-foot array from the previous example. That means we need a flow rate of 850 cfm. At 0.08 inches of water and 850 cfm, Figure 4.122 indicates a duct size of about 13½ inches, with a duct speed of between 800 and 900 feet per minute. That duct size refers to the diameter of round galvanized ducts. Very often rectangular ducts are more convenient. ASHRAE comes to the rescue again and provides us with Table 4.48, which lets you find rectangular ducts with equivalent pressure drops to their circular counterparts. For example, suppose we only have room to accommodate a 9-inch-high duct; the table indicates a 9-by-18-inch rectangular duct is equivalent to a 13.7-inch round duct, so let's use that.

We can now comment on the design of the rock storage unit, an example of which is shown in Figure 4.123. The container itself can be constructed with 2-by-4-inch

Table 4.48 Circular Equivalents of Rectangular Ducts for Equal Friction and Capacity

Side Rectangular Duct	4.0	4.5	5.0	5.5	6.0	6.5	7.0	7.5	8.0	9.0	10.0	11.0	12.0	13.0	14.0	15.0	16.0
3.0	3.8	4.0	4.2	4.4	4.6	4.8	4.9	5.1	5.2	5.5	5.7	6.0	6.2	6.4	6.6	6.8	7.0
3.5	4.1	4.3	4.6	4.8	5.0	5.2	5.3	5.5	5.7	6.0	6.3	6.5	6.8	7.0	7.2	7.4	7.6
4.0	4.4	4.6	4.9	5.1	5.3	5.5	5.7	5.9	6.1	6.4	6.8	7.1	7.3	7.6	7.8	8.1	8.3
4.5	4.6	4.9	5.2	5.4	5.6	5.9	6.1	6.3	6.5	6.9	7.2	7.5	7.8	8.1	8.4	8.6	8.9
5.0	4.9	5.2	5.5	5.7	6.0	6.2	6.4	6.7	6.9	7.3	7.6	8.0	8.3	8.6	8.9	9.1	9.4
5.5	5.1	5.4	5.7	6.0	6.3	6.5	6.8	7.0	7.2	7.6	8.0	8.4	8.7	9.0	9.4	9.6	9.8

Side Rectangular Duct	6	7	8	9	10	11	12	13	14	15	16	17	18	19	20	22	24	26	28	30	Side Rectangular Duct
6	6.6																				6
7	7.1	7.7																			7
8	7.5	8.2	8.8																		8
9	8.0	8.6	9.3	9.9																	9
10	8.4	9.1	9.8	10.4	10.9																10
11	8.8	9.5	10.2	10.8	11.4	12.0															11
12	9.1	9.9	10.7	11.3	11.9	12.5	13.1														12
13	9.5	10.3	11.1	11.8	12.4	13.0	13.6	14.2													13
14	9.8	10.7	11.5	12.2	12.9	13.5	14.2	14.7	15.3												14
15	10.1	11.0	11.8	12.6	13.3	14.0	14.6	15.3	15.8	16.4											15
16	10.4	11.4	12.2	13.0	13.7	14.4	15.1	15.7	16.3	16.9	17.5										16
17	10.7	11.7	12.5	13.4	14.1	14.9	15.5	16.1	16.8	17.4	18.0	18.6									17
18	11.0	11.9	12.9	13.7	14.5	15.3	16.0	16.6	17.3	17.9	18.5	19.1	19.7								18
19	11.2	12.2	13.2	14.1	14.9	15.6	16.4	17.1	17.8	18.4	19.0	19.6	20.2	20.8							19
20	11.5	12.5	13.5	14.4	15.2	15.9	16.8	17.5	18.2	18.8	19.5	20.1	20.7	21.3	21.9						20
22	12.0	13.1	14.1	15.0	15.9	16.7	17.6	18.3	19.1	19.7	20.4	21.0	21.7	22.3	22.9	24.1					22
24	12.4	13.6	14.6	15.6	16.6	17.5	18.3	19.1	19.8	20.6	21.3	22.1	22.6	23.2	23.9	25.1	26.2				24
26	12.8	14.1	15.2	16.2	17.2	18.1	19.0	19.8	20.6	21.4	22.1	22.8	23.5	24.1	24.8	26.1	27.2	28.4			26
28	13.2	14.5	15.6	16.7	17.7	18.7	19.6	20.5	21.3	22.1	22.9	23.6	24.4	25.0	25.7	27.1	28.2	29.5	30.6		28
30	13.6	14.9	16.1	17.2	18.3	19.3	20.2	21.1	22.0	22.9	23.7	24.4	25.2	25.9	26.7	28.0	29.3	30.5	31.6	32.8	30
32	14.0	15.3	16.5	17.7	18.8	19.8	20.8	21.8	22.7	23.6	24.4	25.2	26.0	26.7	27.5	28.9	30.1	31.4	32.6	33.8	32
34	14.4	15.7	17.0	18.2	19.3	20.4	21.4	22.4	23.3	24.2	25.1	25.9	26.7	27.5	28.3	29.7	31.0	32.3	33.6	34.8	34
36	14.7	16.1	17.4	18.6	19.8	20.9	21.9	23.0	23.9	24.8	25.8	26.6	27.4	28.3	29.0	30.5	32.0	33.0	34.6	35.8	36
38	15.0	16.4	17.8	19.0	20.3	21.4	22.5	23.5	24.5	25.4	26.4	27.3	28.1	29.0	29.8	31.4	32.8	34.2	35.5	36.7	38
40	15.3	16.8	18.2	19.4	20.7	21.9	23.0	24.0	25.1	26.0	27.0	27.9	28.8	29.7	30.5	32.1	33.6	35.1	36.4	37.6	40
42	15.6	17.1	18.5	19.8	21.1	22.3	23.4	24.5	25.6	26.6	27.6	28.5	29.4	30.4	31.2	32.8	34.4	35.9	37.3	38.6	42
44	15.9	17.5	18.9	20.2	21.5	22.7	23.9	25.0	26.1	27.2	28.2	29.1	30.0	31.0	31.9	33.5	35.2	36.7	38.1	39.5	44
46	16.2	17.8	19.2	20.6	21.9	23.2	24.3	25.5	26.7	27.7	28.7	29.7	30.6	31.6	32.5	34.2	35.9	37.4	38.9	40.3	46
48	16.5	18.1	19.6	20.9	22.3	23.6	24.8	26.0	27.2	28.2	29.2	30.2	31.2	32.2	33.1	34.9	36.6	38.2	39.7	41.2	48
50	16.8	18.4	19.9	21.3	22.7	24.0	25.2	26.4	27.6	28.7	29.8	30.8	31.8	32.8	33.7	35.5	37.3	38.9	40.4	42.0	50
52	17.0	18.7	20.2	21.6	23.1	24.4	25.6	26.8	28.1	29.2	30.3	31.4	32.4	33.4	34.3	36.2	38.0	39.6	41.2	42.8	52
54	17.3	19.0	20.5	22.0	23.4	24.8	26.1	27.3	28.5	29.7	30.8	31.9	32.9	33.9	34.9	36.8	38.7	40.3	42.0	43.6	54
56	17.6	19.3	20.9	22.4	23.8	25.2	26.5	27.7	28.9	30.1	31.2	32.4	33.4	34.5	35.5	37.4	39.3	41.0	42.7	44.3	56
58	17.8	19.5	21.1	22.7	24.2	25.5	26.9	28.2	29.3	30.5	31.7	32.9	33.9	35.0	36.0	38.0	39.8	41.7	43.4	45.0	58
60	18.1	19.8	21.4	23.0	24.5	25.8	27.3	28.7	29.8	31.0	32.2	33.4	34.5	35.5	36.5	38.6	40.4	42.3	44.0	45.8	60
62	18.3	20.1	21.7	23.3	24.8	26.2	27.6	29.0	30.2	31.4	32.6	33.8	35.0	36.0	37.1	39.2	41.0	42.9	44.7	46.5	62
64	18.6	20.3	22.0	23.6	25.2	26.5	27.9	29.3	30.6	31.8	33.1	34.2	35.5	36.5	37.6	39.7	41.6	43.5	45.4	47.2	64
66	18.8	20.6	22.3	23.9	25.5	26.9	28.3	29.7	31.0	32.2	33.5	34.7	35.9	37.0	38.1	40.2	42.2	44.1	46.0	47.8	66
68	19.0	20.8	22.5	24.2	25.8	27.3	28.7	30.1	31.4	32.6	33.9	35.1	36.3	37.5	38.6	40.7	42.8	44.7	46.6	48.4	68
70	19.2	21.0	22.8	24.5	26.1	27.6	29.1	30.4	31.8	33.1	34.3	35.6	36.8	37.9	39.1	41.3	43.3	45.3	47.2	49.0	70
72															39.6	41.8	43.8	45.9	47.8	49.7	72
74															40.0	42.3	44.4	46.4	48.4	50.3	74
76															40.5	42.8	44.9	47.0	49.0	50.8	76
78															40.9	43.3	45.5	47.5	49.5	51.5	78
80															41.3	43.8	46.0	48.0	50.1	52.0	80
82															41.8	44.2	46.4	48.6	50.6	52.6	82
84															42.2	44.6	46.9	49.2	51.1	53.2	84
86															42.6	45.0	47.4	49.6	51.6	53.7	86
88															43.0	45.4	47.9	50.1	52.2	54.3	88
90															43.4	45.9	48.3	50.6	52.8	54.8	90
92															43.8	46.3	48.7	51.1	53.4	55.4	92
96															44.6	47.2	49.5	52.0	54.4	56.3	96

Equation for Circular Equivalent of a Rectangular Duct:[10]

$$D_e = 1.30 \left[(ab)^{0.625}/(a+b)^{0.250} \right] = 1.30 \sqrt[8]{(ab)^5/(a+b)^2}$$

where

a = length of one side of rectangular duct, inches.
b = length of adjacent side of rectangular duct, inches.
D_e = circular equivalent of rectangular duct for equal friction and capacity, inches.

or 2-by-6-inch stud walls filled with fiberglass insulation and covered with ½-inch plywood. Alternatively, a reinforced concrete box with 2 inches of rigid fiberglass board insulation on the interior can be used. Above and below the actual rock volume an air chamber, or plenum, must be provided to help the air distribute itself more evenly as it passes through the pile. The top plenum is provided by simply leaving about an 8-inch air space between the rocks and the lid. The bottom plenum is created by laying metal lath on top of two- or three-web bond beam blocks which are spaced every few inches across the floor. The lath and blocks hold the rock off the floor and allow relatively free circulation within the bottom plenum.

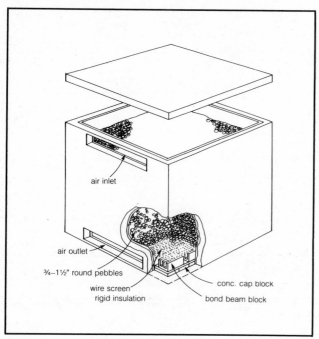

Figure 4.123 Rock bed heat storage unit (from Colorado State University, 1977).

The recommended volume of rock pile is between ½ and 1 cubic foot of rock per square foot of collector area. If we use ¾-foot per square foot as a norm, then our 425-square-foot collector array would require a rock bin of about 320 cubic feet. If the bin were a perfect cube, it would be nearly 7 feet on a side. While the actual dimensions are somewhat flexible, the maximum depth of the rock pile should be no less than about 2½ feet to assure good thermal stratification.

The speed with which the air moves through the rocks should be no less than about 6 feet per minute (fpm) or else the heat-transfer rate will be poor and the cross-sectional area required will be awkwardly large. On the other hand, flow speeds should not be in excess of about 25 feet per minute or the pressure drop will be high, causing excessive power consumption by the fan. Since the air speed (called "superficial velocity") is just the air flow rate in cfm divided by the cross-sectional area perpendicular

to the flow, these guidelines place some bounds on the dimensions of the overall unit. For example, with our air flow rate of 850 cfm, a 6-fpm velocity would result from an area of 141 square feet (850 ÷ 6) and a 25-fpm velocity would result from an area of 34 square feet (850 ÷ 25). If we made our box 7 by 7 feet across, it would have a superficial velocity of about 17 fpm, which is a good rate, and the resulting box height would be 6½ feet.

The rocks themselves should be hard and dense. Round riverbed granite rock is the best, though crushed gravel aggregates normally used for concrete may also be used. The rocks should be relatively uniform in size so that little ones don't fill up the necessary air spaces between the bigger ones. Rocks that will pass through a 1½-inch screen but not a ¾-inch screen are ideally sized. Larger rocks aren't as efficient in capturing and releasing heat and smaller ones pack too densely, which unnecessarily increases the power required to force air through the bin. The rocks should be washed before they are put in the bin.

The remaining component to be sized is the fan. The technique is similar to that used in the sizing of pumps in liquid systems and involves determining the overall pressure drop through the ducting, collectors, and rock bin and matching it to the fan characteristics. The collector manufacturer can help you there.

If you are interested in the design details for air systems, the best reference is the *Design/Application Engineering Manual,* available from Solaron Corporation (300 Galleria Tower, 720 South Colorado Blvd., Denver, Colorado 80222).

The Economics of Solar Energy Systems

There are several approaches that we might take to evaluating the economics of a given solar energy system that vary from extremely simple to extremely complex. At the simple end of the scale, we might ask "how much does it cost, how much will it save me in fuel in the first year, and at that rate, how many years will it take to pay for itself?" That sort of payback analysis is understandable to anyone and is the usual way lay people think about solar economics. It is, unfortunately, the least effective way to view solar savings. If the payback is longer than about five years, most people don't think it is a good investment. They would rather buy stocks or something and earn 10 to 15 percent interest on their money even though, in reality, the solar investment gives a much greater rate of return.

If you must deal in payback periods, you should add at least two important parameters into your calculation. The first is fuel escalation. If, by having installed a solar system, you save $100 in fuel bills this year, then next year you will undoubtedly save more, and so on through each succeeding year. Let's use *r* to stand for the annual rate of increase in the cost of the conventional fuel that you are displacing with solar. Let's leave it as a parameter that we can change at will. We may think that fuel oil is going to increase at 30 percent per year, but someone else may think only 10 percent, so we will leave this as something to be plugged in at the end.

The second variable that needs to be included is the time value of money, or interest, i. By taking money out of the bank or some other investment to pay for the solar equipment, you are going to lose the interest that you could have been earning. That is an added, hidden cost of the solar system that needs to be included. And, of course, if you borrow the money instead of taking it out of another investment, you still have an interest charge to contend with.

If we neglect fuel escalation and lost interest, the payback period is simply the initial cost, call it C_i, divided by the first year's fuel savings, call it S_1. If we include fuel escalation and interest the payback period, N_p (years) becomes

E. 4.80 $$N_p = \frac{\log[1 + \frac{C_i}{S_1} \cdot (r - i)]}{\log R}$$

where

E. 4.81 $$R = \frac{1 + r}{1 + i}$$

Before we can plug into these equations, we need to say something about inflation. Inflation affects both the fuel escalation rate and the interest rate. The real value of an investment is not what interest rate it earns, but what interest rate it earns in excess of the inflation rate. And while the cost of fuel may go up next year, what is most important is how much it goes up beyond the general rate of inflation. We are talking about what economists call "constant dollars." What it boils down to is that the values we use for i and r in Equations 4.80 and 4.81 should have inflation rates subtracted out before being used.

Example: A solar hot-water heating system costs $2,000 and saves $200 in electric costs in the first year. Electric rates are predicted to go up at 18 percent per year, the best alternative investment would earn 12 percent, and inflation is running at 10 percent. If these rates hold, what would be the payback period?

Solution: In simple terms, the payback is just $2,000 divided by $200 a year savings, or 10 years. Including the other factors, we have

$$r = 0.18 - 0.10 = 0.08$$
$$i = 0.12 - 0.10 = 0.02$$
$$R = \frac{1 + r}{1 + i} = \frac{1.08}{1.02} = 1.059$$

and plugging into Equation 4.80, the payback period would be

$$N_p = \frac{\log \left[1 + \frac{C_i}{S_1}(r - i)\right]}{\log R}$$
$$= \frac{\log \left[1 + \frac{2000}{200} \times (0.08 - 0.02)\right]}{\log 1.059} = 8.1 \text{ years}$$

So the payback declined by a few years because of the rapidly rising costs of electricity.

To simplify this procedure, we have prepared a plot of payback versus the cost-to-first-year's-savings ratio (real payback versus "simple" payback) in Figure 4.124. Notice that the parameter on the graph is $(r - i)$, which simplifies matters while introducing only slight errors in the solution.

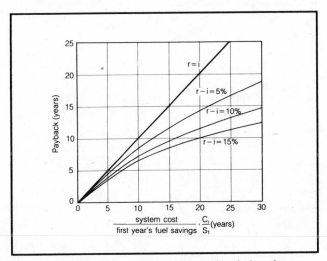

Figure 4.124   Payback periods are shorter when fuel escalation exceeds interest.

While payback periods are perhaps the most understandable, they are the least effective way to present the economic advantages of solar. Other approaches include life-cycle costing, wherein costs of using solar are compared to the cost of not using it over the life of the system. Sizable savings are generally easy to show, but the case is still less than convincing. Saying that the system saves $5,847 over the next 20 years is likely to meet with the response, "What good does that do me if I move three years from now?"

The annual cash flow approach to showing solar economics is generally the most effective. It also allows many additional factors such as operation and maintenance costs, tax deductible interest payments, loan payments, tax rebates, down payments, property taxes, insurance costs, and so on to be clearly spelled out. The process involves setting up a table with year-by-year listings for all of the factors involved with a total net cash flow for each year.

Let's set up an example to give you the idea. Suppose

you decide to have a $2,500 solar hot-water heater added to a house at the time of purchase. The $2,500 becomes part of the total cost of the house and so gets thrown in with your mortgage. If we assume the loan terms are 20 percent down with 30-year financing at 12 percent interest, then we must come up with an extra $500 down payment.

Our additional annual mortgage payments can be found using the capital recovery factors (CRF) introduced in the last chapter (Table 3.11) or by the Equation

$$A = P \left[\frac{i}{(1 + i)^n - 1} + i \right] = P \times CRF$$

where A is the annual payment on a principal of P, borrowed at interest rate i for a term of n years. The added amount of our loan is $2,500 less the $500 down payment, or $2,000. The CRF is 0.1241 so our extra mortgage payments amount to

$$A = 2000 \times 0.1241 = \$248 \text{ per year}$$

The interest portion of that payment in the first year is 12 percent of the $2,000, or $240. Now interest is deductible from your income when it comes to paying your federal and state taxes, so your tax obligation is reduced by an amount that corresponds to your tax bracket. If you are in the 35 percent tax bracket, for example, then reducing your taxable income by $240 will save you $84 in taxes in the first year.

The next year your loan balance is down to $1,992 (you paid off $8 in principal in the first year), so the interest portion of the second year's payment is $239. As you can see, interest accounts for the biggest chunk of your loan payment for a good number of years.

Let's assume the cost of maintenance of the system is 1 percent or $25 in the first year, which we will escalate at 20 percent per year (including inflation). Let's assume the system saves $200 in fuel in the first year and that this figure escalates by 20 percent per year (including inflation). Finally, we will include the federal tax credit of 40

percent, which we will also throw into the first year's calculation. That is $1,000. Table 4.49 shows the combination of all these factors. Notice that with this presentation, the system has a positive cash flow every single year! Compare that to a simple payback analysis, which would have said it takes 7½ years to break even. Which is more convincing?

Concluding Remarks

Where can you go from here? Given the rapidity of change in the solar field, a list of articles or manufacturers and dealers would be out of date by the time you read this, so it seems more important to help you tap into the flow of information rather than give you specifics.

For a list of local businesses involved in the design and sale of solar systems, you can't beat the yellow pages of your phone directory. Just look under "Solar." (At the rate that solar companies emerge and then fade back into

---

Table 4.49   An Example of a Cash Flow Presentation[a]

Year	Fuel Savings	Loan Payment	Loan Interest	Tax Savings	O&M	Tax Credit	Down Payment	Net Cash Benefit
1	+200	−248	240	+84	−25	+1000	−500	516
2	240	248	239	84	30	—	—	46
3	288	248	238	83	36	—	—	87
4	346	248	237	83	43	—	—	138
5	414	248	235	82	52	—	—	198
.	.	.	.	.	.			.
.	.	.	.	.	.			.
.	.	.	.	.	.			.

Notes: a. $2,500 system cost; 20% down, 30-year, 12% loan; 35% tax bracket; $200 first year savings, escalating at 20%; 40% federal tax credit.

the bushes, you'd better get the very latest edition.)

To keep up on new products and tips on everything from solar legislation to design and installation of systems, there are some very good magazines around, including *Solar Age* (Box 4934, Manchester, New Hampshire 03108) and *Solar Engineering Magazine* (GPO Box 1736, Brooklyn, New York 11202). Other magazines such as *Sunset, Popular Science,* and *Co-Evolution Quarterly* regularly feature articles on innovative solar applications. If you are interested in more technical literature, *the* journal in the solar field is called simply *Solar Energy* (Pergamon Press, Maxwell House, Fairview Park, Elmsford, New York 10523).

There are annual conferences of the International Solar Energy Society with published proceedings that should be available in a good university library. Many regions of the country have their own local solar energy associations with periodic meetings, newsletters, and tours of local installations.

Local, state, and federal government agencies involved in energy are good sources of information. The National Solar Heating and Cooling Information Center, for example, maintains a toll-free telephone number to help you with solar-related questions (800/523-2929).

If your interest is in the quantitative side of this chapter, there are several good textbooks out now that cover this material much more carefully and in much greater depth, including K. Kreith and J. Kreider, *Principles of Solar Engineering,* 1978; P. J. Lunde, *Solar Thermal Engineering,* 1980; J. Duffie and W. Beckman, *Solar Engineering of Thermal Processes,* 1980; and A. Meinel and M. Meinel, *Applied Solar Energy,* 1976. And, of course, the ASHRAE *Handbook of Fundamentals, Applications,* and *Systems* are the bibles for designers of heating, ventilating, and air-conditioning systems.

With what you have picked up in this chapter, you should be able to read the literature, critically evaluate solar products and claims, and most of all, do a darn good job of specifying exactly the kind of system that most closely meets your needs.

State and Station	Lat. °	Median of Annual Extremes	Winter 99%	97½%	Coincident Wind Velocity
ALABAMA					
Alexander City	33	12	16	20	L
Anniston AP	33	12	17	19	L
Auburn	32	17	21	25	L
Birmingham AP	33	14	19	22	L
Decatur	34	10	15	19	L
Dothan AP	31	19	23	27	L
Florence AP	34	8	13	17	L
Gadsden	34	11	16	20	L
Huntsville AP	34	8	13	17	L
Mobile AP	30	21	26	29	M
Mobile CO	30	24	28	32	M
Montgomery AP	32	18	22	26	L
Selma-Craig AFB	32	18	23	27	L
Talladega	33	11	15	19	L
Tuscaloosa AP	33	14	19	23	L
ALASKA					
Anchorage AP	61	−29	−25	−20	VL
Barrow	71	−49	−45	−42	M
Fairbanks AP	64	−59	−53	−50	VL
Juneau AP	58	−11	− 7	− 4	L
Kodiak	57	4	8	12	M
Nome AP	64	−37	−32	−28	L
ARIZONA†					
Douglas AP	31	13	18	22	VL
Flagstaff AP	35	−10	0	5	VL
Fort Huachuca AP	31	18	25	28	VL
Kingman AP	35	18	25	29	VL
Nogales	31	15	20	24	VL
Phoenix AP	33	25	31	34	VL
Prescott AP	34	7	15	19	VL
Tucson AP	33	23	29	32	VL
Winslow AP	35	2	9	13	VL
Yuma AP	32	32	37	40	VL
ARKANSAS					
Blytheville AFB	36	6	12	17	L
Camden	33	13	19	23	L
El Dorado AP	33	13	19	23	L
Fayetteville AP	36	3	9	13	M
Fort Smith AP	35	9	15	19	M
Hot Springs Nat. Pk.	34	12	18	22	M
Jonesboro	35	8	14	18	M
Little Rock AP	34	13	19	23	M
Pine Bluff AP	34	14	20	24	L
Texarkana AP	33	16	22	26	M
CALIFORNIA					
Bakersfield AP	35	26	31	33	VL
Barstow AP	34	18	24	28	VL
Blythe AP	33	26	31	35	VL
Burbank AP	34	30	36	38	VL
Chico	39	23	29	33	VL
Concord	38	27	32	36	VL
Covina	34	32	38	41	VL
Crescent City AP	41	28	33	36	L
Downey	34	30	35	38	VL
El Cajon	32	26	31	34	VL
El Centro AP	32	26	31	35	VL
Escondido	33	28	33	36	VL
Eureka/Arcata AP	41	27	32	35	L
Fairfield-Travis AFB	38	26	32	34	VL
Fresno AP	36	25	28	31	VL
Hamilton AFB	38	28	33	35	VL
Laguna Beach	33	32	37	39	VL

State and Station	Lat. °	Median of Annual Extremes	Winter 99%	97½%	Coincident Wind Velocity
CALIFORNIA (continued)					
Livermore	37	23	28	30	VL
Lompoc, Vandenburg AFB	34	32	36	38	VL
Long Beach AP	33	31	36	38	VL
Los Angeles AP	34	36	41	43	VL
Los Angeles CO	34	38	42	44	VL
Merced-Castle AFB	37	24	30	32	VL
Modesto	37	26	32	36	VL
Monterey	36	29	34	37	VL
Napa	38	26	31	34	VL
Needles AP	34	27	33	37	VL
Oakland AP	37	30	35	37	VL
Oceanside	33	33	38	40	VL
Ontario	34	26	32	34	VL
Oxnard AFB	34	32	35	37	VL
Palmdale AP	34	18	24	27	VL
Palm Springs	33	27	32	36	VL
Pasadena	34	31	36	39	VL
Petaluma	38	24	29	32	VL
Pomona CO	34	26	31	34	VL
Redding AP	40	25	31	35	VL
Redlands	34	28	34	37	VL
Richmond	38	28	35	38	VL
Riverside-March AFB	33	26	32	34	VL
Sacramento AP	38	24	30	32	VL
Salinas AP	36	27	32	35	VL
San Bernardino, Norton AFB	34	26	31	33	VL
San Diego AP	32	38	42	44	VL
San Fernando	34	29	34	37	VL
San Francisco AP	37	32	35	37	L
San Francisco CO	37	38	42	44	VL
San Jose AP	37	30	34	36	VL
San Luis Obispo	35	30	35	37	VL
Santa Ana AP	33	28	33	36	VL
Santa Barbara CO	34	30	34	36	VL
Santa Cruz	37	28	32	34	VL
Santa Maria AP	34	28	32	34	VL
Santa Monica CO	34	38	43	45	VL
Santa Paula	34	28	33	36	VL
Santa Rosa	38	24	29	32	VL
Stockton AP	37	25	30	34	VL
Ukiah	39	22	27	30	VL
Visalia	36	26	32	36	VL
Yreka	41	7	13	17	VL
Yuba City	39	24	30	34	VL
COLORADO					
Alamosa AP	37	−26	−17	−13	VL
Boulder	40	− 5	4	8	L
Colorado Springs AP	38	− 9	− 1	4	L
Denver AP	39	− 9	− 2	3	L
Durango	37	−10	0	4	VL
Fort Collins	40	−1o	− 9	− 5	L
Grand Junction AP	39	− 2	8	11	VL
Greeley	40	−18	− 9	− 5	L
La Junta AP	38	−14	− 6	− 2	M
Leadville	39	−18	− 9	− 4	VL
Pueblo AP	38	−14	− 5	− 1	L
Sterling	40	−15	− 6	− 2	M
Trinidad AP	37	− 9	1	5	L

Notes: a. From ASHRAE *Handbook of Fundamentals*.

b. AP indicates airport; AFB indicates Air Force base; CO indicates cosmopolitan area; other may be taken to be semi-rural.

c. Wind velocity: VL = Very Light, 70% or more of cold extreme hours at less than 7 mph; L = Light, 50-69% cold extreme hours less than 7 mph; M = Moderate, 50-74% cold extreme hours more than 7 mph; H = High, 75% or more of cold extreme hours more than 7 mph, 50% more than 12 mph.

State and Station	Lat. °	Median of Annual Extremes	Winter 99%	Winter 97½%	Coincident Wind Velocity
CONNECTICUT					
Bridgeport AP	41	− 1	4	8	M
Hartford, Brainard Field	41	− 4	1	5	M
New Haven AP	41	0	5	9	H
New London	41	0	4	8	H
Norwalk	41	− 5	0	4	M
Norwich	41	− 7	− 2	2	M
Waterbury	41	− 5	0	4	M
Windsor Locks, Bradley Field	42	− 7	− 2	2	M
DELAWARE					
Dover AFB	39	8	13	15	M
Wilmington AP	39	6	12	15	M
DISTRICT OF COLUMBIA					
Andrews AFB	38	9	13	16	M
Washington National AP	38	12	16	19	M
FLORIDA					
Belle Glade	26	31	35	39	M
Cape Kennedy AP	28	33	37	40	L
Daytona Beach AP	29	28	32	36	L
Fort Lauderdale	26	37	41	45	M
Fort Myers	26	34	38	42	M
Fort Pierce	27	33	37	41	M
Gainesville AP	29	24	28	32	L
Jacksonville AP	30	26	29	32	L
Key West AP	24	50	55	58	M
Lakeland CO	28	31	35	39	M
Miami AP	25	39	44	47	M
Miami Beach CO	25	40	45	48	M
Ocala	29	25	29	33	L
Orlando AP	28	29	33	37	L
Panama City, Tyndall AFB	30	28	32	35	M
Pensacola CO	30	25	29	32	M
St. Augustine	29	27	31	35	L
St. Petersburg	28	35	39	42	M
Sanford	28	29	33	37	L
Sarasota	27	31	35	39	M
Tallahassee AP	30	21	25	29	L
Tampa AP	28	32	36	39	M
West Palm Beach AP	26	36	40	44	M
GEORGIA					
Albany, Turner AFB	31	21	26	30	L
Americus	32	18	22	25	L
Athens	34	12	17	21	L
Atlanta AP	33	14	18	23	H
Augusta AP	33	17	20	23	L
Brunswick	31	24	27	31	L
Columbus, Lawson AFB	32	19	23	26	L
Dalton	34	10	15	19	L
Dublin	32	17	21	25	L
Gainesville	34	11	16	20	L
Griffin	33	13	17	22	L
La Grange	33	12	16	20	L
Macon AP	32	18	23	27	L
Marietta, Dobbins AFB	34	12	17	21	L
Moultrie	31	22	26	30	L
Rome AP	34	11	16	20	L
Savannah-Travis AP	32	21	24	27	L
Valdosta-Moody AFB	31	24	28	31	L
Waycross	31	20	24	28	L
HAWAII					
Hilo AP	19	56	59	61	L
Honolulu AP	21	58	60	62	L
Kaneohe	21	58	60	61	L
Wahiawa	21	57	59	61	L

State and Station	Lat. °	Median of Annual Extremes	Winter 99%	Winter 97½%	Coincident Wind Velocity
IDAHO					
Boise AP	43	0	4	10	L
Burley	42	− 5	4	8	VL
Coeur d'Alene AP	47	− 4	2	7	VL
Idaho Falls AP	43	−17	−12	− 6	VL
Lewiston AP	46	1	6	12	VL
Moscow	46	−11	− 3	1	VL
Mountain Home AFB	43	− 3	2	9	L
Pocatello AP	43	−12	− 8	− 2	VL
Twin Falls AP	42	− 5	4	8	L
ILLINOIS					
Aurora	41	−13	− 7	− 3	M
Belleville, Scott AFB	38	0	6	10	M
Bloomington	40	− 7	− 1	3	M
Carbondale	37	1	7	11	M
Champaign/Urbana	40	− 6	0	4	M
Chicago, Midway AP	41	− 7	− 4	1	M
Chicago, O'Hare AP	42	− 9	− 4	0	M
Chicago, CO	41	− 5	− 3	1	M
Danville	40	− 6	− 1	4	M
Decatur	39	− 6	0	4	M
Dixon	41	−13	− 7	− 3	M
Elgin	42	−14	− 8	− 4	M
Freeport	42	−16	−10	− 6	M
Galesburg	41	−10	− 4	0	M
Greenville	39	− 3	3	7	M
Joliet AP	41	−11	− 5	− 1	M
Kankakee	41	−10	− 4	1	M
La Salle/Peru	41	− 9	− 3	1	M
Macomb	40	− 5	− 3	1	M
Moline AP	41	−12	− 7	− 3	M
Mt. Vernon	38	0	6	10	M
Peoria AP	40	− 8	− 2	2	M
Quincy AP	40	− 8	− 2	2	M
Rantoul, Chanute AFB	40	− 7	− 1	3	M
Rockford	42	−13	− 7	− 3	M
Springfield AP	39	− 7	− 1	4	M
Waukegan	42	−11	− 5	− 1	M
INDIANA					
Anderson	40	− 5	0	5	M
Bedford	38	− 3	3	7	M
Bloomington	39	− 3	3	7	M
Columbus, Bakalar AFB	39	− 3	3	7	M
Crawfordsville	40	− 8	− 2	2	M
Evansville AP	38	1	6	10	M
Fort Wayne AP	41	− 5	0	5	M
Goshen AP	41	−10	− 4	0	M
Hobart	41	−10	− 4	0	M
Huntington	40	− 8	− 2	2	M
Indianapolis AP	39	− 5	0	4	M
Jeffersonville	38	3	9	13	M
Kokomo	40	− 6	0	4	M
Lafayette	40	− 7	− 1	3	M
La Porte	41	−10	− 4	0	M
Marion	40	− 8	− 2	2	M
Muncie	40	− 8	− 2	2	M
Peru, Bunker Hill AFB	40	− 9	− 3	1	M
Richmond AP	39	− 7	− 1	3	M
Shelbyville	39	− 4	2	6	M
South Bend AP	41	− 6	− 2	3	M
Terre Haute AP	39	− 3	3	7	M
Valparaiso	41	−12	− 6	− 2	M
Vincennes	38	− 1	5	9	M

State and Station	Lat. °	Median of Annual Extremes	Winter 99%	97½%	Coincident Wind Velocity
IOWA					
Ames	42	−17	−11	− 7	M
Burlington AP	40	−10	− 4	0	M
Cedar Rapids AP	41	−14	− 8	− 4	M
Clinton	41	−13	− 7	− 3	M
Council Bluffs	41	−14	− 7	− 3	M
Des Moines AP	41	−13	− 7	− 3	M
Dubuque	42	−17	−11	− 7	M
Fort Dodge	42	−18	−12	− 8	M
Iowa City	41	−14	− 8	− 4	M
Keokuk	40	− 9	− 3	1	M
Marshalltown	42	−16	−10	− 6	M
Mason City AP	43	−20	−13	− 9	M
Newton	41	−15	− 9	− 5	M
Ottumwa AP	41	−12	− 6	− 2	M
Sioux City AP	42	−17	−10	− 6	M
Waterloo	42	−18	−12	− 8	M
KANSAS					
Atchison	39	− 9	− 2	2	M
Chanute AP	37	− 3	3	7	H
Dodge City AP	37	− 5	3	7	M
El Dorado	37	− 3	4	8	H
Emporia	38	− 4	3	7	H
Garden City AP	38	−10	− 1	3	M
Goodland AP	39	−10	− 2	4	M
Great Bend	38	− 5	2	6	M
Hutchinson AP	38	− 5	2	6	H
Liberal	37	− 4	4	8	M
Manhattan, Fort Riley	39	− 7	− 1	4	H
Parsons	37	− 2	5	9	H
Russell AP	38	− 7	0	4	M
Salina	38	− 4	3	7	H
Topeka AP	39	− 4	3	6	H
Wichita AP	37	− 1	5	9	H
KENTUCKY					
Ashland	38	1	6	10	L
Bowling Green AP	37	1	7	11	L
Corbin AP	37	0	5	9	L
Covington AP	39	− 3	3	8	L
Hopkinsville, Campbell AFB	36	4	10	14	L
Lexington AP	38	0	6	10	M
Louisville AP	38	1	8	12	L
Madisonville	37	1	7	11	L
Owensboro	37	0	6	10	L
Paducah AP	37	4	10	14	L
LOUISIANA					
Alexandria AP	31	20	25	29	L
Baton Rouge AP	30	22	25	30	L
Bogalusa	30	20	24	28	L
Houma	29	25	29	33	L
Lafayette AP	30	23	28	32	L
Lake Charles AP	30	25	29	33	M
Minden	32	17	22	26	L
Monroe AP	32	18	23	27	L
Natchitoches	31	17	22	26	L
New Orleans AP	30	29	32	35	M
Shreveport AP	32	18	22	26	M
MAINE					
Augusta AP	44	−13	− 7	− 3	M
Bangor, Dow AFB	44	−14	− 8	− 4	M
Caribou AP	46	−24	−18	−14	L
Lewiston	44	−14	− 8	− 4	M
Millinocket AP	45	−22	−16	−12	L
Portland AP	43	−14	− 5	0	L
Waterville	44	−15	− 9	− 5	M

State and Station	Lat. °	Median of Annual Extremes	Winter 99%	97½%	Coincident Wind Velocity
MARYLAND					
Baltimore AP	39	8	12	15	M
Baltimore CO	39	12	16	20	M
Cumberland	39	0	5	9	L
Frederick AP	39	2	7	11	M
Hagerstown	39	1	6	10	L
Salisbury	38	10	14	18	M
MASSACHUSETTS					
Boston AP	42	− 1	6	10	H
Clinton	42	− 8	− 2	2	M
Fall River	41	− 1	5	9	H
Framingham	42	− 7	− 1	3	M
Gloucester	42	− 4	2	6	H
Greenfield	42	−12	− 6	− 2	M
Lawrence	42	− 9	− 3	1	M
Lowell	42	− 7	− 1	3	M
New Bedford	41	3	9	13	H
Pittsfield AP	42	−11	− 5	− 1	M
Springfield, Westover AFB	42	− 8	− 3	2	M
Taunton	41	− 9	− 4	0	H
Worcester AP	42	− 8	− 3	1	M
MICHIGAN					
Adrian	41	− 6	0	4	M
Alpena AP	45	−11	− 5	− 1	M
Battle Creek AP	42	− 6	1	5	M
Benton Harbor AP	42	− 7	− 1	3	M
Detroit Met. CAP	42	0	4	8	M
Escanaba	45	−13	− 7	− 3	M
Flint AP	43	− 7	− 1	3	M
Grand Rapids AP	42	− 3	2	6	M
Holland	42	− 4	2	6	M
Jackson AP	42	− 6	0	4	M
Kalamazoo	42	− 5	1	5	M
Lansing AP	42	− 4	2	6	M
Marquette CO	46	−14	− 8	− 4	L
Mt. Pleasant	43	− 9	− 3	1	M
Muskegon AP	43	− 2	4	8	M
Pontiac	42	− 6	0	4	M
Port Huron	43	− 6	− 1	3	M
Saginaw AP	43	− 7	− 1	3	M
Sault Ste. Marie AP	46	−18	−12	− 8	L
Traverse City AP	44	− 6	0	4	M
Ypsilanti	42	− 3	− 1	5	M
MINNESOTA					
Albert Lea	43	−20	−14	−10	M
Alexandria AP	45	−26	−19	−15	L
Bemidji AP	47	−38	−32	−28	L
Brainerd	46	−31	−24	−20	L
Duluth AP	46	−25	−19	−15	M
Faribault	44	−23	−16	−12	L
Fergus Falls	46	−28	−21	−17	L
International Falls AP	48	−35	−29	−24	L
Mankato	44	−23	−16	−12	L
Minneapolis/St. Paul AP	44	−19	−14	−10	L
Rochester AP	44	−23	−17	−13	M
St. Cloud AP	45	−26	−20	−16	L
Virginia	47	−32	−25	−21	L
Willmar	45	−25	−18	−14	L
Winona	44	−19	−12	− 8	M
MISSISSIPPI					
Biloxi, Keesler AFB	30	26	30	32	M
Clarksdale	34	14	20	24	L
Columbus AFB	33	13	18	22	L
Greenville AFB	33	16	21	24	L

State and Station	Lat. °	Winter Median of Annual Extremes	99%	97½%	Coincident Wind Velocity	State and Station	Lat. °	Winter Median of Annual Extremes	99%	97½%	Coincident Wind Velocity
MISSISSIPPI (continued)						**NEVADA (continued)**					
Greenwood	33	14	19	23	L	Reno AP	39	− 2	2	7	VL
Hattiesburg	31	18	22	26	L	Reno CO	39	8	12	17	VL
Jackson AP	32	17	21	24	L	Tonopah AP	38	2	9	13	VL
						Winnemucca AP	40	− 8	1	5	VL
Laurel	31	18	22	26	L	**NEW HAMPSHIRE**					
McComb AP	31	18	22	26	L	Berlin	44	−25	−19	−15	L
Meridian AP	32	15	20	24	L	Claremont	43	−19	−13	− 9	L
Natchez	31	18	22	26	L	Concord AP	43	−17	−11	− 7	M
Tupelo	34	13	18	22	L	Keene	43	−17	−12	− 8	M
Vicksburg CO	32	18	23	26	L	Laconia	43	−22	−16	−12	M
MISSOURI						Manchester, Grenier AFB	43	−11	− 5	1	M
Cape Girardeau	37	2	8	12	M	Portsmouth, Pease AFB	43	− 8	− 2	3	M
Columbia AP	39	− 4	2	6	M	**NEW JERSEY**					
Farmington AP	37	− 2	4	8	M	Atlantic City CO	39	10	14	18	H
Hannibal	39	− 7	− 1	4	M	Long Branch	40	4	9	13	H
Jefferson City	38	− 4	2	6	M	Newark AP	40	6	11	15	M
Joplin AP	37	1	7	11	M	New Brunswick	40	3	8	12	M
Kansas City AP	39	− 2	4	8	M	Paterson	40	3	8	12	M
						Phillipsburg	40	1	6	10	L
Kirksville AP	40	−13	− 7	− 3	M	Trenton CO	40	7	12	16	M
Mexico	39	− 7	− 1	3	M	Vineland	39	7	12	16	M
Moberly	39	− 8	− 2	2	M	**NEW MEXICO**					
Poplar Bluff	36	3	9	13	M	Alamagordo, Holloman AFB	32	12	18	22	L
Rolla	38	− 3	3	7	M	Albuquerque AP	35	6	14	17	L
						Artesia	32	9	16	19	L
St. Joseph AP	39	− 8	− 1	3	M	Carlsbad AP	32	11	17	21	L
St. Louis AP	38	− 2	4	8	M	Clovis AP	34	2	14	17	L
St. Louis CO	38	1	7	11	M	Farmington AP	36	− 3	6	9	VL
Sedalia, Whiteman AFB	38	− 2	4	9	M						
Sikeston	36	4	10	14	L	Gallup	35	−13	− 5	− 1	VL
Springfield AP	37	0	5	10	M	Grants	35	−15	− 7	− 3	VL
MONTANA						Hobbs	32	9	15	19	L
Billings AP	45	−19	−10	− 6	L	Las Cruces	32	13	19	23	L
Bozeman	45	−25	−15	−11	L	Los Alamos	35	− 4	5	9	L
Butte AP	46	−34	−24	−16	VL	Raton AP	36	−11	− 2	2	L
Cut Bank AP	48	−32	−23	−17	L						
Glasgow AP	48	−33	−25	−20	L	Roswell, Walker AFB	33	5	16	19	L
Glendive	47	−28	−20	−16	L	Santa Fe CO	35	− 2	7	11	L
Great Falls AP	47	−29	−20	−16	L	Silver City AP	32	8	14	18	VL
						Socorro AP	34	6	13	17	L
Havre	48	−32	−22	−15	M	Tucumcari AP	35	1	9	13	L
Helena AP	46	−27	−17	−13	L	**NEW YORK**					
Kalispell AP	48	−17	− 7	− 3	VL	Albany AP	42	−14	− 5	0	L
Lewiston AP	47	−27	−18	−14	L	Albany CO	42	− 5	1	5	L
Livingston AP	45	−26	−17	−13	L	Auburn	43	−10	− 2	2	M
Miles City AP	46	−27	−19	−15	L	Batavia	43	− 7	− 1	3	M
Missoula AP	46	−16	− 7	− 3	VL	Binghamton CO	42	− 8	− 2	2	L
NEBRASKA											
Beatrice	40	−10	− 3	1	M	Buffalo AP	43	− 3	3	6	M
Chadron AP	42	−21	−13	− 9	M	Cortland	42	−11	− 5	− 1	M
Columbus	41	−14	− 7	− 3	M	Dunkirk	42	− 2	4	8	M
Fremont	41	−14	− 7	− 3	M	Elmira AP	42	− 5	1	5	L
						Geneva	42	− 8	− 2	2	M
Grand Island AP	41	−14	− 6	− 2	M						
Hastings	40	−11	− 3	1	M	Glens Falls	43	−17	−11	− 7	L
Kearney	40	−14	− 6	− 2	M	Gloversville	43	−12	− 6	− 2	L
Lincoln CO	40	−10	− 4	0	M	Hornell	42	−15	− 9	− 5	L
McCook	40	−12	− 4	0	M	Ithaca	42	−10	− 4	0	L
Norfolk	42	−18	−11	− 7	M	Jamestown	42	− 5	1	5	M
North Platte AP	41	−13	− 6	− 2	M	Kingston	42	− 8	− 2	2	L
Omaha AP	41	−12	− 5	− 1	M	Lockport	43	− 4	2	6	M
Scottsbluff AP	41	−16	− 8	− 4	M	Massena AP	45	−22	−16	−12	M
Sidney AP	41	−15	− 7	− 2	M						
NEVADA						Newburgh-Stewart AFB	41	− 4	2	6	M
Carson City	39	− 4	3	7	VL	NYC-Central Park	40	6	11	15	H
Elko AP	40	−21	−13	− 7	VL	NYC-Kennedy AP	40	12	17	21	H
Ely AP	39	−15	− 6	− 2	VL	NYC-LaGuardia AP	40	7	12	16	H
Las Vegas AP	36	18	23	26	VL	Niagara Falls AP	43	− 2	4	7	M
Lovelock AP	40	0	7	11	VL	Olean	42	−13	− 8	− 3	L

State and Station	Lat. °	Median of Annual Extremes	99%	97½%	Coincident Wind Velocity
NEW YORK (continued)					
Oneonta	42	−13	− 7	− 3	L
Oswego CO	43	− 4	2	6	M
Plattsburg AFB	44	−16	−10	− 6	L
Poughkeepsie	41	− 6	− 1	3	L
Rochester AP	43	− 5	2	5	M
Rome-Griffiss AFB	43	−13	− 7	− 3	L
Schenectady	42	−11	− 5	− 1	L
Suffolk County AFB	40	4	9	13	H
Syracuse AP	43	−10	− 2	2	M
Utica	43	−12	− 6	− 2	L
Watertown	44	−20	−14	−10	M
NORTH CAROLINA					
Asheville AP	35	8	13	17	L
Charlotte AP	35	13	18	22	L
Durham	36	11	15	19	L
Elizabeth City AP	36	14	18	22	M
Fayetteville, Pope AFB	35	13	17	20	L
Goldsboro, Seymour AFB	35	14	18	21	M
Greensboro AP	36	9	14	17	L
Greenville	35	14	18	22	M
Henderson	36	8	12	16	L
Hickory	35	9	14	18	L
Jacksonville	34	17	21	25	M
Lumberton	34	14	18	22	L
New Bern AP	35	14	18	22	L
Raleigh/Durham AP	35	13	16	20	L
Rocky Mount	36	12	16	20	L
Wilmington AP	34	19	23	27	L
Winston-Salem AP	36	9	14	17	L
NORTH DAKOTA					
Bismarck AP	46	−31	−24	−19	VL
Devil's Lake	48	−30	−23	−19	M
Dickinson AP	46	−31	−23	−19	L
Fargo AP	46	−28	−22	−17	L
Grand Forks AP	48	−30	−26	−23	L
Jamestown AP	47	−29	−22	−18	L
Minot AP	48	−31	−24	−20	M
Williston	48	−28	−21	−17	M
OHIO					
Akron/Canton AP	41	− 5	1	6	M
Ashtabula	42	− 3	3	7	M
Athens	39	− 3	3	7	M
Bowling Green	41	− 7	− 1	3	M
Cambridge	40	− 6	0	4	M
Chillicothe	39	− 1	5	9	M
Cincinnati CO	39	2	8	12	L
Cleveland AP	41	− 2	2	7	M
Columbus AP	40	− 1	2	7	M
Dayton AP	39	− 2	0	6	M
Defiance	41	− 7	− 1	1	M
Findlay AP	41	− 6	0	4	M
Fremont	41	− 7	− 1	3	M
Hamilton	39	− 2	4	8	M
Lancaster	39	− 5	1	5	M
Lima	40	− 6	0	4	M
Mansfield AP	40	− 7	1	3	M
Marion	40	− 5	1	6	M
Middletown	39	− 3	3	7	M
Newark	40	− 7	− 1	3	M
Norwalk	41	− 7	− 1	3	M
Portsmouth	38	0	5	9	L
Sandusky CO	41	− 2	4	8	M
Springfield	40	− 3	3	7	M
OHIO (continued)					
Steubenville	40	− 2	4	9	M
Toledo AP	41	− 5	1	5	M
Warren	41	− 6	0	4	M
Wooster	40	− 7	− 1	3	M
Youngstown AP	41	− 5	1	6	M
Zanesville AP	40	− 7	− 1	3	M
OKLAHOMA					
Ada	34	6	12	16	H
Altus AFB	34	7	14	18	H
Ardmore	34	9	15	19	H
Bartlesville	36	− 1	5	9	H
Chickasha	35	5	12	16	H
Enid-Vance AFB	36	3	10	14	H
Lawton AP	34	6	13	16	H
McAlester	34	7	13	17	H
Muskogee AP	35	6	12	16	M
Norman	35	5	11	15	H
Oklahoma City AP	35	4	11	15	H
Ponca City	36	1	8	12	H
Seminole	35	6	12	16	H
Stillwater	36	2	9	13	H
Tulsa AP	36	4	12	16	H
Woodward	36	− 3	4	8	H
OREGON					
Albany	44	17	23	27	VL
Astoria AP	46	22	27	30	M
Baker AP	44	−10	− 3	1	VL
Bend	44	− 7	0	4	VL
Corvallis	44	17	23	27	VL
Eugene AP	44	16	22	26	VL
Grants Pass	42	16	22	26	VL
Klamath Falls AP	42	− 5	1	5	VL
Medford AP	42	15	21	23	VL
Pendleton AP	45	− 2	3	10	VL
Portland AP	45	17	21	24	L
Portland CO	45	21	26	29	L
Roseburg AP	43	19	25	29	VL
Salem AP	45	15	21	25	VL
The Dalles	45	7	13	17	VL
PENNSYLVANIA					
Allentown AP	40	− 2	3	5	M
Altoona CO	40	− 4	1	5	L
Butler	40	− 8	− 2	2	L
Chambersburg	40	0	5	9	L
Erie AP	42	1	7	11	M
Harrisburg AP	40	4	9	13	L
Johnstown	40	− 4	1	5	L
Lancaster	40	− 3	2	6	L
Meadville	41	− 6	0	4	M
New Castle	41	− 7	− 1	4	M
Philadelphia AP	39	7	11	15	M
Pittsburgh AP	40	− 1	5	9	M
Pittsburgh CO	40	1	7	11	M
Reading CO	40	1	6	9	M
Scranton/Wilkes-Barre	41	− 3	2	6	L
State College	40	− 3	2	6	L
Sunbury	40	− 2	3	7	L
Uniontown	39	− 1	4	8	L
Warren	41	− 8	− 3	1	L
West Chester	40	4	9	13	M
Williamsport AP	41	− 5	1	5	L
York	40	− 1	4	8	L
RHODE ISLAND					
Newport	41	1	5	11	H
Providence AP	41	0	6	10	M

State and Station	Lat. °	Winter Median of Annual Extremes	99%	97½%	Coincident Wind Velocity
SOUTH CAROLINA					
Anderson	34	13	18	22	L
Charleston AFB	32	19	23	27	L
Charleston CO	32	23	26	30	L
Columbia AP	34	16	20	23	L
Florence AP	34	16	21	25	L
Georgetown	33	19	23	26	L
Greenville AP	34	14	19	23	L
Greenwood	34	15	19	23	L
Orangeburg	33	17	21	25	L
Rock Hill	35	13	17	21	L
Spartanburg AP	35	13	18	22	L
Sumter-Shaw AFB	34	18	23	26	L
SOUTH DAKOTA					
Aberdeen AP	45	−29	−22	−18	L
Brookings	44	−26	−19	−15	M
Huron AP	44	−24	−16	−12	L
Mitchell	43	−22	−15	−11	M
Pierre AP	44	−21	−13	− 9	M
Rapid City AP	44	−17	− 9	− 6	M
Sioux Falls AP	43	−21	−14	−10	M
Watertown AP	45	−27	−20	−16	L
Yankton	43	−18	−11	− 7	M
TENNESSEE					
Athens	33	10	14	18	L
Bristol-Tri City AP	36	6	11	16	L
Chattanooga AP	35	11	15	19	L
Clarksville	36	6	12	16	L
Columbia	35	8	13	17	L
Dyersburg	36	7	13	17	L
Greenville	35	5	10	14	L
Jackson AP	35	8	14	17	L
Knoxville AP	35	9	13	17	L
Memphis AP	35	11	17	21	L
Murfreesboro	35	7	13	17	L
Nashville AP	36	6	12	16	L
Tullahoma	35	7	13	17	L
TEXAS					
Abilene AP	32	12	17	21	M
Alice AP	27	26	30	34	M
Amarillo AP	35	2	8	12	M
Austin AP	30	19	25	29	M
Bay City	29	25	29	33	M
Beaumont	30	25	29	33	M
Beeville	28	24	28	32	M
Big Spring AP	32	12	18	22	M
Brownsville AP	25	32	36	40	M
Brownwood	31	15	20	25	M
Bryan AP	30	22	27	31	M
Corpus Christi AP	27	28	32	36	M
Corsicana	32	16	21	25	M
Dallas AP	32	14	19	24	H
Del Rio, Laughlin AFB	29	24	28	31	M
Denton	33	12	18	22	H
Eagle Pass	28	23	27	31	L
El Paso AP	31	16	21	25	L
Fort Worth AP	32	14	20	24	H
Galveston AP	29	28	32	36	M
Greenville	33	13	19	24	H
Harlingen	26	30	34	38	M
Houston AP	29	23	28	32	M
Houston CO	29	24	29	33	M
Huntsville	30	22	27	31	M
TEXAS (continued)					
Killeen-Gray AFB	31	17	22	26	M
Lamesa	32	7	14	18	M
Laredo AFB	27	29	32	36	L
Longview	32	16	21	25	M
Lubbock AP	33	4	11	15	M
Lufkin AP	31	19	24	28	M
McAllen	26	30	34	38	M
Midland AP	32	13	19	23	M
Mineral Wells AP	32	12	18	22	H
Palestine CO	31	16	21	25	M
Pampa	35	0	7	11	M
Pecos	31	10	15	19	L
Plainview	34	3	10	14	M
Port Arthur AP	30	25	29	33	M
San Angelo, Goodfellow AFB	31	15	20	25	M
San Antonio AP	29	22	25	30	L
Sherman-Perrin AFB	33	12	18	23	H
Snyder	32	9	15	19	M
Temple	31	18	23	27	M
Tyler AP	32	15	20	24	M
Vernon	34	7	14	18	H
Victoria AP	28	24	28	32	M
Waco AP	31	16	21	26	M
Wichita Falls AP	34	9	15	19	H
UTAH					
Cedar City AP	37	−10	− 1	6	VL
Logan	41	− 7	3	7	VL
Moab	38	2	12	16	VL
Ogden CO	41	− 3	7	11	VL
Price	39	− 7	3	7	L
Provo	40	− 6	2	6	L
Richfield	38	−10	− 1	3	L
St. George CO	37	13	22	26	VL
Salt Lake City AP	40	− 2	5	9	L
Vernal AP	40	−20	−10	− 6	VL
VERMONT					
Barre	44	−23	−17	−13	L
Burlington AP	44	−18	−12	− 7	M
Rutland	43	−18	−12	− 8	L
VIRGINIA					
Charlottesville	38	7	11	15	L
Danville AP	36	9	13	17	L
Fredericksburg	38	6	10	14	M
Harrisonburg	38	0	5	9	L
Lynchburg AP	37	10	15	19	L
Norfolk AP	36	18	20	23	M
Petersburg	37	10	15	18	L
Richmond AP	37	10	14	18	L
Roanoke AP	37	9	15	18	L
Staunton	38	3	8	12	L
Winchester	39	1	6	10	L
WASHINGTON					
Aberdeen	47	19	24	27	M
Bellingham AP	48	8	14	18	L
Bremerton	47	17	24	29	L
Ellensburg AP	47	− 5	2	6	VL
Everett-Paine AFB	47	13	19	24	L
Kennewick	46	4	11	15	VL
Longview	46	14	20	24	L
Moses Lake, Larson AFB	47	−14	− 7	− 1	VL
Olympia AP	47	15	21	25	L
Port Angeles	48	20	26	29	M
Seattle-Boeing Fld	47	17	23	27	L

State and Station	Lat. °	Median of Annual Extremes	Winter		Coincident Wind Velocity
			99%	97½%	
WASHINGTON (*continued*)					
Seattle CO...............	47	22	28	32	L
Seattle-Tacoma AP.......	47	14	20	24	L
Spokane AP.............	47	− 5	− 2	4	VL
Tacoma-McChord AFB...	47	14	20	24	L
Walla Walla AP..........	46	5	12	16	VL
Wenatchee..............	47	− 2	5	9	VL
Yakima AP..............	46	− 1	6	10	VL
WEST VIRGINIA					
Beckley................	37	− 4	0	6	L
Bluefield AP............	37	1	6	10	L
Charleston AP...........	38	1	9	14	L
Clarksburg.............	39	− 2	3	7	L
Elkins AP..............	38	− 4	1	5	L
Huntington CO..........	38	4	10	14	L
Martinsburg AP.........	39	1	6	10	L
Morgantown AP.........	39	− 2	3	7	L
Parkersburg CO.........	39	2	8	12	L
Wheeling...............	40	0	5	9	L
WISCONSIN					
Appleton...............	44	−16	−10	− 6	M
Ashland................	46	−27	−21	−17	L
Beloit..................	42	−13	− 7	− 3	M
Eau Claire AP...........	44	−21	−15	−11	L
Fond du Lac............	43	−17	−11	− 7	M
Green Bay AP...........	44	−16	−12	− 7	M
La Crosse AP...........	43	−18	−12	− 8	M
Madison AP............	43	−13	− 9	− 5	M
Manitowoc.............	44	−11	− 5	− 1	M
Marinette..............	45	−14	− 8	− 4	M
Milwaukee AP..........	43	−11	− 6	− 2	M
Racine.................	42	−10	− 4	0	M
Sheboygan..............	43	−10	− 4	0	M
Stevens Point...........	44	−22	−16	−12	M
Waukesha..............	43	−12	− 6	− 2	M
Wausau AP.............	44	−24	−18	−14	M
WYOMING					
Casper AP..............	42	−20	−11	− 5	L
Cheyenne AP...........	41	−15	− 6	− 2	M
Cody AP...............	44	−23	−13	− 9	L
Evanston...............	41	−22	−12	− 8	VL
Lander AP..............	42	−26	−16	−12	VL
Laramie AP.............	41	−17	− 6	− 2	M
Newcastle..............	43	−18	− 9	− 5	M
Rawlins................	41	−24	−15	−11	L
Rock Springs AP........	41	−16	− 6	− 1	VL
Sheridan AP............	44	−21	−12	− 7	L
Torrington.............	42	−20	−11	− 7	M

Appendix 4B Average Monthly and Yearly Degree-Days for the United States[a][b][c]

State	Station	Avg. Winter Temp	July	Aug.	Sept.	Oct.	Nov.	Dec.	Jan.	Feb.	Mar.	Apr.	May	June	Yearly Total
Ala.	Birmingham............A	54.2	0	0	6	93	363	555	592	462	363	108	9	0	2551
	Huntsville.............A	51.3	0	0	12	127	426	663	694	557	434	138	19	0	3070
	Mobile................A	59.9	0	0	0	22	213	357	415	300	211	42	0	0	1560
	Montgomery...........A	55.4	0	0	0	68	330	527	543	417	316	90	0	0	2291
Alaska	Anchorage.............A	23.0	245	291	516	930	1284	1572	1631	1316	1293	879	592	315	10864
	Fairbanks.............A	6.7	171	332	642	1203	1833	2254	2359	1901	1739	1068	555	222	14279
	Juneau................A	32.1	301	338	483	725	921	1135	1237	1070	1073	810	601	381	9075
	Nome.................A	13.1	481	496	693	1094	1455	1820	1879	1666	1770	1314	930	573	14171
Ariz.	Flagstaff..............A	35.6	46	68	201	558	867	1073	1169	991	911	651	437	180	7152
	Phoenix...............A	58.5	0	0	0	22	234	415	474	328	217	75	0	0	1765
	Tucson................A	58.1	0	0	0	25	231	406	471	344	242	75	6	0	1800
	Winslow..............A	43.0	0	0	6	245	711	1008	1054	770	601	291	96	0	4782
	Yuma.................A	64.2	0	0	0	0	108	264	307	190	90	15	0	0	974
Ark.	Fort Smith.............A	50.3	0	0	12	127	450	704	781	596	456	144	22	0	3292
	Little Rock............A	50.5	0	0	9	127	465	716	756	577	434	126	9	0	3219
	Texarkana.............A	54.2	0	0	0	78	345	561	626	468	350	105	0	0	2533
Calif.	Bakersfield............A	55.4	0	0	0	37	282	502	546	364	267	105	19	0	2122
	Bishop................A	46.0	0	0	48	260	576	797	874	680	555	306	143	36	4275
	Blue Canyon...........A	42.2	28	37	108	347	594	781	896	795	806	597	412	195	5596
	Burbank...............A	58.6	0	0	6	43	177	301	366	277	239	138	81	18	1646
	Eureka................C	49.9	270	257	258	329	414	499	546	470	505	438	372	285	4643
	Fresno................A	53.3	0	0	0	84	354	577	605	426	335	162	62	6	2611
	Long Beach............A	57.8	0	0	9	47	171	316	397	311	264	171	93	24	1803
	Los Angeles...........A	57.4	28	28	42	78	180	291	372	302	288	219	158	81	2061
	Los Angeles...........C	60.3	0	0	6	31	132	229	310	230	202	123	68	18	1349
	Mt. Shasta............C	41.2	25	34	123	406	696	902	983	784	738	525	347	159	5722
	Oakland...............A	53.5	53	50	45	127	309	481	527	400	353	255	180	90	2870
	Red Bluff.............A	53.8	0	0	0	53	318	555	605	428	341	168	47	0	2515
	Sacramento............A	53.9	0	0	0	56	321	546	583	414	332	178	72	0	2502
	Sacramento............C	54.4	0	0	0	62	312	533	561	392	310	173	76	0	2419
	Sandberg..............C	46.8	0	0	30	202	480	691	778	661	620	426	264	57	4209
	San Diego.............A	59.5	9	0	21	43	135	236	298	235	214	135	90	42	1458
	San Francisco..........A	53.4	81	78	60	143	306	462	508	395	363	279	214	126	3015
	San Francisco..........C	55.1	192	174	102	118	231	388	443	336	319	279	239	180	3001
	Santa Maria...........A	54.3	99	93	96	146	270	391	459	370	363	282	233	165	2967
Colo.	Alamosa...............A	29.7	65	99	279	639	1065	1420	1476	1162	1020	696	440	168	8529
	Colorado Springs.......A	37.3	9	25	132	456	825	1032	1128	938	893	582	319	84	6423
	Denver................A	37.6	6	9	117	428	819	1035	1132	938	887	558	288	66	6283
	Denver................C	40.8	0	0	90	366	714	905	1004	851	800	492	254	48	5524
	Grand Junction.........A	39.3	0	0	30	313	786	1113	1209	907	729	387	146	21	5641
	Pueblo................A	40.4	0	0	54	326	750	986	1085	871	772	429	174	15	5462
Conn.	Bridgeport.............A	39.9	0	0	66	307	615	986	1079	966	853	510	208	27	5617
	Hartford..............A	37.3	0	12	117	394	714	1101	1190	1042	908	519	205	33	6235
	New Haven............A	39.0	0	12	87	347	648	1011	1097	991	871	543	245	45	5897
Del.	Wilmington............A	42.5	0	0	51	270	588	927	980	874	735	387	112	6	4930
D. C.	Washington............A	45.7	0	0	33	217	519	834	871	762	626	288	74	0	4224
Fla.	Apalachicola...........C	61.2	0	0	0	16	153	319	347	260	180	33	0	0	1308
	Daytona Beach.........A	64.5	0	0	0	0	75	211	248	190	140	15	0	0	879
	Fort Myers............A	68.6	0	0	0	0	24	109	146	101	62	0	0	0	442
	Jacksonville...........A	61.9	0	0	0	12	144	310	332	246	174	21	0	0	1239
	Key West.............A	73.1	0	0	0	0	0	28	40	31	9	0	0	0	108
	Lakeland..............C	66.7	0	0	0	0	57	164	195	146	99	0	0	0	661
	Miami................A	71.1	0	0	0	0	0	65	74	56	19	0	0	0	214

Notes: a. From ASHRAE *Guide and Data Book*; base temperature 65°F.
b. A indicates airport; C indicates city.
c. Average winter temperatures for October through April, inclusive.

State	Station	Avg. Winter Temp	July	Aug.	Sept.	Oct.	Nov.	Dec.	Jan.	Feb.	Mar.	Apr.	May	June	Yearly Total
Fla. (Cont'd)	Miami Beach............C	72.5	0	0	0	0	0	40	56	36	9	0	0	0	141
	Orlando...............A	65.7	0	0	0	0	72	198	220	165	105	6	0	0	766
	Pensacola..............A	60.4	0	0	0	19	195	353	400	277	183	36	0	0	1463
	Tallahassee.............A	60.1	0	0	0	28	198	360	375	286	202	36	0	0	1485
	Tampa.................A	66.4	0	0	0	0	60	171	202	148	102	0	0	0	683
	West Palm Beach.......A	68.4	0	0	0	0	6	65	87	64	31	0	0	0	253
Ga.	Athens................A	51.8	0	0	12	115	405	632	642	529	431	141	22	0	2929
	Atlanta................A	51.7	0	0	18	124	417	648	636	518	428	147	25	0	2961
	Augusta...............A	54.5	0	0	0	78	333	552	549	445	350	90	0	0	2397
	Columbus..............A	54.8	0	0	0	87	333	543	552	434	338	96	0	0	2383
	Macon.................A	56.2	0	0	0	71	297	502	505	403	295	63	0	0	2136
	Rome..................A	49.9	0	0	24	161	474	701	710	577	468	177	34	0	3326
	Savannah..............A	57.8	0	0	0	47	246	437	437	353	254	45	0	0	1819
	Thomasville............C	60.0	0	0	0	25	198	366	394	305	208	33	0	0	1529
Hawaii	Lihue..................A	72.7	0	0	0	0	0	0	0	0	0	0	0	0	0
	Honolulu...............A	74.2	0	0	0	0	0	0	0	0	0	0	0	0	0
	Hilo...................A	71.9	0	0	0	0	0	0	0	0	0	0	0	0	0
Idaho	Boise..................A	39.7	0	0	132	415	792	1017	1113	854	722	438	245	81	5809
	Lewiston...............A	41.0	0	0	123	403	756	933	1063	815	694	426	239	90	5542
	Pocatello...............A	34.8	0	0	172	493	900	1166	1324	1058	905	555	319	141	7033
Ill.	Cairo..................C	47.9	0	0	36	164	513	791	856	680	539	195	47	0	3821
	Chicago (O'Hare)........A	35.8	0	12	117	381	807	1166	1265	1086	939	534	260	72	6639
	Chicago (Midway).......A	37.5	0	0	81	326	753	1113	1209	1044	890	480	211	48	6155
	Chicago................C	38.9	0	0	66	279	705	1051	1150	1000	868	489	226	48	5882
	Moline.................A	36.4	0	9	99	335	774	1181	1314	1100	918	450	189	39	6408
	Peoria.................A	38.1	0	6	87	326	759	1113	1218	1025	849	426	183	33	6025
	Rockford...............A	34.8	6	9	114	400	837	1221	1333	1137	961	516	236	60	6830
	Springfield.............A	40.6	0	0	72	291	696	1023	1135	935	769	354	136	18	5429
Ind.	Evansville..............A	45.0	0	0	66	220	606	896	955	767	620	237	68	0	4435
	Fort Wayne.............A	37.3	0	9	105	378	783	1135	1178	1028	890	471	189	39	6205
	Indianapolis............A	39.6	0	0	90	316	723	1051	1113	949	809	432	177	39	5699
	South Bend............A	36.6	0	6	111	372	777	1125	1221	1070	933	525	239	60	6439
Iowa	Burlington..............A	37.6	0	0	93	322	768	1135	1259	1042	859	426	177	33	6114
	Des Moines............A	35.5	0	6	96	363	828	1225	1370	1137	915	438	180	30	6588
	Dubuque...............A	32.7	12	31	156	450	906	1287	1420	1204	1026	546	260	78	7376
	Sioux City.............A	34.0	0	9	108	369	867	1240	1435	1198	989	483	214	39	6951
	Waterloo..............A	32.6	12	19	138	428	909	1296	1460	1221	1023	531	229	54	7320
Kans.	Concordia..............A	40.4	0	0	57	276	705	1023	1163	935	781	372	149	18	5479
	Dodge City.............A	42.5	0	0	33	251	666	939	1051	840	719	354	124	9	4986
	Goodland..............A	37.8	0	6	81	381	810	1073	1166	955	884	507	236	42	6141
	Topeka................A	41.7	0	0	57	270	672	980	1122	893	722	330	124	12	5182
	Wichita...............A	44.2	0	0	33	229	618	905	1023	804	645	270	87	6	4620
Ky.	Covington..............A	41.4	0	0	75	291	669	983	1035	893	756	390	149	24	5265
	Lexington..............A	43.8	0	0	54	239	609	902	946	818	685	325	105	0	4683
	Louisville..............A	44.0	0	0	54	248	609	890	930	818	682	315	105	9	4660
La.	Alexandria.............A	57.5	0	0	0	56	273	431	471	361	260	69	0	0	1921
	Baton Rouge...........A	59.8	0	0	0	31	216	369	409	294	208	33	0	0	1560
	Lake Charles...........A	60.5	0	0	0	19	210	341	381	274	195	39	0	0	1459
	New Orleans...........A	61.0	0	0	0	19	192	322	363	258	192	39	0	0	1385
	New Orleans...........C	61.8	0	0	0	12	165	291	344	241	177	24	0	0	1254
	Shreveport............A	56.2	0	0	0	47	297	477	552	426	304	81	0	0	2184
Me.	Caribou...............A	24.4	78	115	336	682	1044	1535	1690	1470	1308	858	468	183	9767
	Portland...............A	33.0	12	53	195	508	807	1215	1339	1182	1042	675	372	111	7511
Md.	Baltimore..............A	43.7	0	0	48	264	585	905	936	820	679	327	90	0	4654
	Baltimore..............C	46.2	0	0	27	189	486	806	859	762	629	288	65	0	4111
	Frederich.............A	42.0	0	0	66	307	624	955	995	876	741	384	127	12	5087
Mass.	Boston................A	40.0	0	9	60	316	603	983	1088	972	846	513	208	36	5634
	Nantucket.............A	40.2	12	22	93	332	573	896	992	941	896	621	384	129	5891
	Pittsfield..............A	32.6	25	59	219	524	831	1231	1339	1196	1063	660	326	105	7578
	Worcester.............A	34.7	6	34	147	450	774	1172	1271	1123	998	612	304	78	6969

State	Station	Avg. Winter Temp	July	Aug.	Sept.	Oct.	Nov.	Dec.	Jan.	Feb.	Mar.	Apr.	May	June	Yearly Total
Mich.	Alpena.................A	29.7	68	105	273	580	912	1268	1404	1299	1218	777	446	156	8506
	Detroit (City)...........A	37.2	0	0	87	360	738	1088	1181	1058	936	522	220	42	6232
	Detroit (Wayne)........A	37.1	0	0	96	353	738	1088	1194	1061	933	534	239	57	6293
	Detroit (Willow Run)....A	37.2	0	0	90	357	750	1104	1190	1053	921	519	229	45	6258
	Escanaba..............C	29.6	59	87	243	539	924	1293	1445	1296	1203	777	456	159	8481
	Flint..................A	33.1	16	40	159	465	843	1212	1330	1198	1066	639	319	90	7377
	Grand Rapids..........A	34.9	9	28	135	434	804	1147	1259	1134	1011	579	279	75	6894
	Lansing...............A	34.8	6	22	138	431	813	1163	1262	1142	1011	579	273	69	6909
	Marquette.............C	30.2	59	81	240	527	936	1268	1411	1268	1187	771	468	177	8393
	Muskegon.............A	36.0	12	28	120	400	762	1088	1209	1100	995	594	310	78	6696
	Sault Ste. Marie........A	27.7	96	105	279	580	951	1367	1525	1380	1277	810	477	201	9048
Minn.	Duluth................A	23.4	71	109	330	632	1131	1581	1745	1518	1355	840	490	198	10000
	Minneapolis...........A	28.3	22	31	189	505	1014	1454	1631	1380	1166	621	288	81	8382
	Rochester.............A	28.8	25	34	186	474	1005	1438	1593	1366	1150	630	301	93	8295
Miss.	Jackson...............A	55.7	0	0	0	65	315	502	546	414	310	87	0	0	2239
	Meridian..............A	55.4	0	0	0	81	339	518	543	417	310	81	0	0	2289
	Vicksburg.............C	56.9	0	0	0	53	279	462	512	384	282	69	0	0	2041
Mo.	Columbia..............A	42.3	0	0	54	251	651	967	1076	874	716	324	121	12	5046
	Kansas City...........A	43.9	0	0	39	220	612	905	1032	818	682	294	109	0	4711
	St. Joseph.............A	40.3	0	6	60	285	708	1039	1172	949	769	348	133	15	5484
	St. Louis..............A	43.1	0	0	60	251	627	936	1026	848	704	312	121	15	4900
	St. Louis..............C	44.8	0	0	36	202	576	884	977	801	651	270	87	0	4484
	Springfield............A	44.5	0	0	45	223	600	877	973	781	660	291	105	6	4900
Mont.	Billings...............A	34.5	6	15	186	487	897	1135	1296	1100	970	570	285	102	7049
	Glasgow..............A	26.4	31	47	270	608	1104	1466	1711	1439	1187	648	335	150	8996
	Great Falls............A	32.8	28	53	258	543	921	1169	1349	1154	1063	642	384	186	7750
	Havre.................A	28.1	28	53	306	595	1065	1367	1584	1364	1181	657	338	162	8700
	Havre.................C	29.8	19	37	252	539	1014	1321	1528	1305	1116	612	304	135	8182
	Helena................A	31.1	31	59	294	601	1002	1265	1438	1170	1042	651	381	195	8129
	Kalispell..............A	31.4	50	99	321	654	1020	1240	1401	1134	1029	639	397	207	8191
	Miles City.............A	31.2	6	6	174	502	972	1296	1504	1252	1057	579	276	99	7723
	Missoula..............A	31.5	34	74	303	651	1035	1287	1420	1120	970	621	391	219	8125
Neb.	Grand Island..........A	36.0	0	6	108	381	834	1172	1314	1089	908	462	211	45	6530
	Lincoln...............C	38.8	0	6	75	301	726	1066	1237	1016	834	402	171	30	5864
	Norfolk...............A	34.0	9	0	111	397	873	1234	1414	1179	983	498	233	48	6979
	North Platte...........A	35.5	0	6	123	440	885	1166	1271	1039	930	519	248	57	6684
	Omaha...............A	35.6	0	12	105	357	828	1175	1355	1126	939	465	208	42	6612
	Scottsbluff............A	35.9	0	0	138	459	876	1128	1231	1008	921	552	285	75	6673
	Valentine.............A	32.6	9	12	165	493	942	1237	1395	1176	1045	579	288	84	7425
Nev.	Elko..................A	34.0	9	34	225	561	924	1197	1314	1036	911	621	409	192	7433
	Ely...................A	33.1	28	43	234	592	939	1184	1308	1075	977	672	456	225	7733
	Las Vegas.............A	53.5	0	0	0	78	387	617	688	487	335	111	6	0	2709
	Reno.................A	39.3	43	87	204	490	801	1026	1073	823	729	510	357	189	6332
	Winnemucca..........A	36.7	0	34	210	536	876	1091	1172	916	837	573	363	153	6761
N. H.	Concord..............A	33.0	6	50	177	505	822	1240	1358	1184	1032	636	298	75	7383
	Mt. Washington Obsv....	15.2	493	536	720	1057	1341	1742	1820	1663	1652	1260	930	603	13817
N. J.	Atlantic City...........A	43.2	0	0	39	251	549	880	936	848	741	420	133	15	4812
	Newark...............A	42.8	0	0	30	248	573	921	983	876	729	381	118	0	4589
	Trenton...............C	42.4	0	0	57	264	576	924	989	885	753	399	121	12	4980
N. M.	Albuquerque...........A	45.0	0	0	12	229	642	868	930	703	595	288	81	0	4348
	Clayton...............A	42.0	0	6	66	310	699	899	986	812	747	429	183	21	5158
	Raton................A	38.1	9	28	126	431	825	1048	1116	904	834	543	301	63	6228
	Roswell...............A	47.5	0	0	18	202	573	806	840	641	481	201	31	0	3793
	Silver City............A	48.0	0	0	6	183	525	729	791	605	518	261	87	0	3705
N. Y.	Albany................A	34.6	0	19	138	440	777	1194	1311	1156	992	564	239	45	6875
	Albany................C	37.2	0	9	102	375	699	1104	1218	1072	908	498	186	30	6201
	Binghamton...........A	33.9	22	65	201	471	810	1184	1277	1154	1045	645	313	99	7286
	Binghamton...........C	36.6	0	28	141	406	732	1107	1190	1081	949	543	229	45	6451
	Buffalo...............A	34.5	19	37	141	440	777	1156	1256	1145	1039	645	329	78	7062
	New York (Cent. Park)..	42.8	0	0	30	233	540	902	986	885	760	408	118	9	4871
	New York (La Guardia)..A	43.1	0	0	27	223	528	887	973	879	750	414	124	6	4811

State	Station	Avg. Winter Temp	July	Aug.	Sept.	Oct.	Nov.	Dec.	Jan.	Feb.	Mar.	Apr.	May	June	Yearly Total
	New York (Kennedy)....A	41.4	0	0	36	248	564	933	1029	935	815	480	167	12	5219
	Rochester...........A	35.4	9	31	126	415	747	1125	1234	1123	1014	597	279	48	6748
	Schenectady...........C	35.4	0	22	123	422	756	1159	1283	1131	970	543	211	30	6650
	Syracuse...........A	35.2	6	28	132	415	744	1153	1271	1140	1004	570	248	45	6756
N. C.	Asheville...........C	46.7	0	0	48	245	555	775	784	683	592	273	87	0	4042
	Cape Hatteras...........	53.3	0	0	0	78	273	521	580	518	440	177	25	0	2612
	Charlotte...........A	50.4	0	0	6	124	438	691	691	582	481	156	22	0	3191
	Greensboro...........A	47.5	0	0	33	192	513	778	784	672	552	234	47	0	3805
	Raleigh...........A	49.4	0	0	21	164	450	716	725	616	487	180	34	0	3393
	Wilmington...........A	54.6	0	0	0	74	291	521	546	462	357	96	0	0	2347
	Winston-Salem...........A	48.4	0	0	21	171	483	747	753	652	524	207	37	0	3595
N. D.	Bismarck...........A	26.6	34	28	222	577	1083	1463	1708	1442	1203	645	329	117	8851
	Devils Lake...........C	22.4	40	53	273	642	1191	1634	1872	1579	1345	753	381	138	9901
	Fargo...........A	24.8	28	37	219	574	1107	1569	1789	1520	1262	690	332	99	9226
	Williston...........A	25.2	31	43	261	601	1122	1513	1758	1473	1262	681	357	141	9243
Ohio	Akron-Canton...........A	38.1	0	9	96	381	726	1070	1138	1016	871	489	202	39	6037
	Cincinnati...........C	45.1	0	0	39	208	558	862	915	790	642	294	96	6	4410
	Cleveland...........A	37.2	9	25	105	384	738	1088	1159	1047	918	552	260	66	6351
	Columbus...........A	39.7	0	6	84	347	714	1039	1088	949	809	426	171	27	5660
	Columbus...........C	41.5	0	0	57	285	651	977	1032	902	760	396	136	15	5211
	Dayton...........A	39.8	0	6	78	310	696	1045	1097	955	809	429	167	30	5622
	Mansfield...........A	36.9	9	22	114	397	768	1110	1169	1042	924	543	245	60	6403
	Sandusky...........C	39.1	0	6	66	313	684	1032	1107	991	868	495	198	36	5796
	Toledo...........A	36.4	0	16	117	406	792	1138	1200	1056	924	543	242	60	6494
	Youngstown...........A	36.8	6	19	120	412	771	1104	1169	1047	921	540	248	60	6417
Okla.	Oklahoma City...........A	48.3	0	0	15	164	498	766	868	664	527	189	34	0	3725
	Tulsa...........A	47.7	0	0	18	158	522	787	893	683	539	213	47	0	3860
Ore.	Astoria...........A	45.6	146	130	210	375	561	679	753	622	636	480	363	231	5186
	Burns...........C	35.9	12	37	210	515	867	1113	1246	988	856	570	366	177	6957
	Eugene...........A	45.6	34	34	129	366	585	719	803	627	589	426	279	135	4726
	Meacham...........A	34.2	84	124	288	580	918	1091	1209	1005	983	726	527	339	7874
	Medford...........A	43.2	0	0	78	372	678	871	918	697	642	432	242	78	5008
	Pendleton...........A	42.6	0	0	111	350	711	884	1017	773	617	396	205	63	5127
	Portland...........A	45.6	25	28	114	335	597	735	825	644	586	396	245	105	4635
	Portland...........C	47.4	12	16	75	267	534	679	769	594	536	351	198	78	4109
	Roseburg...........A	46.3	22	16	105	329	567	713	766	608	570	405	267	123	4491
	Salem...........A	45.4	37	31	111	338	594	729	822	647	611	417	273	144	4754
Pa.	Allentown...........A	38.9	0	0	90	353	693	1045	1116	1002	849	471	167	24	5810
	Erie...........A	36.8	0	25	102	391	714	1063	1169	1081	973	585	288	60	6451
	Harrisburg...........A	41.2	0	0	63	298	648	992	1045	907	766	396	124	12	5251
	Philadelphia...........A	41.8	0	0	60	297	620	965	1016	889	747	392	118	40	5144
	Philadelphia...........C	44.5	0	0	30	205	513	856	924	823	691	351	93	0	4486
	Pittsburgh...........A	38.4	0	9	105	375	726	1063	1119	1002	874	480	195	39	5987
	Pittsburgh...........C	42.2	0	0	60	291	615	930	983	885	763	390	124	12	5053
	Reading...........C	42.4	0	0	54	257	597	939	1001	885	735	372	105	0	4945
	Scranton...........A	37.2	0	19	132	434	762	1104	1156	1028	893	498	195	33	6254
	Williamsport...........A	38.5	0	9	111	375	717	1073	1122	1002	856	468	177	24	5934
R. I.	Block Island...........A	40.1	0	16	78	307	594	902	1020	955	877	612	344	99	5804
	Providence...........A	38.8	0	16	96	372	660	1023	1110	988	868	534	236	51	5954
S. C..	Charleston...........A	56.4	0	0	0	59	282	471	487	389	291	54	0	0	2033
	Charleston...........C	57.9	0	0	0	34	210	425	443	367	273	42	0	0	1794
	Columbia...........A	54.0	0	0	0	84	345	577	570	470	357	81	0	0	2484
	Florence...........A	54.5	0	0	0	78	315	552	552	459	347	84	0	0	2387
	Greenville-Spartenburg...A	51.6	0	0	6	121	399	651	660	546	446	132	19	0	2980
S. D.	Huron...........A	28.8	9	12	165	508	1014	1432	1628	1355	1125	600	288	87	8223
	Rapid City...........A	33.4	22	12	165	481	897	1172	1333	1145	1051	615	326	126	7345
	Sioux Falls...........A	30.6	19	25	168	462	972	1361	1544	1285	1082	573	270	78	7839
Tenn.	Bristol...........A	46.2	0	0	51	236	573	828	828	700	598	261	68	0	4143
	Chattanooga...........A	50.3	0	0	18	143	468	698	722	577	453	150	25	0	3254
	Knoxville...........A	49.2	0	0	30	171	489	725	732	613	493	198	43	0	3494
	Memphis...........A	50.5	0	0	18	130	447	698	729	585	456	147	22	0	3232

State or Prov.	Station	Avg. Winter Temp	July	Aug.	Sept.	Oct.	Nov.	Dec.	Jan.	Feb.	Mar.	Apr.	May	June	Yearly Total
	Memphis..............C	51.6	0	0	12	102	396	648	710	568	434	129	16	0	3015
	Nashville..............A	48.9	0	0	30	158	495	732	778	644	512	189	40	0	3578
	Oak Ridge..............C	47.7	0	0	39	192	531	772	778	669	552	228	56	0	3817
Tex.	Abilene..............A	53.9	0	0	0	99	366	586	642	470	347	114	0	0	2624
	Amarillo..............A	47.0	0	0	18	205	570	797	877	664	546	252	56	0	3985
	Austin..............A	59.1	0	0	0	31	225	388	468	325	223	51	0	0	1711
	Brownsville..............A	67.7	0	0	0	0	66	149	205	106	74	0	0	0	600
	Corpus Christi..........A	64.6	0	0	0	0	120	220	291	174	109	0	0	0	914
	Dallas..............A	55.3	0	0	0	62	321	524	601	440	319	90	6	0	2363
	El Paso..............A	52.9	0	0	0	84	414	648	685	445	319	105	0	0	2700
	Fort Worth..............A	55.1	0	0	0	65	324	536	614	448	319	99	0	0	2405
	Galveston..............A	62.2	0	0	0	6	147	276	360	263	189	33	0	0	1274
	Galveston..............C	62.0	0	0	0	0	138	270	350	258	189	30	0	0	1235
	Houston..............C	61.0	0	0	0	6	183	307	384	288	192	36	0	0	1396
	Houston..............C	62.0	0	0	0	0	165	288	363	258	174	30	0	0	1278
	Laredo..............A	66.0	0	0	0	0	105	217	267	134	74	0	0	0	797
	Lubbock..............A	48.8	0	0	18	174	513	744	800	613	484	201	31	0	3578
	Midland..............A	53.8	0	0	0	87	381	592	651	468	322	90	0	0	2591
	Port Arthur..............A	60.5	0	0	0	22	207	329	384	274	192	39	0	0	1447
	San Angelo..............A	56.0	0	0	0	68	318	536	567	412	288	66	0	0	2255
	San Antonio..............A	60.1	0	0	0	31	204	363	428	286	195	39	0	0	1546
	Victoria..............A	62.7	0	0	0	6	150	270	344	230	152	21	0	0	1173
	Waco..............A	57.2	0	0	0	43	270	456	536	389	270	66	0	0	2030
	Wichita Falls..........A	53.0	0	0	0	99	381	632	698	518	378	120	6	0	2832
Utah	Milford..............A	36.5	0	0	99	443	867	1141	1252	988	822	519	279	87	6497
	Salt Lake City..........A	38.4	0	0	81	419	849	1082	1172	910	763	459	233	84	6052
	Wendover..............A	39.1	0	0	48	372	822	1091	1178	902	729	408	177	51	5778
Vt.	Burlington..............A	29.4	28	65	207	539	891	1349	1513	1333	1187	714	353	90	8269
Va.	Cape Henry..............C	50.0	0	0	0	112	360	645	694	633	536	246	53	0	3279
	Lynchburg..............A	46.0	0	0	51	223	540	822	849	731	605	267	78	0	4166
	Norfolk..............A	49.2	0	0	0	136	408	698	738	655	533	216	37	0	3421
	Richmond..............A	47.3	0	0	36	214	495	784	815	703	546	219	53	0	3865
	Roanoke..............A	46.1	0	0	51	229	549	825	834	722	614	261	65	0	4150
Wash.	Olympia..............A	44.2	68	71	198	422	636	753	834	675	645	450	307	177	5236
	Seattle-Tacoma..........A	44.2	56	62	162	391	633	750	828	678	657	474	295	159	5145
	Seattle..............C	46.9	50	47	129	329	543	657	738	599	577	396	242	117	4424
	Spokane..............A	36.5	9	25	168	493	879	1082	1231	980	834	531	288	135	6655
	Walla Walla..............C	43.8	0	0	87	310	681	843	986	745	589	342	177	45	4805
	Yakima..............A	39.1	0	12	144	450	828	1039	1163	868	713	435	220	69	5941
W. Va.	Charleston..............A	44.8	0	0	63	254	591	865	880	770	648	300	96	9	4476
	Elkins..............A	40.1	9	25	135	400	729	992	1008	896	791	444	198	48	5675
	Huntington..............A	45.0	0	0	63	257	585	856	880	764	636	294	99	12	4446
	Parkersburg..............C	43.5	0	0	60	264	606	905	942	826	691	339	115	6	4754
Wisc.	Green Bay..............A	30.3	28	50	174	484	924	1333	1494	1313	1141	654	335	99	8029
	La Crosse..............A	31.5	12	19	153	437	924	1339	1504	1277	1070	540	245	69	7589
	Madison..............A	30.9	25	40	174	474	930	1330	1473	1274	1113	618	310	102	7863
	Milwaukee..............A	32.6	43	47	174	471	876	1252	1376	1193	1054	642	372	135	7635
Wyo.	Casper..............A	33.4	6	16	192	524	942	1169	1290	1084	1020	657	381	129	7410
	Cheyenne..............A	34.2	28	37	219	543	909	1085	1212	1042	1026	702	428	150	7381
	Lander..............A	31.4	6	19	204	555	1020	1299	1417	1145	1017	654	381	153	7870
	Sheridan..............A	32.5	25	31	219	539	948	1200	1355	1154	1051	642	366	150	7680

Appendix 4C Solar Positions and Insolation Values for Various Latitudes[a]

Table I 24 Degrees North Latitude

(JAN 21 – JUL 21)

DATE	AM	PM	SOLAR POSITION ALT	SOLAR POSITION AZM	NORMAL	HORIZ.	14	24	34	54	90
JAN 21	7	5	4.8	65.6	71	10	17	21	25	28	31
	8	4	16.9	58.3	239	83	110	126	137	145	127
	9	3	27.9	48.8	288	151	188	207	221	228	176
	10	2	37.2	36.1	308	204	246	268	282	287	207
	11	1	43.6	19.6	317	237	283	306	319	324	226
	12		46.0	0.0	320	249	296	319	332	336	232
	SURFACE DAILY TOTALS				2766	1622	1984	2174	2300	2360	1766
FEB 21	7	5	9.3	74.6	158	35	44	49	53	56	46
	8	4	22.3	67.2	263	116	135	145	150	151	102
	9	3	34.4	57.6	298	187	213	225	230	228	141
	10	2	45.1	44.2	314	241	273	286	291	287	168
	11	1	53.0	25.0	321	276	310	324	328	323	185
	12		56.0	0.0	324	288	323	337	341	335	191
	SURFACE DAILY TOTALS				3036	1998	2276	2396	2446	2424	1476
MAR 21	7	5	13.7	83.8	194	60	63	64	62	59	27
	8	4	27.2	76.8	267	141	150	152	149	142	64
	9	3	40.2	67.9	295	212	226	229	225	214	95
	10	2	52.3	54.8	309	266	285	288	283	270	120
	11	1	61.9	33.4	315	300	322	326	320	305	135
	12		66.0	0.0	317	312	334	339	333	317	140
	SURFACE DAILY TOTALS				3078	2270	2428	2456	2412	2298	1022
APR 21	6	6	4.7	100.6	40	7	5	4	4	3	2
	7	5	18.3	94.9	203	83	77	70	62	51	10
	8	4	32.0	89.0	256	160	157	149	137	122	16
	9	3	45.6	81.9	280	227	227	220	206	186	41
	10	2	59.0	71.8	292	278	282	275	259	237	61
	11	1	71.1	51.6	298	310	316	309	293	269	74
	12		77.6	0.0	299	321	328	321	305	280	79
	SURFACE DAILY TOTALS				3036	2454	2458	2374	2228	2016	488
MAY 21	6	6	8.0	108.4	86	22	15	12	12	9	5
	7	5	21.2	103.2	203	98	85	73	59	44	12
	8	4	34.6	98.5	248	171	159	145	127	106	15
	9	3	48.3	93.6	269	233	224	210	190	165	16
	10	2	62.0	87.7	280	281	275	261	239	211	22
	11	1	75.5	76.9	286	311	307	293	270	240	34
	12		86.0	0.0	288	322	317	304	281	250	37
	SURFACE DAILY TOTALS				3032	2556	2447	2286	2072	1800	246
JUN 21	6	6	9.3	111.6	97	29	20	12	12	9	7
	7	5	22.3	106.8	201	103	87	73	58	41	13
	8	4	35.5	102.6	242	173	158	142	122	99	16
	9	3	49.0	98.7	263	234	221	204	182	155	18
	10	2	62.6	95.0	274	280	269	253	229	199	18
	11	1	76.3	90.8	279	309	300	283	259	227	19
	12		89.4	0.0	281	319	310	294	269	236	22
	SURFACE DAILY TOTALS				2994	2574	2422	2230	1992	1700	204
JUL 21	6	6	8.2	109.0	81	23	16	11	10	9	6
	7	5	21.4	103.8	195	98	85	73	59	44	13
	8	4	34.8	99.2	239	169	157	143	125	104	16
	9	3	48.4	94.5	261	231	221	207	187	161	18
	10	2	62.1	89.0	272	278	270	256	235	206	21
	11	1	75.7	79.2	278	307	302	287	265	235	32
	12		86.6	0.0	280	317	312	298	275	245	36
	SURFACE DAILY TOTALS				2932	2526	2412	2250	2036	1766	246

Headings: BTUH/SQ. FT. TOTAL INSOLATION ON SURFACES — NORMAL, HORIZ., and SOUTH FACING SURFACE ANGLE WITH HORIZ. (14, 24, 34, 54, 90).

(AUG 21 – DEC 21)

DATE	AM	PM	SOLAR POSITION ALT	SOLAR POSITION AZM	NORMAL	HORIZ.	14	24	34	54	90
AUG 21	6	6	5.0	101.3	35	7	5	4	4	4	2
	7	5	18.5	95.6	186	82	76	69	60	50	11
	8	4	32.2	89.7	241	158	154	146	134	118	16
	9	3	45.9	82.9	265	223	222	214	200	181	39
	10	2	59.3	73.0	278	273	275	268	252	230	58
	11	1	71.6	53.2	284	304	309	301	285	261	71
	12		78.3	0.0	286	315	320	313	296	272	75
	SURFACE DAILY TOTALS				2864	2408	2402	2316	2168	1958	470
SEP 21	7	5	13.7	83.8	173	57	60	60	59	56	26
	8	4	27.2	76.8	248	136	144	146	143	136	62
	9	3	40.2	67.9	278	205	218	221	217	206	93
	10	2	52.3	54.8	292	258	275	278	273	261	116
	11	1	61.9	33.4	299	291	311	315	309	295	131
	12		66.0	0.0	301	302	323	327	321	306	136
	SURFACE DAILY TOTALS				2878	2194	2342	2366	2322	2212	992
OCT 21	7	5	9.1	74.1	138	32	40	45	48	50	42
	8	4	22.0	66.7	247	111	129	139	144	145	99
	9	3	34.1	57.1	284	180	206	217	223	221	138
	10	2	44.7	43.8	301	234	265	277	282	279	165
	11	1	52.5	24.7	309	268	301	315	319	314	182
	12		55.5	0.0	311	279	314	328	332	327	188
	SURFACE DAILY TOTALS				2868	1928	2198	2314	2346	2364	1442
NOV 21	7	5	4.9	65.8	67	10	16	20	24	27	29
	8	4	17.0	58.4	232	82	108	123	135	142	124
	9	3	28.0	48.9	282	150	186	205	217	224	172
	10	2	37.3	36.3	303	203	244	265	278	283	204
	11	1	43.8	19.7	312	236	280	302	316	320	222
	12		46.2	0.0	315	247	293	315	328	332	228
	SURFACE DAILY TOTALS				2706	1610	1962	2146	2268	2324	1730
DEC 21	7	5	3.2	62.6	30	3	9	11	11	12	14
	8	4	14.9	55.3	225	71	99	116	129	139	130
	9	3	25.5	46.0	281	137	176	198	214	223	184
	10	2	34.3	33.7	304	189	234	258	275	283	217
	11	1	40.4	18.2	314	221	270	295	312	320	236
	12		42.6	0.0	317	232	282	308	325	332	243
	SURFACE DAILY TOTALS				2624	1474	1852	2058	2204	2286	1808

Headings: BTUH/SQ. FT. TOTAL INSOLATION ON SURFACES — NORMAL, HORIZ., and SOUTH FACING SURFACE ANGLE WITH HORIZ. (14, 24, 34, 54, 90).

Notes: a. From ASHRAE *Transactions*; ground reflection not included.

Appendix 4C—Continued

Table II 32 Degrees North Latitude

DATE	SOLAR TIME AM	SOLAR TIME PM	ALT	AZM	NORMAL	HORIZ.	22	32	42	52	90
JAN 21	7	5	1.4	65.2	1	0	0	0	0	1	1
	8	4	12.5	56.5	203	56	93	106	116	123	115
	9	3	22.5	46.0	269	118	175	193	206	212	181
	10	2	30.6	33.1	295	167	235	256	269	274	221
	11	1	36.1	17.5	306	198	273	295	308	312	245
	12		38.0	0.0	310	209	285	308	321	324	253
	SURFACE DAILY TOTALS				2458	1288	1839	2008	2118	2166	1779
FEB 21	7	5	7.1	73.5	121	22	34	37	40	42	38
	8	4	19.0	64.4	247	95	127	136	140	141	108
	9	3	29.9	53.4	288	161	206	217	222	220	158
	10	2	39.1	39.4	306	212	266	278	283	279	193
	11	1	45.6	21.4	315	244	304	317	321	315	214
	12		48.0	0.0	317	255	316	330	334	328	222
	SURFACE DAILY TOTALS				2872	1724	2188	2300	2345	2332	1644
MAR 21	7	5	12.7	81.9	185	54	60	60	59	56	32
	8	4	25.1	73.0	260	129	146	147	144	137	78
	9	3	36.8	62.1	290	194	222	224	220	209	119
	10	2	47.3	47.5	304	245	280	283	278	265	150
	11	1	55.0	26.8	311	277	317	321	315	300	170
	12		58.0	0.0	313	287	329	333	327	312	177
	SURFACE DAILY TOTALS				3012	2084	2378	2403	2358	2246	1276
APR 21	6	6	6.1	99.9	66	14	9	6	6		3
	7	5	18.8	92.2	206	86	78	71	62	51	10
	8	4	31.5	84.0	255	158	156	148	136	120	35
	9	3	43.9	74.2	278	220	225	217	203	183	68
	10	2	55.7	60.3	290	267	279	272	256	234	95
	11	1	65.4	37.5	295	297	313	306	290	265	112
	12		69.6	0.0	297	307	325	318	301	276	118
	SURFACE DAILY TOTALS				3076	2390	2444	2356	2206	1994	764
MAY 21	6	6	10.4	107.2	119	36	21	13	13	12	7
	7	5	22.8	100.1	211	107	88	75	60	44	13
	8	4	35.4	92.9	250	175	159	145	127	105	15
	9	3	48.1	84.7	269	233	223	209	188	163	33
	10	2	60.6	73.3	280	277	273	259	237	208	56
	11	1	72.0	51.9	285	305	305	290	268	237	72
	12		78.0	0.0	286	315	315	301	278	247	77
	SURFACE DAILY TOTALS				3112	2582	2454	2284	2064	1788	469
JUN 21	6	6	12.2	110.2	131	45	26	16	15	14	9
	7	5	24.3	103.4	210	115	91	76	59	41	14
	8	4	36.9	96.8	245	180	159	143	122	99	16
	9	3	49.6	89.4	264	236	221	204	181	153	19
	10	2	62.2	79.7	274	279	268	251	227	197	41
	11	1	74.2	60.9	279	306	299	282	257	224	56
	12		81.5	0.0	280	315	309	292	267	234	60
	SURFACE DAILY TOTALS				3084	2634	2436	2234	1990	1690	370
JUL 21	6	6	10.7	107.7	113	37	22	14	13	12	8
	7	5	23.1	100.6	203	107	87	75	60	44	14
	8	4	35.7	93.6	241	174	158	143	125	104	16
	9	3	48.4	85.5	261	231	220	205	185	159	31
	10	2	60.9	74.3	271	274	269	254	232	204	54
	11	1	72.4	53.3	277	302	300	285	262	232	69
	12		78.6	0.0	279	311	310	296	273	242	74
	SURFACE DAILY TOTALS				3012	2558	2422	2250	2030	1754	458

DATE	SOLAR TIME AM	SOLAR TIME PM	ALT	AZM	NORMAL	HORIZ.	22	32	42	52	90
AUG 21	6	6	6.5	100.5	59	14	9	7	6	6	4
	7	5	19.1	92.8	190	85	77	69	60	50	12
	8	4	31.8	84.7	240	156	152	144	132	116	33
	9	3	44.3	75.0	263	216	220	212	197	178	65
	10	2	56.1	61.3	276	262	272	264	249	226	91
	11	1	66.0	38.4	282	292	305	298	281	257	107
	12		70.3	0.0	284	302	317	309	292	268	113
	SURFACE DAILY TOTALS				2902	2352	2388	2296	2144	1934	756
SEP 21	7	5	12.7	81.9	163	51	56	56	55	52	30
	8	4	25.1	73.0	240	124	140	141	138	131	75
	9	3	36.8	62.1	272	188	213	215	211	201	114
	10	2	47.3	47.5	287	237	270	273	268	255	145
	11	1	55.0	26.8	294	268	306	309	303	289	164
	12		58.0	0.0	296	278	318	321	315	300	171
	SURFACE DAILY TOTALS				2808	2014	2288	2308	2264	2154	1226
OCT 21	7	5	6.8	73.1	99	19	29	32	34	36	32
	8	4	18.7	64.0	229	90	120	128	133	134	104
	9	3	29.5	53.0	273	155	198	208	213	212	153
	10	2	38.7	39.1	293	204	257	269	273	270	188
	11	1	45.1	21.1	302	236	294	307	311	306	209
	12		47.5	0.0	304	247	306	320	324	318	217
	SURFACE DAILY TOTALS				2696	1654	2100	2208	2252	2232	1588
NOV 21	7	5	1.5	65.4	2	0	0	0	1	1	1
	8	4	12.7	56.6	196	55	91	104	113	119	111
	9	3	22.6	46.1	263	118	173	190	202	208	176
	10	2	30.8	33.2	289	166	233	252	265	270	217
	11	1	36.2	17.6	301	197	270	291	303	307	241
	12		38.2	0.0	304	207	282	304	316	320	249
	SURFACE DAILY TOTALS				2406	1280	1816	1980	2084	2130	1742
DEC 21	8	4	10.3	53.8	176	41	77	90	101	108	107
	9	3	19.8	43.6	257	102	161	180	195	204	183
	10	2	27.6	31.2	288	150	221	244	259	267	226
	11	1	32.7	16.4	301	180	258	282	298	305	251
	12		34.6	0.0	304	190	271	295	311	318	259
	SURFACE DAILY TOTALS				2348	1136	1704	1888	2016	2086	1794

Column headers: BTUH/SQ. FT., TOTAL INSOLATION ON SURFACES — NORMAL, HORIZ., SOUTH FACING SURFACE ANGLE WITH HORIZ. (22, 32, 42, 52, 90)

Appendix 4C—Continued

Table III   40 Degrees North Latitude

JAN 21 – JUL 21

DATE	AM	PM	ALT	AZM	NORMAL	HORIZ	30	40	50	60	90
JAN 21	8	4	8.1	55.3	142	28	65	74	81	85	84
	9	3	16.8	44.0	239	83	155	171	182	187	171
	10	2	23.8	30.9	274	127	218	237	249	254	223
	11	1	28.4	16.0	289	154	257	277	290	293	253
	12		30.0	0.0	294	164	270	291	303	306	263
SURFACE DAILY TOTALS					2182	948	1660	1810	1906	1944	1726
FEB 21	7	5	4.8	72.7	69	10	19	21	23	24	22
	8	4	15.4	62.2	224	73	114	122	126	127	107
	9	3	25.0	50.2	274	132	195	205	209	208	167
	10	2	32.8	35.9	295	178	256	267	271	267	210
	11	1	38.1	18.9	305	206	293	306	310	304	236
	12		40.0	0.0	308	216	306	319	323	317	245
SURFACE DAILY TOTALS					2640	1414	2060	2162	2202	2176	1730
MAR 21	7	5	11.4	80.2	171	46	55	55	54	51	35
	8	4	22.5	69.6	250	114	140	141	138	131	89
	9	3	32.8	57.3	282	173	215	217	213	202	138
	10	2	41.6	41.9	297	218	273	276	271	258	176
	11	1	47.7	22.6	305	247	310	313	307	293	200
	12		50.0	0.0	307	257	322	326	320	305	208
SURFACE DAILY TOTALS					2916	1852	2308	2330	2284	2174	1484
APR 21	6	6	7.4	98.9	89	20	11	8	7	4	4
	7	5	18.9	89.5	206	87	77	70	61	50	12
	8	4	30.3	79.3	252	152	153	145	133	117	53
	9	3	41.3	67.2	274	207	221	213	199	179	93
	10	2	51.2	51.4	286	250	275	267	252	229	126
	11	1	58.7	29.2	292	277	308	301	285	260	147
	12		61.6	0.0	293	287	320	313	296	271	154
SURFACE DAILY TOTALS					3092	2274	2412	2320	2168	1956	1022
MAY 21	5	7	1.9	114.7	1	0	0	0	0	0	0
	6	6	12.7	105.6	144	49	25	15	14	13	9
	7	5	24.0	96.6	216	114	89	76	60	44	13
	8	4	35.4	87.2	250	175	158	144	125	104	25
	9	3	46.8	76.0	267	227	221	206	186	160	60
	10	2	57.5	60.9	277	267	270	255	233	205	89
	11	1	66.2	37.1	283	293	301	287	264	234	108
	12		70.0	0.0	284	301	312	297	274	243	114
SURFACE DAILY TOTALS					3160	2552	2442	2264	2040	1760	724
JUN 21	5	7	4.2	117.3	22	4	3	3	2	2	1
	6	6	14.8	108.4	155	60	30	18	17	16	10
	7	5	26.0	99.7	216	123	92	77	59	41	14
	8	4	37.4	90.7	246	182	159	142	121	97	16
	9	3	48.8	80.2	263	233	219	202	179	151	47
	10	2	59.8	65.8	272	272	266	248	224	194	74
	11	1	69.2	41.9	277	296	296	278	253	221	92
	12		73.5	0.0	279	304	306	289	263	230	98
SURFACE DAILY TOTALS					3180	2648	2434	2224	1974	1670	610
JUL 21	5	7	2.3	115.2	2	0	0	0	0	0	0
	6	6	13.1	106.1	138	50	26	17	15	14	9
	7	5	24.3	97.2	208	114	89	75	60	44	14
	8	4	35.8	87.8	241	174	157	142	124	102	24
	9	3	47.2	76.7	259	225	218	203	182	157	58
	10	2	57.9	61.7	269	265	266	251	229	200	86
	11	1	66.7	37.9	275	290	296	281	258	228	104
	12		70.6	0.0	276	298	307	292	269	238	111
SURFACE DAILY TOTALS					3062	2534	2409	2230	2006	1728	702

AUG 21 – DEC 21

DATE	AM	PM	ALT	AZM	NORMAL	HORIZ	30	40	50	60	90
AUG 21	6	6	7.9	99.5	81	21	12	12	8	7	5
	7	5	19.3	90.0	191	87	76	69	60	49	12
	8	4	30.7	79.9	237	150	150	141	129	113	50
	9	3	41.8	67.9	260	205	216	207	193	173	89
	10	2	51.7	52.1	272	246	267	259	244	221	120
	11	1	59.3	29.7	278	273	300	292	276	252	140
	12		62.3	0.0	280	282	311	303	287	262	147
SURFACE DAILY TOTALS					2916	2244	2354	2258	2104	1894	978
SEP 21	7	5	11.4	80.2	149	43	51	51	49	47	32
	8	4	22.5	69.6	230	109	133	134	131	124	84
	9	3	32.8	57.3	263	167	206	208	203	193	132
	10	2	41.6	41.9	280	211	262	265	260	247	168
	11	1	47.7	22.6	287	239	298	301	295	281	192
	12		50.0	0.0	290	249	310	313	307	292	200
SURFACE DAILY TOTALS					2708	1788	2210	2228	2182	2074	1416
OCT 21	7	5	4.5	72.3	48	7	14	15	17	17	16
	8	4	15.0	61.9	204	68	106	113	117	118	100
	9	3	24.5	49.8	257	126	185	195	200	198	160
	10	2	32.4	35.6	280	170	245	257	261	257	203
	11	1	37.6	18.7	291	199	283	295	299	294	229
	12		39.5	0.0	294	208	295	308	312	306	238
SURFACE DAILY TOTALS					2454	1348	1962	2060	2098	2074	1654
NOV 21	8	4	8.2	55.4	136	28	63	72	78	82	81
	9	3	17.0	44.1	232	82	152	167	178	183	167
	10	2	24.0	31.0	268	126	215	233	245	249	219
	11	1	28.6	16.1	283	153	254	273	285	288	248
	12		30.2	0.0	288	163	267	287	298	301	258
SURFACE DAILY TOTALS					2128	942	1636	1778	1870	1908	1686
DEC 21	8	4	5.5	53.0	89	14	39	45	50	54	56
	9	3	14.0	41.9	217	65	135	157	164	171	163
	10	2	20.7	29.4	261	107	200	221	235	242	221
	11	1	25.0	15.2	280	134	239	262	276	283	252
	12		26.6	0.0	285	143	253	275	290	296	263
SURFACE DAILY TOTALS					1978	782	1480	1634	1740	1796	1646

Appendix 4C—Continued

Table IV 48 Degrees North Latitude

DATE	AM	PM	ALT	AZM	NORMAL	HORIZ.	38	48	58	68	90
JAN 21	8	4	3.5	54.6	37	4	17	19	21	22	22
	9	3	11.0	42.6	185	46	120	132	140	145	139
	10	2	16.9	29.4	239	83	190	206	216	220	206
	11	1	20.7	15.1	261	107	231	249	260	263	243
		12	22.0	0.0	267	115	245	264	275	278	255
	SURFACE DAILY TOTALS				1710	596	1360	1478	1550	1578	1478
FEB 21	7	5	2.4	72.2	12	1	4	4	4	4	4
	8	4	11.6	60.5	188	49	95	102	105	106	96
	9	3	19.7	47.7	251	100	178	187	191	190	167
	10	2	26.2	33.3	278	139	240	251	255	251	217
	11	1	30.5	17.2	290	165	278	290	294	288	247
		12	32.0	0.0	293	173	291	304	307	301	258
	SURFACE DAILY TOTALS				2330	1080	1880	1972	2024	1978	1720
MAR 21	7	5	10.0	78.7	153	35	49	49	47	45	35
	8	4	19.5	66.8	236	96	131	132	129	122	96
	9	3	28.2	53.4	270	147	205	207	203	193	152
	10	2	35.4	37.8	287	187	263	266	261	248	195
	11	1	40.3	19.8	295	212	300	303	297	283	223
		12	42.0	0.0	298	220	312	315	309	294	232
	SURFACE DAILY TOTALS				2780	1578	2208	2228	2182	2074	1632
APR 21	6	6	8.6	97.8	108	27	7	9	8	7	5
	7	5	18.6	86.7	205	85	76	69	59	48	21
	8	4	28.5	74.9	247	142	149	141	129	113	69
	9	3	37.8	61.2	268	191	216	208	194	174	115
	10	2	45.8	44.6	280	228	268	260	245	223	152
	11	1	51.5	24.0	286	252	301	294	278	254	177
		12	53.6	0.0	288	260	313	305	289	264	185
	SURFACE DAILY TOTALS				3076	2106	2358	2266	2114	1902	1262
MAY 21	5	7	5.2	114.3	41	10	4	4	4	4	3
	6	6	14.7	103.7	162	61	27	16	15	13	10
	7	5	24.6	93.0	219	118	89	75	60	43	13
	8	4	34.7	81.6	248	171	156	142	123	101	45
	9	3	44.3	68.3	264	217	217	202	182	156	86
	10	2	53.0	51.3	274	252	265	251	229	200	120
	11	1	59.5	28.6	279	274	296	281	258	228	141
		12	62.0	0.0	280	281	306	292	269	238	149
	SURFACE DAILY TOTALS				3254	2482	2418	2234	2010	1728	982
JUN 21	5	7	7.9	116.5	77	21	8	9	8	7	5
	6	6	17.2	106.2	172	74	33	19	18	16	12
	7	5	27.0	95.8	220	129	93	77	59	39	15
	8	4	37.1	84.6	246	181	157	140	119	95	35
	9	3	46.9	71.6	261	225	216	198	175	147	74
	10	2	55.8	54.8	269	259	262	244	220	189	105
	11	1	62.7	31.2	274	280	291	273	248	216	126
		12	65.5	0.0	275	287	301	283	258	225	133
	SURFACE DAILY TOTALS				3312	2626	2420	2204	1950	1644	874
JUL 21	5	7	5.7	114.7	43	10	5	5	5	5	3
	6	6	15.2	104.1	156	62	28	18	16	15	11
	7	5	25.1	93.5	211	118	89	75	59	42	14
	8	4	35.1	82.1	240	171	154	140	121	99	43
	9	3	44.8	68.8	256	215	214	199	178	153	83
	10	2	53.5	51.9	266	250	261	246	224	195	116
	11	1	60.1	29.0	271	272	291	276	253	223	137
		12	62.6	0.0	272	279	301	286	263	232	144
	SURFACE DAILY TOTALS				3158	2474	2386	2200	1974	1694	956

DATE	AM	PM	ALT	AZM	NORMAL	HORIZ.	38	48	58	68	90
AUG 21	6	6	9.1	98.3	99	28	14	10	9	8	6
	7	5	19.1	87.2	190	85	75	67	58	47	20
	8	4	29.0	75.4	232	141	145	137	125	109	65
	9	3	38.4	61.8	254	189	210	201	187	168	110
	10	2	46.4	45.1	266	225	260	252	237	214	146
	11	1	52.2	24.3	272	248	293	285	268	244	169
		12	54.3	0.0	274	256	304	296	279	255	177
	SURFACE DAILY TOTALS				2898	2086	2300	2200	2046	1836	1208
SEP 21	7	5	10.0	78.7	131	35	44	44	43	40	31
	8	4	19.5	66.8	215	92	124	124	121	115	90
	9	3	28.2	53.4	251	142	196	197	193	183	143
	10	2	35.4	37.8	269	181	251	254	248	236	185
	11	1	40.3	19.8	278	205	287	289	284	269	212
		12	42.0	0.0	280	213	299	302	296	281	221
	SURFACE DAILY TOTALS				2568	1522	2102	2118	2070	1966	1546
OCT 21	7	5	2.0	71.9	4	0	1	1	1	1	1
	8	4	11.2	60.2	165	44	86	91	95	95	87
	9	3	19.3	47.4	233	94	167	176	180	178	157
	10	2	25.7	33.1	262	133	228	239	242	239	207
	11	1	30.0	17.1	274	157	266	277	281	276	237
		12	31.5	0.0	278	166	279	291	294	288	247
	SURFACE DAILY TOTALS				2154	1022	1774	1860	1890	1866	1626
NOV 21	8	4	3.6	54.7	36	5	17	19	21	22	22
	9	3	11.2	42.7	179	46	117	129	137	141	135
	10	2	17.1	29.5	233	83	186	202	212	215	201
	11	1	20.9	15.1	255	107	227	245	255	258	238
		12	22.2	0.0	261	115	241	259	270	272	250
	SURFACE DAILY TOTALS				1668	596	1336	1448	1518	1544	1442
DEC 21	9	3	8.0	40.9	140	27	87	98	105	110	109
	10	2	13.6	28.2	214	63	164	180	192	197	190
	11	1	17.3	14.4	242	86	207	226	239	244	231
		12	18.6	0.0	250	94	222	241	254	260	244
	SURFACE DAILY TOTALS				1444	446	1136	1250	1326	1364	1304

Column groups: SOLAR TIME (AM, PM); SOLAR POSITION (ALT, AZM); BTUH/SQ. FT. TOTAL INSOLATION ON SURFACES — NORMAL, HORIZ., SOUTH FACING SURFACE ANGLE WITH HORIZ. (38, 48, 58, 68, 90).

Appendix 4C—Continued

Table V   56 Degrees North Latitude

DATE	SOLAR TIME AM	SOLAR TIME PM	SOLAR POSITION ALT	SOLAR POSITION AZM	NORMAL	HORIZ.	46	56	66	76	90
JAN 21	9	3	5.0	41.8	78	11	50	55	59	60	60
	10	2	9.9	28.5	170	39	135	146	154	156	153
	11	1	12.9	14.5	207	58	183	197	206	208	201
	12		14.0	0.0	217	65	198	214	222	225	217
	SURFACE DAILY TOTALS				1126	282	934	1010	1058	1074	1044
FEB 21	8	4	7.6	59.4	129	25	65	69	72	72	69
	9	3	14.2	45.9	214	65	151	159	162	161	151
	10	2	19.4	31.5	250	98	215	225	228	224	208
	11	1	22.8	16.1	266	119	254	265	268	263	243
	12		24.0	0.0	270	126	268	279	282	276	255
	SURFACE DAILY TOTALS				1986	740	1640	1716	1742	1716	1598
MAR 21	7	5	8.3	77.5	128	28	40	40	39	37	32
	8	4	16.2	64.4	215	75	119	120	117	111	97
	9	3	23.3	50.3	253	118	192	193	189	180	154
	10	2	29.0	34.9	272	151	249	251	246	234	205
	11	1	32.7	17.9	282	172	285	288	282	268	236
	12		34.0	0.0	284	179	297	300	294	280	246
	SURFACE DAILY TOTALS				2586	1268	2066	2084	2040	1938	1700
APR 21	5	7	1.4	108.8	0	0	0	0	0	0	0
	6	6	9.6	96.5	122	32	14	9	8	7	6
	7	5	18.0	84.1	201	81	74	66	57	46	29
	8	4	26.1	70.9	239	129	143	135	123	108	82
	9	3	33.6	56.3	260	169	208	200	186	167	133
	10	2	39.9	39.7	272	201	259	251	236	214	174
	11	1	44.1	20.7	278	220	292	284	268	245	200
	12		45.6	0.0	280	227	303	295	279	255	209
	SURFACE DAILY TOTALS				3024	1892	2282	2186	2038	1830	1458
MAY 21	4	8	1.2	125.5	0	0	0	0	0	0	0
	5	7	8.5	113.4	93	25	10	9	8	7	6
	6	6	16.5	101.5	175	71	28	17	15	13	11
	7	5	24.8	89.3	219	119	88	74	58	41	16
	8	4	33.1	76.3	244	163	153	138	119	98	63
	9	3	40.9	61.6	259	201	212	197	176	151	109
	10	2	47.6	44.2	268	231	259	244	222	194	146
	11	1	52.3	23.4	273	249	288	274	251	222	170
	12		54.0	0.0	275	255	299	284	261	231	178
	SURFACE DAILY TOTALS				3340	2374	2374	2188	1962	1682	1218
JUN 21	4	8	4.2	127.2	21	4	2	2	2	2	1
	5	7	11.4	115.3	122	40	14	13	11	10	8
	6	6	19.3	103.6	185	86	34	19	17	15	12
	7	5	27.6	91.7	222	132	92	76	57	38	15
	8	4	35.9	78.8	243	175	154	137	116	92	55
	9	3	43.8	64.1	257	212	211	193	170	143	98
	10	2	50.7	46.4	265	240	255	238	214	184	133
	11	1	55.6	24.9	269	258	284	267	242	210	156
	12		57.5	0.0	271	264	294	276	251	219	164
	SURFACE DAILY TOTALS				3458	2562	2388	2166	1910	1606	1120
JUL 21	4	8	1.7	125.8	0	0	0	0	0	0	0
	5	7	9.0	113.7	91	27	11	10	9	8	6
	6	6	17.0	101.9	169	72	30	18	16	14	12
	7	5	25.3	89.7	212	119	88	74	58	41	15
	8	4	33.6	76.7	237	163	151	137	117	96	61
	9	3	41.4	62.0	252	201	208	193	173	147	106
	10	2	48.2	44.6	261	230	254	239	217	189	142
	11	1	52.9	23.7	265	248	283	268	245	216	165
	12		54.6	0.0	267	254	293	278	255	225	173
	SURFACE DAILY TOTALS				3240	2372	2342	2152	1926	1646	1186

DATE	SOLAR TIME AM	SOLAR TIME PM	SOLAR POSITION ALT	SOLAR POSITION AZM	NORMAL	HORIZ.	46	56	66	76	90
AUG 21	5	7	2.0	109.2	1	3	0	0	0	0	0
	6	6	10.2	97.0	112	34	16	11	10	9	7
	7	5	18.5	84.5	187	82	73	65	56	45	28
	8	4	26.7	71.3	225	128	140	131	119	104	78
	9	3	34.3	56.7	246	168	202	193	179	160	126
	10	2	40.5	40.0	258	199	251	242	227	206	166
	11	1	44.8	20.9	264	218	282	274	258	235	191
	12		46.3	0.0	266	225	293	285	269	245	200
	SURFACE DAILY TOTALS				2850	1884	2218	2118	1966	1760	1392
SEP 21	7	5	8.3	77.5	107	25	36	36	34	32	28
	8	4	16.2	64.4	194	72	111	111	108	102	89
	9	3	23.3	50.3	233	114	181	182	178	168	147
	10	2	29.0	34.9	253	146	236	237	232	221	193
	11	1	32.7	17.9	263	166	271	273	267	254	223
	12		34.0	0.0	266	173	283	285	279	265	233
	SURFACE DAILY TOTALS				2368	1220	1950	1962	1918	1820	1594
OCT 21	8	4	7.1	59.1	104	20	53	57	59	59	57
	9	3	13.8	45.7	193	60	138	145	148	147	138
	10	2	19.0	31.3	231	92	201	210	213	210	195
	11	1	22.3	16.0	248	112	240	250	253	248	230
	12		23.5	0.0	253	119	253	263	266	261	241
	SURFACE DAILY TOTALS				1804	688	1516	1586	1612	1588	1480
NOV 21	9	3	5.2	41.9	76	12	49	54	57	59	58
	10	2	10.0	28.5	165	39	132	143	149	152	148
	11	1	13.1	14.5	201	58	179	193	201	203	196
	12		14.2	0.0	211	65	194	209	217	219	211
	SURFACE DAILY TOTALS				1094	284	914	986	1032	1046	1016
DEC 21	9	3	1.9	40.5	5	0	3	4	4	4	4
	10	2	6.6	27.5	113	19	86	95	101	104	103
	11	1	9.5	13.9	166	37	141	154	163	167	164
	12		10.6	0.0	180	43	159	173	182	186	182
	SURFACE DAILY TOTALS				748	156	620	678	716	734	722

Appendix 4C—Concluded

Table VI   64 Degrees North Latitude

DATE	SOLAR TIME AM	SOLAR TIME PM	SOLAR POSITION ALT	SOLAR POSITION AZM	NORMAL	HORIZ.	54	64	74	84	90
JAN 21	10	2	2.8	28.1	22	2	17	19	20	20	20
	11	1	5.2	14.1	81	12	72	77	80	81	81
		12	6.0	0.0	100	16	91	98	102	103	103
	SURFACE DAILY TOTALS				306	45	268	290	302	306	304
FEB 21	8	4	3.4	58.7	35	4	17	19	19	19	19
	9	3	8.6	44.8	147	31	103	108	111	110	107
	10	2	12.6	30.3	199	55	170	178	181	178	173
	11	1	15.1	15.3	222	71	212	220	223	219	213
		12	16.0	0.0	228	77	225	235	237	232	226
	SURFACE DAILY TOTALS				1452	400	1230	1286	1302	1282	1252
MAR 21	7	5	6.5	76.5	95	18	30	29	29	27	25
	8	4	12.7	62.6	185	54	101	102	99	94	89
	9	3	18.1	48.1	227	87	171	172	169	160	153
	10	2	22.3	32.7	249	112	227	229	224	213	203
	11	1	25.1	16.6	260	129	262	265	259	246	235
		12	26.0	0.0	263	134	274	277	271	258	246
	SURFACE DAILY TOTALS				2296	932	1856	1870	1830	1736	1656
APR 21	5	7	4.0	108.5	27	5	2	2	2	2	1
	6	6	10.4	95.1	133	37	15	9	8	7	6
	7	5	17.0	81.6	194	76	70	63	54	43	37
	8	4	23.3	67.5	228	112	136	128	116	102	91
	9	3	29.0	52.3	248	144	197	189	176	158	145
	10	2	33.5	36.0	260	169	246	239	224	203	188
	11	1	36.5	18.4	266	184	278	270	255	233	216
		12	37.6	0.0	268	190	289	281	266	243	225
	SURFACE DAILY TOTALS				2982	1644	2176	2082	1936	1736	1594
MAY 21	4	8	5.8	125.1	51	11	5	4	4	3	3
	5	7	11.6	112.1	132	42	13	11	10	9	8
	6	6	17.9	99.1	185	79	29	16	14	12	11
	7	5	24.5	85.7	218	117	86	72	56	39	28
	8	4	30.9	71.5	239	152	148	133	116	94	80
	9	3	36.8	56.1	252	182	204	190	170	145	128
	10	2	41.6	38.9	261	205	249	235	213	186	167
	11	1	44.9	20.1	265	219	278	264	242	213	193
		12	46.0	0.0	267	224	288	274	251	222	201
	SURFACE DAILY TOTALS				3470	2236	2312	2124	1898	1624	1436
JUN 21	3	9	4.2	139.4	21	4	2	2	2	2	1
	4	8	9.0	126.4	93	27	10	9	8	7	6
	5	7	14.7	113.6	154	60	16	15	13	11	10
	6	6	21.0	100.8	194	96	34	19	17	14	13
	7	5	27.5	87.5	221	132	91	74	55	36	23
	8	4	34.0	73.3	239	166	150	133	112	88	73
	9	3	39.9	57.8	251	195	204	187	164	137	119
	10	2	44.9	40.4	258	217	247	230	206	177	157
	11	1	48.3	20.9	262	231	275	258	233	202	181
		12	49.5	0.0	263	235	284	267	242	211	189
	SURFACE DAILY TOTALS				3650	2488	2342	2118	1862	1558	1356

DATE	SOLAR TIME AM	SOLAR TIME PM	SOLAR POSITION ALT	SOLAR POSITION AZM	NORMAL	HORIZ.	54	64	74	84	90
JUL 21	4	8	6.4	125.3	53	13	6	5	5	4	4
	5	7	12.1	112.4	128	44	14	13	11	10	9
	6	6	18.4	99.4	179	81	30	17	16	13	12
	7	5	25.0	86.0	211	118	86	72	56	38	28
	8	4	31.4	71.8	231	152	146	131	113	91	77
	9	3	37.3	56.3	245	182	201	186	166	141	124
	10	2	42.2	39.2	253	204	245	230	208	181	162
	11	1	45.4	20.2	257	218	273	258	236	207	187
		12	46.6	0.0	259	223	282	267	245	216	195
	SURFACE DAILY TOTALS				3372	2248	2280	2090	1864	1588	1400
AUG 21	5	7	4.6	108.8	29	6	3	3	2	2	2
	6	6	11.0	95.5	123	39	16	11	10	8	7
	7	5	17.6	81.9	181	77	69	61	52	42	35
	8	4	23.9	67.8	214	113	132	123	112	97	87
	9	3	29.6	52.6	234	144	190	182	169	150	138
	10	2	34.2	36.2	246	168	237	229	215	194	179
	11	1	37.2	18.5	252	183	268	260	244	222	205
		12	38.3	0.0	254	188	278	270	255	232	215
	SURFACE DAILY TOTALS				2808	1646	2108	2008	1860	1662	1522
SEP 21	7	5	6.5	76.5	77	16	25	24	24	23	21
	8	4	12.7	62.6	163	51	92	92	90	85	81
	9	3	18.1	48.1	206	83	159	159	156	147	141
	10	2	22.3	32.7	229	108	212	213	209	198	189
	11	1	25.1	16.6	240	124	246	248	243	230	220
		12	26.0	0.0	244	129	258	260	254	241	230
	SURFACE DAILY TOTALS				2074	892	1726	1736	1696	1608	1532
OCT 21	8	4	3.0	58.5	17	2	9	9	10	10	10
	9	3	8.1	44.6	122	26	86	91	93	92	90
	10	2	12.1	30.2	176	50	152	159	161	159	155
	11	1	14.6	15.2	201	65	193	201	203	200	195
		12	15.5	0.0	208	71	207	215	217	213	208
	SURFACE DAILY TOTALS				1238	358	1088	1136	1152	1134	1106
NOV 21	10	2	3.0	28.1	23	3	18	20	21	21	21
	11	1	5.4	14.2	79	12	70	76	79	80	79
		12	6.2	0.0	97	17	89	96	100	101	100
	SURFACE DAILY TOTALS				302	46	266	286	298	302	300
DEC 21	11	1	1.8	13.7	4	0	3	3	4	4	4
		12	2.6	0.0	16	2	14	15	16	17	17
	SURFACE DAILY TOTALS				24	2	20	22	24	24	24

Table I Conductivities (k), Conductances (C), and Resistances (R) of Various Construction Materials

Material	Description	Density (Lb per Cu Ft)	Mean Temp F	Conductivity (k)	Conductance (C)	Resistance (R) Per inch thickness (1/k)	Resistance (R) For thickness listed (1/C)	Specific Heat, Btu per (lb) (F deg)
BUILDING BOARD Boards, Panels, Subflooring, Sheathing, Woodbased Panel Products	Asbestos-cement board.............	120	75	4.0	—	0.25	—	
	Asbestos-cement board..........⅛ in.	120	75	—	33.00	—	0.033	
	Asbestos-cement board..........¼ in.	120	75	—	16.50	—	0.07	
	Gypsum or plaster board........⅜ in.	50	75	—	3.10	—	0.32	
	Gypsum or plaster board........½ in.	50	75	—	2.25	—	0.45	
	Plywood........................	34	75	0.80	—	1.25	—	0.29
	Plywood.......................¼ in.	34	75	—	3.20	—	0.31	0.29
	Plywood.......................⅜ in.	34	75	—	2.13	—	0.47	0.29
	Plywood.......................½ in.	34	75	—	1.60	—	0.62	0.29
	Plywood or wood panels.........¾ in.	34	75	—	1.07	—	0.93	0.29
	Insulating board							
	Sheathing, regular density.....½ in.	18	75	—	0.76	—	1.32	0.31
	...........................²⁵⁄₃₂ in.	18	75	—	0.49	—	2.06	0.31
	Sheathing intermediate density.½ in.	22	75	—	0.82	—	1.22	0.31
	Nail-base sheathing...........½ in.	25	75	—	0.88	—	1.14	0.31
	Shingle backer...............⅜ in.	18	75	—	1.06	—	0.94	0.31
	Shingle backer..............⁵⁄₁₆ in.	18	75	—	1.28	—	0.78	0.31
	Sound deadening board........½ in.	15	75	—	0.74	—	1.35	0.30
	Tile and lay-in panels, plain or acoustic....................	18	75	0.40	—	2.50	—	0.32
	...........................½ in.	18	75	—	0.80	—	1.25	0.32
	...........................¾ in.	18	75	—	0.53	—	1.89	0.32
	Laminated paperboard..........	30	75	0.50	—	2.00	—	
	Homogeneous board from repulped paper...............	30	75	0.50	—	2.00	—	0.28
	Hardboard							
	Medium density siding.......⁷⁄₁₆ in.	40	75	—	1.49	—	0.67	0.28
	Other medium density...........	50	75	0.73	—	1.37	—	0.31
	High density, service temp. service, underlay...................	55	75	0.82	—	1.22	—	0.33
	High density, std. tempered.......	63	75	1.00	—	1.00	—	0.33
	Particleboard							
	Low density...................	37	75	0.54	—	1.85	—	0.31
	Medium density................	50	75	0.94	—	1.06	—	0.31
	High density..................	62.5	75	1.18	—	0.85	—	0.31
	Underlayment................⅝ in.	40	75	—	1.22	—	0.82	0.29
	Wood subfloor................¾ in.		75	—	1.06	—	0.94	0.34
BUILDING PAPER	Vapor—permeable felt.............	—	75	—	16.70	—	0.06	
	Vapor—seal, 2 layers of mopped 15 lb felt......................	—	75	—	8.35	—	0.12	
	Vapor—seal, plastic film...........	—	75	—	—	—	Negl.	
FINISH FLOORING MATERIALS	Carpet and fibrous pad.............	—	75	—	0.48	—	2.08	
	Carpet and rubber pad.............	—	75	—	0.81	—	1.23	0.34
	Cork tile.....................⅛ in.	—	75	—	3.60	—	0.28	
	Terrazzo.....................1 in.	—	75	—	12.50	—	0.08	
	Tile—asphalt, linoleum, vinyl, rubber.	—	75	—	20.00	—	0.05	0.30
INSULATING MATERIALS Blanket and Batt	Mineral Fiber, fibrous form processed from rock, slag, or glass							
	approx. 2–2¾ in................	—	75	—	—	—	7	0.18
	approx. 3–3½ in................	—	75	—	—	—	11	0.18
	approx. 5¼–6½ in..............	—	75	—	—	—	19	0.18
Board and Slabs	Cellular glass....................	9	75	0.40	—	2.50	—	0.24
	Glass fiber, organic bonded..........	4–9	75	0.25	—	4.00	—	0.19
	Expanded rubber (rigid).............	4.5	75	0.22	—	4.55	—	
	Expanded polystyrene extruded, plain......................	1.8	75	0.25	—	4.00	—	0.29
	Expanded polystyrene extruded, (R-12 exp.).................	2.2	75	0.20	—	5.00	—	0.29
	Expanded polystyrene extruded, (R-12 exp.) (Thickness 1 in. and greater)..	3.5	75	0.19	—	5.26	—	0.29
	Expanded polystyrene, molded beads.	1.0	75	0.28	—	3.57	—	0.29
	Expanded polyurethane (R-11 exp.)	1.5	75	0.16	—	6.25	—	0.38
	(Thickness 1 in. or greater)........	2.5						0.38
	Mineral fiber with resin binder.......	15	75	0.29	—	3.45	—	0.17
	Mineral fiberboard, wet felted Core or roof insulation............	16–17	75	0.34	—	2.94	—	

Notes: a. From ASHRAE *Handbook of Fundamentals*.

Table I—*Continued*

Material	Description	Density (Lb per Cu Ft)	Mean Temp F	Conductivity (k)	Conductance (C)	Resistance (R) Per inch thickness (1/k)	Resistance (R) For thickness listed (1/C)	Specific Heat, Btu per (lb)(F deg)
BOARD AND SLABS (*Continued*)	Acoustical tile..................	18	75	0.35	—	2.86	—	
	Acoustical tile..................	21	75	0.37	—	2.73	—	
	Mineral fiberboard, wet molded							
	Acoustical tile	23	75	0.42	—	2.38	—	
	Wood or cane fiberboard							
	Acoustical tile ....½ in.	—	75	—	0.80	—	1.25	0.30
	Acoustical tile ....¾ in.	—	75	—	0.53	—	1.89	0.30
	Interior finish (plank, tile)	15	75	0.35	—	2.86	—	0.32
	Insulating roof deck							
	Approximately............1½ in.	—	75	—	0.24	—	4.17	
	Approximately............2 in.	—	75	—	0.18	—	5.56	
	Approximately............3 in.	—	75	—	0.12	—	8.33	
	Wood shredded (cemented in							
	preformed slabs)...............	22	75	0.60	—	1.67	—	0.38
LOOSE FILL	Cellulose insulation (milled paper or							
	wood pulp)...................	2.5–3	75	0.27	—	3.70	—	0.33
	Sandust or shavings...............	0.8–1.5	75	0.45	—	2.22	—	0.33
	Wood fiber, softwoods.............	2.0–3.5	75	0.30	—	3.33	—	0.33
	Perlite, expanded.............	5.0–8.0	75	0.37	—	2.70	—	
	Mineral fiber (rock, slag or glass)							
	approx. 3 in................	—	75	—	—	9	—	0.18
	approx. 4½ in................	—	75	—	—	13	—	0.18
	approx. 6¼ in................	—	75	—	—	19	—	0.18
	approx. 7¼ in................	—	75	—	—	24	—	0.18
	Silica aerogel................	7.6	75	0.17	—	5.88	—	
	Vermiculite (expanded).............	7.0–8.2	75	0.47	—	2.13	—	
		4.0–6.0	75	0.44	—	2.27	—	
ROOF INSULATION	Preformed, for use above deck							
	Approximately............½ in.	—	75	—	0.72	—	1.39	
	Approximately............1 in.	—	75	—	0.36	—	2.78	
	Approximately............1½ in.	—	75	—	0.24	—	4.17	
	Approximately............2 in.	—	75	—	0.19	—	5.56	
	Aoproximately............2½ in.	—	75	—	0.15	—	6.67	
	Approximately............3 in.	—	75	—	0.12	—	8.33	
	Cellular glass................	9	75	0.40	—	2.50	—	0.24
MASONRY MATERIALS CONCRETES	Cement mortar...................	116		5.0	—	0.20	—	
	Gypsum-fiber concrete 87½% gypsum,							
	12½% wood chips................	51		1.66	—	0.60	—	
	Lightweight aggregates including ex-	120		5.2	—	0.19	—	
	panded shale, clay or slate; expanded	100		3.6	—	0.28	—	
	slags; cinders; pumice; vermiculite;	80		2.5	—	0.40	—	
	also cellular concretes	60		1.7	—	0.59	—	
		40		1.15	—	0.86	—	
		30		0.90	—	1.11	—	
		20		0.70		1.43		
	Sand and gravel or stone aggregate							
	(oven dried)................	140		9.0	—	0.11	—	
	Sand and gravel or stone aggregate							
	(not dried)...................	140		12.0	—	0.08	—	
	Stucco......................	116		5.0	—	0.20	—	
MASONRY UNITS	Brick, common	120	75	5.0	—	0.20	—	
	Brick, face	130	75	9.0	—	0.11	—	
	Clay tile, hollow:							
	1 cell deep...................3 in.	—	75	—	1.25	—	0.80	
	1 cell deep...................4 in.	—	75	—	0.90	—	1.11	
	2 cells deep...................6 in.	—	75	—	0.66	—	1.52	
	2 cells deep...................8 in.	—	75	—	0.54	—	1.85	
	2 cells deep...................10 in.	—	75	—	0.45	—	2.22	
	3 cells deep...................12 in.	—	75	—	0.40	—	2.50	
	Concrete blocks, three oval core:							
	Sand and gravel aggregate.....4 in.	—	75	—	1.40	—	0.71	
	.....8 in.	—	75	—	0.90	—	1.11	
	....12 in.	—	75	—	0.78	—	1.28	
	Cinder aggregate............3 in.	—	75	—	1.16	—	0.86	
	.........4 in.	—	75	—	0.90	—	1.11	
	.........8 in.	—	75	—	0.58	—	1.72	
	.........12 in.	—	75	—	0.53	—	1.89	
	Lightweight aggregate {3 in.	—	75	—	0.79	—	1.27	
	(expanded shale, clay, slate 4 in.	—	75	—	0.67	—	1.50	
	or slag; pumice) 8 in.	—	75	—	0.50	—	2.00	
	{12 in.	—	75	—	0.44	—	2.27	

Table I—*Concluded*

Material	Description	Density (Lb per Cu Ft)	Mean Temp F	Conductivity (k)	Conductance (C)	Resistance (R) Per inch thickness (1/k)	Resistance (R) For thickness listed (1/C)	Specific Heat Btu per (lb) (F deg)
	Concrete blocks, rectangular core.							
	Sand and gravel aggregate							
	2 core, 8 in. 36 lb.	—	45	—	0.96	—	*1.04*	
	Same with filled cores	—	45	—	0.52	—	*1.93*	
	Lightweight aggregate (expanded shale, clay, slate or slag, pumice):							
	3 core, 6 in. 19 lb.	—	45	—	0.61	—	*1.65*	
	Same with filled cores	—	45	—	0.33	—	*2.99*	
	2 core, 8 in. 24 lb.	—	45	—	0.46	—	*2.18*	
	Same with filled cores	—	45	—	0.20	—	*5.03*	
	3 core, 12 in. 38 lb.	—	45	—	0.40	—	*2.48*	
	Same with filled cores	—	45	—	0.17	—	*5.82*	
	Stone, lime or sand	—	75	12.50	—	*0.08*	—	
	Gypsum partition tile:							
	3 × 12 × 30 in. solid	—	75	—	0.79	—	*1.26*	
	3 × 12 × 30 in. 4-cell	—	75	—	0.74	—	*1.35*	
	4 × 12 × 30 in. 3-cell	—	75	—	0.60	—	*1.67*	
METALS	(See Chapter 30, Table 3)							
PLASTERING MATERIALS	Cement plaster, sand aggregate	116	75	5.0	—	*0.20*	—	
	Sand aggregate ... 3/8 in.	—	75	—	13.3	—	*0.08*	
	Sand aggregate ... 3/4 in.	—	75	—	6.66	—	*0.15*	
	Gypsum plaster:							
	Lightweight aggregate ... 1/2 in.	45	75	—	3.12	—	*0.32*	
	Lightweight aggregate ... 5/8 in.	45	75	—	2.67	—	*0.39*	
	Lightweight agg. on metal lath. 3/4 in.	—	75	—	2.13	—	*0.47*	
	Perlite aggregate	45	75	1.5	—	*0.67*	—	
	Sand aggregate	105	75	5.6	—	*0.18*	—	
	Sand aggregate ... 1/2 in.	105	75	—	11.10	—	*0.09*	
	Sand aggregate ... 5/8 in.	105	75	—	9.10	—	*0.11*	
	Sand aggregate on metal lath .. 3/4 in.	—	75	—	7.70	—	*0.1*	
	Vermiculite aggregate	45	75	1.7	—	*0.59*	—	
ROOFING	Asbestos-cement shingles	120	75	—	4.76	—	*0.21*	
	Asphalt roll roofing	70	75	—	6.50	—	*0.15*	
	Asphalt shingles	70	75	—	2.27	—	*0.44*	
	Built-up roofing ... 3/8 in.	70	75	—	3.00	—	*0.33*	0.35
	Slate ... 1/2 in.	—	75	—	20.00	—	*0.05*	
	Wood shingles, plain a plastic film faced	—	75	—	1.06	—	*0.94*	0.31
SIDING MATERIALS (ON FLAT SURFACE)	Shingles							
	Asbestos-cement	120	75	—	4.76	—	*0.21*	
	Wood, 16 in., 7½ exposure	—	75	—	1.15	—	*0.87*	0.31
	Wood, double, 16-in., 12-in. exposure	—	75	—	0.84	—	*1.19*	0.31
	Wood, plus insul. backer board. 5/16 in.	—	75	—	0.71	—	*1.40*	0.31
	Siding							
	Asbestos-cement, 1/4 in., lapped	—	75	—	4.76	—	*0.21*	
	Asphalt roll siding	—	75	—	6.50	—	*0.15*	
	Asphalt insulating siding (1/2 in. bd.)	—	75	—	0.69	—	*1.46*	
	Wood, drop, 1 × 8 in.	—	75	—	1.27	—	*0.79*	0.31
	Wood, bevel, 1/2 × 8 in., lapped	—	75	—	1.23	—	*0.81*	0.31
	Wood, bevel, 3/4 × 10 in., lapped	—	75	—	0.95	—	*1.05*	0.31
	Wood, plywood, 3/8 in., lapped	—	75	—	1.59	—	*0.59*	0.29
	Aluminum or Steel -, over sheathing							
	Hollow-backed	—	—	—	1.61	—	*0.61*	
	Insulating-board backed nominal 3/8 in.	—	—	—	0.55	—	*1.82*	
	Insulating-board backed nominal 3/8 in. foil backed	—	—	—	0.34	—	*2.96*	
	Architectural glass	—	75	—	10.00	—	*0.10*	
WOODS	Maple, oak, and similar hardwoods	45	75	1.10	—	*0.91*	—	0.30
	Fir, pine, and similar softwoods	32	75	0.80	—	*1.25*	—	0.33
	Fir, pine, and similar softwoods ... 3/4 in.	32	75	—	1.06	—	*0.94*	0.33
	.. 1½ in.	32	75	—	0.53	—	*1.89*	0.33
	.. 2½ in.	32	75	—	0.32	—	*3.12*	0.33
	.. 3½ in.	32	75	—	0.23	—	*4.35*	0.33

Table II Thermal Conductivity (k) of Various Construction Materials[a]

Form	Material (Composition)	Accepted Max Temp for Use, F	Typical Density (lb/cu ft)	Typical Conductivity k at Mean Temp F													
				−100	−75	−50	−25	0	25	50	75	100	200	300	500	700	900
BLANKETS & FELTS	MINERAL FIBER (Rock, Slag, or Glass) Blanket, Metal Reinforced	1200	6–12									0.26	0.32	0.39	0.54		
		1000	2.5–6									0.24	0.31	0.40	0.61		
	Mineral Fiber, Glass Blanket, Flexible, Fine-Fiber Organic Bonded	350	0.65				0.25	0.26	0.28	0.30	0.33	0.36	0.53				
			0.75				0.24	0.25	0.27	0.29	0.32	0.34	0.48				
			1.0				0.23	0.24	0.25	0.27	0.29	0.32	0.43				
			1.5				0.21	0.22	0.23	0.25	0.27	0.28	0.37				
			2.0				0.20	0.21	0.22	0.23	0.25	0.26	0.33				
			3.0				0.19	0.20	0.21	0.22	0.23	0.24	0.31				
	Blanket, Flexible, Textile-Fiber Organic Bonded	350	0.65				0.27	0.28	0.29	0.30	0.31	0.32	0.50	0.68			
			0.75				0.26	0.27	0.28	0.29	0.31	0.32	0.48	0.66			
			1.0				0.24	0.25	0.26	0.27	0.29	0.31	0.45	0.60			
			1.5				0.22	0.23	0.24	0.25	0.27	0.29	0.39	0.51			
			3.0				0.20	0.21	0.22	0.23	0.24	0.25	0.32	0.41			
	Felt, Semi-Rigid Organic Bonded	400	3–8					0.24	0.25	0.26	0.27	0.35	0.44				
	Laminated & Felted	850	3	0.16	0.17	0.18	0.19	0.20	0.21	0.22	0.23	0.24	0.35	0.55			
	Without Binder	1200	7.5										0.35	0.45	0.60		
	VEGETABLE & ANIMAL FIBER Hair Felt or Hair Felt plus Jute	180	10					0.26	0.28	0.29	0.30						
BLOCKS, BOARDS & PIPE INSULATION	ASBESTOS Laminated Asbestos Paper	700	30									0.40	0.45	0.50	0.60		
	Corrugated & Laminated Asbestos Paper																
	4-ply	300	11–13							0.54	0.57	0.68					
	6-ply	300	15–17							0.49	0.51	0.59					
	8-ply	300	18–20							0.47	0.49	0.57					
	MOLDED AMOSITE & BINDER	1500	15–18									0.32	0.37	0.42	0.52	0.62	0.72
	85% MAGNESIA	600	11–12									0.35	0.38	0.42			
	CALCIUM SILICATE	1200	11–13									0.38	0.41	0.44	0.52	0.62	0.72
		1800	12–15												0.63	0.74	0.95
	CELLULAR GLASS	800	9				0.32	0.33	0.35	0.36	0.38	0.40	0.42	0.48	0.55		
	DIATOMACEOUS SILICA	1600	21–22												0.64	0.68	0.72
		1900	23–25												0.70	0.75	0.80
	MINERAL FIBER Glass, Organic Bonded, Block and Boards Non-Punking Binder	400	3–10	0.16	0.17	0.18	0.19	0.20	0.22	0.24	0.25	0.26	0.33	0.40			
		1000	3–10									0.26	0.31	0.38	0.52		
	Pipe Insulation, slag or glass	350	3–4					0.20	0.21	0.22	0.23	0.24	0.29				
		500	3–10					0.20	0.22	0.24	0.25	0.26	0.33	0.40			
	Inorganic Bonded-Block	1000	10–15									0.33	0.38	0.45	0.55		
		1800	15–24									0.32	0.37	0.42	0.52	0.62	0.74
	Pipe Insulation slag or glass	1000	10–15									0.33	0.38	0.45	0.55		
	MINERAL FIBER Resin Binder		15				0.23	0.24	0.25	0.26	0.28	0.29					
	Rigid Polystyrene Extruded, R-12 exp	170	3.5	0.16	0.16	0.15	0.16	0.16	0.17	0.18	0.19	0.20					
	Extruded, R-12 exp	170	2.2	0.16	0.16	0.17	0.16	0.17	0.18	0.19	0.20						
	Extruded	170	1.8	0.17	0.18	0.19	0.20	0.21	0.23	0.24	0.25	0.27					
	Molded Beads	170	1	0.18	0.20	0.21	0.23	0.24	0.25	0.26	0.28						
	Polyurethane R-11 exp	210	1.5–2.5	0.16	0.17	0.18	0.18	0.18	0.17	0.16	0.16	0.17					
	RUBBER, Rigid Foamed	150	4.5					0.20	0.21	0.22	0.23						
	VEGETABLE & ANIMAL FIBER Wool Felt (Pipe Insulation)	180	20					0.28	0.30	0.31	0.33						
INSULATING CEMENTS	MINERAL FIBER (Rock, Slag, or Glass) With Colloidal Clay Binder	1800	24–30									0.49	0.55	0.61	0.73	0.85	
	With Hydraulic Setting Binder	1200	30–40									0.75	0.80	0.85	0.95		
LOOSE FILL	Cellulose insulation (Milled pulverized paper or wood pulp)		2.5–3							0.26	0.27	0.29					
	Mineral fiber, slag, rock or glass		2–5			0.19	0.21	0.23	0.25	0.26	0.28	0.31					
	Perlite (expanded)		5–8	0.25	0.27	0.29	0.30	0.32	0.34	0.35	0.37	0.39					
	Silica aerogel		7.6			0.13	0.14	0.15	0.15	0.16	0.17	0.18					
	Vermiculite (expanded)		7–8.2			0.39	0.40	0.42	0.44	0.45	0.47	0.49					
			4–6			0.34	0.35	0.38	0.40	0.42	0.44	0.46					

Appendix 4E—Coefficients of Transmission (U) for Various Structural Elements[a][b]

Table I   Coefficients of Transmission (U) of Frame Walls[c]

These coefficients are expressed in Btu per (hour) (square foot) (degree Fahrenheit) difference in temperature between the air on the two sides), and are based on an outside wind velocity of 15 mph

Replace Air Space with 3.5-in. R-11 Blanket Insulation (New Item 4)

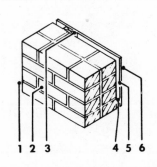

Construction	1 Resistance (R)		2	
	Between Framing	At Framing	Between Framing	At Framing
1. Outside surface (15 mph wind)	0.17	0.17	0.17	0.17
2. Siding, wood, 0.5 in.× 8 in. lapped (average)	0.81	0.81	0.81	0.81
3. Sheathing, 0.5-in. asphalt impregnated	1.32	1.32	1.32	1.32
4. Nonreflective air space, 3.5 in. (50 Fmean; 10 deg F temperature difference)	1.01	—	11.00	—
5. Nominal 2-in. × 4-in. wood stud	—	4.38	—	4.38
6. Gypsum wallboard, 0.5 in.	0.45	0.45	0.45	0.45
7. Inside surface (still air)	0.68	0.68	0.68	0.68
Total Thermal Resistance (R)	R_i=4.44	R_s=7.81	R_i=14.43	R_s=7.81

Construction No. 1: $U_i = 1/4.44 = 0.225$; $U_s = 1/7.81 = 0.128$. With 20% framing (typical of 2-in. × 4-in. studs @ 16-in. o.c.), $U_{av} = 0.8 (0.225) + 0.2 (0.128) = 0.206$ (See Eq 9)

Construction No. 2: $U_i = 1/14.43 = 0.069$; $U_s = 0.128$. With framing unchanged, $U_{av} = 0.8(0.069) + 0.2(0.128) = 0.081$

Table II   Coefficients of Transmission (U) of Solid Masonry Walls

Coefficients are expressed in Btu per (hour) (square foot) (degree Fahrenheit difference in temperature between the air on the two sides), and are based on an outside wind velocity of 15 mph

Replace Furring Strips and Air Space with 1-in. Extruded Polystyrene (New Item 4)

Construction	1 Resistance (R)		2
	Between Furring	At Furring	
1. Outside surface (15 mph wind)	0.17	0.17	0.17
2. Common brick, 8 in.	1.60	1.60	1.60
3. Nominal 1-in. ×3-in. vertical furring	—	0.94	—
4. Nonreflective air space, 0.75 in. (50 F mean; 10 deg F temperature difference)	1.01	—	5.00
5. Gypsum wallboard, 0.5 in.	0.45	0.45	0.45
6. Inside surface (still air)	0.68	0.68	0.68
Total Thermal Resistance (R)	$R_i = 3.91$	$R_s = 3.84$	$R_i = 7.90 = R_s$

Construction No. 1: $U_i = 1/3.91 = 0.256$; $U_s = 1/3.84 = 0.260$. With 20% framing (typical of 1-in. × 3-in. vertical furring on masonry @ 16-in. o.c.) $U_{av} = 0.8 (0.256) + 0.2 (0.260) = 0.257$

Construction No. 2: $U_i = U_s = U_{av} = 1/7.90 = 0.127$

Table III   Coefficients of Transmission (U) of Frame Partitions or Interior Walls[d]

Coefficients are expressed in Btu per (hour) (square foot) (degree Fahrenheit difference in temperature between the air on the two sides), and are based on still air (no wind) conditions on both sides

Replace Air Space with 3.5-in. R-11 Blanket Insulation (New Item 3)

Construction	1 Resistance (R)		2	
	Between Framing	At Framing	Between Framing	At Framing
1. Inside surface (still air)	0.68	0.68	0.68	0.68
2. Gypsum wallboard, 0.5 in.	0.45	0.45	0.45	0.45
3. Nonreflective air space, 3.5 in. (50 F mean; 10 deg F temperature difference)	1.01	—	11.00	—
4. Nominal 2-in. × 4-in. wood stud	—	4.38	—	4.38
5. Gypsum wallboard0.5 in.	0.45	0.45	0.45	0.45
6. Inside surface (still air)	0.68	0.68	0.68	0.68
Total Thermal Resistance (R)	R_i= 3.27	R_s= 6.64	R_i=13.26	R_s= 6.64

Construction No. 1: $U_i = 1/3.27 = 0.306$; $U_s = 1/6.64 = 0.151$. With 10% framing (typical of 2-in. × 4-in. studs @ 24-in. o.c.), $U_{av} = 0.9 (0.306) + 0.1 (0.151) = 0.290$

Construction No. 2: $U_i = 1/13.26 = 0.075$, $U_s = 1/6.64 = 0.151$. With framing unchanged, $U_{av} = 0.9(0.075) + 0.1(0.151) = 0.083$

Notes: a. From ASHRAE *Handbook of Fundamentals, 1977.*
　　　b. *U*-values are expressed in Btu/hr-ft²-°F.

c. Outside wind velocity of 15mph.
d. Still air conditions on both sides.
e. Winter conditions, upward flow.

Table IV Coefficients of Transmission (U) of Masonry Walls[c]

Coefficients are expressed in Btu per (hour) (square foot) (degree Fahrenheit difference in temperature between the air on the two sides), and are based on an outside wind velocity of 15 mph

Replace Cinder Aggregate Block with 6-in. Light-weight Aggregate Block with Cores Filled (New Item 4)

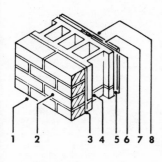

| Construction | 1 Resistance (R) | | 2 | |
	Between Furring	At Furring	Between Furring	At Furring
1. Outside surface (15 mph wind)	0.17	0.17	0.17	0.17
2. Face brick, 4 in.	0.44	0.44	0.44	0.44
3. Cement mortar, 0.5 in.	0.10	0.10	0.10	0.10
4. Concrete block, cinder aggregate, 8 in.	1.72	1.72	2.99	2.99
5. Reflective air space, 0.75 in. (50 F mean; 30 deg F temperature difference)	2.77	—	2.77	—
6. Nominal 1-in. × 3-in. vertical furring	—	0.94	—	0.94
7. Gypsum wallboard, 0.5 in., foil backed	0.45	0.45	0.45	0.45
8. Inside surface (still air)	0.68	0.68	0.68	0.68
Total Thermal Resistance (R)	R_i = 6.33·	R_s = 4.50	R_i = 7.60	R_s = 5.77

Construction No. 1: U_i = 1/6.33 = 0.158; U_s = 1/4.50 = 0.222. With 20% framing (typical of 1-in. × 3-in. vertical furring on masonry @ 16-in. o.c.), U_{av} = 0.8 (0.158) + 0.2 (0.222) = 0.171

Construction No. 2: U_i = 1/7.60 = 0.132, U_s = 1/5.77 = 0.173. With framing unchanged, U_{av} = 0.8(0.132) + 0.2(0.173) = 1.40

Table V Coefficients of Transmission (U) of Masonry Cavity Walls[c]

Coefficients are expressed in Btu per (hour) (square foot) (degree Fahrenheit difference in temperature between the air on the two sides), and are based on an outside wind velocity of 15 mph

Replace Furring Strips and Gypsum Wallboard with 0.625-in. Plaster (Sand Aggregate) Applied Directly to Concrete Block-Fill 2.5-in. Air Space with Vermiculite Insulation (New Items 3 and 7.

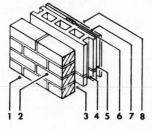

| Construction | 1 Resistance (R) | | 2 |
	Between Furring	At Furring	
1. Outside surface (15 mph wind)	0.17	0.17	0.17
2. Common brick, 8 in.	0.80	0.80	0.80
3. Nonreflective air space, 2.5 in. (30 F mean; 10 deg F temperature difference)	1.10*	1.10*	5.32**
4. Concrete block, stone aggregate, 4 in.	0.71	0.71	0.71
5. Nonreflective air space 0.75 in. (50 F mean; 10 deg F temperature difference)	1.01	—	—
6. Nominal 1-in. × 3-in. vertical furring	—	0.94	—
7. Gypsum wallboard, 0.5 in.	0.45	0.45	0.11
8. Inside surface (still air)	0.68	0.68	0.68
Total Thermal Resistance (R)	R_i = 4.92	R_s = 4.85	R_i = R_s = 7.79

Construction No. 1: U_i = 1/4.92 = 0.203; U_s = 1/4.85 = 0.206. With 20% framing (typical of 1-in. × 3-in. vertical furring on masonry @16-in. o.c.), U_{av} = 0.8(0.203) + 0.2(0.206) = 0.204

Construction No. 2: U_i = U_s = U_{av} = 1.79 = 0.128

* Interpolated value from Table 2.

** Calculated value from Table 3.

Table VI Coefficients of Transmission (U) of Masonry Partitions.

Coefficients are expressed in Btu per (hour) (square foot) (degree Fahrenheit difference in temperature between the air on the two sides), and are based on still air (no wind) conditions on both sides

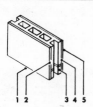

Replace Concrete Block with 4-in. Gypsum Tile (New Item 3) Construction	1	2
1. Inside surface (still air)	0.68	0.68
2. Plaster, lightweight aggregate, 0.625 in.	0.39	0.39
3. Concrete block, cinder aggregate, 4 in.	1.11	1.67
4. Plaster, lightweight aggregate, 0.625 in.	0.39	0.39
5. Inside surface (still air)	0.68	0.68
Total Thermal Resistance(R)	3.25	3.81

Construction No. 1: U = 1/3.25 = 0.308

Construction No. 2: U = 1/3.81= 0.262

Table VII   Coefficients of Transmission (*U*) of Frame Construction of Ceilings and Floors[d]

Coefficients are expressed in Btu per (hour) (square foot) (degree Fahrenheit difference between the air on the two sides), and are based on still air (no wind) on both sides

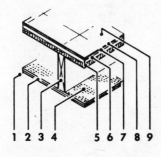

Assume Unheated Attic Space above Heated Room with Heat Flow Up—Remove Tile, Felt, Plywood, Sub-floor and Air Space—Replace with R-19 Blanket Insulation (New Item 4)

Heated Room Below Unheated Space Construction (Heat Flow Up)	1 Resistance (R) Between Floor Joists	At Floor Joist	2 Between Floor Joists	At Floor Joists
1. Bottom surface (still air)	0.61	0.61	0.61	0.61
2. Metal lath and lightweight aggregate, plaster, 0.75 in.	0.47	0.47	0.47	0.47
3. Nominal 2-in. × 8-in. floor joist	—	9.06	—	9.06
4. Nonreflective airspace, 7.25-in.	0.93*	—	19.00	—
5. Wood subfloor, 0.75 in.	0.94	0.94	—	—
6. Plywood, 0.625 in.	0.78	0.78	—	—
7. Felt building membrane	0.06	0.06	—	—
8. Resilient tile	0.05	0.05	—	—
9. Top surface (still air)	0.61	0.61	0.61	0.61
Total Thermal Resistance (R)	R_i = 4.45	R_s = 12.58	R_i = 20.69	R_s = 10.75

Construction No. 1 U_i = 1/4.45 = 0.225; U_s = 1/12.58 = 0.079. With 10% framing (typical of 2-in. joists @ 16-in. o.c.), U_{av} = 0.9 (0.225) + 0.1 (0.079) = 0.210

Construction No. 2 U_i = 1/20.69 = 0.048; U_s = 1/10.75 = 0.093. With framing unchanged, U_{av} = 0.9 (0.048) + 0.1 (0.093) = 0.053

*Use largest air space (3.5 in.) value shown in Table 2.

Table VIII   Coefficients of Transmission (*U*) of Flat Masonry Roofs with Built-up Roofing, with and without Suspended Ceilings[ce]

These Coefficients are expressed in Btu per (hour) (square foot) (degree Fahrenheit difference in temperature between the air on the two sides), and are based upon an outside wind velocity of 15 mph

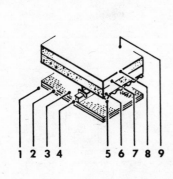

Add Rigid Roof Deck Insulation, C = 0.24 (R = 1/C) (New Item 7) Construction (Heat Flow Up)	1	2
1. Inside surface (still air)	0.61	0.61
1. Metal lath and lightweight aggregate plaster, 0.75 in.	0.47	0.47
3. Nonreflective air space, greater than 3.5 in. (50 F mean; 10 deg F temperature difference)	0.93*	0.93*
4. Metal ceiling suspension system with metal hanger rods	0**	0**
5. Corrugated metal deck	0	0
6. Concrete slab, lightweight aggregate, 2 in.	2.22	2.22
7. Rigid roof deck insulation (none)	—	4.17
8. Built-up roofing, 0.375 in.	0.33	0.33
9. Outside surface (15 mph wind)	0.17	0.17
Total Thermal Resistance (R).	4.73	8.90

Construction No. 1: U_{av} = 1/4.73 = 0.211

Construction No. 2: U_{av} = 1/8.90 = 0.112

[b] To adjust *U* values for the effect of added insulation between framing members, see Table 5 or 6.

*Use largest air space (3.5 in.) value shown in Table 2.

**Area of hanger rods is negligible in relation to ceiling area.

Table IX Coefficients of Transmission (U) of Wood Construction of Flat Roofs and Ceilings[ce]

Coefficients are expressed in Btu per (hour) (square foot) (degree Fahrenheit difference in temperature between the air on the two sides), and are based upon an outside wind velocity of 15 mph

Replace Roof Deck Insulation and 7.25-in. Air Space with 6-in. R-19 Blanket Insulation and 1.25-in. Air Space (New Items 5 and 7)

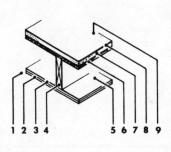

Construction (Heat Flow Up)	1 Resistance (R) Between Joists	At Joists	2 Between Joists	At Joists
1. Inside surface (still air)	0.61	0.61	0.61	0.61
2. Acoustical tile, fiberboard, glued, 0.5 in.	1.25	1.25	1.25	1.25
3. Gypsum wallboard, 0.5 in.	0.45	0.45	0.45	0.45
4. Nominal 2-in. × 8-in. ceiling joists	—	9.06	—	9.06
5. Nonreflective air space, 7.25 in. (50 F mean; 10 deg F temperature difference)	0.93*	—	1.05**	—
6. Plywood deck, 0.625 in.	0.78	0.78	0.78	0.78
7. Rigid roof deck insulation, c = 0.72, (R = 1/C)	1.39	1.39	19.00	—
8. Built-up roof	0.33	0.33	0.33	0.33
9. Outside surface (15 mph wind)	0.17	0.17	0.17	0.17
Total Thermal Resistance (R)	R_i=5.91	R_s=14.04	R_i=23.64	R_s=12.65

Construction No. 1 U_i = 1/5.91 = 0.169; U_s = 1/14.04 = 0.071. With 10% framing (typical of 2-in. joists @ 16-in. o.c.), U_{av} = 0.9 (0.169) + 0.1 (0.071) = 0.159

Construction No. 2 U_i = 1/23.64 = 0.042; U_s = 1/12.65 = 0.079. With framing unchanged, U_{av} = 0.9 (0.042) + 0.1 (0.079) = 0.046

*Use largest air space (3.5 in.) value shown in Table 2.
**Interpolated value (0 F mean; 10 deg F temperature difference).

Table X Coefficients of Transmission (U) of Metal Construction of Flat Roofs and Ceilings[ce]

Coefficients are expressed in Btu per (hour) (square foot) (degree Fahrenheit difference in temperature between the air on the two sides), and are based on upon outside wind velocity of 15 mph

Replace Rigid Roof Deck Insulation (C = 0.24) and Sand Aggregate Plaster with Rigid Roof Deck Insulation, C = 0.36 and Lightweight Aggregate Plaster (New Items 2 and 6)

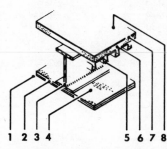

Construction (Heat Flow Up)	1	2
1. Inside surface (still air)	0.61	0.61
2. Metal lath and sand aggregate plaster, 0.75 in	0.13	0.47
3. Structural beam	0.00*	0.00*
4. Nonreflective air space (50 F mean; 10 deg F temperature difference	0.93**	0.93**
5. Metal deck	0.00*	0.00*
6. Rigid roof deck insulation, C = 0.24(R = 1/c)	4.17	2.78
7. Built-up roofing, 0.375 in.	0.33	0.33
8. Outside surface (15 mph wind)	0.17	0.17
Total Thermal Resistance (R)	6.34	5.29

Construction No. 1: U = 1/6.34 = 0.158
Construction No. 2: U = 1/5.29 = 0.189

*If structural beams and metal deck are to be considered, the technique shown in _Examples 1 and 2,_ and Fig. 3 may be used to estimate total R. Full scale testing of a suitable portion of the construction is, however, preferable.
**Use largest air space (3.5 in.) value shown in Table 2.

Table XI Coefficients of Transmission (*U*) of Pitched Roofs[f]

Coefficients are expressed in Btu per (hour) (square foot) (degree Fahrenheit difference in temperature between the air on the two sides), and are based on an outside wind velocity of 15 mph for heat flow upward and 7.5 mph for heat flow downward

Find U_{av} for same Construction 2 with Heat Flow Down (Summer Conditions)

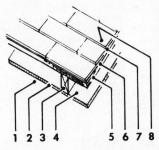

Construction 1 (Heat Flow Up) (Reflective Air Space)	1		2	
	Between Rafters	At Rafters	Between Rafters	At Rafters
1. Inside surface (still air)	0.62	0.62	0.76	0.76
2. Gypsum wallboard 0.5 in., foil backed	0.45	0.45	0.45	0.45
3. Nominal 2-in. × 4-in. ceiling rafter	—	4.38	—	4.38
4. 45 deg slope reflective air space, 3.5 in. (50 F mean, 30 deg F temperature difference)	2.17	—	4.33	—
5. Plywood sheathing, 0.625 in.	0.78	0.78	0.78	0.78
6. Felt building membrane	0.06	0.06	0.06	0.06
7. Asphalt shingle roofing	0.44	0.44	0.44	0.44
8. Outside surface (15 mph wind)	0.17	0.17	0.25**	0.25**
Total Thermal Resistance (R)	R_i=4.69	R_s=6.90	R_i=7.07	R_s=7.12

Construction No. 1: U_i=1/4.69= 0.213; U_s = 1/6.90 = 0.145. With 10% framing (typical of 2-in. rafters @16-in. o.c.), U_{av} = 0.9 (0.213) + 0.1 (0.145) = 0.206

Construction No. 2: U_i=1/7.07 = 0.141; U_s = 1/7.12 = 0.140. With framing unchanged, U_{av}= 0.9 (0.141) + 0.1 (0.140) = 0.141

Find U_{av} for same Construction 2 with Heat Flow Down (Summer Conditions)

Construction 1 (Heat Flow Up) (Non-Reflective Air Space)	3		4	
	Between Rafters	At Rafters	Between Rafters	At Rafters
1. Inside surface (still air)	0.62	0.62	0.76	0.76
2. Gypsum wallboard, 0.5 in.	0.45	0.45	0.45	0.45
3. Nominal 2-in. × 4-in. ceiling rafter	—	4.38	—	4.38
4. 45 deg slope, nonreflective air space, 3.5 in. (50 F mean; 10 deg F temperature difference)	0.96	—	0.90*	—
5. Plywood sheathing, 0.625 in.	0.78	0.78	0.78	0.78
6. Felt building membrane	0.06	0.06	0.06	0.06
7. Asphalt shingle roofing	0.44	0.44	0.44	0.44
8. Outside surface (15-mph wind)	0.17	0.17	0.25**	0.25**
Total Thermal Resistance (R)	R_i=3.48	R_s=6.90	R_i=3.64	R_s=7.12

Construction No. 3: U_i= 1/3.48 = 0.287; U_s = 1/6.90 = 0.145. With 10% framing typical of 2-in. rafters @ 16-in. o.c.), U_{av}= 0.9 (0.287)+ 0.1 (0.145) = 0.273

Construction No. 4: U_i= 1/3.64 = 0.275; U_s = 1/7.12 = 0.140. With framing unchanged, U_{av}= 0.9 (0.275) + 0.1 (0.140) = 0.262

[b] Pitch of roof—45 deg.

*Air space value at 90 F meann, 10 F dif. temperature difference.

**7.5-mph wind.

($\bar{H}$ = Monthly average daily total radiation on a horizontal surface, Btu/day-ft²; $\bar{K}_t$ = the fraction of the extra terrestrial radiation transmitted through the atmosphere; t_0 = ambient temperature, deg F.)

		Jan	Feb	Mar	Apr	May	Jun	July	Aug	Sep	Oct	Nov	Dec
Albuquerque, N. M.	$\bar{H}$	1150.9	1453.9	1925.4	2343.5	2560.9	2757.5	2561.2	2387.8	2120.3	1639.8	1274.2	1051.6
Lat. 35°03′ N.	$\bar{K}_t$	0.704	0.691	0.719	0.722	0.713	0.737	0.695	0.708	0.728	0.711	0.684	0.704
El. 5314 ft	t_0	37.3	43.3	50.1	59.6	69.4	79.1	82.8	80.6	73.6	62.1	47.8	39.4
Annette Is., Alaska	$\bar{H}$	236.2	428.4	883.4	1357.2	1634.7	1638.7	1632.1	1269.4	962	454.6	220.3	152
Lat. 55°02′ N.	$\bar{K}_t$	0.427	0.415	0.492	0.507	0.484	0.441	0.454	0.427	0.449	0.347	0.304	0.361
El. 110 ft	t_0	35.8	37.5	39.7	44.4	51.0	56.2	58.6	59.8	54.8	48.2	41.9	37.4
Apalachicola, Florida	$\bar{H}$	1107	1378.2	1654.2	2040.9	2268.6	2195.9	1978.6	1912.9	1703.3	1544.6	1243.2	982.3
Lat. 29°45′ N.	$\bar{K}_t$	0.577	0.584	0.576	0.612	0.630	0.594	0.542	0.558	0.559	0.608	0.574	0.543
El. 35 ft	t_0	57.3	59.0	62.9	69.5	76.4	81.8	83.1	83.1	80.6	73.2	63.7	58.5
Astoria, Oregon	$\bar{H}$	338.4	607	1008.5	1401.5	1838.7	1753.5	2007.7	1721	1322.5	780.4	413.6	295.2
Lat. 46°12′ N.	$\bar{K}_t$	0.330	0.397	0.454	0.471	0.524	0.466	0.551	0.538	0.526	0.435	0.336	0.332
El. 8 ft	t_0	41.3	44.7	46.9	51.3	55.0	59.3	62.6	63.6	62.2	55.7	48.5	43.9
Atlanta, Georgia	$\bar{H}$	848	1080.1	1426.9	1807	2018.1	2102.6	2002.9	1898.1	1519.2	1290.8	997.8	751.6
Lat. 33°39′ N.	$\bar{K}_t$	0.493	0.496	0.522	0.551	0.561	0.564	0.545	0.559	0.515	0.543	0.510	0.474
El. 976 ft	t_0	47.2	49.6	55.9	65.0	73.2	80.9	82.4	81.6	77.4	66.5	54.8	47.7
Barrow, Alaska	$\bar{H}$	13.3	143.2	713.3	1491.5	1883	2055.3	1602.2	953.5	428.4	152.4	22.9	—
Lat. 71°20′ N.	$\bar{K}_t$	—	0.776	0.773	0.726	0.553	0.533	0.448	0.377	0.315	0.35	—	—
El. 22 ft	t_0	−13.2	−15.9	−12.7	2.1	20.5	35.4	41.6	40.0	31.7	18.6	2.6	−8.6
Bismarck, N. D.	$\bar{H}$	587.4	934.3	1328.4	1668.2	2056.1	2173.8	2305.5	1929.1	1441.3	1018.1	600.4	464.2
Lat. 46°47′ N.	$\bar{K}_t$	0.594	0.628	0.565	0.565	0.588	0.579	0.634	0.606	0.581	0.584	0.510	0.547
El. 1660 ft	t_0	12.4	15.9	29.7	46.6	58.6	67.9	76.1	73.5	61.6	49.6	31.4	18.4
Blue Hill, Mass.	$\bar{H}$	555.3	797	1143.9	1438	1776.4	1943.9	1881.5	1622.1	1314	941	592.2	482.3
Lat. 42°13′ N.	$\bar{K}_t$	0.445	0.458	0.477	0.464	0.501	0.516	0.513	0.495	0.492	0.472	0.406	0.436
El. 629 ft	t_0	28.3	28.3	36.9	46.9	58.5	67.2	72.3	70.6	64.2	54.1	43.3	31.5
Boise, Idaho	$\bar{H}$	518.8	884.9	1280.4	1814.4	2189.3	2376.7	2500.3	2149.4	1717.7	1128.4	678.6	456.8
Lat. 43°34′ N.	$\bar{K}_t$	0.446	0.533	0.548	0.594	0.619	0.631	0.684	0.660	0.656	0.588	0.494	0.442
El. 2844 ft	t_0	29.5	36.5	45.0	53.5	62.1	69.3	79.6	77.2	66.7	56.3	42.3	33.1
Boston, Mass.	$\bar{H}$	505.5	738	1067.1	1355	1769	1864	1860.5	1570.1	1267.5	896.7	635.8	442.8
Lat. 42°22′ N.	$\bar{K}_t$	0.410	0.426	0.445	0.438	0.499	0.495	0.507	0.480	0.477	0.453	0.372	0.400
El. 29 ft.	t_0	31.4	31.4	39.9	49.5	60.4	69.8	74.5	73.8	66.8	57.4	46.6	34.9
Brownsville, Texas	$\bar{H}$	1105.9	1262.7	1505.9	1714	2092.2	2288.5	2345	2124	1774.9	1536.5	1104.8	982.3
Lat. 25°55′ N.	$\bar{K}_t$	0.517	0.500	0.505	0.509	0.584	0.627	0.650	0.617	0.566	0.570	0.468	0.488
El. 20 ft	t_0	63.3	66.7	70.7	76.2	81.4	85.1	86.5	86.9	84.1	78.9	70.7	65.2
Caribou, Maine	$\bar{H}$	497	861.6	1360.1	1495.9	1779.7	1779.7	1898.1	1675.6	1254.6	793	415.5	398.9
Lat. 46°52′ N.	$\bar{K}_t$	0.504	0.579	0.619	0.507	0.509	0.473	0.522	0.527	0.506	0.455	0.352	0.470
El. 628 ft	t_0	11.5	12.8	24.4	37.3	51.8	61.6	67.2	65.0	56.2	44.7	31.3	16.8
Charleston, S. C.	$\bar{H}$	946.1	1152.8	1352.4	1918.8	2063.4	2113.3	1649.4	1933.6	1557.2	1332.1	1073.8	952
Lat. 32°54′ N.	$\bar{K}_t$	0.541	0.521	0.491	0.584	0.574	0.567	0.454	0.569	0.525	0.554	0.539	0.586
El. 46 ft	t_0	53.6	55.2	60.6	67.8	74.8	80.9	82.9	82.3	79.1	69.8	59.8	54.0
Cleveland, Ohio	$\bar{H}$	466.8	681.9	1207	1443.9	1928.4	2102.6	2094.4	1840.6	1410.3	997	526.6	427.3
Lat. 41°24′ N.	$\bar{K}_t$	0.361	0.383	0.497	0.464	0.543	0.559	0.571	0.559	0.524	0.491	0.351	0.371
El. 805 ft.	t_0	30.8	30.9	39.4	50.2	62.4	72.7	77.0	75.1	68.5	57.4	44.0	32.8
Columbia, Mo.	$\bar{H}$	651.3	941.3	1315.8	1631.3	1999.6	2129.1	2148.7	1953.1	1689.6	1202.6	839.5	590.4
Lat. 38°58′ N.	$\bar{K}_t$	0.458	0.492	0.514	0.514	0.559	0.566	0.585	0.588	0.606	0.562	0.491	0.457
El. 785 ft	t_0	32.5	36.5	45.9	57.7	66.7	75.9	81.1	79.4	71.9	61.4	46.1	35.8
Columbus, Ohio	$\bar{H}$	486.3	746.5	1112.5	1480.8	1839.1	(2111)	2041.3	1572.7	1189.3	919.5	479	430.2
Lat. 40°00′ N.	$\bar{K}_t$	0.356	0.401	0.447	0.470	0.515	(0.561)	0.555	0.475	0.433	0.441	0.302	0.351
El. 833 ft	t_0	32.1	33.7	42.7	53.5	64.4	74.2	78	75.9	70.1	58	44.5	34.0
Davis, Calif.	$\bar{H}$	599.2	945	1504	1959	2368.6	2619.2	2565.6	2287.8	1856.8	1288.5	795.6	550.5
Lat. 38°33′ N.	$\bar{K}_t$	0.416	0.490	0.591	0.617	0.662	0.697	0.697	0.687	0.664	0.598	0.477	0.421
El. 51 ft	t_0	47.6	52.1	56.8	63.1	69.6	75.7	81	79.4	76.7	67.8	57	48.7
Dodge City, Kan.	$\bar{H}$	953.1	1186.3	1565.7	1975.6	2126.5	2459.8	2400.7	2210.7	1841.7	1421	1065.3	873.8
Lat. 37°46′ N.	$\bar{K}_t$	0.639	0.598	0.606	0.618	0.594	0.655	0.652	0.663	0.654	0.650	0.625	0.652
El. 2592 ft	t_0	33.8	38.7	46.5	57.7	66.7	77.2	83.8	82.4	73.7	61.7	46.5	36.8
East Lansing, Michigan	$\bar{H}$	425.8	739.1	1086	1249.8	1732.8	1914	1884.5	1627.7	1303.3	891.5	473.1	379.7
Lat. 42°44′ N.	$\bar{K}_t$	0.35	0.431	0.456	0.406	0.489	0.508	0.514	0.498	0.493	0.456	0.333	0.349
El. 856 ft	t_0	26.0	26.4	35.7	48.4	59.8	70.3	74.5	72.4	65.0	53.5	40.0	29.0

Notes: a. Liu, B. Y. H. and Jordan, R. C., 1963. "A Rational Procedure for Predicting the Long-Term Performance of Flat Plate Solar Energy Collectors." *Solar Energy*. Vol. 7, No. 2, pp. 71–74.

		Jan	Feb	Mar	Apr	May	Jun	July	Aug	Sep	Oct	Nov	Dec
East Wareham, Mass.	$\bar{H}$	504.4	762.4	1132.1	1392.6	1704.8	1958.3	1873.8	1607.4	1363.8	996.7	636.2	521
Lat. 41°46′ N.	$\bar{K}_t$	0.398	0.431	0.469	0.449	0.480	0.520	0.511	0.489	0.508	0.496	0.431	0.461
El. 18 ft	t_0	32.2	31.6	39.0	48.3	58.9	67.5	74.1	72.8	65.9	56	46	34.8
Edmonton, Alberta	$\bar{H}$	331.7	652.4	1165.3	1541.7	1900.4	1914.4	1964.9	1528	1113.3	704.4	413.6	245
Lat. 53°35′ N.	$\bar{K}_t$	0.529	0.585	0.624	0.564	0.558	0.514	0.549	0.506	0.506	0.504	0.510	0.492
El. 2219 ft	t_0	10.4	14	26.3	42.9	55.4	61.3	66.6	63.2	54.2	44.1	26.7	14.0
El Paso, Texas	$\bar{H}$	1247.6	1612.9	2048.7	2447.2	2673	2731	2391.1	2350.5	2077.5	1704.8	1324.7	1051.6
Lat. 31°48′ N.	$\bar{K}_t$	0.686	0.714	0.730	0.741	0.743	0.733	0.652	0.669	0.693	0.695	0.647	0.626
El. 3916 ft	t_0	47.1	53.1	58.7	67.3	75.7	84.2	84.9	83.4	78.5	69.0	56.0	48.5
Ely, Nevada	$\bar{H}$	871.6	1255	1749.8	2103.3	2322.1	2649	2417	2307.7	1935	1473	1078.6	814.8
Lat. 39°17′ N.	$\bar{K}_t$	0.618	0.660	0.692	0.664	0.649	0.704	0.656	0.695	0.696	0.691	0.658	0.64
El. 6262 ft	t_0	27.3	32.1	39.5	48.3	57.0	65.4	74.5	72.3	63.7	52.1	39.9	31.1
Fairbanks, Alaska	$\bar{H}$	66	283.4	860.5	1481.2	1806.2	1970.8	1702.9	1247.6	699.6	323.6	104.1	20.3
Lat. 64°49′ N.	$\bar{K}_t$	0.639	0.556	0.674	0.647	0.546	0.529	0.485	0.463	0.419	0.416	0.47	0.458
El. 436 ft	t_0	−7.0	0.3	13.0	32.2	50.5	62.4	63.8	58.3	47.1	29.6	5.5	−6.6
Fort Worth, Texas	$\bar{H}$	936.2	1198.5	1597.8	1829.1	2105.1	2437.6	2293.3	2216.6	1880.8	1476	1147.6	913.6
Lat. 32°50′ N.	$\bar{K}_t$	0.530	0.541	0.577	0.556	0.585	0.654	0.624	0.653	0.634	0.612	0.576	0.563
El. 544 ft.	t_0	48.1	52.3	59.8	68.8	75.9	84.0	87.7	88.6	81.3	71.5	58.8	50.8
Fresno, Calif.	$\bar{H}$	712.9	1116.6	1652.8	2049.4	2409.2	2641.7	2512.2	2300.7	1897.8	1415.5	906.6	616.6
Lat. 36°46′ N.	$\bar{K}_t$	0.462	0.551	0.632	0.638	0.672	0.703	0.682	0.686	0.665	0.635	0.512	0.44
El. 331 ft.	t_0	47.3	53.9	59.1	65.6	73.5	80.7	87.5	84.9	78.6	68.7	57.3	48.9
Gainesville, Fla.	$\bar{H}$	1036.9	1324.7	1635	1956.4	1934.7	1960.9	1895.6	1873.8	1615.1	1312.2	1169.7	919.5
Lat. 29°39′ N.	$\bar{K}_t$	0.535	0.56	0.568	0.587	0.538	0.531	0.519	0.547	0.529	0.515	0.537	0.508
El. 165 ft	t_0	62.1	63.1	67.5	72.8	79.4	83.4	83.8	84.1	82	75.7	67.2	62.4
Glasgow, Mont.	$\bar{H}$	572.7	965.7	1437.6	1741.3	2127.3	2261.6	2414.7	1984.5	1531	997	574.9	428.4
Lat. 48°13′ N.	$\bar{K}_t$	0.621	0.678	0.672	0.597	0.611	0.602	0.666	0.630	0.629	0.593	0.516	0.548
El. 2277 ft	t_0	13.3	17.3	31.1	47.8	59.3	67.3	76	73.2	61.2	49.2	31.0	18.6
Grand Junction, Colorado	$\bar{H}$	848	1210.7	1622.9	2002.2	2300.3	2645.4	2517.7	2157.2	1957.5	1394.8	969.7	793.4
Lat. 39°07′ N.	$\bar{K}_t$	0.597	0.633	0.643	0.632	0.643	0.704	0.690	0.65	0.705	0.654	0.59	0.621
El. 4849 ft	t_0	26.9	35.0	44.6	55.8	66.3	75.7	82.5	79.6	71.4	58.3	42.0	31.4
Grand Lake, Colo.	$\bar{H}$	735	1135.4	1579.3	1876.7	1974.9	2369.7	2103.3	1708.5	1715.8	1212.2	775.6	660.5
Lat. 40°15′ N.	$\bar{K}_t$	0.541	0.615	0.637	0.597	0.553	0.63	0.572	0.516	0.626	0.583	0.494	0.542
El. 8389 ft	t_0	18.5	23.1	28.5	39.1	48.7	56.6	62.8	61.5	55.5	45.2	30.3	22.6
Great Falls, Mont.	$\bar{H}$	524	869.4	1369.7	1621.4	1970.8	2179.3	2383	1986.3	1536.5	984.9	575.3	420.7
Lat. 47°29′ N.	$\bar{K}_t$	0.552	0.596	0.631	0.551	0.565	0.580	0.656	0.627	0.626	0.574	0.503	0.518
El. 3664 ft	t_0	25.4	27.6	35.6	47.7	57.5	64.3	73.8	71.3	60.6	51.4	38.0	29.1
Greensboro, N. C.	$\bar{H}$	743.9	1031.7	1323.2	1755.3	1988.5	2111.4	2033.9	1810.3	1517.3	1202.6	908.1	690.8
Lat. 36°05′ N.	$\bar{K}_t$	0.469	0.499	0.499	0.543	0.554	0.563	0.552	0.538	0.527	0.531	0.501	0.479
El. 891 ft	t_0	42.0	44.2	51.7	60.8	69.9	78.0	80.2	78.9	73.9	62.7	51.5	43.2
Griffin, Georgia	$\bar{H}$	889.6	1135.8	1450.9	1923.6	2163.1	2176	2064.9	1961.2	1605.9	1352.4	1073.8	781.5
Lat. 33°15′ N.	$\bar{K}_t$	0.513	0.517	0.528	0.586	0.601	0.583	0.562	0.578	0.543	0.565	0.545	0.487
El. 980 ft	t_0	48.9	51.0	59.1	66.7	74.6	81.2	83.0	82.2	78.4	68	57.3	49.4
Hatteras, N. C.	$\bar{H}$	891.9	1184.1	1590.4	2128	2376.4	2438	2334.3	2085.6	1758.3	1337.6	1053.5	798.1
Lat. 35°13′ N.	$\bar{K}_t$	0.546	0.563	0.593	0.655	0.661	0.652	0.634	0.619	0.605	0.58	0.566	0.535
El. 7 ft	t_0	49.9	49.5	54.7	61.5	69.9	77.2	80.0	79.8	76.7	67.9	59.1	51.3
Indianapolis, Ind.	$\bar{H}$	526.2	797.4	1184.1	1481.2	1828	2042	2039.5	1832.1	1513.3	1094.4	662.4	491.1
Lat. 39°44′ N.	$\bar{K}_t$	0.380	0.424	0.472	0.47	0.511	0.543	0.554	0.552	0.549	0.520	0.413	0.391
El. 793 ft	t_0	31.3	33.9	43.0	54.1	64.9	74.8	79.6	77.4	70.6	59.3	44.2	33.4
Inyokern, Calif.	$\bar{H}$	1148.7	1554.2	2136.9	2594.8	2925.4	3108.8	2908.8	2759.4	2409.2	1819.2	1376.1	1094.4
Lat. 35°39′ N.	$\bar{K}_t$	0.716	0.745	0.803	0.8	0.815	0.830	0.790	0.820	0.834	0.795	0.743	0.742
El. 2440 ft	t_0	47.3	53.9	59.1	65.6	73.5	80.7	87.5	84.9	78.6	68.7	57.3	48.9
Ithaca, N. Y.	$\bar{H}$	434.3	755	1074.9	1322.9	1779.3	2025.8	2031.3	1736.9	1320.3	918.4	466.4	370.8
Lat. 42°27′ N.	$\bar{K}_t$	0.351	0.435	0.45	0.428	0.502	0.538	0.554	0.530	0.497	0.465	0.324	0.337
El. 950 ft	t_0	27.2	26.5	36	48.4	59.6	68.9	73.9	71.9	64.2	53.6	41.5	29.6
Lake Charles, La.	$\bar{H}$	899.2	1145.7	1487.4	1801.8	2080.4	2213.3	1968.6	1910.3	1678.2	1505.5	1122.1	875.6
Lat. 30°13′ N.	$\bar{K}_t$	0.473	0.492	0.521	0.542	0.578	0.597	0.538	0.558	0.553	0.597	0.524	0.494
El. 12 ft	t_0	55.3	58.7	63.5	70.9	77.4	83.4	84.8	85.0	81.5	73.8	62.6	56.9
Lander, Wyo.	$\bar{H}$	786.3	1146.1	1638	1988.5	2114	2492.2	2438.4	2120.6	1712.9	1301.8	837.3	694.8
Lat. 42°48′ N.	$\bar{K}_t$	0.65	0.672	0.691	0.647	0.597	0.662	0.665	0.649	0.647	0.666	0.589	0.643
El. 5370 ft	t_0	20.2	26.3	34.7	45.5	56.0	65.4	74.6	72.5	61.4	48.3	33.4	23.8

		Jan	Feb	Mar	Apr	May	Jun	July	Aug	Sep	Oct	Nov	Dec
Las Vegas, Nev.	$\bar{H}$	1035.8	1438	1926.5	2322.8	2629.5	2799.2	2524	2342	2062	1602.6	1190	964.2
Lat. 36°05′ N.	$\bar{K}_t$	0.654	0.697	0.728	0.719	0.732	0.746	0.685	0.697	0.716	0.704	0.657	0.668
El. 2162 ft	t_0	47.5	53.9	60.3	69.5	78.3	88.2	95.0	92.9	85.4	71.7	57.8	50.2
Lemont, Illinois	$\bar{H}$	(590)	879	1255.7	1481.5	1866	2041.7	1990.8	1836.9	1469.4	1015.5	(639)	(531)
Lat. 41°40′ N.	$\bar{K}_t$	(0.464)	0.496	0.520	0.477	0.525	0.542	0.542	0.559	0.547	0.506	(0.433)	(0.467
El. 595 ft	t_0	28.9	30.3	39.5	49.7	59.2	70.8	75.6	74.3	67.2	57.6	43.0	30.6
Lexington, Ky.	$\bar{H}$	—	—	—	1834.7	2171.2	—	2246.5	2064.9	1775.6	1315.8	—	681.5
Lat. 38°02′ N.	$\bar{K}_t$	—	—	—	0.575	0.606	—	0.610	0.619	0.631	0.604	—	0.513
El. 979 ft	t_0	36.5	38.8	47.4	57.8	67.5	76.2	79.8	78.2	72.8	61.2	47.6	38.5
Lincoln, Neb.	$\bar{H}$	712.5	955.7	1299.6	1587.8	1856.1	2040.6	2011.4	1902.6	1543.5	1215.8	773.4	643.2
Lat. 40°51′ N.	$\bar{K}_t$	0.542	0.528	0.532	0.507	0.522	0.542	0.547	0.577	0.568	0.596	0.508	0.545
El. 1189 ft	t_0	27.8	32.1	42.4	55.8	65.8	76.0	82.6	80.2	71.5	59.9	43.2	31.8
Little Rock, Ark.	$\bar{H}$	704.4	974.2	1335.8	1669.4	1960.1	2091.5	2081.2	1938.7	1640.6	1282.6	913.6	701.1
Lat. 34°44′ N.	$\bar{K}_t$	0.424	0.458	0.496	0.513	0.545	0.559	0.566	0.574	0.561	0.552	0.484	0.463
El. 265 ft	t_0	44.6	48.5	56.0	65.8	73.1	76.7	85.1	84.6	78.3	67.9	54.7	46.7
Los Angeles, Calif. (WBAS)	$\bar{H}$	930.6	1284.1	1729.5	1948	2196.7	2272.3	2413.6	2155.3	1898.1	1372.7	1082.3	901.1
Lat. 33°56′ N.	$\bar{K}_t$	0.547	0.596	0.635	0.595	0.610	0.608	0.657	0.635	0.641	0.574	0.551	0.566
El. 99	t_0	56.2	56.9	59.2	61.4	64.2	66.7	69.6	70.2	69.1	66.1	62.6	58.7
Los Angeles, Calif. (WBO)	$\bar{H}$	911.8	1223.6	1640.9	1866.8	2061.2	2259	2428.4	2198.9	1891.5	1362.3	1053.1	877.8
Lat. 34°03′ N.	$\bar{K}_t$	0.538	0.568	0.602	0.571	0.573	0.605	0.66	0.648	0.643	0.578	0.548	0.566
	t_0	57.9	59.2	61.8	64.3	67.6	70.7	75.8	76.1	74.2	69.6	65.4	60.2
Madison, Wis.	$\bar{H}$	564.6	812.2	1232.1	1455.3	1745.4	2031.7	2046.5	1740.2	1443.9	993	555.7	495.9
Lat. 43°08′ N.	$\bar{K}_t$	0.49	0.478	0.522	0.474	0.493	0.540	0.559	0.534	0.549	0.510	0.396	0.467
El. 866 ft	t_0	21.8	24.6	35.3	49.0	61.0	70.9	76.8	74.4	65.6	53.7	37.8	25.4
Matanuska, Alaska	$\bar{H}$	119.2	345	—	1327.6	1628.4	1727.6	1526.9	1169	737.3	373.8	142.8	56.4
Lat. 61°30′ N.	$\bar{K}_t$	0.513	0.503	—	0.545	0.494	0.466	0.434	0.419	0.401	0.390	0.372	0.364
El. 180 ft	t_0	13.9	21.0	27.4	38.6	50.3	57.6	60.1	58.1	50.2	37.7	22.9	13.9
Medford, Oregon	$\bar{H}$	435.4	804.4	1259.8	1807.4	2216.2	2440.5	2607.4	2261.6	1672.3	1043.5	558.7	346.5
Lat. 42°23′ N.	$\bar{K}_t$	0.353	0.464	0.527	0.584	0.625	0.648	0.710	0.689	0.628	0.526	0.384	0.313
El. 1329 ft	t_0	39.4	45.4	50.8	56.3	63.1	69.4	76.9	76.4	69.6	58.7	47.1	40.5
Miami, Florida	$\bar{H}$	1292.2	1554.6	1828.8	2020.6	2068.6	1991.5	1992.6	1890.8	1646.8	1436.5	1321	1183.4
Lat. 25°47′ N.	$\bar{K}_t$	0.604	0.616	0.612	0.600	0.578	0.545	0.552	0.549	0.525	0.534	0.559	0.588
El. 9 ft	t_0	71.6	72.0	73.8	77.0	79.9	82.9	84.1	84.5	83.3	80.2	75.6	72.6
Midland, Texas	$\bar{H}$	1066.4	1345.7	1784.8	2036.1	2301.1	2317.7	2301.8	2193	1921.8	1470.8	1244.3	1023.2
Lat. 31°56′ N.	$\bar{K}_t$	0.587	0.596	0.638	0.617	0.639	0.622	0.628	0.643	0.642	0.600	0.609	0.611
El. 2854 ft	t_0	47.9	52.8	60.0	68.8	77.2	83.9	85.7	85.0	78.9	70.3	56.6	49.1
Nashville, Tenn.	$\bar{H}$	589.7	907	1246.8	1662.3	1997	2149.4	2079.7	1862.7	1600.7	1223.6	823.2	614.4
Lat. 36°07′ N.	$\bar{K}_t$	0.373	0.440	0.472	0.514	0.556	0.573	0.565	0.554	0.556	0.540	0.454	0.426
El. 605 ft	t_0	42.6	45.1	52.9	63.0	71.4	80.1	83.2	81.9	76.6	65.4	52.3	44.3
Newport, R. I.	$\bar{H}$	565.7	856.4	1231.7	1484.8	1849	2019.2	1942.8	1687.1	1411.4	1035.4	656.1	527.7
Lat. 41°29′ N.	$\bar{K}_t$	0.438	0.482	0.507	0.477	0.520	0.536	0.529	0.513	0.524	0.512	0.44	0.460
El. 60 ft	t_0	29.5	32.0	39.6	48.2	58.6	67.0	73.2	72.3	66.7	56.2	46.5	34.4
New York, N. Y.	$\bar{H}$	539.5	790.8	1180.4	1426.2	1738.4	1994.1	1938.7	1605.9	1349.4	977.8	598.1	476
Lat. 40°46′ N.	$\bar{K}_t$	0.406	0.435	0.480	0.455	0.488	0.53	0.528	0.486	0.500	0.475	0.397	0.403
El. 52 ft	t_0	35.0	34.9	43.1	52.3	63.3	72.2	76.9	75.3	69.5	59.3	48.3	37.7
Oak Ridge, Tenn.	$\bar{H}$	604	895.9	1241.7	1689.6	1942.8	2066.4	1972.3	1795.6	1559.8	1194.8	796.3	610
Lat. 36°01′ N.	$\bar{K}_t$	0.382	0.435	0.471	0.524	0.541	0.551	0.536	0.534	0.542	0.527	0.438	0.422
El. 905 ft	t_0	41.9	44.2	51.7	61.4	69.8	77.8	80.2	78.8	74.5	62.7	50.4	42.5
Oklahoma City, Oklahoma	$\bar{H}$	938	1192.6	1534.3	1849.4	2005.1	2355	2273.8	2211	1819.2	1409.6	1085.6	897.4
Lat. 35°24′ N.	$\bar{K}_t$	0.580	0.571	0.576	0.570	0.558	0.629	0.618	0.656	0.628	0.614	0.588	0.608
El. 1304 ft	t_0	40.1	45.0	53.2	63.6	71.2	80.6	85.5	85.4	77.4	66.5	52.2	43.1
Ottawa, Ontario	$\bar{H}$	539.1	852.4	1250.5	1506.6	1857.2	2084.5	2045.4	1752.4	1326.6	826.9	458.7	408.5
Lat. 45°20′ N.	$\bar{K}_t$	0.499	0.540	0.554	0.502	0.529	0.554	0.560	0.546	0.521	0.450	0.359	0.436
El. 339 ft	t_0	14.6	15.6	27.7	43.3	57.5	67.5	71.9	69.8	61.5	48.9	35	19.6
Phoenix, Ariz.	$\bar{H}$	1126.6	1514.7	1967.1	2388.2	2709.6	2781.5	2450.5	2299.6	2131.3	1688.9	1290	1040.9
Lat. 33°26′ N.	$\bar{K}_t$	0.65	0.691	0.716	0.728	0.753	0.745	0.667	0.677	0.722	0.708	0.657	0.652
El. 1112 ft	t_0	54.2	58.8	64.7	72.2	80.8	89.2	94.6	92.5	87.4	75.8	63.6	56.7
Portland, Maine	$\bar{H}$	565.7	874.5	1329.5	1528.4	1923.2	2017.3	2095.6	1799.2	1428.8	1035	591.5	507.7
Lat. 43°39′ N.	$\bar{K}_t$	0.482	0.524	0.569	0.500	0.544	0.536	0.572	0.554	0.546	0.539	0.431	0.491
El. 63 ft	t_0	23.7	24.5	34.4	44.8	55.4	65.1	71.1	69.7	61.9	51.8	40.3	28.0

		Jan	Feb	Mar	Apr	May	Jun	July	Aug	Sep	Oct	Nov	Dec
Rapid City, S. D.	$\bar{H}$	687.8	1032.5	1503.7	1807	2028	2193.7	2235.8	2019.9	1628	1179.3	763.1	590.4
Lat. 44°09′ N.	$\bar{K}_t$	0.601	0.627	0.649	0.594	0.574	0.583	0.612	0.622	0.628	0.624	0.566	0.588
El. 3218 ft	t_0	24.7	27.4	34.7	48.2	58.3	67.3	76.3	75.0	64.7	52.9	38.7	29.2
Riverside, Calif.	$\bar{H}$	999.6	1335	1750.5	1943.2	2282.3	2492.6	2443.5	2263.8	1955.3	1509.6	1169	979.7
Lat. 33°57′ N.	$\bar{K}_t$	0.589	0.617	0.643	0.594	0.635	0.667	0.665	0.668	0.665	0.639	0.606	0.626
El. 1020 ft	t_0	55.3	57.0	60.6	65.0	69.4	74.0	81.0	81.0	78.5	71.0	63.1	57.2
Saint Cloud, Minn.	$\bar{H}$	632.8	976.7	1383	1598.1	1859.4	2003.3	2087.8	1828.4	1369.4	890.4	545.4	463.1
Lat. 45°35′ N.	$\bar{K}_t$	0.595	0.629	0.614	0.534	0.530	0.533	0.573	0.570	0.539	0.490	0.435	0.504
El. 1034 ft	t_0	13.6	16.9	29.8	46.2	58.8	68.5	74.4	71.9	62.5	50.2	32.1	18.3
Salt Lake City, Utah	$\bar{H}$	622.1	986	1301.1	1813.3	—	—	—	—	1689.3	1250.2	—	552.8
Lat. 40°46′ N.	$\bar{K}_t$	0.468	0.909	0.529	0.578	—	—	—	—	0.621	0.610	—	0.467
El. 4227 ft	t_0	29.4	36.2	44.4	53.9	63.1	71.7	81.3	79.0	68.7	57.0	42.5	34.0
San Antonio, Tex.	$\bar{H}$	1045	1299.2	1560.1	1664.6	2024.7	814.8	2364.2	2185.2	1844.6	1487.4	1104.4	954.6
Lat. 29°32′ N.	$\bar{K}_t$	0.541	0.550	0.542	0.500	0.563	0.220	0.647	0.637	0.603	0.584	0.507	0.528
El. 794 ft	t_0	53.7	58.4	65.0	72.2	79.2	85.0	87.4	87.8	82.6	74.7	63.3	56.5
Santa Maria, Calif.	$\bar{H}$	983.8	1296.3	1805.9	2067.9	2375.6	2599.6	2540.6	2293.3	1965.7	1566.4	1169	943.9
Lat. 34°54′ N.	$\bar{K}_t$	0.595	0.613	0.671	0.636	0.661	0.695	0.690	0.678	0.674	0.676	0.624	0.627
El. 238 ft	t_0	54.1	55.3	57.6	59.5	61.2	63.5	65.3	65.7	65.9	64.1	60.8	56.1
Sault Ste. Marie, Michigan	$\bar{H}$	488.6	843.9	1336.5	1559.4	1962.3	2064.2	2149.4	1767.9	1207	809.2	392.2	359.8
Lat. 46°28′ N.	$\bar{K}_t$	0.490	0.560	0.606	0.526	0.560	0.549	0.590	0.554	0.481	0.457	0.323	0.408
El. 724 ft	t_0	16.3	16.2	25.6	39.5	52.1	61.6	67.3	66.0	57.9	46.8	33.4	21.9
Sayville, N. Y.	$\bar{H}$	602.9	936.2	1259.4	1560.5	1857.2	2123.2	2040.9	1734.7	1446.8	1087.4	697.8	533.9
Lat. 40°30′ N.	$\bar{K}_t$	0.453	0.511	0.510	0.498	0.522	0.564	0.555	0.525	0.530	0.527	0.450	0.447
El. 20 ft	t_0	35	34.9	43.1	52.3	63.3	72.2	76.9	75.3	69.5	59.3	48.3	37.7
Schenectady, N. Y.	$\bar{H}$	488.2	753.5	1026.6	1272.3	1553.1	1687.8	1662.3	1494.8	1124.7	820.6	436.2	356.8
Lat. 42°50′ N.	$\bar{K}_t$	0.406	0.441	0.433	0.413	0.438	0.448	0.454	0.458	0.426	0.420	0.309	0.331
El. 217 ft	t_0	24.7	24.6	34.9	48.3	61.7	70.8	76.9	73.7	64.6	53.1	40.1	28.0
Seattle, Wash.	$\bar{H}$	282.6	520.6	992.2	1507	1881.5	1909.4	2110.7	1688.5	1211.8	702.2	386.3	239.5
Lat. 47°27′ N.	$\bar{K}_t$	0.296	0.355	0.456	0.510	0.538	0.508	0.581	0.533	0.492	0.407	0.336	0.292
El. 386 ft	t_0	42.1	45.0	48.9	54.1	59.8	64.4	68.4	67.9	63.3	56.3	48.4	44.4
Seattle, Wash.	$\bar{H}$	252	471.6	917.3	1375.6	1664.9	1724	1805.1	1617	1129.1	638	325.5	218.1
Lat. 47°36′ N.	$\bar{K}_t$	0.266	0.324	0.423	0.468	0.477	0.459	0.498	0.511	0.459	0.372	0.284	0.269
El. 14 ft	t_0	38.9	42.9	46.9	51.9	58.1	62.8	67.2	66.7	61.6	54.0	45.7	41.5
Seabrook, N. J.	$\bar{H}$	591.9	854.2	1195.6	1518.8	1800.7	1964.6	1949.8	1715	1445.7	1071.9	721.8	522.5
Lat. 39°30′ N.	$\bar{K}_t$	0.426	0.453	0.476	0.481	0.504	0.522	0.530	0.517	0.524	0.508	0.449	0.416
El. 100 ft	t_0	39.5	37.6	43.9	54.7	64.9	74.1	79.8	77.7	69.7	61.2	48.5	39.3
Spokane, Wash.	$\bar{H}$	446.1	837.6	1200	1764.6	2104.4	2226.5	2479.7	2076	1511	844.6	486.3	279
Lat. 47°40′ N.	$\bar{K}_t$	0.478	0.579	0.556	0.602	0.603	0.593	0.684	0.656	0.616	0.494	0.428	0.345
El. 1968	t_0	26.5	31.7	40.5	49.2	57.9	64.6	73.4	71.7	62.7	51.5	37.4	30.5
State College, Pa.	H	501.8	749.1	1106.6	1399.2	1754.6	2027.6	1968.2	1690	1336.1	1017	580.1	443.9
Lat. 40°48′ N.	$\bar{K}_t$	0.381	0.413	0.451	0.448	0.493	0.539	0.536	0.512	0.492	0.496	0.379	0.376
El. 1175 ft	t_0	31.3	31.4	39.8	51.3	63.4	71.8	75.8	73.4	66.1	55.6	43.2	32.6
Stillwater, Okla.	$\bar{H}$	763.8	1081.5	1463.8	1702.6	1879.3	2235.8	2224.3	2039.1	1724.3	1314	991.5	783
Lat. 36°09′ N.	$\bar{K}_t$	0.484	0.527	0.555	0.528	0.523	0.596	0.604	0.607	0.599	0.581	0.548	0.544
El. 910 ft	t_0	41.2	45.6	53.3	64.2	71.6	81.1	85.9	85.9	77.5	67.6	52.6	43.9
Tampa, Fla.	$\bar{H}$	1223.6	1461.2	1771.9	2016.2	2228	2146.5	1991.9	1845.4	1687.8	1493.3	1328.4	1119.5
Lat. 27°55′ N.	$\bar{K}_t$	0.605	0.600	0.606	0.602	0.620	0.583	0.548	0.537	0.546	0.572	0.590	0.589
El. 11 ft	t_0	64.2	65.7	68.8	74.3	79.4	83.0	84.0	84.4	82.9	77.2	69.6	65.5
Toronto, Ontario	$\bar{H}$	451.3	674.5	1088.9	1388.2	1785.2	1941.7	1968.6	1622.5	1284.1	835	458.3	352.8
Lat. 43°41′ N.	$\bar{K}_t$	0.388	0.406	0.467	0.455	0.506	0.516	0.539	0.500	0.493	0.438	0.336	0.346
El. 379 ft	t_0	26.5	26.0	34.2	46.3	58	68.4	73.8	71.8	64.3	52.6	40.9	30.2
Tucson, Arizona	$\bar{H}$	1171.9	1453.8	—	2434.7	—	2601.4	2292.2	2179.7	2122.5	1640.9	1322.1	1132.1
Lat. 32°07′ N.	$\bar{K}_t$	0.648	0.646	—	0.738	—	0.698	0.625	0.640	0.710	0.672	0.650	0.679
El. 2556 ft	t_0	53.7	57.3	62.3	69.7	78.0	87.0	90.1	87.4	84.0	73.9	62.5	56.1
Upton, N. Y.	$\bar{H}$	583	872.7	1280.4	1609.9	1891.5	2159	2044.6	1789.6	1472.7	1102.6	686.7	551.3
Lat. 40°52′ N.	$\bar{K}_t$	0.444	0.483	0.522	0.514	0.532	0.574	0.557	0.542	0.542	0.538	0.448	0.467
El. 75 ft	t_0	35.0	34.9	43.1	52.3	63.3	72.2	76.9	75.3	69.5	59.3	48.3	37.7
Washington, D. C. (WBCO)	$\bar{H}$	632.4	901.5	1255	1600.4	1846.8	2080.8	1929.9	1712.2	1446.1	1083.4	763.5	594.1
Lat. 38°51′ N.	$\bar{K}_t$	0.445	0.470	0.496	0.504	0.516	0.553	0.524	0.516	0.520	0.506	0.464	0.460
El. 64 ft	t_0	38.4	39.6	48.1	57.5	67.7	76.2	79.9	77.9	72.2	60.9	50.2	40.2
Winnipeg, Man.	$\bar{H}$	488.2	835.4	1354.2	1641.3	1904.4	1962	2123.6	1761.2	1190.4	767.5	444.6	345
Lat. 49°54′ N.	$\bar{K}_t$	0.601	0.636	0.661	0.574	0.550	0.524	0.587	0.567	0.504	0.482	0.436	0.503
El. 786 ft	t_0	3.2	7.1	21.3	40.9	55.9	65.3	71.9	69.4	58.6	45.6	25.2	10.1

The following collector design, developed and tested at The Evergreen State College, combines reasonable cost with high performance and durability. (The cost is about one hundred dollars if all parts are bought at retail stores. This price can be reduced significantly if you already have some of the materials or scavenge them from such places as old buildings, etc.)

The collector incorporates a wood box frame of 1 × 6 mahogany or redwood about three feet wide and six and one-half feet long. See figure 4G–1. One sheet of tempered glass on top of the box covers an array of one-half inch copper tubing soldered to 0.010 inch copper sheet fins. A space of about one inch is required between the glazing and the array. The array is "free floating" above three and one-half inches of normal household insulation separated by a sheet of plywood. Free floating means that the array of fins and tubing does not rest directly on the plywood flooring but actually is raised about one-half inch above, supported at the head, middle and foot. Aluminum foil is placed over the floor to reflect heat back onto the array. Finally, a sheet of plywood closes the bottom of the box.

Dimensions for this collector have been determined solely by the 34″ × 76″ size of the glazing that we could obtain. Anyone designing or building a collector should take limiting factors such as glazing and copper sheeting sizes into account. It seems reasonable that most collectors will be designed around the glass as most other materials can easily be fitted to it.

A. Materials:

Description	Unit Cost	Amount	Price
1. Glazing — 34″ × 76″	$10.00/sheet	1 sheet	$10.00
2. Copper sheeting — 0.010″	$1.40/sq. foot	19½ sq. ft.	$27.30
3. Copper tubing — ½″	$0.39/ft.	36 ft.	$14.04
4. Copper tubing — ¾″	$0.59/ft.	5 ft.	$ 2.95
5. Copper tees — ¾″ × ¾″ × ½″	$0.51/tee	12 tees	$ 6.12
6. Copper caps — ¾″	$0.30/cap	2 caps	$ 0.60
7. Solder	$7.50/lb.	½ lb.	$ 3.75
8. Flux	$0.79/jar	1 jar	$ 0.79
9. Mahogany — 1 × 6	$0.45/ft.	20 ft.	$ 9.00
10. Plywood	$5.00/4 × 8 sheet	2 sheets	$10.00
11. Fiberglass insulation 3½″ × 1¼′ R-11	$0.20/sq. ft.	18 sq. ft.	$ 3.60
12. Butyl rubber caulking	$2.00/tube	1 tube	$ 2.00
13. Marine varnish	$7.00/qt.	1 qt.	$ 7.00
14. Temperature resistant flat-black paint	$3.00/can	1 can	$ 3.00
15. Miscellaneous (nails, screws, glue, aluminum foil, etc.)			$ 2.00
		TOTAL	$102.15
		COST/SQ. FOOT	$5.68

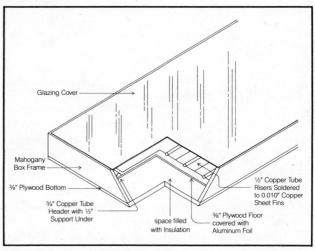

Figure 4G-1   Collector details

B. Box Construction:

The dimensions for our box are given in figure 4G–2 but again the design was dependent on our glass size. All

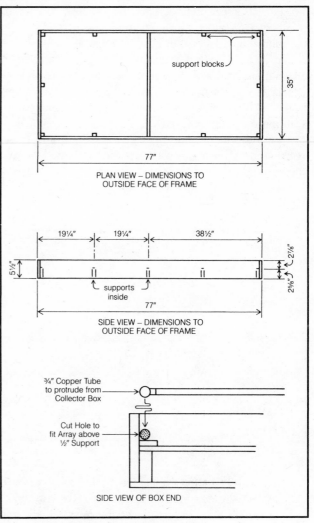

Figure 4G-2   Dimensions and Frame Details

joints and overlapped areas should be cemented with a good waterproof glue and screwed or nailed. This is important for durability.

The frame is constructed first with the end pieces overlapping the side lengths. To keep the box as straight as possible for better fit of the glass, the box frame should be constructed first with the bottom then immediately being put on. In this way any warps in the frame can easily be taken out by aligning the frame on the straight edges of the bottom and nailing and glueing them together.

The middle support frame should be put in next along with all the floor support blocks. All of the support pieces should extend up from the bottom of the frame to support the floor and leave a two inch gap between the top of the floor and the bottom of the glass. Be sure to caulk around the whole bottom and around all supports and seams up to floor level using a high temperature caulk (above 200°F) to seal it from any possible moisture that might seep in through the edges.

Insulation can then be placed in the box, foil side up to reflect heat back towards the array. In general, the more insulation, the better, but in most areas three and one-half inches of standard household fiberglass insulation (R-11) is quite sufficient. If you are planning to mount your collectors so that the bottoms of the boxes may be exposed to the outside, you might consider designing a box with more insulation space.

With the insulation in place, mark the frame above each support piece and place the floor into the box onto the supports. The floor should not be glued in but only screwed down in case access is ever needed to the insulation.

on all sides leaving three-eighths inches for holding the glass at the edge. One eighth inch is left on all sides of the glass for expansion and contraction of the glass and box. One-sixteenth to one-eighth inch should be left in the depth of the groove with the glass so that sealer can be placed above and below it. After grooving the top of the box, caulk around the floor and up the sides at each corner to the point where the glass will be.

Finally, three lengths of one-half inch array support blocks should be glued onto the floor at the head, middle and foot of the collector. Roll out sheets of aluminum foil over the floor, shinier side up, and staple it down along its edges. Covering the floor with foil will reflect more heat back onto the fins.

C. Construction of Array

To begin, there is one fundamental rule: maximize the area of the collector array surface to the size of the glazing and box. On our collectors, we allow one-eighth inch between the interior of the box frame and the header pipes. The more collector surface area there is, the higher the efficiency of the collector will be. Keeping this in mind when designing, measure the depths of the fittings (usually one-half inch) to see how far the pipes will go into them, then maximize the length of the risers in the box. Our sizes are shown in figure 4G–4 which also shows how the pipes are assembled. Five and one-half inches from center to center of risers is a good spacing compromise between efficiency and economics. Also allow about 4 inches between the center of the side risers and the inside edge of the box. This should save trimming of the fins later on. Make sure that the openings into the array are on opposite sides and corners.

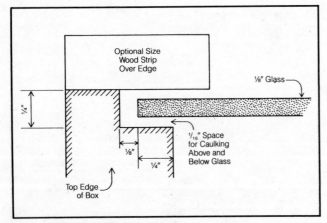

Figure 4G-3   Glass Support

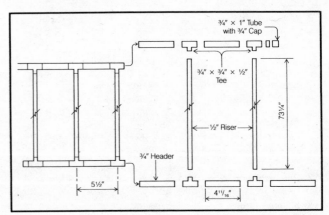

Figure 4G-4   Collector Piping

Figure 4G–3 shows a section of the glass support. Our boxes were designed so that we grooved the top of the frame with a router and placed the glass actually into the frame. One-quarter inch of frame supports the glass

Carefully cut the tubes with a tubing cutter and piece the array together. It may be worthwhile to cut the first riser, put on its two tees and actually see if it will fit in the box.

242

The next step involves cutting the copper sheeting and putting it on the riser tubes. The first thing to do if you are designing your own is to figure out how to best use the copper sheeting without wasting any. Our fins were made by unrolling the two foot wide roll and cutting off six and one-half inch pieces. Because each fin is bent around a riser tube, plan to cut long, thin pieces that can be bent around one riser only for much easier assembly. About one to one and one-quarter inches is needed to bind halfway around a one-half inch nominal copper pipe. Remember that one-half inch of the pipe must be exposed on each end of the riser so that it will go into its fitting. Metal shears are excellent for cutting the copper sheeting and may also be used for any trimming that may be needed later.

After all the fins are cut, a jig must be made to bend them around the pipes. The key to a good bond is tight metal to metal contact with little solder. Solder is a poor thermal conductor compared to copper, so the less you can use, the better efficiency you can obtain. See figure 4G–5.

To make the jig, rout out a groove lengthwise down a 2 × 6 at least six inches longer than the fins. The groove should be five-eighths inches wide and three eighths inches deep. In another 2 × 6 of the same length, rout out a similar groove but not as deep. This channel should be five-eighths inches wide and only one-quarter inch deep. Glue a wooden dowel of one half inch diameter into the quarter inch groove of the 2 × 6. See figure 4G–6.

By placing a cut fin lengthwise down the length of the jig and pressing, a good groove in the fin can be made. Begin pushing the jig together, slowly at first, and then

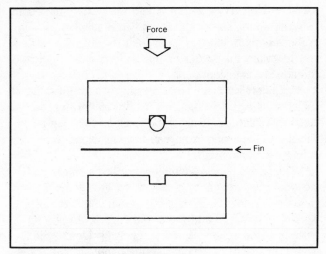

Figure 4G-6 The jig for bending the fins

beat it hard with a wooden mallet or jump on it. The more groove there is, the better the thermal contact will be. Check the fit of each fin on a piece of tubing. The best fins will fit quite snugly when pushed on the tube.

The next step is to solder the fins onto the risers and again tight contact between the tubing and the fins is crucial. Another simple jig helps. Clamp a pair of 2 × 4 or similar wood to a table or nail them to a piece of plywood so their lengths are three inches apart. If possible, cover the wood with asbestos to help prevent the wood from burning up.

It is very important to clean each riser and fin groove carefully and completely with steel wool and solvent before soldering. Make sure to wipe off all the solvent and keep fingers off the area to be soldered. Coat the riser and fin groove with flux and put the two pieces together so that enough room is left on the end of the riser for the fitting. Center the pieces over the jig groove and have someone or two push down hard on the tube with wooden blocks to protect their hands from the heat of the torch. See figure 4G–7. It is essential that the people push hard and steady until the fin is completely soldered to the tube.

To solder, start at one end of the fin and heat the top of the tube only with a small propane torch about an inch

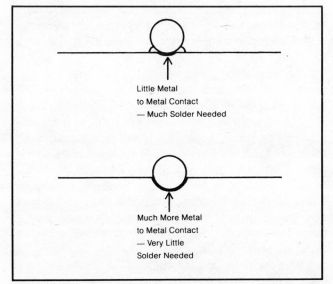

Figure 4G-5 Better thermal contact can be obtained by pressing the tubes into the fins.

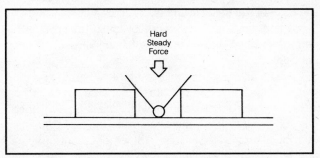

Figure 4G-7 Another jig for soldering the tubes to the fins.

away, moving the torch back and forth along its length about three inches. Solder is applied only when the flux in the area is boiling. A good joint should only require you to touch the solder to the gap on each side. You shouldn't have to continually run the solder down the gap. It should flow by itself. The heat required for this kind of soldering is very low (you don't want to burn up all the flux), so adjust the flame of the torch so the blue part is about one inch long. You may have to experiment with different adjustments.

The whole fin is soldered on in this manner by working your way down in about three inch lengths. You should see solder fill the gap by itself. If you find that you have to fill the gap and the solder isn't flowing by itself, use a little more heat. When you finish soldering the fin, keep pressure on it for at least one minute so the solder can cool down. There is the possibility that the joint may crack if it is moved too soon.

It is a good idea to check the ends of each fin to see how good a solder job was done. Each joint end should have a small amount of solder extending all the way around the connection. Butt up the next fin when you finish and continue until all the fins are soldered on their risers.

Remember: it is most important to have tubes and fin grooves that are shiny clean for a good solder joint. Also, use lots of flux and push the pieces together with a constant and hard force.

When all the fins are soldered on, bend the fins perpendicular to the pipe and clean all the pipe ends and fitting interiors with steel wool. Flux every piece and assemble the array with the exposed pipe facing towards the glass. It is better to have the tube exposed to the sun's rays. You might want to solder the array together on the floor. Put some 2 × 4s under the array to prop it off the ground or table and push the pipes hard into the fittings. Check by measuring and square the array. It's easy to cut fins off the sides but nearly impossible to adjust the length. It must fit in the box!

To solder, start at a tee in one end and heat the back of the fitting only. When the flux in all the joints bubbles, touch the solder to each joint until it flows all the way around the pipe. Again, let the solder flow. When you can see it go all the way around by itself, you know it will be a good connection. Don't move or touch the array until you are finished and let it cool a few minutes when you are done.

After soldering, you must test for leaks and to do this you may have to come up with your own ideas for hardware. We use rubber stoppers with a glass tube inserted through them to hook the array up to the faucet, joined by rubber surgical tubing. Cap the other end of the pipe and hold or wire the stoppers in place. With water line pressure (usually between 80-130 lbs/sq. inch) you can see if any joints leak by the drops of water that will come off.

Mark any leaky joints and disconnect and drain the array. Reheat the marked joints, again at the back of the tee. It is important to fix all three joints at each marked tee because reheating may open one up. Apply solder to the joints. Because the water may not all drain from the array, it may take a while to get the tees hot enough to solder. If so, increase the heat of the flame and heat a larger area all around the tee. When all joints are done, pressure test again. The array must hold water at line pressure.

The final step in the assembly of the array is to paint it black but first it must be cleaned and all the old flux removed. Steel wool the whole collector surface that will face the glass, fin and tube, until it shines. Then apply a solution of baking soda and water, especially scrubbing the joint areas with a brush. Hose off the array and let it dry.

Paint the upper surface of the array with a good quality flat black paint that is heat resistant to at least between two hundred and four hundred degrees fahrenheit. The lower surface of the array facing the insulation need not be painted. A couple of thin coats is far better than one thick one.

D. Putting It All Together

After the paint has dried completely, carefully place it on the collector box. It won't fit in because of the two extruding tubes that connect it with the outside of the box. Support the array on the box top with 2 × 4s and center it to its position in the box. Mark the centers of the extruding pipes on the outside of the box frame and remove the array. Measure down into the box from the top to the collector supports where the collector will rest and mark these on the outside of the box frame. Drill a seven-eighths inch hole so the bottom of the hole is aligned with the support mark and centered to the array tube. See bottom of figure 4G-2.

Carefully try to fit the array through the holes and into the box. It may not go. If it does not, saw a slot from the top of the box down to one of the holes and save the piece. Place the array into the box and secure it down onto the supports at the head and foot of the collector box with wire screwed down around the half inch side of each tee. An alternative is to nail in U–shaped staples over the same areas. Be careful not to scratch the paint or hit the plates or tubing.

With the piece you cut out, make a small insert that takes up the gap of the saw blade and insert it into the gap along with the old piece. Use lots of water proof glue and, when it dries, reform the top edge of the box for the glazing. Seal the inside crack edges and then seal around both pipe extrusions from the inside and outside.

The next step is critical and requires a few good hot days with lots of sunshine. The collector must be baked in the sun to dry out any moisture in the box and to cure the paint. If the moisture is not removed from the box, condensation will occur on the glass and efficiency will suffer. Also, paint releases fumes when it dries and they may collect on the glass too.

Take the collector outside in a space where it can get sun all day. Lay the glass into its place and let it sit until the afternoon. Remove the glass, clean off any condensation and take the collector back inside for the night. Do the same the following day but in the afternoon, remove and clean the glass with solvent and window cleaner. Staying in the sun, spread caulk around the edging of the box and place the glass onto its space. Caulk around the edges of the glass as well as over it and screw down three-eighths inch by one inch edging wood over the glass and box.

Put the collector on sawhorses or prop it up somewhere and paint all exposed wood areas with a good quality marine varnish. At least two coats are necessary but three or four would be best.

Bibliography

American Society of Heating, Refrigerating, and Air Conditioning Engineers. 1972. *Handbook of Fundamentals.* New York: ASHRAE.

―――― 1977. *ASHRAE Handbook and Product Directory, 1977 Fundamentals.* New York: ASHRAE.

Anderson, B. 1976. *The Solar Home Book.* Harrisville, N.H.: Cheshire Books.

Balcomb, J. D. and McFarland, R. D. 1978. "A Simple Empirical Method for Estimating the Performance of a Passive Solar Heated Building of the Thermal Storage Wall Type." *Proceedings of the Second National Passive Solar Conference,* Philadelphia. March 1978.

Beckman, W. A., Klein, S. A., and Duffie, J. A. 1977. *Solar Heating Design by the f-Chart Method.* New York: John Wiley & Sons.

Berdahl, P. 1978. *California Solar Data Manual.* Sacramento, California: California Energy Commission.

Bliss, R. W. Jr. 1959. "The Derivation of Several 'Plate Efficiency Factors' Useful in the Design of Flat Plate Solar Heat Collectors." *Solar Energy,* Vol. 3, No. 4, 1959. pp. 55–64.

Campbell, S. 1980. *The Underground House Book.* Charlotte, Vermont: Garden Way Publishing.

Colorado State University. 1977. *Solar Heating and Cooling of Residential Buildings, Design of Systems.* Washington, D.C.: U.S. Department of Commerce.

Copper Development Association. 1979. *Solar Energy Systems.* 405 Lexington Avenue, New York 10017: Copper Development Association.

―――― 1973. *Copper Tube Handbook.* New York: Copper Development Association.

deWinter, F. 1973. *How to Design and Build a Solar Swimming Pool Heater.* New York: Copper Development Association.

Dallaire, G. 1980. "Zero-Energy House: Bold, Low-Cost Breakthrough that may Revolutionize Housing." *Civil Engineering-ASCE,* May 1980.

Duffie, J. A. and Beckman, W. A. 1980. *Solar Engineering of Thermal Processes.* New York: John Wiley & Sons.

Farallones Institute. 1979. *The Integral Urban House.* San Francisco: Sierra Club Books.

Fisher, R. and Yanda, B. 1976. *The Food and Heat Producing Solar Greenhouse.* Santa Fe, New Mexico: John Muir Publications.

Franklin Research Center. 1979. *Installation Guidelines for Solar DHW Systems.* Washington, D.C.: U.S. Department of Housing and Urban Development.

Kreith, F. and Kreider, J. F. 1978. *Principles of Solar Engineering.* New York: McGraw Hill.

Labs, K. 1979. "Underground Building Climate." *Solar Energy.* October 1979.

Liu, B. Y. H. and Jordan, R. C. 1963. "A Rational Procedure for Predicting the Long-Term Performance of Flat-Plate Solar-Energy Collectors." *Solar Energy.* Vol. 7, No. 2, pp 71–74, 1963.

Lunde, P. J. 1980. *Solar Thermal Engineering.* New York: John Wiley & Sons.

Mazria, E. 1979. *The Passive Solar Energy Book.* Emmaus, Pennsylvania: Rodale Press.

McCullagh, J. C., ed. 1978. *The Solar Greenhouse Book.* Emmaus, Pennsylvania: Rodale Press.

Meinel, A. B. and Meinel, M. P. 1976. *Applied Solar Energy, An Introduction.* Reading, Massachusetts: Addison-Wesley Publishing.

National Oceanic and Atmospheric Administration. 1968. *Climatic Atlas of the United States.* Washington, D.C.: U.S. Department of Commerce.

Nevins, R. G. 1965. *Criteria for Thermal Comfort.* Manhattan, Kansas: Institute for Environmental Research, Kansas State University.

Office of Appropriate Technology. 1980. *Solar Gain: Winners of the Passive Solar Design Competition.* Sacramento: California Energy Commission.

Olivieri, J. B. 1970. *How To Design Heating-Cooling Comfort Systems.* Birmingham, Michigan: Business News Publishing.

Root, D. E. Jr., 1959. "A Simplified Approach to Swimming Pool Heating." *Solar Energy,* Vol. 3, No. 1, pp 60–63, 1959.

Sandia Laboratory. 1979. *Passive Solar Buildings.* SAND 79-0824. Albuquerque, New Mexico: Los Alamos Scientific Laboratory.

Shurcliff, W. A. 1980. *Superinsulated Houses and Double-Envelope Houses.* 19 Appleton Street, Cambridge, Massachusetts 02138.

―――― 1980. *Thermal Shutters and Shades.* Andover, Massachusetts: Brick House Publishing.

Sunset Books. 1978. *Sunset Homeowner's Guide to Solar Heating.* Menlo Park: Lane Publishing Company.

Underground Space Center, University of Minnesota. 1978. *Earth Sheltered Housing Design.* New York: Van Nostrand Reinhold.

Wilson, A. 1979. *Thermal Storage Wall Design Manual.* P.O. Box 2004, Santa Fe, New Mexico 87501 ($4): New Mexico Solar Energy Association.

Wray, W. O., Balcomb, J. D., and McFarland, R. D. 1979. "A Semi-Empirical Method for Estimating the Performance of Direct Gain Passive Solar Heated Buildings." *Proceedings of the Third Annual Passive Solar Conference,* San Jose, California, January 1979.

Wright, D. 1978. *Natural Solar Architecture: A Passive Primer.* New York: Van Nostrand Reinhold.

WASTE

Wastes as resources

The methane digester:
why, how it works, its products
and what to do with them

Grey water systems

The Clivus Multrum: what and how

Outhouses and septic tanks

Oxidation ponds: why, when, and how

Deciding which method is best for you

WASTE-HANDLING SYSTEMS

Introduction

Our sewage and solid waste problems are a good reminder that it's usually easier in the long run to avoid problems than to correct them. Yet "out of sight, out of mind" simply does not work when we are talking about the day-to-day production of wastes. In controlled municipal settings, the disposal problem is an ever-growing headache, and with ever increasing energy costs it is becoming a very expensive problem. In more rural environments, inadequate or inappropriate waste-handling techniques often have led to poisoned water and grave sicknesses. In either place, we cannot escape our wastes.

We are talking, as you may gather, about more than litter and junk, which are avoidable through conservative use and recycling. We are talking about animal manures, food scraps, harvest dross, about the water that is lost each time we flush the toilet and the human excreta that go with it. No matter how conscientiously conservative we are, there still will be wastewater and solid wastes to dispose of. To say the least, it is a historical problem.

No amount of adjustment can make an inappropriate system work well, particularly when a large number of options have been developed. There are many ways of handling the disposal of human and animal wastes. What we would like to show you is how to deal with your wastes in a manner which can allow you to gain some positive benefit from them—to turn your wastes into resources. We have taken the approach here of providing basic information in a context and format which will allow you to make responsible, intelligent choices for yourself. We have gathered together information and data in a manner

designed to allow computations, for example, on any possible combination of circumstances in the case of a methane digester. We consider the type of raw material available to the digester, appropriate nutrient balance, and expected gas production. In addition to the methane digester, such waste-handling techniques as greywater systems, waterless toilets (Clivus Multrum), outhouses, septic tanks, and oxidation ponds are considered. Composting, another excellent technique, is dealt with in Chapter 7.

Obviously, you cannot develop your own waste-handling facilities without paying a price. The cost is a combination of dollars and physical and mental effort, and there are certainly going to be trade-offs between them. You may not have had any previous experience with methane digesters, pumps, and oxidation ponds, and it may not be among the easiest of your experiences—but you can do it! Once you master the concepts, the calculations are simple and relatively straightforward.

Methane Digesters

Methane digestion has been used by sanitary engineers in the treatment of domestic sewage sludge and organic wastes for decades, but as a process found in nature, it is far older than man. Recently, its usefulness for waste reduction has received new attention among farmers here and abroad. Human excreta, animal manures, garbage, and even refuse—all previously thought of as undesir-

249

able, troublesome "wastes" of raw materials—can be digested under suitable conditions, resulting in the production of valuable bio-gas and fertilizer. So magic survives in the twentieth century: complete the cycle, close the loop, and "wastes" are transformed into new raw materials.

Why a Digester?

What is a methane digester anyway? A methane digester is nothing more than a container which holds our organic wastes in a manner which allows natural bacterial degradation of the organic matter to occur in the absence of oxygen. By causing this anaerobic (oxygen-free) process to occur in a container, we can control the conditions inside and outside the container to promote the efficiency of the process and capture the bio-gas product. The fact is that the methane digestion process will occur quite naturally without our interference—all we do is try to improve the process somewhat. What else can a digester do for us besides provide some bio-gas? First, it rids us of our organic wastes—horse manure, human excreta, vegetable wastes, and so forth; and second, it converts these wastes into resources. These resources are (in addition to the bio-gas) sludge and effluent, both excellent fertilizing materials.

But bio-gas and sludge are only resources if you both need and are in a position to utilize them. What this means is that digesters basically are only suitable for a rural or semi-rural setting. If this is your situation and you are interested in building a digester, you will want to consider the costs and the potential returns before embarking on a digester trip.

Bio-gas consists of methane mixed with carbon dioxide, approximately two parts methane to one part carbon dioxide by volume, and with very small additional amounts of oxygen, nitrogen, hydrogen, carbon monoxide, and hydrogen sulfide. Any appliance that runs on natural gas, which is primarily methane, runs well on bio-gas pressurized in the proper range [2 to 8 inches of water or 0.07 to 0.3 pounds per square inch (psi)], including gas stoves, refrigerators, hot-water heaters, lamps, incubators, and space heaters. Butane and propane appliances also have been run on bio-gas, and it can be used to operate steam and internal-combustion engines, both of which can operate electrical generators. In *Mother Earth News,* Keith Gilbert reports: "There are currently available from Japan several models of steam engines which can be used for any number of things on the farm or in a small factory. They are quite inexpensive (the starting cost is about $200 for a small one), and will operate a wide variety of equipment including such things as: electric generators, hammer mills, shredders, pumps, power saws for producing lumber, compressors, irrigation pumps, combines for threshing grain and beans, and other power machinery. One Japanese steam plant I observed was being used to operate a small saw mill and it did an effective job. It was a wood burner and cost only $100. Contact the Japanese Trade Legation for further information."

A small-scale digester will produce relatively small amounts of energy. We must maintain a perspective when we plan how to make use of the methane produced. As a point of reference, per capita consumption of natural gas in the United States is about 350 cubic feet per day. This represents about 30 percent of the total consumption of energy in this country for all purposes. It is clearly unreasonable, at normal consumption levels, to expect to drive a car or to take care of space heating with the output of a small digester, as you can see from the rates at which various appliances use methane (Table 5.1).

If we want to use a methane digester to provide all or some of our gas-related energy needs, we need to know what our present consumption is or is likely to be in the near future. An average family of five, using natural gas for cooking, heating water, drying clothes, and space heating, will consume on the order of 8000 to 10,000 cubic feet per month during the winter in California (mild winters). If space and water heating are handled by solar energy or by a wood-burning stove, and clothes are dried

Table 5.1 Rates of Use of Methane[a]

Use	Rate (ft^3)
Lighting, Methane	2.5 per mantle per hour
Cooking, Methane	8–16 per hour per 2- to 4-inch burner
	12–15 per person per day
Incubator, Methane	0.5–0.7 per hour per cubic foot of incubator
Gas Refrigerator, Methane	1.2 per hour per cubic foot of refrigerator
Gasoline Engine (25 percent efficiency)	
Methane	11 per brake horsepower per hour
Bio-Gas	16 per brake horsepower per hour
As Gasoline Alternative	
Methane	135–160 per gallon
Bio-Gas	180–250 per gallon
As Diesel Oil Alternative	
Methane	150–188 per gallon
Bio-Gas	200–278 per gallon

Notes: a. Adapted from *Methane Digester for Fuel Gas and Fertilizer,* by Merrill and Fry.

in the sun, the winter monthly consumption can be cut to about 2000 to 4000 cubic feet, easily within the range of a digester of moderate size.

If you presently use natural gas, you can estimate your requirements by looking at your utility bills for the last year (if you can't locate your bills, the utility company will usually provide you with copies). Then you can estimate cubic feet of natural gas used per month over an annual cycle, as well as the maximum monthly use (usually during winter). Once you have this estimate and when you are able to calculate the quantity of methane available from your waste materials, you can evaluate the level of self-sufficiency you can achieve. Even if you are able only to satisfy half of your estimated needs, you may still consider it worth your while to build a digester as a waste-handling unit and energy supplement.

Natural gas in the United States now costs on the order of 3 to 5 cents per 10 cubic feet (in 1980). If we compare raw gas from a methane digester to natural gas, we find that natural gas has about 1000 Btu/ft^3 while bio-gas has about 600 Btu/ft^3; thus, it takes roughly one-third more bio-gas to give the same heat value as natural gas. If we consider a small digester producing on the order of 50 cubic feet of bio-gas per day (two-thirds methane), we save about $33 to $55 per year at current prices. It becomes obvious that small-scale digesters are not built primarily for savings on gas alone. If we consider other aspects of digesters—the value of the sludge and supernatant as fertilizer—our benefits are somewhat more apparent. If you are located in a remote area, the value of the gas as well as the fertilizer would be significantly increased because of transportation costs or the absence of a steady gas supply.

In quantity, commercial dried-sludge fertilizer costs close to $2 per 100 pounds. This is equivalent to about 100 gallons of wet sludge effluent from a digester, since a gallon weighs about 10 pounds and the effluent is almost 10 percent solids. Besides this modest return, you then have the added comfort of knowing that sludge from methane digesters operating on concentrated slurries is known to have a superior fertilizer value compared to sludges from municipal sewage-treatment plants (which operate on a very dilute input). Another factor you may consider is that, for many locations, the cost and labor involved in installing a septic tank and leaching field are avoided.

It is very difficult to estimate the cost of building a digester, as expenses vary with the ingenuity of the builder, the good fortune of finding used or surplus equipment, and the amount of labor hired out. Ram Bux Singh suggests a design for a digester capable of producing 100 cubic feet of gas per day, and calculates that it would cost $400 to build, as the construction is largely of concrete and masonry (in 1971). William Olkowski built a 300-gallon digester for $150, out of surplus tanks, valves, and hoses. John Fry was able to produce about 8000 cubic

feet of methane per day with a digester initially costing $10,000. With gas at a value of 10 cents per 100 cubic feet, the value of Fry's daily gas production is about $8, giving an annual value of $2920. At this rate, he was able to pay for the cost of his digester within three years, giving him "free" gas from then on.

Even though our main concern in this book is not economics, the costs and returns of each potential energy source cannot be ignored and, in fact, must be weighed very carefully before you embark on a given project. If you are thinking seriously about designing a methane digester for a small-scale application, you must ask yourself one basic question: is a small-scale digester practical? Will the methane digester provide you with enough gas and fertilizer to make it worth your time and money to build and maintain it? The answer to this question depends upon your available wastes and money and your willingness to alter your lifestyle to make the time to maintain the digester properly. The larger the scale of its operation, the more practical and feasible a methane digester becomes. Thus, what might not be practical for a single family may well be practical for a large farm or a small group of families. The ideal, of course, is an integrated energy-resource system. Figure 5.1 depicts such a system, where the methane digester constitutes a focal point for the other energy sources as a waste-to-resource converter.

The present state-of-the-art in methane digesters for small-scale operations is limited to homebuilt and owner-operated units. There are no commercially available units at the present time—you will have to design and build your own methane digester if you want one. Your decision to build or not build a digester rests with an evaluation of your basic needs—waste-disposal and energy needs, fertilizer requirements, and any other appropriate consid-

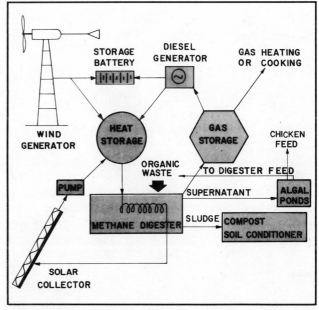

Figure 5.1 An integrated energy and resource system utilizing a digester.

erations related to your particular situation. We can't give you a ready-made guide for evaluating your needs and requirements—you must do that. What we can say, however, is that if you do not own one or two horses or cows, or several hundred chickens, a methane digester is not going to be worth your investment. Beyond this lower limit, you must do some careful estimating. The design considerations in this chapter should help you out and there are several excellent publications on the construction and operation of small digesters for home or farm use. One of the most recent, *Methane Digesters for Fuel Gas and Fertilizer,* was produced in 1973 by the members of the New Alchemy Institute (NAI). The NAI work is based in part on an earlier, extremely helpful publication, *Bio-Gas Plant* (1971), produced under the direction of the Indian investigator Ram Bux Singh. A third very practical resource is *Practical Building of Methane Power Plants,* by L. John Fry. All three publications are strongly recommended source material for anyone interested in evaluating, building, and operating a digester.

The Digestion Process

Methane digestion is an *anaerobic* process; it occurs in the absence of oxygen. In anaerobic digestion, organic waste is mixed with large populations of microorganisms under conditions where air is excluded. Under these conditions, bacteria grow which are capable of converting the organic waste to carbon dioxide (CO_2) and methane gas (CH_4). The anaerobic conversion to methane gas yields relatively little energy to the microorganisms themselves. Thus, their rate of growth is slow and only a small portion of the degradable waste is converted to new microorganisms; most is converted to methane gas (for animal manures, about 50 percent is converted to methane). Since this gas is insoluble, it escapes from the digester fluid and can then be collected and burned to carbon dioxide and water for heat. It turns out that as much as 80 to 90 percent of the degradable organic portion of a waste can be stabilized in this manner, even in highly loaded systems.

Anaerobic treatment of complex organic materials is normally considered to be a two-stage process, as indicated in Figure 5.2. In the first stage, there is no methane production. Instead the complex organics are changed in form by a group of bacteria commonly called the "acid formers." Such complex materials as fats, proteins, and carbohydrates are biologically converted to more simple organic materials—for the most part, organic fatty acids. Acid-forming bacteria bring about these initial transformations to obtain small amounts of energy for growth and reproduction. This first phase is required to transform the organic matter to a form suitable for the second stage of the process.

It is in the second stage of anaerobic digestion that methane is produced. During this phase, the organic acids

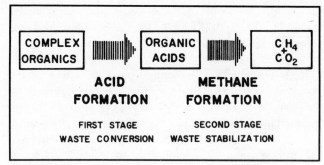

Figure 5.2 The two stages of anaerobic methane digestion.

are converted by a special group of bacteria called the "methane formers" into gaseous carbon dioxide and methane. The methane-forming bacteria are strictly anaerobic and even small amounts of oxygen are harmful to them. There are several different types of these bacteria, and each type is characterized by its ability to convert a relatively limited number of organic compounds into methane. Consequently, for complete digestion of the complex organic materials, several different types are needed. The most important variety, which makes its living on acetic and propionic acids, grows quite slowly and hence must be retained in the digester for four days or longer; its slow rate of growth (and low rate of acid utilization) normally represents one of the limiting steps around which the anaerobic process must be designed.

The methane-forming bacteria have proven to be very difficult to isolate and study, and relatively little is known of their basic biochemistry. The conversion of organic matter into methane no doubt proceeds through a long sequence of complex biochemical steps. These complexities, however, need not concern us here; we can represent the overall process schematically (Figure 5.3) and derive the level of understanding necessary for our purposes. The two major volatile acids formed during the anaerobic treatment, as we implied a moment ago, are acetic acid and propionic acid. The importance of these two acids is indicated in Figure 5.4, which shows the pathways by which mixed complex organic materials are converted to methane gas.

Digester Design Process

There are two basic designs for the anaerobic process. One is the "conventional" process most widely used for the digestion of such concentrated wastes as animal manures and primary and secondary sludges at municipal treatment plants. The other process is one designed to handle more dilute wastes and has been termed the "anaerobic contact" process. These two process designs are depicted schematically in Figure 5.5. We will concentrate our discussion on the conventional process since most of our waste materials will come in concentrated form.

The conventional anaerobic treatment setup consists

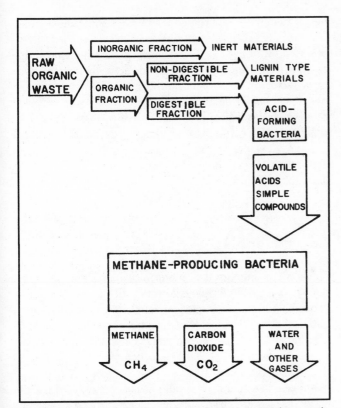

Figure 5.3 The biological breakdown of organic material in a methane digester.

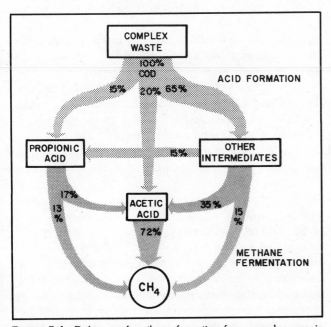

Figure 5.4 Pathways of methane formation from complex organic wastes.

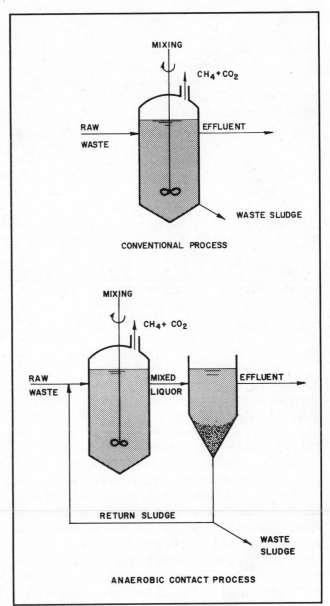

Figure 5.5 The two basic methane digester designs.

of a digestion tank containing waste and the bacteria responsible for the anaerobic process. Raw waste is introduced either periodically or continuously and is preferably mixed with the digester contents. The treated waste and microorganisms are usually removed together as treated sludge. Sometimes this mixture is introduced into a second tank where the suspended material is allowed to settle and concentrate before the sludge is removed.

There are many variations on a theme possible for methane digesters. A digester can be fed either on a batch basis (the simplest) or on a continuous basis, depending upon the trade-offs between initial cost, sophistication of design, and the cost of maintenance and operation. Any decision as to feed type also will depend on the projected scale of the operation. Another factor that you will need to consider is heat for the digester (to optimize the rate of methane production) and insulation of the digester tank (to reduce heat loss). These are cost considerations and will require you to do some estimating on your own spe-

253

cific design details once you have arrived at a tank size for your needs. A design decision which you will need to make early in the design process is whether you want a single-stage or a multiple-stage digestion system. This is really a question of how many tanks you want in series and is related to the residence time of the materials in the digestion system—details we will cover. Mixing of the digester contents is desirable since this agitation helps to increase the rate of methane production. The decision to mix mechanically or to allow natural mixing (much slower) depends again on a cost/benefit analysis which you must perfom for yourself. A final consideration has to do with the manner in which you add your feed and remove your supernatant effluent (liquid by-product). There are basically only two possibilities: digesters with fixed covers and ones with floating covers.

Like any other design process, there are many interrelated factors involved in the design of a methane digester. Let us assume for purposes of discussion that we want to evaluate the design of a methane digester for a small five-acre farm—say, several cows, horses, and goats, and maybe fifty chickens. What kind of information must we have available before we can sit down and make our calculations? The first and most obvious consideration is the type and quantity of organic waste which can be used as feed for the digester. There will be a number of wastes—cow manure, chicken droppings, goat turds, and maybe the green trimmings from the vegetable garden (in late summer, early fall)—and we will need to know something about the composition of the various waste materials to insure that our friendly bacteria have a well-balanced diet (with special attention paid to nutrients such as nitrogen). Knowing the quantity and quality (composition) of the waste materials available as feed for the digester, we can calculate the mixture and size of our actual input into the digester (slurry feed). Then we can estimate the required size of the digester tank for specified conditions of temperature and residence time of waste in the tank—the average time that the waste is in the digester before leaving as sludge or supernatant liquid.

Once we know the quantity and quality of our organic wastes and the temperature and residence time of wastes in the digester tank, we will be in a position to estimate the amount of gas which will be produced—thus allowing us to pick a size for the gas collection tank. Your gas tank should be of sufficient size (several days' use) to insure that you will have gas available for occasional high-consumption use.

Notice that our attitude toward the methane digester is slightly different from the design procedures involved with deriving power from wind, water, or sun. We do not start out with design considerations to develop a methane digester to cover *all* your power needs; instead, we concentrate on your available resources in the way of waste products and investigate how much benefit you can derive from them. This is a reasonable attitude not only because

here we are concerned with waste-handling, but also because of the economics involved. As we will see later, two cows and a horse can provide around 10 percent of an average individual's methane needs; if we then multiplied by a factor of 10 to accommodate 100 percent of our needs, we have a small ranch! So, all in all, we attempt to provide you with data to analyze what you have available right now; this same data, of course, *can* be used to calculate a 100 percent self-sufficient household or small community, if you have the requisite time, money, and waste already at hand.

Raw Materials

As we mentioned earlier, anaerobic organisms—bacteria that grow in the complete absence of oxygen—are responsible for converting the various organic raw materials into useful methane gas (CH_4), with carbon dioxide (CO_2) and water (H_2O) as by-products. Chemical analyses of anaerobic bacteria show the presence of carbon, oxygen, hydrogen, nitrogen, phosphorus, potassium, sodium, magnesium, calcium, and sulfur. This formidable list of elements, along with a number of organic and inorganic trace materials usually present in most raw materials used in methane fermentation, is essential for the growth of anaerobic bacteria; the hard-working bacteria must have a well-balanced diet if you expect them to perform at their best. Here, a well-balanced diet means adequate quantities of such nutrients as nitrogen and phosphorus. Nitrogen is generally the most important because it is the nutrient most likely to limit bacterial growth and, therefore, the rate and efficiency of methane production. A well-balanced diet for anaerobic bacteria also requires about thirty times more carbon than nitrogen, so you will need to know something about the carbon and nitrogen composition of the waste materials you are feeding your digester.

Phosphorus is third in importance only because smaller amounts are commonly needed. Although phosphorus and other elements that are found in even smaller percentages are necessary for growth, digesters are rarely inhibited by a lack of any of them because normal waste materials contain sufficient amounts to satisfy the bacteria's needs. (Interestingly enough, most detergents are "polluting" because they contain relatively large amounts of phosphorus compounds and other growth nutrients which stimulate growth of microorganisms and algae in receiving waters, leading to overproduction and stagnation.)

Assuming sufficient food is available in the proper form, other environmental conditions must also be satisfied for bacterial growth. The size and amount of the solid particles feeding the digester, the amount of water present in the feed slurry, how well the contents of the digester are mixed, the temperature range, and the acidity or alkalinity of the digesting mixture must all be favorable. Also, there are several kinds of waste that you must *not* use or your digester will cease to function properly. Let's start our discussion by looking into the composition of various organic wastes, and then we can talk about how to prepare a nourishing diet for your bacteria.

General Composition of Wastes

Table 5.2 is intended to give you a *general* idea of what to expect from animals as sources of energy. At least three variables (size of animal, degree of livestock confinement, and portion of manure collected) make this data nothing more than a series of rough approximations, but nevertheless it can be useful. Table 5.3 shows more specifically how the production of wet manure can vary (proportionally, in this case) with the weight of the animal.

Table 5.2 Production of Raw Materials[a]

Average Adult Animal	Urine Portion[b]	Fecal Portion[b]	Livestock Units
Bovine (1000 lbs)	20.0	52.0	
Bulls			130.0–150.0
Dairy cow			120.0
Under 2 years			50.0
Calves			10.0
Horses (850 lbs)	8.0	36.0	
Heavy			130.0–150.0
Medium			100.0
Pony			50.0– 70.0
Swine (160 lbs)	4.0	7.5	
Boar, sow			25.0
Pig, over 160 lbs			20.0
Pig, under 160 lbs			10.0
Weaners			2.0
Sheep (67 lbs)	1.5	3.0	
Ewes, rams			8.0
Lambs			4.0
Humans (150 lbs)			5.0
Urine	2.2		
Feces		0.5	
Poultry			
Geese, turkey (15 lbs)		0.5[c]	2.0
Ducks (6 lbs)		—	1.5
Layer chicken (3.5 lbs)		0.3[c]	1.0

Notes: a. Adapted from *Methane Digesters for Fuel Gas and Fertilizer* (Merrill and Fry) and "Anaerobic Digestion of Solid Wastes" (Klein).
 b. Pounds of wet manure per animal per day.
 c. Total production.

Table 5.3 Hog Manure Production vs. Weight[a]

Hog Weight (lbs)	Feces[b]	Urine[b]	Total Manure[b]
40–80	2.7	2.9	5.6
80–120	5.4	6.1	11.5
120–160	6.5	8.1	14.6
160–200	8.5	9.1	17.6

Notes: a. From "Properties of Farm Animal Excreta" (Taiganides and Hazen).
 b. Pounds per day.

Manure deposited in open fields is obviously hard to collect and transport to the digester. NAI figures that open grazing during the day with confinement at night will yield about one-half of the total output as collectable raw material.

The *portion* of manure collected is important because urination is an animal's way of disposing of excess nitrogen and the nitrogen content of the raw material is a primary design consideration. Fecal material collected from cattle, horses, swine, and sheep in confinement may contain some or all of the urine output. You must make some judgment as to about how much urine is contained in the collected raw material. Human wastes are easily combined or separated, while poultry waste is produced in one combined load.

It is difficult to estimate the output of a garbage grinder in the kitchen. When sanitary engineers design treatment facilities for a city in which most people use garbage disposals, they increase the projected per capita output of sewage solids by 60 percent. If you have a garbage grinder, it might be practical to increase your daily output by about one-half (instead of 0.6) of the total sewage output of the household.

NAI uses a useful term called the *Livestock Unit* as a means of comparison of outputs between different kinds of animals (see Table 5.2). Taking the smallest tabulated output (that of a standard 3.5-pound layer chicken) as the unit of comparison, all other outputs are calculated as multiples of the chicken standard. Under this system, a common dairy cow is seen to be as valuable as 120 chickens from the standpoint of manure production. The Livestock Unit system is based on output of *digestible solids*, a term we must now define.

Wet manure or raw material is composed of both water and solids. We define the solid portion (*total solids*) as the "dry weight" of the raw material, or the portion which would remain if the wet material were dried at a temperature of 212°F until no more weight was lost by drying (sun-dried manure still contains up to 30 percent water). It turns out that, of the total solids (TS), the fraction which would be digested by bacteria in a normal digester is proportional to the portion which would be *burned off* if it (total solids) were again heated, this time to about 1100°F, and kept at that temperature until once again there was no more weight loss. This digestible portion is called *volatile solids* (or VS). The remaining portion (after the water is evaporated and the volatile solids are burned off) is called the *fixed solids*. Figure 5.6 demonstrates these relationships for horse manure.

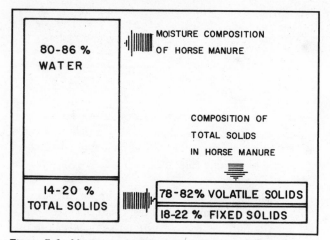

Figure 5.6 Moisture and solids content of horse manure.

Table 5.4 gives approximate values for the digestible portions of a variety of raw materials. These figures must be used realizing that the values have been arrived at under specific experimental conditions which may differ from those present in any other case.

The first part of the table (green garbage, kraft paper, newspaper, garden debris, white fir, average refuse, chicken manure, and steer-manure fertilizer) is drawn from an article by S. A. Klein (see Bibliography). Notice that his values for percent moisture are *extremely* low (green garbage has only 1 percent moisture). Except for the steer-manure fertilizer, all of his raw materials were freeze-dried before examination. His percentages of volatile solids are

usable directly because volatile solids are taken as a percentage of dry *total solids,* not wet raw material. However, unless you can duplicate Klein's *freeze-dried* initial conditions (unlikely), his values for total solids should not be applied directly to your wet raw material.

There is a further complication with calculation of total solids of raw materials. If we assume that the raw manure is collected from animal enclosures, it is reasonable to assume that fresh fecal material will contain some urine as liquid. This urine content will raise the percentage of moisture in the manure above the "normal" level if the urine does not evaporate before the manure is used in the digester. A bit later we will detail the chemical significance of this addition of urine. The values in the rest of Table 5.4 are calculated with the assumption that the manure is used as a raw material for the digester *before* the urine component has evaporated significantly. If a rough separation of fecal material and urine is assumed, 20 percent total solids can be used as a good approximation for the fecal material for steers (fresh), horses, swine, and sheep. Separate values are given for human urine and fecal material because separation is more practical, and chicken manure will always contain the animal's urine excreta because, as we mentioned, the two components are deposited in the same load.

If you are an adventuresome experimenter, you can perform your own laboratory analysis for total solids by drying a known weight of wet manure in a kitchen oven at 212°F and measuring the weight lost (evaporated water). This weight loss is divided by the original wet weight and multiplied by 100 to give the percentage of moisture content in the original wet manure:

E. 5.1   *% moisture + % total solids = 100%*

Table 5.4 Composition of Raw Materials[a]

Material	%Moisture	%Total Solids (TS)	Volatile Solids (% of TS)	%C	%N	C/N Ratio
Green garbage	1.0	99.0	77.8	54.7	3.04	18
Kraft paper	6.0	94.0	99.6	40.6	0	∞
Newspaper	7.0	93.0	97.1	40.6	0.05	813
Garden debris	24.8	75.2	87.0	–	–	–
White fir	9.3	90.7	99.5	46.0	0.06	767
Average refuse	7.3	92.7	63.6	33.4	0.74	45
Chicken manure	9.8	90.2	56.2	23.4	3.2	7
Steer manure (prepared fertilizer)	45.7	54.3	68.5	34.1	1.35	25
Steer manure (fresh)[b]	86.0	14.0	80.0	30.8	1.7	18
Horse manure[b]	84.0	16.0	80.0	57.5	2.3	25
Swine manure[b]	87.0	13.0	85.0	–	3.8	–
Sheep manure[b]	89.0	11.0	80.0	–	3.8	–
Human urine	94.0	6.0	75.0	14.4	18.0	0.8
Human feces	73.0	27.0	92.0	36.0–60.0	6.0	6–10
Chicken manure (fresh)	65.0	35.0	65.0	–	–	–

Notes: a. From "Anaerobic Digestion of Solid Wastes" (Klein) and *Methane Digesters for Fuel Gas and Fertilizer* (Merrill and Fry).
b. Includes urine.

Figure 5.6 demonstrates this point.

We also should note that Klein's value for percentage of volatile solids for steer fertilizer is lower than the value for fresh steer manure (from NAI) because he is using manure which has been partially digested before examination, during the composting/preparation process involved in fertilizer production. His chicken manure (% total solids) is also high in comparison to the fresh manure value (NAI) because his extremely dry starting material will naturally have a higher content of total solids.

Tables 5.5 and 5.6 can be used to get a rough idea of the potential production of bio-gases (60 percent methane, 40 percent carbon dioxide) from typical raw materials if the volatile-solids content of the raw material is known. Equations presented in a later section can be used to determine the production of methane from other materials, if you know or can determine their volatile-solids content.

Example: Let's calculate the cubic feet of methane per pound of raw chicken manure we can reasonably expect on the basis of information given in Table 5.5.

Solution: First we need information on percent TS and percent VS for fresh chicken manure given in Table 5.4. The cubic feet of methane per pound of fresh chicken manure is given by

E. 5.2
$$\frac{cubic\ feet\ of\ methane}{pound\ of\ raw\ material} = 1 \times \%TS \times \%VS$$
$$\times \frac{ft^3 gas}{lb} \times \frac{\%\ methane}{gas}$$
$$= 1 \times 0.35 \times 0.65$$
$$\times \frac{5\ ft^3}{lb} \times 0.598$$
$$= 0.68\ ft^3/lb$$

This gives us a rough estimate of the quantity of gas we can expect from a pound of fresh chicken manure, but

Table 5.5   Gas Production as a Function of Volatile Solids[a]

Material	Proportion (%)	Cubic Feet of Gas [b]	Methane Content of Gas
Chicken manure	100	5.0	59.8
Chicken manure	31	7.8	60.0
& paper pulp	69		
Chicken manure	50	4.1	66.1
& newspaper	50		
Chicken manure	50	5.9	68.1
& grass clippings	50		
Steer manure	100	1.4	65.2
Steer manure	50	4.3	51.1
& grass clippings	50		
Steer manure	50	3.4	61.9
& chicken manure	50		
Steer manure	50	5.0	63.9
& sewage sludge	50		
Grass clippings	50	7.8	69.5
& sewage sludge	50		
White fir (wood)	10	9.3	68.9
& sewage sludge	90		
White fir (wood)	60	4.3	69.7
& sewage sludge	40		
Newspaper	10	9.9	67.1
& sewage sludge	90		
Newspaper	20	8.8	69.0
& sewage sludge	80		
Newspaper	30	7.5	69.5
& sewage sludge	70		

Notes: a. From "Anaerobic Digestion of Solid Wastes," by S.A. Klein.
b. Per pound of volatile solids (VS) added.

Table 5.6   Gas Production as a Function of Total Solids[a]

Material	Bio-gas (ft³)[b]
Pig manure	6.0–8.0
Cow manure (India)	3.1–4.7
Chicken manure	6.0–13.2
Conventional sewage	6.0–9.0

Notes: a. From *Methane Digesters for Fuel Gas and Fertilizer* (Merrill and Fry). Note that *total solids* rather than *volatile solids* is used as the determinant of produced gas volume.
b. Per pound of total solids (TS) added.

what we eventually want is to be able to calculate the gas production for a mixture of raw wastes in a general way. Knowing specific information on gas production per pound of waste is helpful, but limited to the specific waste material.

Ram Bux Singh has recorded outputs of gas from vegetable matter that were seven times the output from common manures. NAI also found great increases in gas production brought about by the addition of fluids pressed from succulents (cacti). However, because the carbon content of plant material (compared to nitrogen content) is very high, the digestion of plant material releases a far greater percentage of carbon dioxide than the digestion of manures. Since carbon dioxide does not burn, we must view it as an impurity, and plant-generated bio-gas is therefore qualitatively inferior to manure-generated bio-gas.

Substances Inhibiting Digester Operation

Plant material also contains a high percentage of fixed solids, thus leaving a lower fraction of volatile solids. If the material itself is used instead of the pressed juices, scum formation in the digester will be greatly accelerated and can cause problems. McNary and Walford found that citrus peels ruined their digesters, due to the presence in the peels of the chemical inhibitor, d-limonene. Other substances that are known to inhibit the digestion process include heavy metals (zinc, lead, mercury, copper), high amounts of ammonia (above 1500 parts per million), and the alkali elements (sodium, potassium, calcium, and magnesium). Another serious problem is the presence of sulfides, observed in many sewage-treatment digesters. Sulfides are easily detectable by their distinctive rotten-egg odor. It is very unlikely that any toxic materials will be present in small digester units utilizing manures and household wastes. If, however, toxicity is suspected, further study in the matter is required. P. McCarty has presented problems of digester toxicity in simple and concise terms and he is recommended for further reading on this aspect (see Bibliography). Later in the chapter, we also consider the digestibility of algae.

Carbon/Nitrogen Ratios

Our bacteria use carbon and nitrogen in the production of new cells and methane, and most people agree that, since carbon and nitrogen are used in the cells in the approximate ratio (C/N) of 30:1, the optimum ratio in the feed slurry also should be 30:1. By altering the composition of the inflow slurry, the digester can be "tuned" for efficient output. And, since the percentage of methane is in some ways determined by the carbon/nitrogen ratio of the feed, the quality of the gas also can be regulated.

The C/N ratio is difficult to establish for a general category of raw material because of the difficulty in testing for the *available* quantities and because the actual content of a material can vary with the maturity of the plants in-

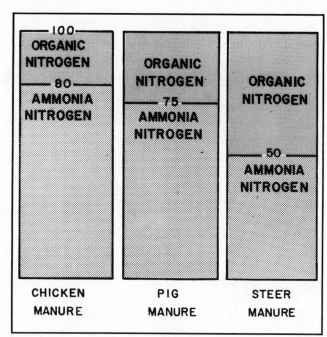

Figure 5.7 Variations in organic and inorganic nitrogen in different manures. The nitrogen of ammonia is more readily available.

volved or the storage time of the manure. For these reasons, the figures given in our tables must be taken as approximations and guides rather than exact design parameters. It is the best we can do at this time.

Nitrogen is present in waste in many chemical forms, not all of which are equally available to anaerobic bacteria. The nitrogen in ammonia, for example, is more readily available (see Figure 5.7). Also, since urination is an animal's method of eliminating excess nitrogen, the amount of urine present in the manure will strongly affect the C/N ratio. Poultry waste is high in available nitrogen because urine and feces are excreted in the same load. Cattle and other ruminants (cud chewers) produce manure with an especially low nitrogen content since the bacteria essential to their digestion process live in one of their two stomachs and consume much of the nitrogen contained in the animal's diet. Vegetable waste is typically quite low in nitrogen content, while algae is quite high. Stable manure will usually be higher in nitrogen because it contains more urine than pasture manure (however, the straw included in stable manure can act to offset this increase because of its *low* nitrogen content).

Tables 5.4 and 5.7 give values for percent of *dry weight* (total solids) for nitrogen, since both volatile-solids and fixed-solids sources of nitrogen are available to the bacteria. The carbon percentages are for volatile or non-lignin portions whenever possible, again using dry weight. Using the weights of various raw materials and their C/N ratios, a recipe for a total-inflow C/N ratio of 30:1 can be derived from Tables 5.4 and 5.7. Further qualitative information about the importance of the C/N ratio in determining the quality of the bio-gas produced is provided in Table 5.8. Be sure that you are working with the *di-*

	Table 5.7 Nitrogen Content and C/N Ratio[a]	
Material	**Total Nitrogen (% dry weight)**	**C/N Ratio**
Animal wastes		
Urine	16.0	0.8
Blood	12.0	3.5
Bone meal	—	3.5
Animal tankage	—	4.1[b]
Dry fish scraps	—	5.1[b]
Manure		
Human feces	6.0	6.0–10.0
Human urine	18.0	—
Chicken	6.3	15.0
Sheep	3.8	
Pig	3.8	
Horse	2.3	25.0[b]
Cow	1.7	18.0[b]
Steer	1.35	25.3
Sludge		
Milorganite	—	5.4[b]
Activated sludge	5.0	6.0
Fresh sewage	—	11.0[b]
Plant meals		
Soybean	—	5.0
Cottonseed	—	5.0[b]
Peanut hull	—	36.0[b]
Plant wastes		
Green garbage	3.0	18.0
Hay, young grass	4.0	12.0
Hay, alfalfa	2.8	17.0[b]
Hay, blue grass	2.5	19.0
Seaweed	1.9	19.0
Nonleguminous vegetables	2.5–4.0	11.0–19.0
Red clover	1.8	27.0
Straw, oat	1.1	48.0
Straw, wheat	0.5	150.0
Sawdust	0.1	200.0–500.0
White fir wood	0.06	767.0
Other wastes		
Newspaper	0.05	812.0
Refuse	0.74	45.0

Notes: a. From "Anaerobic Digestion of Solid Wastes" (Klein) and *Methane Digesters for Fuel Gas and Fertilizer* (Merrill and Fry).
   b. Nitrogen is the percentage of total dry weight while carbon is calculated from either the total carbon percentage of dry weight or the percentage of dry weight of nonlignin carbon.

Table 5.8 C/N Ratio and Composition of Bio-gas[a]

Material	Methane	CO₂	Hydrogen	Nitrogen
		Gas		
C/N low (high nitrogen)	little	much	little	much
Blood				
Urine				
C/N high (low nitrogen)	little	much	much	little
Sawdust				
Straw				
Sugar and starch				
potatoes				
corn				
sugar beets				
C/N balanced (near 30:1)	much	some	little	little
Manures				
Garbage				

Notes: a. Adapted from *Methane Digesters for Fuel Gas and Fertilizer* (Merrill and Fry).

digester helps to protect the system from failure due to overloading.

Example: If we have 50 pounds of cow manure and 20 pounds of horse manure, what is the C/N ratio of the mixture?

Solution: Cow manure is 86 percent water and 14 percent solids (Table 5.4). So its dry weight (50 × 0.14) equals 7 pounds of total solids. These dry solids are 1.7 percent nitrogen (also from Table 5.4) and so the weight of nitrogen (7 × 0.017) is *0.119 pounds.* Cow manure's C/N ratio is 18:1; so, since it contains 18 times as much carbon as nitrogen, it has (0.119 × 18) *2.14 pounds of carbon,* dry weight.

Using the same procedure for horse manure (84 percent water, 16 percent solids, 2.3 percent nitrogen by dry weight, and C/N ratio of 25:1—Tables 5.4 and 5.7), we find that horse manure has a dry weight of 3.2 pounds, and contains 0.074 pounds of nitrogen and 1.85 pounds of carbon, dry weight.

The total carbon content, then, is 2.14 pounds plus 1.85 pounds, or 3.99 pounds, dry weight. The total nitrogen content of the mixture is 0.193 pounds, dry weight. Thus, the total C/N ratio of the mixture is:

$$\frac{3.99 \text{ lb}}{0.193 \text{ lb}} = \frac{21}{1}$$

A C/N ratio of 21:1 isn't all that bad, but it's lower than the 30:1 we would like. A little bit of thinking will reveal the fact that we can never do better than a C/N ratio of 25:1, that of horse manure, because each time raw material is added, both the carbon and nitrogen components will be added proportionately. Obviously, the less cow manure we use (18:1), the better our C/N total will be; but we would lose total volume unless we found some horses to replace the cows.

gestible portion of the raw materials in your calculations. Singh recommends that the C/N ratio never exceed 35:1, but NAI notes that a level of 46:1 would be acceptable if it were unavoidable.

Although the addition of plant waste raises the carbon content of the inflow slurry significantly and aggravates the scum problem, it also tends to buffer the system at an alkaline level, protecting against a dangerous drop in pH to the acid level. Since overloading the digester with too much raw material lowers the pH and stops digestion if allowed to continue, the presence of plant material in the

Our hope for improving the C/N total beyond 25:1 lies in adding some raw material with a C/N of *greater than* 25:1 (or better yet, greater than 30:1)—wheat straw, for example (C/N = 150:1).

Assuming that we want to use all of our cow and horse manure and that we have some wheat straw to spare, take the total dry solids (10.2 pounds) with a total C/N ratio of 21:1 and combine it with some amount of wheat straw (you can guess at a figure for percent moisture; how about 10 percent?). Then use the above procedures to get the C/N ratio for your new mixture. Run through the calculations more than once to get a feel for the principles and an idea of how much wheat straw would be required to bring the total C/N up to around 30:1. (Try 1.5 pounds of wheat straw; you should get a C/N ratio of just about 30:1.)

Feed Slurry

Moisture Content, Volume, and Weight

For proper digestion, the raw materials must contain a certain amount of water, and experience with operating digesters has shown that a feed slurry containing 7 to 9 percent solids is optimum for digestion. To calculate the amount of water that must be combined with our raw materials to give this consistency, the moisture content of the raw material must be known.

Moisture values for various feed materials often used in digestion appear in Table 5.4. If there is any doubt as to the correctness of these values, or if the raw materials under consideration do not appear in this table, a direct determination of the moisture is usually feasible: we require only a small balance and an oven set at 212°F.

First, a small pan or plate is weighed and filled with a sample of the raw material. Care should be taken that the portion of the material used in this determination is representative of the entire batch to be used in the digestion process. Pan and raw material are then weighed together. After this step, pan and material are placed in the oven and allowed to dry until all the water has evaporated. When drying is completed, the pan and contents are allowed to cool in a dry place and are weighed once more.

Percent moisture is given by

$$\text{E. 5.3} \qquad \%M = \frac{W_i - W_f}{W_i - W_p} \times 100$$

where %M equals the percent moisture of the raw material; W_p equals the weight of the pan or plate (lbs); W_i equals the initial weight of the pan and sample, before drying (lbs); and W_f equals the final weight of the pan and sample, after drying (lbs).

Say the weight of your pan is 0.1 pounds, the initial weight is 2.1 pounds, and the final weight is 0.7 pounds. Then the percent moisture is

$$\begin{aligned}
\%M &= \frac{W_i - W_f}{W_i - W_p} \times 100 \\
&= \frac{2.1 - 0.7}{2.1 - 0.1} \times 100 \\
&= 70\%
\end{aligned}$$

Once the moisture content of the feed material(s) is known, the amount of water that must be added in order to give an 8 percent slurry (midway between 7 and 9 percent) can be calculated.

Let's first deal with the situation when the total weight of raw material we intend to put in the digester is known (by either weighing or estimation). We are going to introduce a long list of definitions and a very formidable-looking series of equations, but don't worry—we arrive at the other end with a few fairly simple formulas. Here are the definitions:

$\%M$ = *percent moisture content of raw material*
M = *moisture content of raw material as decimal fraction*
$\%TS$ = *percent total solids of raw material*
TS = *total solids as decimal fraction of weight of raw material*
W_r = *total weight of raw material*
W_s = *weight of total solids in raw material*
W'_w = *weight of water already in raw material*
W''_w = *total weight of water in 8 percent slurry*
W_w = *weight of water to be added to make 8 percent slurry*
V_w = *volume of water to be added to make 8 percent slurry*
W_{sl} = *total weight of slurry*
V_{sl} = *total volume of slurry*
V_r = *volume of raw material*
D_r = *apparent density of raw material*

The moisture content of the raw material can be equated with the percentage of total solids in the raw material, either as percentages or as decimal fractions:

$$\text{E. 5.4} \qquad \%TS = 100 - \%M$$

$$\text{E. 5.5} \qquad M = \frac{\%M}{100}$$

$$\text{E. 5.6} \qquad TS = 1 - M$$

The weight of solids in the raw material is given by the following two relationships:

$$\begin{aligned}
\text{E. 5.7} \quad W_s &= W_r TS \\
&= W_r \times (1 - M)
\end{aligned}$$

To produce an 8 percent slurry, 8 pounds of solids should be mixed with 92 pounds of water, including, of course, the water already present in the raw materials:

$$\text{E. 5.8} \qquad W'_w = W_r M$$

The total amount of water contained in an 8 percent slurry is

$$\begin{aligned}
\text{E. 5.9} \qquad W''_w &= 92\frac{W_s}{8} \\
&= 11.5 W_s
\end{aligned}$$

and the amount of water which you will need to add is the difference between the total moisture needed and the moisture already present:

$$\begin{aligned}
\text{E. 5.10} \quad W_w &= W''_w - W'_w \\
&= 11.5\, W_s - W_r M \\
&= 11.5\, W_r \times (1 - M) - W_r M \\
&= 11.5\, W_r - 12.5\, W_r M
\end{aligned}$$

The volume of water to be added is

$$\begin{aligned}
\text{E. 5.11} \quad V_w &= \frac{W_w}{62.3} \\
&= 0.1845\, W_r - 0.2\, W_r M
\end{aligned}$$

since water weighs 62.3 pounds per cubic foot at 60 to 70°F.

The weight of the 8 percent slurry can be calculated by adding the weight of water added to the original weight of raw material:

$$\begin{aligned}
\text{E. 5.12} \quad W_{sl} &= W_w + W_r \\
&= 12.5\, W_r \times (1 - M)
\end{aligned}$$

and this must be equal to the sum of total water and total solids:

$$\text{E. 5.13} \qquad W_{sl} = W''_w + W_s$$

By using 65 pounds per cubic foot as an average

density of the 8 percent slurry, the volume of the slurry is

E. 5.14
$$V_{sl} = \frac{W_{sl}}{65}$$
$$= 0.192\ W_r \times (1 - M)$$

where V_{sl} is in cubic feet (1 gal = 7.5 ft³).

So, using Equations 5.10, 5.11, 5.12, and 5.14, we can figure out the weight and volume of the water to be added and the weight and volume of our 8 percent slurry, once we know the total weight of raw material and the moisture content (don't mix up M with $\%M$!):

$$W_w = 11.5\ W_r - 12.5\ W_r M$$
$$V_w = 0.1845\ W_r - 0.2\ W_r M = \frac{W_w}{62.3}$$
$$W_{sl} = 12.5\ W_r \times (1 - M)$$
$$V_{sl} = 0.192\ W_r \times (1 - M)$$

When the volume, density, and moisture content of a raw material are known (instead of the total weight), calculation of the volume of 8 percent slurry can be done in the following manner. The weight of raw material can be estimated by multiplying volume times density:

E. 5.15
$$W_r = V_r D_r$$

where D_r is in pounds per cubic foot. The volume of slurry then becomes

E. 5.16
$$V_{sl} = 0.192\ V_r D_r \times (1 - M)$$

The apparent density of the raw material can be estimated by weighing a known volume of material (without compacting the raw material) and dividing the weight by the volume.

When a mixture of, say, three materials ($\%A + \%B + \%C = 100\%$) is to be used in a digester, the moisture content of the mixture can be computed by

E. 5.17
$$M_{mix} = \frac{\%A \times \%M_a}{100} + \frac{\%B \times \%M_b}{100}$$
$$+ \frac{\%C \times \%M_c}{100}$$

where the subscripts denote the individual components of the mixture, A, B, and C. The weight of the mixture is

E. 5.18
$$W_{mix} = W_a + W_b + W_c$$

and the volume of the mixture is computed in a similar manner:

E. 5.19
$$V_{mix} = V_a + V_b + V_c$$

This same procedure can be followed for any number of mixture components.

Example: From two cows and a horse, you have 50 pounds of cow manure ($\%M = 86\%$) and 20 pounds of horse manure ($\%M = 84\%$). What is the volume of the slurry?

Solution: We must first compute the moisture content of the mixture. Total weight of mixture is

$$W_a + W_b = 50 + 20 = 70\ lbs$$

Percent cow manure in the mixture is

$$\%A = \frac{50}{70} \times 100 = 71.5\%$$

Percent horse manure in the mixture is

$$\%B = \frac{20}{70} \times 100 = 28.5\%$$

The percent moisture of the mixture is

$$\%M_{mix} = \frac{71.5 \times 86}{100} + \frac{28.5 \times 84}{100}$$
$$= 85.5\%$$

The volume of water to be added (from Equation 5.11) is

$$V_w = 0.1845 \times 70 - (0.2 \times 70 \times 0.855)$$
$$= 0.95\ ft^3$$

The weight of water to be added (also from Equation 5.11) is the volume times the density of water:

$$W_w = V_w \times 62.3$$
$$= 59.2\ lbs$$

The volume of the 8 percent slurry (from Equation 5.14) is

$$V_{sl} = 0.192 \times 70 \times (1.0 - 0.855)$$
$$= 1.95\ ft^3$$

Now we have come to a potentially confusing point. The raw material contains a lot of void spaces and when water is added to make up the slurry, it is "soaked" up by the raw manure—thus, the volume of added water and the volume of raw material *cannot* simply be added to find the volume of slurry.

Particle Size

The solids in your slurry should be in small particles so that bacterial action can proceed at a maximum rate (the previous calculations of the water needed to produce an 8 percent slurry assume that the solids are of sufficiently small size so that a slurry *is* produced!). Reducing the particle size also will facilitate transport of the slurry in pumps and pipes if these are used.

Manure does not require much reduction in the size of its solids—thorough mixing with water is sufficient in most cases. But when garbage, garden debris, or other kinds of refuse are to be digested, they should be shredded or chopped up by hand if a shredder is not available.

A good way to judge the proper particle size in a slurry is to observe how fast the solids settle out or if there are many solids floating on the surface after the water has been added. If there is a fast settling, the solids will accumulate on the bottom of the digester too quickly and make it difficult for the bacteria to do their work. In the case of floating material, the bacteria may never reach the solids to degrade them. With the raw materials normally used in digestion operations, flotation might be more of a problem than rapid settling. If the mixture is viscous enough, flotation can be avoided by proper mixing to entrap the particles. If flotation takes place, scum problems will appear in the working digester. John Fry has studied the scum problem and has offered some useful information on handling the scum in digesters (see Bibliography).

Acid/Base Considerations (pH)

The term *pH* refers to the amount of acid or base present in solution. Too much of either can kill the methane-producing bacteria. As we described earlier, methane production is a two-stage process. In the first stage, one group of bacteria (the acid formers) utilize the organic matter of the feed solution (slurry) as a food source and produce organic acids. These acids are utilized in the second stage of digestion by another group of bacteria called methane formers. The methane formers utilize organic acids as food and produce methane. A balance of these two groups of bacteria must be maintained inside the digester at all times.

The methane formers multiply much more slowly than the acid formers, and this fact can result in an acidic environment that inhibits the growth of the methane formers. When you first start up your digester, such an imbalance is very likely. To help the situation, artificial means for raising the pH (to make the solution neutral—pH 7.0) of the feed have been successfully employed. Bicarbonate of soda can be used for this purpose at about 0.003 to 0.006 pounds per cubic foot of feed solution. This should be added to the slurry routinely during start-up and only when necessary while the digester is in full operation. Lime also can be used, but it is not as safe as bicarbonate and should be avoided if at all possible.

The pH of the feed slurry or the supernatant liquor can be determined in a number of ways. The most inexpensive ways are *pH paper* and the indicator *bromthymol blue*. Both may be obtained from a chemical supply house. The pH paper is easier to use, but it does not work well in the presence of sulfides, a common substance in anaerobic digesters.

Methane digestion will proceed quite well when the pH lies in the range 6.6–7.6. The optimum range is 7.0–7.2. In this range, a drop of bromthymol blue indicator will be dark blue-green in color (about one drop of indicator to ten drops of solution). If the mixture becomes more green, an acidic environment exists and bicarbonate of soda should be added. A deep blue color indicates a basic solution. In this case the cure is patience; in time, the digester will return to normal by itself.

Calculating Detention Time

Now that we have calculated the components of our feed slurry, we must find out *how long* the feed will need to remain in the digester to be processed. Temperature considerations play a large factor, so we will need to discuss them a bit. Then we can add in a safety factor and find out exactly how large a tank we will require. In order to find out the digestion time, we must return to a discussion of volatile solids and do a few preliminary calculations.

Chemical Oxygen Demand (*COD*)

Volatile solids, you will remember, are that portion of the total solids which burn off at a temperature of about 1100°F, and they represent the organic fraction of the total solids. Organics which can be decomposed by bacteria are called biodegradable. This portion is what the bacteria will use as a food source. It is also the portion responsible for methane production during digestion.

To calculate the minimum time required for digestion of certain raw materials, the *chemical oxygen demand* (*COD*) of the feed slurry is required. This quantity represents the amount of oxygen required to oxidize—that is, to degrade or destroy—the organics by chemical means. In order to make the best use of available data and formulas, it is more convenient to express the *COD* in parts per million (ppm) than in pounds per cubic foot (where 1 pound per cubic foot equals 16,000 ppm). We also require the moisture content and percentage of volatile solids of the raw material (both appear in Table 5.4). For mixtures of raw materials, the amount of volatile solids in pounds for each component A is given by

E. 5.20 $\quad VS_a = W_a \times (1 - M_a) \times \dfrac{\%VS_a}{100}$

where VS_a equals the weight of volatile solids of component A (lbs); W_a equals the weight of raw A used (lbs); M_a equals the moisture content of A as a decimal fraction; and $\%VS_a$ equals the percent of total solids that are volatile (from Table 5.4). The total amount of volatile solids then can be found by adding up the amounts of volatile solids of each component.

The concentration of volatile solids in the feed slurry (VS_{con}) is equal to the total amount of volatile solids present in the feed (VS_{total}) divided by the volume of the feed (which we calculated in the previous section):

E. 5.21
$$VS_{con} = \frac{VS_{total}}{V_{sl}}$$

The COD concentration of most materials can be approximated as equal to 1.5 times the volatile-solids concentration (or, of any specific sample, the total COD equals 1.5 times the volatile-solids total). But we must also account for the fact that only about 50 percent of the volatile solids are biodegradable:

E. 5.22 $COD = 0.5 \times 1.5 \times VS_{con}$

If we want to express the COD in parts per million (after measuring the VS_{con} in pounds per cubic foot), the conversion equation is

E. 5.23 $COD = 0.5 \times 1.5 \times 16,000 \times VS_{con}$
$$= 12,000 \times VS_{con}$$

These last equations can also give us the *total COD* of a particular batch of feed, which we will need in later calculations.

Example: If 50 pounds of cow manure with 86 percent moisture and 80 percent VS is mixed with 20 pounds of horse manure having 84 percent moisture and 80 percent VS to produce, upon addition of water, an 8 percent slurry, calculate the biodegradable COD (in ppm).

Solution: As we calculated previously, the volume of this particular slurry is 1.95 cubic feet. Using Equation 5.20, the volatile solids of cow manure is

$$VS_{cm} = W_{cm} \times (1 - M_{cm}) \times \frac{\%VS_{cm}}{100}$$
$$= 50 \times (1 - 0.86) \times \left(\frac{80}{100}\right)$$
$$= 50 \times (0.14) \times (0.80)$$
$$= 5.6 \ lb$$

The volatile solids of horse manure, by the same equation, is

$$VS_{hm} = 20 \times (1 - 0.84) \times \left(\frac{80}{100}\right)$$
$$= 2.56 \ lb$$

so, the total amount of volatile solids in the mixture is

$$VS_{total} = 5.6 + 2.56 = 8.16 \ lb$$

The concentration of volatile solids in pounds per cubic foot (from Equation 5.21) is

$$VS_{con} = \frac{VS_{total}}{V_{sl}}$$
$$= \frac{8.16}{1.95} = 4.18 \ lb/ft^3$$

Then the biodegradable COD of the feed slurry in ppm is

$$COD = 12,000 \times VS_{con}$$
$$= 12,000 \times 4.18$$
$$= 50,300 \ ppm$$

Solids Retention Time

Now that we have the COD of our slurry mixture, we are in a position to figure out how long it must remain in the digester. The solids retention time (SRT) is the average time that the incoming solids stay in the tank. We assume here that the mechanical design of our digester—its inflow and outflow schemes—is such that when new raw materials are introduced into the digester, they will replace old and digested material (a bottom inflow and top outflow arrangement, for example).

The SRT relates the digestion operation to the age and quantity of microorganisms in the system, and it is a sound parameter for design. An SRT of at least 10 days is a good rule-of-thumb value for the conventional digestion process. There also is a *minimum SRT* which reflects the ability of the microorganisms to consume the food source and reproduce themselves. If the SRT is less than the minimum SRT, you will literally wash out the bacteria faster than they can reproduce themselves and the digester will begin to lose efficiency. If the SRT is not increased, eventually the digestion process will stop. The minimum SRT is given by the following equation:

E. 5.24 $\dfrac{1}{SRT_m} = \left[a \times k \times [1 - \left(\dfrac{K_c}{K_c + COD}\right)^{1/2}] \right] - b$

where SRT_m equals the minimum solids retention time (days); COD equals the biodegradable chemical oxygen demand (ppm); a equals a constant showing how many bacteria can be produced per amount of food (COD) available (equal to about 0.04); b equals a constant showing how fast the bacteria die (equal to about 0.015); k is a factor for how fast the bacteria will consume food (depending on the temperature of digestion); and K_c equals the minimum amount of food required before bacteria can start multiplying (also dependent upon the temperature of digestion).

Values of k and K_c for the temperature range 59 to 95°F appear below:

Temperature	k	K_c
59°F	3.37	18,500
68°F	3.97	10,400
77°F	4.73	6,450
86°F	5.60	3,800
95°F	6.67	2,235

You can see from this table that favorable conditions for digestion increase with increasing temperature. If the digestion time is well above the minimum retention time, it has been found experimentally that the efficiency of the process (how much methane is produced) is about the same for digester temperatures ranging from 77 to 86°F. At 68°F it is a little lower and at 59°F it is about one-fourth the efficiency of the range from 77 to 86°F. Below 59°F very little if any methane appears to be produced. For the raw materials in our last example (50 pounds cow manure and 20 pounds horse manure) the COD was calculated as 50,300 ppm. Then, at 68°F for instance, the SRT_m of these raw materials is

$$\frac{1}{SRT_m} = \left[0.04 \times 3.97 \right.$$
$$\left. \times \left[1 - \left(\frac{10,400}{10,400 + 50,300} \right)^{1/2} \right] \right] - 0.015$$
$$= 0.108$$

and the SRT_m is the inverse of this quantity:

$$SRT_m = \frac{1}{0.108}$$
$$= 9.25 \text{ days}$$

Therefore it will take about 9 days at a minimum to have the digestion of 70 pounds of combined manure going full blast.

Temperature Considerations

We just saw that temperature plays a very significant role in the digestion process. Anaerobic bacteria can operate either in a low or in a high temperature range. Bacteria that grow well in the range of from 77 to 95°F are called *mesophilic,* while bacteria that grow at higher temperatures (120 to 140°F) are called *thermophilic.* The higher temperatures required by thermophilic bacteria make them economically prohibitive for the small digesters we are considering here. Moreover, digestion within the thermophilic range produces a supernatant effluent much higher in colloidal (hard to settle out) solids, as shown below:

Characteristics of Supernatant from Laboratory Digesters	Thermophilic Range (130°F ± 10)	Normal Range (90°F ± 10)
Total solids (ppm)	0.309	0.231
Volatile solids (%)	67.1	58.5
Settleable solids (ml/l)	17.2	12.0
Suspended solids (ppm)	1490.0	773.0
Nonsettleable solids (ppm)	451.0	107.0

Therefore, only mesophilic bacteria are considered, and you should take the time to get to know your bacteria.

Mesophilic bacteria are very sensitive to temperature and temperature variations. This sensitivity, in turn, has a very noticeable effect on digester design and operation. As an example, consider the minimum solids retention time we just calculated, based on a temperature of digester operation of 68°F. At that temperature, the minimum solids retention time was calculated as approximately 9 days. By keeping all conditions of that example constant except for the temperature, you can calculate that the minimum-solids retention time at 95°F is approximately 3 days! In other words, a 27°F increase in the digester operating temperature results in a reduction of the minimum solids retention time by two-thirds. This kind of impact in the minimum solids retention time will have an obvious impact on how fast the process can go and therefore on the size of the digestion and gas storage tanks needed. The higher temperatures result in a decreased detention time while more methane also is produced. So, the digestion tank will be smaller while the gas storage tank is larger. These considerations must be included in the selection of a safety factor, which we will discuss in a moment.

Any increase in temperature increases the rate of gas ebullition (bubbling) and so increases the solids bubbling about in the supernatant. There is not an appreciable change in this solids content over the temperature range of 70 to 95°F, but an unheated tank warming in the summer months may have rapid enough temperature changes and consequent changes in tank activity to show a high overflow of solids and even a complete overturn of the tank! Uniformity of tank temperature through controlled heating and insulation can reduce the possibility of any such unpleasantness.

Remember that, unless the digester is to be located in a tropical climate, temperatures of 95°F (optimum gas production) require artificial heating and/or insulation of the digester tank. The most common method of heating the tank uses methane-burning heaters, and this drain of methane production should be included in your calculations of total gas output. The heat losses and heat requirements of your digester must be calculated; if, for example, all methane produced has to be used for heating your digester, heating should not be employed. (For detailed calculations, see listings under Metcalf and Eddy, Eckenfelder and O'Connor, and Perry in the Bibliography.)

An alternate method might involve the use of solar heating, although we've never seen it done.

Insulating the digester in some fashion will help to reduce extreme temperature variations. A number of digester designs place the digester totally or partially underground, so that the surrounding soil provides some insulation. Housing the digester inside a building also provides some protection against extreme temperature variations. This approach is, however, handicapped by the fact that feed slurry and sludge and supernatant products then have to be transported in and out of some structure, which might interfere with its other uses. Another pitfall of this approach is that the storage tank for the bio-gas should be located *outside* the building, to minimize explosion hazards inside.

Safety Factor

As in most design operations, a minimum is never taken as the basis for final calculations—it is multiplied by a safety factor before it is used to calculate other design parameters. Because it is difficult and time-consuming to get a methane digester operating properly, but it is easy to "kill" the digester operation by overloading, our safety factor is used to prevent accidental overloading.

The magnitude of a safety factor for the digestion process lies in the range of 5 to 100 and depends on the following considerations: (1) expected variations in temperature—the greater the variation, the greater the safety factor; (2) expected variations in raw materials (flow concentration and type of material)—dealt with as temperature variations; (3) other raw-material characteristics (C/N ratio, presence of phosphorus and other nutrients)—increase the safety factor as the C/N ratio moves away from 30 or the nutrient content drops; (4) competence of operators and attendance of the process; and (5) confidence in SRT_m value and the numbers used in calculating it.

We can express the use of the safety factor in the following equation:

E. 5.25 $DT = SF \times SRT_m$

where DT equals the digester detention time (days); SF equals the safety factor; and SRT_m equals the minimum solids retention time (days).

Unfortunately, no precise value can be given for the safety factor. Its usefulness rests on the fact that, as the degree of variation and uncertainty increases in factors important to the design and operation of any digester, the greater the potential for digester failure. We can only make some qualitative recommendations here and suggest that you do some experimentation and observe the results of your own digester. A reasonable rule of thumb for the safety factor is a minimum of 5 for a well-controlled digester with constant feed rate and composition, and a stable temperature of about 90°F. A safety factor of 10 would be advisable for a system with fluctuations in feed rate and composition, but a rather stable temperature at about 90°F. And finally, a safety factor of 20 or more for systems poorly controlled as to feed rate, composition, C/N ratio, or temperature.

Example: For the example considered thus far (50 pounds of cow manure and 20 pounds of horse manure), let us say that it is known that temperature variations will occur, but that the raw materials will not change appreciably as to nature and amounts. Further, let us suppose that methane production is employed only when these raw materials are available and that the digester is not attended extensively.

Solution: Based on these considerations, a reasonable choice of a safety factor will be about 20. Then

$$DT = SF \times SRT_m$$
$$= 20 \times 9.25 = 185 \ days$$

Digester Characteristics

Calculating Tank Volume

Once the digester detention time is determined for our available raw materials, the volume of the digester tank can be calculated. In the case of a batch-system operation, the volume of the feed slurry (which we calculated previously) is equal to the volume of the digester. But in the case of a continuous or semi-continuous feeding system, the amount of raw materials processed per unit time must be known before we can determine the volume of the digester required. In either case, the following calculations *do not include* the volume of the methane gas produced. As we speak of it here, the digester volume is the volume that the slurry occupies excluding the gas that is produced during the process. Provisions obviously must be made to take care of this gas volume—a separate gas-collection tank or a floating-top digestion tank, for example—and we will consider these systems a bit later.

We should add that a reduction in liquid volume occurs in the digester once methane is being produced. This reduction will create volume variations inside the digester, but their effect is insignificant.

The equation we use to determine the volume of a digester tank (slurry feed, supernatant effluent, and sludge) for a continuous-feed operation is

E. 5.26 $V_t = V_{sl} \times DT$

where V_t equals the volume of the tank; V_{sl} equals the daily volume of the slurry concocted from the raw materials (from Equation 5.14); and DT equals the detention time (Equation 5.25).

Example: For the case of two cows and a horse we have been using as a sample, it is known that 70 pounds of combined manure is produced *daily* and that the volume of the 8 percent slurry is 1.95 cubic feet. The required digestion (detention) time also has been estimated as 185 days (with a safety factor of 20). What is the volume of the required digester tank?

Solution: The volume of the digester is

$$V_t = V_{sl} \times DT$$
$$= 1.95 \times 185$$
$$= 360 \, ft^3$$

At 7.5 gallons per cubic foot, the tank should be able to hold 2700 gallons.

Now let's change our safety factor from 20 to 10 (that is, assume we have a much better controlled system). The new detention time is then 92.5 days, and the digester tank volume is then

$$V_t = 1.95 \times 92.5$$
$$= 180 ft^3 = 1352 \, gal$$

Thus, for the same feed rate, the tank volume is a simple function of the detention time—double the detention time, double the tank volume.

Operation and Types of Digesters

First of all, digesters should be located to minimize the distances for transporting manure and wastes, for piping the gas, and for transporting the sludge and supernatant effluents. Secondly, since the digestion process can continue only under anaerobic conditions and since combinations of 5 to 15 percent methane in air are highly explosive, it is of the utmost importance that no air enter your digester with the incoming slurry. If the outside opening of the inflow pipe is well above the *highest possible* level of the liquid in the tank *and* the inside opening of the pipe to the tank is well below the *lowest possible* level of liquid in the tank *and* the inflow pipe is open to the atmosphere *only* during periods of slurry addition, the chances for air/methane mixing are minimized. Indian experimenters also have found that an 8 percent slurry is more dense than the digesting sludge in the tank. If the slurry is added at the bottom of the tank, its density will keep it below the older sludge until it, in turn, begins to digest and is pushed upward by new additions. This mode of addition affords the digestion process a natural mixing which supplements any mechanical techniques.

A pipe 3 inches in diameter should be sufficient for the inflow of the slurry. The pipe should be straight and without bends or the slurry is apt to cake on the inside and clog it, requiring periodic reaming to allow free flow.

An 8 percent slurry is very similar in consistency to cream. The raw material must be reduced to an adequate

particle size and then must be well dispersed in the water medium before it is added to the tank. This mixing process may require a sturdy basin or trough to allow vigorous stirring.

Certain design characteristics determine your control over the quality of the supernatant in your digester. Single-stage (one tank) digesters can incorporate either fixed covers, floating covers, or multiple outflow valves (see Figures 5.8 and 5.9).

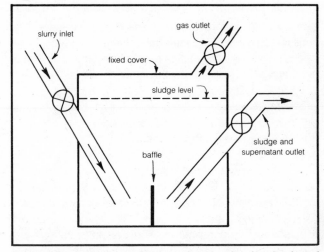

Figure 5.8 A fixed-cover digester with outlet placed at the desired sludge level in the digester.

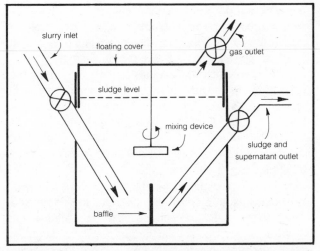

Figure 5.9 A floating-cover digester. For a two-tank system, simply connect two tanks in series. Mixing devices are useful, but optional.

Fixed-cover digesters require that supernatant, or perhaps sludge, be removed for the introduction of fresh slurry. If the supernatant is removed simply by overflow through an outflow pipe, then the rate and time of excess liquid removal is obviously identical to the fresh slurry introduced (if no sludge is withdrawn at the same time). And, by the way, since continuous agitation or agitation due to the addition of raw slurry causes an increase in solids in the supernatant (due merely to mechanical action), slurry input should be slow and constant for the highest quality supernatant.

Supernatant preferably should be removed using an outflow valve at a more convenient and advantageous time—for example, before feed addition. Removal flow rates have to be high to prevent clogging of the valve. Floating-cover tanks offer the best timing control of supernatant removal: the supernatant need not be removed each time slurry is fed into the digester.

Two-stage digesters provide a far superior quality of supernatant. Here, the first tank is agitated and heated and the consequent overflow, full of suspended solids, runs into an unagitated tank for settling. The second tank need not be very large since it only serves the purpose of separating the solids from the mixture. Once the solids have settled, they can be recycled into the first tank to promote biological activity. Obviously, the two-stage digester system is preferred if your resources allow for construction of the second tank. However, problems can arise due to the septic properties of the supernatant. These properties can cause particle suspension in the settling tank if the settled solids are not removed periodically.

Overloading of a digester can cause serious impairment of sludge-supernatant separation. Rudolfs and Fontenelli (see Bibliography) studied the problem of overloading and we can summarize some of their findings here. They found an optimum loading rate for a two-stage digester operating at 82 to 84°F to be about 0.1 pounds of volatile solids per cubic foot of primary (the first tank) digester capacity per day. Doubling this loading rate increased the solids content in the supernatant to a point where sludge-supernatant separation was not easily achieved. For single-stage digesters, it was determined that even at loading rates of only 0.042 pounds of volatile solids per cubic foot per day, the supernatant contained about 3 percent solids. In sanitary-engineering practice, loading rates of 0.03 to 0.1 pounds of volatile solids per cubic foot per day are used for single-stage digesters with detention times on the order of 90 days. These figures will give you an idea of the range of loading rates which have been found experimentally to give reliable performance from a digester. The engineering book by Metcalf and Eddy has a lot of useful detailed information if you are keen to go into greater depth, and L.J. Fry has collected the best set of practical notes and experiences presently available concerning operation and maintenance of small-scale digesters (see Bibliography).

The importance of good sludge-supernatant separation is manifested first in terms of the effective capacity of the digester. With poor separation, solids—particularly fresh undigested solids—are much more likely to escape by overflow in the effluent. Because these solids are then no longer available as a fuel source, there is a decrease in digester efficiency and gas production. These factors, too, should be considered when selecting a safety factor

for the digester. Poor separation also results in thinner and larger volumes of sludge. A sludge of 5 percent solids will contain twice as much water as a sludge of 10 percent solids and this excess water can create a handling problem, particularly in drying the digested sludge.

The sludge can be pumped out or, more simply, an outlet pipe 2 to 4 inches in diameter can be fitted as near to the bottom as possible, to allow for the periodic removal of the digested sludge into a dolly or wheelbarrow. Or, given the proper initial elevation, a large-diameter pipe can carry sludge directly into your garden or fields. A sludge outlet is not essential in batch digesters, though it simplifies unloading.

Start-up Considerations

A very important aspect of digester operation is the initial development of a good gas-producing sludge. You cannot overestimate the importance of this phase of digester operation.

It is advantageous to start the digester with a "seed" containing anaerobic bacteria. A sample of digester sludge from a properly operating municipal sewage-treatment facility or sludge from another methane digester would be ideal. Anaerobic muds from swamps or lake bottoms also can serve the purpose. If none of these is avilable, it would be wise to prepare a tightly sealed container of soil, water, and organic matter. This should sit in a warm place, about 95°F, for a few weeks. When the digester is ready to begin operation, everything but the gritty particles of soil should be decanted into the digester with as little exposure to air as possible.

We also must remind you about pH considerations. During start-up, the digester is often too acidic for the methane-forming bacteria. Review the section on pH for testing and rectifying techniques.

Products of a Digester

A normal unmixed digester will separate into layers as shown in Figure 5.10. Each of these layers can be used as a resource if the proper opportunities are available. Methane gas, supernatant liquor or effluent (the liquid product of the digestion process), and sludge are withdrawn in a continuous or semi-continuous digester setup, at a volume rate equal to that of feed after an initial detention time period has elapsed.

Bio-gas and Gas Storage

Given the COD (assuming proper pH, temperature, and C/N ratio), an estimate of gas production can be made. We use the formula

E. 5.27 $C = 5.62 \times [(e \times COD) - 1.42W_2]$

where C equals the cubic feet of methane produced at 32°F and 14.7 psi (lbs/in²) pressure; e equals the efficien-

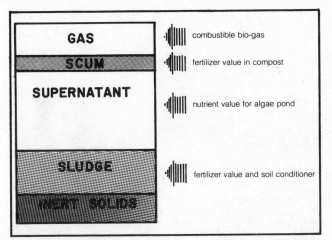

Figure 5.10 Stratification in a methane digester and uses of its products.

cy of raw-material utilization—how efficient the bacteria are in converting raw material to methane—with 6.0 being a recommended value; *COD* equals the total biodegradable chemical oxygen demand of the raw materials (this time we have a total, not a concentration: in pounds); and W_2 equals the weight of solids produced due to bacteria (lbs). This last factor we have not spoken of yet and, indeed, we *still* don't have to (see "Sludge"). The reason? For anaerobic decomposition the second term in the equation ($1.42W_2$) is small compared to the first term; and because of this comparative smallness, we can approximate our production using the shortened equation

E. 5.28 $C = 5.62 \times e \times COD$

You may recall from Equation 5.22 that the *COD* equals $0.75\ VS_{total}$; therefore

E. 5.29 $C = 5.62 \times 0.6 \times 0.75\ VS_{total}$
              $= 2.5 VS_{total}$

A nice, neat way to estimate the volume of methane gas!

For our 50 pounds of cow manure and 20 pounds of horse manure, the VS_{total} was 8.16 pounds. The methane produced will be

$$C = 2.5 \times 8.16$$
$$= 20.4\ ft^3$$

Remember, this is *methane* produced and bio-gas is only about two-thirds methane. The volume of bio-gas can be obtained by multiplying C by a factor of 1.5. Certain materials and their gas productions were listed in Table 5.6; also remember that the quality of the bio-gas will vary (see Table 5.8).

So, now we know that when the digester continuously is fed 70 pounds of combined manure daily (of a specified 50/20 mix), it will produce about 20 cubic feet of methane

per day, after an initial period of time equal to the detention time. (At current prices for natural gas, this total is equivalent to 10 cents a day and would satisfy maybe 10 percent of the needs of an average individual.) The inherent assumption here is that all previously mentioned conditions—size solids, water content of feed slurry, etc.—are met. We also assume that the *C/N* ratio is favorable and that there are enough nutrients present. If the digester is not producing approximately the above calculated volume of methane, you should try to eliminate any possible malfunctions and insure that all assumed conditions are met. A bit later we will present a trouble-shooting summary. But now let's speak of how to collect and store the gas.

As methane is insoluble in water, it bubbles to the top of the digester tank. In order to maximize methane production and help eliminate oxygen from the system, the digester tank should be kept fairly full. Depending on your digester design, an additional tank for gas storage may be needed. Singh also suggests a few possible designs for gas storage tanks (see Bibliography).

A balance will have to be struck between the daily production of methane and the rate at which the methane is used. Since methane is a very dilute fuel, a compressor will have to be employed if periodic production of methane in considerable excess of the daily capacity to use it is anticipated. However, this seldom is the case. Ideally, the storage tank should be sufficiently large to hold at least several days' worth of optimal daily gas production. This capacity will allow some leeway in your rate of consumption as well as provide sufficient bio-gas for any short-term task that requires a high rate of energy input. Storage capacity certainly should be in excess of the anticipated peak daily demand. In the case of batch digestion, a few digesters with staggered digestion periods should be operated in order to maintain a relatively uniform rate of gas production.

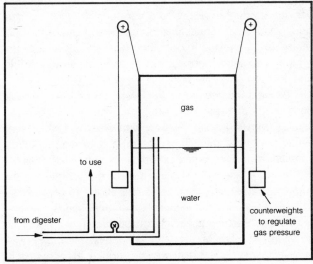

Figure 5.11 Floating-cover gas collection tank.

For purposes of keeping oxygen out of the system and for maintaining a slight positive gas pressure, a floating-tank setup is best (see Figure 5.11). This is a concrete or steel tank filled with water on which the gas-holding tank floats. If concrete is used, the tank should be sunk in the ground to be able to withstand the pressure of the liquid inside. In any case, a below-ground design is desirable in colder climates to prevent freezing of the water; a thin oil layer on top of the water also helps to prevent freezing. The water-holding tank should be taller than the gas-holding tank, so that all the air can be flushed out of the gas-holding tank (by opening the top valve and pushing down on the floating tank until the top of the tank reaches the water level) before methane production begins. If you want, a few cups of lime can be added to the water in order to increase the fuel value of the gas by removing inert carbon dioxide—alkaline water will dissolve a larger quantity of carbon dioxide than water at neutral pH.

A simple apparatus can be set up to monitor the gas pressure in the gas storage tank (see Merrill and Fry). Or, a standard pressure gauge can be mounted on the gas line. The pressure can be controlled within a broad range by adding weight to the cover of the float tank or by using counterweights on pulleys. A compressor may be needed if large quantities of gas are needed at distances too far for piping (perhaps 100 feet, when we use weights on the cover to increase pressure) or to fuel a moving machine such as a car or rototiller. Small quantities of gas also can be made mobile by storing them in inner tubes.

Supernatant

For all practical purposes, the supernatant produced is approximately equal to the amount of water added to produce the 8 percent slurry that feeds the digester (see Equation 5.10). For removal techniques, see "Operation and Types of Digesters."

This supernatant can vary in color from clear, through various shades of yellow, to a very unsightly black. The odor may be unnoticeable or extremely offensive and nauseating. A properly operating digester has a clear (to slightly yellow) supernatant with few suspended solids and with no offensive odor.

As we discussed earlier in digester operations, various parameters can affect the quality of the supernatant resulting from digestion. As you would suspect, the characteristics of the raw slurry affect the supernatant: solids increase in the supernatant with the fineness of division of the slurry, and they also increase as the volatile-matter content of the slurry increases. This is due to greater activity and agitation in the digestion of these solids. Neither of these two factors is easily controllable. The amount of water in the slurry is, however, a controllable factor. Excessive volumes of slurry water produce excessive volumes of supernatant.

As we also have mentioned, two-stage digesters provide a far superior quality of supernatant. Single-stage, fixed-cover digesters are less expensive, but two-stage digesters offer vast improvements for a minimal extra cost. There are also temperature parameters, which we mentioned in the section "Temperature Considerations."

Supernatant has its uses—fertilizer for your fields, material for your compost pile, feed for your algae (see "Oxidation Ponds" in this chapter and also Chapter 7). But if you have an excess quantity, you must know what to do with it. In the past, supernatant was viewed primarily as a disposal problem rather than as a utilizable resource, and several methods were evolved for the liquor's disposal. For example, the supernatant was disposed of on sand beds. This method is unsatisfactory because of prohibitive costs due to clogging and odor problems. Centrifugation also has been used, but, on a small-scale basis, this is neither practical nor economical.

In large-scale digesters, the predominant method of disposal is to return the supernatant to the input of the digester. A.J. Fischer reports that this can cause problems in these digesters if the total-solids content exceeds 30 to 50 percent (see Bibliography), but this still is probably the most practical method for supernatant disposal in a small-scale, manual-fed digester: without perfect separation of the supernatant, the liquors can be recycled into the digester as solvent for making dry waste into slurry.

Sludge

The sludge produced in a digester is a combination of the nonbiodegradable portion of the solids introduced into the digester and the amount of bacteria produced during the digestion process. After operation has started and the digester is running continuously, the amount of sludge solids produced by nonbiodegradable solids (W_l) is given by

E. 5.30
$$W_1 = W \times \left[1 - (0.5)\left(\frac{\%VS}{100}\right) \right]$$

$$= W_s \times (1 - M) \times \left[1 - (0.5)\left(\frac{\%VS}{100}\right) \right]$$

where W_s equals the weight of sludge solids produced due to initial solids (lbs); W_r equals the weight of raw material added (lbs); M equals moisture of raw material as a decimal fraction; and $\%VS$ equals the percent of volatile solids of the raw material. In case mixtures of raw materials are used, both M and $\%VS$ must be those of the mixture, as calculated previously.

The amount of sludge solids produced in the form of bacteria is

E. 5.31
$$W_2 = \frac{0.04 \times COD}{1 + (0.015 \times DT)}$$

where W_2 equals the weight of sludge solids of bacterial origin (lbs); COD equals the total biodegradable chemical oxygen demand (lbs); and DT equals the detention time of the digester (days).

The total amount of sludge solids produced is then

E. 5.32
$$W_{ss} = W_1 + W_2$$

Since the digested sludge is approximately 10 percent solids by weight, the amount of total sludge (10 percent solids + 90 percent water) is

E. 5.33
$$W_{sludge} = 10 W_{ss}$$

If we assume an average density of 65 pounds per cubic foot for the digested sludge, its volume is

E. 5.34
$$V_{sludge} = \frac{W_{sludge}}{65}$$

Example: In the example considered thus far (50 pounds of cow manure mixed with 20 pounds of horse manure, with an average moisture of 85.5 percent, a $\%VS$ of 80 percent, and a VS_{total} of 8.16 pounds, digested for 185 days), how much sludge will be produced?

Solution: The amount of sludge solids produced due to incoming solids is

$$W_1 = W_r \times (1 - M) \times \left[1 - (0.5)\left(\frac{\%VS}{100}\right) \right]$$

$$= 70 \times (1 - 0.855) \times \left[1 - (0.5)\left(\frac{80}{100}\right) \right]$$

$$= 70 \times 0.145 \times [1 - (0.5 \times 0.8)]$$

$$= 70 \times 0.145 \times 0.6 = 6.09 \; lb$$

The biodegradable COD is given by

$$COD = 0.75 VS_{total}$$
$$= 0.75 \times 8.16$$
$$= 6.12 \; lb$$

The sludge solids due to bacteria are

$$W_2 = \frac{0.04 \times COD}{1 + (0.015 \times DT)}$$
$$= \frac{0.04 \times 6.12}{1 + (0.015 \times 185)}$$
$$= \frac{0.245}{3.775}$$
$$= 0.065 \; lb$$

The total weight of sludge solids is

$$W_{ss} = W_1 + W_2$$
$$= 6.09 + 0.065$$
$$= 6.155 \; lb$$

The total weight of sludge is

$$W_{sludge} = 10 W_{ss}$$
$$= 10 \times 6.155$$
$$= 61.55 \; lb$$

The total volume of the sludge is

$$V_{sludge} = \frac{W_{sludge}}{65}$$
$$= \frac{61.55}{65}$$
$$= 0.947 \; ft^3 = 7.1 \; gal$$

The above figures are for a single load in one day. If the digester is run continuously with 70 pounds of combined manure a day, the production figures represent production per day (for removal techniques, see "Operation and Types of Digesters"). And depending on the degree of agitation, the digestion period, and other factors, poor separation of the sludge and supernatant may occur. This larger volume of dilute sludge will require more labor to produce usable fertilizer.

Containing nitrogen (principally as ammonium ion NH_4), phosphorus, potassium, and trace elements, the digested sludge is an excellent fertilizer—it has a higher quality than the digested sludge from sewage plants, which use very dilute waste. It is also a very good soil conditioner. Recently, ammonium has been found to be superior to nitrate (an oxidized form of nitrogen and a standard nitrogen fertilizer) since it adsorbs well to soil particles and is therefore not as easily leached away, a serious problem with nitrate fertilizers. When exposed to air, the nitrogen in sludge is lost by the evaporation of ammonia (NH_3). Adsorption to soil particles can prevent this evaporative loss, and so the fresh sludge should be blended or mixed into the soil by shovel, fork, or tilling. If not used promptly, it should be stored in a covered container, or else stored temporarily in a hole in the ground and covered with a thick layer of straw.

The capacity of soils to take up sludge varies considerably. For example, sludge has to be spread more thinly on clay soils than on loamy soils, at least until the soil structure is improved. In any case, the soil should not be allowed to become waterlogged; waterlogging prevents aerobic microorganisms and processes from eliminating any disease-producing organisms which might not have been destroyed in the digester (if human waste was used).

Digested sludges produced from human waste should be used with some caution. Though the area is not well studied and no firm information is available, it is suggested by K. Gilbert (see Bibliography) that when batch digestion is carried out, a digestion period of at least three months is desirable so that adequate destruction of pathogenic organisms and parasites occurs. However, the minimum digestion period required for adequate sanitation has not yet been definitely demonstrated. And since mixing occurs in a continuous-flow digester, there is no way to insure that all introduced material will undergo a lengthy digestion period.

Incorporation of the sludge into the soil provides a set of conditions unfavorable for pathogenic organisms that thrive in the human body, but common sense dictates that sludge should not be used on soil growing food (excluding orchards) to be eaten raw. The fertilization of these soils with sludge should be done several months before planting and preferably used on land not to be cultivated for at least a year to insure complete exposure to aerobic conditions.

Digestibility of Algae

Because of a growing interest in the subject, we include a few separate remarks about algae. Difficulty has been encountered in the anaerobic digestion of algae. This is due to several factors. Firstly, algal material is highly proteinaceous. As a result, high ammonia concentrations arise in the culture media, pH increases, and bacterial activity decreases. Other problems arise due to the resistance of living algal cells to bacterial attacks. However, if algae is not the only feed source (mix it with manure, for example) for the digester, these problems virtually disappear. Algae also is a good source of carbon for balancing the nutrients of your slurry.

Further promising aspects of algae digestion are that alum-flocculated algae (see "Harvesting and Processing of Algae" in this chapter) digest just as well as algae that do not contain the 4 percent inorganic aluminum. Detention times as short as 11 days are possible, and variation of the detention time from 11 to 30 days has little effect on gas production. Loading rates can be as high as 0.18

pounds of volatile solids per cubic foot of digester capacity per day without deleterious effects. Digesters using algae also are much less affected by variations in loading rates.

For raw sewage sludge, there are 9.2 to 9.9 cubic feet of gas produced per pound of volatile matter introduced. For algae at mesophilic temperatures, only 6.1 to 7.0 cubic feet of gas is produced per pound of volatile solids.

The sludge produced by algae has undesirable characteristics due to the fact that it is not completely digested. There is an odor problem not encountered in sewage sludges. The algal sludge is highly colloidal and gelatinous. As a result, it dewaters poorly and disposal becomes a problem.

The use of algae to capture energy from the digester supernatant and the sun has some future possibilities (see "Oxidation Ponds"). Major problems now involve the conversion of energy stored in algae to usable forms. Digestion seems marginally applicable to such conversions.

Summary of Methodology

So far we have considered the various aspects of digester design separately. Now if we are to pull everything together, we can summarize the design process in a series of steps as follows:

1. Knowing the daily weight of available wastes to be used as digester feed, calculate the characteristics of the waste mixture, W_{mix}, $\%M_{mix}$, VS_{mix}, using Tables 5.4 through 5.7.

2. Calculate the C/N ratio for the mixed waste and make any adjustments which are necessary to achieve a reasonably balanced diet ($C/N = 30{:}1$ optimal).

3. Compute the COD, choose a projected digestion temperature, and then compute a minimum solids retention time.

4. Pick a safety factor appropriate to the situation and compute the detention time and then the volume of the digester.

5. Make your design decisions about the nature of your digester (one-tank or two-tank, fixed-cover or floating-cover, etc.).

6. Estimate the daily rate of gas production from VS_{total}, subtract gas necessary to heat tank (if applicable), and size collection or storage tank.

Indications of Poor Performance and How to Avoid It

A good indication of poor performance is the amount and quality of bio-gas your digester produces. If gas production is well below the value calculated using VS_{total}, the digestion is not proceeding at the optimum rate. When the carbon dioxide (CO_2) content of the bio-gas exceeds 50 percent, the digester is performing poorly. In both cases, corrections can be made to improve the digester operation.

The percentage of CO_2 in your bio-gas can be found either by devising a homemade gas analysis unit or by purchasing a commercial kit. A rather simple, easy-to-use manual gas analyzer is made by the Brenton Equipment Company (P.O. Box 34300, San Francisco, California 94134), called the Bacharach Duplex Kit. This analyzer is available in a form for measuring CO_2 in the 0 to 60 percent range, perfect for digester analysis.

If you prefer to devise a system for yourself, you will need some way of measuring the gas volume. Displacement of water inside a container of known volume can be employed if the container is marked at different volume capacities. If a known volume of bio-gas is bubbled through a lime solution, the carbon dioxide of the bio-gas will react with the lime and thus will be removed from the bio-gas mixture. If the volume of the gas remaining after bubbling through the lime solution is measured, the percentage of carbon dioxide in the bio-gas mixture is given by

$$\text{E. 5.35} \quad \%CO_2 = \frac{V_{bb} - V_{ab}}{V_{bb}} \times 100$$

where V_{bb} equals the volume of bio-gas before bubbling through lime and V_{ab} equals the volume after bubbling.

Factors that cause poor digester performance or even complete failure include:

1. Sudden change in temperature (either due to climatic changes or failure of the heating system if one is used).

2. Sudden change in the rate of loading (how fast raw materials are introduced into the digester).

3. Sudden change in the nature of raw materials (materials or mixtures of raw materials other than what is routinely added).

4. Presence of toxic materials.

5. Extreme drop in pH (the digester has become acidic).

6. Slow bacterial growth during the start-up (especially important at initial stages of operation).

In case of poor performance or failure, the following steps should be followed:

1. Provide pH control.

2. Determine the cause of the upset: improper environmental conditions (pH, temperature); nutrient insufficiencies (C/N ratio, phosphorus); or toxic materials present (limonene, heavy metals, sulfides).

3. Correct the cause of the imbalance.

Poor operation can cause foul odors in the bio-gas, sludge, and supernatant. With proper and careful operation, such problems are minimized. The case of poor performance and failure is a whole study in itself and hardly enough material can be presented here on the subject. P.L. McCarty (see Bibliography) gives a good review that is concerned mainly with sewage-treatment digesters, but also is applicable in every case.

Safety Considerations

Methane/air mixtures are explosive when methane is present in 5 to 15 percent by volume. In an atmosphere of an inert gas (such as the carbon dioxide in bio-gas), oxygen must be present at least to the extent of about 13 percent before an explosion can occur. Obviously, you must take precautions to prevent explosive mixtures from occurring. Although no accidents have been reported in the literature for small digestion units (they rarely are), it is highly advisable that the entire gas-handling system—piping, valves, storage tank, and so on—be designed with the utmost care. You should give special consideration to any possible leaks that might develop at any point of gas transport or storage. Needless to say, methane is merely another name for the natural gas commonly used for home cooking and heating. It therefore should be handled and used with the same caution. There are numerous examples of asphyxiation and death due to gas leakage from stoves and other household devices.

How supernatant and sludge are used becomes critical when human excreta are used as raw materials. Very little is known about the fate of pathogenic organisms during an anaerobic digestion process. The direct application of sludge and supernatant as fertilizer material is not recommended on vegetables or any other plants which are consumed by humans. Using them in orchards is quite safe, however. If no human excreta are used, both sludge and supernatant are safe for use anywhere as fertilizer material. In the case of pig manure, the precautions stated for human excreta apply, since certain pathogens common to pigs are transmittable to humans.

In case the water table is near the surface of application, sludge and supernatant should not be used as fertilizer but rather transported where there is no possibility of the sludge and/or supernatant leaching through soils into the groundwater. If this is not possible, provisions should be made for drying these products in impermeable basins and using the reulting dry solids in a manner that avoids groundwater contamination.

Final Thoughts

Your decision to build or not to build a methane digester ultimately will be based upon an analysis of the costs and benefits to you and your willingness to alter your lifestyle sufficiently to be compatible with the day-to-day operation of a digester. If you construct a digester, it should be planned and designed in a manner that takes into consideration the potential impacts—visual, physical, and chemical—on the environment. A digester potentially can free you from total dependence on your local utility company, but it surely will tie you to the routine maintenance and operation of the digester itself. Digesters are not for everyone, but if they fit into your lifestyle, we wish you well and hope that you produce the best gas around!

Other Waste-Handling Techniques

In the first section we considered the use of a methane digester as both a waste-handling technique and as a potential waste-to-resource converter. But a digester does not fit into everyone's plans and alternative approaches to waste handling must be considered. Several alternatives are explored in this section, including recycling greywater, outhouses, septic tanks, oxidation ponds, and waterless toilets such as the Clivus Multrum. Composting is also an excellent technique; it is discussed at some length in Chapter 7.

The types of wastes considered are those commonly produced by any normal household: human excreta, food wastes, etc. Solid wastes such as paper, plastics, and wood are not considered here. The type of setting where these alternative waste-handling techniques might be used is more rural than urban. We assume that sewer hook-ups are generally unavailable, but that land availability is not a problem. The one exception is the waterless toilet, which is being used successfully in urban settings as described in *The Integral Urban House* (Farallones Institute).

Before moving on to a discussion of specifics, it is worth taking a few moments to look at the current state of affairs regarding household wastes. Tables 5.9 and 5.10 summarize data on the average waste concentration and volume generated by present methods of disposal using a water-carried sewage system. Note that a family of four requires on the order of 50 gallons of water per person per day, most of which ends up as wastewater; if we somehow can utilize the toilet in a manner which does not require water, we will have saved about 40 percent of our normal water requirements. Alternatively, if we can recycle or reuse the greywater portion of our wastewater for irrigation of gardens or lawns, we could obtain substantial savings in water. Moreover, since it is easier to treat concentrated wastes, a good portion of our waste-handling problems are then also solved.

Greywater Systems

Domestic wastewater is made up of two parts, *blackwater*, referring to all wastewater from toilets carrying human excreta, and *greywater*, referring to all the wastewater

Table 5.9 Average Waste Loads and Wastewater Volume from a Domestic Household with Four Members[a]

Wastewater Event	Number per day	Water Vol. per use (gal)	Total Water Use (gal)	BOD (lb/day)	Suspended Solids (lb/day)
Toilet	16	5	80	0.208	0.272
Bath/Shower	2	25	50	0.078	0.050
Laundry	1	40	40	0.085	0.065
Dishwashing	2	7	14	0.052	0.026
Garbage disposal	3	2	6	0.272	0.384
Total			190	0.695	0.797

Notes: a. Adapted from "Household Wastewater Characterization," by K. Ligman, et al.

Table 5.10 Water Use in Domestic Households[a]

Use	Percentage of Total
Bath	37
Toilet	41
Kitchen	6
Laundry	4
Cleaning	3
Drinking	5
Car wash	1
Lawn sprinkling	3

Notes: a. Adapted from "Household Wastewater Characterization," by K. Ligman, et al.

from nontoilet plumbing fixtures and appliances in the home. Greywater generally comes from baths, basins, showers, clothes washers, dishwashers, and the kitchen sink. These lightly polluted wastewaters contain less nutrients, disease-carrying organisms, and pollutants than blackwater effluents. Although we may remove the need for a flush toilet by substituting one of the dry varieties discussed below, we still have the problem of satisfactory disposal of greywater. Our approach here is that of an onsite recycling system for greywater, which can save at both ends of the system. Thus, for example, if household use is 1000 gallons per week, and if 300 gallons is recycled—by irrigating lawns or using shower water to flush toilets—then both the freshwater supply and wastewater are reduced by 300 gallons. You immediately save the cost of the reduced freshwater demand but probably won't realize any savings from the reduced load on the sewer because of the tax structure in most communities.

At present, the only accepted disposal of greywater in most health jurisdictions is through the sewer or a septic tank system. However, due to seasonal water shortages and the need to conserve water in some regions, local ordinances are being relaxed or altered to allow selective use of homesite greywater recycling systems. You must remember, however, that greywater is wastewater—sewage—and must be reused with proper concern and foresight. The discussion below will provide you with some guidelines and recommendations for safe and sanitary reuse of greywater, but you must check with your local health authorities before undertaking extensive plumbing modifications. You can find extensive experience and information on greywater systems summarized in *Residential Water Re-Use* (Milne) and *The Integral Urban House* (Farallones Institute).

Greywater Use

If you are interested in considering a greywater recycle system, the first decision you must make is how you will use the greywater. Once you know the use you can proceed to questions concerned with treatment and/or the characteristics of the soil on your property and whether the soil is compatible with applications for greywater irrigation.

Obviously the most cost-effective way to recycle greywater in a home is to eliminate the need for treatment between uses. By "cascading" the greywater in a sequence of applications which can use progressively less sanitary water, we might be able to achieve this goal. For example, water from the shower might be reused in a toilet. Greywater reused in the toilet should not contain organic solids, food particles, or grease from the kitchen sink. This problem is most easily eliminated by not connecting the kitchen sink to the greywater recycling system, but if it is connected, the solids and grease can be removed by several different types of devices discussed below.

One of the oldest and most logical means of reusing domestic wastes has been to condition and fertilize soils and to irrigate gardens and lawns. The use of composting as a means of using kitchen wastes is time-honored, and even today in many rural areas washwater is routinely used in the nearby garden. The use of greywater for irrigating gardens and lawns has a number of distinct advantages: it conserves water thus saving money, it utilizes the nutrients, particularly phosphates, for plant growth that would otherwise be lost, and it reduces wastewater flow to your septic tank or the local municipal sewage treatment plant.

If you decide to use greywater for irrigation the success of your application will depend on the interaction of the soil, the climate, the quality of the greywater, and the type of plants selected for irrigation. Under natural conditions each of these factors is balanced one against the other so that indigenous plants, which are best matched to the soil, rainfall, and climate, prevail.

The use of greywater for irrigation is different from normal irrigation in at least two important ways. First, the composition of the greywater—soaps, detergents, phosphates, sodium salts—can be either beneficial or deleterious to your garden plants and soil. Second, greywater may be produced in volumes and at frequencies not matched to your garden's needs. Although you might not notice anything unusual about a garden specifically de-

signed to be irrigated with greywater, there are some questions you must consider before actually proceeding. These issues are discussed in more detail below, and you are encouraged to benefit by the experience of the Farallones Institute's Rural Center and Integral Urban House in Berkeley, which has been experimenting with greywater recycling for a number of years—see *The Integral Urban House* (Farallones Institute). You will also find *Residential Water Re-Use* by Murray Milne of great help.

Soils

How can you evaluate a soil for possible use of greywater irrigation? Soil characteristics are the major determinants of the frequency and amount of water required for irrigation and the type of plants that can be grown. Because soil is such an excellent filter and treatment medium, it is also the key factor in renovation of the applied greywater. You can not overestimate the importance of understanding the characteristics of your soil in planning and practicing greywater irrigation. Soils are very complex materials; fortunately, the evaluation of soils for greywater use is concerned with only a few key characteristics. The critical soil characteristics and their functions are: the soil texture or particle size distribution, which is a key factor in filtration and removal of water contaminants; the organic content of the soil, which affects its fertility and moisture content; soil structure, or how particles stick together, which affects the permeability of soil to air and water; and percolation and infiltration rates.

For our purposes the two most critical factors affecting potential use of greywater for irrigation are the rate of surface infiltration and the rate of percolation. The rate of infiltration refers to the speed with which water moves into the surface of a soil. In contrast, percolation rate is the measure of water movement through deep subsurface soil. To use greywater it is essential that all the greywater enter the soil and none be allowed to leave the irrigation site as surface runoff.

The following factors control the rate of movement of water into soil: (1) the fraction of sand, silt, and clay in the soil, with coarse sands giving highest infiltration rates (Table 5.11); (2) soil structure, with soils having large, water-stable aggregates having higher infiltration rates; (3) organic matter content, with the more coarse organic matter content yielding higher infiltration rates; (4) the depth of the soil to an impervious layer, with deep soils holding more water than shallow soils; (5) moisture content, with drier soils generally having higher infiltration rates.

The rate of infiltration can be approximated by a simple test outlined by Milne in *Residential Water Re-Use*. Remove both ends from a large can (at least 8 inches long). Push one end at least two inches into the soil in the area to be tested. Remember that we want to test undisturbed soil. Fill the can with water to a level of about 6 inches, noting the initial water level, and measure the de-

Table 5.11 Size Classification of Soil Particles and Soils by Decreasing Particle Size

Soil Separate	Size Range, μm (micrometers)
Very coarse sand	2000–1000
Coarse sand	1000–500
Medium sand	500–250
Fine sand	250–100
Very fine sand	100–50
Silt	50–2.0
Clay	less than 2.0

Soil Classifications

Decreasing Particle Size

Sand
Loamy sand
Sandy loam
Loam
Silty loam
Silt
Sandy clay loam
Clay loam
Silty clay loam
Sandy clay
Silty clay
Clay

crease after one hour. This is a first approximation of your rate of infiltration.

The rate of percolation through subsurface soil will determine how fast greywater will move through the soil and, therefore, the quantity of greywater which can be applied before the soil becomes saturated. Hydraulic conductivity or permeability is the capacity of a soil to transmit water through subsurface soil and is the common measure of percolation rate.

Soils with impermeable layers very near the surface cannot be used for greywater irrigation. The preferred type of soil is a deep, well-drained loam. Soils of moderate permeability are better than soils with either very slow permeability, such as clays, or very rapid permeability, such as coarse sand.

The permeability of a test soil can be estimated by conducting a very simple test as outlined by Warshall (1979). By comparing your results to Table 5.12 you can estimate the general range of permeability for your soil. The permeability test is as follows. First, dig or bore two holes with hand tools either 12 inches square or 13 to 14 inches in diameter. One hole should be dug to about 12 inches deeper than the depth of the intended greywater irrigation system (this includes surface irrigation systems).

Table 5.12 Hydraulic Conductivity or Permeability Classifications

Permeability Classes	Rate (inches per hour)
Very rapid	Greater than 6.0
Rapid	2.0–6.0
Moderate	0.60–2.0
Slow	0.20–0.60
Very slow	less than 0.20

Dig a second hole in the same vicinity to a depth of about 48 inches. Second, remove any smeared surfaces from the sides of the holes to provide as natural a soil interface as practical to infiltrating waters. Remove loose material from the bottom of the hole and add an inch or two of coarse sand or fine gravel to prevent the bottom from scouring. Then, presoak the hole carefully, never filling it deeper than about 8 inches with clean water. Do not drop the water into the hole from much distance. Ease it in gently. If it is known that the soil has low shrink-swell potential and clay content is low (perhaps less than 15 percent), proceed with the test. If not, let the hole rest overnight. Finally, fill the empty hole with clean water to exactly 6 inches above the soil bottom of the hole (do not consider the layer of protective gravel as the bottom of the hole). The level of water can be most easily gauged with a wooden yardstick held vertically in the hole. Wait one hour and measure the amount of drop in the water level in the hole. This will be the percolation rate or permeability so long as the water level at least still covers the top of the gravel in the bottom of the hole.

Greywater tends to be slightly alkaline, and extended use of greywater for irrigation can cause soil to become progressively more alkaline. When soil becomes alkaline, trace metals such as copper, nickel, and cobalt become fixed in solid form and become unavailable to plants. An additional hazard to watch for is the buildup of salt in the topsoil. Salts are the white crusty substances that build up on the top of soil around plants and on the outside of pots. These salts are carried into the soil in greater concentration by greywater than by most tap waters. As water evaporates it leaves the salts behind in the soil. The buildup of sodium in soil can drastically alter its physical characteristics and can be toxic to many plants. If a water softener is used in your home it will contribute very large quantities of sodium to the water, and we recommend that you not use the greywater for plant irrigation. If salt accumulation is a continuing problem you must alternate application of greywater with tap water frequently to leach out the salts and prevent their further accumulation. Of course, use of salt-tolerant plants would obviate the need to alternate types of irrigation water, but accumulation of salts over long time periods can seriously alter the quality of your soil and we do not recommend it. Finally, the use of soaps rather than detergents will help reduce buildup of alkalinity, and under no circumstances should products with high boron content be used or added to greywater. Boron is very injurious to plants. If you plan on recycling washing machine water, minimize or eliminate the use of bleach. When diapers are being washed, of course, the wash water should be discharged to the sanitary sewer.

A Few Systems

If you have now decided to recycle a fraction of your greywater, you will need to consider the various systems others have had experience with. These systems fall into two main categories: proprietary commercial systems and experimental systems. We do not explore the full range of possibilities but describe only a few of the basic systems here. Details on many other systems are available in *Residential Water Re-Use* (Milne).

A system using greywater to flush the toilet is shown in Figure 5.12. Only laundry and bath greywaters are recycled. Although disinfection is not included there are several types of chlorinators which might be included in the system (see Chapter 6 for details). If no disinfection is included a toilet bowl disinfectant will help minimize health and odor problems. If kitchen sink greywater is to be recycled you will need a grease trap (Figure 5.13) and a filter system. A storage tank is needed on all systems (Figure 5.14) since volumes and frequency of greywater production usually do not match up to use.

Numerous proprietary commercial systems for greywater reuse are now available on the market. The scale of the proprietary systems covers the entire spectrum from simple kits for temporary operation to complex systems requiring special maintenance attention. We present only two types here for your consideration.

The Clivus Multrum Washwater Roughing Filter is a simple trickling filter (Figure 5.15) designed to pretreat greywater for an irrigation disposal system. The filter removes particulates and acts as a partial grease trap and a partial heat sink to reduce the temperature of the treated greywater. Details on this device and its use in a greenhouse context can be obtained from Clivus Multrum USA, Inc., 14A Eliot Street, Cambridge, Massachusetts 02138. Present costs are about $500 per unit.

The Aquasaver System (Figure 5.16) is typical of the more complex systems available. This system processes wastewater from the tub, shower, bathroom sinks, and washing machine. It is not intended to treat greywater from the kitchen sink. According to the manufacturer,

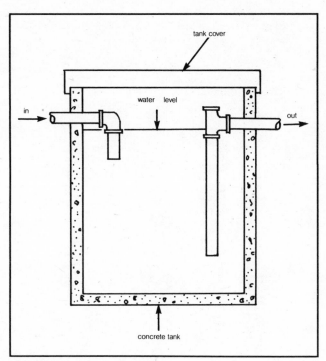

Figure 5.13 Typical grease trap.

greywater recycled through this system is odorless, free of discoloration, and contains no particulates larger than 25 micrometers in size. Maintenance requirements are minimal, including replacement of filter cartridges and clean-

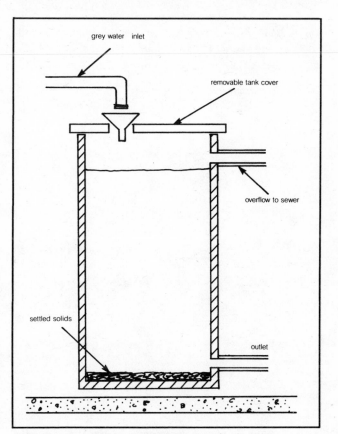

Figure 5.14 Greywater storage tank.

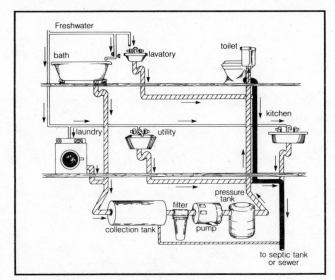

Figure 5.12 General greywater toilet system.

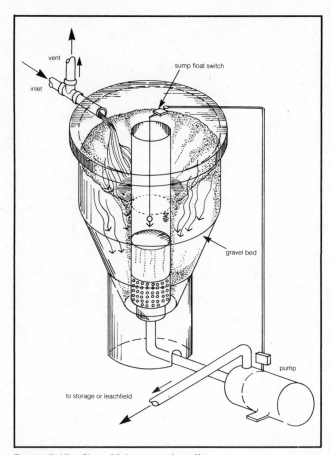

Figure 5.15 Clivus Multrum roughing filter.

ing of the storage tank. These operations must be attended to about every 90 days. Initial costs of about $3,000 for the system are significant but not overwhelming. An-

nual maintenance costs would be about $60 to $120 depending on the volume of greywater. Further information can be obtained from Aquasaver, Inc., 7902 Belair Rd., Baltimore, Maryland 21236.

Other systems have been tried. These systems range from simple storage systems (Figure 5.17) and partially treated systems (Figure 5.18) to more complex systems (Figure 5.19), all of which are simple combinations of readily available components. The best source we have seen on both details of systems as well as where to get components and how to assemble them is Milne's *Residential Water Re-Use*. Happy recycling!

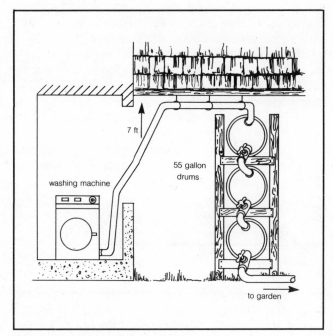

Figure 5.17 Simple storage system.

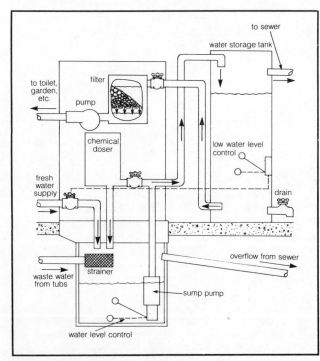

Figure 5.16 The aquasaver system.

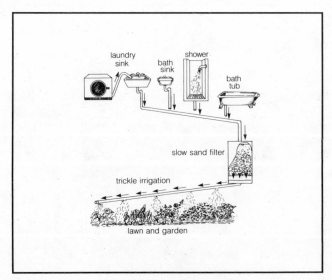

Figure 5.18 Greywater recycling system with filter.

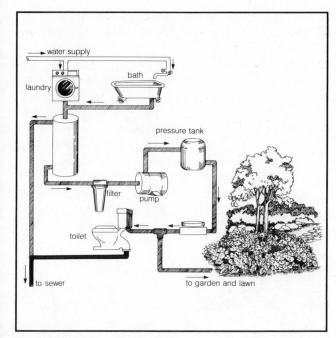

Figure 5.19 More complex greywater recycling system.

Clivus Multrum

The Clivus Multrum waterless toilet was introduced in Sweden some twenty-five years ago by Richard Lindstrom, but, although the unit is simple, inexpensive, and fairly easy to install, the Clivus is generally unknown in the United States. Perhaps the affluent American, being accustomed to water-flushed toilets, is turned off by the prospect of having his wastes decomposed directly beneath him in the cellar.

Public examples of successful use of the Clivus Multrum include the Integral Urban House in Berkeley, California (Farallones Institute) and Naturhset (Nature House) in Stockholm.

The Clivus Multrum (literally "inclined tank") is primarily intended for use in single-family houses. Each unit is capable of handling the wastes of about four or five people. The unit consists of a large container with a sloping bottom (30 degrees), and center and top sections (see Figure 5.20). The length of the Clivus container is partially divided by vertical baffles into three sections interconnected at the bottom. The excrement and refuse chambers are equipped with vertical tubes, one leading to the toilet (specially designed) and the other to a garbage chute. The decomposition products eventually find their way to the third (lowest) chamber, where aerobic decomposition continues. The inclined slope promotes slow movement towards the last chamber while the baffles prevent any short-circuiting—that is, prevent new material from tumbling over the old and arriving at the bottom chamber before decomposition is complete. Approximately twenty-four to thirty-six months' retention time is required before materials enter the last chamber. This

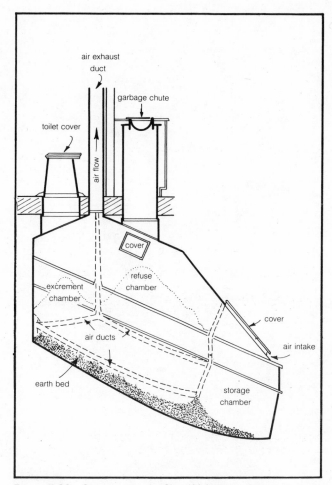

Figure 5.20 Cross section of a Clivus Multrum in place.

length of time is required for the composting processes to proceed to completion.

The Clivus Multrum container has openings which admit air, and the air moves through the channels into the waste mass. The air inlet is situated in the end wall of the storage chamber and is usually provided with a damper to regulate air flow. The air outlet is at the highest point in the container and is connected to an exhaust duct which extends above the roof. The exhaust duct opening should be larger than the air inlet to assure continuous ventilation.

During the decomposition process, the waste material generates heat which, in turn, warms the passing air, causing the air to rise through the exhaust duct. For thorough ventilation and to prevent water vapor from condensing on the duct walls, it is essential that the heat be conserved by insulating the Clivus container as well as the entire exhaust duct. The exhaust duct must not be exposed to temperatures lower than those inside the duct; that is, it should not run through an unheated attic or above the roof of your building. In colder regions, you can maintain a warm temperature in the exhaust duct by locating it next to a heater duct or inside a chimney (Figure 5.21). Also, the exhaust duct must be of sufficient height to insure a proper pressure drop for draft requirements.

279

At least one author contends that a two-story house provides the necessary height, leaving split-level homes with a problem.

Another potential problem with the Clivus Multrum seems to be the presence of unpleasant odors. Some gases inadvertently produced during decomposition—hydrogen sulfide, ammonia, and various mercaptains—are within the washroom safety limits established by the National Institute of Occupational Safety and Health, according to the manufacturer. With the ducts arranged as we described above, natural ventilation should take all odors out through the exhaust duct. However, this seems to be a rather fragile process, subject to periodic difficulties. Toilet and garbage-disposal covers must be tightly closed when not in use to maintain the normal flow of air through the system. Although a down draft should theoretically exist, air entering from an open disposal cover will directly replace (into your home) the gases above the waste. And the channels that are specifically designed to facilitate aeration of the compost do not work if there is continual leakage of air through the disposal lids.

Pests should not pose much of a problem, since fine-meshed nets cover all air and gas intakes and outlets. However, these nets need constant inspection or your cellar could turn into a breeding ground for flies, worms, and other creatures. According to Lindstrom, a year at 90°F generally kills any undesirables in a Clivus; this seems to be an unproven statement, however, and warrants attention before you actually install one.

Cold locales seem to be at a disadvantage because the composting process is temperature-dependent and natural drafts often bring in air of subfreezing temperatures. Consequently, electric heaters often must be used to control the temperature and these accessories increase the cost. You must also watch them carefully: the heat cannot be inordinately high or the mediating bacteria will be unable to function. Additionally, the house itself must be well insulated from cold air drawn in from below.

Greywater cannot be discharged to the Clivus. Lindstrom and Rockefeller (see Bibliography) describe a greywater system (Washwater Rough Filter) now offered by Clivus Multrum, Inc., as mentioned in the greywater section above.

The compost produced by the Clivus has the consistency of peat moss and is a good soil conditioner of the following approximate composition:

Water	19.32%
Nitrogen	2.13%
Phosphorus	0.36%
Potash	1.04%
Organics	24.49%
Ash	52.26%

By using the Clivus Multrum system, human wastes are kept out of waterways, thus reducing eutrophication, and a 45 percent saving in water consumption can be

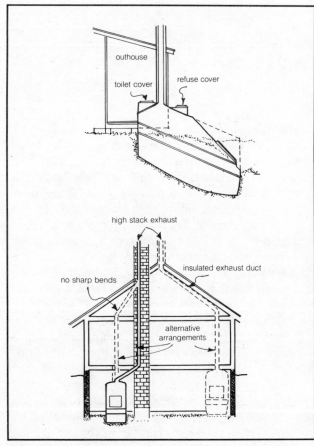

Figure 5.21 Alternative arrangement for placement of the Clivus Multrum.

280

realized since no water is used to carry away the wastes. In addition, the expense of underground pipe networks and of periodic solid waste collection is reduced. And while the Clivus seems quite specific as to applicability, and the process itself appears quite fragile and dependent on many factors which can easily fail and produce drastic results from both aesthetic and health points of view, with proper design and operation these negative factors can be eliminated. Finally, while the capital cost of $2000 to $3000 (including the Washwater Roughing Filter) is substantial, it is not prohibitive. For additional information, write: Clivus Multrum USA, Inc., 14A Eliot Street, Cambridge, Massachusetts 02138.

Other Waterless Toilets

Many types of waterless toilets are now commercially available. Waterless or composting toilets have some very substantial advantages over conventional flush toilets. Besides conserving water and making excellent use of the nutrient content in human wastes, composting toilets reduce our impact on the general environment. However, composting toilets have some very important limitations you should know about. First and foremost, they require a significant alteration of your lifestyle and how you see yourself in terms of your living context. Gone is the "out of sight, out of mind" syndrome present in flush-conscious America. Instead you must accept the fact that to live is to produce waste—human waste in this case. Second, these devices require maintenance, since the wastes are composting in the toilet container itself.

This type of toilet is just making a comeback after decades of inattention. Consequently, many state and lo-

cal health authorities are not familiar with these devices and you need to check with your local county or regional department of health concerning regulations before you invest in a composting toilet.

If you decide you wish to pursue this issue further, we suggest you consult both *The Integral Urban House* (Farallones Institute) and *Stop The Five Gallon Flush!* (Minimum Cost Housing Group) for details on the advantages and disadvantages of the many commercial devices available.

Outhouses

Pit Privy　The pit privy is by far the most widely used type of outhouse, due to its dependability and simplicity of design and construction. The system consists of a superstructure built over a pit into which the human wastes are deposited. The outhouse is built outside and downwind from the main dwelling, and preferably is placed distant and downhill from any water source, to prevent possible seepage and contamination.

A pit privy cannot be used if the water table is close enough to the pit to cause concern for possible contamination. Naturally, the soil type is of primary importance: too porous a soil allows seepage of the waste to great depths, possibly to groundwater level, while an impervious soil such as clay is totally unacceptable because the waste cannot undergo natural filtration. Especially dangerous is a pit over limestone or fissured rock, for the waste can seep into cracks and travel great distances unchecked. In a moderately pervious soil, the depth of penetration is generally about 3 feet; if the groundwater is at a sufficiently greater depth (10 feet), there is little worry of contamination.

Assuming wastes of approximately 2 pounds per person per day, the pit privy is constructed with a capacity of 1.5 cubic feet per person per year where liquids are allowed to leach away, and 19.5 cubic feet per person per year where watertight vaults are used. There are many construction designs, ranging from very elaborate types accentuating comfort, to the simplest, consisting of four walls, a roof, a seat, and a hole in the ground (see Figure 5.22). Of course, you also can choose to locate two or more latrines within the same building (over the same pit) and divide the building into individual compartments, thus permitting complete privacy and the separation of sexes. Brick or concrete floors are recommended since daily cleaning is essential. You also should make provisions to keep insects and animals out of the pit. Complete construction specifications are available in many of the references in the Bibliography.

Table 5.13	Data for a Pit Privy[a]	
Service Life (yrs)	Volume[b] (ft³)	Depth (ft)
4 (minimum)	41	4.6
8	81	9.0
15 (maximum)	150	16.6

Notes: a. Adapted from *Excreta Disposal for Rural Areas and Small Communities* (Wagner and Lanoix). Data for a family of five.
b. Cross-sectional area of 9 ft².

The pit privy has a life of 5 to 15 years, depending upon its capacity (see Table 5.13). When the level of excreta rises to within approximately 20 inches of ground level, the waste should be covered with dirt and the structure moved over a new pit. After a period of about one year, the old waste pit should have completely decomposed anaerobically, leaving an end product that may be used as a soil conditioner in acreage which will not be used for food crops. Of course, after the humus has been removed, the pit may be used for the same purpose once again, thus requiring only two pits for a serviceable system.

Aqua Privy Aqua privies, another widely used outhouse type, have the advantage of being permanent structures. A watertight tank replaces the earthen pit as the receptacle of the excreta. A slightly larger tank volume is needed compared to the pit privy, since liquids do not leach out. A drop pipe extends from the toilet seat into the liquid in the tank; the outlet is thus submerged, preventing any major quantity of gas from escaping into the interior of the outhouse. A vent is provided to allow the escape of these foul-smelling and toxic gases (see Figure 5.23). Care must be taken to keep the water level at a sufficient height; otherwise, in addition to foul odors, flies will reach and breed in the waste.

As with the pit privy, the sludge is considerably reduced in volume through the decomposition process, but, after approximately 6 to 8 years of use by an average family (four people), the tank will be approximately 40 percent full and should be emptied. The contents are removed through a manhole. This manhole should provide easy access not only to the sludge but also to the outlet tee and ventilation opening, both of which may need periodic cleaning; the manhole cover naturally should fit tightly to prevent the entrance of flies and mosquitoes.

Several problems, however, beset the aqua privy. Cleaning water is necessary on a daily basis and the unit is not workable in cold climates. A drainage trench also is necessary since approximately a gallon per day per person must be removed from the tank. Moreover, the drop pipe often becomes clogged and so presents a surface upon which flies can deposit their eggs.

While the cost of a pit privy can be made about as low as you desire through your choice of materials, such

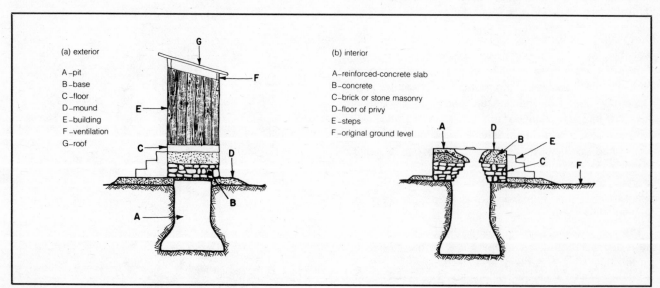

Figure 5.22 A rural pit privy.

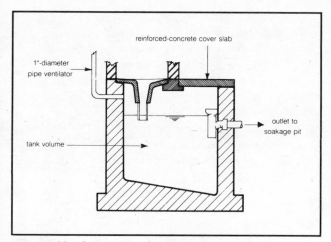

Figure 5.23 Cross section of an aqua privy.

is not the case with the aqua privy. Materials must be purchased for the superstructure, for the leakproof tank, and for an outlet pipeline leading to the seepage pit. This cost is generally around several hundred dollars.

Septic Tanks

The septic tank is a most useful and dependable method for disposal of excreta and liquid wastes in a rural environment. The system is composed of a covered settling tank into which the waste flows and a drainage field for final disposal. After a sufficient detention time, the liquid waste flows out of the tank to a distribution box which apportions it to different areas of the drainage field, where it undergoes natural "secondary" treatment (see Figure 5.24).

Settling Tank

The detention time inside the tank generally runs from 3 to 5 days. The heavier solids settle to the bottom while the lighter wastes, including grease and fats, accu-

mulate at the liquid surface and form a scum layer; the rest is carried away to the disposal area. The solids accumulating in the tank undergo anaerobic decomposition; this reduces the volume of the sludge and lengthens the period between cleanings of the tank to from 2 to 5 years. The effluent has a putrid odor, is slightly turbid, has a moderately high *BOD* (biochemical oxygen demand— the oxygen required by aerobic bacteria to oxidize waste material), and may contain pathogens, bacteria, cysts, or worm eggs. Obviously, it is a potential health hazard and you must give some thought to the design of the drainage field.

As the sludge decomposes, gases bubble up to the surface and carry with them organic particles which are vital to the putrefaction process. These particles eventually enlarge the scum layer. Once the scum becomes so thick and heavy that it sinks slightly, it impinges on the main sewage current; bounded below by the sludge, the flow area then becomes so narrow that adequate sedimentation becomes impossible. Consequently, your tank should be inspected and cleaned at regular intervals or the system will cease to operate properly.

The size and shape of the tank are very important, since these factors determine detention time, effective flow area, sludge space, dead space, and capacity. In addition, the tank volume must be large enough to keep turbulence and surge flows at a minimum, for these phenomena play havoc with the settling process. And finally, since the bubbling up of the sludge gas interferes with sedimentation, it is not uncommon to divide the tank into two compartments in series. In this arrangement, the bulk of the sludge decomposes in the first chamber, while the lighter suspended solids flow through to the second chamber where, with a minimum of bubbling interference, they settle out. Figure 5.25 shows a cross section of both a single- and double-chamber septic tank.

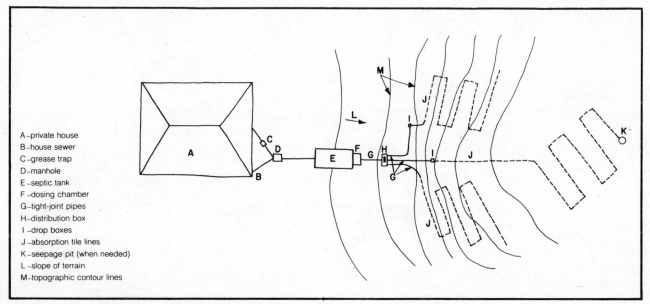

A—private house
B—house sewer
C—grease trap
D—manhole
E—septic tank
F—dosing chamber
G—tight-joint pipes
H—distribution box
I—drop boxes
J—absorption tile lines
K—seepage pit (when needed)
L—slope of terrain
M—topographic contour lines

Figure 5.24 A septic-tank system with drainage field.

The design of septic tanks is relatively simple, and, since septic tanks have been in use for many years, there is considerable tabulated information concerning the volume required per person, drainage area, and other design parameters. Based on an assumption of 50 gallons per person per day, a tank capacity of 1500 gallons is needed for 16 people. Wagner and Lanoix have tabulated the dimensions of a tank to maximize efficiency—for a 1500-gallon tank, these dimensions are 4.5 feet wide, 10 feet long, and 5.5 feet deep. However, their estimate of daily wastewater production may be quite conservative; it is preferable to build a larger tank rather than risk the effects of surge charges, overloading, and turbulence.

There are several inlet and outlet techniques that may be used for septic tanks. The simple baffle arrangement shown in Figure 5.25 is most often used and plays an important role in the process: the depth of penetration of the baffles into the liquid helps control the volumes of clear space and sludge accumulation. Experience has shown that the inlet baffle should extend approximately 12 inches below water level while the outlet baffle should penetrate to about 40 percent of the liquid depth. Both baffles should extend no higher than an inch from the covers of the tank, to allow adequate tank ventilation. The inlet pipe should be 3 inches above water level, while an el pipe is used to allow flow between the compartments.

The tank should be buried approximately 18 inches below ground level and preferably located downhill from any water source or dwelling in case of leakage. Adequate inspection manholes must be provided. The covers of these manholes should be round rather than rectangular, to prevent you from accidentally dropping the cover into the tank.

Every 12 to 18 months, check that the distance from the bottom of the scum to the bottom of the baffle (scum-clear space) is greater than 3 inches and measure the depth of accumulation of sludge over the tank bottom; the total depth of the scum plus sludge should not exceed 20 inches. When cleaning is necessary, you can either bail out the sludge with a long-handled dipper bucket or else pump it out. This excess sludge then should be buried rather than used as fertilizer, since it will contain an undigested portion.

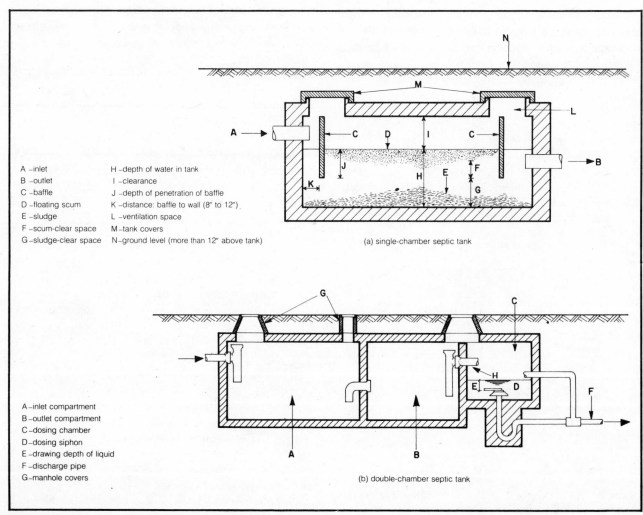

A – inlet
B – outlet
C – baffle
D – floating scum
E – sludge
F – scum-clear space
G – sludge-clear space
H – depth of water in tank
I – clearance
J – depth of penetration of baffle
K – distance: baffle to wall (8″ to 12″)
L – ventilation space
M – tank covers
N – ground level (more than 12″ above tank)

(a) single-chamber septic tank

A – inlet compartment
B – outlet compartment
C – dosing chamber
D – dosing siphon
E – drawing depth of liquid
F – discharge pipe
G – manhole covers

(b) double-chamber septic tank

Figure 5.25 Two types of septic tanks.

Drainage Field

Under noncleaning conditions, what becomes of the effluent after leaving the tank? It is vital that this effluent be evenly distributed throughout a drainage field. The device accomplishing this task is called the distribution box (Figure 5.26), and all its drainage lines should leave the box at the same level. The distribution box regulates the flow among the drainage tiles. If one area becomes oversaturated or clogged, the flow to that area can be either reduced or cut off entirely.

After leaving the distribution box, the effluent is divided among several tile lines laid at a slope of 2 to 4 inches per 100 feet. None of these lines should be longer than 100 feet or uneven distribution will result. Generally, a 4-inch tile laid with open jointing (0.5 to 0.25 inches) is sufficient to disperse an effluent from an average family within a reasonable area. If vehicles cross over the line, vitrified tile, which affords greater strength, should be used. The trenches in which the tiles are laid are 18 to 36 inches deep and approximately 24 inches wide at the bottom. As the pipe is being laid, tar paper or other suitable material must be placed over the joints to prevent the entrance of sand or other substances that might block the line. About 6 inches of coarse rock should be laid on the floor of the trench, followed by the pipe, and then 2 inches of drainage material (crushed rock or road sand); the

trench is then filled to the surface with sand or loam.

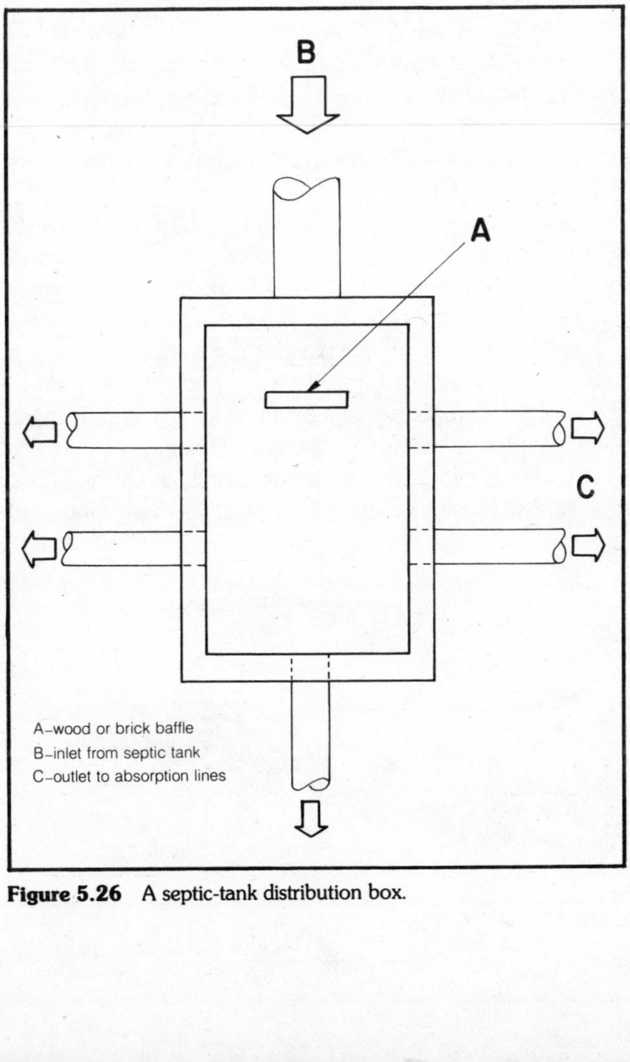

Multiple tile lines must be used as the quantity of waste increases. The actual length and number of your tile lines must be determined by a test of the absorptive properties of the soil. See *Excreta Disposal for Rural Areas and Small Communities* (Wagner and Lanoix) for specific testing and evaluation details. A rule of thumb is to limit the length of tile lines to less than 100 feet, with a distance between lines of at least three times the trench bottom width, assuming a minimum of 6 feet.

If the water table is very low, drain tiles might not be necessary at all; here you can use, for example, a sand filter. If possible, tile pipes should be at least 10 feet from the water table; at any lesser distance, the soil may become saturated by capillary action, thus preventing air from entering. Since the decomposition requires oxygen, we must avoid this condition to operate properly. Assuming that your tile line is properly laid, overloading generally results from poor soil or a faulty tank.

The septic tank, when operated properly, is a very convenient, dependable, and practical manner of disposing of human excreta. Its main drawbacks are that it requires great quantities of flush water, the proper type and size of drainage area, and considerable amounts of materials and labor to install, consequently increasing the capital cost (which, by the way, can run from $1000 to $3000). Also, if clogging does occur, getting the system back into operation can be a sizable and expensive headache. See *Septic Tank Practices* by Peter Warshall for excellent practical information on design, installation, and maintenance of septic tank systems.

Oxidation Ponds

The oxidation-pond process offers a very good low-cost, low-maintenance treatment method for domestic wastewater. Oxidation ponds are shallow basins used to treat wastewater by storage under conditions that favor the growth of algae. The process takes advantage of algae's ability to trap solar energy through photosynthesis and to accomplish this capture in a symbiotic relationship with bacteria in the pond which utilize organic waste as their energy source.

There has been considerable use of oxidation ponds throughout the world to treat raw wastewater, but most of these setups are fairly large. How can we utilize this technique on a small-scale basis? And what are some of the advantages and disadvantages of these ponds?

First, the good news: using an oxidation pond we can dispose of our wastewater; use the pond as an equalizing basin to absorb rapid fluctuations in the flow and strength of wastewater; produce algae for use as chicken feed; under appropriate conditions, provide ourselves with a duck and fish pond or a wildlife refuge; and accomplish all this at a low initial cost, when conditions are favorable and land is available.

Figure 5.26   A septic-tank distribution box.

285

But, in exchange for these advantages, we are stuck with a potential health hazard; with aesthetically unappealing conditions when maintenance is not proper; with possible contamination of groundwater and adjacent surface waters (pollution of surface waters can result from the accidental overflow or flooding of the pond); with the cost of maintenance and harvesting our algae; and, under certain conditions, with silting, overgrowth of algae and aquatic weeds, and the prolific breeding of mosquitoes and other flying insects.

Some of these problems are more easily dealt with than others. For example, the breeding of insects—particularly mosquitoes—can be prevented or controlled by raising top-feeding minnows in the pond (assuming there is sufficient oxygen available in the water). And we can avoid some of the dangers of using raw sewage by using only the effluent from a septic tank or methane digester; thus, we dispose of this treatment waste and yet capture the nutrient value still held in the waste effluent (see Figure 5.27). But under no circumstances should a small group consider using *raw sewage* as a *direct source* for the pond; the health hazards are too great.

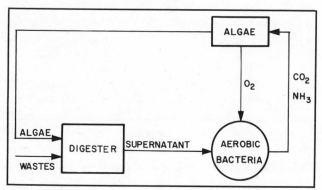

Figure 5.27 Flow diagram of an oxidation pond/anaerobic digester system.

Because of this risk, let's assume that we are utilizing the effluent from a digester as our main flow source for the oxidation pond. We also assume that the size of the community is about 10 families with a total of maybe 40 people. But before moving on to any specific design details, we should spend a little more time exploring some of the process features to get a better conceptual idea of how this system works.

Bacteria and Algae

In shallow ponds, bacterial growth is supported by aerated water and the presence of organic waste. The bacteria aerobically oxidize the waste organics in the water, producing carbon dioxide and different mineral-nitrogen compounds. In the presence of light, algae will grow in the pond by using the bacterial by-products of carbon dioxide and mineral nutrients. The algae, in turn, release oxygen into the water. This process is known as photosynthesis and is shown in Figure 5.28.

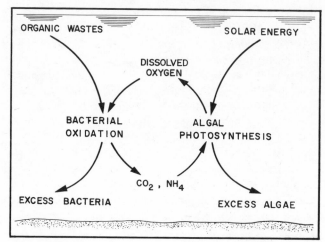

Figure 5.28 The symbiotic process of bacteria and algae in oxidation ponds.

Since photosynthesis can proceed only with sufficient solar radiation, it is obvious that the symbiosis cannot operate during the night. Because photosynthetic efficiency changes with the intensity of light, seasonal effects also are important.

During the day, aerobic decomposition of the waste occurs. At night, however, as the amount of carbon dioxide increases in the water, anaerobic oxidation takes place and the pH decreases (CO_2 in the water increases acidity) if the load of wastes in the pond is too heavy. When light returns, the algae consume the CO_2 and restore a favorable pH for aerobic action. By producing oxygen, these plants stop possible anaerobic oxidation.

Another source of oxygen is a daily cycle of gentle mixing and destratification by the actions of wind and

temperature. The ratio of aeration by daily cycle to aeration by photosynthesis increases with the dimensions of the pond. Since we are considering a pond for a small community, it is assumed that the major source of oxygen is the oxygen produced by the algae. And, since we only consider aeration by photosynthesis in our design, there will be excess oxygen due to gas transfer from the air. This excess may allow the cultivation of fish in the pond (see Chapter 7 for further details).

Because algae play such a vital role, we must pay some attention to their requirements and the rewards they bestow on us. Nitrogen and phosphorus both stimulate algal growth and these two nutrients are important for favorable operation of oxidation ponds. A study of the nutritional requirements of algae in oxidation ponds by Oswald and Gotaas (1955; see Bibliography) determined that normal domestic sewage contains enough phosphorus to support an algae culture concentration of 400 ppm. Nor are magnesium and potassium limiting elements, since normal domestic sewage contains sufficient magnesium and potassium to support a 500-ppm concentration of algae. These workers found that carbon is the usual limiting element. This condition is partially alleviated by the culture becoming basic due to photosynthesis, which in turn causes absorption of atmospheric carbon dioxide, a usable source of carbon. Nutrition seems to be the limiting factor up to 300-ppm concentrations of algae. Beyond that, the limiting factor is the amount of available light for photosynthesis.

The biochemical oxygen demand (BOD) is the amount of oxygen required to degrade or destroy organic material via bacterial action. Figure 5.29 (from Oswald and Gotaas) relates algal yield to the BOD of a cultural medium. An average BOD of 250 ppm can be assumed for our oxidation pond and this would produce concentrations of algae of 280 ppm, just below the limiting values imposed by nutritional or photosynthetic light demands (we will discuss the BOD more fully in a while).

The ability of algae to scavenge phosphorus, nitrogen, and BOD from effluents is highly useful to prevent contamination of water sources close to waste-treatment facilities. During high photosynthetic activity, both nitrogen and phosphorus are removed efficiently, providing an effluent water of a quality generally acceptable for most of the sources into which it may flow. But it is best and most safely used for irrigation purposes.

The quantity of water required to produce a pound of protein by using algae as feed can be less than a hundredth of that required by conventional agricultural methods. Wastewater-grown algae have been fed to a number of animals with no evidence of unsatisfactory results. For example, the value of this kind of food as a supplement to chicken feed is now approximately $400 per ton. The rate of algal yield may vary from 1 ton per acre per month in winter to 5 tons in summer. If we compare this yield to that of field crops, we find that it is twenty times the agricultural average.

The high protein content (more than 50 percent) is not the only important property of the algae. They may become an important source of vitamins, of raw products for organic synthesis, and also of such elements as germanium (which algae concentrate). Moreover, the fuel characteristics of dry algae are similar to those of medium-grade bituminous coal, although their heat content is somewhat less (ranging up to 10,000 Btu/pound). Algae also may be used as a carbon source for digesters producing methane by fermentation.

Wastewater and the BOD

Before we can begin our design calculations, we need to know some basic information about our wastewater characteristics and the quantity of flow. Earlier we mentioned the BOD (biochemical oxygen demand), because wastewater strength is generally measured in terms of the amount of oxygen required by aerobic bacteria to oxidize organic wastes biologically (to CO_2 and H_2O). The amount of oxygen required to completely oxidize the organic matter in a wastewater is called the *ultimate* or *maximum BOD*. For a family of four, the average waste load is about 0.695 pounds of BOD per day, and the wastewater volume produced is around 200 gallons; the concentration then is about 300 to 400 ppm of BOD. After the raw wastewater has been processed by a digester or septic tank, the effluent contains a concentration on the order of 75 to 150 ppm of BOD. (If animal wastes and other materials are being added to the digester, the concentration in the effluent may be higher, around 300 to 400 ppm.)

We can estimate the volume of wastewater flow at about 50 gallons per day per person. In the design we are considering, we have 10 families with around 40 people; this gives us an average daily flow of about 2000 gallons per day.

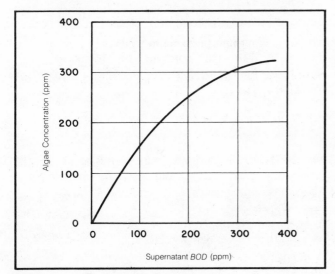

Figure 5.29 The relationship of BOD to algae in an oxidation pond.

Climatic Considerations of Design

In temperate areas, winter temperatures can be low enough so that the rates of all biological reactions (photosynthesis, aerobic and anaerobic oxidation) fall severely, even if no ice cover occurs—little waste stabilization takes place beyond sedimentation. For an oxidation pond, consequently, concentration of wastes in winter remains higher than in summer. Because anaerobic oxidation (the primary source of odors, by the way) is also reduced, we design the pond for the winter period.

By way of contrast, in a tropical area during the summer (temperature over 73°F), stratification is intense and anaerobic conditions and fermentation are dominant in the lower two-thirds of the pond. If winter temperatures are high, stratification is absent and waste stabilization is high. In this case, the pond should be aerated mechanically during the summer.

As we have mentioned, a large oxidation pond receives the main part of its oxygen from the air; in a small pond, the oxygen comes from the biological process of photosynthesis. Concentrated wastes require a dense algal growth (which needs lots of light) and so the depth of the pond has to be shallow to allow a sufficient penetration of the light; dilute domestic wastewater may be processed at greater depth. In order to provide a detention period suitable for effective photosynthetic oxygen production during both winter and summer, certain compromises are necessary.

Perhaps a few broader remarks are now in order. We must design for the winter months because that is the period of slowest biological activity. In the summer, the efficiency of a pond designed for winter months is very low. Without proper variations in operating procedures, the result can be overproduction of algae, a part of which may die, decompose, and produce a pond effluent with a high supernatant *BOD*. On the other hand, if we design for midsummer months, our detention time will be very low (about a day or so) and, during the winter, the algae will be unable to grow fast enough to prevent being washed out of the pond. So, in order to provide a detention period suitable for effective photosynthetic oxygen production in both winter and summer and with some capacity to sustain changes in light, temperature, and shock loading, we reiterate: certain compromises are necessary.

In general, we can note that, for most conditions, detention times should not be less than a day for summer conditions nor more than 10 to 12 days for winter conditions. A pond having a detention period of about 3 days and a depth of 12 inches should, for example, satisfactorily produce adequate oxygen by photosynthesis more than 80 percent of the time (latitudes up to 40°N), so long as continuous ice cover does not occur.

Now we must get acquainted with the design equations and the various parameters necessary for a successful design calculation.

Computation of Depth

We can obtain an approximation of the depth of an oxidation pond by using the following formula:

E. 5.36
$$d = \frac{\ln (I_i)}{C_c \alpha}$$

where d equals the depth (cm); I_i equals the incident light intensity (footcandles); $\ln$ indicates a mathematical operation—the natural logarithm of I_i; C_c equals the concentration of algal matter; and α equals a specific absorption coefficient.

The estimation of $\ln(I_i)$ can be obtained by the following steps:

1. Find the maximum and minimum total solar radiation for the relevant latitude from Table 5.14.

2. Make necessary corrections for cloudiness and elevation (see Equations 5.37 and 5.38).

3. Multiply the resulting value by 10.

4. Multiply the result of the third step by the fraction of time the sun is visible for the approximate latitude and month as determined from Figure 5.30. This gives us a value for I_i.

5. Refer to Table 5.15 for logarithmic values, using I_i as the value of N. The listed value gives us $\ln(I_i)$ for use in Equation 5.36.

The correction for cloudiness—that is, what percent of the time we actually have clear weather and thus available solar radiation—is given by

E. 5.37
$$total\ radiation = min + (max - min) \times \left(\frac{\%\ time\ clear}{100}\right)$$

where minimum and maximum values also are given in Table 5.14 (use "total," not "visible"). This gives the corrected total for sea level. The correction for a particular elevation is given by

E. 5.38
$$total\ radiation = (total\ at\ sea\ level) \times [1 + (0.0185 \times elevation)]$$

where elevation is expressed in thousands of feet: that is, an elevation of 2500 feet would be 2.5 in the above equation. And summarizing from steps 3 and 4 above, we can express, I_i as

E. 5.39
$$I_i = 10 \times \left(\frac{\%\ time\ sun\ above\ horizon}{100}\right) \times total\ radiation$$

Table 5.14 Solar Radiation: Probable Average of Insolation[a,b,c]

North Latitude Degree	Range	January vis[c]	tot[d]	February vis	tot	March vis	tot	April vis	tot	May vis	tot	June vis	tot	July vis	tot	August vis	tot	September vis	tot	October vis	tot	November vis	tot	December vis	tot	Range	North Latitude Degree
0	max	255	685	266	700	271	708	266	690	249	645	236	626	238	630	252	666	269	690	265	694	256	683	253	667	max	0
0	min	210	580	219	583	206	536	188	462	182	480	103	274	137	368	167	432	207	533	203	530	202	543	195	527	min	0
2	max	250	670	263	693	271	706	267	697	253	655	241	642	244	646	255	673	269	693	262	688	251	666	249	646	max	2
2	min	206	560	213	560	204	534	188	464	184	484	108	288	141	375	169	432	206	530	203	530	198	526	189	505	min	2
4	max	244	650	259	688	270	704	268	701	258	665	247	656	250	657	258	678	269	695	260	680	246	650	244	628	max	4
4	min	200	540	206	543	202	532	187	466	187	492	113	300	146	385	171	448	204	524	196	523	194	510	183	480	min	4
6	max	238	630	254	675	268	702	270	705	262	675	252	668	255	669	261	683	269	697	256	670	240	634	238	610	max	6
6	min	193	540	199	530	200	530	186	467	189	500	118	310	150	395	172	452	202	520	191	510	188	494	176	460	min	6
8	max	230	610	249	665	267	700	270	709	266	685	258	678	260	680	263	688	267	695	252	660	234	616	231	590	max	8
8	min	187	495	192	510	196	523	185	467	191	506	124	320	154	405	174	456	200	518	186	500	182	478	169	440	min	8
10	max	223	595	244	655	264	694	271	711	270	694	262	688	265	690	266	693	266	693	248	650	228	600	225	570	max	10
10	min	179	475	184	490	193	513	183	464	192	512	129	330	158	414	176	462	196	507	181	490	176	462	162	420	min	10
12	max	216	572	239	645	262	690	271	710	273	702	267	700	269	700	267	697	264	691	244	640	221	585	217	550	max	12
12	min	172	455	176	470	189	500	181	462	193	518	133	343	161	421	176	464	193	502	176	462	169	446	154	400	min	12
14	max	208	555	233	630	258	680	271	709	276	710	272	710	273	710	269	700	262	688	240	627	214	567	209	536	max	14
14	min	163	430	167	450	184	487	177	460	194	524	137	354	164	429	177	467	189	496	170	449	162	430	146	380	min	14
16	max	200	530	226	610	255	670	272	707	279	718	276	720	277	715	270	704	259	684	234	615	206	550	200	520	max	16
16	min	154	400	159	430	180	473	172	456	194	528	141	363	167	435	177	469	185	489	164	434	154	410	138	360	min	16
18	max	192	500	220	590	250	664	272	705	282	723	280	728	280	723	272	706	256	680	229	605	198	538	192	500	max	18
18	min	146	380	150	410	174	459	174	452	194	530	145	375	170	442	177	471	182	479	157	418	146	390	129	340	min	18
20	max	184	500	213	575	246	652	271	703	284	730	284	738	282	729	272	708	252	674	224	596	190	520	182	480	max	20
20	min	134	360	140	390	168	440	170	447	194	532	148	383	172	450	177	472	176	467	150	400	138	370	120	320	min	20
22	max	174	480	206	560	241	644	270	701	286	734	286	747	285	736	273	707	248	668	218	582	183	500	172	460	max	22
22	min	123	335	132	370	162	426	167	440	193	530	152	392	173	454	176	472	170	455	143	380	128	350	110	300	min	22
24	max	166	460	200	545	236	625	268	697	288	738	290	753	287	742	273	708	244	659	212	568	175	480	161	440	max	24
24	min	111	310	123	340	156	410	164	433	191	525	155	403	176	459	174	471	165	443	136	360	118	326	101	280	min	24
26	max	156	440	192	530	230	615	266	690	288	741	292	760	288	749	272	706	240	652	205	552	166	460	149	420	max	26
26	min	103	335	111	315	149	390	160	420	189	518	158	409	177	463	173	469	160	429	128	337	109	300	90	260	min	26
28	max	146	420	184	510	224	603	264	683	289	743	294	764	288	755	272	704	236	635	199	537	157	440	138	400	max	28
28	min	99	310	106	290	142	373	156	415	187	506	161	418	178	467	169	466	154	415	120	310	99	278	80	236	min	28
30	max	136	400	176	490	218	587	261	675	290	744	296	768	289	759	271	702	231	625	192	524	148	420	126	380	max	30
30	min	87	250	96	260	134	362	151	405	184	490	163	425	178	469	166	462	147	399	113	290	90	256	70	210	min	30
32	max	126	380	169	470	212	570	258	663	290	744	296	772	289	761	269	700	226	615	185	510	138	400	114	360	max	32
32	min	63	180	87	180	126	340	146	395	181	475	166	431	178	472	163	458	140	385	104	250	80	224	60	184	min	32
34	max	114	360	160	450	204	553	254	657	290	743	297	775	289	763	267	696	221	602	176	490	128	380	101	338	max	34
34	min	53	155	72	215	118	320	141	385	176	462	168	439	178	472	159	448	134	368	96	230	72	202	47	158	min	34
36	max	103	335	150	430	196	538	250	650	288	741	298	776	289	765	264	690	215	590	170	470	118	360	88	314	max	36
36	min	44	133	62	200	111	300	136	375	172	444	170	443	177	470	155	438	127	358	88	230	61	180	39	134	min	36
38	max	90	310	140	415	189	520	246	640	287	738	298	778	288	766	262	684	210	576	162	450	106	336	77	290	max	38
38	min	35	120	50	180	103	280	131	365	166	428	171	448	175	464	152	429	120	330	80	216	50	158	30	111	min	38
40	max	80	280	130	390	181	500	241	630	286	732	298	778	288	765	258	680	203	562	152	430	95	313	66	270	max	40
40	min	28	105	40	160	95	270	125	355	162	415	173	450	172	455	147	416	112	310	72	202	42	134	24	94	min	40
42	max	68	255	119	370	172	485	236	618	283	728	298	777	287	761	254	670	196	547	144	410	84	289	56	244	max	42
42	min	24	90	45	140	88	250	120	344	157	405	174	451	167	442	143	403	105	290	65	187	34	112	19	78	min	42
44	max	55	228	106	340	165	470	230	607	280	722	298	777	285	755	250	660	189	530	132	390	72	263	43	218	max	44
44	min	20	80	30	130	80	230	114	325	153	395	175	453	164	430	139	530	95	270	47	173	25	98	12	62	min	44
46	max	45	200	94	315	156	450	224	598	278	716	298	776	284	749	245	650	181	512	122	370	61	238	32	194	max	46
46	min	16	74	25	110	72	210	108	315	150	385	176	455	150	420	134	512	90	250	39	158	20	62	9	48	min	46
48	max	35	180	82	290	149	430	218	582	274	710	297	776	282	740	241	640	174	500	111	350	50	210	21	170	max	48
48	min	12	64	20	90	64	190	102	307	146	378	176	458	148	410	129	496	81	230	32	134	15	48	9	37	min	48
50	max	28	164	70	265	141	410	210	568	271	703	297	776	280	733	236	625	166	480	100	329	40	183	11	144	max	50
50	min	10	54	15	80	58	173	97	300	134	371	175	460	146	403	125	342	73	210	40	130	15	60	6	30	min	50
52	max	22	140	60	240	134	390	202	555	267	695	296	776	278	725	232	615	158	460	87	307	32	160	21	121	max	52
52	min	8	45	14	62	51	158	92	295	141	366	176	460	153	398	120	326	65	190	34	92	12	53	1	27	min	52
54	max	16	120	50	215	126	370	194	542	263	687	296	776	276	720	224	602	150	440	78	285	25	140	16	99	max	54
54	min	6	40	11	45	46	145	88	289	139	360	176	460	150	394	116	312	58	170	29	106	9	43	4	23	min	54
56	max	12	102	43	200	120	350	188	528	258	680	295	775	273	714	218	587	141	420	69	261	20	120	13	78	max	56
56	min	4	35	6	35	41	132	85	283	136	352	175	460	148	390	110	297	51	150	24	95	7	36	3	18	min	56
58	max	7	80	37	170	113	330	182	516	254	670	294	774	270	710	212	575	134	402							max	58
58	min	3	28	4	28	37	118	82	277	134	346	175	460	146	385	106	285	44	132							min	58
60	max	5	60	32	150	107	310	176	500	249	660	294	773	268	708	205	556	126	386							max	60
60	min	2	20	2	24	33	105	79	270	132	340	174	460	144	380	100	270	38	116							min	60

Notes:
a. From "Photosynthesis in Sewage Treatment" (1957) by W.J. Oswald and H.B. Gataas.
b. Direct and diffuse insolation on a horizontal surface at sea level (Langleys per day).
c. Visible: Radiation of wave lengths 4000 to 7000Å penetrating a smooth water surface.
d. Total: all wave lengths in solar spectrum.
e. For corrections due to elevation up to 10,000 feet and for cloudiness, see Equations 5.37, 5.38, and 5.42.

Table 5.15   Logarithmic Values (0-999)

N	0	1	2	3	4	5	6	7	8	9
0	− ∞	0.00000	0.69315	1.09861	.38629	.60944	.79176	.94591	*.07944	*.19722
1	2.30259	.39790	.48491	.56495	.63906	.70805	.77259	.83321	.89037	.94444
2	.99573	*.04452	*.09104	*.13549	*.17805	*.21888	*.25810	*.29584	*.33220	*.36730
3	3.40120	.43399	.46574	.49651	.52636	.55535	.58352	.61092	.63759	.66356
4	.68888	.71357	.73767	.76120	.78419	.80666	.82864	.85015	.87120	.89182
5	.91202	.93183	.95124	.97029	.98898	*.00733	*02535	*.04305	*.06044	*.07754
6	4.09434	.11087	.12713	.14313	.15888	.17439	.18965	.20469	.21951	.23411
7	.24850	.26268	.27667	.29046	.30407	.31749	.33073	34381	.35671	.36945
8	.38203	.39445	.40672	.41884	.43082	.44265	.45435	.46591	.47734	.48864
9	.49981	.51086	.52179	.53260	.54329	.55388	.56435	.57471	.58497	.59512
10	4.60517	.61512	.62497	.63473	.64439	.65396	.66344	.67283	.68213	.69135
11	.70048	.70953	.71850	.72739	.73620	.74493	.75359	.76217	.77068	.77912
12	.78749	.79579	.80402	.81218	.82028	.82831	.83628	.84419	.85203	.85981
13	.86753	.87520	.88280	.89035	.89784	.90527	.91265	.91998	.92725	.93447
14	.94164	.94876	.95583	.96284	.96981	.97673	.98361	.99043	.99721	*.00395
15	5.01064	.01728	.02388	.03044	.03695	.04343	.04986	.05625	.06260	.06890
16	.07517	.08140	.08760	.09375	.09987	.10595	.11199	.11799	.12396	.12990
17	.13580	.14166	.14749	.15329	.15906	.16479	.17048	.17615	.18178	.18739
18	.19296	.19850	.20401	.20949	.21494	.22036	.22575	.23111	.23644	.24175
19	.24702	.25227	.25750	.26269	.26786	.27300	.27811	.28320	.28827	.29330
20	5.29832	.30330	.30827	.31321	.31812	.32301	.32788	.33272	.33754	.34233
21	.34711	.35186	.35659	.36129	.36598	.37064	.37528	.37990	.38450	.38907
22	.39363	.39816	.40268	.40717	.41165	.41610	.42053	.42495	.42935	.43372
23	.43808	.44242	.44674	.45104	.45532	.45959	.46383	.46806	.47227	.47646
24	.48064	.48480	.48894	.49306	.49717	.50126	.50533	.50939	.51343	.51745
25	.52146	.52545	.52943	.53339	.53733	.54126	.54518	.54908	.55296	.55683
26	.56068	.56452	.56834	.57215	.57595	.57973	.58350	.58725	.59099	.59471
27	.59842	.60212	.60580	.60947	.61313	.61677	.62040	.62402	.62762	.63121
28	.63479	.63835	.64191	.64545	.64897	.65249	.65599	.65948	.66296	.66643
29	.66988	.67332	.67675	.68017	.68358	.68698	.69036	.69373	.69709	.70044
30	5.70378	.70711	.71043	.71373	.71703	.72031	.72359	.72685	.73010	.73334
31	.73657	.73979	.74300	.74620	.74939	.75257	.75574	.75890	.76205	.76519
32	.76832	.77144	.77455	.77765	.78074	.78383	.78690	.78996	.79301	.79606
33	.79909	.80212	.80513	.80814	.81114	.81413	.81711	.82008	.82305	.82600
34	.82895	.83188	.83481	.83773	.84064	.84354	.84644	.84932	.85220	.85507
35	.85793	.86079	.86363	.86647	.86930	.87212	.87493	.87774	.88053	.88332
36	.88610	.88888	.89164	.89440	.89715	.89990	.90263	.90536	.90808	.91080
37	.91350	.91620	.91889	.92158	.92426	.92693	.92959	.93225	.93489	.93754
38	.94017	.94280	.94542	.94803	.95064	.95324	.95584	.95842	.96101	.96358
39	.96615	.96871	.97126	.97381	.97635	.97889	.98141	.98394	.98645	.98896
40	5.99146	.99396	.99645	.99894	*.00141	*.00389	*.00635	*.00881	*.01127	*.01372
41	6.01616	.01859	.02102	.02345	.02587	.02828	.03069	.03309	.03548	.03787
42	.04025	.04263	.04501	.04737	.04973	.05209	.05444	.05678	.05912	.06146
43	.06379	.06611	.06843	.07074	.07304	.07535	.07764	.07993	.08222	.08450
44	.08677	.08904	.09131	.09357	.09582	.09807	.10032	.10256	.10479	.10702
45	.10925	.11147	.11368	.11589	.11810	.12030	.12249	.12468	.12687	.12905
46	.13123	.13340	.13556	.13773	.13988	.14204	.14419	.14633	.14847	.15060
47	.15273	.15486	.15698	.15910	.16121	.16331	.16542	.16752	.16961	.17170
48	.17379	.17587	.17794	.18002	.18208	.18415	.18621	.18826	.19032	.19236
49	.19441	.19644	.19848	.20051	.20254	.20456	.20658	.20859	.21060	.21261

Notes: a. Taken from *Standard Mathematical Tables*, 21st Edition, edited by S.M. Selby.

Table 5.15—*Concluded*

N	0	1	2	3	4	5	6	7	8	9
50	6.21461	.21661	.21860	.22059	.22258	.22456	.22654	.22851	.23048	.23245
51	.23441	.23637	.23832	.24028	.24222	.24417	.24611	.24804	.24998	.25190
52	.25383	.25575	.25767	.25958	.26149	.26340	.26530	.26720	.26910	.27099
53	.27288	.27476	.27664	.27852	.28040	.28227	.28413	.28600	.28786	.28972
54	.29157	.29342	.29527	.29711	.29895	.30079	.30262	.30445	.30628	.30810
55	.30992	.31173	.31355	.31536	.31716	.31897	.32077	.32257	.32436	.32615
56	.32794	.32972	.33150	.33328	.33505	.33683	.33859	.34036	.34212	.34388
57	.34564	.34739	.34914	.35089	.35263	.35437	.35611	.35784	.35957	.36130
58	.36303	.36475	.36647	.36819	.36990	.37161	.37332	.37502	.37673	.37843
59	.38012	.38182	.38351	.38519	.38688	.38856	.39024	.39192	.39359	.39526
60	6.39693	.39859	.40026	.40192	.40357	.40523	.40688	.40853	.41017	.41182
61	.41346	.41510	.41673	.41836	.41999	.42162	.42325	.42487	.42649	.42811
62	.42972	.43133	.43294	.43455	.43615	.43775	.43935	.44095	.44254	.44413
63	.44572	.44731	.44889	.45047	.45205	.45362	.45520	.45677	.45834	.45990
64	.46147	.46303	.46459	.46614	.46770	.46925	.47080	.47235	.47389	.47543
65	.47697	.47851	.48004	.48158	.48311	.48464	.48616	.48768	.48920	.49072
66	.49224	.49375	.49527	.49677	.49828	.49979	.50129	.50279	.50429	.50578
67	.50728	.50877	.51026	.51175	.51323	.51471	.51619	.51767	.51915	.52062
68	.52209	.52356	.52503	.52649	.52796	.52942	.53088	.53233	.53379	.53524
69	.53669	.53814	.53959	.54103	.54247	.54391	.54535	.54679	.54822	.54965
70	6.55108	.55251	.55393	.55536	.55678	.55820	.55962	.56103	.56244	.56386
71	.56526	.56667	.56808	.56948	.57088	.57228	.57368	.57508	.57647	.57786
72	.57925	.58064	.58203	.58341	.58479	.58617	.58755	.58893	.59030	.59167
73	.59304	.59441	.59578	.59715	.59851	.59987	.60123	.60259	.60394	.60530
74	.60665	.60800	.60935	.61070	.61204	.61338	.61473	.61607	.61740	.61874
75	.62007	.62141	.62274	.62407	.62539	.62672	.62804	.62936	.63068	.63200
76	.63332	.63463	.63595	.63726	.63857	.63988	.64118	.64249	.64379	.64509
77	.64639	.64769	.64898	.65028	.65157	.65286	.65415	.65544	.65673	.65801
78	.65929	.66058	.66185	.66313	.66441	.66568	.66696	.66823	.66950	.67077
79	.67203	.67330	.67456	.67582	.67708	.67834	.67960	.68085	.68211	.68336
80	6.68461	.68586	.68711	.68835	.68960	.69084	.69208	.69332	.69456	.69580
81	.69703	.69827	.69950	.70073	.70196	.70319	.70441	.70564	.70686	.70808
82	.70930	.71052	.71174	.71296	.71417	.71538	.71659	.71780	.71901	.72022
83	.72143	.72263	.72383	.72503	.72623	.72743	.72863	.72982	.73102	.73221
84	.73340	.73459	.73578	.73697	.73815	.73934	.74052	.74170	.74288	.74406
85	.74524	.74641	.74759	.74876	.74993	.75110	.75227	.75344	.75460	.75577
86	.75693	.75809	.75926	.76041	.76157	.76273	.76388	.76504	.76619	.76734
87	.76849	.76964	.77079	.77194	.77308	.77422	.77537	.77651	.77765	.77878
88	.77992	.78106	.78219	.78333	.78446	.78559	.78672	.78784	.78897	.79010
89	.79122	.79234	.79347	.79459	.79571	.79682	.79794	.79906	.80017	.80128
90	6.80239	.80351	.80461	.80572	.80683	.80793	.80904	.81014	.81124	.81235
91	.81344	.81454	.81564	.81674	.81783	.81892	.82002	.82111	.82220	.82329
92	.82437	.82546	.82655	.82763	.82871	.82979	.83087	.83195	.83303	.83411
93	.83518	.83626	.83733	.83841	.83948	.84055	.84162	.84268	.84375	.84482
94	.84588	.84694	.84801	.84907	.85013	.85118	.85224	.85330	.85435	.85541
95	.85646	.85751	.85857	.85961	.86066	.86171	.86276	.86380	.86485	.86589
96	.86693	.86797	.86901	.87005	.87109	.87213	.87316	.87420	.87523	.87626
97	.87730	.87833	.87936	.88038	.88141	.88244	.88346	.88449	.88551	.88653
98	.88755	.88857	.88959	.89061	.89163	.89264	.89366	.89467	.89568	.89669
99	.89770	.89871	.89972	.90073	.90174	.90274	.90375	.90475	.90575	.90675

Example: N = 92 ln(92) = 4.52179   N = 403 ln(403) = 5.99894

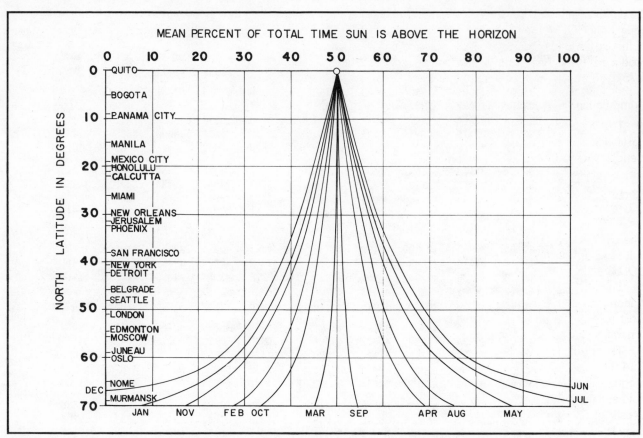

Figure 5.30 The mean percent total time the sun is above the horizon as a function of latitude for the northern hemisphere.

It also turns out that we have available figures for C_c and α: C_c is usually from 100 to 300 ppm; α is generally taken to be 0.0015. So, let's try an example to get a feel for all these equations and numbers.

Example: Designing for winter temperatures, we want to estimate the depth of an oxidation pond to be built near San Francisco (latitude 37°N) at an elevation of 1000 feet with clear weather 50 percent of the time in December.

Solution: From Table 5.14, we get maximum total radiation equals 290 Langleys per day and the minimum total radiation equals 111 Langleys per day. Using Equation 5.37 to correct for clear weather only 50 percent of the time, we find

$$total\ radiation = 111 + (290 - 111)\left(\frac{50}{100}\right)$$
$$= 200.5\ Langleys/day$$

The correction for elevation is made using Equation 5.38:

$$total\ radiation = (200.5)$$
$$\times\ [1 + (0.0185 \times 1)]$$
$$= 204.21\ Langleys/day$$

Now using Equation 5.39, we must multiply our result by

10 and by the fraction of the time the sun is visible above the horizon (from Figure 5.30 we see that this fraction for December is nearly 40 percent):

$$I_i = 10 \times \frac{40\%}{100} \times 204.21$$
$$= 816.8\ footcandles$$

If you check for $ln\ (I_i)$ in Table 5.15, you find that the natural logarithm of 816.8 is about 6.705. Now we can calculate the depth of the pond, using 0.0015 for α and 200 ppm for C_c with Equation 5.36:

$$d = \frac{ln\ (I_i)}{C_c} = \frac{6.705}{200 \times 0.0015}$$
$$= 22.35\ cm = 8.80\ in$$

where 1 inch equals 2.54 centimeters.

Computation of Algal Concentration

The concentration of algal cells can be estimated from the following equation:

E. 5.40 $$C_c = \frac{L_t}{P}$$

where C_c equals the concentration of algae cells (ppm; in

292

the depth calculation, we used only an average figure); L_t equals the *BOD* removal (ppm); and *P* equals the ratio of the weight of oxygen produced to the weight of algae produced. *P* has been found to be in the range 1.25 to 1.75, with a value of 1.64 recommended.

Computation of Detention Time and Area

The detention time is the average length of time the wastewater will stay in the oxidation pond and is given by the following formula:

E. 5.41 $\quad DT = \dfrac{h \times L_t \times d}{F \times P \times T_c \times S} \times 0.001$

where *DT* equals the detention time (days); *h* equals the unit heat combustion of algae (6 cal/mg); L_t equals the *BOD* 5.14.

The efficiency of light conversion (*F*) in outdoor oxidation ponds ranges between 1 and 10 percent, with most values in the narrow range of 3 to 7 percent. In general 6 percent is a good approximation.

The *visible* solar radiation (*S*) can be found in Table 5.14. For example, in Sacramento (38°N) in December, *S* equals 34 cal/day-cm² (Langleys per day). Corrections still need to be made for percent clearness and elevation. We still use Equation 5.37 for cloudiness corrections, but there is another formula for elevation corrections for visible radiation:

E. 5.42 $\quad S = (total\ visible\ at\ sea\ level)$
$\qquad \times\ [1 + (0.00925 \times elevation)]$

Example: Consider a small group of 40 people using flush toilets and a methane digester where the digester effluent has a *BOD* of about 125 ppm. We want to design an oxidation pond for the winter conditions used in the previous example (the depth calculation in San Francisco, at 37°N latitude and an elevation of 1000 feet; clear weather 50 percent of the time in December). Let us also suppose that the mean temperature is 50°F.

Table 5.16   Temperature Coefficients for Chlorella

Mean Temperature (°F)	Photosynthetic Temperature Coefficient (T_c)
32	—
41	0.26
50	0.49
59	0.87
68	1.00
77	0.91
86	0.82
95	0.69
104	—

Notes: a. From "Photosynthesis in Sewage Treatment" (1957) by W.J. Oswald and H.B. Gataas. Data determined in pilot-plant studies.

Solution: We can compute C_c by knowing L_t and using the value for *P* of 1.64. In this case, let's suppose L_t equals 125 ppm. Then

$$C_c = \frac{L_t}{P} = \frac{125}{1.64} = 76.2\ ppm$$

The depth of the oxidation pond can now be computed as before from Equation 5.36:

$$d = \frac{ln\ (816.8)}{76.2 \times 0.0015}$$
$$= 58.71\ cm = 23.11\ in$$

Quite a change! The depth has gone from less than 9 inches to over 23 inches. Now we need to compute the detention time (*DT*) of the pond. Using Equations 5.37 and 5.42 with the value for *visible* radiation at 38°N latitude from Table 5.14, we correct for an elevation of 1000 feet for 50 percent cloudiness:

$$S = min + (max - min)\left(\frac{\%\ time\ clear}{100}\right)$$
$$= 30 + (77 - 30)\left(\frac{50}{100}\right)$$
$$= 53.5\ Langleys/day$$

Now correcting for altitude where elevation is in thousands of feet:

$$S = (visible\ at\ sea\ level)$$
$$\times\ [1 + (0.00925 \times elevation)]$$
$$= 53.5 \times [1 + (0.00925 \times 1)]$$
$$= 54.0\ Langleys/day$$

From Table 5.16, we find T_c equals 0.49 for 50°F mean temperature. Assuming we remove 80 percent of the *BOD* (a good average value) from our effluent, we can now compute the detention time with Equation 5.41:

$$DT = \frac{6 \times 100 \times 58.71}{0.06 \times 1.64 \times 0.49 \times 54.0} \times 0.001$$
$$= 13.5\ days$$

From Table 5.9, we estimate the average flow *Q* to be 2000 gallons per day for a community of 40.

We now know the detention time (*DT*), the depth (*d*), and the flow (*Q*); the surface area of the pond can be computed from the volume (*V*), which is given by the equation

E. 5.43 $\quad V = Q \times DT$
$\qquad = 2000 \times 13.5$
$\qquad = 27,000\ gal = 3609.6\ ft^3$

The area (A) is then given by

$$\textbf{E. 5.44} \qquad A = \frac{V}{d}$$

$$= \frac{3610}{23.1} \times 12$$

$$= 1875 \; ft^2$$

or roughly a square 43 feet on a side—a fair-sized pond. Notice that the volume was given in cubic feet and the depth in inches; that is why we multiplied V/d by 12.

Construction and Maintenance

The ideal soil for pond construction is relatively impervious so that there will not be excessive seepage (concrete-lined ponds are actually best). Embankments around ponds should be constructed of compacted impervious material and have inside slopes of 2.5:1 as a maximum and 4:1 as a minimum, with outside slopes 2:1 as a minimum. The inside surface should be sodded as well as the outside; for small oxidation ponds, a plastic coat can be used. Top width should not be less than 8 feet and the freeboard should be 2 feet at a minimum, with more where considerable agitation is expected. Overflows may be constructed at the side. Care should be taken to prevent bank erosion at outlets or inlets if these also are in the embankments. The pond bottom should be level. As a final suggestion, you might enclose the pond to hinder access to animals and children. (For further information on construction details, see Chapters 3 and 7 and the literature listed in the Bibliography.)

Detention times should be kept near 3 or 4 days in the winter and 2 or 3 days in the summer. Ponds should be kept at a depth of 8 to 10 inches in the winter and 12 to 18 inches in the summer. Cultures should be mixed thoroughly once a day, but not continually. These figures assume climatic conditions of Richmond, California, but give a general idea of the ranges you will encounter. Average algal yield under these conditions is about a pound of dry algae per 500 gallons of supernatant from your digester.

Other maintenance consists of elimination of emergent vegetation, care of embankments, and control of possible insects.

Another aspect of the use of oxidation ponds is a reduction in the number of pathogenic organisms in waste. In the case of a single pond, it has been reported that 90 percent of the bacteria are killed during the first 6 days of detention time. But this is for *raw* sewage, not the already-treated effluent of a digester or septic tank. Even though we recommend detention times shorter than 6 days the prior use of the digester and/or septic tank has reduced the hazard significantly.

For those instances when the oxidation pond is fed raw sewage, the only way to obtain a better efficiency figure is to build ponds in series, which takes the waste-water of several thousand people to be viable. If, instead, we try to increase the detention time to treat the wastes longer, we run the risk of creating anaerobic conditions. Under such conditions, mortality of pathogenic fecal organisms appears to be very low. Rapid oxidation of organic matter accelerates the accumulation of sludge in a pond, especially in a small one. We can offset this sludging, which is a source of anaerobic conditions, by increasing the dilution factor of our supernatant input, controlling our algae crop, distributing the load through multiple inlets or through one in the middle of the pond, and orienting the pond to obtain the maximum benefit of wind mixing and aeration. Normally, the water at the output of the oxidation pond can be used for irrigation, or it can be placed in a stream or receiving water, if necessary; but we recommend you have a bacteriological test done on it first.

Harvesting and Processing Algae

Methods of harvesting and processing depend on the uses to which the algae will be applied. For example, a high-grade algae is required for use in a digester, and a higher grade yet is necessary when algae are used as a livestock feed.

Processing involves three steps: initial concentration or removal, dewatering, and final drying. The difficulty with harvesting algae lies in the small size and low specific gravity of the particles, characteristics which give them a slow settling rate.

Concentration can be accomplished most easily by precipitation and there are several means available. Cationic flocculants under the trade names Purifloc 601 and Purifloc 602 can be used to gather algae into a cohesive mass. At concentrations of 10 ppm (at pennies per ton of harvest), 100 percent removal of the algae is possible; at 3 ppm, 95 percent removal is possible. In terms of speed, with concentrations of 10 ppm, 90 percent removal is possible with a 4-hour settling time, while 98 percent removal is possible for a 24-hour settling time. The use of lime to raise pH above 11 causes a gelatinous coagulation of the algae. Use of 40 ppm of ferric sulphate and 120 ppm of lime gives the best harvesting results, but the slurry and supernatant then contain objectionable amounts of iron. Alum also can be used at neutral pH for precipitation; concentrations of 90 ppm give 98 percent removal with settling complete in 2 to 3 hours.

Dewatering, the second step, can be accomplished by centrifugation, filtering, or by use of a sand bed (ranked in descending order of expense). Centrifugation involves far too substantial a cost for a small-scale operation. But industrial nylon filters give concentrations of 8 to 14 percent solids within 24 hours; the speed of filtering, however, rapidly decreases as an algae cake forms on the nylon. Also, a 2-inch slurry on paper filters on a sand bed dewatered and dried to 12 to 15 percent solids in 24 hours.

A sand bed can be used for both dewatering and drying through drainage evaporation. The amount of sand embedded in the dried product increases with sand particle size. Golueke and Oswald (1965) used sand which passed through a 50-mesh screen (opening 0.297 mm); with a slurry depth of 5 inches, they obtained 7 to 10 percent solids after 24 to 48 hours, and after 5 to 7 days the algae contained only 15 to 20 percent water. The dry algae chips then were collected by raking. These chips were sieved over a 0.16-cm mesh screen to remove most of the sand, 2 to 3 percent of the total dry weight. For a slurry of 1.6 percent solids, Golueke and Oswald estimated that a square foot of drying bed would be needed for each 7 square feet of pond area. Although sand dewatering and drying was the most economical of the processes they considered, they indicated that cost increased substantially for all processes as the scale of the operation decreased.

Final Comments

Enough now has been said to allow you to select the most appropriate waste-handling technique or process for your needs—be it digester, septic tank, or Clivus Multrum. You will undoubtedly work through several designs as you evaluate the trade-offs between costs, benefits, convenience, and reliability; these systems are most suitable for a rural or suburban setting. But no matter which design (if any) you select, there are always a few things to keep in mind. Always design from a conservative position—overestimate your needs and underestimate your supply, be it your water supply or your gas or disposal needs. A second point is that when you move to the operation and maintenance of your systems, you must always be concerned with factors of health and safety. The potential for explosion with a methane digester is always present and contamination of a water supply is always possible—proper operation and maintenance procedures minimize, but do not remove, dangerous possibilities. With these few points in mind, you should be able to move toward a higher degree of self-sufficiency both safely and efficiently.

Bibliography

Methane Digesters

Barker, H. A. 1965. "Biological Formation of Methane." *Industrial and Engineering Chemistry* 48:1438–42.

Buswell, A. M. 1947. "Microbiology and Theory of Anaerobic Digestion." *Sewage Works Journal* 19:28–36.

———. 1954. "Fermentations in Waste Treatment." In *Industrial Fermentations*, eds. L. A. Underkofter and R. J. Hickey. New York: Chemical Publishing Co.

Buswell, A. M., and Mueller, H. F. 1952. "Mechanism of Methane Fermentation." *Industrial and Engineering Chemistry* 44:550–52.

DeTurk, E. E. 1935. "Adaptability of Sewage Sludge as a Fertilizer." *Sewage Works Journal* 7:597–610.

Eckenfelder, W. W., and O'Connor, D. J. 1961. *Biological Waste Treatment*. London: Pergamon Press.

Erickson, C. V. 1945. "Treatment and Disposal of Digestion Tank Supernatant Liquor." *Sewage Works Journal* 17:889–905.

Fischer, A. J. 1934. "Digester Overflow Liquor—Its Character and Effect on Plant Operation." *Sewage Works Journal* 6:956–65.

Fry, L. J. 1974. *Practical Building of Methane Power Plants for Rural Energy Independence*. Santa Barbara, Calif.: Standard Printing.

Gilbert, K. 1971. "How to Generate Power from Garbage." *Mother Earth News* 3.

Greely, S., and Valzy, C. R. 1936. "Operation of Sludge Gas Engines." *Sewage Works Journal* 8:57–63.

Kappe, S. E. 1958. "Digester Supernatant: Problems, Characteristics and Treatment." *Sewage and Industrial Wastes* 30:937–52.

Kelly, E. M. 1937. "Supernatant Liquor—A Separate Sludge Digestion Operating Problem." *Sewage Works Journal* 9:1038–42.

Klein, S. A. 1972. "Anaerobic Digestion of Solid Wastes." *Compost Science* 13:6–11.

McCabe, B. J., and Eckenfelder, W. W., Jr. 1958. *Biological Treatment of Sewage and Industrial Wastes*, vol 2. New York: Reinhold.

McCarty, P. L. 1964. "Anaerobic Waste Treatment Fundamentals." A series of monthly articles in *Public Works*, September–December 1964.

McNary, R. R., and Walford, L. 1951. "Methane Digestion Inhibition by Limonene." *Food Technology* 5.

Merrill, R., and Fry, L. J. 1973. *Methane Digesters for Fuel Gas and Fertilizer*. Santa Barbara, Calif.: New Alchemy Institute.

Merrill, R., Missar, C., Garge, T., and Bukey, J., eds. 1974. *Energy Primer*. Menlo Park, Calif.: Portola Institute.

Metcalf and Eddy, Inc. 1972. *Wastewater Engineering—Collection, Treatment, Disposal*. New York: McGraw-Hill.

Morris, G. 1973. "Methane for Home Power Use." *Compost Science* 14:11.

Nishihara, S. 1935. "Digestion of Human Fecal Matter, with pH Adjustment by Air Control (Experiments with and without Garbage)." *Sewage Works Journal* 7:798–809.

O'Rouke, J. T. 1968. *Kinetics of Anaerobic Waste Treatment at Reduced Temperatures*. Ph.D. Dissertation, Stanford University.

Perry, J. H. 1963. *Chemical Engineers Handbook*. New York: McGraw-Hill.

Rudolfs, W., and Fontenelli, L. J. 1945. "Relation Between Loading and Supernatant Liquor in Digestion Tanks." *Sewage Works Journal* 17:538–49.

Sanders, F. A., and Bloodgood, D. E. 1965. "The Effect of Nitrogen-to-Carbon Ratio on Anaerobic Decomposition." *Journal Water Pollution Control Federation* 37:1741–52.

Sawyer, C. N., and McCarty, P. L. 1978. *Chemistry for Environmental Engineers.* 3rd ed. New York: McGraw-Hill.

Singh, R. B. 1971. *Bio-gas Plant—Generating Methane from Organic Wastes.* Ajitmal, Etawah (U.P.) India: Gobar Gas Research Station.

Speece, R. E., and McCarty, P. L. 1964. "Nutrients Requirements and Biological Solids Accumulation in Anaerobic Digestion." *First International Conference on Water Pollution Research.* London: Pergamon Press.

Standard Methods. 1971. *Standard Methods for the Examination of Water and Wastewater.* 13th ed. Washington, D.C.: American Public Health Association.

Taiganides, E., and Hazen, T. 1966. "Properties of Farm Animal Excreta." *Transactions of American Society Agricultural Engineering* 9.

Other Waste-Handling Techniques

American Institute of Chemical Engineers. 1975. *Proceedings of the Second National Conference of Complete Water Reuse.* Chicago.

American Chemical Society. 1978. *Cleaning Our Environment: A Chemical Perspective,* 2nd ed. Washington, D.C.

Babbit, H. E. 1937. *Engineering in Public Health.* New York: John Wiley and Sons.

Babbit, H. E., and Bauman, E. 1958. *Sewerage and Sewage Treatment.* New York: John Wiley and Sons.

Basbore, H. B. 1905. *The Sanitation of a Country House.* New York: John Wiley and Sons.

Baver, L. D., Gardner, W. H., and Gardner, W. R. 1972. *Soil Physics,* 4th ed. New York: John Wiley & Sons.

Bear, J. Zaslovsky, D. and Irmay, S. 1968. *Physical Principles of Water Percolation and Seepage.* Paris: UNESCO.

Bernhardt, A. P. 1973. *Treatment and Disposal of Waste from Homes by Soil Infiltration and Evapotranspiration.* Toronto: University of Toronto Press.

Berry, B. J. L., and Horton, F. E. 1974. *Urban Environmental Management: Planning for Pollution Control.* Englewood Cliffs, New Jersey: Prentice-Hall, Inc.

Caldwell, D. H. 1946. "Sewage Oxidation Ponds Performance, Operation and Design." *Sewage Works Journal* 18:433–58.

California State Water Resources Control Board. 1977. "Rural Wastewater Disposal Alternatives." Final Report—Phase 1, SCWRCB.

Canale, R. P., ed. 1971. *Biological Waste Treatment.* New York: Wiley-Interscience.

Clark, J. W., Viessman, W., and Hammer, M. 1971. *Water Supply and Pollution Control.* Scranton, Pa.: International Textbook Co.

Cox, C. R. 1946. *Laboratory Control of Water Purification.* New York: Case-Sheppard-Mann.

Darrow, K., and Pam, R. 1976. *Appropriate Technology Sourcebook: A Guide to Practical Books and Plans for Village and Small Community Technology.* Stanford, California: Volunteers in Asia.

Donahue, R. L. 1971. *Soils: An Introduction to Soils and Plant Growth.* 3rd ed. New York: Prentice-Hall, Inc.

Ehler, V. M. 1927. *Municipal and Rural Sanitation.* New York: F. D. Davis Co.

Ehler, V. M., and Steele, E. W. 1950. *Municipal and Rural Sanitation.* 4th ed. New York: McGraw-Hill.

Fair, G. M., and Geyer, J. C. 1954. *Water Supply and Waste-Water Disposal.* New York: John Wiley and Sons.

Fair, G. M.; Geyer, J. C.; and Okun, D. A. 1968. *Water and Wastewater Engineering.* New York: John Wiley and Sons.

Farallones Institute. 1979. *The Integral Urban House.* San Francisco: Sierra Club Books.

Feachem, R., McGarry, M., and Mara, D. 1977. *Water, Wastes and Health in Hot Climates.* New York: John Wiley and Sons.

Gainey, P. L., and Lord, H. 1952. *Microbiology of Water and Sewage.* New York: Prentice-Hall.

Gloyna, E. F. 1971. *Waste Stabilization Ponds.* Geneva: World Health Organization.

Goldstein, J. 1977. *Sensible Sludge.* Emmaus, Pennsylvania: Rodale Press, Inc.

Golueke, C. G. 1970. *Comprehensive Studies of Solid Waste Management; First and Second Annual Reports.* Washington, D.C.: Bureau of Solid Waste Management, Public Health Service, U.S. Department of Health, Education and Welfare.

——— . 1972. *Composting: A Study of the Process and its Principles.* Emmaus, Pa.: Rodale Press, Inc.

Golueke, C. G., and Oswald, W. J. 1957. "Anaerobic Digestion of Algae." *Applied Microbiology* 5:47–55.

——— . 1959. "Biological Conversion of Light Energy to the Chemical Energy of Methane." *Applied Microbiology* 7:219–27.

——— . 1963. "Power from Solar Energy—Via Algae-Produced Methane." *Solar Energy* 7:86.

——— . 1965. "Harvesting and Processing Sewage-Grown Planktonic Algae." *Journal Water Pollution Control Federation* 37:471–98.

Gotaas H. B. 1956. *Composting.* Geneva: World Health Organization.

Herring, S. A. 1909. *Domestic Sanitation and Plumbing.* New York: Gumey and Jackson.

Hills, L. D. 1972. "Sanitation for Conservation." *Ecologist,* November 1972.

Hopkins, E. S., and Elder, F. B. 1951. *The Practice of Sanitation.* 1st ed. Baltimore: Williams and Wilkins Co.

Hopkins, E. S., and Schulze, W. H. 1954. *The Practice of Sanitation.* 2nd ed. Baltimore: Williams and Wilkins Co.

Imhoff, C. 1956. *Sewage Treatment.* New York: John Wiley and Sons.

Jayangoudar, I. S., Kothandaraman, V., Thergaonkar, V. P., and Shaik, S. G. 1970. "Rational Process Design Standards for Aerobic Oxidation Ponds in Ahmedabad." *Journal Water Pollution Control Federation* 42:1501–14.

Kibbey, C. H. 1965. *The Principles of Sanitation.* New York: McGraw-Hill.

Ligman, K., Hutzler, N., Boyle, W. C. 1974. "Household Wastewater Characterization." *Journal of the Environmental Engineering Division, ASCE* 100:201–13.

Lindstrom, C., and Rockefeller, A. 1977. "Greywater for the Greenhouse." *Proceedings of the Conference on Energy Conserving Solar Heated Greenhouses.* Marlboro, Vermont: Marlboro College.

Loehr, R. C. 1979. *Land Application of Wastes.* Vol. 1 and 2. New York: Van Nostrand Reinhold.

McClelland, N. I. 1977. *Individual Onsite Wastewater Systems.* Ann Arbor: Ann Arbor Science Publishers.

Marais, G. R. 1974. "Fecal Bacterial Kinetics in Stabilization Pond." *Journal of the Environmental Engineering Division, ASCE* 100:119–39.

Milne, M. 1979. *Residential Water Re-Use.* California Water Resources Center Report No. 46, University of California, Davis.

Minimum Cost Housing Group. 1973. "Stop the Five Gallon Flush." Available from: School of Architecture, McGill University, P.O. Box 6070, Montreal 101, Quebec, Canada.

Mitchell, R. 1972. *Water Pollution Microbiology.* New York: Wiley-Interscience.

Moran, E. 1978. "Waterless Toilets—Modern Home Systems." *Popular Science,* January.

Ogden, H. R. 1911. *Rural Hygiene.* New York: MacMillan.

Oswald, W. J., and Gataas, H. B. 1955. "Photosynthesis in Sewage Treatment." *Proceedings American Society Civil Engineers,* Separate no. 686.

———. 1957. "Photosynthesis in Sewage Treatment." *Transactions American Society Civil Engineers* 122:73–79.

Rich, G. 1963. *Unit Processes of Sanitary Engineering.* New York: John Wiley and Sons.

Scott, R. F. 1963. *Principles of Soil Mechanics.* Reading, Massachusetts: Addison-Wesley.

Skinner, S. A., and Sykes, G., eds. 1972. *Microbial Aspects of Pollution.* Society for Applied Biology Symposium Series, no. 1. New York: Academic Press.

Steel, E. W. 1960. *Water Supply and Sewerage.* New York: McGraw-Hill.

Van der Ryn, S. 1978. *The Toilet Papers.* Santa Barbara: Capra Press.

Wagner, E. G., and Lanoix, J. N. 1958. *Excreta Disposal for Rural Areas and Small Communities.* Geneva, Switzerland: World Health Organization.

Warshall, P., "Greywater Re-Use." *The Co-Evolution Quarterly,* Spring 1977.

———. 1979. *Septic Tank Practices: A Guide to the Conservation and Re-Use of Household Wastewater.*

Wiley, J. S., and Kochtitzky, O. W. 1965. "Composting Developments in the U.S." International Research Group on Refuse Disposal, Bulletin no. 25. Washington, D.C.: U.S. Department of Health, Education and Welfare.

Winneberger, J. T. 1967. "Practical Uses of New Septic Tank Technology." *Journal of Environmental Health* 30(3):250–262.

———. 1974. *Manual of Greywater Treatment Practice, Part I: On-Site Treatment and Sub-Surface Disposal.* Monogram Industries, Inc.

———. 1976. *The Principle of Alternation of Subsurface Wastewater Disposal Fields.* Finley, Ohio: Hancore, Inc.

———. 1976. *Manual of Greywater Treatment Practice.* Ann Arbor, Michigan: Ann Arbor Science Press.

Winneberger, J. R., and Anderman, W. H. 1972. "Public Management of Septic Tank Systems Is a Practical Method of Maintenance." *Journal of Environmental Health* 35(2).

Wolf, R. 1977. "Greywater in the Garden." *Organic Gardening and Farming* 24(7).

Wolman, A. 1967. *Water, Health and Society.* Bloomington: Indiana University Press.

WATER

Water and where to find it

Capture and storage techniques

Solar distillation and hydraulic rams

Figuring your water requirements

Making it fit to drink

WATER SUPPLY

In this section we discuss several alternative water supply systems, providing you with basic information required to evaluate your available water sources. No attempt has been made to be totally complete; rather, emphasis here is placed on very simple systems which can generate a small supply adequate for up to 20 or 25 people.

As you would expect, water-quality requirements vary considerably depending upon the expected use. If you are going to use the water as a domestic drinking supply, then the water must be free of water-borne diseases, toxic materials, or noxious mineral and organic matter. For the irrigation of crops, on the other hand, water-quality requirements are much lower and more easily met. Even here, however, there are cautions you must be aware of; for instance, high concentrations of sodium can be detrimental to some types of soils, causing them to become impermeable to water. The best approach in making a decision on the quality of a given water source for a particular use is to seek out the advice of a competent authority and then decide whether you can use the water source directly or whether the water must be treated. Later in this section we will discuss some simple treatment techniques.

Along with establishing the quality requirements for a water supply and assessing how far existent conditions meet these requirements, you must determine *how much* water is needed. Some typical requirements for different household and farm uses are given in Table 6.1. There is no foolproof method of determining the quantity of water needed per capita. Consumption fluctuates for different locations, climates, and conditions. For example, a person will use less water if she has to pump it by hand. But the estimates drawn from this table should be adequate to establish the basic size requirements for the water supply and distribution system.

Table 6.1 Water Quantity Requirements[a]

Type of Use	Gallons Per Day
Domestic Use [b]	
Household with	
1 hand pump	10
1 pressure faucet	15
Hot and cold running water	50
Camps and schools	
Work camp, hot and cold running water	45
Camps, with flush toilets	25
Camps, without running water or flush toilets	5
Small dwellings and cottages	50
Single family dwelling	75
Farm Use (animal consumption)	
Horses or mules[c]	12
Sheep or goats[c]	2
Swine [c]	4
Brood sows, nursing[c]	6
Dairy cows, average[c]	20
Calves [c]	7
Chickens [d]	6
Turkeys [d]	20
Ducks [d]	22
Flushing floors for sanitation [e]	10

Notes: a. From *Planning for an Individual Water System* (AAVIM) and *Water Supply for Rural Areas and Small Communities* (Wagner and Lanoix).
     b. Per person.
     c. Per head.
     d. Per hundred birds.
     e. Per hundred square feet.

Several additional pieces of information might be useful. First, if you have a garden and irrigate it using a three-quarter-inch hose with a quarter-inch nozzle, you need approximately 300 gallons per hour for this task alone. Sprinkling lawns will require another 600 gallons per day for every 1000 square feet. Another important consideration is fire protection. To fight a small fire you should always have available an adequate "first-aid" water supply giving a discharge of about 3 to 10 gal/min; 10 gal/min is sufficient for one quarter-inch nozzle and a storage tank of 600 gallons can supply water at that rate for an hour.

Once you have made a preliminary assessment of the amount of water needed, you must figure out whether there is enough water available to meet your needs. To answer this question may take more time and understanding than to evaluate the amount of water needed; but until you arrive at the answers to *both* questions, planning cannot proceed. It would be wise, too, to check into what state laws might apply in your area, at this time. Assuming you have arrived at a reasonable estimate of the quantity of water required to meet your expected needs (from Table 6.1), we can proceed to an analysis of the various sources of water supply and the criteria for making the best source available.

Sources

The two basic criteria for the selection of a water source for your water supply are the quality of the water source and the relative location of the water source with respect to the area of intended use. Using these criteria, we can weigh water sources in general terms and rank them accordingly: (1) water which requires no treatment to meet bacteriological, physical, or chemical requirements, and can be delivered through a gravity system; (2) water which requires no treatment to meet bacteriological, physical, or chemical requirements, but must be pumped to consumers (well supplies fall into this category); (3) water which requires simple treatment before it meets requirements, but can be delivered by a gravity system; and (4) water which requires simple treatment, and must be pumped to the consumer (obviously the most expensive). These rankings are very general in nature and your actual costs in time, labor, and money must be examined carefully before a final decision is made.

Groundwater

Every time it rains, part of the rainfall percolates into the soil and is deposited in formations of pervious materials. These water-bearing formations are called *groundwater aquifers* or just *aquifers*. Aquifers may be confined between two impervious layers or may be unconfined, and the upper water surface of an unconfined aquifer is called the *water table*. The water table in most aquifers is not constant; it rises during rainy seasons and falls during dry seasons. Consequently, it is not unusual for a well to go dry during extended rainless periods. Another common cause of a low water table is excessive pumping of the well.

Groundwater is one of the main water sources in rural areas; in earlier times, an adequate supply was the limiting factor in many homestead regions. Groundwater has many advantages as a water supply. It is likely to be free of pathogenic bacteria and, in most cases, it can be used directly without further treatment. Groundwater aquifers can also be used as reservoirs to store excess water. Certain water districts in California use this technique to minimize evaporation losses of water normally stored behind dams.

Locating aquifers is often not an easy or inexpensive job. You can get a good indication of the existence of groundwater by examining the depth and productivity of other wells in the vicinity of your land. In addition, geological studies done by state and federal agencies (e.g., U.S. Geological Survey) can provide useful information. Proximity to rivers and lakes indicates a water table close to the ground surface. But in any case, you should seek the advice of an expert in this matter. Sinking a dry well can be a very expensive learning experience! Engineers have such special aids as seismic and resistivity surveys to help them locate aquifers.

Once a good groundwater source has been located, there are several ways of tapping the aquifer, including wells, infiltration galleries, and—if you are really fortunate—springs; your choice will depend upon the location and formation of the aquifer (Figure 6.1).

Wells

Drilled wells are the most common means of extracting water from aquifers. However, wells may also be constructed by such techniques as digging, jetting, and driving. Special equipment and experienced personnel are required for drilling, jetting, or driving a well.

Dug wells are relatively cheap, requiring simple equipment and little experience. They are seldom deeper than 50 feet, and a minimum diameter of 3 feet is required for construction purposes: all dug wells require a lining to protect the water source and to prevent the walls from collapsing, and usually this lining is built as the construction proceeds. Lining materials may be masonry, brickwork, steel, or timber. The construction of dug wells is a slow, tedious process, and it can be difficult to penetrate some hard strata or layers in the soil. An additional problem is the difficulty of digging far enough below the water table to allow a sufficiently high yield.

Driven wells are constructed by driving (literally

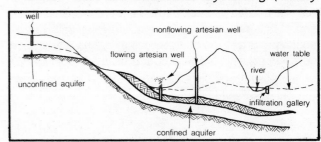

Figure 6.1 A variety of water sources.

300

pounding) a perforated pipe (2.5 inches or smaller in diameter) into an aquifer. These types of wells are typically constructed in unconsolidated materials (soft earth) and may be as deep as 60 feet.

Drilled wells, with which you are probably most familiar, are constructed using special machinery and techniques to drill holes from 2 to 60 inches in diameter and from a few feet to thousands of feet in depth. The cost, of course, is dependent upon the diameter, depth, and type of material to be penetrated. You will have to get cost estimates for specific sites and, in general, it is best to get at least two independent estimates—they can vary considerably from firm to firm.

Gravel-packed wells are very efficient and easily constructed once you have decided to drill for your water. These types of wells are constructed by drilling a hole larger than actually required for the pipe; a screened pipe casing then is placed into the drilled hole and gravel is packed between the casing and the well walls, as shown in Figure 6.2.

There are a number of precautions which must be observed in the siting, maintenance, and operation of a well, to insure that contamination does not occur. Many incidents of typhoid fever and other water-borne diseases have been caused by polluted wells. Keep your well at least 50 to 100 feet from any potential source of bacterial pollution; this means that animals should be kept clear of the well area. Lengthy discussions on details of this subject are given in *Water Supply for Rural Areas and Small Communities* (Wagner and Lanoix) and in *Planning for an Individual Water System* (AAVIM).

All outhouses, septic-tank lines, and sewer lines must be placed well away and downhill (if possible) from the well site. Although bacteria are usually removed from water percolating through soils, there is always the chance of short-circuiting and, hence, contamination of the water source. Wells can also become contaminated from surface water. Refuse, compost, and animal-feeding areas must be situated to avoid drainage toward the well. No chemicals, toxic materials, or petroleum products can be stored on the ground near the well site. You must be sure to seal the top of the well to protect it from possible surface contamination. Since a well can become contaminated during construction, it is common practice to disinfect it before use by adding chlorine so that a concentration of about 10 parts per million (ppm) is attained—at least four hours contact time is required to assure adequate disinfection. After this initial treatment, the first few gallons of pumped water will be undrinkable because of excess chlorine compounds and they should be discarded: use your own taste as a guide, and when the taste of chlorine has subsided to the point where it is aesthetically drinkable, your water should be all right.

Infiltration Galleries

Infiltration galleries were first used over a hundred

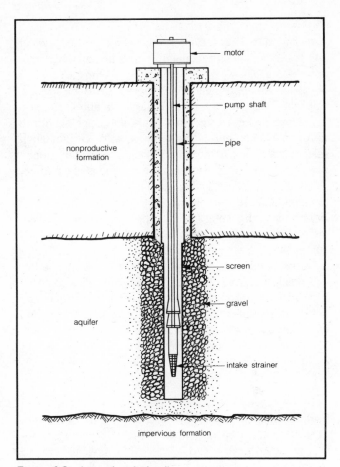

Figure 6.2 A gravel-packed well.

years ago. They are horizontal wells which collect water over practically their entire length and are constructed almost always in close proximity to rivers, streams, or lakes. By digging a tunnel parallel to a river, but a safe distance inland from the shore, you use the sand and soil between the river and the tunnel as a kind of filtration medium for the water as it flows through the soil towards the gallery. If the gallery is located at a distance of 50 feet or more from the river or lake shore, you can collect good-quality water since this distance is sufficient to remove particulates, including bacteria. A typical cross section of an infiltration gallery is shown in Figure 6.3.

To construct a gallery, you must first dig a trench in which it will be located. The trench should be dug carefully and special care must be taken to support the side walls during work. Since the trench must be below the water table, you will probably require pumps during the construction phase. The gallery walls can be built of either masonry or concrete; or, you might wish to use a large perforated pipe instead of actually building a gallery. The length of the gallery or pipe depends upon the quantity of water to be collected and the rate at which infiltration occurs. Careful testing of the potential capacity of the gallery should be conducted before deciding to build. See the listing in the Bibliography under Wagner and Lanoix for details.

Springs

Natural flowing springs can be one of the best water sources if the flow is adequate. Springs are either *gravity-flow* or *artesian* in nature. In gravity springs, the water flows over an impermeable layer or stratum to the surface. The yield of a gravity spring will vary with any fluctuation in the height of the water table. It is not unusual for springs to run dry by the end of the summer, so be careful when selecting a spring as a primary source for water supply: you should know what the minimum yield is likely to be.

Springs, especially the gravity type, are subject to contamination unless adequate precautions are taken. Before using the water from a spring, you should have it tested for bacterial contamination and general chemical composition. Both public health agencies and independent companies can do these tests at little or no expense.

Safety measures similar to those for wells also apply to springs. A typical protection and collection structure is shown in Figure 6.4. Placing a ditch around the spring will divert surface runoff and thus protect it from possible contamination by surface waters; it is also advisable to exclude animals and buildings within about 300 feet.

Surface Water

Surface water originates primarily from the runoff portion of rainfall, although groundwater makes some contribution in certain locales. Those sources of surface water used to supply our needs can vary from a small stream, fed either by runoff or a spring, to a river, pond, or lake. You might also consider systems for the collection of rainfall.

The surface area draining into a stream is called the *watershed* for that particular stream. The geological and topographical features of the watershed, along with the type and density of vegetation and the human activities thereon, significantly affect the quantity and quality of the surface runoff. As water flows over the ground, it may pick up silt, organic matter, and bacteria from the topsoil. In inhabited watersheds, the water may contain industrial wastes and fecal material containing pathogenic organisms. Additional pollution results from pesticides used in the watershed. And the water will contain dissolved salts in amounts which depend upon the time of contact with and the type of soil, as well as the mineral content of any groundwater contributions. Rivers are often turbid and sometimes contain color from natural organic matter; in most cases, rivers should be considered polluted by both industrial and domestic wastes. Water from lakes is usually clearer (less turbid), but is not necessarily free of pollution. Obviously each case must be considered individually with appropriate tests.

If you decide to rely on a stream for your water needs, it is wise to take measurements at various times of the year so that you can evaluate the rate of flow during both the wet and dry seasons of the year. Techniques for these measurements are given in Chapter 3.

You can collect surface waters in artificial ponds and small reservoirs by building a dam. Dams and ponds are also discussed in some detail in the water-power section of Chapter 3. It is particularly important to prepare the reservoir site as it is there described; otherwise the water will acquire undesirable tastes and odors from decaying

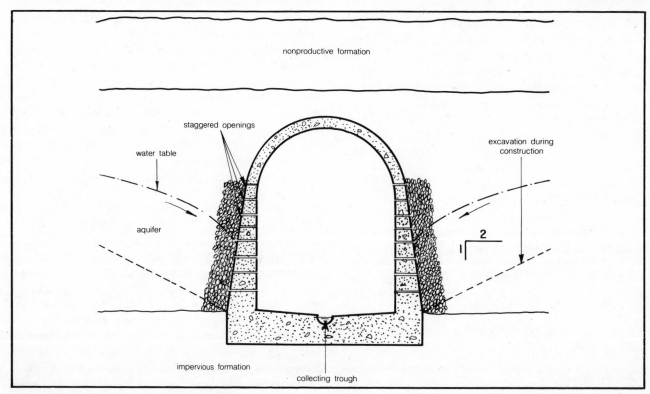

Figure 6.3 Cross section of an infiltration gallery.

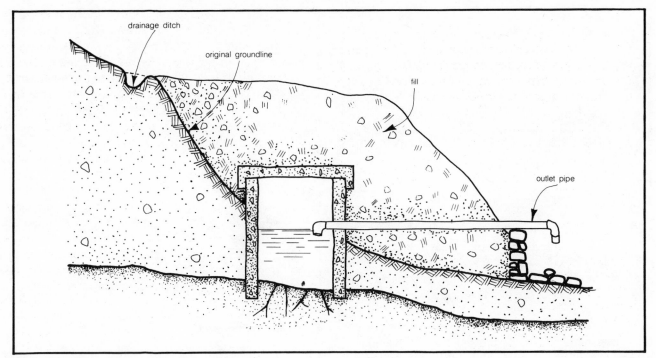

Figure 6.4 Protection and collection for a spring.

organic matter. As with streams, you should check for any sources of pollution or contamination in the watershed area. Actually, you will *always* want to be informed of any developments in the watershed, since it is possible that new pollution sources may appear after the construction of your pond.

Another way of providing yourself with small quantities of water is to collect rainfall from the roof of your home. This is an old technique still used in some rural areas in the United States and quite common in other countries. It is easy to estimate the average quantity to be expected if you have rainfall data for your area. This data is compiled by the U.S. National Weather Service in more than 13,000 stations throughout the United States, and is published monthly (see your local library). For example, if you live in an area where the rainfall is 30 inches per year on the average and your home has a roof with a total surface area of about 900 square feet (this is about right for a three-room house), then the quantity of water you can expect to collect over the year is

$$(900 \ ft^2) \left(\frac{30 \ in}{12 \ in/ft} \right) = 2250 \ ft^3 = 16,800 \ gal$$

Assuming that you may have about 5 percent losses, the net available water (0.95 × 16,800) is about 16,000 gallons. This corresponds to a daily supply of 44 gallons—not bad, considering the *ease* of collection! This amount would cover a significant part of your domestic needs. The best practical guide we have seen on this subject is *Planning for an Individual Water System*, by the American Association for Vocational Instructional Materials (AAVIM).

Solar Distillation

Of the earth's total water mass, 97 percent is in the oceans of the world and about 2.5 percent is found in inland brackish waters. This leaves only about 0.5 percent as fresh water to be used and reused through the various methods of purification. Since solar energy is abundant in many places where fresh water is scarcest, the use of solar energy to obtain drinking water from saline sources is an attractive possibility. Mankind long ago started thinking about making the seas drinkable and Aristotle, in the fourth century B.C., described a method of evaporating ocean water to produce potable water. Much effort has been expended since then to develop desalination methods, but one characteristic of all proposed methods is the significant amount of energy required per unit of water produced. The possibility of using the endless and renewable energy of the sun to produce potable water is consequently intriguing. By the simple expedient of trapping solar energy in an enclosure containing brackish water, evaporating the water (which leaves the impurities behind), and then recondensing the water vapor in a collectable manner, we can have the sun do most of the work for us. In very simple terms, we have just described solar distillation; a detailed discussion of the availability of solar energy can be found in Chapter 4.

All solar stills share the same basic concept. Figure 6.5 shows a basin solar still. The sun's rays pass through a glass cover and are absorbed by a blackened basin holding saline water. This water is heated by the energy reradiating from the basin. As the water vapor pressure increases from this heat, the liquid water evaporates and is condensed on the underside of the roof enclosure, from

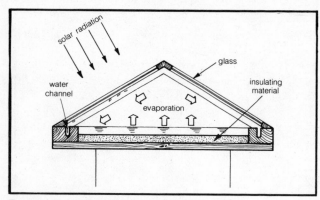

Figure 6.5 A solar still utilizing a basin.

which it runs down into collection troughs.

Fresh water produced from a solar still is best removed by gravity flow to a storage tank of some sort, to keep the mechanical system as simple as possible. The depth of the water in the basin can vary from an inch to a foot, but since the bottom of the basin must be black in order to absorb solar radiation, you must flush out the brine from time to time to prevent the precipitation of light-reflecting salts. A reasonable rule of thumb is to replenish the brackish supply when half the volume has been evaporated.

There are a number of factors you must consider when thinking about solar distillation. The higher the latitude, the less the solar radiation that is intercepted by horizontal surfaces; unless you tilt your still toward the sun to intercept the radiation, it will lose efficiency. You may well ask, "How can we tilt a water surface?" Well, tilting a water surface can be done by providing a porous wick or cloth (preferably black to absorb radiation) on an incline oriented toward the sun; Figure 6.6 shows an example. An inclined still with a wick or cloth allows evaporation to occur over the equivalent of a thin sheet of water as it flows down the incline. The inclined still depicted in Figure 6.7 consists of a series of shallow horizontal black trays. Brackish water overflows from tray to tray and is evaporated in the process. This last variety of stills is less efficient than the wick type and it is mostly used for brackish water rather than sea water.

Yet another type of solar still is shown in Figure 6.8. The parabolic mirror acts as a concentration reflector and provides a focusing effect for solar energy; the resulting high temperatures evaporate water rapidly. These stills must have a continuous supply of salt water to the central evaporating unit. Note that the water vapor goes into a condenser for cooling. Parabolic stills have an average productivity of about 0.5 to 0.6 gal/day-ft², but they are much more costly to build yourself (both in terms of time and money) and are presented here primarily as an indication of what is possible rather than what is likely.

Trombe and Foëx (see Bibliography) have come up with an interesting design of a solar house which incorporates solar distillation for both a water supply and air conditioning (Figure 6.9 shows a cross section). The roof

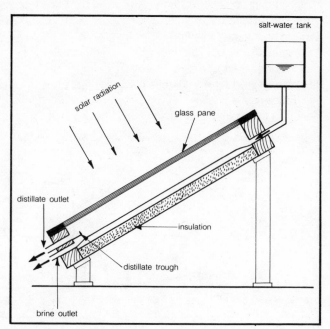

Figure 6.6 A tilted-wick solar still.

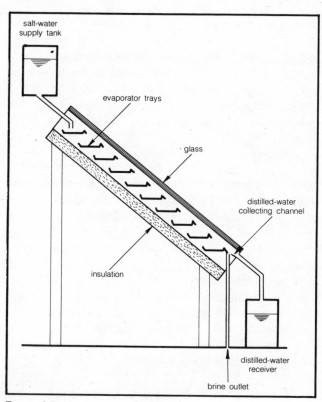

Figure 6.7 A multiple-tray tilted still.

is covered with a transparent plastic or glass, and immediately below are tanks filled with brackish water. Both illumination and temperature can be regulated by increasing or decreasing the surface of the tanks, through movable covers of either the tanks or the roof.

Efficiency and Production

You might think that efficiency considerations for a solar still would not be necessary because solar energy is "free." But when you stop to think about the fact that this form of energy is of low intensity and requires a lot of area to produce a usable quantity of water, it becomes clear that we had better pay some attention to the factors which can give us the highest possible efficiency for our system.

Efficiency is defined as the ratio of fresh water produced to the energy expended in producing it. Two of the important factors, our location and the salinity of our water, we are basically stuck with. Chapter 4 gives information for determining the available solar radiation of your specific locale. Areas with frequent dense cloudiness obviously will cause problems and the distillation process may become practically unfeasible.

The type of still that you choose is related to your particular needs and resources. Howe and Tleimat achieved 50 percent efficiency with a tilted-tray still yielding 0.12 gal/day-ft²; they also claim that this unit is the most efficient design. However, the relatively complicated and expensive nature of this still has precluded common use. Current research is also investigating the use of multieffect stills. The multieffect still is composed of a number of stills in series that have a decreasing depth of water from top to bottom. This stepping produces a temperature gradient which increases the yield of fresh water. But again, while the efficiency increases, so does the cost. More information on this design is available from C. Gomella (see Bibliography).

There are several design features which can maximize efficiency for any particular type of still. Although the exact distance has not yet been pinned down, generally the closer your vaportight transparent cover is to the surface of the water, the greater the efficiency of the unit. And the higher the temperature of this glass or plastic cover, the better the efficiency. Glass temperature should be highest for units having the smallest ratio of glass area to evaporating area and also for those units with the best insulation

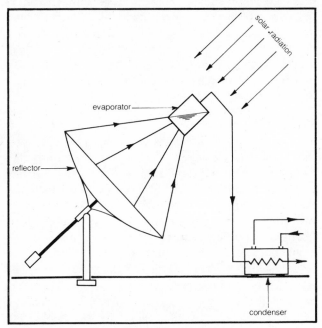

Figure 6.8 A solar still using a parabolic mirror.

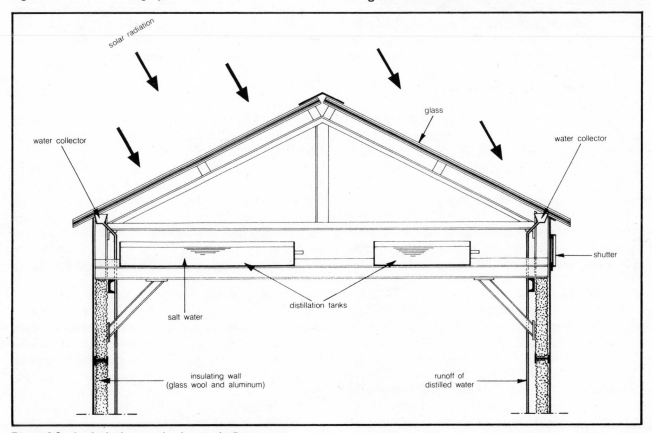

Figure 6.9 A solar hothouse with salt-water distillation system.

305

Table 6.2 Solar Still Construction Data[a]

Component and Material	Test Period (years)	Rating[b]	Life Expectancy (years)	Remarks
Side members				
Galv. iron	3	NR	2–10	Corrodes
Concrete	6	R	20+	
Asbestos	1	?	15+	
Basin liner				
Polyethylene	4	NR	1–4	Cracks
Butyl rubber	3	R	15+	
Distillate Trough				
Galv. iron	1	NR	1	Corrodes
Al. alloy 50/52	3	A	10+	
Al. alloy 1100	3	A	10+	
St. steel 316	3	A	10+	
St. steel 321	3	A	10+	
Cover				
Glass	13	R	20+	
Sealant				
Butyl molding	3	NR	10	
Butyl calk	3	NR	10	
Silicon	5	R	10+	
Insulation				
Polystyrene	3	A	10+	
Polyurethane	1	A	15+	

Notes: a. From *Design Philosophy and Operating Experience for Australian Solar Stills*, by P. Cooper and W. Read.
  b. NR—not recommended; A—acceptable; R—recommended.

under the tray bottom.

The greater the heat capacity of the still, the higher its efficiency. Choosing proper construction materials is thus critical. Table 6.2 lists a few commonly available materials with suitable remarks. There is, however, a sizable amount of research in progress that is devoted to finding materials of greater thermal capacity, and you should check the literature frequently for the newest developments.

Reductions in efficiency also can arise from shading caused by opaque supports or neighboring stills. And if your construction is sloppy, leaks due to insufficient sealing can reduce your efficiency by half. In general, efficiencies of a solar still will range from an average of 35 percent to a maximum of 60 percent.

How large a still to construct is difficult to determine without the context of a specific plan, particularly when considering larger yields on the order of 1000 gallons per day. But in general, for a yield of 1 gal/day of fresh water, an area of 8 to 14 square feet is required; 10 square feet will provide a day's drinking water for one person. When we consider that the average per capita domestic use of fresh water in the United States is 50 gal/day, it becomes clear that a rooftop still on the order of 100 square feet, providing 10 gal/day, can hardly supply a household's per capita demand for water. On small islands in the Pacific, where fresh water is scarce and supply is dependent upon rainfall, the per capita demand is as low as 1.33 gal/day. Solar stills can play a significant part in supplying water to these isolated areas. On the other hand, where a non-

potable water supply is available for most nondrinking purposes, you can use a solar still to good advantage as a supplementary water supply. Another possible consideration is the production of high-quality water (high purity) for special uses.

The productivity of solar stills depends on the geographic location as well as the still type. On the average, glasshouse-type stills can have average annual yields of from 35 to 50 gallons per square foot. Figure 6.10 gives the daily productivity of two solar stills in Florida as a function of solar radiation. From these curves, you can estimate productivity (gal/ft²-day); knowing your water demand you can then estimate the size of the still required to meet your needs.

Construction and Economy

The construction of a basin solar still is relatively simple. Do-it-yourself kits are available for individual stills from Solar Sunstill (Setauket, New York 11733) and Sunwater Company (1112 Pioneer Way, El Cajon, CA 92020). Materials for construction have been improved over the last ten years. For the roofs, horticultural glass, fiberglass, and new hard plastics are available. Glass is highly durable and, in the process of distillation, the distillate will form a continuous film on the inside of the glass and thus will maintain a continuous flow into the collection trough; but glass is also heavy and relatively difficult to seal. Plastics, on the other hand, are less durable and tend to tear in high winds. The transmittance of plastic is less than that of glass, mainly because plastic is a hydrophobic material. The distillate forms beads on the roof which tend to drip back into the undistilled water, reducing efficiency by about 10 percent. However, chemicals such as Sun Clear (available from Solar Sunstill) can be used to produce a wet film on the plastic rather than droplets, allowing for increased light transmittance. It appears that present designs should use glass, but that future designs will take advantage of the low cost and weight of plastic covers.

Polystyrene or foamed glass insulation is optional in the design of your still. Insulation increases material costs by about 16 percent, but the advantage is a decrease in heat loss to the ground (and hence, greater efficiency). For *all* stills, you need a black cover for the bottom of your basin or tray, to absorb the sun's radiant heat. You can paint the bottom or else line it with black earth, pebbles, sand, or cloth. Supports for your still should be kept to a minimum; metal along the ridges or concrete around the base can form shadows in the still and decrease the absorption of light. This is especially true of smaller stills.

Horace McCracken has researched various available still pans. Of the five types—wood and wood-fiber products with coatings or impregnates, thermosetting plastics, thermoplastic materials, asbestos-cement with impregnates and coatings, and metals with coatings—he concluded that porcelain-enameled steel is the optimum choice. It imposes little taste on the water, it is least af-

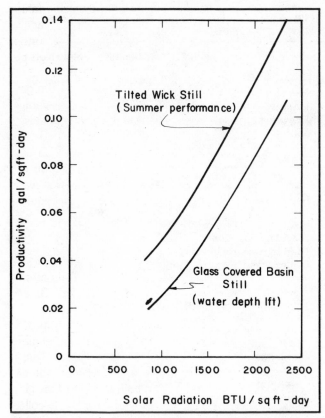

Figure 6.10 Productivity of solar stills as a function of solar radiation.

life, higher efficiencies, and mass production of still units are the necessary general factors for cost reduction.

In the Bibliography are listings which provide cost data for particular designs. William Edmondson, for example, offers a still design with a fiberglass cover and a useful life of 20 years, giving an estimated crude unit-construction cost of 42 cents a square foot (these and all prices immediately following are for 1975). Strobel gives a deep-basin still design of 3000 square feet with a useful life expectancy of 30 years, for an estimated cost of $4.75 per square foot and a unit production cost of $10.72 per 1000 gallons. And Daniels gives cost comparisons for three solar stills that were exposed to the same conditions and yielded equal amounts of fresh water:

Still Type	Life Expectancy (years)	Unit Cost ($/ft²)
Glass-covered basin	50	$3.94
Tilted tray	10	$2.56
Plastic-covered	3	$0.87

Finally you should probably be aware of several general economic considerations which favor the solar distillation process: (1) unit construction is not appreciably affected by the size of the still; (2) power considerations are almost nonexistent, with the possible exception of pumps; (3) solar stills can be constructed on-site with semi-skilled labor and you can handle the operation and maintenance without any technical training; (4) you can readily find the materials necessary for construction and they are generally very durable; and (5) still designs are modular and easily handled by anyone.

fected by the water's corrosive properties (durability of 10 years or more), and its weight is a minor obstacle. In Table 6.2, you should note that durability is emphasized since life expectancy is a major factor in incurred costs.

The economics of solar distillation are for the most part based on capital investment. While taxes, land costs, financing, and labor vary from case to case, nevertheless existing setups cost on the order of $3 to $6 per 1000 gallons. Is it worthwhile for you to invest in a solar still? Consider the following simple example: if a solar still of 10 square feet produces 1 gal/day for 333 days a year, it will produce 1000 gallons in 3 years. Let's assume the still we are considering has a life expectancy of 15 years and we estimate it will cost us $25 to build. It is clear that we are paying $25 for 5000 gallons, or $5/1000 gallons, plus labor and operating expenses to keep our still functioning properly. The usefulness of computing cost per 1000 gallons is for comparison with other sources of water and between various still designs.

Sometimes the costs for a still design are given in dollars per square foot. This unit cost for our example above ($25 per 10 square feet) would be $2.50 per square foot.

The factors that you will have to balance are your water requirements, how much water is produced per square foot of still (in your climatic conditions) to meet these needs, how much it will cost to build a still of this required size, and how long the whole setup can be expected to keep producing at the levels you require. Longer

Transport and Storage

Sizing a Pump

If you have a well or your house is located above a lake or river, you will need some type of pumping device to move the water to the point of use. In order to select the proper pump for your water supply system, you must first determine what pumping capacity is required to meet your needs. The pump capacity depends upon both your rate of water consumption and the size of the storage tank you have in your system. If you have no substantial storage capacity in your system, your pump must be able to deliver water at a rate commensurate with your greatest need—usually called the *peak demand*.

For many years there was no satisfactory method of determining the pump capacity needed to supply adequate water for a particular set of conditions. At best, there was considerable guessing. The guessing now has been reduced to a minimum due to studies conducted by the U.S. Department of Agriculture regarding water use for the home, for appliances, for watering livestock and poultry, for irrigation, and for general cleaning purposes outside the home. It is now possible to determine the pump capacity needed with considerable accuracy.

There are two kinds of water usage—intermittent (5 minutes or less) and sustained (more than 10 minutes). You can determine the peak demand for your situation by adding up the various rates of water demand for all the uses you expect to encounter simultaneously. Table 6.3 gives the peak demand allowances for various uses as well as the average individual-fixture flow rate. In arriving at a peak demand for your pump, the procedures can be divided into three related groups of uses, each requiring a slightly different set of steps: (1) pump capacity needed for household uses; (2) pump capacity needed for irrigation, cleaning, and miscellaneous uses; and (3) pump capacity needed for watering livestock and poultry. As you design your system, you will need to select the group (or groups) of uses that fits your needs and follow the procedures given below for each category.

First, determine the pump capacity needed for your household uses by listing all of your home uses and the peak demand allowance for each from Table 6.3. Let's say you end up with the following list:

Home Use	Peak Demand Allowance (gal/min)
Tub and shower	2.0
Toilet	0.75
Kitchen sink	1.0
Clotheswasher	2.0
Total:	5.75

Make sure that all demands are accounted for, including duplicates (for example, *all* sinks). The total demand allowance for the uses listed above is 5.75 gallons per minute. If you are designing a system for a cluster of houses, use the same procedure for each house; but, after you have determined the demand allowance for each house, divide the total by 2. (Each additional house will tend to spread out the peak demand over time; this division accounts for the time spread.)

Now list all the lawn, garden, and miscellaneous uses you have or expect to have and the water demand for each use. Let's suppose you have a small rural home with several acres available for gardening. Again using Table 6.3, for your estimated peak demand allowance you have:

Irrigation Uses	Peak Demand Allowance (gal/min)
Garden irrigation (3 sprinklers)	7.5
Lawn irrigation (1 sprinkler)	2.5
Hose cleaning barn floors, ramps, etc.	5.0
Tractor and equipment washing	2.5
Total:	17.5

Table 6.3 Peak Demand Allowance and Individual-Fixture Flow Rate for Various Uses[a]

Water Uses	Peak Demand Allowance (gal/min)	Individual-Fixture Flow Rate (gal/min)
1. *Household*		
Lavatory	0.5	2.0
Dishwasher	0.5	2.0
Toilet	0.75	3.0
Sink (no garbage disposal)	1.0	4.0
Shower only	1.0	4.0
Laundry sink	1.5	6.0
Bathtub or tub-shower combo	2.0	8.0
Clotheswasher	2.0	8.0
2. *Irrigation and Cleaning*		
Swimming pool	2.5	5.0
Lawn irrigation (per sprinkler)	2.5	5.0
Garden irrigation (per sprinkler)	2.5	5.0
Automobile washing	2.5	5.0
Equipment washing (tractor)	2.5	5.0
Cleaning milling equipment and storage areas	4.0	8.0
Flushing driveways and walkways	5.0	10.0
Hose cleaning barn floors, ramps, etc.	5.0	10.0
3. *Livestock Drinking Demands* (All open-lot housing)		
Horse, mule or steer (10 per watering space)	0.75 per space	1.5
Dairy cows (8 per watering space)	0.75 per space	1.5
Hogs (25 per watering space)	0.25 per space	0.5
Sheep (40 per watering space	0.25 per space	0.5
Chickens (100 per waterer)	0.12 per waterer	0.25
Turkeys (100 per waterer)	0.4 per waterer	0.8
4. *Garden, Fire Extinction and Other*		
Garden Hose—⅝ inch	3.5	
Garden Hose—¾ inch ¼-inch nozzle)	5.0	
Fire Hose—1½ inch (½-inch nozzle)	40.0	
Continuous flow drinking fountain	1.25	

Notes: a. Adapted from *Water Supply for Rural Areas and Small Communities* (Wagner and Lanoix) and *Planning for an Individual Water System* (AAVIM).

For this category of usage, your total is 17.5 gal/min. But now you must determine which of the listed uses are *competing* with each other. Your judgment is very important here in determining which of the demands overlap each other. For example, you must consider whether both lawn and garden sprinkler systems will be operated at the same time, and whether, in addition, you will be running your hose cleaning units simultaneously. Once you have estimated the likely overlap, you can ignore the other noncompeting demands in the rest of the analysis. Let us assume that three sprinklers are likely to be on at the same time as the barn cleaning operation. We then modify our list to arrive at the following:

Irrigation Uses (competing)	Peak Demand Allowance (gal/min)
3 sprinklers	7.5
Barn cleaning use	5.0
Total:	12.5

Now let us assume that you have some livestock on your small acreage and you must determine the required pump capacity for this use as well. List all of the watering units you have in use or expect to have in use and the corresponding demand for each (again from Table 6.3). Let us assume you have a small operation to start with (you can expand it if you like!):

Livestock	Peak Demand Allowance (gal/min)
2 horses (open lot)	0.75
1 dairy cow (open lot)	0.75
30 laying hens	0.12
Total:	1.62

Notice that the table is set up per watering space or per waterer. But even though we have only one cow or two horses, we still use the figure for one entire watering space.

The next step is to determine, for each category, which use requires the *greatest fixture flow*. This step is somewhat tricky. We go back, say, to household uses and look at the second column of Table 6.2. There we see that *both* the bath/shower combination *and* the clotheswasher have individual flow rates of 8 gal/min. In the replacement step to follow, we will only replace *one* of them (it doesn't matter which). For purposes of irrigation and cleaning, the largest (competing) fixture flow is 10 gal/min for cleaning the barn. And for watering your livestock the largest fixture flow is 1.5 gal/min for the horses and cow. We then modify our list again, by putting in these values for our greatest fixture flow in place of our demand allowances:

Use	Peak Demand Allowance (gal/min)
Home	
Tub and shower	8.0
Toilet	0.75
Kitchen sink	1.0
Clotheswasher	2.0
Irrigation (competing)	
3 sprinklers	7.5
Barn cleaning use	10.0
Livestock	
2 horses (open lot)	1.5
1 dairy cow (open lot)	0.75
30 laying hens	0.12
Total:	31.62

So the total peak demand on this particular pump will be 31.62 gallons per minute. If you follow these steps carefully, you should be able to determine the pump capacity required for your own special case.

Since most household uses do not last longer than 5 minutes, a small storage tank can cover most of your needs during the short peak demand periods and thus prevent any overload in the future. A storage tank also helps to deliver water during any small fire emergency. In fact, if you consider *real* fire protection in your pump sizing calculations, it will be the dominant requirement (see Table 6.3).

There are many kinds of pumps available and selecting one may be troublesome if you are not familiar with the advantages and disadvantages of the various types. This is the time to seek the advice of someone with lengthy practical experience in dealing with pumps (a repairman or mechanic, for instance).

Pumps can be classified according to the mode of power used to move the water: hand-powered, motor-powered, wind-powered (windmills), and water-powered (hydraulic ram). Let's consider a few of the design and efficiency aspects of these various types.

Hand-powered Pumps

The most popular hand-powered pump is the piston type shown in Figure 6.11. The two basic operational

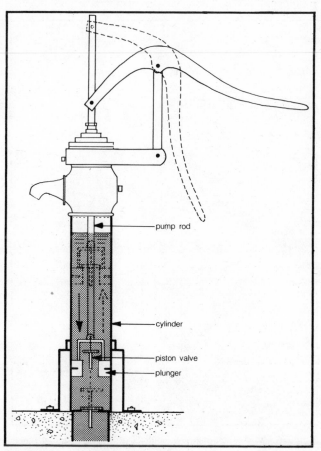

Figure 6.11 A hand-operated pump.

309

steps are also shown. During the downstroke, the valve in the plunger opens and the cylinder above the plunger is filled with water. At the same time, a vacuum is formed below the plunger, drawing the water into the suction pipe to open the check valve and fill the cylinder from below. This process is repeated each stroke. If the distance between the pump and water surface in your well is less than 15 or 20 feet, the cylinder can be used above ground level as the figure shows; otherwise the cylinder must be placed down the well shaft (Figure 6.12). Although plunger-type pumps have low efficiencies (from about 25 to 60 percent), they operate in a positive manner, have low maintenance requirements, and can deliver up to 10 to 15 gallons per minute.

There are many other kinds of hand-powered systems for moving water. Some of these designs are thousands of years old and are still used extensively in those places where energy has always been expensive for the common man. In many cases, animal power (horse, mule, or ox) is used to activate the system. The most simple mechanical device is probably the rope and bucket sys-

tem (Figure 6.13). The design shown uses a hook to catch and tilt the bucket, discharging the water into a trough. Another simple system is the continuous belt-bucket design, shown in Figure 6.14, where a series of metal buckets is attached to a chain. The buckets are emptied as they reach the top of the chain. Many variations on this theme are evident in rural areas worldwide.

Motor-powered Pumps

There are a large number of different designs and sizes available in motor-powered pump units. We will discuss briefly three basic types: reciprocating pumps, centrifugal pumps, and jet pumps. More detailed information is available in specialty books for those intrigued by such things (see, for example, the listing for Hicks and Edwards in the Bibliography). Performance data are available from pump manufacturers or retailers and should be consulted for specific information.

The operation of reciprocating pumps is based on the same principle as that of the plunger-type hand-powered pumps. Simple single-action reciprocal pumps discharge water only on alternate piston strokes, while improved double-action pumps discharge water on each stroke, thus providing a more uniform flow. The cylinder can either sit on the ground or be seated in the well itself, depending on the depth of the water surface in your well. The efficiency of reciprocating pumps is low (25 to 60 percent) and they are usually used for relatively low flow rates of from 10 to 30 gallons per minute. Despite their poor efficiency, these pumps are simple, and thus easy to operate and maintain.

Centrifugal pumps operate quite differently. They have a rapidly rotating part (the impeller) which transforms kinetic energy into pressure. There are many different

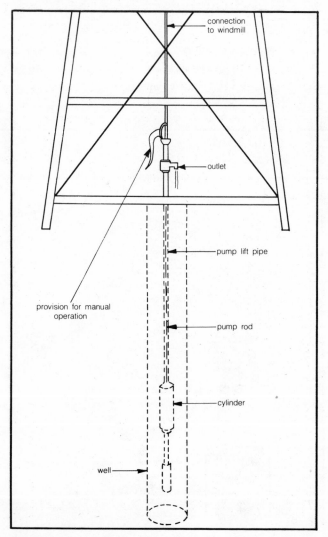

Figure 6.12 A water-pumping windmill with hand-operated pump unit.

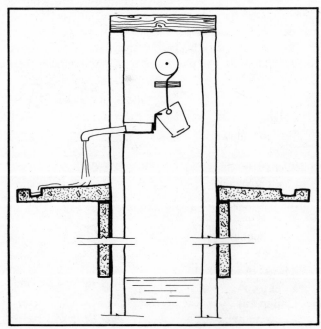

Figure 6.13 A rope and bucket system for lifting water.

impeller designs. Centrifugal pumps which move water to great heights above the pump have two or more impellers, one above the other, and are termed multistage pumps. Operation of centrifugal pumps requires that they start with the casing full of water; that is, you have to prime the pump to make it work. Priming the pump removes any air trapped in the pump casing. The efficiency of centrifugal pumps varies from 50 to 95 percent and they may be used for a great range of lifts, pushing water up to 1500 feet above the level of the pump.

In jet pumps, the water is discharged from a nozzle at high velocity and is forced through a conical apparatus called a diffuser (Figure 6.15). The water velocity is increased significantly as it passes through the diffuser and this results in a drop in pressure in the pipe. The drop in pressure creates a suction, thus drawing water up into the pipe. The efficiency of these pumps is relatively low, varying from 40 to 60 percent. Jet pumps can be combined with centrifugal pumps (as shown in the figure) to increase the lift or height to which water may be driven. Used by themselves, they can move water to only relatively low heights above the pump.

Wind-Powered Pumps

The cost of energy to drive an electric pump or gasoline to run an engine-driven pump will very rapidly con-

stitute the major single part of the cost of pumping. And, of course, the deeper the well, the higher the energy costs will be. In view of the limited economic resources available to many people living in rural areas and small communities, it is very important that careful consideration be given to the selection of a power source. In Chapter 3 we discussed how we can use the wind to generate electricity. However, long before man thought to use wind to produce electrical energy, he was using the wind to pump water out of the ground mechanically. Wind is a very cheap source of power—given that you are in an area where there is sufficient wind. Wind-driven pumps or windmills usually require the availability of winds at sustained speeds of more than 5 miles per hour. Towers are typically used to raise the windmill 15 to 20 feet above the surrounding obstacles in order to provide a clear sweep of wind to the mill.

Several types of windmills are available. A typical arrangement for a wind-driven pump is shown in Figure 6.16. Here the energy of the wind is transformed into mechanical movement to drive a rod and piston assembly up and down in a well shaft. Although most windmills are fixed on stationary towers, Sparco makes two portable windmill models, a piston type described above and a diaphragm type designed to pump water from a nearby spring, stream, lake, or shallow well (Figure 6.17). The Sparco piston type windmill can draw water from a well, boring, bridge, or pier, lifting the water a maximum of 33 feet. The Sparco diaphragm type windmill can lift water

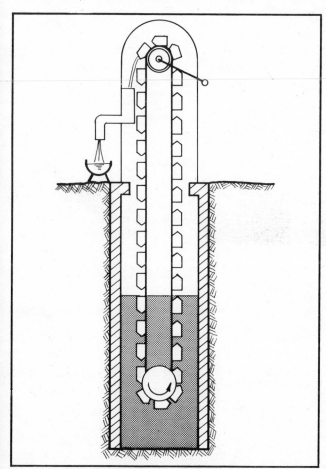

Figure 6.14 A continuous belt-bucket system.

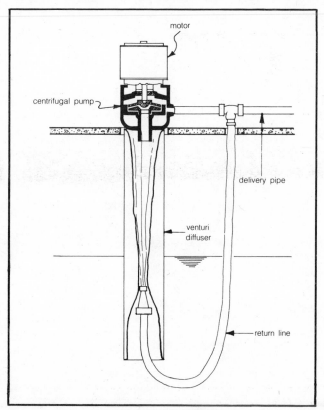

Figure 6.15 A jet pump providing pumping action.

13 feet over a horizontal distance of 30 feet. Although these portable types of windmills might have only special applications, the advantages are their cost (about $400), ease of installation, and low maintenance requirements. Sparco wind-powered water pumps can be obtained from Sencenbaugh Wind Electric, Palo Alto, California 94306.

Larger fixed windmills are typically multibladed mills designed in such a manner as to ensure that the windwheels will pivot freely and answer quickly to changes in the direction of the wind. They are also equipped with a "pull-out" system which will automatically turn the windwheel off to one side when the wind velocity becomes excessive (30 to 35 miles per hour). Lubrication is typically by an oil-pump system or crankcase type reservoir which needs at least annual maintenance. The ratio of piston strokes per revolution of the windwheel can be varied from 1 stroke per revolution for high wind velocities to 1 stroke per 4 revolutions for lower wind speeds. If you consider putting in a windmill, you might also consider providing a handle on the pump (at the base) so that water can be drawn by hand when there is no wind. The water-pumping capacity of a windmill varies with its design and size; typical capacities for traditional multibladed windwheels are given in Table 6.4.

Example: You have a six-acre farm and your average daily water requirements are 500 gallons per day. Your well is 100 feet deep and you have estimated your average wind speed at 12 miles per hour for 70 hours per month. Can you use a wind-driven pump to provide for your water needs?

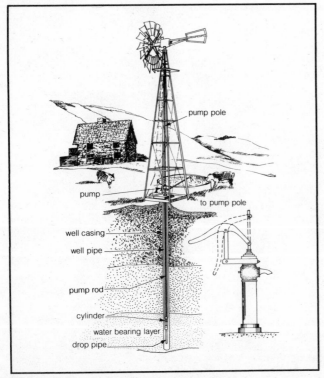

Figure 6.16 Typical windmill installation.

Solution: From Table 6.4, at 12 miles per hour our rated capacity is reduced to 80 percent of listed value. Now we must make a decision on size. Your monthly water requirement is

30 days/month × 500 gal/day = 15,000 gal/month

You get 70 hours of average wind velocity each month, so your pumping rate will need to be

$$\frac{15,000 \ gal/month}{70 \ hr} = 214.3 \ gal/hr$$

Now checking Table 6.4 we see that we have several choices of windmill size for a lift of 100 feet and a pumping capacity of at least 214.3 gallons per hour. You could select an 8-foot mill with a 7½ inch stroke (capacity about

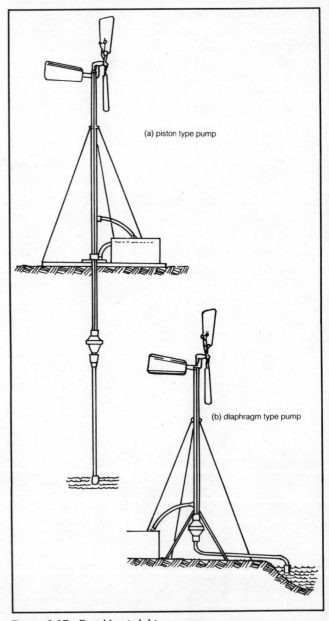

(a) piston type pump

(b) diaphragm type pump

Figure 6.17 Portable wind-driven pumps.

248 gallons per hour for a 107-foot lift) or a 10-foot mill with the same stroke (capacity 357 gallons per hour for a 102-foot lift).

If you select the larger (10-foot) windmill you will have extra pumping capacity which would allow you to use a larger storage tank to provide a safety margin for those dry spells of both wind and water. Fifteen thousand gallons per month are required, and on the average the 10-foot mill will pump

$$0.8 \times 357 \times 70 = 19{,}992 \ gal/mo$$

or an excess beyond needs of

$$19{,}992 - 15{,}000 = 4992 \ gal$$

If your storage tank is 8000 gallons you will have sufficient storage capacity to last 16 days of no wind.

Several suppliers of wind-driven pumps have equipment readily available. Prices vary with design and size of the windmill. For current information on prices and available models you should contact Dempster Industries Inc., Beatrice, Nebraska 68310 or KMP Lake Pump Mfg. Co., Inc., P.O. Box 441, Earth, Texas 79031.

Hydraulic Rams

If you have a fairly large stream or have access to a river, you can take advantage of one of the truly fine engineering holdovers from the nineteenth century—the hydraulic ram (Figure 6.18). Here, power is derived from the inherent energy of flowing water itself. The force of the water is captured in a chamber where air is compressed; when the compressed air expands, it pushes a small amount of the water to a higher elevation than that from which it originally came. The water which provided the energy is then released to flow on its way downstream.

A typical hydraulic ram installation consists of two pipes (supply and delivery), an air chamber, and two valves (waste and delivery). You set the hydraulic ram into motion by merely opening the waste valve and allowing the water to run through the ram unit. As the flow is accelerated, the force exerted on the waste valve causes it to close, causing a so-called "water hammer" or pressure build-up. This pressure buildup forces open the delivery valve and water flows into the air chamber, compressing the air inside. Because water is flowing into the air chamber, the pressure on the waste valve is lessened; it then opens, and the delivery valve consequently closes, trapping behind it a small quantity of water and compressed air. As the compressed air expands, it shoves this water into the delivery pipe and, as this process is repeated endlessly, you find—presto!—the water is at a higher elevation, ready to use.

Rife Hydraulic Engine Manufacturing Company (P.O. Box 367, Millburn, New Jersey 07041) is the only American-based supplier of hydraulic-ram pumps. They can provide you with pumps taking inlet and outlet pipe sizes from 1.25 to 8 inches. Costs run between $500 and $5000 (FOB factory).

A few comments concerning the use of the hydraulic ram are in order. First of all, there is a spring on the waste valve of most hydraulic rams which regulates the pressure required to close the waste valve. You can regulate the quantity of water and the height you raise it by varying the tension on this spring. You will have to make a few experimental runs at first to decide what the best setting is for your particular needs. You can compute the quantity of water pumped by a hydraulic ram using the following equation:

E. 6.1 $$\frac{Q_p}{Q_s} = \frac{H_s}{H_p}e$$

where Q_p is the flow pumped to a new location (gal/min); Q_s is the flow supplied to the hydraulic ram (gal/min); H_p is the pumping head, i.e., the vertical distance between

Table 6.4 Pumping Capacities for Multibladed Back-geared Windmills[a]

Cylinder Size	6 ft 5" Stroke		8 ft "A" 7½" Stroke		10 ft 7½" Stroke		12 ft 12" Stroke		14 ft 12" Stroke	
	Elev.	gph	Elev.	gph	Elev.	gph	Elev.	gph	Elev.	gph
1⅞	120	115	172	173	256	140	388	180	580	159
2	95	130	135	195	210	159	304	206	455	176
2¼	75	165	107	248	165	202	240	260	360	222
2½	62	206	89	304	137	248	200	322	300	276
2¾	54	248	77	370	119	300	173	390	260	334
3	45	294	65	440	102	357	147	463	220	396
3¼	39	346	55	565	86	418	125	544	187	465
3½	34	400	48	600	75	487	108	630	162	540
3¾	29	457	42	688	65	558	94	724	142	620
4	26	522	37	780	57	635	83	822	124	706

Notes: a. These capacities are based on a 15-mile-per-hour wind for small mills and 18- to 20-mile-per-hour winds for larger mills. Capacities are based on longest stroke of Dempster mills. If short stroke used, capacities will be reduced in proportion to length stroke used. If the wind velocity be increased or decreased, the pumping capacity of the windmill will also be increased or decreased. Capacities will be reduced approximately as follows if wind velocity is less than 15 miles per hour: 12-mile-per-hour wind, capacity reduced approximately 20 percent; 10-mile-per-hour wind, capacity reduced approximately 38 percent.

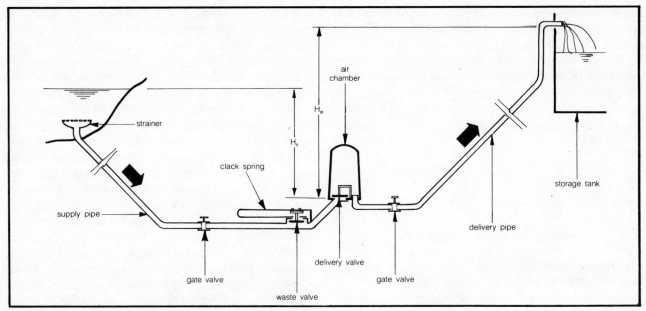

Figure 6.18 A typical hydraulic-ram installation.

the ram and the water surface in the tank where the water is pumped (in feet); H_s is the power head, i.e., the vertical distance between the free water surface of the supply water and the ram (in feet); and e is the efficiency of the ram, usually about 50 percent.

Figure 6.19 gives directly the ratio Q_p/Q_s as a function of the ratio H_p/H_s for typical hydraulic rams. If the supply and delivery pipes are long, you must take into consideration the hydraulic losses in these pipes (described in the water-power section of Chapter 3). H_s should be reduced by the equivalent losses in the supply pipe and H_p should be increased by the equivalent losses in the delivery pipe. Here we essentially are accounting for the energy lost due to friction in the pipes.

Example: You have a stream flowing at 10 gal/min on your property and you want to pump water to a tank 8 feet above the level of the stream. If you put the hydraulic ram 2 feet below the surface of the stream, how many gallons per minute can your hydraulic ram deliver to the tank?

Solution: The power head, H_s, is 2 feet and the pumping head, H_p, is 10 feet (8 + 2). From Figure 6.19 you find that for

$$\frac{H_p}{H_s} = \frac{10}{2} = 5$$

you have

$$\frac{Q_p}{Q_s} = 0.1$$

and

$$Q_p = 0.1 \times Q_s = 0.1 \times 10 = 1 \text{ gal/min}$$

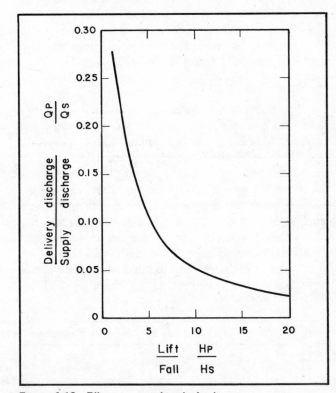

Figure 6.19 Efficiency curve for a hydraulic ram.

Thus we see that we must use 10 gal/min to pump 1 gal/min to a height of 8 feet; the other 9 gallons per minute are returned to the stream. If your ram is allowed to pump continuously, you will pump daily (1 × 60 × 24) about 1440 gallons per day. Not bad considering that the water provides its own energy for pumping!

As you can see from this example, the hydraulic ram requires a lot of water to operate. The higher the ratio of the pumping head to the power head, the more water the ram uses for energy purposes. However, if large flows are available, the hydraulic ram may be a very good choice for your pumping needs: it is durable and inexpensive, requires little maintenance, and can be operated continuously. You should be aware of the fact that the ram is fairly noisy; but with proper siting, this should not be a major problem.

Storage Systems

The amount of water you must have in storage depends upon both a realistic assessment of your needs and a good estimate of the period of time during which your source can be expected to be dry or unavailable. The average value for domestic daily water consumption is about 50 gallons per person, 49 of which are devoted to washing and waste disposal; we drink and cook with the sole remaining gallon. Thus, for example, if you expect your water source to be dry for a maximum of one month at a time, you will need to have a storage volume capable of meeting your normal demands for 30 days. Assuming you have a family of four and use, on the average, 50 gallons per day per person, your required storage volume will be

$$30 \text{ days} \times 50 \text{ gallons/day-person} \times 4 \text{ persons}$$
$$= 6000 \text{ gallons}$$

The area required to store this quantity of water is

$$6000 \text{ gallons} \times 0.1337 \text{ ft}^3/\text{gallon} = 802 \text{ ft}^3$$

So you will need a tank capable of storing at least 800 cubic feet of water—a tank 10 feet square and 8 feet deep would give the minimum capacity required.

A storage tank is one way of storing water; a reservoir or pond is another (both Chapters 3 and 7 discuss certain aspects of dam construction and maintenance). Of course, there are problems associated with open-surface bodies of water. For instance, the growth of algae may cause deterioration of water quality over the summer months; and the inadvertent introduction of materials into the water by animals, birds, or wind also can reduce its purity. Because of these problems it is almost always necessary to treat surface water to insure that the water is hygienically acceptable.

In order to avoid pollution, it is advisable to store your drinking water in a covered tank of some sort. A water storage system must be kept reliably watertight to prevent leakage or contamination. This means that seepage, warping, and corrosion must be guarded against and that pipelines to and from the storage container must be sound. To avoid odors, tastes, or toxic materials in the water, the appropriate surfaces need to be constructed or coated with inert materials such as wood or some plastics and paints. In addition, there must be provision for easy access to the storage container above the maximum water height, to permit visual checks of the water level and convenient maintenance when necessary.

Water storage tanks come in a variety of sizes, shapes, and materials. The three main construction materials are wood, steel, and concrete. Wooden tanks are virtually maintenance-free and leave no taste or odor in the water. However, they must be kept from drying out for more than two months at a time; the wood may otherwise warp and allow leakage after refill. Steel tanks are also available. These containers tend to corrode or leave a metallic taste in the water if not properly lined; but minimum maintenance and proper lining can eliminate these problems. New steel tanks can be fabricated to meet specific criteria, while used ones are also available. The third type available, concrete tanks, are usually constructed in place. They are quite inert and require little upkeep. Some small concrete tanks are available commercially.

Before you select any container, you should consult several sources to get comparative prices and construction methods. Your best source of tanks is generally a local supplier; sometimes good bargains can be made by checking with local salvage companies. Although prices change very rapidly these days, it is still of some use for you to have a rough idea of the price range for different sizes and types of tanks—Table 6.5 gives prices for redwood tanks of various sizes. These prices do not include installation costs, which can vary considerably from site to site. If a special foundation is required for the tank, the cost will be significantly more. This is especially true for installations on slopes or areas subject to slides or slippage. Although pressure tanks are available, they are not recommended because of the added cost and maintenance; however, if your location is not readily suited to a gravity-type tank, you may not have any choice.

Gravity tanks are located at a higher elevation than the point where the water is to be used. The added height gives the water the necessary pressure for your supply system to work conveniently. The pressure (P) in pounds per square inch (psi) at a given point in your system is given by the formula

E. 6.2 $$P = \frac{H}{2.3}$$

where H is the elevation difference or head (in feet) between the water surface in the tank and the point where you want to know the pressure. If you have a long pipe from the tank to the point at which you wish to know the pressure (or, more likely, where you wish to use the water) you will need to reduce H in the above equation; this reduction accounts for friction and methods to estimate this loss of head described in the water-power section of Chapter 3. You will need to maintain a minimum pressure of 15 to 20 psi if you have any automatic water-using machines in your home (such as a dishwasher). The minimum elevation difference for such a pressure is about 35

Table 6.5 Redwood Storage Tanks[a]

| Standard 2" Redwood Tanks With Chime Joists | | | | | Flat Covers | |
Gallons	Dia.	Height	Weight (lbs)	Price ($)	Weight (lbs)	Price ($)
200	4'0"	3'	260	344	65	95
300	4'0"	4'	330	410	65	95
400	4'8"	4'	410	468	75	115
500	5'2"	4'	470	553	85	123
600	5'0"	5'	525	591	85	123
900	6'0"	5'	660	812	100	153
1000	6'0"	6'	760	925	100	153
1500	7'0"	6'	930	1145	175	181
2000	8'0"	6'	1095	1240	225	257
2500	8'4"	7'	1400	1490	260	267
3000	9'0"	7'	1600	1566	300	300
4000	10'0"	8'	1965	1892	365	347
5000	11'0"	8'	2235	2080	435	395
5000	10'0"	9'	2100	2080	365	347
6000	12'0"	8'	2460	2404	510	410
8000	12'0"	10'	2850	2730	510	410
10,000	13'8"	10'	3550	3283	625	564
12,000	13'8"	12'	4050	3655	625	564

| Standard 3" Redwood Tanks With Chime Joists | | | | | Flat Covers | |
Gallons	Dia.	Height	Weight (lbs)	Price ($)	Weight (lbs)	Price ($)
10,000	14'0"	10'	5500	4756	670	564
12,000	14'0"	12'	6350	5460	670	564
15,000	15'6"	12'	7100	6032	800	598
20,000	18'0"	12'	8700	7330	1060	878
20,000	16'6"	14'	8600	7330	940	802
25,000	18'0"	14'	9700	8380	1060	878
30,000	20'0"	14'	10200	9454	1450	955
40,000	23'0"	14'	13650	11,100	1910	1137
50,000	24'0"	16'	15900	13,480	2140	1594
60,000	26'0"	16'	17900	15,235	2370	1814
70,000	28'0"	16'	20000	17,080	2850	2000
75,000	29'0"	16'	21100	17,770	3070	2200
80,000	30'0"	16'	22300	18,710	3200	2329
90,000	30'0"	18'	24400	20,530	3200	2329
100,000	32'0"	18'	28700	22,556	3660	2558
100,000	30'0"	20'	26400	22,556	3200	2329

Notes: a. All dimensions are outside measurements: exact stave length is 1" shorter than the normal length in feet. Capacities are approximate; weights are estimated. 3" × 4" chime joists are used tanks 2000 gallons and smaller; 4" × 6" chime joists are used with larger tanks. Approximate prices as of January 1, 1980. T. E. Brown, Inc., 14361 Washington Ave, San Leandro, California.

to 45 feet, which you can verify from Equation 6.2. As we mentioned a moment ago, you may have to use a pressure tank if your location does not allow a natural elevation difference of 40 feet or so; in this case, you will need to check with other references for details [see, for instance, the very fine discussion in *Planning for an Individual Water System (AAVIM)*].

Quality and Control

First of all, let's recognize that water quality varies by degrees, not by absolutes. That is to say, we never have pure water in the true meaning of the word *pure*. What we essentially have are acceptable levels of impurities; when these levels are exceeded, it can often lead to health problems.

We should start this discussion by considering first those characteristics most easily recognized. Many rivers and lakes contain particulate material that makes their waters turbid. The turbidity may be due to silt and clay particles, but this condition also can be caused by organic matter. Organic matter is often responsible for taste and odor problems, as well.

Natural waters contain many dissolved salts, most of which have no deleterious effects. A common characteristic of most groundwaters and some surface waters is *hardness*. Hardness is caused by an excess of dissolved calcium and magnesium, metal ions which tend to interfere with the use of soaps by combining with the soap molecules. An additional problem sometimes associated with hard water is scaling in hot-water heaters, thus reducing their heat-transfer efficiency. When you use hard water, you find that you cannot easily form a lather with soap and your skin tends to roughen from washing. However, hard water is not harmful to your health.

Iron and manganese in a water source can cause staining of clothes and give water a characteristic metallic taste. Even when iron is present in low concentrations, red stains in clothes and on porcelain plumbing may appear. Manganese typically causes a brownish-black stain. Preparing your coffee and tea with water containing substantial manganese may result in a bitter tasting brew! Obviously you are going to want to remove these materials if you find them in your water supply.

It is worth mentioning a few other substances which are commonly found in natural waters to varying degrees. Sulfate is always found in water to some extent. However, a high sulfate concentration can have laxative effects if your body is not accustomed to it. There is very little you can do easily to correct this condition, so if your body objects too strenuously, you may have to choose another water source. Another common constituent of natural waters is carbon dioxide. Excess carbon dioxide imparts a degree of acidity to the water and may increase the rate of corrosion of metal pipes and fixtures in your supply system.

There are many potentially toxic or hazardous substances which can be found in a natural water—such things as arsenic, barium, cadmium, lead, and zinc. Water supply sources close to, or coming from, industrial areas or mining regions require careful examination by experts to insure that the water is healthful before it is developed as a drinking source. (If not, again look elsewhere; these conditions are untreatable by our methods.) This warning includes, of course, the most obvious danger—bacteria or microorganisms capable of transmitting diseases.

Several water-borne diseases can arise from untreated water and you should be aware of them. Troublesome bacterial or protozoan diseases include typhoid fever and both bacillary and amoebic dysentery. Of the viral infections that can contaminate water supplies, infectious hepatitis and poliomyelitis are the most likely. Salmonella-caused diarrhea can also result from drinking polluted waters.

Water is dangerous only when contaminated by some external source, and almost invariably pathogens are spread through the feces of infected hosts. This fact is important to remember in any community which also is involved with alternative methods of waste disposal. Since pathogenic bacteria do not normally multiply in water, they present a hazard only through recent or continuous contamination. Have your water tested *regularly* and *professionally* to assure that it meets safe standards.

Water testing is based on the assumption that any water which is contaminated by feces contains intestinal pathogens and is therefore unpotable. It would be too costly and time-consuming to test for all possible pathogens. In the United States, *Escherichia coli* is used as an indicator of fecal contamination because it only occurs in feces and is never free-living in nature. If water tests do show the presence of *E. coli,* it is advisable to find another water supply or to obtain professional help in treating it.

Other microorganisms can pollute water supplies without causing contamination. When algae are present in large quantities, they may cause turbidity and change the water color. Algae cause no known human diseases, but, as we have mentioned, they can contribute unpleasant tastes and odors.

Occasionally water contains small worms, blood-red or greyish in color. The red worms are the larvae of Chironomus flies; the others are larvae of related midge flies. Remedial measures involve draining and cleaning your basins to eliminate existing larvae; you must then use insect-tight covers on the basins to prevent reinfestation.

Disinfection

We have spent some time discussing what the water-quality problems might be; now let's turn to a few techniques that can help us, if necessary, to solve them.

Disinfection of water does not mean *sterilization;* we mean by disinfection the adequate destruction of water-borne pathogenic microorganisms including bacteria, viruses, and protozoa. (Sterilization also destroys certain bacterial spores; disinfection does not.) There are many ways to disinfect water but only a few of them have any real practical application for the development of your own water supply system.

We should start with the easiest technique for small quantities of water—simply boil it. Heating water to a temperature of 140°F for 15 minutes is sufficient for disinfecting; boiling for a longer period tends to sterilize it unnecessarily and wastes fuel. Because of the energy required and the small quantities of water that can be handled easily, boiling can only be considered as an emergency technique.

The most reliable type of disinfectant for small-scale applications is chlorine or a chlorine compound. Chlorine solutions must be kept in brown or green bottles and stored in the dark to prevent photodecomposition of the active agent. Storage of chlorine solutions for long periods is not recommended since they can lose over half their activity in one year. Laundry bleaches should not be used as a chlorine source since most commercial products contain other additives which may cause taste and odor problems. And solutions containing more than 10 percent chlorine by weight are unstable and should not be used under any circumstances.

Now we can begin to make a few specific suggestions. But first we need to discuss some of the types of materials available and how to use them.

If you need to disinfect a small quantity of water for some reason—say, 20 gallons—and you don't have a regular disinfection system operating, you can use chlorinated lime. A stock solution of chlorinated lime can be mixed at home by adding a teaspoon of chlorinated lime (40 percent chlorine by weight) to a quart of water. After it is well mixed, one teaspoon of this stock solution for *every two gallons* of water usually provides adequate disinfection after half an hour. So, for 20 gallons, you would use 10 teaspoons of stock.

Calcium hypochlorite is one of the best and most common chlorine compounds around. It is available commercially in powder and tablet form containing 30 to 75 percent active chlorine by weight; usually the percentage of chlorine is found on the container. Common trade names are B-K Powder, Percholoron, and Pittchlor. If you purchase this material you will need to store the cans in a cool, dark area—away from any direct sunlight. The calcium hypochlorite powder can be used to make up stock solutions for disinfection in the same manner (same proportions) as with chlorinated lime compounds.

Now, how do we go about disinfecting a large volume of water on a batch basis? First, we need to know that the required concentration of chlorine in solution for adequate disinfection is about 1 to 5 parts per million (ppm). Typically you will mix up a stock solution of about 5 percent chlorine (about the same strength as found in common laundry bleach). The volume of water that can be disinfected by a specific volume of stock chlorine solution is given by the following equation:

E. 6.3 $$V_w = \frac{10,000 \, PV_{Cl}}{C}$$

where V_w is the volume of water disinfected (gallons); V_{Cl} is the volume of stock chlorine solution (gallons); P is the percent, by weight, of chlorine in solution; and C is the concentration of chlorine in the final mixture (usually about 1 to 5 ppm).

Example: What quantity of water can you disinfect with one gallon of 5 percent chlorine solution if you want a chlorine concentration in the disinfected water to be 2 ppm?

Solution: Using Equation 6.3 with P equal to 5 percent, C at 2 ppm, and V_{Cl} at 1 gallon, we have

$$V_w = \frac{10,000 \times 5 \times 1}{2} = 25,000 \, gal$$

Now that is a whole lot of water! It is obvious that a little stock chlorine solution can go a long way in disinfection processes.

One application of batch disinfection might be in your storage tank, especially when you first start up your system. The process also cannot hurt if applied after any situation which you think might possibly have contaminated your source, such as after a big storm.

What do you do if you want the disinfection process to be automatic? Small chlorination units have been designed for use by individuals or small living groups. The main types are the so-called pump, injector, and tablet types. The pump type is designed to deliver a predetermined amount of chlorine solution at each stroke of a chlorination pump. A chlorinator of the injector type consists of a nozzle at some point along the pipe between pump and storage tank. As the water flows through the nozzle at high velocity, a suction develops in a line connected to the chlorine solution container and chlorine solution is injected into the main pipe in proportion to the flow in the main. The tablet form of chlorinator consists of a tank of calcium hypochlorite tablets through which water is circulated. Figure 6.20 shows the bypass line running through the calcium hypochlorite tablets. The best working information we have seen on this type of chlorinator can be found in *Planning for an Individual Water System* (AAVIM).

Filtration of Turbid Water

Filtration is probably the oldest and most easily understood process of water treatment available. It is used to remove suspended particles from water and also to remove some bacteria, although it cannot be counted upon to do this effectively. The most commonly used filters in household water supplies are sand and ceramic varieties.

You can easily build a sand filter at home; a design by the U.S. Department of Agriculture for home use is shown in Figure 6.21. The filter is made from two 10-inch-diameter sections of vitrified tile pipe set in concrete.

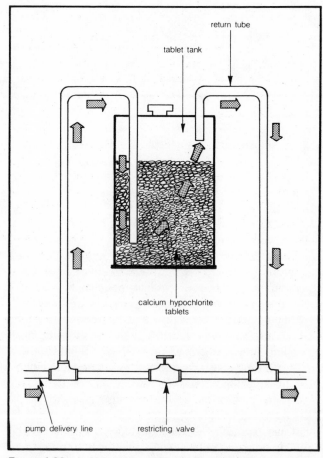

Figure 6.20 A chlorination unit using calcium hypochlorite tablets.

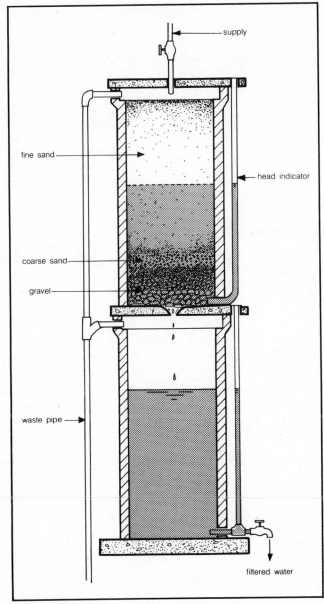

Figure 6.21 A slow sand filter made from clay pipe.

The upper section contains the filter material (sand) and the lower section is used to collect the filtered water. It is important to note that the sand varies in grain size: it is finer in the upper part of the filter and becomes coarser as you get deeper into the filter bed. You can use either fine and coarse sand (your local sand and gravel man can help you here), or fine sand and crushed charcoal or coal. If you use activated charcoal in your filter, you will have the additional benefit of taste and odor removal.

The filter shown in Figure 6.21 has an overflow pipe on the left side and a glass tube on the right side to show pressure losses in the filter due to clogging. When the filter is clean, the level in the tube is the same as the level in the tile pipe. As the sand becomes clogged, resistance builds up to flow through the filter and the level in the glass tube becomes lower than the water level in the filter.

To clear a clogged filter, you have to backwash it by flushing clean water back through the sand; this flush water is drained off above the filter material. You may have to repeat this washing process several times until you get the same water levels in the glass tube and the filter. If you use charcoal in your filter, you will have to replace it occasionally (about once a year); if you are filtering organically laden surface water, more frequent replacement is necessary because bacteria may collect in the charcoal and reproduce there. The capacity of sand filters depends mainly on the surface area, height, and grain size of the sand. For example, the 30-inch-high sand filter shown in Figure 6.21 has a capacity of about 4 gallons per hour.

The pressure filter or rapid sand filter (Figure 6.22) operates on a slightly different basis: it is a closed tank containing sand of various grain sizes and the water comes in from the pump under pressure. The capacity of the rapid sand filter is high, about 2 to 3 gal/min per square foot of surface area, but its effectiveness in removing very small particles is limited and it is not recommended for waters with large quantities of fine matter.

Ceramic filters constitute a class of filters well suited to small-scale operations. Figure 6.23 shows a typical ceramic filter. Water is filtered as it flows through a ceramic medium (candle) of very small pore size. The filter candle is contained in a tank which may or may not be under pressure. These filters are very efficient in removing fine particles, but we do not recommend their use with very turbid water since clogging then occurs very rapidly. Ceramic filter candles are made of various clays (including porcelain) and sometimes can be coated with diatomaceous earth. The Berkefeld filter is shown in Figure 6.23. The ceramic candles come in coarse, normal, and fine pore sizes. Careful maintenance of ceramic filters is important to avoid short-circuiting of water through cracks. With the exception of the porcelain variety, water processed through any type of filter should be disinfected before use.

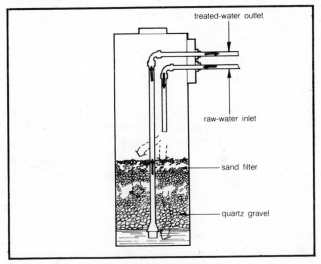

Figure 6.22 A pressurized rapid sand filter.

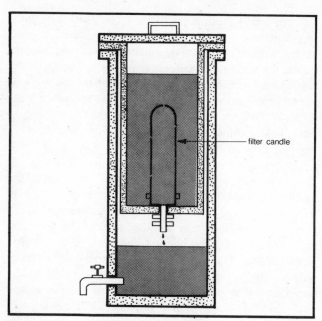

Figure 6.23 A Berkefeld ceramic filter with ceramic candle in place.

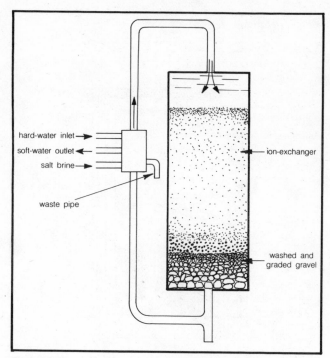

Figure 6.24 A small-scale ion-exchange unit appropriate for home use.

Ion-Exchange Process

Problems with water quality associated with hard water—dissolved ions such as calcium and magnesium—are rather common, especially in groundwater sources. The presence of dissolved iron and manganese is also not unusual. There are numerous ways of dealing with these unwanted materials but, unfortunately, most of these processes are not suitable for small-scale home application. One gratifying exception is the ion-exchange process.

Figure 6.24 shows a typical ion-exchange unit. These units operate on the principle of exchanging one kind of ion (usually sodium) provided by the exchanger for another, unwanted kind of ion in solution in the water (calcium, for example); troublesome ions are thus replaced with a type more generally acceptable, and the water is "softened."

When all the sodium ions in the ion-exchanger have been replaced by calcium, the exchanger must be recharged—a process which requires a very concentrated solution of sodium chloride, common table salt. The ion-exchange units are generally placed directly before that point in the water line where softened or treated water is to be used—before the kitchen or bathroom, for example—to avoid unnecessarily treating water used for gardening and other such purposes. Small units available from local suppliers are capable of treating moderately hard water (60 to 80 ppm of calcium; 20 to 40 ppm of magnesium) on an economical basis, *if* you use them to treat only the water you need for washing and cooking. An example may be helpful here: for a family of four using 1000 gallons of water per month (for cooking and washing), this water containing 40 ppm of calcium, then one cubic foot of ion-exchange resin would need to be recharged only once a month, two cubic feet of resin would last two months, and so forth.

We are not presenting design calculations here because they can get very cumbersome. However, once testing has determined the particulate composition of your water in parts per million, a consultation with a local supplier should enable you to size an ion-exchange unit fairly easily. For those of you interested in doing it all yourself, we suggest you look into the publications put out by the American Water Works Association and also into *Planning for an Individual Water System* (AAVIM). You should be forewarned that the use of an ion-exchanger will raise the sodium ion content of the water to concentration levels which might preclude greywater irrigation as a means of disposal. See Chapter 5 for a discussion of this potential problem.

If you have a small piece of land in the country and a source for a water supply, you may have found some useful information and suggestions here. We hope that you will consider carefully your needs and your resources before deciding to alter your landscape. And whether you use groundwater or a lake or a stream for your water source, remember that it is always cheaper and safer to protect a good, clean source of water than it is to treat the water to make it acceptable. With a little foresight and care, you should be able to enjoy a healthy, adequate supply of fine-tasting water.

Bibliography

Ameen, J. S. *Community Water Systems*. 5th ed. Available from Technical Proceedings, P.O. Box 5041, High Point, North Carolina 27262.

American Association for Vocational Instructional Materials (AAVIM). 1973. *Planning for an Individual Water System*. Athens, Georgia: AAVIM.

American Water Works Association. 1941. *Manual of Water Quality and Treatment*. New York: AWWA.

———. 1969. *Water Treatment Plant Design*. New York: AWWA.

———. 1971. *Water Quality and Treatment*. 3rd ed. New York: AWWA.

Anderson, K. E. 1966. *Water Well Handbook*. Rolla, Missouri: Missouri Water Well Drillers Association.

Baum, V. A. 1961. "Solar Distillers." From *Proceedings of the U.N. Conference on New Sources of Energy*, Rome, vol. 6. New York: United Nations.

Bloemer, J. W. 1965. "A Practical Basin-Type Solar Still." *Solar Energy* 9:197.

Brinkworth, B. J. 1972. *Solar Energy for Man*. New York: John Wiley and Sons.

Cooper, P. I. 1969. "Digital Simulation of Transient Solar Still Processes." *Solar Energy* 12:313.

———. 1972. "Some Factors Affecting the Absorption of Solar Radiation in Solar Stills." *Solar Energy* 13:373.

Cooper, P. I., and Read, W. R. W. 1974. "Design Philosophy and Operating Experience for Australian Solar Stills." *Solar Energy* 16:1–8.

Daniels, F. 1964. *Direct Use of the Sun's Energy*. New Haven, Conn.: Yale University Press.

Duffie, A., and Beckman, W. 1974. *Solar Energy and Thermal Processes*. New York: John Wiley and Sons.

Edmondson, W. B. 1974. "Vertical Floating Solar Stills." *Solar Energy Digest*. 3:12.

———. 1974. "Solar Water Stills." *Solar Energy Digest* 3:25.

Environmental Protection Agency, Office of Water Supply. 1976. *Manual of Water Well Construction Practices*. EPA-570/9-75-001, U.S. Government Printing Office.

Gary, H. P., and Mann, H. S. 1976. "Effect of Climatic, Operational and Design Parameters on the Year Round Performance of Single-Sloped and Double-Sloped Solar Stills Under Indian Arid Zone Conditions." *Solar Energy* 18:159–164.

———. 1978. "Reply to the Comments on the Performance of Solar Stills." *Solar Energy* 20:363.

Gibson, U. P., and Singer, R. D. 1971. *Water Well Manual*. Berkeley, Calif.: Premier Press.

Gomella, C. 1961. "Use of Solar Energy for the Production of Fresh Water." From *Proceedings of the U.N. Conference on New Sources of Energy*, Rome, vol. 6. New York: United Nations.

Grune, W. N. 1961. "Forced-Convection, Multiple-Effect Solar Still for Desalting Sea and Brackish Waters." From *Proceedings of the U.N. Conference on New Sources of Energy*, Rome, vol. 6. New York: United Nations.

Harr, M. E. 1962. *Groundwater and Seepage*. New York: McGraw-Hill.

Hazen, A. 1916. *Clean Water and How to Get It*. New York: John Wiley and Sons.

Hem, J. D. 1970. *Study and Interpretation of the Chemical Characteristics of Natural Water*. Washington, D.C.: U.S. Government Printing Office.

Hicks, T. G. and Edwards, T. 1971. *Pump Application Engineering*. New York: McGraw-Hill.

Holdren, W. S. 1970. *Water Treatment and Examination*. Baltimore: Williams and Wilkins.

Howe, E. D. 1961. "Solar Distillation Research at the University of California." From *Proceedings of the U.N. Conference on New Sources of Energy*, Rome, vol. 6. New York: United Nations.

———. 1964. "A Combined Solar Still and Rainfall Collector." *Solar Energy* 8:23.

Howe, E. D., and Tleimat, B. W. 1974. "Twenty Years of Work on Solar Distillation at the University of California." *Solar Energy* 16:97.

Howood, M. P. 1932. *The Sanitation of Water Supply*. New York: C. C. Thomas.

Hummel, R. L. 1961. "A Large Scale, Low Cost, Solar Heat Collector and Its Application to Sea Water Conversion." From *Proceedings of the U.N. Conference on New Sources of Energy*, Rome, vol. 6. New York: United Nations.

Karim, M. 1978. "Comments on the Performance of Solar Stills." *Solar Energy* 20:361.

Lawand, T. A. 1965. *Simple Solar Still for the Production of Distilled Water*. Test Report No. 17, Brace Research Institute. Quebec: McGill University Press.

Leopold, L. B. 1974. *Water: A Primer*. San Francisco: W. H. Freeman and Co.

Löf, G. O. G. 1961. "Application of Theoretical Principles in Improving the Performance of Basin-type Solar Distillers." From *Proceedings of the U.N. Conference on New Sources of Energy*, Rome, vol. 6. New York: United Nations.

———. 1966. "Solar Distillation." From *Principles of Desalination*, ed. K. S. Spiegler. New York: Academic Press.

McCracken, H. 1964. "Solar Still Pans." *Solar Energy* 9:201.

Mann, H. T., and Williamson, D. 1976. *Water Treatment and Sanitation: Simple Methods for Rural Areas*. London: Intermediate Technology Publications Ltd.

Moustafa, S. M. A., and Brusewitz, G. H. 1979. "Direct Use of Solar Energy for Water Desalination." *Solar Energy* 22:141–149.

New York State Department of Health. 1966. *Rural Water Supply*. Albany, New York: State Department of Health.

Selcuk, M. K. 1964. "A Multiple-Effect Tilted Solar Distillation Unit." *Solar Energy* 8:23.

Skeat, W. O. 1969. *Manual of British Water Engineering Practise*. London: W. Heffer and Sons, Ltd.

Strobel, J. J. 1961. "Developments in Solar Distillation." From *Proceedings of the U.N. Conference on New Sources of Energy*, Rome, vol. 6. New York: United Nations.

Trombe, F., and Foëx, M. 1964. "Utilization of Solar Energy for Simultaneous Distillation of Brackish Water and Air-Conditioning of Hot-Houses in Arid Regions." *Proceedings of the U.N. Conference on New Sources of Energy*, Rome, vol. 6. New York: United Nations.

United Nations. 1970. *Solar Distillation as a Means of Meeting Small Water Demands*. Sales No. E 70.11.B.1 from Sales Section, United Nations, N.Y. 10017.

Wagner, E., and Lanoix, J. 1959. *Water Supply for Rural Areas and Small Communities*. Geneva, Switzerland: World Health Organization.

Watt, S. B., and W. E. Wood. 1977. *Hand Dug Wells and Their Construction*. London: Intermediate Technology Publications, Ltd.

Williams, J. R. 1977. *Solar Energy Technology and Applications*. Ann Arbor: Ann Arbor Science Publishers.

AGRICULTURE/AQUACULTURE

Food chains

Farming, by land and sea

On the transcendence
and transformation of garbage

Gardens for both tenements
and the great outdoors

The purchase and care of livestock

Fishpond construction and
the bounties therefrom

AGRICULTURE AND AQUACULTURE

Introduction

Everything is connected to everything else is the first "law" of ecology coined by the ecologist Barry Commoner. This chapter is no different. Like electricity and solar heating, agriculture and aquaculture are also processes of energy conversion, transforming light and chemicals into food for our consumption. Those converted forms which we don't utilize (both before and after consumption) are of direct concern in the waste and water chapters. And, of course, like architecture, the practical aspects of the process of food raising cannot be separated from the aesthetic quality it adds to our homes and our lives.

We start by looking briefly at two ecological principles which are important for anyone wanting to work with the natural environment. The chapter then surveys basic information you'll need to farm both the land (agriculture) and also the lakes, streams, or oceans (aquaculture). In each case, your individual situation, whether it be urban, suburban, or rural, will determine what information is directly applicable. Since the wealth of information has expanded in the last few years, we attempt to give the essentials with pointers to where the details can be found in the literature.

For example, vegetables literally can be grown *anywhere,* in containers on a terrace or a flat rooftop, even on the window ledge of an apartment. And if you're fortunate enough to have a sunny spot of ground, the tiniest plot can produce impressive yields with the Biodynamic/ French Intensive method of crop production. Even urban animals can be raised in other than sylvan surroundings. Rabbits need as much room as it would take to store two bicycles. Gil Masters raises chickens in downtown Menlo Park, and the roof of an apartment is a perfect location for a beehive—out of the way, but accessible.

Of course, if you own land, whether it be a large backyard or several acres, the possibilities multiply: both agriculture and aquaculture become available. Simple practices—blocking off a small inlet along the coast (which may require a permit from various agencies such as the Department of Fish and Game) or constructing several rock pools in a mountain stream—can yield increases in your fish harvest. If enough land is available, a low-maintenance fish pond for recreation and food-producing purposes can be stocked free of charge by the state or federal government; with proper management, this source can yield 200 pounds or more per acre every year. We discuss the farm pond possibilities in some detail because of its low-maintenance, low-cost attributes. We also provide some general information on fish species and culturing for both freshwater and marine habitats. We encourage you to be imaginative and include in our chapter an outline of experimental aquaculture systems which are presently under development. They are significant in their attempt to integrate several concepts—food growth with waste-water handling, and the combined use of recycled water, solar heating, and windmill power.

Because the literature is vast, we attempt here to provide you with a collection of basic information, highlighting methods which are energy-conservative, low in waste, and adaptable to individual needs and locations. Although these individual needs can range from total self-sufficiency to supplemental food raising, we hope this chapter will be useful no matter what your situation.

Let us begin by looking at two fundamental concepts of ecology which are important to both agricultural and aquacultural practices. The first is the concept of the food chain, which refers to a specific and sequential transfer of the energy available in food from one organism to another. The first members of the chain, plants or algae ("primary producers"), are consumed by a group of animals ("consumer level 1"), which in turn is consumed by a second group ("consumer level 2"), and so on. The primary producers are the most important members of this sequence. Only they have the unique capacity to transform solar energy or incident light into food energy or plant tissue through the fixation of inorganic CO_2. The basic chemical reaction is

$$CO_2 + H_2O \xrightarrow{\text{solar energy}} (CH_2O) + O_2$$
$$\text{plant tissue}$$

All other organisms essentially depend upon this transformation for their energy. Of the solar energy available to primary producers, only about 1 percent is captured in plant tissue. Of this 1 percent, only about 0.1 to 0.5 percent is available to the first level of consumers; the remainder has been used by the plant for its own respiration. With each subsequent transfer in the food chain, a major portion (about 90 percent) of the remaining available energy is lost, mostly as heat and respiration. Consequently, the longer the food chain, the less energy available from a given number of primary producers. For example, Figure 7.1 illustrates that one pound of vegetables or rice can provide from 165 to 1650 kilocalories of energy. If the pound were fed to rabbits or chickens, only about 16 to 165 kilocalories would be conserved and hence would be available for our own consumption. If we ourselves had consumed the vegetables or rice, we would have had available the original 165 to 1650 kilocalories.

A second concept to keep in mind is that, generally, a diverse system tends to be more stable than a simple system. For example, if only one species of fish inhabits

a fish pond, the invasion of a single parasite can rapidly and completely eliminate the fish population. On the other hand, if polyculture is practiced, and several compatible species are grown together, the pathogenic organism, which tends to be specific for each species, can only attack a fraction of the total population. In addition, since the number of individuals of the victimized species is fewer, the disease would tend to spread more slowly. Large areas of land planted with a single genetic strain of but one crop also tend to be less stable when faced with a stress such as disease. Consequently, variety is not only the spice of life; it's also a healthy component.

Agriculture

The objectives of the agriculture section are many. Of course, the most important aims are to produce high-quality, nutritious, and delicious food for the household, and to recycle its solid and liquid wastes. But there are others—the beautification of the home, sun and wind protection—which also must be considered in the agricultural realm. These objectives must be balanced against three important factors: the labor cost, in terms of both quantity and quality; the economic expense; and perhaps most importantly, the ecological costs.

We have attempted to present the information necessary to allow the readers to plan for themselves what will work best in their particular situation. The focus and the sizing considerations were determined for the use of a small living group; intensive agriculture of large acreage was not considered, and practices requiring high-maintenance, specialized techniques and energy-consuming machinery were also de-emphasized.

We consider production of food from both plants and animals. Because of the vast amount of literature on the subject, no effort was made to describe the step-by-step procedures of traditional cultivation. However, since we consider them important, such techniques as composting and the Biodynamic/French Intensive method are described in more detail. The material is presented in a simple (hopefully coherent) manner, and should be both an adequate introduction to "small-time" agriculture and also a reference guide for the more experienced. It goes without saying that you should experiment with other plants, different species, and various techniques to find what best suits your own backyard.

Crops

Much of our information was drawn from *First-Time Farmer's Guide* by B. Kaysing and from texts by J. I. Rodale (see Bibliography). We recommend you consult them if you want more data.

If You Have No Land

We also wish to point out information specifically relating to container gardening. With a resurgence of inter-

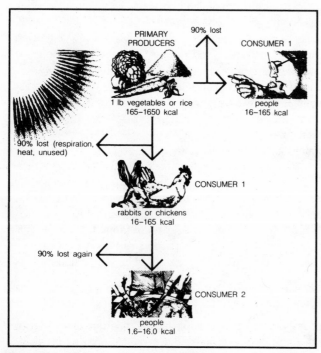

Figure 7.1 Energy transfer through a food chain.

est in growing your own food and the concentration of populations in city centers, we recognize that the urban dweller has special needs. *The Integral Urban House* by the Farallones Institute is a resource book that directly addresses these needs if you wish more specifics. In general, shallow-rooted vegetables and fruits such as short carrots, cabbage, chard, celery, beets, lettuce, radishes, and strawberries do best in containers. Yields from bushy vegetables such as tomatoes, peppers, squash, and beans will be a function of the amount of root space available, i.e. the bigger the container, the more harvest you will reap. A big boon to the urban farmer is the availability of dwarf strains developed by the seed companies which are particularly compact and suitable for small spaces.

Vegetables

Several major considerations go into the planning of a vegetable garden. Climate, soil, and a host of various environmental factors must be taken into account in the choice of plants. Nutritional value should be not ignored, in terms of calories, protein, and vitamin and mineral content. And, of course, personal preference may be the deciding factor in many cases. Hundreds of books, each hundreds of pages long, have been written on the topic of vegetable gardening. In order to present a great deal of information concisely, we have used a number of tables, while specific plants are discussed with an eye towards pointers. Although they appear later, Tables 7.6 and 7.7 on "companion planting" are also relevant here.

Alfalfa Sprouts or Bean Sprouts: Great for salads and sandwiches. Soak alfalfa seeds, soybeans, or mung beans overnight at room temperature. Rinse in a wide-mouthed jar with cheesecloth fastened over the mouth, then drain by inverting jar. Wash at least three times a day. It's ready to eat in three or four days—quick and nutritious.

Lima Beans: Beans are easy to grow, have both a high yield and a high caloric content, and are an excellent source of protein. Lima beans may be grown up a pole or as a bush, with comparable yields. Because a bush takes up more area, the pole variety would yield more per square foot. To grow pole beans, any convenient pole, fence, or even cornstalk may be used. Care should be taken to avoid shading other plants.

Snap Beans: Also called string beans, they come in either green or yellow varieties, with either flat or round pods. Culturing of bush beans is the same as pole beans, but without any poles. Keep in mind that all beans grow well in nitrogen-poor soil since they have nitrogen-fixing bacteria growing in nodules on their roots. Because of this, bean plants are excellent compost material after harvesting; or they can be tilled directly back into the soil for the next year's planting.

Beets: A useful plant since both the red root and the green tops can be eaten. Beets are good indicators of soil acidity; a good beet crop is evidence that your soil is not too acid. They grow quickly, so that crops can be successively replanted several times during the growing season. They can be easily transplanted, are relatively free of disease and pests, can be grown into the winter, and are good crops for container planting. Consequently, beets are a highly desirable crop.

Broccoli: A large plant, usually two feet high. Besides the flowering heads, stems and leaves are also edible. I find the secret to preparing the stems for eating is to strip off the tough outer skin before cooking. In this way you can easily double the amount of food from a broccoli plant. After cutting the central flower stalk, new flower heads will develop. But watch out for cabbage worm.

Cabbage: Easy to grow, store, and cook. It is nutritious, a hardy plant which plays an important role in many gardens. Cabbage likes a lot of sun, but does not like tomatoes nearby. Unfortunately, it is a prime target for insects, but can be grown in containers successfully.

Carrots: A sure thing for your garden. They are easy to grow, resistant to insects and disease, and very nutritious. Plant some every month for a continuous harvest. Carrots can be grown year round in warmer climates and do well in container gardens. These and all other plants which can be grown through the winter are good candidates for greenhouse crops in colder climates and for winter planters having a southern exposure.

Celery: A bit choosy, with a preference for cool surroundings and rich soils. They have a fairly shallow root system and need to be kept moist. Good container crop.

Chard: Another fast and easy-to-grow plant with a long growing season. Chard can be harvested continuously one leaf at a time. They are susceptible to the same worms that eat cabbage, so don't put these two kinds of plants next to each other. Good container crop.

Corn: In addition to its obvious aesthetic appeal, corn is not hard to grow and has a high caloric content. Stalks may be used for cattle fodder or as poles for pole beans. Its only drawback is a low yield per square foot. Corn should be planted in adjacent rows to insure pollination and may be planted in succession for a continuous harvest. More to come about corn when we discuss grain.

Cucumber: A rapid-growing, warm-season vegetable which needs lots of water. The vine can grow up onto a fence to save space and the cucumber may appear overnight, so be prepared for a pleasant surprise. The new dwarf variety is a bush plant which takes up one-third the space of the vine.

Eggplant: One of the most attractive plants and vegetables to look at, from its lavender flowers to its deep-magenta fruit. It likes a long, hot growing season and a rich soil. Just a few plants provide more than enough eggplant for a family.

Lettuce: Easy to grow and full of vitamins. Plant in succession for a continuous crop, or grow the loose-leaf variety and continuously pick off the outer leaves. Good for containers. Who can eat a salad without lettuce?

Melons: A vegetable not to forget. The melon needs sun, heat, and a lot of space in which to grow. A good place might be around cornstalks. Don't be in a hurry—they need three or four months.

Onions: A hardy and readily grown plant. The simplest and quickest method is from bulbs. Onions have few pests and don't mind cold weather. An onion has stopped growing when its top falls over, but it need not be dug up right away. For green onions, pick them before they form bulbs. Easily grown in containers and window boxes.

Peas: A gourmet treat that rapidly deteriorates as it is stored. Peas should be planted early in the spring, and at ten-day intervals through the summer for a continuous crop. Trouble with pests is largely avoided by picking the peas when young and tender. Don't overlook the Snow Peas and Sugar Peas, which are eaten with their tender pods and thus create less wastage.

Peppers: Very nutritious and relatively free of diseases and insect pests. Plants can be started either in a hotbed, in a bed of rich soil covered with glass, or in pots indoors. They are transplanted in from eight to ten weeks, once the frost danger is past.

Radishes: An infallible crop that requires little care, grows rapidly, and can be planted just about anywhere. Their shallow roots need nutrients and moisture near the surface. These can readily be grown in containers and are a satisfying crop since you can harvest in a month or less.

Spinach: A vigorous and attractive plant that contains a lot of vitamins and iron. It grows quickly (40 days from seed to maturity), prefers cool temperatures, and can be a winter crop in temperate regions. It is sown early and, like other leafy crops, can be seeded in succession to provide virtually a year-round crop. Harvest the whole plant, or individual leaves one at a time. Another good container crop.

Soybeans: The most complete protein source of all vegetables. They are easily grown like other beans and have few insect enemies, but watch out for rabbits. They can be picked green, to shell and eat like peas; or pick them already dried on the stalk for storage, milling, sprouting, and eating. The entire plant is an excellent animal feed and nitrogen source for composting.

Squash: Produces phenomenal yields of nutritious food. The traditional Hubbard squash is a sure bet for most gardens. Squash need elbow-room and, like melons, can be grown interspersed with corn. It is worthwhile to know that squash can be eaten at any stage of development (though the summer squashes tend to be best eaten young), and all varieties keep very well. New bush varieties take up one-quarter to one-third the space and are suitable for small gardens.

Table 7.1   Vegetable Planting Periods[a]

Season	Vegetable	Planting Period
Sp	Asparagus	1/1–3/1
Sp/Su	Beans, Bush	3/10–8/1
Sp/Su	Beans, Lima	3/15–7/15
Sp/Su	Beans, Pole	3/10–7/15
A	Beets	All year
Sp/F	Broccoli	2/1–3/1 & 8/1–11/15
Sp/F	Brussels Sprouts	2/1–3/1 & 8/1–11/15
Sp/F	Cabbage, Early	1/15–2/25 & 8/1–11/15
Sp/F	Cabbage, Late	1/15–2/25 & 8/1–11/15
Sp	Cantaloupes	3/15–5/15
A	Carrots	All year
Sp/F	Cauliflower	1/20–2/20 & 8/1–11/15
Sp/F	Celery	2/1–3/1 & 8/1–11/15
A	Chard	All year
Sp	Chives	1/1–2/15[d]
Sp/F	Collards	1/15–3/15 & 8/1–11/15
Sp/Su	Corn	3/1–7/1[e]
Sp/Su	Cucumbers	3/1–7/1
Sp	Eggplant	3/10–4/15
Sp/F	Garlic	2/1–3/1 & 8/1–11/15
Sp	Horseradish	3/1–4/1
Sp/F	Kale	2/1–2/20 & 8/1–11/15
Sp/F	Kohlrabi	2/1–2/20 & 8/1–11/15
Sp/F	Leeks	1/15–2/15 & 8/1–11/15
Sp/F	Lettuce, Head	1/15–2/15 & 8/1–11/15
A	Lettuce, Leaf	All year[b]
Sp/F	Mustard	2/1–3/1 & 8/1–11/15
Sp	Okra	3/10–6/1
Sp	Onions	1/1–2/15 & 8/1–11/15
Sp/F	Parsnips	1/15–2/15 & 8/1–11/15
Sp/F	Peas, Bush	1/15–3/1 & 8/1–11/15
Sp/F	Peas, Pole	1/15–3/1 & 8/1–11/15
Sp	Peppers	3/15–5/1
Sp	Potatoes	1/15–3/1
Sp	Potatoes, Sweet	3/20–6/1
Sp	Pumpkins	3/15–5/15
A	Radishes	All year[c]
Sp	Rhubarb	2/1–3/7
A	Rutabagas	All year
A	Salsify	All year
Sp	Scallions	1/1–2/15[d]
Sp	Shallots	1/1–2/15[d]
Sp	Soybeans	3/20–6/30
Sp/F	Spinach	1/1–3/1 & 8/1–11/15
Sp/Su	Squash, Summer	3/15–7/1
Sp	Squash, Winter	3/15–5/15
Sp	Tomatoes	3/10–6/1[f]
A	Turnips	All year
Sp	Watermelons	3/15–5/15

Notes: a. From Common Ground Organic Supply, Palo Alto, Calif. Data relevant for climates similar to Palo Alto.
   b. Some protection may be required in winter and summer.
   c. Some protection may be required in summer.
   d. March 1 for sets.
   e. August 1 for early varieties.
   f. July 1 for early varieties.

Tomatoes: Because of the many ways in which tomatoes are used, they will probably figure prominently in any garden. Insect pests pose a real problem, but one that can be overcome. If chickens are available, they make ideal hunters for the tomato horn worm. Tomatoes can be started as seedlings in either glassed-in seedbeds or indoor pots. They are transplanted when two inches tall into separate pots and should be moved into the ground when all danger of frost is past. They can be either staked or unstaked. In the latter case, it is advisable to use a lot of mulch (an insulating layer of wood chips, sawdust, or vegetable matter) to keep the fruit clean and dry. Don't overwater; flowers drop, and so does your yield. Varieties have been developed by the seed companies specifically for small spaces and containers.

This is not a comprehensive list; it deals with a few of the more common, reliable vegetables. Table 7.1 summarizes the approximate planting periods for a variety of vegetables and may help you plan your garden for the year (data applicable to all climates similar to Palo Alto, California). Anyone doing gardening is advised to buy and keep for reference any of the fine books on organic gardening (see Bibliography), and to ascertain planting periods for your specific climatic situation. Another source is the seed catalogues, which have quite a bit of information when read carefully.

Berries

Berries are an important element in your garden, as anyone who has ever eaten blueberry pie or peanut butter and jelly sandwiches can attest. And if you're a thirsty winebibber. . . .

Strawberries: Strawberries grow best in a slightly acidic environment (pH 6), with rich organic soil. It is a shallow-rooted plant; good drainage is important, as well as lots of moisture when the fruits are growing. Strawberries *need* sun; they should not be near trees or other plants with extensive roots (such as grapes). If different types of species are intermixed—early-season, mid-season, and late-season varieties, for example—a long harvest is possible. Plants will cost about $18–$30 per hundred (this and all other prices quoted herein are estimates; prices vary according to where and when purchased, the quality and age of the plant, and the quantity). Some varieties can be grown from seeds which are quite inexpensive. Strawberries should be planted on a cloudy spring day to protect them from drying. The roots should always be kept moist; spread them well when you plant them in the soil. Pruning is suggested for the first year to insure good rooting. Strawberries will send out runners to propagate, and a few score plants will soon turn into a few hundred!

These berries are a good choice for an urban garden of limited size. Not much space is needed if a tiered pyramid of soil is fashioned for the strawberry patch. They can even be grown on a sunny patio in a strawberry pot or a barrel with holes uniformly spaced along the sides;

the individual plants are each placed in a hole. Good drainage is very important, and the pot or barrel should be rotated so that all plants get sufficient sunlight.

Blueberries: Blueberry bushes need a lot of sun, a rich, loose, acidic (pH 5) soil, and fair amounts of water. They grow slowly and bear the most fruit after eight or ten years.

When buying blueberry bushes, be certain of two things: buy three-year-old plants, and buy at least two different types to insure cross-pollination. Three-year-old plants (12 to 18 inches) will cost about $5.00 each. Spring planting is best; water immediately after planting, then mulch with sawdust if the soil is too alkaline. It is more important in the first year for the plant to develop good roots than to blossom: all the blossoms should be pruned off the first year, and any suckers (shoots growing from the roots or stem) should also be cut. Mulching each year keeps the soil acid, and pruning each year increases yield. The bush will bear two years after transplanting. Yield will be about 10 quarts per bush, although the first harvest will probably be smaller.

Blackberries and Raspberries: These tough and hardy bramble bushes grow happily almost anywhere, but more fruit is harvested when they are planted in deep, loamy soils (having porous consistency and good drainage) at pH 6. They prefer some shade and protection from winds, and also need extra water when the berries are maturing.

Buy one-year-old stock from a local nursery and plant in the early spring. The costs run about $35 for 25 small blackberry plants and $30 for an equal number of small raspberry plants. Plants should be placed from 3 to 10 feet apart since they have extensive root systems. Mulching should be performed after planting, using 10 inches of straw or rotted leaves, or 3 inches of sawdust.

Pruning for raspberries and blackberries is highly recommended. Left alone, they can take over your entire garden. All shoots should be cut back to 10 inches in length after planting; each year, after harvesting, the fruit-bearing canes should be pruned entirely away, since they will no longer bear fruit. It is best to prune back to about half a dozen of the sturdiest year-old canes after the winter. Blackberries and raspberries self-propagate by sending up root suckers. To slow down the propagation, simply treat a sucker as you would any weed. One last thing: there is virtually no pest damage if you have good soil drainage.

Grapes: Grapes grow best in rich, well-drained, neutral soil (pH 6 to 8). They need plenty of sun and air, but can withstand dry weather very well because they are a deep-rooting vine, delving down from 6 to 8 feet. They are long-lived (50 to 60 years) and require from three to five years for full productivity.

Buy one- or two-year-old plants. The cost for five plants will range from $10 to $20, with the seedless varieties being more expensive. Plants should be spaced from 4 to 10 feet apart, depending on the pruning and training procedures. They do well in sunny, urban gardens when trained for trellises or patios, but remember: it will take several years. It's also nice to know that they are relatively pest-free.

Careful pruning is not as critical for a decorative grape arbor as it is for a bountiful grape harvest. Pruning controls the old branches since fruits are carried only by new growth. Among the many methods, one example is described here and illustrated in Figure 7.2—the four-arm Kniffen method. Just before or after planting, trim away all the shoots until only one remains. This will form the trunk of the vine. Then, late the next winter, after the plant has grown out some, choose four canes, two growing in each direction, and prune away all other canes. These four canes should then be attached to a wire strung between the stakes. After the second winter, prune away all but twelve buds from the four canes; but also leave one spur, with one bud, next to each cane. A spur is a smaller branch, cut back almost to the trunk. It is these spurs which will form the secondary canes or laterals. Each successive year, leave a few more laterals on the plant; by the fifth year, the plant will be at its most desirable size.

Trees

When people think of gardening, they usually think

Table 7.2 Nutritional Value of Fresh Fruits and Nuts[a]

Fruit or Nuts	Quantity	Calories (Energy Value)	Protein (gm)	Fat (gm)	Calcium (mg)	Iron (mg)	Vitamin A (Internat. Units)	Vitamin B₁ Thiamin (mg)	Vitamin B₂ Riboflavin (mg)	Niacin (mg)	Vitamin C Ascorbic Acid (mg)
Almonds	1 cup (shelled)	850	26.0	77.0	232	6.7	—	0.34	1.31	5.0	—
Apples	1 medium	76	0.4	0.5	8	0.4	120	0.05	0.04	0.2	6
Apricots	3	54	1.1	0.1	17	0.5	2990	0.03	0.05	0.9	7
Avocados	1/2 (peeled)	279	1.9	30.1	11	0.7	330	0.07	0.15	1.3	18
Bananas	1 large	119	1.6	0.3	11	0.8	570	0.06	0.06	1.0	13
Blackberries	1 cup	82	1.7	1.4	46	1.3	280	0.05	0.06	0.5	30
Blueberries	1 cup	85	0.8	0.8	22	1.1	400	0.04	0.03	0.4	23
Cashews	1 cup (shelled)	1312	41.0	110.0	104	11.2	—	1.40	0.40	4.8	—
Cherries	1 cup	65	1.2	0.5	19	0.4	660	0.05	0.06	0.4	9
Currants	1 cup	60	1.3	0.2	40	1.0	130	0.04	0	0	40
Dates (fresh or dried)	1 cup (pitted)	505	3.9	1.1	128	3.7	100	0.16	0.17	3.9	0
Figs	4 large	79	1.4	0.4	54	0.6	80	0.06	0.05	0.5	2
Grapefruit	1/2 medium	75	0.9	0.4	41	0.4	20	0.07	0.04	0.4	76
Grapes (American)	1 cup (raw)	84	1.7	1.7	20	0.7	90	0.07	0.05	0.3	5
Guavas	1 medium	49	0.7	0.4	21	0.5	180	0.05	0.03	0.8	212
Lemons	1 medium	20	0.6	0.4	25	0.4	0	0.03	tr.[b]	0.1	31
Limes	1 medium	18	0.4	0.1	21	0.3	0	0.02	tr.[b]	0.1	14
Loganberries	1 cup	90	1.4	0.9	50	1.7	280	0.04	0.10	0.1	34
Mangoes	1 medium	87	0.9	0.3	12	0.3	8380	0.08	0.07	1.2	55
Oranges	1 medium	70	1.4	0.3	51	0.6	290	0.12	0.04	0.4	77
Papayas	1 cup	71	1.1	0.2	36	0.5	3190	0.06	0.07	0.5	102
Peaches	1 medium	46	0.5	0.1	8	0.6	880	0.02	0.05	0.9	8
Peanuts	1 cup (shelled)	1272	61.0	100.0	168	4.0	—	0.72	0.32	37.0	—
Pears	1 (peeled)	95	1.1	0.6	20	0.5	30	0.03	0.06	0.2	6
Pecans	1 cup (shelled halves)	696	9.4	73.0	74	2.4	50	0.72	0.11	0.9	2
Persimmons	1 medium (seedless)	95	1.0	0.5	7	0.4	3270	0.06	0.05	tr.[b]	13
Pineapple	1 cup (diced)	74	0.6	0.3	22	0.4	180	0.12	0.04	0.3	33
Plums	1 medium	29	0.4	0.1	10	0.3	200	0.04	0.02	0.3	3
Prunes (dried)	4 medium (unsulfured)	73	0.6	0.2	15	1.1	510	0.03	0.04	0.5	1
Raisins (dried)	1 cup (unsulfured)	429	3.7	0.8	125	5.3	80	0.24	0.13	0.5	tr.[b]
Raspberries (black)	1 cup	74	1.5	2.1	54	1.2	0	0.03	0.09	0.4	32
Raspberries (red)	1 cup	70	1.5	0.5	49	1.1	160	0.03	0.08	0.4	29
Strawberries	1 cup	54	1.2	0.7	42	1.2	90	0.04	0.10	0.4	89
Tangerines	1 medium	35	0.6	0.2	27	0.3	340	0.06	0.02	0.2	25
Walnuts (English)	100 gm.	650	15.0	64.0	99	3.1	30	0.33	0.13	0.9	3

Notes: a. From *The Encyclopedia of Organic Gardening* and *How to Grow Vegetables and Fruits by the Organic Method*, by J.I. Rodale. b. Trace.

only of plants which must be planted every year. There is no reason why trees can't be included in a backyard garden if the area is sufficiently large; dwarf varieties are perfect for these backyard situations. With enough land, of course, you can plan a nice orchard. Fruit- and nut-bearing trees should not be overlooked when you consider landscaping or wind and sun protection; beyond beauty and shelter, they provide a regular source of highly nutritional food. Table 7.2 provides a summary of the nutritional aspects of a variety of fruits and nuts.

Fruit Trees: There are two very common methods for setting up an orchard: straight rows, or rows which curve along the contours of a hill. No matter which method you choose, the following recommendations should be followed. Fruit trees should be planted on higher land to prevent frost from killing the fruit and to insure adequate water drainage. They need well-drained soil (important for air circulation to the roots), a medium loam rich in organic material (3 to 5 percent), and a pH of about 6. Deep soil is also a must; depth can be determined by taking a boring with a soil tube. Plant on a northern slope to delay the blooming season and a southern slope to hasten it. Planting distances for the various trees are listed in Table 7.3.

All fruit trees should be watered only once a week; overwatering delays maturity of young trees and damages the fruits. Composting and mulching are essential for good growth. Make a ring of compost around the tree (but out away from the trunk to prevent rodent destruction) and then cover this ring with a foot of hay, leaves, or orchard-grass mulch. Pruning is also essential to increase the crop, improve fruit quality, and repair damages. Figure 7.3 summarizes the four basic pruning steps, along with some other techniques important for tree maintenance.

Purchase your stock from a local nursery; be sure to obtain types which do best in your area. It is important to remember that for the best-quality fruit (and for most trees to develop fruit at all), more than one variety must be planted in the same vicinity to insure cross-pollination, necessary for most fruit trees. Peach, nectarine, and fig, however, can self-pollinate. Nursery stock usually are two- and three-year-old trees. The average cost will be about $6 to $12 per tree.

Propagation of most trees can be accomplished by layering; pears, apples, cherries, peaches, and plums are exceptions. Layering consists of bending and burying part of the length of a branch from three to six inches in the ground. The top of the branch becomes the new plant. Roots will form where it is buried; the connection with the parent tree then can be cut. This technique produces a new seedling quickly. Pear, apple, cherry, peach, and plum trees can be propagated by growing seedlings and then budding or grafting them onto a root stock (a length of root taken from an adult plant). Detailed information on these propagation techniques can be found in almost every reference on orchards and trees. Harvesting, of

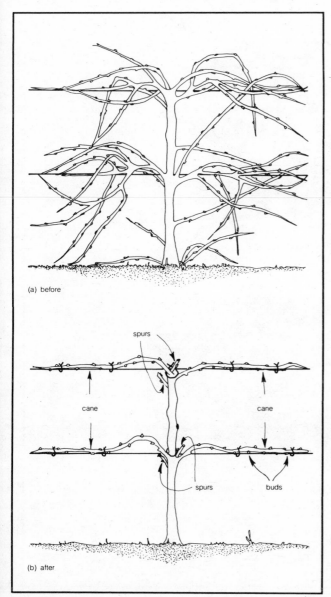

(a) before

spurs

cane

cane

spurs

buds

(b) after

Figure 7.2 The four-arm Kniffen method of pruning.

Table 7.3 Fruit Tree Data[a]			
	Min. Distance Between Plants (feet)	Approx. Yield per Plant (bushels)	Bearing Age (years)
Apple, standard	35	8.0	6–10
Apple, double dwarf	20	2.0	4–6
Apple, dwarf	12	0.5	2–3
Pear, standard	25	3.0	5–8
Pear, dwarf	12	0.5	3–4
Peach	20	4.0	3–4
Plum	20	2.0	4–5
Quince	15	1.0	5–6
Cherry, sour	20	2.0	4–5
Cherry, sweet	25	2.5	5–7

Notes: a. From J.I. Rodale, *How to Grow Vegetables and Fruits by the Organic Method.* Prepared by Virginia Polytechnic Institute.

course, is the most fun; optimum ripeness is determined by your taste. The approximate yields and bearing ages of various fruit trees are listed in Table 7.3.

Dwarf Trees: Many species of fruit trees also can be obtained as dwarf trees which are from five to eight feet tall; there are even smaller "double dwarf" trees which are from four to six feet tall. They produce, however, the same size fruit as a standard tree. The advantages of dwarf trees are many: they save space if land is at a premium (in urban gardens); they can be grown in large containers;

they fruit sooner (see Table 7.3); and yield is sometimes better than that from a regular tree, because dwarf trees are easier to care for and easier to harvest, with less consequent waste and fallen fruit. However, dwarf trees have less extensive root systems and so are more susceptible to wind damage. They also have shorter bearing lifespans (20 to 30 years) than standard trees (40 to 50 years), and they cost more initially.

The trees from a local nursery will run about $10 to $15 apiece. Soil and climatic requirements are the same as for normal trees, but planting is a bit different. The

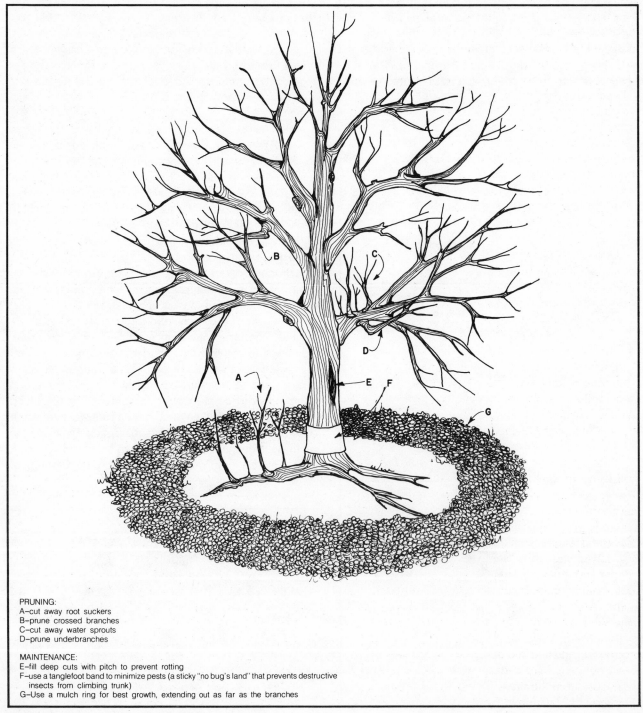

PRUNING:
A–cut away root suckers
B–prune crossed branches
C–cut away water sprouts
D–prune underbranches

MAINTENANCE:
E–fill deep cuts with pitch to prevent rotting
F–use a tanglefoot band to minimize pests (a sticky "no bug's land" that prevents destructive insects from climbing trunk)
G–Use a mulch ring for best growth, extending out as far as the branches

Figure 7.3 Tree pruning and maintenance.

dwarf tree must be planted with the graft-union above ground—the graft-union is a small knob on the trunk where the bark is a different color. These trees also need cross-pollination: more than two species *must* be planted. After planting, trim off any suckers or branches within a foot of the ground at the trunk. Maintenance, mulching, and harvesting are the same as for the regular trees, and the approximate yields are given in Table 7.3.

Nut Trees: The best trees for edible nuts are Chinese chestnut, hickory, pecan, walnut, and filbert. Certain types grow better in specific climates, as do certain species of each type, so check in advance with your local nursery or Agricultural Extension Service.

Some basic advice will suffice for all the many types and species. A northern slope with deep soil and good drainage is best. Trees should be planted from 20 to 30 feet apart; this distance is adequate for their deep, extensive root system, yet close enough for cross-pollination to occur. Again, to insure cross-pollination, at least two species of any single type must be planted. Planting requires a large hole for the extensive taproot (the main root which grows straight down). Pack soil around the tree; it then should be watered and a mulch of straw or rotted leaves spread around the trunk. Maintenance and pruning are the same as for fruit trees, and propagation can be achieved by layering.

One final note: these trees grow very slowly and do not always bear. Even when they bear, the yield is small unless conditions are almost perfect, so don't plant these trees with exaggerated hopes. Approximate costs vary from $7 to $15 depending on the species and the size.

Grain

If your farm is to be self-sufficient, it will need at least a few acres of grain. The grain is used not only for human consumption, but also for fodder, winter bedding for your animals, covercropping, mulching, and feed for your methane digester. Obviously, it is not a good choice for the urban garden of limited size.

Except for corn, the procedures for planting and harvesting the different grains are very similar. Grain is planted by two basic methods: either get a grain drill, drill holes, and drop the seed in; or simply broadcast the seeds uniformly over the ground and rake to cover them over. Harvesting for any grain (except corn) is a back-breaking, time-consuming labor. Stiff muscles may cause you to wonder just how self-sufficient you really want to be. Grain-bearing grass is cut with either a normal or cradle scythe. A cradle scythe is one with an arrangement of fingerlike rods which catch the grass and enable you to lay it evenly on the ground; alternatively, the grass can be propped up and tied into bundles. For threshing, the grass is laid out on a hard surface, and a flail is used to beat grain loose from the straw. To separate the grain from the straw, you must winnow: the threshed grass is thrown up in the air when the wind is blowing, and the straw is blown away as the heavier grain drops straight down. The grain can then be stored until milling. It should be well protected from insects.

Buckwheat: Buckwheat can be used as an ingredient in breads or for livestock feed. It grows best in a cool, moist climate; but it also grows on soil which does not support other grains very well because of buckwheat's ability to utilize nutrients from the soil more effectively. The two major varieties are the Japanese and the silverhull, which are often sown together; but check with your local Agricultural Extension Service to determine the proper types for your area. Be sure the seeds you purchase are certified disease-free. The best planting time is ten weeks before the first fall frost. If you have a grain drill, or can borrow one, drilling is preferred. Use about 4 pecks (1 peck = 0.25 bushel = 8 quarts) per acre. After harvesting, allow your grain to field-dry for ten days. It can then be stored for winter fodder or else be threshed in preparation for milling. After threshing, the straw can be used for mulch or bedding. Yield is between 20 and 30 bushels per acre.

Oats: Oats can be used for bedding, for fodder, and, of course, for cereals and breads to eat yourself. Make certain you buy the right type for your area. You will need about 5 to 10 pecks per acre, depending on regional conditions. Spring seeding is preferred, and should take place about a week before the last spring frost. Adequate water is very important. Harvest the oats when the kernels are soft enough to be dented slightly by your fingernail. Cut it with a cradle scythe, let it dry for a day, and then bind it into 12-inch-diameter bundles; stand these bundles upright to field-cure for two weeks. Yield will be about 25 to 40 bushels per acre.

Rye: Because rye will grow in almost any type of soil, it is useful as a cover crop or as green manure (a plant which is plowed back into the soil so that it will decompose into fertilizer). Rye also can be used for making bread. Plant rye in either fall or spring, at about the time of the first or last frost, respectively. Use 2 bushels of seed per acre for green manuring, and 1 bushel per acre for grain. Harvest as you would wheat; yield will be about 15 bushels per acre.

Wheat: Wheat does best where there is a cool, moist growing season followed by a warm, dry period for curing. Spring wheat is usually planted in the northern United States, and winter wheat in the South. There are many types of wheat—hard red, soft red, winter, hard red spring, and durum, among others. Buy the one that best suits your growing area. Since wheat is self-fertilizing, you will be able to use your own seed the next year. Use about 6 pecks per acre when sowing. Plant winter wheat about the time of the first frost, and spring wheat about the time of the last killing frost. Harvest, as with rye and oats, when you can dent the grain kernel with your fingernail. Yield will be about 20 bushels per acre. To harvest, cut the wheat using a cradle scythe, bind it into bundles 10 inches in diameter, and let it field-dry for ten days. For flour, thresh and winnow the grain, and then grind it as needed to make bread. The straw can be used either for mulch or for bedding your livestock.

Corn: Plant dent corn or flint corn for stock feed, ground meal, and silage (green fodder preserved in a silo until it ferments). Plant sweet corn for yourself. All these types grow best in deep, rich, neutral-pH soil with lots of loam and adequate water.

Buy yellow corn seeds as opposed to white varieties, and open-pollinated types as opposed to hybrids. With the nonhybrid varieties, you will be able to use your own homegrown seeds for the following year's planting. In addition, the open-pollinated varieties tend to be sweeter and higher in protein. Use three different varieties in one planting to insure a long harvest, or else plant rows a week apart for from four to six weeks.

You should plant your corn a week after the last spring frost. The soil temperature required for germination is 60°F. Seeds should be deposited about 1.5 inches into the soil, in at least several rows to insure pollination. Rows should be spaced from 30 to 40 inches apart. Mulch with hay when the sprouts are 8 inches tall; or, if you prefer, cultivate in between the cornstalks such low-growing plants as melons or beans. Varieties with prickly stems and leaves are a good deterrent to raccoons, who may otherwise enjoy the corn as much as you would. Corn should be fed with compost or organic fertilizer when the lower leaves begin to lose their color. Harvest as soon as it is ripe; ripeness is indicated by brown silk and the appearance of a milky liquid when the kernel is dented with your fingernail. Yield is about 30 ears for a 50-foot row.

Livestock

As we pointed out earlier, all animals ultimately derive their energy from plants. In theory, energy conservation could be best effected by eating only plants. But we consider small farm livestock as an integral part of any agricultural system both because of their useful conversion to palatable food of plant materials (grass, garbage, chicken feed) most of us find unappetizing and also because they are a good source of manure, indispensable to a good organic garden.

For the most part, unfortunately, raising animals is not as viable as gardening on small urban "homesteads." But this is not to say there are no urban possibilities; these will be pointed out along the way. There are also a number of pamphlets put out by the state and federal governments which are useful, concise, and free (see Bibliography).

Chickens

Raising chickens for eggs and meat, as well as for their highly valuable manure, is relatively inexpensive and easy.

With your own homemade feed, you can say goodbye to the hormone-injected monsters weighed out in today's markets. To have an efficient, steadily producing flock rather than half-wild birds, it is important to have a good breed, good food and shelter, regular cleaning, and accurate laying records.

A dozen good laying hens will produce an average of six eggs per day. An easily managed project would be to start off with 50 one-day-old chicks and raise them, gradually selecting a dozen good pullets (young hens) for egg production and using the rest as fryers. The next year you start a new flock of egg layers by buying and raising a new brood of day-old chicks. Year-old hens lose about 15 to 30 percent of their egg-laying ability in their second year; they should be replaced gradually by newly selected pullets. This procedure presents a problem in housing since both groups need a coop; but if the chick raising is performed in the spring, extensive shelter will not be needed.

The shelter should take into consideration climate, feeding, egg collection, and maintenance. Based on a figure of 4 square feet per laying hen, a dozen laying hens will need a 6-by-8-foot house, with a small yard for exercise.

A chicken roost 18 inches high, with slats to provide a frame and covered with 1-inch chicken mesh, can be used within the coop (see Figure 7.4). The use of this roost can cut cleaning to three or four times a year, unless odors and flies become objectionable. This may not work very well in an urban environment where your own living quarters and those of neighbors are close by. In such a case, it would be best to consider a deep litter system or a tray and composting system as described in the *Integral Urban House*. Only three nests are required for 12 hens. To ease disturbance during egg collection, a rear hinged door can be installed for each nest so that you can reach into the coop quickly and quietly.

Breeds and Brooding: The breeds that you select should be the best ones available for year-round egg production and also for meat. The Rhode Island Red is good in this respect, with the Barred Plymouth Rock as a close second. Cross-breeding between these two breeds also provides excellent results.

To prevent the development of fatal pullorum disease in chicks, the breed selected should be rated "USDA pullorum-clean." To obtain the best egg layers, the chicks should be rated "U.S. Record of Performance Chicks" or "U.S. Certified Chicks." The latter two are National Poultry Improvement Plan ratings.

High-quality chicks run about 50 cents apiece and up, so that a flock of 50 will cost at least $25. It is best to buy a flock of both sexes as the cockerels (young males) can be used for meat at the end of three months, when they weigh around three pounds.

The most self-sufficient plan for raising chickens is to acquire both an incubator for hatching and a brooder for raising the chicks. (You will need a rooster only if fertile eggs are desired. They also make fewer friends among your neighbors.) Provided that adequate energy is available, an incubator can be used for the 20-day hatching period. The hens also can be used to hatch the eggs; however, this maternal care takes up egg-laying time. In most cases, it may be better to purchase day-old chicks each April when starting a new flock rather than hatch your own. Brooders (heated shelters—see Figure 7.5) should be used for about six weeks with increased space provided according to the size of the chicks. The brooder is set inside an enclosure with accessible water jars and

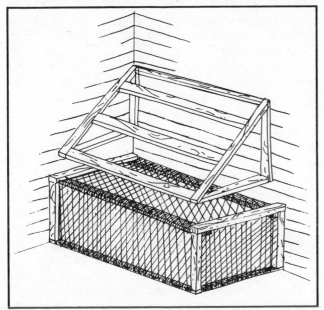

Figure 7.4 The chicken roost should be located away from drafts and against a wall. It can be constructed of supporting slats and chicken wire; if desired, a pit can be dug under the roosting area.

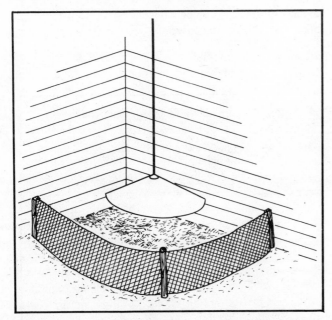

Figure 7.5 A brooder should be located in an area well protected from drafts. The area needs to be fenced to keep the little chicks in and the larger chickens out. Provide food, water, and heat from a hover.

feeders. A 60- to 100-watt bulb, a gallon jug of hot water, or hot-water pipes can provide adequate heat to the brooder. The area should be free from drafts. The temperature is right when the chicks stretch out uniformly under the hover (a heat-producing cover). The amount of heat should be reduced as rapidly as possible since lower temperatures help the chicks to feather faster. Some heat, however, is generally required for the first six weeks. Litter—peat moss, sand, wood shavings, and so on—should be placed underneath the brooder to absorb waste. It is advisable that the chicks be brooded away from older hens to prevent possible disease transmission. A basement or side room in your house will provide adequate warmth to maintain the 90°F temperature under the hover.

Feeding: For the first three days, the chicks can be fed a chick grain of finely cut corn, wheat, and oats, with chick-size insoluble grit or coarse sand also available in a feeder alongside. They then should be switched to starter mash—a mixture of corn, oats, and warm water, supplemented with grain meal and vitamins. About six weeks later, scratch—a mixture of corn, wheat, and oats without water—should be added in increasing proportions until, at four months, the chicks are receiving equal servings of scratch and mash. Calcium is an important nutrient for laying hens and is supplied by additions of ground limestone or oyster shells to the mash. The mash and scratch should be kept before the chickens in self-feeding hoppers nearby to gallon-size waterers. Save on purchased feed by using such kitchen wastes as leftover bread, vegetable peelings, leftover meat, fish, cheese, and culled potatoes. These scraps can be fed directly or boiled in a minimum of water and mixed with a sufficient amount of mash to make a crumbly mixture that is an excellent feed. Surplus greens—lawn clippings, kale, cabbage—can also be used as a feed supplement. If they are allowed to wander in your garden they are good pest predators and delight in consuming such delectables as snails and that juicy worm eating up the tomato plant. For scratch feed, an acre of field corn produces 75 percent of the total feed requirements for 25 chickens. A small corn sheller and feed grinder or a small feed mill can be purchased for $10. The feed items that you will have to buy are ground oats, bran, soybean oil meal, corn gluten meal, limestone, and salt; these items are far cheaper to purchase than to grow on a small farm. Over the year, you will need about 45 or 50 pounds each of both mash and grain for every fowl. Generally, a good hen will produce between 200 and 240 eggs a year. Keep in mind that some hens end up as nonlayers; these should be weeded out and used as fryers.

It is advisable not to feed the fowl during the 12 hours before slaughter. A small hand guillotine is the most humane and cleanest method; a stretch and twist of the neck is also fast.

Because of their relatively small size and their adaptability to enclosures, chickens can be raised in a large

333

backyard. Their manure is a source of essential nitrogen for the compost pile. The amount of space available will limit the number of chickens which can be accommodated. Remember, also, that a dozen or so chickens can get noisy and may not win friends among your neighbors. It's probably a good idea to check for community restrictions; you may not be "zoned" for poultry. For further information, see listings for J. Morley and G. Klein in the Bibliography.

Rabbits

Rabbits are among the easiest animals to raise and care for; they are also quite suitable for both rural and urban regions. Irate neighbors are certainly less probable than with chickens. The medium and large breeds are best for food requirements. Some breeds to consider are the French Angora, which grows to over 8 pounds and can be sheared for wool every ten weeks; California rabbits, which grow to 8 or 10 pounds; the American Chinchilla, which grows to 10 pounds; and the New Zealand breed, which grows to a comparable size. As with goats or poultry, you should check on the reliability of your dealer when you go into rabbit raising; that is, he or she should stand behind the product and guarantee the health and productivity of the animals. One buck and from two to four does are sufficient for a starting herd. The gestation period is very short, 30 days, and a good doe can produce four litters (five to eight young each litter) every year. Consequently, you have either a steady supply of food or a rapidly increasing rabbit herd! The young are marketable at four pounds, attained in about two months.

Shelter: Adequate shelter from the rain and occasional frost should be provided, as well as adequate shade and ventilation during the summer months. The dimensions for a medium-sized hutch (three to six rabbits) are generally 2 feet high, 2.5 feet wide, and 3 to 5 feet long (see Figure 7.6). Two hutches with a central storage compartment form a portable unit that can be taken under a larger

shelter or put outside for better ventilation. The floors should be slatted or wire meshed on one side for easier cleaning and for the collection of manure. Wire construction, if available, is preferable to wood since it does not retain odors. If chickens have access to rabbit droppings, they can control the breeding of maggots, making the final product less undesirable. A slight slope is best for good drainage. Nest boxes should be provided for seclusion when a doe gives birth; strong cardboard boxes with a small nest of hay will do. These should be placed in the hutch a few days before the doe gives birth.

Feeding: In order to minimize your labor, the holders should have the capacity for several feedings. The use of a central hay manger is very efficient. Grain hoppers made from five-gallon cans are also excellent, especially for pregnant does, since you want to minimize disturbances during gestation. Fresh water should be in continuous supply, particularly in hot weather, when a doe and her litter can drink up to a gallon a day.

The best hays to feed rabbits are such broad-leafed, green, short-stemmed hays as alfalfa, clover, lespedeza, and peanut; all of these are high in protein and need no supplement. Stemmier grasses—timothy, prairie, Johnson, Sudan, or carpet grasses—are fine, but you will need to add additional protein. High-protein diets may be necessary if your herd is doing poorly. For example, cracked grains can be supplemented with a soybean meal. Salt, too, should be provided; you can use blocks or else add it to the meals in a 0.5 or 1 percent concentration. Vegetable table scraps are excellent feed supplements and what the rabbits can't finish, the compost heap can. In fact, it has been pointed out that the feeding of bulky, fibrous table scraps to rabbits and chickens might be considered an initial process which makes the material more readily compostable, since it results in ground-up material that is partially decomposed.

Breeding: The medium-sized breeds can be mated between the ages of five and six months and the does will

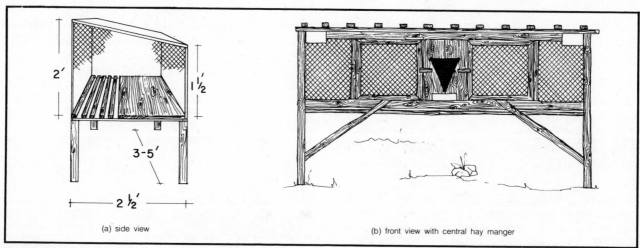

(a) side view

(b) front view with central hay manger

Figure 7.6 Rabbit shelters.

continue to reproduce for up to thirty months thereafter. Each litter requires a four-week gestation period and two months of nursing; as we mentioned, a healthy doe can produce four litters a year.

Slaughter: Rabbits grow rapidly and will be ready for slaughter after eight weeks. Killing is best effected by a stretch and twist of the neck or a sharp blow to the base of the skull. To skin the carcass, it should be hooked through the right rear leg. The tail, head, front feet, and free rear leg (up to the hock joint) should be severed. A slit is cut across the rear and the skin is pulled off like a glove with as much fat left on the carcass as possible. To clean the meat, the belly should be opened and the entrails and gall bladder removed. The carcass is then washed off and kept cool. The skin must be stretched while it is still warm. The use of barrel stretchers and patient work in a ventilated area will produce good results.

For further information on rabbits in general, see the listings under B. Angier, B. Kaysing, U.S. Department of Agriculture in the Bibliography and *The Integral Urban House,* by the Farallones Institute.

Goats

Goats are a good source of milk and cheese on a small farm. The better dairy goats provide 2 to 4 quarts per day for ten months of the year, eat less than a cow, and are easier to care for. The two dry months are taken up by pregnancy.

When selecting a particular breed, check with several dealers so that you see a variety of animals. There are five main milking breeds in the United States: American La Mancha, Nubian, Saanen, French Alpine, and Loggenburg. You should purchase two does, both to insure a continuous flow of milk and to give your goat company. A good doe costs from $35 to $75 and two provide enough milk for eight or ten people.

Housing: Special housing is not required, although any simple shelter should take into consideration dryness, cleanliness, and adequate warmth and shade. You must have space to handle hay, grain, water, and manure, and about 15 square feet of moving room per animal. For most of the year, however, goats can be put out to pasture.

Breeding: Unless you care to raise a larger herd, it is advisable to have the does bred at the dealer rather than raise a buck. Bucks can develop objectionable odors and they give little return for their feed. Also, a well-recorded buck insures excellent milkers in its offspring, and dealers keep such records. The gestation period is about 150 days and each doe generally produces two kids. They breed between September and February and give no milk for two months in early pregnancy.

Feeding: Goats are perhaps the best of all livestock for feeding on unimproved pasture. They should not be let out, however, on spring pasture until there is at least three or four inches of growth. The best range includes alfalfa, brome grass, clover, Sudan grass, or millet, the latter two being adequate for summer feed. An excellent spring or fall pasture is rye, wheat, or barley.

Goats need loose salt mixed in with their feed since they do not eat sufficient amounts of salt if it is in block form. Also, if the pasture is predominantly grass, they will need calcium and phosphorus supplements.

A milking doe will need about 450 pounds of grain and 500 pounds of hay each year, as well as vegetable scraps and any available root crops such as carrots, beets, and parsnips. When she is on a good pasture that is balanced in grasses and legumes, she should be fed one pound of grain for every four pounds of milk that she gives. To be on the safe side, equal quantities of salt and di-calcium phosphate should be easily available in separate, weatherproof containers. Yearlings should be given enough hay and grain to keep them content, but not so much that they become fat and you can no longer feel their ribs.

For the Best Milk: To obtain the best-tasting milk, the following guidelines should be followed:

1. Don't feed strong-flavored feeds (onions, silage, cabbage) within four hours of milking.

2. The udders and flanks should be clipped to prevent hair from getting in the milk.

3. Wash udders with warm water and iodophor or a solution of quaternary ammonium prior to each milking.

4. Use a milking stand with a stanchion (a bar that holds the animal's head in place) and stainless-steel milking pails.

5. The milk should be strained when poured into the milk cans.

6. To retard bacterial growth, the cans should be immersed in coolers that are at a temperature of 33 to 35°F.

7. Pasteurization can be done easily by rapid heating to from 150 to 180°F over the stove and then cooling.

For further information, see the listings in the Bibliography under B. Colby and U.S. Department of Agriculture.

Cows

The advantages of raising a cow need hardly be recounted—all the milk, cream, yoghurt, and butter you can eat. In addition, cow manure is one of the finest additions your garden or compost heap can ever see. You will have the best results if pasture and hay are plentiful, shelter and daily care can be given, and breeding is available.

Dairy cows vary in the amount of milk they can produce. A cow with moderate production can be purchased for $400 to $500, kept five years, and then sold for $100; this would amount to about $60 or $80 of "depreciation" each year. This animal will produce from 3000 to 5000 quarts per year, roughly enough milk for from 8 to 16 people. An estimate of total yearly costs, including the cost for feed and bedding, would be $650—roughly 20 cents per quart! Actual costs might even be less.

Housing: The cow needs only a simple shelter with a small amount of moving space. A three-sided stable with sunny southern exposure is probably adequate in a moderate climate. The cow can be either stanchioned or left untied in a box stall about 10 feet square. Bedding of straw, cornstalks, or similar material is required—about 800 to 1600 pounds a year.

Feeding: A milk cow can eat up to 25 pounds of hay per day, which adds up to 3 or 4 tons per year. She also needs 1 or 2 tons of grain supplements each year. These costs can run about $60 to $100 a ton for hay, and around $80 to $120 a ton for grain; naturally, you can save money if you grow feed grain and hay yourself. Two acres of pastureland supplying about six months of food can cut the cost in half. A rough estimate of yearly food and bedding costs for a cow is from $300 to $650.

Care: A cow must be tended every day and generally is milked both morning and evening; the guidelines for goat's milk also apply here. A small electric home pasteurizer costs about $80 and can be used for either goat's or cow's milk. For further information, see listings for B. Angier and B. Kaysing in the Bibliography.

Bees

Beekeeping (apiculture) is a venture that requires only a small initial investment and a minimal amount of labor, and is adaptable to both urban and rural settings. From very modest efforts, you can expect a yield of approximately 75 to 100 pounds of honey a year per hive. In addition to being a source of food, bees also pollinate flowering crops and play an important part in increasing crop yields. And, they sting! To produce a honey crop, you need to make about 20 visits to the hives a year; in contrast to raising animals, no feed need be provided.

There are five basic pieces of "equipment" to which you will need access: a hive, bees, protective clothing, a smoker, and an extractor. For a start, you can buy the bees for from $20 to $30 from a supplier (who can certify that they are disease-free), invest in one hive, and then rent the extractor.

Housing: Bees and a large secondhand hive can be purchased for around $70 to $80. The standard hive produced in the United States is called a ten-frame Langstroth. As illustrated in Figure 7.7, it includes a cover, two honey supers, a queen excluder, a brood chamber, and a bottom stand. Ten wax frames, embossed with a pattern of hexagonal cells to provide a base for the bees to build regular cells, are placed perpendicularly into each of the honey supers and the brood chamber. These are reusable and can last up to 40 years. The queen excluder is a sievelike screen that allows the smaller workers to pass through, but confines the queen to the brood chamber. This isolation insures that no eggs will be laid in the honey supers.

When handling the hive, you should wear light-colored, smooth clothing because this attire seems to calm angry bees. Wear hightop boots with the cuffs of your pants tucked in securely. A fine mesh or screen should be used to protect your face and neck. But bear in mind that no matter how good your protective clothing is or how careful you are, you still can expect to get stung occasionally.

Care: The best time to start beekeeping is in the spring. If the bees are properly managed, the major honey flow will occur in late June or early July. A second honey flow will occur in the fall. The bees should have access both to water and to 15 or 20 pounds of reserve honey at any time during the year. Since a single frame of honeycomb usually contains from 5 to 7 pounds of honey, this means three frames should be left in the hive as surplus. But to over-winter a hive in cold climates, your bees will need approximately 60 pounds of honey or supplementary sugar water to last until spring.

Bees are subject to diseases that can reduce honey yields. These diseases generally appear in the hive when the bees are under stress. Consequently, removing the stress usually eliminates the disease. If you suspect a problem, it is a good idea to consult the local apiary inspector.

To extract honey, first use the smoker to blow smoke into the hive; this pacifies the bees. Then the frames are removed and placed in the extractor. The extractor spins around and centrifugal force throws the honey against the walls. The honey then can be collected from the bottom of the extractor.

After gaining experience and discovering your limitations, you might expand until you have up to four hives. Unless you are going into business, four hives produce about as much honey as most small groups can consume. For further information, see listings in the Bibliography for R. A. Morse and A. I. Root.

Compost and Fertilizer

The concept of fertilization is fundamental to the process of recycling nutrients through the biosphere. As a plant grows, it extracts nutrients from the soil, the most important ones being nitrogen, phosphorus, and potassium. Without restoration of its nutrients, the soil would eventually be depleted and be unable to support plant growth.

There are four arguments against the use of chemical fertilizers to resupply the soil. First, the nutrients found in chemical fertilizers have been "displaced" from some other "home" in the natural world; the redistribution of these nutrients (away from their home) somewhere disturbs the balance of natural, complex cycling processes. Secondly, chemical fertilizers do not improve soil texture or soil's ability to hold moisture. Nutrients are leached away by rainfall; large runoffs of nitrogen fertilizer can cause algal blooms in rivers and streams, which lead to lower dissolved-oxygen levels in the water, which can, in turn, kill fish. Thirdly, the manufacture of chemical fertilizer consumes great quantities of valuable energy. And finally, the use of chemical fertilizers implies that natural sources of fertilizer are not being exploited and, most probably, are being disposed of in some polluting manner.

A typical municipal sewer system is an example of real waste and pollution through the disposal of "wastes" that, properly handled, could have been utilized as fertilizer. Human, animal, and vegetable wastes can be recycled through a field of food crops repeatedly without seriously upsetting the natural mineral balance of the soil.

Composting

Composting is one of the most commonly practiced methods of recycling nutrients through crop lands on a small scale and is useful for both urban and rural gardens. Although there are many techniques, the most commonly practiced composting process is the mixture of organic wastes and soil into a pile where the temperature can be maintained at around 140 to 160°F. This high temperature enables bacteria and fungi from the soil to decompose the organic wastes into chemical nutrients that can be used by plants.

Almost any organic matter can be used as composting material (see Table 7.4). Exceptions include such hard calcareous organic matter as bone or seashell. The primary sources of material for the compost pile are animal wastes (manure), vegetable or crop wastes, kitchen wastes, and soil. All green material should be partially withered.

Most materials will be dry or, at most, damp. Each component must be sprinkled with water for the process to occur. It is important, however, not to make the pile too wet, as excessive moisture will hinder the process. If the materials are quite wet, they should be spread out to dry somewhat before adding to the compost heap.

Besides these basic ingredients, additives can improve the pH and the nutrient content of the final product. Ground limestone, commercial lime, or ashes can be mixed in to increase the pH (lower the acidity) of the compost; satisfactory compost has a pH between 7 and 8. There are also nitrogen-rich additives—blood meal or sewage sludge—that can increase its nitrogen content, while bone meal can be used to increase the compost's phosphorus content. Seaweed and ashes provide trace minerals. Unless there is reason to believe these specific components are lacking, these additives may not be necessary. Many of these additives can be obtained for free from certain industries; or, you can gather them easily from nature. In a small living group, you can use your vegetable wastes, yard cuttings, manure from your livestock, and your household wastes in the form of garbage and excrement. (Human excrement probably is most safely handled with initial treatment by a Clivus Multrum or methane digester; see Chapter 5.) These available ingredients, plus additives and soil, are the components of a recycling system that can be supplied almost entirely by the living processes of a single small community.

A sheltered site with a windbreak for the north and west is best—particularly for smaller piles—since strong winds cool the pile and stop fermentation. For

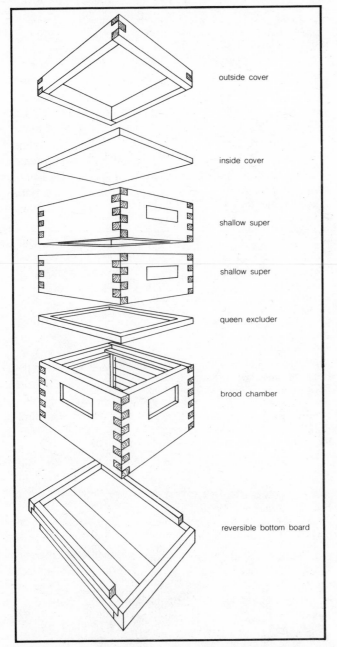

outside cover

inside cover

shallow super

shallow super

queen excluder

brood chamber

reversible bottom board

Figure 7.7 A ten-frame Langstroth beehive; each of the honey supers and the brood chamber can hold ten wax frames hung vertically.

337

Table 7.4 Composition of Various Materials for Compost[a]

Material	Nitrogen (%)	Phosphoric Acid (%)	Potash (%)	Material	Nitrogen (%)	Phosphoric Acid (%)	Potash (%)
Alfalfa hay	2.45	0.50	2.10	Incinerator ash	0.24	5.15	2.33
Apple (fruit)	0.05	0.02	0.10	Kentucky bluegrass (green)	0.66	0.19	0.71
Apple (leaves)	1.00	0.15	0.35	Kentucky bluegrass (hay)	1.20	0.40	1.55
Apple pomace	0.20	0.02	0.15	King crab (dried and ground)	10.00	0.26	0.06
Apple skins (ash)	—	3.08	11.74	King crab (fresh)	2.0–2.5	—	—
Banana skins (ash)	—	3.25	41.76	Leather (acidulated)	7.0–8.0	—	—
Banana stalk (ash)	—	2.34	49.40	Leather (ground)	10.0–12.0	—	—
Barley (grain)	1.75	0.75	0.50	Leather, scrap (ash)	—	2.16	0.35
Bat guano	1.0–12.0	2.5–16.0	—	Lemon culls, California	0.15	0.06	0.26
Beet roots	0.25	0.10	0.50	Lemon skins (ash)	—	6.30	31.00
Bone (ground, burned)	—	34.70	—	Lobster refuse	4.50	3.50	—
Brewer's grains (wet)	0.90	0.50	0.05	Lobster shells	4.60	3.52	—
Brigham tea (ash)	—	—	5.94	Milk	0.50	0.30	0.18
Cantaloupe rinds (ash)	—	9.77	12.21	Mussels	0.90	0.12	0.13
Castor-bean pomace	5.0–6.0	2.0–2.5	1.0–1.25	Molasses residue in manufacturing of alcohol	0.70	—	5.32
Cattail reed and stems of water lily	2.02	0.81	3.43	Oak leaves	0.80	0.35	0.15
Cattail seed	0.98	0.39	1.71	Oats, grain	2.00	0.80	0.60
Coal ash (anthracite)	—	0.1–0.15	0.1–0.15	Olive pomace	1.15	0.78	1.26
Coal ash (bituminous)	—	0.4–0.5	0.4–0.5	Olive refuse	1.22	0.18	0.32
Cocoa-shell dust	1.04	1.49	2.71	Orange culls	0.20	0.13	0.21
Coffee grounds	2.08	0.32	0.28	Orange skins (ash)	—	2.90	27.00
Coffee grounds (dried)	1.99	0.36	0.67	Pea pods (ash)	—	1.79	9.00
Common crab	1.95	3.60	0.20	Peanuts, seeds or kernels	3.60	0.70	0.45
Corncobs (ground, charred)	—	—	2.01	Peanut shells	0.80	0.15	0.50
Corncob (ash)	—	—	50.00	Peanut shells (ash)	—	1.23	6.45
Corn (grain)	1.65	0.65	0.40	Pigeon manure (fresh)	4.19	2.24	1.41
Corn (green forage)	0.30	0.13	0.33	Pigweed, rough	0.60	0.16	—
Cottonseed	3.15	1.25	1.15	Pine needles	0.46	0.12	0.03
Cottonseed-hull (ash)	—	7.0–10.0	15.0–30.0	Potatoes, tubers	0.35	0.15	0.50
Cowpeas (green forage)	0.45	0.12	0.45	Potatoes, leaves and stalks	0.60	0.15	0.45
Cowpeas (seed)	3.10	1.00	1.20	Potato skins, raw (ash)	—	5.18	27.50
Crab grass (green)	0.66	0.19	0.71	Prune refuse	0.18	0.07	0.31
Cucumber skins (ash)	—	11.28	27.20	Pumpkin, flesh	0.16	0.07	0.26
Dog manure	1.97	9.95	0.30	Pumpkin seeds	0.87	0.50	0.45
Dried jellyfish	4.60	—	—	Rabbit-brush ashes	—	—	13.04
Dried mussel mud	0.72	0.35	—	Ragweed, great	0.76	0.26	—
Duck manure (fresh)	1.12	1.44	0.49	Red clover, hay	2.10	0.50	2.00
Eggs	2.25	0.40	0.15	Redtop hay	1.20	0.35	1.00
Eggshells (burned)	—	0.43	0.29	Residuum from raw sugar	1.14	8.33	—
Eggshells	1.19	0.38	0.14	Rockweed	1.90	0.25	3.68
Feathers	15.30	—	—	Roses, flower	0.30	0.10	0.40
Field bean (seed)	4.00	1.20	1.30	Rhubarb, stems	0.10	0.04	0.35
Field bean (shells)	1.70	0.30	0.35	Rock and mussel deposits from sea	0.22	0.09	1.78
Fire-pit ashes from smokehouses	—	—	4.96	Salt-marsh hay	1.10	0.25	0.75
Fish scrap (red snapper and grouper)	7.76	13.00	0.38	Salt mud	0.40	—	—
Fish scrap (fresh)	2.0–7.5	1.5–6.0	—	Sardine scrap	7.97	7.11	—
Freshwater mud	1.37	0.26	0.22	Seaweed (Atlantic City, N.J.)	1.68	0.75	4.93
Garbage rubbish (New York City)	3.4–3.7	0.1–1.47	2.25–4.25	Sewage sludge from filter beds	0.74	0.33	0.24
Greasewood ashes	—	—	12.61	Shoddy and felt	4.0–12.0	—	—
Garden beans (beans and pods)	0.25	0.08	0.30	Shrimp heads (dried)	7.82	4.20	—
Gluten feed	4.0–5.0	—	—	Shrimp waste	2.87	9.95	—
Greensand	—	1.6–2.0	5.00	Siftings from oyster-shell mound	0.36	10.38	0.09
Grapes, fruit	0.15	0.07	0.30	Silkworm cocoons	9.42	1.82	1.08
Grapefruit skins (ash)	—	3.58	30.60	Soot from chimney flues	0.5–11.0	1.05	0.35
Hair	12.0–16.0	—	—	Spanish moss	0.60	0.10	0.55
Harbor mud	0.99	0.77	0.05	Starfish	1.80	0.20	0.25
Hoof meal and horn dust	10.0–15.0	1.5–2.0	—	String bean strings and stems (ash)	—	4.99	18.03

Table 7.4—Continued

Material	Nitrogen (%)	Phosphoric Acid (%)	Potash (%)
Sunflower seeds	2.25	1.25	0.79
Sweet potato skins, boiled (ash)	—	3.29	13.89
Sweet potatoes	0.25	0.10	0.50
Tanbark ash	—	0.24	0.38
Tanbark ash (spent)	—	1.5–2.0	1.5–2.5
Tea grounds	4.15	0.62	0.40
Tea-leaf ash	—	1.60	0.44
Timothy hay	1.25	0.55	1.00
Tobacco leaves	4.00	0.50	6.00
Tobacco stalks	3.70	0.65	4.50
Tobacco stems	2.50	0.90	7.00
Tomatoes, fruit	0.20	0.07	0.35
Tomatoes, leaves	0.35	0.10	0.40
Tomatoes, stalks	0.35	0.10	0.50
Waste from hares and rabbits	7.00	1.7–3.1	0.60
Waste from felt-hat factory	13.80	—	0.96
Waste product from paint manufacture	0.028	39.50	—
Waste silt	8.0–11.0	—	—
Wheat, bran	2.65	2.90	1.60
Wheat, grain	2.00	0.85	0.50
Wheat, straw	0.50	0.15	0.60
White clover (green)	0.50	0.20	0.30
White sage (ashes)	—	—	13.77
Wood ashes (leached)	—	1.0–1.5	1.0–3.0
Wood ashes (unleached)	—	1.0–2.0	4.0–10.0
Wool waste	5.0–6.0	2.0–4.0	1.0–3.0

Notes: a. From *How to Grow Vegetables and Fruits by the Organic Method*, by J.I. Rodale.

these smaller piles, protection should be given on three sides by means of walls or hedges where possible, but the compost must never be banked up against a wall. The site also should have good drainage on all sides so that rain does not create a giant vegetable mud pie!

Compost piles are built either into or above the ground. Above-ground compost piles are enclosed by some supporting structure (of brick or wood) or else formed in natural mounds. The minimum size of a pile should be three feet high by three feet square. This sizing is necessary to insure proper insulation so the pile can maintain the high temperatures required by the decomposition process. The pile should not be heaped too high; otherwise, it will become compacted due to its own weight. When a pile is built into the ground, it is necessary to cover the pit with either a plastic tarp or a wire screen to keep out vermin. If plastic is used, the decomposition process is called *anaerobic* (without oxygen). It is important to maintain the proper moisture balance, about that of a squeezed-out sponge; in an above-ground pile, this is accomplished by covering it with a protective material. A layer of straw or sawdust works well and also acts to insulate the pile.

Since the compost from an above-ground pile is formed by *aerobic* (with free oxygen available) decomposition, it is important that the pile be well ventilated. Aeration can be provided by either regular turning of the material undergoing decomposition, a forced aeration system, or a combination of both. The pile breathes from above and below, and also at the sides. It must not, of course, be trampled on or pressed down. To increase air access from the bottom, a thin layer of twigs or branch material can be used to lift the heap a little. Or, you can thrust a few metal pipes open to the air into the core of the pile. If abundant oxygen is not present, putrefaction may occur. A properly constructed compost pile should never putrefy, and it should never breed maggots or flies, or emit an unpleasant smell. If these do occur, they are infallible signs of faulty conditions. The cause is usually excessive wetness or some form of imperfect aeration. The cure is to re-admit air by turning. Above-ground compost is best for a permanent household because it has several advantages: it is easier to turn, easier to move when you want to spread it on the fields, and, when decomposing, it obtains higher temperatures than pit setups. This higher temperature speeds decomposition, kills pathogens from waste material, and aids in the elimination of pests. The minimum condition for pathogen destruction is 18 to 21 days at temperatures consistently above 130°F. Such temperatures are reached in normal operation, and temperatures of up to 170°F are reached in larger piles.

To service your compost pile you will need plastic bags to store the composting material until it is time to construct a pile; a shovel and pitchfork to load the compost and turn the pile; and a wheelbarrow to transport the compost to its ultimate destination. A shredder is a useful (but not essential) item. Shredding the composting material speeds the decomposition process by exposing more surface area to the activities of decomposing bacteria. There are both power and manual shredders, but, as a matter of fact, a manual rotary mower serves the purpose well.

There are numerous methods of composting that advocate different mixtures of composting materials and types of additives to supplement the compost. For example, the Biodynamic method calls for 70 percent green matter, 20 percent manure, and 10 percent soil. Four of the most widely used techniques include the Indore, the Rodale, the aforementioned Biodynamic, and the Santa Cruz French Intensive (we will discuss these last two in more detail soon). All these methods require from two to three months and yield approximately 1000 pounds per cubic yard, enough to cover 2000 square feet of garden. The differences in these methods seem to involve basically "cultish" preferences; none has a proven advantage in terms of efficiency of recycling or increased crop yield. The basic concept of composting is that anything organic can be composted and, although some composted materials—shredded paper, for example—have few concrete benefits, they do no harm and are disposed of in a satisfactory manner. Excessive amounts of shredded paper should not be used since it can unbalance the carbon-nitrogen ratio of the pile, and inks (as in newsprint) may contain some toxic materials. For all methods, the decomposition process can be accelerated by increasing the aeration of the pile, by adding nitrogenous materials, and by shredding the materials to increase the surface area exposed to decomposition bacteria. The important thing to remember is that nitrogen, usually in the form of manure (fresh grass clippings are also a good source), is essential.

Two somewhat different methods of composting are *sheet composting* and *green manuring*. Sheet composting involves the spread of garbage, vegetation, and manure on crop land (usually in late summer) and then the tillage of these wastes into the soil; they decompose right in the crop land. For green manuring, you till a crop (usually a legume) into the soil and let the crop decompose. Both of these methods require either power machinery or intense labor. They are also more applicable when acres of crops are being grown rather than square feet.

The best time to start a compost pile is at the end of a growing season, when plenty of vegetable wastes are available. Also, if the pile is started at the end of a growing season, it can be ready to apply before the next year's growing season begins; it is easiest to apply compost to a bare field during a slack period, when you are not otherwise busy. Even so, labor on a compost pile averages only five person-hours a week, including construction, gathering material, tending, and spreading the final product.

Although timing varies, the composting process should last about three months. The most intense activity occurs during the first three weeks, at the end of which time the pile should be turned (with a pitchfork) so that all parts are thoroughly mixed. This turning assists and accelerates the process. About five weeks later, the pile should be turned again. That's all that needs to be done! If everything has gone well, you needn't thrust in any metal pipes or poke any holes (for aeration), although it wouldn't hurt. Four weeks later, or about three months after the process began, the compost is ready to use and can be applied to the soil. Compost is ready to apply when it is dark and crumbly; not all of its component materials need to be broken down completely.

Orchard crops and perennials (plants which live for more than one year, like asparagus and artichokes) can be fertilized at any time of the year. With annual crops (plants which must be planted every year—most garden crops are annuals), it is best to apply compost before they are planted; this way you don't disturb any seeds while you make nutrients available for the important seedling stage. If you have enough, apply compost twice a year to crop lands. Spread from one to three inches over the soil (approximately 50 pounds per 100 square feet). The compost then should be mixed with the top four inches of topsoil, so chemicals and nutrients don't evaporate. This treatment will improve soil aeration and moisture-holding ability, as well as make nutrients available to the crops. It thus can be used to upgrade marginally produc-

tive land for future gardens. For further general information, see the listings under B. Kaysing, J. I. Rodale, and R. Merrill et al. in the Bibliography.

Small-volume composting for urban dwellers can be carried out in covered plastic buckets. Kitchen wastes and plant clippings can be layered with sawdust. Aeration of the pile is carried out by turning it into another bucket every couple of days. Do not oversaturate with water. Since the volume of material is smaller, the high temperature is harder to maintain. Hence, during cold winter months, the buckets should not be left outdoors unprotected. See *The Integral Urban House* for more suggestions.

Clivus Multrum

A device known as the Clivus Multrum presents another opportunity to dispose of organic household wastes in a productive way. Details regarding its usage, design, and construction can be found in Chapter 5. The Clivus requires a fairly large initial investment ($2000 purchased; less if constructed), but so do septic tanks and pipes to plug into a municipal disposal system. A Clivus will last indefinitely; there are no moving parts to wear out or complex pipe systems to get choked or broken. Moreover, it recycles nutrients efficiently without pollution, does not use water (an important point), and produces an odor-free compost. Before installing one, however, it is best to check for any problems with local health and building codes.

The residue produced in the unit is a stabilized organic compost which can be used as a soil conditioner. The Multrum's composting process is a slow one, taking from 2 to 4 years. Once the process is established, it can produce approximately 3 to 10 gallons of compost per person per year. The chemical characteristics of the residue compare very favorably with organic garden compost in terms of nutrients (nitrogen, phosphorus, and potassium) and trace elements (such as boron, manganese, and iron) needed for plant growth. From a health safety standpoint, use of the residue should be limited to ornamental plants and trees where there is little likelihood of coming into contact with food material.

Digester Effluent

Another source of recycled fertilizer comes from the anaerobic decomposition which occurs in a methane digester. The sludge that accumulates in a methane digester is similar to municipal sewage sludge, which has been widely used as a fertilizer. Physical and chemical characteristics of both the liquid effluent and the solid sludge are described in detail in Chapter 5. Like the Clivus, the digester requires a fairly large initial investment. Potential health problems have created state regulations controlling its use. It should be used as a source of fertilizer only for crops where the actual food crop does not come in direct contact with the sludge or effluent. Application to orchards or to crops which are to be plowed under for green manure would be acceptable.

Greywater

Since it takes energy to pump and distribute water from a central reservoir miles away, water conservation is also energy conservation. Water conservation around the home is also a way to reduce the total volume of waste produced. When the availability of water is sharply reduced, as was clearly the case during the 1977 drought in California, recycling household water becomes a necessity as well as an ecologically sound choice. Greywater constitutes all household water *other* than that from the toilet (referred to in this context as blackwater). This means everything from sinks, baths, laundry, and dishwasher. Discussion on its characteristics, handling, and distribution is found in Chapter 5. We will refer only to its usefulness in the garden.

Because of health safety and perhaps local health regulations, greywater is best limited to watering trees, non-food-producing plants, and lawns. The coliform standards (an indicator of fecal contamination) recommended by the National Technical Advisory Committee for recreational bathing water is less than 200 coliforms per 100 milliliters, and that for drinking water is less than 1 coliform per 100 milliliters. Local and state standards may be different, as illustrated by the California Environmental Health Code regarding the usage of any reclaimed water for surface irrigation or public use (Table 7.5). Other than the last category shown in Table 7.5, the coliform counts for household greywater generally exceed these standards. Since there are discrepancies between the federal and the state requirements, it is not clear how this affects the private household user. Furthermore, coliforms can multiply in greywater and any volume left standing could have increased levels. Alternatives which could be considered are chlorination (requires monitoring, and high levels may affect plants) and subsurface irrigation. The latter in particular would add cost and complexity and would require a continuous source of greywater. For any system,

thought should be given to clogging of distribution lines, quality of soil and the effect of greywater components, tolerance of plants, and effect on their growth and productivity.

Assuming that greywater is to be used, consideration must be given to plants which would be tolerant to eventual buildup of salts and alkaline conditions. Generally, plants that like acid conditions, such as citrus trees, azaleas, and rhododendrons, would not thrive well with greywater. An excellent user of greywater is lawn grass, which is highly tolerant to the salts and is also a heavy consumer of water in any case. Plants native to the desert and near ocean environments, such as sea grapes and iceplants, are also good candidates. As for food crops, broccoli, tomato, and melons such as cantaloupe are fairly salt-tolerant. On the other hand beans and fruit trees such as peaches and apricots are not tolerant of greywater.

Other than sodium and chloride the components in greywater are useful nutrients for plants, but not in amounts or ratios which would be considered fertilizer quality. For example, comparison of greywater with tapwater for some of the major constituents is given in Table 7.6. Boron is a constituent found in high amounts in boron or boraxo detergents and can damage plant foliage, so these products should be avoided, as should cleaning agents with chlorine bleach. If sodium levels become too high germination can be inhibited, growth may be stunted, leaf burn can result, and the water retention of the soil may be reduced. Several strategies may be employed to counteract these problems. One is to minimize the problem by avoiding as much as possible the use of cleaning agents with high amounts of boron, chlorine, or sodium. For example, it is better to use soap than detergents. Another is to dilute the greywater with another water source. If this is not possible, application of the greywater to a sandy soil would be less of a problem than to a highly organic one. If treatment of the soil is necessary, calcium sulfate or calcium polysulfide (gypsum or lime sulfur) can be applied. The calcium displaces the sodium

Table 7.5 California Environmental Health Code Standards for Reclaimed Water

Usage	Requirement
Food crops: spray or surface irrigation / Recreational lake, public contact	Median coliform count 2.2 per 100 ml
Landscape irrigation, lawn, parks, playgrounds, or dairy pastures / Landscape lake, no public contact	Median coliform count 23.0 per 100 ml
Orchards, vineyards, fodder, fiber, seed crop, surface irrigation	Primary treatment

Table 7.6 Comparison of Greywater, Tapwater, and Suggested Irrigation Water Standards

Component	Tapwater	Greywater	Irrigation Standards
Ammonia	0.06 mg/l	0.80 mg/l	—
Arsenic	<0.01	<0.01	0.05 mg/l
Barium	<1	<1	1.0
Cadmium	<0.01	0.01	0.01
Chloride	19	30	500
Chromium	<0.05	<0.05	0.05
Copper	0.08	0.16	1.0
Fluoride	0.75	0.95	6.0
Iron	0.18	0.20	1.0
Lead	<0.01	0.05	0.05
Manganese	<0.05	<0.05	0.5
Nitrate	0.2	2.1	180
Phosphate	1.0	68	—
Sodium	8.0	93	—
Sulfate	40	160	500

attached to the soil particles and the sodium is eventually leached away.

A greywater system which has been fully incorporated into the living unit and also into an attached greenhouse is described in *Compost Science* by A. Rockefeller and C. Lindstrom (see Figure 7.8). All household washwater goes through a roughing filter which removes most of the particles, lint, and hair. The water then goes into the soil in the greenhouse via PVC pipes with ¼-inch holes drilled on the bottom side. The pipes are placed 3 inches under the soil surface. The soil boxes are 2 feet wide and 4 feet deep. The deep soil layer essentially serves as a leaching field and treatment process for the greywater. The growing plants also serve a function by removing the useful nutrients in the greywater. Excess water drains out of the system with a reduced pollutional load. For additional information on greywater, see the listing for M. Milne in the Bibliography.

Biodynamic/French Intensive Method

To increase the self-sufficiency of a living group in an ecologically sound manner, your methods of fertilizing and nutrient regeneration need to take into account the type of community in which you are living. On a farm or in a rural area, it is possible to use composting, the Clivus, and the methane digester simultaneously. Garden and animal waste can go into compost and/or the methane digester, while household waste can be decomposed in the Clivus. This integrated program would provide a steady supply of fertilizers for your crops.

Figure 7.8 A greywater system in a greenhouse.

On the other hand, in an urban or suburban area, the Clivus and methane digester may not be feasible. Composting, however, can be easily used and provides excellent garden nutrients.

Fertilizer collected from compost piles, a Clivus, or a digester is fundamental to the Biodynamic/French Intensive method (B/FI) of crop production. This highly productive, nontraditional method, developed over the last decade by combining two slightly older practices, is here given a more detailed discussion because of its adaptability to any type of community. Since the B/FI method is based on the principle of intensive cultivation of small land areas, it is particularly useful in the urban backyard. One outstanding and important aspect is that its yields (determined for annual vegetable crops) are reported to be 1.5 to 7 times greater than by traditional methods. It requires a little more dedication and intensive labor, but the results appear to be well worth it.

The Biodynamic/French intensive method is based on the theory that natural biological control is better for agriculture than man-made chemical control: modern agriculture is thought to extract nutrients from the soil (which inorganic fertilizers do not replace correctly), while organic fertilizers are thought to keep the nutrients balanced. The B/FI method also incorporates the practice of growing plants on raised beds of loosened and fertilized soil. A natural weeding process is encouraged by growing plants very close together, so that the foliage of your crop shades the ground and forms a "living mulch." Another worthy aspect of the method is that water conservation is promoted; estimates indicate that about half as much watering is needed, compared to conventional gardening, since the closely grown plants tend to discourage evaporation from the soil. Insect pests are controlled by companion planting and by encouraging predaceous insects.

Preparations: Preparing the raised bed is the most exhausting part of this farming method. The theory is that a mound warms quickly and also drains and aerates the soil best. Beds are from 3 to 5 feet wide and about 20 feet long; they should run north and south. One such bed can provide the vegetable needs for four people (one pound per day each) indefinitely.

The first step is to prepare the site. Hard and dry soils should be well watered (about one or two hours), then allowed to drain for a few days. Loosen the soil on the plot (down to 12 inches deep) and add from 1 to 3 inches of compost or manure (remember that manure must age a few months before use to get rid of some of its ammonia). The suggested B/FI proportions for compost are equal portions of green vegetation, kitchen scraps, and soil; the nitrogen is provided by the green vegetation. However, other ways of composting should do fine.

Now the digging starts. As illustrated in Figure 7.9, ideally a trench 12 inches square (cross section) should be dug across the head of the bed. If the soil is too hard,

Table 7.7 Biodynamic/French Intensive Bed Preparation

1. Initial preparation: soak 1–2 hours for dry, hard soils; drain and dry 1–2 days; loosen soil to 12″ and add texturizers—manure and/or seed.

2. Double digging: spread 1–3″ compost; dig and remove soil from trench 12″ wide by 12″ deep, extending across end of bed; double dig by loosening soil 12″ deeper at trench bottom; dig second trench by filling first trench; double dig; continue to end; add soil from first trench to the very last trench.

3. Finishing touches: level and shape raised bed; add 2–4 lbs bone meal, 2–4 lbs wood ash; 2–4 ft³ aged manure.

4. Plant and sow.

5. Repeat from Step 2 for continuing bed.

(a) the beginning of a trench

(b) "double digging"

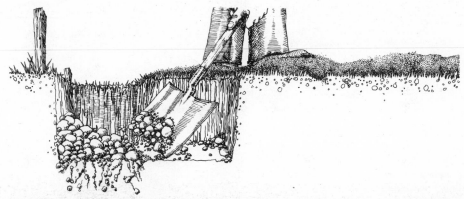

(c) digging a second trench behind the first

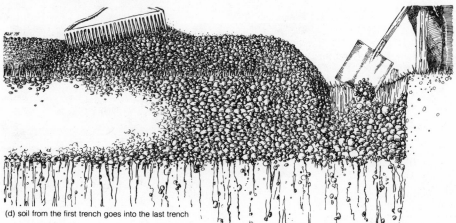

(d) soil from the first trench goes into the last trench

Figure 7.9 Bed preparation for Biodynamic/French Intensive gardening (see Table 7.7 for complete summary).

343

then dig as deep as possible; put the soil you've dug out into a wheelbarrow. Now, along the entire bottom of the trench, drive your shovel or fork into the ground and wiggle it back and forth. Don't take any soil out, just loosen it. Ideally your shovel should loosen the soil to a depth of another foot. This procedure is called "double digging."

Next dig another trench directly behind the first and push the soil from the second trench forward into the first trench. Double dig! Dig a third trench behind the second with double digging and continue this back-breaking labor until you reach the foot of the bed. Dump the soil from the wheelbarrow into your last trench. Then spread from 2 to 4 pounds each of both bone meal and wood ash and from 2 to 4 cubic feet of aged manure over the entire bed, mix the top few inches with a fork, level and shape, and (voila!) you have a raised bed. Put a flat board over the bed if you must walk on it. This process needs to be repeated after every crop, but it should get easier each time: new bed preparations take from six to twelve hours and repeat bed preparations take only from four to six hours. Preparation steps are summarized in Table 7.7.

Planting: Before sowing your seed, you should study *companion planting* possibilities. Some plants get along well with other plants: each grows better in the presence of the other. Some plants repel insect pests, lure pests away from a more vulnerable crop, or attract insect predators. Some plants provide nutrients for other plants. Still other plants are grown together because they make an efficient use of space (one example is growing shallow-rooted plants together with deep-rooted plants). Tables 7.8 and 7.9 summarize the information on who likes whom and the effect of herbs.

Now it's time for planting. Requirements vary for different plants, but the key is to place them close enough so that their full-grown leaves just touch. Plant in staggered rows so that each plant has six nearest neighbors which are the same distance away (see Figure 7.10). Putting a chicken-wire "template" over the mound and planting in the meshes might help your spacing technique. After some experience, you can throw the seeds on the mound like a real farmer. If your plants do grow too closely, they can always be thinned; but you can't do anything if they're too far apart.

Table 7.8 Companion Planting[a]

Vegetables	Likes	Dislikes	Vegetables	Likes	Dislikes
Asparagus	Tomato, parsley, basil		Lettuce	Carrot, radish (lettuce, carrots, and radishes make a strong team grown together), strawberry, cucumber	
Bean	Potato, carrot, cucumber, cauliflower, cabbage, summer savory, most other vegetables and herbs	Onion, garlic, gladiolus			
Bush Bean	Potato, cucumber, corn, strawberry, celery, summer savory	Onion	Onion (and garlic)	Beet, strawberry, tomato, lettuce, summer savory, camomile (sparsely)	Pea, bean
			Parsley	Tomato, asparagus	
Pole Bean	Corn, summer savory	Onion, beet, kohlrabi, sunflower	Pea	Carrot, turnip, radish, cucumber, corn, bean, most vegetables and herbs	Onion, garlic, gladiolus, potato
Beet	Onion, kohlrabi	Pole bean			
Cabbage Family (cabbage, cauliflower, kale, kohlrabi, broccoli)	Aromatic plants, potato, celery, dill, camomile, sage, peppermint, rosemary, beet, onion	Strawberry, tomato, pole bean	Potato	Bean, corn, cabbage, horseradish (should be planted at corners of patch), marigold, eggplant (as a lure for Colorado potato beetle)	Pumpkin, squash, cucumber, sunflower, tomato, raspberry
Carrot	Pea, leaf lettuce, chive, onion, leek, rosemary, sage, tomato	Dill			
			Pumpkin	Corn	Potato
			Radish	Pea, nasturtium, lettuce, cucumber	
Celery	Leek, tomato, bush bean, cauliflower, cabbage		Soybean	Grows with anything, helps everything	
Chive	Carrot	Pea, bean	Spinach	Strawberry	
Corn	Potato, pea, bean, cucumber, pumpkin, squash		Squash	Nasturtium, corn	
			Strawberry	Bush bean, spinach, borage, lettuce (as a border)	Cabbage
Cucumber	Bean, corn, pea, radish, sunflower	Potato, aromatic herbs			
Eggplant	Bean		Sunflower	Cucumber	Potato
Leek	Onion, celery, carrot		Tomato	Chive, onion, parsley, asparagus, marigold, nasturtium, carrot	Kohlrabi, potato, fennel, cabbage
			Turnip	Pea	

Notes: a. From *Organic Gardening and Farming,* February 1972, p. 54.

Seedlings can be transplanted, but don't plant them near seeds; the seedlings will gobble up all the nutrients and your seeds won't germinate. Also, be careful with their roots. It is recommended that planting be done by phases of the moon; this precaution might actually help, but its logic is today still somewhat controversial.

Care: Water daily with a sprinkler a few hours before sunset; if you've watered enough, the soil stays shiny for around five seconds before the water sinks in. Because of plant placement and shading, weeds shouldn't be much of a problem after the plants are grown; but some weeds will always grow even where it doesn't seem light can penetrate.

As we mentioned, companion planting discourages pests. In general, growing a variety of plants on one bed encourages insect predators and inhibits insect pests (an example of how diversity can promote health). Insect pests are best discouraged by keeping plants healthy, but you can always pick them off plants by hand, put up sticky, impassable insect barriers, spray garlic juice on infested portions, or set up deterrent fences of fresh ash.

The B/FI method of crop production should be easier to do each time. For further information, see *How to Grow More Vegetables (than you ever thought possible on less land than you can imagine),* put out for $4 by Ecology Action (2225 El Camino, Palo Alto, CA 94306). This and the progress report put out by J. Jeavons are listed in the Bibliography.

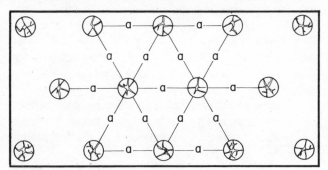

Figure 7.10 Plant spacing for Biodynamic/French Intensive gardening. Staggered rows provide each plant with an even distance from each neighboring plant.

Table 7.9   Herbal Companions and Effects[a]

Herb	Companions and Effects	Herb	Companions and Effects
Basil	Companion to tomatoes; dislikes rue intensely; improves growth and flavor; repels flies and mosquitoes.	Nasturtium	Companion to radishes, cabbage, and cucurbits[b]; plant under fruit trees; deters aphids, squash bugs, striped pumpkin beetles, improves growth and flavor.
Borage	Companion to tomatoes, squash, and strawberries; deters tomato worm; improves growth and flavor.	Petunia	Protects beans.
Caraway	Plant here and there; loosens soil.	Peppermint	Planted among cabbages, it repels the white cabbage butterfly.
Catnip	Plant in borders; deters flea beetle.	Pigweed	One of the best weeds for pumping nutrients from the subsoil; especially beneficial to potatoes, onions, and corn; keep these weeds thinned.
Camomile	Companion to cabbages and onions; improves growth and flavor.		
Chervil	Companion to radishes; improves growth and flavor.	Pot Marigold	Companion to tomatoes, but also plant elsewhere; deters asparagus beetle, tomato worm, and general garden pests.
Chive	Companion to carrots; improves growth and flavor.		
Dead Nettle	Companion to potatoes; deters potato bug; improves growth and flavor.	Rosemary	Companion to cabbage, bean, carrots, and sage; deters cabbage moth, bean beetles, and carrot fly.
Dill	Companion to cabbage; dislikes carrots; improves growth and health of cabbage.	Rue	Keep far away from Sweet Basil; plant near roses and raspberries; deters Japanese beetle.
Fennel	Plant away from gardens; disliked by most plants.	Sage	Plant with rosemary, cabbage, and carrots; keep away from cucumbers; deters cabbage moth, carrot fly.
Flax	Companion to carrots, potatoes; deters potato bug; improves growth and flavor.		
Garlic	Plant near roses and raspberries; deters Japanese beetle; improves growth and health.	Southernwood	Plant here and there in garden; companion to cabbage, improves growth and flavor; deters cabbage moth.
Henbit	General insect repellent.		
Horseradish	Plant at corners of potato patch to deter potato bug.	Sowthistle	This weed in moderate amounts can help tomatoes, onions, and corn.
Hyssop	Deters cabbage moth; companion to cabbage and grapes; keep away from radishes.	Summer Savory	Plant with beans and onions; improves growth and flavor; deters bean beetles.
Lamb's Quarters	This edible weed should be allowed to grow in moderate amounts in the garden, especially in corn.	Tansy	Plant under fruit trees; companion to roses and raspberries; deters flying insects, Japanese beetles, striped cucumber beetles, squash bugs, ants.
Lemon Balm	Sprinkle throughout garden.		
Marigold	The workhorse of the pest deterrents; plant throughout garden to discourage Mexican bean beetles, nematodes, and other insects.	Tarragon	Good throughout garden.
		Thyme	Here and there in garden; it deters cabbage worm.
Marjoram	Here and there in garden; improves flavors.	Valerian	Good anywhere in garden.
Mint	Companion to cabbage and tomatoes; improves health and flavor; deters white cabbage moth.	Wormwood	As a border, it keeps animals from the garden.
		Yarrow	Plant along borders, paths, near aromatic herbs; enhances essential oil production.
Mole Plant	Deters moles and mice if planted here and there.		

Notes: a. From *Organic Gardening and Farming,* February 1972, pp. 52–53. Also includes a few weeds and flowers. b. Plants in the gourd family.

Hydroponics

Now that you've been thoroughly convinced of the benefits of organic farming, and now that you've been told how it's best to let natural biological controls solve all your problems, let's look at another highly productive method of farming which is *not* natural and, in its pure form, uses nothing but chemicals. Hydroponics may be taken loosely to include all forms of agriculture that do not rely on soil as a planting medium. Sand, gravel, cinders, and other such materials can be included as hydroponic media.

The main advantage of hydroponic agriculture is increased production with low maintenance costs. Production is high because growth can be controlled easily through careful regulation of the nutrients applied to the plants. Disadvantages include the high initial cost of plumbing, the use of processed chemical nutrients, and the great volume of water needed. Water can be conserved if a recycling system is designed, but this feature also adds to the initial plumbing costs.

There are as many ways to apply the nutrients as there are types of media. Nutrient solutions may be prepared and applied by hand or by pump. The solution can be sprayed onto the plants, dripped onto the plants, or supplied to the plant bed by irrigation or subirrigation. The beds may be located either outdoors or in greenhouses. Obviously, building a greenhouse would be a significant expense that would have to be balanced against its higher yield.

In general, the more complicated and mechanized the hydroponic system is, the more expensive the installation costs will be. The simplest setup is a sand or gravel system where the nutrients are applied dry and then watered in by a hand-held hose. If gravity is used, no pump will be needed to drain the nutrients. (Feeding should last about fifteen minutes; after this time, the nutrient must be removed somehow, by some form of drainage.) Moderately coarse silicate sand from the beach is ideal as a medium. The sand can be placed directly into a shallow pit lined with a wooden border. Such a setup can be used to grow virtually all plants that are grown in soil, with root crops doing the best. Your major expense is then only the chemical nutrients; industrial grade salts are recommended since they also supply needed trace elements. A typical mixture is:

Sodium nitrate	13.50 oz
Potassium sulphate	4.00 oz
Superphosphate 16% P_2O_5	10.00 oz
Magnesium sulphate	4.00 oz
Ferrous sulphate	0.25 oz
Water	100 gal

Adequate stock solution can be made up once a week; the amount of time involved depends upon your dexterity. The solution should be applied at least once a day. A significant time-saving feature of hydroponics is that almost no time has to be spent weeding.

Small-scale hydroponics can be practiced in urban communities and even in apartments to grow beans, tomatoes, and other small vegetables. The easiest procedure is to place three or four inches of clean gravel into several plastic dishpans (see Figure 7.11). A small-diameter plastic hose is fixed into a side hole along the bottom edge of each pan. The other end of the hose connects up with a pail of nutrient solution. Feeding and watering is done by raising and lowering the pail twice a day. When you raise the pail above the level of your pans, the solution percolates into the gravel; after fifteen minutes, when the pail is lowered below the dishpans, the solution percolates back into your pail and drainage is complete.

If you are not comfortable with using a purely chemical solution, an alternative is to use a nutrient solution derived from natural organic sources. Two examples are listed:

1. An aqueous infusion made from good compost. Use the liquid portion only.

2. Fish emulsion
Liquid seaweed } 1 tablespoon each per gallon of
Blood meal   } water

More information on organic hydroponics can be found under M. Smith. For further information on hydroponic designs, see the listings under R. Bridwell, T. Saunby, and C. E. Ticquet in the Bibliography.

Aquaculture

A good percentage of the food for your household can come from aquaculture, the art of applying agricultural principles to control the raising of aquatic organisms; it

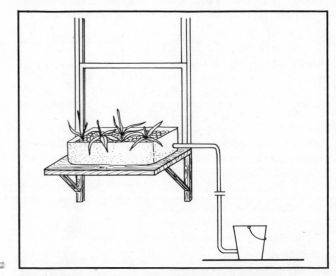

Figure 7.11 A small scale hydroponics setup: Small indoor gravel beds can support healthy growing vegetables. The bucket containing the feed solution is lifted to water the vegetables, then lowered to allow drainage. This is done twice a day.

includes the cultivation of fish, shellfish, and algae. This art has been practiced worldwide for thousands of years, most extensively in the Far East. Aquaculture *does* exist in the United States—primarily in the form of catfish farms and trout hatcheries—but terrestrial agriculture still accounts for most of our food production. We don't mean to insult agriculture, which is a perfectly respectable way to grow food, but aquaculture is generally *more productive* than agriculture and *more efficient* than raising livestock. (Figures for chicken production are comparable to some aquaculture figures, but aquaculture is more efficient at converting feed into biomass.) Any person who is trying to get the maximum food yield out of his land would be wise to consider using part or all of it for an aquaculture operation.

Aquaculture can be more than simply another source of food. It can be a key ingredient which glues together the different components of our garbage-powered home. In addition to the recreational and eye-pleasing benefits of fish ponds in your backyard, they can also be used to supply electricity (Chapter 3), to water livestock, to conserve water for use during dry spells, to convert wastewater into fertilizer and enriched irrigation water (Chapter 5), and, finally, to convert vegetable waste and manure into fish that we can eat.

In Southeast Asia and parts of Africa, waste recycling through aquaculture is well-established. In one system, fruit trees, which anchor the soil, are grown high on a hill and below them is a vegetable garden and chicken coop. Near the bottom of the hill is a pig sty or duck pen, and at the bottom is a pond in which various types of carp are grown. A ditch is dug parallel to the contours of the hill above the fruit trees to prevent excessive rain damage. Rains wash the excess fertilizer, nutrients, dead plant material, and manure into the pond, and this enrichment indirectly feeds the carp. Both the enriched water and mud from the pond bottom can then be applied to fertilize the fruit and vegetables, and the cycle continues.

Aquaculture's superior productivity is due to three characteristics of its medium. First, water absorbs and retains the sun's energy better than land; a pond thus will have more energy available for organisms to use than a comparable land area. Second, water can diffuse material throughout itself, an ability dry land lacks. This ability to mix materials within itself results in a much more even distribution of nutrients than that of soil; on land, one spot might be deficient in a vital nutrient that is at toxic concentration in a spot but a few feet away. The third (and main) advantageous characteristic of water is that it occupies a three-dimensional space: different organisms can live at different depths under the same area of surface. Land is virtually two-dimensional, with life only on, and a short distance above and below, the surface. Thus, an area of water is more productive than an equal area of land because there is more habitable volume. The ancient Chinese found that using all three dimensions of water

made a very productive system. Realizing that different species of fish live at different levels in the water column and eat different food ("occupy different niches" in biological terms; see Figure 7.12), they deduced that it might be possible to culture many different species of fish in the same pond; the fish would not only not interfere with each other, but would even complement each other. For example, an algae-feeding species near the surface and a bottom feeder, both with high reproductive rates, can harmoniously coexist; their young are controlled by a predator species, and the waste products of all three species in turn fertilize the water, thus supporting the growth of algae for the herbivorous species. This culturing of more than one species is called *polyculture*. Obviously, different types of fish must be chosen with care, as two random species do not necessarily complement each other.

In spite of the greater efficiency of polyculture, often economic and social factors confine only one type of fish to a pond. This practice (called *monoculture*) is less efficient with both food and space, and consequently less productive than polyculture.

We've already mentioned twice that aquaculture is "more efficient" than agriculture, but we haven't really explained what we mean. Efficiency, in this case, is the number of pounds of food an animal must be fed for it to grow one pound heavier. It takes more than one pound of food to grow one pound of animal because some food is burned up as the energy the animal uses to live. Aquatic animals need relatively less of this energy than land ani-

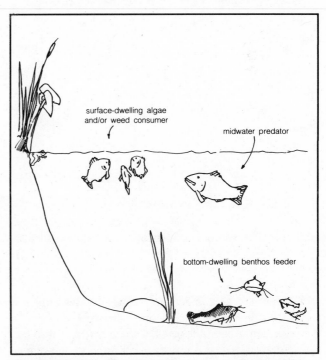

Figure 7.12 Polyculture in a fish pond: efficient utilization of the three-dimensional pond environment can be promoted by culturing compatible, noncompetitive species which have differing feeding niches and habitat niches.

347

mals because energy does not have to be channeled into supporting structures, since the aqueous environment supports their bodies. In addition, most aquatic animals are cold-blooded and domestic land animals are warm-blooded. This means that land animals have to expend much of their energy on maintaining their body temperature, while fish don't. It follows that aquatic animals burn less food into energy than land animals, and can convert more of this food into meat. Thus, in principle, aquaculture is more efficient than culturing land animals.

Another theoretical concept sheds light on this question of efficiency: the food chain. In a generalized ecological system, production occurs when tiny one-celled plants, phytoplankton, use energy from the sun and nutrients from the water to grow and produce more biomass. They are eaten by microscopic animals, zooplankton, which are in turn eaten by bigger and bigger animals until the final consumer is a large fish or land predator. You will remember that organisms at each level use up some (indeed, *most*) of the energy they absorb to carry on their own life functions; thus less energy is available to other consumers higher up the chain. Consequently, the most efficient theoretical way of utilizing the original solar energy input into a system is to cultivate the lower-order consumers: herbivores or zooplankton feeders. But there is a limit to how low you can go before dining becomes unpalatable, or inefficient, or both. Most human societies prefer fish to chironomid larvae and steak to grass; even if you were so inclined, it would take hours to catch a mouthful of copepods. In such circumstances, it's better to let a higher-order consumer convert food to an edible state. A good discussion on energy needs and fish yields for various types of aquaculture practices can be found in the *Energy Primer* (see Bibliography, under Merrill et al.).

The amount of biomass produced is limited by the concentrations of nutrients and vital molecules present in the system, some of the most important being nitrogen, phosphates, carbon dioxide, and oxygen. In a given situation, nitrogen and phosphate concentrations may be too low to permit further production of biomass. When organic waste is added to this limited-nutrient system, bacteria decompose it, releasing nitrogen compounds, phosphates, and other nutrients. Thus, adding *garbage* will add nutrients to a pond, which may stimulate plant growth, which stimulates zooplankton blooms, which in turn increase the food supply and therefore the growth of the organism which the culturist is attempting to raise! (For further information, see "Oxidation Ponds" in Chapter 5.) However, caution must be exercised when applying any such "fertilizer"; the decomposition that produces these nutrients also uses up vital oxygen and makes the water more turbid. It is possible that the end result may be the death of a fish crop, rather than its enhanced growth. Inorganic fertilizers like superphosphates can also stimulate growth and, since bacterial decomposition isn't needed, avert any danger of an induced oxygen shortage.

But inorganic fertilizers cost money, while garbage is cheap and plentiful.

Before going any further, we must differentiate intensive from nonintensive aquaculture. *Intensive aquaculture,* as the name implies, involves feeding the fish, controlling their breeding, and much more; in general, you spend a good deal of your time and labor shaping the environment and life patterns of fish. *Nonintensive culture* is a minimal-labor operation; the fish are not controlled except for an occasional cleanup of debris in the pond, fertilization of the pond, and the harvest of the fish. As you might imagine, nonintensive culture is generally less productive, but it is also less expensive and time-consuming.

Production figures which follow in our discussion are given in kilograms per hectare per year (kg/ha-yr). A kilogram (kg) is 2.2 pounds, and a hectare (ha) is 10,000 square meters or 2.47 acres. Thus, a kg/ha-yr is a little less than a pound/acre-yr.

Please realize that all we can do is summarize some of the information applicable to the question of aquaculture. For a more detailed look at specific problems, you are encouraged to consult other references and sources, many of which are listed in the Bibliography.

Some Fundamental Considerations

One cannot, so to speak, just plunge into an aquaculture operation. There are several important questions which must be faced beforehand. Hopefully, those preceding pages where we described the superiority of aquaculture haven't made you excessively optimistic. Success still requires a great deal of work and the first job is to forget anything you've heard about how easy aquaculture is. If aquaculture were such a sure bet, everyone would be doing it. Although it has great potential, aquaculture requires as much care and maintenance as gardening, and, like gardening, not every site is equally suitable. The weeds must still be pulled, the water checked, and the fish fed. And as an added bonus, fish, too, are menaced by a great variety of predators and diseases just itching to get at them.

A place to start is to decide how large a system can be managed. Let's say that you want to produce enough fish to feed everyone living in your garbage-powered home, and let's say that this comprises a half-dozen full-timers plus a handful of permanent transients, or about 10 people. Assuming that each person eats half a pound of fish per meal, and you eat fish twice a week, you would need 10 pounds per week or about 500 pounds per year, which is about 230 kilograms per year. The kinds of fish we will discuss should produce at least 150 kg/ha-yr; therefore, somewhat less than 2 hectares for aquaculture would be desired.

The next questions you must answer concern the suitability of your site. If a body of water can't exist on a site, obviously aquaculture is impossible. Find a spot that is accessible. Vehicles are needed to plant, maintain, and harvest your pond. Topographical features should allow complete pond drainage, and the legalities of draining into existing streams must be investigated. Avoid areas with high insecticide concentrations and avoid narrow, windless valleys, since you'll want some wind to keep your ponds from stratifying. It is very important to find a spot where the soil holds water. Generally speaking, this soil should be more clayey than sandy, and alluvial or marshy soil is best. To have someone check the sealant properties of your soil, either phone the nearest Soil Conservation Service office or else contact the Deputy Administrator for Technical Services (currently William Johnson), Soil Conservation Service, Department of Agriculture, 14th St. and Jefferson Dr. SW, Washington, D.C. 20250, and ask him how to get in touch with your local conservation district. If your soil doesn't hold water, you can apply chemical sealants, polyvinyl sheets, or concrete, but this is expensive.

Make *sure* that this site has a dependable primary and emergency supply of water, especially in the summer. You can *not* raise fish without plenty of good water. Check the temperature and quality of this water, the organisms present in it, and the likelihood of floods.

Now that you've picked your site, your next problem will be getting permits to install an aquaculture facility. Aquaculture operations may be under the jurisdiction of local, state, or federal agencies that deal with cleanliness of food, purity of water supply, public health, land use, use of navigable waters, or effluent discharges, and all of them may require permits. The Water Pollution Control Act is hazy on effluent standards for aquaculture, but you may have to get a permit from the Environmental Protection Agency to allow you to discharge water from your pond. In some states there are agencies specifically designed to tell users of natural resources about the permits they will need. You should check this out with your state's fish and wildlife department, or with your county extension agent.

To get your permits, you'll need to know how many ponds you want and what size you want them. This depends on your goals. It is much less expensive to build one 1.5-hectare pond than it is to build five 0.3-hectare ponds if land is available. On the other hand, if your goal calls for a continuous supply of fish for home consumption, and you only build one pond, you may go most of the year without fish, and suddenly have more than you can possibly handle at harvest time. (There are ways of managing one pond so that it produces a continuous supply of fish all year, but we'll cover that later.) Furthermore, if something goes wrong in your only pond, you wouldn't have an alternative supply of fish. More information on pond construction is found further on.

We have thus far failed to mention the most important item in your ponds—the fish. No matter what type of fish you raise, you'll need to know where you can get them, how to stock them, how to feed them, how to monitor their physical condition during growth, how to harvest them, and what to do with them after harvest. Obviously, the question of species must be resolved first. Then you must decide whether to initiate the stock with mature breeders or with a younger stage (fry or fingerlings, in the case of fish). Remember that, in many cases, it's better to buy fish that are already hatched than to try to hatch them yourself, even if it means you can't be self-sufficient. Breeding and caring for eggs and fry is an art—an extremely difficult art for some species—and it can require additional expensive equipment. If you want to breed the fish yourself, there must be a supplier from whom you can purchase breeders. Then the age, size, and number of breeders of each sex all need to be determined. Furthermore, the culturist should know at what temperature spawning occurs and how long the breeders must be in breeding surroundings before they spawn, so that you don't harvest them too early and wipe out your stock. And with fingerlings, the culturist must know what size and number to stock and how to stock them without causing thermal shock. The culturist must also do all the necessary preparatory work on the pond water before stocking.

One of the best directories to fish dealers and other suppliers of aquaculture equipment is the annual Buyer's Guide edition of *The Commercial Fish Farmer*. This lists names and addresses of dealers according to the species they sell, and it tells whether they sell eggs, fry, fingerlings, market-sized fish, or brood stock. You could ask your state fish and game department, your county extension agent, or other fish farmers about dealers in your area.

How many fish should you put in your pond? For any species, that depends on the productivity of your pond and on the amount of supplementary feeding and fertilizing you plan to do. The natural productivity of your pond is based mostly on the fertility of the soil. You'll have to guess this, based on the darkness of the soil and on the amount of fertilizer farmers use in your area. If your pond turns out to be more fertile than expected, you can plant more fish next year. If it's less fertile and your fish don't grow very well, plant fewer fish the next year. Fish farming, like land farming or gardening, requires experience with a given site, and you can't expect to get the maximum possible yield on the first try.

Two factors that greatly influence the productivity of your soil are its pH and its alkalinity. You want your pond to have a pH above 7.0 (to be basic) because under acidic conditions nutrients in the soil bind tightly to soil particles and are not released into the water. This means that regardless of how fertile your soil is, or how much fertilizer you add, your water will not be very productive. Your soil will become acidic under low oxygen conditions, which are common on pond bottoms. For this reason, it's wise to drain a pond once in a while, let it dry until deep cracks form, and further aerate it by breaking up the clods. This can best be done in winter, when the fish aren't growing anyway and can all be stored in one pond.

Alkalinity is the buffering capacity of your soil, or its ability to resist changes in pH, and it's measured as the concentration of calcium carbonate (limestone). Under low oxygen conditions, carbon dioxide concentrations drop until there's not enough left for photosynthesis, and production stops. Since carbonate is easily converted to carbon dioxide, alkaline soils essentially have a reservoir of carbon dioxide stored as carbonate. When carbon dioxide levels drop, carbonate is converted to carbon dioxide, and production continues. For this reason, it's a good idea to measure the alkalinity of your soil (procedures are published by the American Public Health Association; see Bibliography). If you have a soft water supply and alkalinity of the soil is below 20 milligrams per milliliter of calcium carbonate, you might consider spreading limestone on the pond. The amount can be determined from measuring the pH and acidity of your soil (see listing for Adams and Evans in the Bibliography).

Regardless of the natural productivity of your pond, you can usually increase production by adding either organic or inorganic fertilizer at one- to two-week intervals during the growing season. Inorganic fertilizers, such as superphosphates and ammonia salts, must be bought (you can produce organic fertilizers right in your own home), and they require energy to manufacture. They do provide a convenience factor if other fertilizers are not readily available at the necessary time. A typical application rate is about 30 to 45 kilograms per hectare of 20–20–0 ($N–P_2O_5–K_2O$) every two weeks. However, this should be adjusted to your needs, such as your fish population and natural fertility of your pond.

Organic fertilizers include plant debris; cow, chicken, duck, and pig manure; and kitchen waste. Some fish, like silver carp, will eat organic fertilizers (garbage) directly. Other fish feed on the worms and insect larvae that feed on the garbage. Most importantly, however, organic fertilizers are decomposed by bacteria. This releases nutrients into the water, which promotes plant production, which in turn promotes animal production. However, bacterial decomposition also uses up oxygen; and too much fertilizer can cause your fish to suffocate, as well as lower the pH of the soil and prevent the release of more nutrients. For this reason, organic fertilizer should be piled in heaps when added to a pond, rather than spread over the bottom, so that decomposition proceeds slowly, and so that the entire bottom doesn't become anoxic. Application rates depend on your supply of garbage, the fish population, natural fertility of the pond, and the oxygen level of your pond. A typical range might also be around 30 to 45 kilograms per hectare every two weeks.

Fertilization is indirect feeding. Production can be further increased by direct supplementary feeding. If your goal is food production rather than profit, however, you should not feed your fish food that you can eat directly because much of that food energy would be lost (see discussion of the food chain at the beginning of this chapter). While it may be profitable to use 15 pounds of low-priced fish meal to produce 1 pound of high-priced eel, this wastes protein and energy. If your pond produces high-protein food such as insects and worms, your fish may grow best with a high-carbohydrate supplementary feed. This is because carbohydrates are converted to energy more efficiently than protein; therefore, if your fish take care of their energy requirements with supplementary feed, all the protein they eat can be converted to growth. In productive ponds, therefore, the best feed would be high-carbohydrate grain products that you yourself wouldn't eat, such as sorghum seeds, rice by-products, and grain hulls.

If you are raising fish such as trout that require clean, well-oxygenated water in a clean pond or tank, the fish's entire diet would have to be provided directly by you. This means buying a feed that satisfies all of the nutrient requirements of your fish. One such feed is the Oregon Moist Pellet (OMP), composed of fish meal, vegetable products, vitamins, and several other ingredients. OMP, which was developed around 1960, has been used mostly for salmonids, but has also been fed to carp and catfish. Fish food distributors are listed in the Buyer's Guide edition of *The Commercial Fish Farmer*.

Be sure not to overfeed. Your fish food distributor can give you a table that applies to his type of feed, but the actual amount you should use will also depend on the productivity and temperature of your pond. In general, young fry might need 20 percent of their body weight per day, while fingerlings might need 5 percent. An easy way to avoid overfeeding a bottom feeder, such as carp, would be to drive a stake into the pond, dump a portion of the daily ration near the stake, and scatter the remainder elsewhere. Before feeding the next day, check to see if there's any food left near the stake. If so, don't feed that day. If not, the ration may be increased. Surface feeders, such as trout, leap for their food when they're hungry; therefore, stop feeding them when the leaping activity slows down.

Regular (for example, weekly) sampling is useful for developing efficient feeding and harvesting strategies. Some hints on sampling: use a seining net; to gather fish together, drop some food in a shallow corner and wait 30 to 60 minutes before seining; collect as many fish as possible into a large bucket and weigh the entire batch, then calculate an average weight per fish.

When the fish reach the desired size it is time to harvest. One method is to drop a baited hook into the water. This is the preferred method for the nonintensive farm pond described later. If, on the other hand, most of the fish are the same age, or you want to start a new crop, or you want to market the fish and harvest the entire crop at once, other methods are needed. Some hints on harvesting: gradually lower the water level in the pond over a period of about three days, allowing the fish to swim to the deep end without getting stranded; have some friends on hand to help; use a seining net; collect the fish into a water tank which has been oxygenated.

If you are raising your fish for market rather than for home consumption, you'll have to harvest and ship all of your fish at one time, because processors will not be interested in buying a few dozen fish at a time. For information on how to market your fish, contact: Marketing Specialist (currently James Ayers), NMFS, No. 1 Union National Plaza, Suite 1160, Little Rock, Arkansas 72201.

What problems can you expect in aquaculture? Your biggest problem might be obtaining the required permits. Once you have the permits, the pond, and the fish, you may find that your fish will not grow. Possibly, they are too crowded and are not getting enough food. The solution would be either to remove some fish or to feed them more. If they still don't grow and there is adequate food and circulation in the pond (there must be some outflow of water because some fish produce a metabolite that retards the growth of other fish), an essential nutrient may be lacking in the diet. If a switch in diet doesn't help, the fish may be sick. The best treatment for disease is prevention. Do not crowd your fish, keep handling to a minimum, be sure the fish receive a balanced diet, and monitor the temperature and oxygen concentration of your pond. Above all, be *sure* that any fish shipped to your pond, especially from out of state, are certified disease free. If this precaution doesn't work, take your sick fish over to the nearest university with a fishery department, or to your state fish and game agency. In spite of any problems you may experience, remember that aquaculture is a trial-and-error art, and once you understand your ponds, the harvests should be very rewarding.

Detailed information regarding stocking, feeding, determining pond fertility, the types and amounts of fertilizer to induce a desired plankton population, feasibility of artificial feed, and what is needed for overwintering is beyond the scope of this chapter. For general reference information, the best English-language encyclopedia is *Aquaculture: the Farming and Husbandry of Freshwater and Marine Organisms* by John Bardach, John Ryther, and William McLarney. It contains a great deal of information on practices throughout the world and information on fish not commonly cultured in the United States. A very good book on trout culture and fish diseases is *Culture and Diseases of Game Fish* by H. S. Davis. These and other books on fish culture are listed at the end of this chapter in the Bibliography.

For more specific questions, help can be obtained from federal and state agencies—fish and game commissions, the Fish and Wildlife Service of the Department of the Interior, and conservation agencies. Other sources might be nearby universities and colleges, especially those involved in Sea Grant programs. Still other sources are those people actively involved in existent commercial ventures: fish farmers, fish-farming associations, and distributors or researchers for fish-food companies. Helpful publications are put out by federal and state governments, universities, and the United Nations Food and Agriculture Organization (FAO). Information is also supplied by such periodicals as *The American Fish Farmer, Farm Pond Harvest,* and *The Progressive Fish-Culturist,* as well as in research reports in scientific and industrial journals. However, one note of caution is necessary. If you have a problem, understand that advice and solutions can vary from one source to another. As a case in point, a fish breeder once had a disease problem he couldn't solve. He asked the state fish and game agency for advice and sent them some diseased fish. Evidently they didn't examine the fish too carefully because each week for several successive weeks they told the breeder to try different solutions, all of which were expensive and none of which worked; the breeder lost most of his fish. He later learned that his problem was due to flukes, a parasite easily controlled by one application of the right chemical. The moral of the story is that aquaculture is an inexact science; don't expect anyone to know all the answers.

Living Quarters for Fish

Don't forget! Fish live in water. This means that successful aquaculture requires an adequate water supply and a container to hold the water. Obvious though this may seem, it is sometimes forgotten, and the results are both costly and embarrassing.

An adequate water supply is one that furnishes water during the driest part of the season, which is usually when it's needed the most. For freshwater aquaculture, this water can come from wells, surface runoff, streams, or springs. Well water has the advantage of being a fairly reliable, relatively pollution-free source, and is also free of undesirable aquatic organisms; however, it needs to be pumped and is low in oxygen. Surface water may not have to be pumped, but it usually contains undesirable fish which are extremely adept at crawling through filters and infesting your pond. Springs are clean water sources that don't need to be pumped and are preferred when available.

Whatever the source, this water must be contained in some manner, in ponds, troughs, raceways, circular ponds, or silos. Fish also can be isolated in larger water bodies by means of floating nets or cages. The type of container you select depends upon local geology, your aesthetic taste, the type of fish you're raising, the amount you want to produce, and your pocketbook. If you want to raise fish in a sylvan setting reminiscent of Walden Pond, concrete circular ponds will never do; you should opt for a farm pond (and lower production). Or, if you live downtown and your backyard only has room for garbage cans and a clothesline, then a farm pond is not practical; you should look into fiberglass silos.

Ponds: Ponds are used mostly for warm-water fish, but they can also be used for trout. For a dirt-bottom pond, the soil must retain water. The Soil Conservation Service of the Department of Agriculture can check the moisture-retaining properties of your soil. If the earth doesn't retain water, a sealant such as bentontite can be used, or a vinyl sheet can be laid between water and ground; but both these methods add considerably to your cost. As we mentioned earlier, be sure that the pond is constructed so that it can be drained completely. Details of construction and illustrations are presented in our discussion of farm pond programs. If there is already a pond present which you wish to use, care must be taken to insure that no undesirable fish are in it. This "care" usually means draining your pond and starting from scratch.

Raceways and Circular Ponds: Pond water, because it is stationary, can be enriched with fertilizer; the pond is thus applicable for warm-water fish which usually live in "productive" water (turbid with phytoplankton, for example). However, salmonid fish (trout and salmon) prefer clear, nonproductive water. Because running water carries away the growth-inhibiting waste products of these fish, the best production of salmonids occurs in either raceways or circular ponds. Expenses can mount up for these types, since they usually need to be constructed and maintained with pumps and filters.

Raceways are long troughs which are slanted or stepped downhill. Water enters through the uphill end and leaves from the downhill end (see Figure 7.13). Since water is continuously flowing through the raceway, great quantities are needed to operate it. American raceways are usually built with concrete, and this material is not cheap. Earth raceways are less expensive and provide natural food for the fish. The soil must retain water, however, and the probability of disease is increased. If you happen to have a clear, cold-water stream on your property, you have a natural raceway and may need only to dam it up a little or build several small pools.

In a circular pond, water is shot out of a pipe on the rim of the pond and the water flows around the pond in a spiral, finally exiting by a drain in the center (see Figure 7.12). This approach uses much less water than a raceway, but it still consumes a considerable amount. Because there must be a permanent slope down to the drain, con-

crete must be used for the bottom and sides, a sacrifice of both natural beauty and many dollars. Construction of a pond 2.5 feet deep and 20 feet in diameter would cost $1500 or more.

If you don't have enough room, water, or money for raceways or circular ponds, high production also has been attained in barrels. In *Aquaculture* (Bardach et al), it is reported that Pennsylvania Fish Commission biologists at Bellefonte, Pennsylvania, once raised 2720 kilograms of trout in a fiberglass silo 5 meters high and 2.3 meters in diameter. It was merely an experimental approach, but you might look into it.

Experimental systems which can be exceedingly productive are the solar-algae ponds being looked at by the New Alchemy Institute. These are described in more detail later in the chapter.

Cages and Nets: Fish are grown inside cages and nets when they are cultured in the ocean, in powerplant effluents, or in large streams. This kind of isolation makes harvesting easy, yet provides a constant supply of circulating water to the fish. The fish, however, must be hatched and raised through early youth in another type of container or else young fry must be collected from some other source. In addition, any use of structures on public waterways first must be cleared with legal authorities.

An experiment with cage culturing has been carried out for the last few years at the New Alchemy Institute in Woods Hole, Massachusetts. Of the catfish, sunfish, and bluegill species used, the yellow bullhead catfish (*Ictalurus natalis*) proved to be the most successful with their particular situation. The natural productivity of the pond they used was supplemented with artificial food, captured flying insects, and cultured midge larvae. The captured juvenile bullheads tripled their weight during three months in the summer, and they calculated the cost of production at 66 cents per pound, including cage construction. Although used by commercial fish farmers, cage culturing has not been widely used by individuals up to now. The experience of the New Alchemy fish farmers, however, is an example of how difficult the process can be. Two seasons of unsuccessful results brought about the changes needed for a successful crop the last time around. (See volumes 4, 5, and 6 of *The Journal of the New Alchemists.*)

Freshwater Aquaculture

Now that we've surveyed the promise, problems, and structures used in aquaculture, we finally can get down to discussing the fish. Much of the data which follows has been drawn from *Aquaculture* by Bardach et al. Bear in mind that great climatic differences occur within the expanse of the United States; some forms of aquaculture which are applicable to one area are wholly inappropriate in another. Most aquaculture activity in this country is carried out in the Southeast, where the warm climate

Figure 7.13 Most frequently found in hatcheries, raceways and circular ponds both require quantities of water and also pumping equipment.

makes possible a long growing season and rapid growth during this season. In the northern part of the United States, the temperature during the summer can be every bit as warm as in the South; but the warm season is shorter, resulting in less annual growth for fish, and the winters are extremely cold, often resulting in *no* growth. Tropical breeds like tilapia, which are very successful in warm climates, cannot survive in the North without special care. And such eurythermic breeds (tolerant of wide temperature ranges) as channel catfish and bass *can* be cultivated in both the North and the South, but grow more slowly in the colder climate.

Do not, however, be misled: aquaculture is still (and equally) feasible in the northern United States. It has been carried on for centuries with great success in the extreme climates of Japan, the north of China, and Eastern Europe. Species native to these regions can survive the local extremes of temperature; years of experience have taught the people which species grow and taste the best and are the most amenable to aquacultural techniques.

For any pond, the fish production is limited by its food production. Some species of fish, however, are more efficient at converting food production to fish biomass than are other species. The most efficient food converters are the plant-eating fish because they are low on the food pyramid. In North America, however, most plant-eating fish are too small for human consumption, and therefore, exotic (meaning non-native) herbivorous fish such as tilapia, grass carp, and silver carp have been imported.

Another efficient way to convert food production to fish biomass is to use all the food produced. The food produced may take the form of detritus, phytoplankton, macroalgae, zooplankton, flowering plants, benthic invertebrates, or small fish. This production is used most efficiently when species that consume all these forms of food are stocked together. Stocking only a species that consumes small fish would not use the production very efficiently. This is why polyculture, in which species with different feeding habits are stocked together in one pond, is more productive than monoculture, in which only one species is stocked.

In Table 7.10 we have listed several species that have good aquaculture potential and have grouped them according to food habits. Theoretically, the most efficient aquaculture system would be a pond stocked with one species from each group. This isn't completely accurate because some feeding groups overlap, some species within a group have sufficiently different preferences that they can be cultured together, and some species live in different regions and prefer different environmental conditions. If you are game, choose one species from several groups and develop your own best combination over time.

Ducks

The first species listed is not even a fish, but it should be included in any pond where natural food production is expected to play a role. In Southeast Asia, ducks are an integral part of many polyculture operations because their manure fertilizes the water and greatly stimulates phytoplankton growth. Ponds produce much more fish when ducks are included than they do without ducks.

The most popular breed in the United States is the White Pekin. This is the all-white duck you see in many parks and farms. It is a meat breed but will produce about 160 eggs per year, although it won't sit on them. Other meat breeds include the Aylesbury and the Muscovy. The best egg producers are the Khaki Campbell and the Indian Runner, but these don't produce much meat.

To raise ducks, you'll need to build a simple one-story shed with windows, ventilation, and 5 to 6 square feet of floor space per duck. No roosts are needed because only Muscovies can fly. You can find duck dealers under "Hatcheries" in the Yellow Pages. Buy your breeders in April or May when the ducks are six to seven weeks old. Select energetic, large ducks (about 2.5 kilograms at six weeks) and get about six females (they honk) per male (they belch) plus a few extras. Spread straw, wood shavings, peat moss, or other dry litter on the floor of the shed and set a few light bulbs in it. Allow each duck 75 square feet of yard space and provide free access to the fish ponds. A fence can keep them from running amok on your property. Periodically scrape up the manure and wet litter, dump it in your fish ponds, and spread out more dry litter.

The ducks will mature after about seven months, and egg laying will start when they get 14 hours of light per day. If the day length is shorter than this, leave the light-bulbs on in the shed to simulate a 14-hour day. Muscovies incubate their eggs but other breeds either require artificial incubation or else broody hens can be borrowed from the chicken coop. Artificially incubated eggs should be gathered before 7:00 A.M. each day, washed in warm (110°-115°F) water, and placed in a chicken incubator for four to five weeks until they hatch. Alternatively, you can avoid this chore (although sacrificing self-sufficiency) by buying day-old ducklings each year. Move the ducklings to a brooder (see section on chickens) for about four weeks, allow 1 square foot per duckling, provide them with plenty of water, and keep the litter dry. After four weeks the ducks can go outside and join the rest of the flock. Ducks can be fed from a hopper with the same feed used for chickens, but keep the hopper near water so that they don't choke on the dry feed. The ducks reach market size in two to four months and can gradually be sent to your kitchen or to your produce stand. Since eggs are produced and hatched throughout the year, you should have a fairly continuous supply of duck meat.

Detritus Feeders

Freshwater clams: Corbicula fluminea, which was imported from Taiwan, and *Lampsilis claibornensis,* which is a native, are both found in stable sand or gravel bottoms of large rivers or lakes in water less than 2 meters deep.

If you happen to find a few of these clams, put them in a sack, take them to your ponds, and drop them in. If they don't survive, you've lost almost nothing. If they do reproduce, they can provide food for you and your fish, they filter excess garbage out of your water, and they never have to be fed. Clams, in short, are the closest things to a free lunch around. Most of them should be harvested each year because if they become too abundant, the larvae, which parasitize the gills of fish, may begin to injure the fish. Another word of caution: the

Table 7.10   Freshwater Aquaculture

Species	Time required to grow to market size without supplementary feeding	Place where growth rate to market size was measured	Current distribution in U.S.	Food	Production rate in U.S. (kg/ha-yr)
Ducks	2–4 months[1]	New York	Nationwide	Chicken Feed	
DETRITUS FEEDERS					
Clam (Lampsilis claibornensis)	—	—	Eastern U.S.	detritus	1000 (with catfish)[2]
Clam (Corbicula fluminea)	7 mos.	Taiwan	Calif, Oregon, Wash.	detritus	—
PHYTOPLANKTON & ALGAE FEEDERS					
Silver Carp (Hypophthalmichthys molitrix)	6 mos.	Israel	Lower Mississippi Basin	phytoplankton	1000 (with catfish)[2]
Gizzard Shad (Dorosoma cepedianum)	1½ yrs.[3]	Lake Erie	Great Plains to Atlantic	algae, phytoplankton, bottom scum	—
Fathead Minnow (Pimephales promelas)	—	—	Central and Eastern U.S.	algae, detritus, zooplankton	300[2]
Tilapia	6 mos.	Israel	Calif, Utah, Col., Okl., Missouri, Miss., Alabama, Fla., Maryland	algae, phytoplankton, flowering plants, detritus	1500 (with catfish)[2]
FLOWERING PLANT EATERS					
Grass Carp (Ctenopharyngodon idella)	5–6 mos.[2]	Hungary	Parts of Mississippi Basin, Fla.,	Flowering plants, leaves	—
Swamp Crayfish (Procambarus clarkii)	6 mos.–1 yr.[2]	Louisiana	Gulf Coast, Nevada, Southern Calif.	Rotting vegetation	225–900[5]
OMNIVORES					
Buffalo Fish (Ictiobus cyprinellus)	1–2 yrs.[3]	Saskatchewan	Mississippi Basin, Lake Erie, Arizona, Southern Calif.	Diatoms for young, planktonic crustaceans, benthic invertebrates	100–1000[5]
Common Carp (Cyprinus carpio)	1 yr.[3]	Ontario	Nationwide	Almost any small planktonic or benthic invertebrates, algae, detritus	300–>4000[2]
Tench (Tinca tinca)	3 yrs.[3]	Great Britain	Pacific Northwest, Maryland	Algae for young, insect larvae, molluscs	20–80[2]
INVERTEBRATE AND SMALL VERTEBRATE FEEDERS					
Sunfish (Lepomis spp.)	1–2 yrs.[4]	Illinois	East & Central U.S., parts of West	Benthic and plankton insects and crustaceans, some algae and small fish	30–150[2]
Black crappie (Pomoxis nigromaculatus)	2 yrs.[3]	Michigan	Nationwide	Invertebrates and minnows	30–150[2]
PISCIVORES					
Bass (Micropterus spp.)	2½–3 yrs[4]	Illinois	Nationwide	Insects, crayfish, fish	10–40[2]
Channel Catfish (Ictalurus punctatus)	1½–2 yrs.[3]	Arkansas	East & Central U.S., parts of West	Benthic invertebrates, fish, some plants	100–1000[2]
Rainbow Trout (Salmo gairdneri)	1–2 yrs.[3]	Minnesota	Nationwide except Gulf states	Insects, larger crustaceans, other invertebrates, fish	50–60,000[2]

References

1. "Raising Ducks" pamphlet. See bibliography, U.S. Dept. of Agriculture.
2. Bardach, Ryther, and McLarney. Aquaculture
3. Scott and Crossman. Freshwater Fishes of Canada. Bulletin Fisheries Research Board of Canada.
4. Lopinot, Pond Fish and Fishing in Illinois.
5. Walsh, D. 1978. Aquaculture in the United States Constraints and Opportunities. A report of the Committee on Aquaculture, National Research Council, National Academy of Sciences, Washington, D.C.

Corbicula clam has no natural predator, and if conditions are favorable, they may become dense enough to be a nuisance in your pond. This was the case in several large irrigation canals in California.

Although marine species have been cultivated in many parts of the world for generations, there is little available material on freshwater clam culture. It is known, however, that some clam species require a fish host at one stage in their larval development. At Auburn University, some *Lampsilis* species were stocked in the polyculture with bluegill, redear sunfish, and bass, and then ignored until the annual harvest. The average yield for clams over six years was 1010 kg/ha-yr (318 kilograms without the shells); the fish contributed 464 kg/ha-yr. In a control pond without clams, 317 kilograms of fish were harvested; clams may promote additional growth in a fish culture by their water-filtering capability. If freshwater clams are native to your area, they might be worth experimenting with.

Phytoplankton and Algae Feeders

Silver Carp (Hypophthalmichthys molitrix): Silver carp are exotics, but in places where they are already established, they would be ideal. They won't spawn in captivity, so 2-gram fry must be bought. Try stocking about 1000 per hectare in a polyculture with 5000 carp (or other bottom feeder) per hectare, 1000 grass carp or gizzard shad per hectare, and maybe 500 to 1000 catfish per hectare. Depending on the temperature, these fish should reach market size in 6 to 18 months. Silver carp especially benefit from duck waste and will feed directly on chicken manure, which can be dumped in a shallow corner of the pond when you intend to sample the fish.

Gizzard Shad (Dorosoma cepedianum): The gizzard shad is the only large plant-eater native to America, and as such it can be used in place of the grass carp. Unfortunately, its flesh is soft, bony, and unmarketable except as crayfish bait. It is probably acceptable for home consumption, but don't try to sell it. It breeds prolifically, and has been used successfully as a forage fish in bass ponds that have been overrun with algae. It got a bad reputation by overpopulating parts of Lake Erie, so polyculture with gizzard shad must include a predator to control the young shad, since breeders are too big for most predators. Check with your state fish and game department to find out how to obtain fingerlings.

Fathead minnow (Pimephales promelas): Fathead minnows grow to about 3 inches long and have been reported to be quite tasty when fried and eaten whole like sardines. They can also be used as a forage fish in polyculture with a predator. The advantage of using fathead minnows instead of gizzard shad is that the adults, as well as the young, can be eaten by predators, while an out-of-control shad population can only be brought back under control by fishing intensively or by draining the pond and starting again.

One-year-old fathead minnows can be planted at about 5000 per hectare in the spring in ponds that have some kind of grass growing along the shore on which eggs can be laid. If no grass is growing, plastic floating mats can be put in the ponds. The minnows spawn naturally and feed on plankton, so addition of fertilizer is important.

Tilapia: Tilapia (*Serotheradon* spp.) are small tropical fish which are generally considered phytoplankton grazers. However, they are quite omnivorous, feeding on plants and as young juveniles also on insects. They require a water temperature above 60°F to survive; and for breeding and maximum growth, the best temperature is in the mid-80s. Hence, overwintering requires heated water in most locations.

For the past several years, experimental pond culturing of tilapia has been carried out at New Alchemy. They have used ponds circulating in series, a dome-covered pond, a bioshelter-enclosed pond, and the solar-algae ponds. Improved fish productivity through supplemental feeding of commercial and home-grown food, through increasing the natural plankton productivity of the pond, and through polyculture with other fish species has been explored.

For example, the bioshelter-enclosed pond is concrete and measures 4.1 meters square by 1.7 meters deep, holding 7700 gallons. During a 3½ month experiment over the summer, 87 adult tilapia totalling 5680 grams and 6 mirror carp totalling 1320 grams were stocked. Commercial feed and vegetable wastes originating from inside the bioshelter itself were used. The results were 60 tilapia at 7600 grams and 10 carp at 5350 grams. In other words, the mean size of tilapia increased from about 1/7 pound to about 1/4 pound, and that of carp from 1/2 pound to 1.2 pounds.

The main disadvantage of tilapia is that they reproduce prolifically thereby overpopulating ponds with lots of little fish and few good-sized specimens for eating. To help get around this problem you can stock males only (more expensive) or determine the sex yourself. To do this requires growth to about 70 grams (about one-seventh of a pound) and some knowledge of the procedure. Also, crosses between *S. aurea* and *S. mossambica* often produce all males, although not always.

Tilapia can also be polycultured with a predator to control the large number of young. One promising procedure is the combination of catfish with tilapia. One discouraging result of the New Alchemy tilapia experiment was the large number of small fish in their harvest. The catfish could use these small fish as a food source and, at the same time, control their population. The tilapia, in turn, could control pond fertility by consuming excess algae and waste matter. In an experiment at Auburn University, 500 tilapia and 1800 catfish were stocked per

355

acre. The result was 400 pounds more catfish per acre than from a pond stocked with catfish alone. On many fish farms, catfish and minnows are raised together for the same reason. One drawback, however, is that catfish do not become active predators until they weigh about a pound.

Tilapia can be planted at the same rates and in the same combinations as silver carp, and like silver carp, they benefit greatly from pond fertilization. *S. aurea, S. mossambica,* and *S. nilotica* have all been cultured successfully in warm climates, but some growers report that *S. nilotica* is more temperamental than the others and more difficult to culture. It is a good species for a small group with limited space to raise, but it may be illegal to import into your state. It's best to check with local state fish and game agencies.

Flowering Plant Eaters

Grass carp (Ctenopharyngodon idella): Grass carp are among the fastest-growing fish in the world, reaching market size in a few months, and they are among the few fish that directly consume flowering plants. They grow well on a diet of grass or garden clippings and, because of this, have been hailed as a near-perfect species for aquaculture. However, they are exotics, having been introduced to the United States in 1963; they have never spawned naturally in the United States (they have in Mexico, though) and therefore probably pose no overpopulation threat. They can cause serious and usually unpredictable changes in ecosystems because they can completely remove all flowering plants from a lake or river. For this reason, grass carp are banned from Canada and over half of the American states. Most other states, except Arkansas, Alabama, Iowa, and South Dakota, require a permit before they can be imported (see the article by Sutton listed in the Bibliography).

If you can legally obtain grass carp, you can plant fingerlings in fertilized ponds at up to 1000 per hectare (depending on how much food you want to produce). They are an excellent species for polyculture because they make use of a seldom-exploited source of food (your kitchen waste), and their waste can fertilize the water or provide food for bottom feeders like the common carp. In warmer climates, it may be possible to get two crops in a pond in one year. Because they don't reproduce naturally, you'll have to buy fingerlings before each planting.

Swamp crayfish (Procambarus clarkii): The only other flowering plant eater widely used for aquaculture in America is a crustacean, the crayfish. Swamp crayfish are raised (and eaten) almost exclusively in Louisiana. Other species, such as pond crayfish (*P. blandingi*), may be suitable for aquaculture farther north, but it may be difficult to buy brood stock and kidnapping wild crayfish for an aquaculture attempt is not a good idea.

Plant brood stock in May at about 25 to 50 kilograms per hectare, depending on the amount of vegetation in the pond. The crayfish will then burrow into the pond bottom and lay eggs. In ponds devoted exclusively to crayfish, the farmers then drain the pond to encourage growth of water plants and to control predators, and reflood it around October when young crayfish are visible in the burrows, but obviously this pond draining is impossible when they are being polycultured with fish. Since crayfish can eat water plants and rotting vegetation, there may be no need to buy supplementary feed. The dissolved oxygen in the pond must be above 3 milligrams per liter, and juveniles grow more quickly in warmer water. They may be mature by December, and they are harvested until May by baiting wire funnel traps with shad heads (draining the pond will not make harvesting any easier). Then the survivors burrow and spawn, so brooders only need to be planted once. The harvesting schedule is a plus for your self-sufficient home because it provides you with a continuous source of food through the winter if your pond doesn't freeze over.

Crayfish crops are often alternated with rice because rice fields are drained after harvest at about the time the crayfish burrow, and the crayfish eat rice stubble. Because crustaceans use a great deal of energy to grow and shed their exoskeletons, crayfish are not efficient at converting food to meat, and their production rates are low. However, the food they consume would usually not be utilized by any other fish in your pond, so any crayfish production you do get can be considered a bonus.

Omnivores

Buffalofish (Ictiobus cyprinellus): Some aquaculture scientists have suggested that there's no reason to import exotic carp and tilapia when an excellent-tasting native, the buffalofish, fills many of the same feeding niches. Buffalofish were once cultured fairly extensively, but catfish culture became more profitable and buffalofish culture declined. They are still grown, however, and they may be a promising species to consider in your polyculture.

They are omnivores that feed on benthic organisms and on midwater plankton. Like carp, they may stir up the bottom in order to suspend bottom organisms in the water column, where they can be eaten. Because they are omnivorous, they will compete to some extent with almost any species with which they are polycultured; however, if food production is sufficient, this competition should be negligible and their presence should permit more efficient use of all available food. For your first stocking, try something on the order of 400 to 1000 fingerlings per hectare and keep some for brood stock the next year.

Common carp (Cyprinus carpio): The bony, scaly carp that American anglers hate is the same species as the meaty, nearly scaleless mirror carp (or Israeli carp) that is cultured and prized throughout the world. Carp, which were the first fish ever domesticated, were natives of East

Asia and were brought to America in the 1870s. They are therefore exotics, but they have become established almost everywhere. In spite of their current unpopularity, there are carp dealers in this country, and they sell native carp as well as imported Israeli carp and koi (ornamental carp).

Carp will spawn in captivity, so it might not be a bad idea to start with breeders. Put above five of each sex in a small pond before the water temperature rises in the spring and put some floating plastic mats in the pond if there aren't emerging reeds growing in it. The carp will lay millions of eggs on their own. Fertilizing the pond will increase the natural food for the fry when they hatch, after which they can be fed powdered grains, such as sorghum, since the natural production will probably be insufficient for the large number of fish. Even with supplementary feeding, the young will probably not grow any larger than 30 grams in one pond. When they reach that size, they can be transplanted to other ponds at a density of about 1000 per hectare. The remainder can be used as a reserve for future transplantings so that you'll be able to plant 30-gram fingerlings from one spring spawning at any time throughout the year. Depending on the water temperature, these carp will reach market size in from six months to two years. When winter approaches, growth will stop. If necessary, then, all the fish can be put in one pond, as long as there's sufficient oxygen. It's best to transfer the fish before they stop growing, so that any wounds they sustain during transfer will have a chance to heal before winter. The other ponds can be drained and dried out to oxygenate the bottom and retard diseases. In the spring you can replant the fish in separate ponds and use some of your larger fish as breeders for the new season, thereby perpetuating your stock.

The ability of carp to spawn in captivity is a mixed blessing. If they spawn in your growing ponds, the young can overrun the pond and prevent growth. For this reason, if you have carp larger than 200 grams in growth ponds in the spring, it would be a good idea to determine their sex and separate them into different ponds.

In America, carp have been polycultured with trout, mostly because they utilize trout waste and the food the trout have missed. They do muddy the water, however, to the detriment of the trout. They have also been polycultured with other carp. Because of their hardiness (they can tolerate considerable handling, low oxygen, high temperatures, and even getting stranded on land for up to 30 minutes), their rapid growth, and their omnivorous feeding habits, they are recommended for small aquaculture operations.

In some parts of the world, subsistence (nonintensive) culture of carp is carried out; breeders and eggs are left alone in the pond and the new fry survive on naturally produced food. Here, as elsewhere, nonintensive yields are less than those of intensive culturing. Polyculture with a predator fish (trout, pike, perch, bass) to control the number of young carp can increase the growth of the survivors. In China, polyculture has produced incredible yields in small ponds. Different species of carp have been bred so that one species feeds on macroalgae, a second feeds on phytoplankton, another on zooplankton, and yet another on bottom detritus. In this highly efficient system, each species complements the others and none are competing. Yields can reach 7500 kg/ha-yr.

On the other hand, subsistence farming in Haiti produced 550 kg/ha-yr. Fingerlings were stocked which took from seven to nine months to reach maturity. With intensive culture in sewage effluent in Java, up to 1,000,000 kg/ha-yr have been produced, a very impressive production figure.

Raising carp, however, does present a few problems. For example, because the temperature fluctuates in the temperate zone, it's possible that carp can be induced to spawn too early and a late cold spell will kill the fry. Competing species usually make survival difficult for young carp. Also, carp eggs are particularly susceptible to fungus outbreaks, and the grown fish easily fall victim to diseases. As with tilapia, metabolites produced by carp limit their own growth (these wastes can be eliminated by filtering systems). In spite of any problems, carp culture, particularly a polyculture arrangement, is worth considering.

Tench (Tinca tinca): Tench are sometimes grown with carp, mostly to provide variety. Since they compete for the same food, a tench-carp combination is not really a polyculture and does not add any efficiency to the utilization of food produced by your pond. They don't convert food to meat as efficiently as carp, but if you're getting tired of eating carp, or like the taste of tench, they can be substituted for common carp on a one-for-one basis (that is, instead of planting 1000 carp per hectare, plant 900 carp and 100 tench).

Invertebrate and Small Vertebrate Feeders

Sunfish (Lepomis spp.): Fish that feed on small invertebrates are often used in polyculture with predator bass. Sunfish, such as bluegill and redear sunfish, are commonly stocked because (1) they fight hard when hooked; (2) they produce great numbers of young naturally, which provide food for bass; (3) they tolerate a wide temperature range; and (4) the Soil Conservation Service may plant them for free as an incentive for more farmers to conserve water by building farm ponds. The major problem with sunfish is that they breed too easily. These mad propagators eat invertebrates and some algae, and their high reproductive rate, if unchecked, causes competition and depletion of food sources; the culturist will end up with many small fish, no one of which can make up a meal.

Reproductive excesses of sunfish can be attacked in various ways. It is possible to breed hybrids which, when crossed, will produce sterile offspring or offspring of only one sex. Another technique is to raise fish in floating cages so that the eggs fall through the mesh; the parents are unable to care for the young, which then die. These methods seem to be both wasteful of life and nonproductive; they also don't encourage a self-sustaining fish population. A better way to control reproduction is to polyculture sunfish with a predator such as the largemouth bass, which eats enough young sunfish to control their numbers and which itself can be harvested for food. (More on this later.)

Black crappie (Pomoxis nigromaculatus): The black crappie can be substituted for sunfish in polyculture on a one-for-one basis. They fill roughly the same feeding niches and are also available from private dealers.

Piscivores

Bass (Micropterus spp): Both the largemouth bass and the smallmouth bass can be used as predator fish in polyculture where you want to control the number of young produced by another fish. Bass, however, as predators high on the food pyramid, have much lower production rates per hectare than other species. Hence, to keep the polyculture system in balance, much fewer numbers of bass than other species should be taken. See the section on the farm pond program.

Bass are generally polycultured with sunfish because of the stocking incentive from the Soil Conservation Service, but they can also be polycultured with carp and tilapia to control runaway reproduction.

Channel catfish (Ictalurus punctatus) and other catfish: Cultivation of channel catfish has been technologically feasible since 1955, and now this species is the most extensively cultured fish in the United States. They do well under intensive culture since they can adapt to crowded conditions.

Spawning is not difficult—stock a few males and females in a small pond in spring and add a few milk cans or sections of pipe. Spawning will begin when temperature rises to over 21°C (70°F). As with carp, a few spawners will probably produce more fry than a small pond can support, even with fertilization; therefore, it will be necessary to supply supplementary powdered feed to the fry, and to stock growth ponds at a lower rate. The fry should be transferred to growth ponds sometime during the first three months. To cut down on insect predators, don't fill the growth ponds until just before stocking. The more insects, the better for the catfish. If you don't intend to provide supplementary feed in the growth ponds, the stocking rate should be on the order of 200 to 300 per hectare. With feeding, the stocking rate can be 1000 to 2000 per hectare. Best growth occurs at between 22° and 30°C (70° and 85°F), and with supplementary feeding catfish can reach market size in six months. Slower growth will continue at temperatures as low as 10°C (15°F).

The main problems in catfish culture are disease and oxygen depletion. The best disease prevention measure is not to overcrowd your ponds. This can also help prevent oxygen depletion.

The dissolved-oxygen content of the water is of vital importance. Greater quantities of fish per acre make heavier demands on available food and oxygen, so management becomes more difficult. A large part of the oxygen in a pond is produced by algae; it is sometimes necessary to use fertilizer to encourage algal growth if you start a new pond. Later, the problem becomes one of controlling excess algae, since at night the algae become oxygen consumers and compete with the fish for the available oxygen. Overfeeding, too, can lead to serious problems in this area, since uneaten food can stimulate algal growth and also consumes oxygen as it decays. Oxygen content is highest late in the afternoon and lowest just before dawn. It is not unusual for the entire population of a pond to die in one night due to oxygen depletion. In the summer, oxygen levels should be measured every day early in the morning and should be kept well above 3 parts per million (consult fish and game agencies for measurement techniques). It's important to monitor the dissolved oxygen in your ponds. To keep the dissolved oxygen high, you can buy commercial aerators, either a paddlewheellike contraption or a kind of fountain. You can also beat the water by hand, raise the oxygen concentration of incoming water by constructing baffles and waterfalls in the inflow ditch, cut down on fertilization, remove excess dead matter or algae scum, or decrease the residence time of water in the pond by lowering the pond and increasing the inflow rate.

For intensive culturing and maximum growth rates, catfish are fed about 3 to 5 percent of their body weight each day. During a seven-month growing period, the cost of feed is about $150 per acre for a pond with 2000 fish per acre. During the winter, only about one-third as much food is consumed per day; the cost is proportionally less.

The amount your fish will grow is directly related to proper diet. The ingredients, of course, can be varied. Catfish have been raised using soybean as the only source of protein, although its utilization is very poor at lower temperatures. Table 7.11 presents a set of diet guidelines, and Table 7.12 illustrates a suggested feed formula. Balance in the feed content is stressed.

Table 7.11 Catfish Diet Guidelines[a]

Diet Element	Percent of Total Feed
Crude protein, more than	30
Digestible protein, more than	25
Animal protein, more than	14
Fish meal protein, more than	5
Crude fat, more than	6
Crude fiber, less than	20
	100

Notes: a. Taken from F. Meyer, *Second Report to the Fish Farmer.*

If you want to avoid commercial fish food, you can raise soybeans as a protein source; but processing to make them acceptable to the fish must be tried out experimentally. Worms and insect larvae also can be raised in a compost pile. Alternate sources of protein are minnows or other herbivorous fish raised in the same pond. Keep in mind that collecting this food requires some effort and growth rates are not likely to be as high.

Harvesting can be done by draining and seining, but this will probably give you more fish than you can use at one time. Catfish can also be harvested by hook and line, a method that will provide smaller quantities over a longer period. After a season of hook and line harvesting, however, the remaining fish might still need to be harvested by draining the pond. Potential breeders can be kept for the next season, so you may only need to stock your ponds once. Since catfish prey on small fish, they have been polycultured with carp, tilapia, and clams.

You might also consider stocking your ponds with bullheads (*Ictalurus* spp.), which are closely related to channel catfish. Since there is little consumer demand for them, much less information on culturing techniques is available. However, they grow to large size quickly, and generally occupy a lower level on the food chain than channel catfish, so experimenting with bullhead culture may show that this species is very suitable for your purposes. It is interesting to note that in the cage-culturing experiments carried out by New Alchemy, the brown bullheads (*I. nebulosus*) were very prone to disease in the system they used, while the yellow bullheads (*I. natalis*) were raised much more successfully. This should not be generalized but is an example of the problems which can arise.

The problems of intensive culturing are many, some of which cannot be handled adequately in a small living unit or backyard. If, for example, you have only a limited supply of electricity, it might be impossible to harvest and preserve the fish all at once. This limitation would mean feeding a large population of nongrowing fish through the winter. There is also the matter of reproduction. Most small-scale catfish farmers find it more economical to buy fingerlings directly from hatcheries than to attempt the

difficult task of raising their own. Large numbers of small fish do not compete well in the same pond with significant numbers of larger fish. And diseases can wipe out the farmer overnight. If you're still interested in catfish, it is best to start with a small pond and then expand as you learn more about it. This, in fact, is a good rule for any aquaculture operation you try. (For more information, see the listing under F. Meyer in the Bibliography.)

Rainbow trout (Salmo gairdneri): Trout are among the most popular game fish in the world. A large proportion of the fish culture in the United States is devoted to trout, which are usually raised for the purpose of stocking fishing grounds. Of all the species considered in this chapter, the salmonids are probably the least suitable for polyculture, because they are the most fussy about water conditions. They require cleaner, clearer, cooler, and more highly oxygenated water than most other cultured species.

Intensive farming in monoculture is a laborious and difficult process. Trout are unusual in that they grow best in cold, sterile water and are more efficient in monoculture than polyculture. Trout won't spawn in captivity without help; they must be artificially fertilized by stripping eggs and sperm. Eggs are hatched in trays, and the fry are raised in shallow raceways and then moved to larger raceways as they grow; circular ponds and silos can also be used. In any case, great quantities of clean water must be available. Water temperatures are normally maintained between 50 and 65°F, and oxygen concentrations must be no less than 5 parts per million. Commercial growers have achieved fantastic production figures for rainbow trout (60,000 kg/ha-yr), but these require tremendous expenditures for concrete raceways, ponds, incubation facilities, and high-protein artificial food, and their methods are not meant to be energy-efficient.

It is also possible to raise trout nonintensively in cold-water ponds. In general, such ponds exist only in the northern tier of states, in Canada, and on the Pacific Coast. To supply your family, a pond should be between one-half to one acre in area, with a degree of both inflow and outflow; at least a quarter of the pond should be from 12 to 15 feet deep if it freezes in winter and also to provide some deep cool pools if summer temperatures get above 21°C (70°F). Rainbow trout are the most suitable salmonids for culture because they are the least fussy about oxygen and water temperature. They can tolerate oxygen levels as low as 3 milligrams per liter and temperatures as high as 24°C (75°F), but they feed less at high temperatures. If your locality is warmer than this, you should deepen your pond to provide some deep, cool pools.

For your purposes, much lower production than that obtained by commercial growers should be expected. You shouldn't attempt to increase production by fertilizing very much, because trout prefer clean, clear water. Production can be increased by using artificial or natural foods. For example, if earthworm cultures are available, pile a load of wormy compost on a styrofoam float with holes

Table 7.12 A Suggested Feed Formula[a]

Ingredients	Percent
Fish meal (menhaden)	12.0
Soybean meal	20.0
Blood meal	10.0
Distillers solubles	8.0
Rice bran	35.0
Rice by-products	10.0
Alfalfa meal	4.5
Vitamin premix	0.5
	100.0

Notes: a. Taken from F. Meyer, *Second Report to the Fish Farmer.*

punched in the bottom. Worms will occasionally poke their heads through the holes and this will make alert trout very happy. Another method is to suspend lights over the pond at twilight to attract insects, which then fall into the water.

Trout rarely spawn in these ponds. Since to induce spawning and to carry out egg incubation requires investment in expensive incubation facilities and a great deal of knowhow, it is best to buy fingerlings from a dealer. Plant them in your pond at about 100 to 200 per hectare, although more is possible if you intend to provide artificial food. Trout planted in spring or summer as fingerlings can begin to be caught with hook and line the next spring. Every two years or so the pond should be drained and completely harvested. Thus, stocking will be necessary again.

With artificial feed, fastest growth is attained with Oregon Moist Pellet (OMP), but these must be stored frozen, and freezers use considerable energy. If you lack freezer facilities, a dry feed might be better. Check with a dealer to find out the pellet size that's appropriate for your fish. When feeding, broadcast the feed lightly and evenly so that all the fish nearby can reach it before it sinks to the bottom. Do not plop big handfuls in one place because once a pellet hits the bottom, trout will not eat it.

This food doesn't have to be wasted, however, if you polyculture trout with a bottom feeder. Carp have been used, but they tend to muddy the water, and trout don't appreciate this. Spreading stones on the bottom of the pond can help keep the water clear, but then harvesting with a net will be difficult. Despite these problems with polyculture, if your water supply remains cold throughout the year, trout might be one of the best species for you to consider from a culinary point of view.

Salmon (Salmo salar, Atlantic salmon; Oncorhyncius spp., *Pacific salmon):* Although this is not on the master list, we mention it since it is such a delicacy. It is not a good species for the home fish farmer. Salmon belong to the same family as trout and, like them, are anadromous (they spawn in freshwater and mature at sea). Although trout *can* grow in freshwater, salmon *must* mature in brine.

Salmon are cultured intensively, if at all. Like trout, spawning is achieved by stripping; unlike trout, the Pacific salmon die after spawning. The fry are raised in raceways until they reach the smolt stage (about two years), after which they must be put out to sea. Fingerlings which have been grown experimentally in cages floating in the ocean are fed on pellet food for six to nine months and then harvested. Growth is rapid and this method shows some promise, but obviously it can be used only in selected areas.

The Farm Pond Program

The nonintensive polyculture systems mentioned above are often used in ponds developed under the farm pond program, a scheme initiated by the government to conserve water and wildlife, which reached its peak popularity in the 1950s but is still used. Under this program, federal or state agencies supply and stock noncommercial ponds one time with bass and bluegill fingerlings, *free of charge*. Sunfish or catfish are legal substitutes. Maintenance and labor is minimal; after a few months, you merely face the challenge of catching your own pan-sized fish! (Actually, it's not quite that easy.)

These ponds are considered "recreational" and, while they can't produce enough for commercial purposes, they can contribute significantly to the food supply for a family living unit. For the purposes of a small self-sufficient living group in temperate climates, a bass-bluegill farm pond culture is considered the best combination. Production figures of 250 to 450 kilograms per hectare have appeared, but it has not been made clear whether or not this is a sustained yield.

Maintenance is minimal once stocking is completed, but there are several problems. A pond of this nature has to be fished regularly or it will become overstocked. Poor pond design has often resulted in too rapid a flow rate or floods which wash out the fish. Weeds, while not too difficult to control, may require some attention.

Constructing the Farm Pond

A farm pond is not a backyard undertaking; an area larger than a quarter of an acre is necessary to produce sufficient fish biomass. Details of pond construction outlined here are also applicable to any other type of aquaculture that uses ponds. For free technical assistance, contact the Soil Conservation Service. They may be especially cooperative if you say that you're planning to use some of the dam water for irrigation.

The best type of site is probably a depression in a somewhat broad, gently sloping field. One mistake often made is selecting a site through which *too much* water flows. This surplus flow carries silt into and fish out of the pond. Depth should be from 2 to 8 feet. Wells or springs are excellent water sources.

The pond can either be excavated or else constructed by building levees or dams around a natural depression. Construction is preferable since drainage can be accomplished without pumping. In general, the dam should be designed with a 2:1 slope on both sides. The width of the base should be about four times the height (plus the width of the top). The top of the dam can be about 7 to 12 feet wide. Soil for this purpose should contain a large percentage of clay. In addition, to prevent water seepage, a clay core wall should be built beneath the dam. This is done by digging a trench 4 to 10 feet wide down to "watertight" soil and then refilling it with a clay soil (see Figures 7.14 and 7.15). Of course, soil for the dam itself can be taken from the pond bed. If your dam is more than 12 feet high, you had better consult a civil engineer. In addition, don't forget to include a drain, and maybe even a spillway. After construction, the dam tends to settle several inches. You also might check in Chapter 3 for further discussion of dams. For visual attractiveness and for erosion control, plant your vegetation as soon as possible. Don't limit yourself to grass; consider all the possibilities—fruit or nut trees, vegetables, berries—however, don't let the trees shade the pond, since it would cut down the solar energy input for heat and photosynthesis.

The cost of a dam varies. Soil can be moved with a dragpan pulled by a team or tractor, or be pushed with bulldozers, or be hauled in trucks. If you own your own equipment, you can construct a pond fairly cheaply. See Chapter 3 for more details.

The pond should be 1 to 2 meters deep, except that there should be a deeper corner to facilitate harvest. If the pond is any shallower than 1 meter, emergent vegetation can take root and turn your pond into a marsh. If it's any deeper, it might stratify (develop a warm, oxygen-rich upper layer, and a cold, oxygen-poor deeper layer). If it stratifies, the poisons will build up in the lower layer, so that when the wind blows again and the pond destratifies, the poisons will get mixed all over the pond and may kill your fish.

Weed Control

Weeds should be kept to a minimum; one suggested figure is 25 percent or less of the surface area. Since young bluegill can escape from bass by hiding in the weeds, excess vegetation tends to slow down the growth of bass and contributes to an overpopulation of competing small bluegill, few of which can grow to edible size. Shallow-water weeds such as cattails and marsh grass must be pulled out by hand. Lily pods, which root in deep water but have leaves that rest on the surface, are best controlled by cutting the leaves; some plants also have leaves beneath the surface of the water, which also need to be cut. Floating plants such as duckweed must be raked out. Filamentous algae can be minimized by successfully controlling the other weeds. And any harvest of unwanted water weeds is an excellent addition to your compost pile.

Water Quality

You don't have to be a chemist to monitor water quality. Several factors are important: temperature, dissolved oxygen (DO), pH, alkalinity, hardness, nutrient levels, ammonia levels, dissolved solids, and so on; but they are interrelated and for most purposes it will be sufficient to monitor temperature and DO (unless you have problems), although pH, as discussed in the beginning of this section, can affect productivity. DO should be measured just before sunrise, when it will be at its lowest. The easiest way to measure DO is to watch the pond and the sky above. If flocks of birds take a sudden interest in your pond because the fish are swimming along the surface with their snouts out, gulping air, you had better start aerating, either by spraying water into the pond, or even by jumping in and beating the water with sticks. More quantitative DO measurements can be obtained with an oxygen probe or by the Winkler test. Oxygen probes, which are made by such firms as Bausch and Lomb or Texas Instruments, are easy to use (but not cheap)—drop one end in the water and read—but the original calibration requires the Winkler test. The Winkler test, and other analyses of water quality, require some laboratory supplies and a place to store concentrated sulfuric acid. For details on procedures of water quality tests, see *Standard Methods for the Examination of Water and Wastewater,* which is published by the American Public Health Association.

Stocking and Fishing

In California, the Department of Fish and Game will provide free first-time stocking for any noncommercial pond (check your own state agency for local regulations). A sand and gravel bottom is best for spawning. If your pond has a mud bottom, good spawning grounds can be created by adding a few bushels of gravel at ten-foot intervals around the margin of the pond.

Stocking must be done correctly the first time around or the pond will never reach its maximum carrying capacity. Largemouth bass should be stocked at a rate of 50 to 100 fingerlings per acre, depending on the pond's fertility; bluegill fingerlings should be stocked at a rate of at least ten times that of the bass. Pond fertility for ponds which are not to be fertilized is based on the soil type. For example, forest soils support the least fertile ponds, light-colored soils are intermediate, and black-colored soils support the most fertile ponds. Table 7.13 summarizes the guidelines for stocking.

Stocking is done in the spring and, as we have mentioned, can be done free of charge by a federal or state agency. It is best not to fish for the first year, and only bluegill should be taken the second year. Bass do not reproduce until they are two years old; they should not be fished until June of the third year—that is, after their

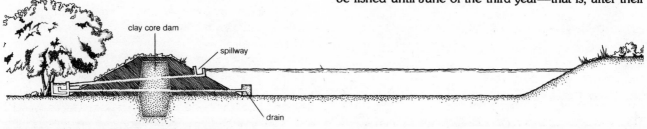

Figure 7.14 A side view of a pond.

clay core dam

spillway

drain

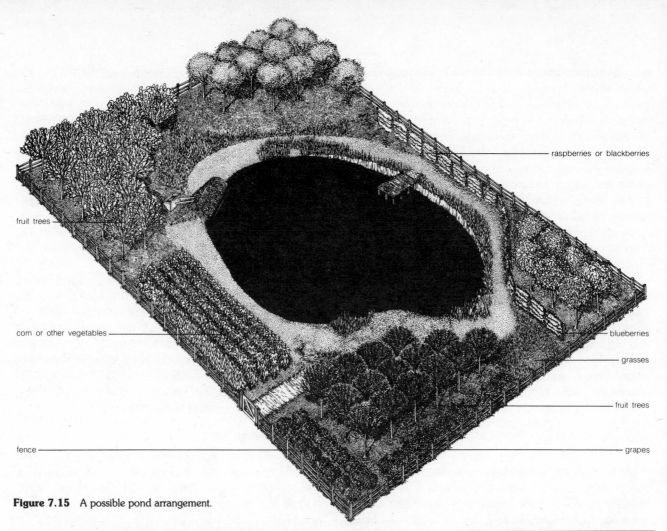

raspberries or blackberries

fruit trees

corn or other vegetables

blueberries

grasses

fruit trees

fence

grapes

Figure 7.15 A possible pond arrangement.

spawning season. Only bass over 12 inches long should be taken because overfishing small bass will result in a high concentration of small bluegill. Table 7.14 provides a guide for harvesting. It is important that fishing be done regularly; in spite of the greater attraction that larger bass have for fishermen, four pounds of bluegill should be taken for every pound of bass, or the population will fluctuate (see Figure 7.16).

The key word is "well-managed"—unless you control the bluegill population, you'll end up with a pond full of stunted bluegill. Because bluegill feed on young bass, you'll also have only a few large bass. If this happens, you'll have no choice but to drain the pond and start over. Therefore, you *must* keep about 20 times as many bluegill as bass when fishing, and you must fish often. Because

Table 7.13   Fish Stocking for Unfertilized Ponds[a]

Fish Species	Black-colored Soils	Light-colored Soils	Forest Soils
Largemouth Bass	100	75	50
Bluegill	1000	750	500
Bluegill	700	500	350
Redear	300	250	150
Channel Catfish	100	75	50

Notes: a. Numbers indicate populations of fingerlings to be stocked per acre; from A. C. Lopinot, *Pond Fish and Fishing in Illinois.*

Table 7.14   Recommended Maximum Angling Harvests[a]

	Species of Fish					
	Largemouth Bass			Bluegill and/or Redear Sunfish		
Carrying Capacity of Pond (pounds per acre)	25	50	100	75	200	400
1st Year harvest						
Total number or	None	None	None	None	None	None
Total pounds	None	None	None	None	None	None
2nd Year harvest						
Total number or	None	None	None	120[b]	320[b]	640[b]
Total pounds	None	None	None	30	80	160
3rd Year harvest						
Total number or	10	20	40	120[b]	320[b]	640[b]
Total pounds	10	20	40	30	80	160
Each succeeding Year harvest						
Total number or	10[c]	20[c]	40[c]	120[b]	320[b]	640[b]
Total pounds	10	20	40	30	80	160

Notes: a. Based on pond size of 1 acre; from A.C. Lopinot, *Pond Fish and Fishing in Illinois.*
b. 6 inches and larger.
c. After quota is reached, all bass over 18 inches can be harvested.

emergent plants help young bluegill hide from bass, you should either remove the plants or lower the level of your pond so that the plants are out of the pond and the bluegills have less space to hide from the bass. Fertilization can help produce invertebrate food for bluegills and can increase your pond's productivity, but if green scum starts to cover your pond, stop fertilizing. Polyculturing plant eaters and bottom feeders with bass and sunfish can take care of any green scum and can utilize your pond's production more efficiently.

If your bass and prey fish seem stunted, there probably isn't enough invertebrate food in the pond. In this case you should either fertilize in an effort to produce more food or, if algae is already abundant, stock a plant-eating minnow such as fathead minnow or gizzard shad. Or you can restock your pond at a lower rate.

Bass-bluegill combinations work best in warm regions and places like eastern Oregon where the bass spawn in spring and the young avoid competition and predation from bluegills, which spawn in summer. Regardless of the region you live in, bass-bluegill combinations can be successful if managed properly. Redear sunfish are sometimes preferred over bluegills because they produce fewer young and pose less of an overpopulation threat.

The stability of the pond population can be measured either by seining and counting or by recording the progress of your fish catch. A desirable population has catches of both bluegill (at least 6 inches) and bass (one to two pounds). Any other yield indicates that one of the species is overcrowded. If you start to catch crappies, bullheads, carp, buffalofish, suckers, or green sunfish, then potential problems may develop since these fish compete with bass and sunfish for food and may also prey on their young. Carp are excellent fish for culture, but they don't contribute to a bass-bluegill system. They can be used, however, as substitutes for bluegill to form a bass-carp polyculture system.

Pond Fertility

To increase the carrying capacity of your pond, fertilizers for algal growth can be used. Since algae form the base of this aquatic food chain, in theory, more algae will yield more and larger fish. Fertilizing is a difficult technique to control, however, whether it be in the form of organic wastes or inorganic compounds. To repeat a few points made earlier, decomposition of organic waste (including organic fertilizer) uses up oxygen and this oxygen depletion may kill fish. Or fertilizing can overstimulate algae and aquatic plants; their subsequent decomposition also causes oxygen depletion and kills fish. Sometimes only a green algal scum (rather than a zooplankton bloom) results. An important point to remember is that carp are much more tolerant of both low oxygen concentration and high turbidity than bass or bluegill; consequently, fertilizer can be used with carp more successfully than with the latter two species.

Using a pump or some similar device to add oxygen to fertilized water would eliminate the problem of oxygen depletion, or so it would seem. Then an unlimited amount of fertilizer could be added safely and fish production

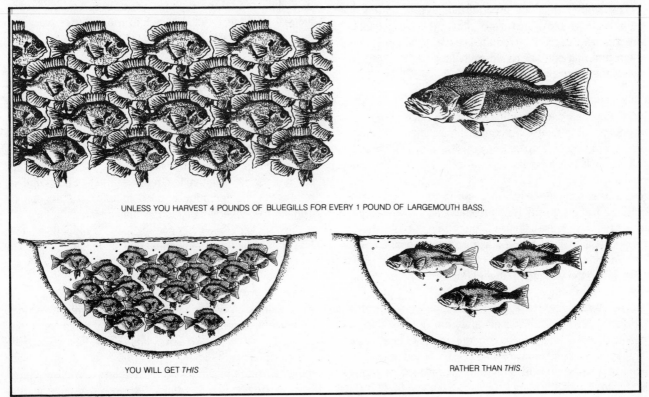

UNLESS YOU HARVEST 4 POUNDS OF BLUEGILLS FOR EVERY 1 POUND OF LARGEMOUTH BASS,

YOU WILL GET *THIS*

RATHER THAN *THIS*.

Figure 7.16 A harvesting pointer.

363

would be correspondingly greater; but, in fact, such success does not follow automatically. As fish become overcrowded, they display a great susceptibility to disease.

Further information on the farm pond program can be found in two publications listed in the Bibliography, by the California Department of Fish and Game and the U.S. Department of Agriculture, from which much of the above material was drawn.

Mariculture

The prospect of farming the oceans for food has been widely discussed for many years. Mariculture is best carried out in protected salt water in a salt-water pond, slough, or protected bay. Tidal flow would be the most likely source of circulation, although pumps could be used in some cases. If circulation is adequate, a pond of only one-quarter of an acre is fine for most mariculture operations, some of which are so productive that we wonder why there isn't more research in this field. In the United States, there are legal restrictions on the use of public waters; this limitation may explain the lagging research, to some degree. By and large, mariculture practices require a combined sense of art, science, and experimentation, and the harvests should be considered useful food supplements rather than staples. Explore the possibilities if you live near the ocean.

Invertebrates

In the United States, more is known about culturing invertebrates than vertebrates. A difficulty with all mariculture, and particularly invertebrate culture, is that the animals undergo a sequence of different larval stages before maturity; each stage requires special (often unknown) environmental conditions. Nonetheless, we can discuss a few of the more prominent crops.

Crustaceans: Crustaceous animals grow by molting (shedding their exoskeleton), a process which wastes a lot of energy; thus their food conversion efficiency is low. In most countries, shrimp culture consists of opening a sluice gate at high tide and letting the water (which hopefully contains shrimp) flow into a pond. The gate is then closed and any shrimp present are trapped. Captured shrimp grow in the pond until they are harvested. Yields of 300 to 800 kg/ha-yr are reported, but these yields can fluctuate dramatically. Only the kuruma shrimp of Japan is cultured intensively, and this culture involves very close attention to the water quality and the feeding at each stage of the shrimp's life cycle.

Malaysian prawns are often mentioned as a promising food source for culturing since they are durable and live in everything from brackish concentrations to fresh water. Unlike many invertebrates, they can be raised in captivity from egg to adulthood. For food, larval prawns require brine shrimp and fish eggs; older prawns eat small pieces of meat. Control of the temperature and salinity of the water is necessary for all life stages. Malaysian prawns can be polycultured with numerous types of herbivorous fish.

Bivalve Mollusks: Bivalves are filter feeders and require no additional feeding. They also are adept at concentrating pollutants in their biomass at toxic levels, so know the quality of your water. The two most popularly cultured bivalves are oysters and mussels. Site selection is vital in bivalve culture; they like areas with high algal productivity, strong tidal currents, and few violent waves.

Free-swimming oyster larvae metamorphose and settle on a solid surface. The young, settled oysters ("spat") then grow to maturity. The trick in oyster farming is to catch the spat, which requires that you be in the right place at the right time; your local government biologist can advise you on improving your chances. Spat are caught by putting out the shells of other bivalves as tempting solid surfaces on which the spat hopefully will settle. These shells are either piled on the bottom or suspended from rafts. Maintenance consists of checking for predators and cleaning off silt. Estimated yields are around 50,000 kg/ha-yr for rafts and 500 kg/ha-yr for bottom culture.

Mussel culture is similar to that of oysters, but the larvae are caught using rope rather than shells. This rope is spiraled around a stake driven into the bottom. Mussels sometimes get so heavy and crowded along it that they fall off; thinning is necessary periodically. Environmental requirements are the same as for oysters. Production in the Galician bays of Spain, where conditions are evidently perfect, reaches the astonishing figure of 600,000 kg/ha-yr. Unless conditions in your neighborhood are really perfect, don't expect yields like that; many other places, in fact, get very low yields.

Fish

Several different species of marine fish have been cultured commercially as a food source. Among these are yellowtail, Pacific mackerel, sardines, anchovies, milkfish, and mullet. The two major species are mullet and yellowtail, and a description of the practices by which they are currently raised adequately illustrates the status of the art. Neither species is native to America (and can't be cultured here), but the techniques used in their culture can be applied to native fish if you're enterprising.

Mullet: Mullet are brackish-water fish which also can survive in fresh water. Spawning can be induced only by injections of carp pituitary, and even if spawning is achieved, the fry seldom last a week. Culturing is still experimental and utterly dependent on getting advanced fry from fishermen. In Israel, these fry are planted in fertilized ponds with carp and tilapia. The best yield from these ponds was 1155 kg/ha-yr, 44 percent of which were mullet. Culture in other countries is less complicated and consists of blocking off bays, letting the fish grow, and then harvesting.

Yellowtail: Yellowtail are pelagic fish of the Western Pacific which also cannot spawn in captivity. Larvae are picked up at sea and sold to fry specialists, who sell the fry in turn to culturists. In Japan, yellowtail are kept in floating nets and are fed reject shrimp and fish. Reported production is incredible, reaching 500,000 kg/ha-yr. The major obstacle to yellowtail culture in the United States is that they aren't available here; consequently, fry cannot be obtained. There are other likely pelagic species off American waters, but it's still an unresolved question whether or not these other crops can be grown in captivity.

Algae

Culturing algae (freshwater or marine) in an enclosure—for example, a small blocked bay or a backyard tank—can add another layer to the recycling operations of a small community. Algae can grow on the soluble nutrients in wastewater from your anaerobic digester. Not only can algae be used to remove certain pollutants from your water, but, when harvested, they can be used as compost, fertilizer, animal feed, or fuel to cycle back into the digester. Such a scheme has been proposed by Golueke and Oswald in Berkeley (see Bibliography). Using algae as a tertiary treatment for secondary effluent of domestic wastewaters has also been proposed by J. H. Ryther and his coworkers. Details of the characteristics of the effluent from the digester, its use in algae production, factors affecting algal yields, and the biochemical characteristics of algae can be found in "Oxidation Ponds" (Chapter 5).

Solar Algae Ponds

Several interesting aquaculture experiments with a strong ecological focus and designed with self-sufficiency in mind are presently in progress. For the last several years, the New Alchemy Institute, on Cape Cod, Massachusetts, has put quite a bit of effort into such explorations. The most conceptually unique one is described below. The following discussion is intended to illustrate one possible future development rather than to outline projects for you to tackle. Details are available from the *Journal of the New Alchemists,* volumes 2 through 6.

Quite suitable for a large backyard, solar algae ponds are basically 5 feet in diameter by 5 feet high and are constructed of fiberglass-reinforced polyester. An important quality is that they are light translucent. For insulation, dead air space is provided by a second cylinder of the same material separated by a circumference of old garden hose. Both the top and bottom can be insulated with styrofoam. Design and construction details are given in volume 6 of the *Journal of the New Alchemists.* The principle behind these above-ground ponds is that within a given volume of water, the surface area available for collecting solar energy is greatly increased since the sides as well as the top are exposed to the light. This should also have a

cascading effect by increasing the ultimate productivity of the body of water. In addition, when used indoors, they also serve as passive solar collectors, especially effective in winter in the higher latitudes when the sun's rays are low.

The outdoor ponds at New Alchemy are placed on top of white marble chips and in front of curved white walls which serve as solar reflectors to increase the amount of solar energy collected in the ponds (Figure 7.17). The indoor ponds are placed adjacent to a rock heat storage unit and face south. They are inside the Ark, a bioshelter conceptually designed to utilize solar energy, contain living space, and produce fish and plant crops, all in an ecologically integrated manner (Figure 7.18).

The ponds support a dense phytoplankton community which supplies the fish with food. In addition, supplemental food is necessary; the recommended list includes comfrey, a leafy plant high in protein (35 percent); insects caught with a bug light; earthworms; rabbit feed (20 percent protein); and trout feed (40 percent protein). Problems requiring management are low dissolved oxygen and accumulation of toxic waste products such as ammonia. Photosynthesis, which produces oxygen, prevents anoxic conditions, but in conventional ponds it occurs only in the upper regions which receive light; if circulation is poor, the lower regions of the pond can become anoxic. Since photosynthesis takes place throughout the water column in these above-ground ponds, low oxygen is less of a problem. Management of low oxygen, when necessary, requires aeration (such as bubbling with an airstone) after sunset. To prevent accumulation of wastes, bottom waters can be siphoned off and replaced with fresh water, or a continuous inflow-outflow system can be devised.

These solar algae ponds have yielded impressively

Figure 7.17 Solar algae ponds paired in front of white wall.

Figure 7.18 Solar algae ponds against rock storage wall.

high production figures. In a polyculture experiment with tilapia, Chinese big head, and Israeli and silver carp, 3.8 kilograms per square meter were produced over a 3 month period. This translates into 152,000 kilograms per hectare per year, 10 times higher than any other documented pond production. Despite these data, unfortunately, the experiment does not yet translate into a satisfying meal, since the size of the individual fish is quite small (most were less than ¼ pound), and this was attained with quite a bit of supplemental feeding. This may be partly due to the very small initial size of the stocked fish (the tilapia were sometimes less than 0.2 grams) and the short growing season (usually June to October).

Worth noting, however, is the fact that temperate water species could be overwintered in the outdoor ponds. Israeli, Chinese big head, and silver carp were grown from November to April, during which time they almost doubled their size. Supplemental feeding was given, but no extraneous source of heat was necessary.

Growth was at a slower rate than in the summer, but they survived very well through a New England winter.

The appealing thing about these aquaculture ponds is their potential manageability. Certainly, a problem with one of these ponds (2.3 cubic meters) that required draining and restocking would be much less of a disaster than with even a small ¼-hectare pond (250 to 500 cubic meters). This is also true regarding any management of the water quality of the pond. Future results from the New Alchemists should be watched for.

For further information relating to specific aquacultural problems, try contacting these sources: the Fish Farming Experimental Station of the U.S. Fish and Wildlife Service (P.O. Box 860, Stuttgart, Arkansas 72160); your county agricultural extension agent; the Extension Fish and Wildlife Specialist at your state's land grant university (even Washington, D.C. has a land grant university); the Marine Advisory Program Extension Agent at the nearest Sea Grant University (contact the Office of Sea Grants, 3300 Whitehaven St. NW, Washington, D.C. 20235 for information on the Marine Advisory Program); and fisheries departments at other nearby universities. Especially useful sources are periodicals such as *The Commercial Fish Farmer, Aquaculture and the Fish Farmer, The Progressive Fish-Culturist,* and *Aquaculture Digest* (which summarizes articles from other periodicals and alphabetizes them by topic). Other sources include consultants, fish farmers, and equipment distributors. As we mentioned earlier, for information on marketing contact Marketing Specialist (currently James Ayers), National Marine Fisheries Service, No. 1 Union National Plaza, Suite 1160, Little Rock, Arkansas 72201.

And so this chapter, like the whole book, is a beginning. Food, with all of its processes, possibilities, delightful mysteries, and ramifications, is a vast subject. You now have some basic information which you can expand through further reading and through the process of "growing your own." There are new avenues to be explored, avenues which will not unbalance any more of this earth than has already been thrown awry, which will not lead to consumption of any more resources than have already been depleted, which will not waste any more "waste." And what is considered "experimental" today may be common practice in a few years. So grow, harvest, and enjoy the fruits of your labor!

Bibliography

Agriculture

Angier, B. 1972. *One Acre and Security.* New York: Vintage Books.

Bell, R. G. 1973. "The Role of Compost and Composting in Modern Agriculture." *Compost Science,* November–December 1973.

Bridwell, R. 1974. *Hydroponic Gardening.* Santa Barbara, Calif.: Woodbridge Press.

Cienciala, M. 1966. "Factors in the Maturing Process of Some Swiss Refuse Composts." International Research Group on Refuse Disposal, Bulletin no. 28. Washington, D.C.: U.S. Dept. of HEW.

Colby, B. 1972. *Dairy Goats: Breeding/Feeding/Management.* Amherst, Mass.: American Dairy Goat Association.

Commoner, B. 1971. *The Closing Circle.* New York: Alfred A. Knopf.

Edinger, P., ed. 1971. *Sunset Guide to Organic Gardening.* Menlo Park, Calif.: Lane Books.

Farallones Institute. 1979. *The Integral Urban House.* San Francisco: Sierra Club Books.

Golueke, C. G. 1973. "Latest Methods in Composting and Recycling." *Compost Science,* July–August 1973.

Heck, A. F. 1931. "The Availability of the Nitrogen in Farm Manure under Field Conditions." *Soil Science* 31:467–81.

Heck, A. F. 1931. "Conservation and Availability of the Nitrogen in Farm Manure." *Soil Science* 31:335–63.

Howard, L. E. 1947. *Earth's Green Carpet.* Emmaus, Pa.: Rodale Press.

Jeavons, J. 1973. *The Lifegiving Biodynamic/French Intensive Method of Agriculture.* Palo Alto, Calif.: Ecology Action of the Midpeninsula.

——— . 1974. *How to Grow More Vegetables.* Palo Alto, Calif.: Ecology Action of the Midpeninsula.

Jeris, J. S., and Regan, R. W. 1973. "Controlling Environmental Parameters for Optimum Composting." *Compost Science,* January–February 1973.

Jull, M. 1961. *Producing Eggs and Chickens with the Minimum of Purchased Feed.* Bulletin no. 16. Charlotte, Vermont: Garden Way Publishing.

Kaysing, B. 1971. *First-Time Farmer's Guide.* San Francisco: Straight Arrow Books.

Klein, G. 1947. *Starting Right with Poultry.* Charlotte, Vermont: Garden Way Publishing.

Merrill, R., Misser, G. C., Gage, T., and Bukey, J. 1975. *Energy Primer.* Menlo Park, Calif.: Portola Institute.

Milne, M. 1979. *Residential Water Re-Use.* California Water Resources Center Report no. 46. Davis, Calif.: University of California.

Morse, R. A. 1972. *The Complete Guide to Beekeeping.* New York: Dutton Press.

Obrist, W. 1967. "Experiments with Window Composting of Cominuted Domestic Refuse." International Research Group on Refuse Disposal, Bulletin no. 29. Washington, D.C.: U.S. Dept. of HEW.

Odum, E. P. 1971. *Fundamentals of Ecology.* 2nd ed. Philadelphia: W. B. Saunders Company.

Philbrick, J., and Philbrick, H. 1971. *Gardening for Health and Nutrition.* New York: Rudolph Steiner Publications.

Poincelot, R. R. 1972. *The Biochemistry and Methodology of Composting.* New Haven, Conn.: Connecticut Agricultural Experiment Station.

Richardson, H. L., and Wang, Y. 1942. "Nitrogen Conservation of Night Soil in Central China." *Soil Science* 54:381–89.

Ried, G. 1948. *Practical Sanitation.* New York: C. Griffin.

Rockefeller, A., and Lindstrom, C. "Greywater for the Greenhouse." *Compost Science.* 18:22–25 (1977).

Rodale, J. I. 1961. *How to Grow Vegetables and Fruits by the Organic Method.* Emmaus, Pa.: Rodale Press.

——— . 1966. *The Complete Book of Composting.* Emmaus, Pa.: Rodale Press.

——— . 1973. *The Encyclopedia of Organic Gardening.* Emmaus, Pa.: Rodale Press.

Rolle, G., and Orsanic, B. 1964. "New Method of Determining Decompostable and Resistant Organic Matter in Refuse and Refuse Compost." International Research Group on Refuse Disposal, Bulletin no. 21. Washington, D.C.: U.S. Dept. of HEW.

Root, A. I. 1973. *Starting Right with Bees: A Beginners Handbook in Beekeeping.* Medina, Ohio: A. I. Root Company.

Root, A. I., and Root, E. R. 1966. *The ABC and XYZ of Beekeeping.* Medina, Ohio: A. I. Root Company.

Rubins, E. J., and Bear, F. E. 1942. "Carbon-Nitrogen Ratios in Organic Fertilizer Materials in Relation to the Availability of Their Nitrogen." *Soil Science* 54:411–23.

Saunby, T. 1953. *Soilless Culture.* New York: Transatlantic Arts.

Smith, M. *Self Reliance 11.* Washington, D.C.: Institute for Local Self-Reliance. (1976).

Sunset Magazine. 1972. "Getting Started with the Biodynamic-French Intensive Gardening." *Sunset,* September 1972, p. 168.

Ticquet, C.. 1956. *Successful Gardening Without Soil.* New York: Chemical Publishing.

U.S. Department of Agriculture. 1966. *Raising Livestock on Small Farms.* Farmers Bulletin no. 2224. Washington, D.C.: Soil Conservation Service, U.S. Department of Agriculture.

——— . 1971. *Beekeeping for Beginners.* Home and Garden Bulletin no. 158. Washington, D.C.: Soil Conservation Service, U.S. Department of Agriculture.

Aquaculture

Adams, F., and Evans, C. E. 1962. "A rapid method for measuring lime requirement of red-yellow podzolic soils." Soil. *Sci Soc. Amer. Proc.* 26:355–357. (This has that table on how much limestone to put in your pond based on pH and acidity.)

American Public Health Association. 1971. *Standard Methods for the Examination of Water and Wastewater.* 13th ed. New York: American Public Health Association.

Arce, R. G., and Boyd, C. E. 1975. "Effects of agricultural limestone on water chemistry, phytoplankton productivity, and fish production in soft water ponds." *Trans. Am. Fish. Soc.* 104:308–312.

Bardach, J. E.; Ryther, J. H.; and McLarney, W. O. 1972. *Aquaculture: The Farming and Husbandry of Freshwater and Marine Organisms.* New York: Wiley-Interscience.

Borrell, A., and Scheffer, P. 1966. *Trout in Farm and Ranch Farms.* Farmers Bulletin no. 2154. Washington, D.C.: Soil Conservation Service, U.S. Department of Agriculture.

Buck, D. H. 1977. The integration of aquaculture with agriculture. *Fisheries* 2(6):11–16.

California Department of Fish and Game. 1965. *The Fish Pond— How to Stock and Manage It.* Sacramento, California: California Department of Fish and Game.

Davis, H. S. 1970. *Culture and Disease of Game Fish.* Berkeley, Calif.: University of California Press.

Dobie, J., et al. 1956. *Raising Bait Fishes.* Circular 35. Washington, D.C.: Fish and Wildlife Service, U.S. Department of Interior.

Edminister, F.C. 1947. *Fish Ponds for the Farm.* New York: Charles Scribner.

Eschmeyer, R.W. 1955. *Fish Conservation Fundamentals.* Washington, D.C.: Sports Fishing Institute.

Golueke, C., and Oswald, W. 1965. "Harvesting and Processing Sewage Grown Plankton Algae." *Journal of Water Pollution Control Federation* 37:471–98.

Hickling, C. F. 1966. *Fish hybridization:* FAO World Symposium on Warm Water Pond Fish Culture FR: IV/R-1.

Jones, W. 1972. "How to Get Started." *American Fish Farmer,* December 1972.

Lopinot, A. C. 1972. *Pond Fish and Fishing in Illinois.* Fishing Bulletin no. 5. Springfield, Ill.: Illinois Department of Conservation.

McLarney, W. O. 1971. "Aquaculture on the Organic Farm and Homestead." *Organic Gardening and Farming,* August 1971, pp. 71–77.

——— . ed. 1973. *The Backyard Fish Farm Workbook for 1973.* Woods Hole, Mass.: New Alchemy Institute.

Maloy, C., and Willoughby, H. 1967. *Marketable Channel Catfish in Ponds.* Resources Publication vol. 31, January 1967. Washington, D.C.: U.S. Department of Interior.

Meyer, F. 1973. *Second Report to the Fish Farmers.* Washington, D.C. Fish and Wildlife Service, U.S. Department of Interior.

The New Alchemy Institute. *The Journal of the New Alchemists,* vols. 2, 3, 4, 5, and 6. Write to the New Alchemy Institute, 237 Hatchville Rd., East Falmouth, Massachusetts 02536.

Ryther, J. H., Dunstan, W. M., Tonore, K. R., and Huguenin, J. E. 1972. "Controlled Eutrophication—Increasing Food Production from the Sea by Recycling Human Wastes." *Bioscience* 22:144–52.

Scott, W. B. and E. J. Crossman. 1973. *Freshwater Fishes of Canada,* Bulletin Fisheries Research Board of Canada, no. 184.

Sutton, D. L. 1977. "Grass carp (*Ctenopharyngodon idella* Val.) in North America." *Aquat. Bot.* 3:157–164.

U.S. Department of Agriculture. 1948. *Farm Fish Ponds.* Farmers Bulletin no. 1983. Washington, D.C.: Soil Conservation Service, U.S. Department of Agriculture.

U.S. Department of Agriculture. March, 1966. *Raising Ducks.* Farmers Bulletin no. 2215. Washington, D.C.: U.S. Government Printing Office.

Wade, N. 1975. "New Alchemy Institute: Search for an Alternative Agriculture." *Science* 187:727–29.

Walsh, D. 1978. *Aquaculture in the United States—Constraints and Opportunities.* A Report of the Committee on Aquaculture, National Research Council. Washington, D.C.: National Academy of Sciences.

TABLE OF CONVERSION FACTORS

Because different conventions historically have been used to measure various quantities, the following tables have been compiled to sort out the different units. This first table identifies the units typically used for describing a particular quantity. For example, speed might be measured in "miles/hour."

Most quantities can also be described in terms of the following three basic dimensions:

length	L
mass	M
time	T

For example, speed is given in terms of length divided by time, which can be written as "L/T". This description, called "dimensional analysis", is useful in determining whether an equation is correct. The product of the dimensions on each side of the equal sign must match. For example:

$$\text{Distance} = \text{Speed} \times \text{Time}$$
$$L = L/T \times T$$

The dimension on the left side of the equal sign is length, L. On the right side of the equal sign, the product of L/T times T is L, which matches the left side of the equation.

The second table is a Conversion Table, showing how to convert from one set of units to another. It might be necessary to take the reciprocal of the conversion factor or to make more than one conversion to get the desired results.

Measured Quantities and Their Common Units

Length(L)	Area(L^2)	Volume(L^3)		
mile(mi.)	sq. mile(mi²)	gallon(gal.)	kilogram(kg.)	kilometer/hr.
yard (yd.)	sq. yard(yd²)	quart(qt.)		kilometer/min.
foot(ft.)	sq. foot(ft²)	pint(pt.)		kilometer/sec.
inch(in.)	sq. inch(in²)	ounce(oz.)		
fathom(fath.)	acre	cu. foot(ft³)	Pressure($M/L/T^2$)	Energy($ML.^2/T^2$)	Power(ML^2/T^3)
kilometer(km.)	sq. kilometer(km²)	cu. yard(yd³)	atmosphere(atm.)	British thermal	Btu./min.
meter(m.)	sq. meter(m²)	cu. inch(in³)	pounds/sq. inch(psi)	unit(Btu.)	Btu./hour
centimeter(cm.)	sq. centimeter(cm²)	liter(l)	inches of mercury	calories(cal.)	watt
micron(μ)		cu. centimeter(cm³)	cm. of mercury	foot-pound	joule/sec.
angstrom(Å)		acre-foot	feet of water	joule	cal./min.
		cord(cd)		kilowatt-hour	horsepower(hp.)
		cord-foot		(kw-hr.)	
		barrel(bbl.)		horsepower-hour	
				(hp.-hr.)	

Mass(M)	Speed(L/T)	Flow Rate(L^3/T)			
pound(lb.)	feet/minute	cu. feet/min.	Time(T)	Energy Density(M/T^2)	Power Density(M/T^3)
ton(short)	(ft./min.)	cu. meter/min.	year(yr)	calories/sq. cm.	cal./sq. cm./min.
ton(long)	feet/sec.	liters/sec.	month	Btu./sq. foot	Btu./sq. foot/hr
ton(metric)	mile/hour	gallons/min.	day	langley	langley/min.
gram(g.)	mile/min.	gallons/sec.	hour(hr.)	watthr./sq. foot	watt/sq. cm.
			minute(min.)		
			second(sec.)		

Table of Conversion Factors

MULTIPLY	BY	TO OBTAIN:
Acres	43560	Sq. feet
"	0.004047	Sq. kilometers
"	4047	Sq. meters
"	0.0015625	Sq. miles
"	4840	Sq. yards
Acre-feet	43560	Cu. feet
"	1233.5	Cu. meters
"	1613.3	Cu. yards
Angstroms(Å)	1×10^{-8}	Centimeters
"	3.937×10^{-9}	Inches
"	0.0001	Microns
Atmospheres(atm.)	76	Cm. of Hg(0°C)
"	1033.3	Cm. of H_2O(4°C)
"	33.8995	Ft. of H_2O(39.2°F)
"	29.92	In. of Hg(32°F)
"	14.696	Pounds/sq. inch(psi)
Barrels(petroleum, U.S.)(bbl.)	5.6146	Cu. feet
"	35	Gallons(Imperial)
"	42	Gallons(U.S.)
"	158.98	Liters
British Thermal Unit(Btu)	251.99	Calories, gm
"	777.649	Foot-pounds
"	0.00039275	Horsepower-hours
"	1054.35	Joules
"	0.000292875	Kilowatt-hours
"	1054.35	Watt-seconds
Btu/hr.	4.2	Calories/min.
"	777.65	Foot-pounds/hr.
"	0.0003927	Horsepower
"	0.000292875	Kilowatts
"	0.292875	Watts(or joule/sec.)
Btu/lb.	7.25×10^{-4}	Cal/gram
Btu/sq. ft.	0.271246	Calories/sq. cm. (or langleys)
"	0.292875	Watt-hour/sq. foot
Btu/sq. ft./hour	3.15×10^{-7}	Kilowatts/sq. meter
"	4.51×10^{-3}	Cal./sq. cm./min(or langleys/min)
"	3.15×10^{-8}	Watts/sq. cm.
Calories(cal.)	0.003968	Btu.
"	3.08596	Foot-pounds
"	1.55857×10^{-6}	Horsepower-hours
"	4.184	Joules (or watt-secs)
"	1.1622×10^{-6}	Kilowatt-hours
Calories, food unit (Cal.)	1000	Calories
Calories/min.	0.003968	Btu/min.
"	0.06973	Watts
Calories/sq. cm.	3.68669	Btu/sq. ft.
"	1.0797	Watt-hr/sq. foot
Cal./sq. cm./min.	796320.	Btu/sq. foot/hr.
"	251.04	Watts/sq. cm.
Candle power (spherical)	12.566	Lumens
Centimeters(cm.)	0.032808	Feet
"	0.3937	Inches
"	0.01	Meters
"	10.000	Microns
Cm. of Hg(0°C)	0.0131579	Atmospheres
"	0.44605	Ft. of H_2O(4°C)
"	0.19337	Pounds/sq. inch
Cm. of H_2O(4°C)	0.0009678	Atmospheres
"	0.01422	Pounds/sq. inch
Cm./sec.	0.032808	Feet/sec.
"	0.022369	Miles/hr.
Cords	8	Cord-feet
"	128(or $4 \times 4 \times 8$)	Cu. feet
Cu. centimeters	3.5314667	Cu. feet
"	0.06102	Cu. inches
Cu. centimeters	1×10^{-6}	Cu. meters
"	0.001	Liters
"	0.0338	Ounces(U.S. fluid)
Cu. feet(ft.³)	0.02831685	Cu. meters
"	7.4805	Gallons(U.S., liq.)
"	28.31685	Liters
"	29.922	Quarts(U.S., liq.)
Cu. ft. of H_2O (60°F)	62.366	Pounds of H_2O
Cu. feet/min.	471.947	Cu. cm./sec.
Cu. inches(in.³)	16.387	Cu. cm.
"	0.0005787	Cu. feet
"	0.004329	Gallons(U.S., liq.)
"	0.5541	Ounces(U.S., fluid)
Cu. meters	1×10^6	Cu. centimeters
"	35.314667	Cu. feet
"	264.172	Gallons(U.S., liq.)
"	1000	Liters
Cu. yard	27	Cu. feet
"	0.76455	Cu. meters
"	201.97	Gallons(U.S., liq.)
Cubits	18	Inches
Fathoms	6	Feet
"	1.8288	Meters
Feet(ft.)	30.48	Centimeters
"	12	Inches
"	0.00018939	Miles(statute)
Feet of H_2O(4°C)	0.029499	Atmospheres
"	2.2419	Cm. of Hg(0°C)
"	0.433515	Pounds/sq. inch
Feet/min.	0.508	Centimeters/second
"	0.018288	Kilometers/hr.
"	0.0113636	Miles/hr.
Foot-candles	1	Lumens/sq. foot
Foot-pounds	0.001285	Btu.
"	0.324048	Calories
"	5.0505×10^{-7}	Horsepower-hours
"	3.76616×10^{-7}	Kilowatt-hours
Furlong	220	Yards
Gallons(U.S., dry)	1.163647	Gallons(U.S., liq.)
Gallons(U.S., liq.)	3785.4	Cu. centimeters
"	0.13368	Cu. feet
"	231	Cu. inches
"	0.0037854	Cu. meters
"	3.7854	Liters
"	8	Pints(U.S., liq.)
"	4	Quarts(U.S., liq.)
Gallons/min.	2.228×10^{-3}	Cu. feet/sec.
"	0.06308	Liters/sec.
Grams	0.035274	Ounces(avdp.)
"	0.002205	Pounds(avdp.)
Grams-cm.	9.3011×10^{-8}	Btu.
Grams/meter²	3.98	Short ton/acre
"	8.92	lbs./acre
Horsepower	42.4356	Btu/min.
"	550	Foot-pounds/sec.
"	745.7	Watts
Horsepower-hrs.	2546.14	Btu.
"	641616	Calories
"	1.98×10^6	Foot-pounds
"	0.7457	Kilowatt-hours
Inches	2.54	Centimeters
"	0.83333	Feet
In. of Hg(32°F)	0.03342	Atmospheres
"	1.133	Feet of H_2O
"	0.4912	Pounds/sq. inch
In. of Water(4°C)	0.002458	Atmospheres
"	0.07355	In. of Mercury(32°F)
"	0.03613	Pounds/sq. inch
Joules	0.0009485	Btu.
"	0.73756	Foot-pounds
"	0.0002778	Watt-hours
"	1	Watt-sec.
Kilo calories/gram	1378.54	Btu/lb

Kilograms	2.2046	Pounds(avdp.)
Kilograms/hectare	.893	lbs/acre
Kilograms/hectare	.0004465	Short ton/acre
Kilometers	1000	Meters
"	0.62137	Miles(statute)
Kilometer/hr.	54.68	Feet/min.
Kilowatts	3414.43	Btu./hr.
"	737.56	Foot-pounds/sec.
"	1.34102	Horsepower
Kilowatt-hours	3414.43	Btu.
"	1.34102	Horsepower-hours
Knots	51.44	Centimeter/sec.
"	1	Mile(nautical)/hr.
"	1.15078	Miles(Statute)/hr.
Langleys	1	Calories/sq. cm.
Liters	1000	Cu. centimeters
"	0.0353	Cu. feet
"	0.2642	Gallons(U.S., liq.)
"	1.0567	Quarts(U.S., liq.)
Lbs./acre	.0005	Short ton/acre
Liters/min.	0.0353	Cu. feet/min.
"	0.2642	Gallons(U.S., liq.)/min.
Lumens	0.079577	Candle power(spherical)
Lumens(at 5550Å)	0.0014706	Watts
Meters	3.2808	Feet
"	39.37	Inches
"	1.0936	Yards
Meters/sec.	2.24	Miles/hr.
Micron	10000	Angstroms
"	0.0001	Centimeters
Miles(statute)	5280	Feet
"	1.6093	Kilometers
"	1760	Yards
Miles/hour	44.704	Centimeter/sec.
"	88	Feet/min.
"	1.6093	Kilometer/hr.
"	0.447	Meters/second
Milliliter	1	Cu. centimeter
Millimeter	0.1	Centimeter
Ounces(avdp.)	0.0625	Pounds(avdp.)
Ounces(U.S., liq.)	29.57	Cu. centimeters
"	1.8047	Cu. inches
"	0.0625(or 1/16)	Pint(U.S., liq.)
Pints(U.S., liq.)	473.18	Cu. centimeters
"	28.875	Cu. inches
"	0.5	Quarts(U.S., liq.)
Pounds(avdp.)	0.45359	Kilograms
"	16	Ounces(avdp.)
Pounds of water	0.01602	Cu. feet of water
"	0.1198	Gallons(U.S., liq.)
Pounds/acre	0.0005	Short ton/acre
Pounds/sq. inch	0.06805	Atmospheres
"	5.1715	Cm. of mercury(0°C)
"	27.6807	In. of water(39.2°F)
Quarts(U.S., liq.)	0.25	Gallons(U.S., liq.)
"	0.9463	Liters
"	32	Ounces(U.S., liq.)
"	2	Pints(U.S., liq.)
Radians	57.30	Degrees
Sq. centimeters	0.0010764	Sq. feet
"	0.1550	Sq. inches
Sq. feet	2.2957×10^{-5}	Acres
"	0.09290	Sq. meters
Sq. inches	6.4516	Sq. centimeters
"	0.006944	Sq. feet
Sq. kilometers	247.1	Acres
"	1.0764×10^{7}	Sq. feet
"	0.3861	Sq. miles
Sq. meters	10.7639	Sq. feet
"	1.196	Sq. yards
Sq. miles	640	Acres
"	2.788×10^{7}	Sq. feet
Sq. miles	2.590	Sq. kilometers
Sq. yards	9(or 3×3)	Sq. feet
"	0.83613	Sq. meters
Tons, long	1016	Kilograms
"	2240	Pounds(avdp.)
Tons(metric)	1000	Kilograms
"	2204.6	Pounds(avdp.)
Tons, metric/hectare	0.446	Short ton/acre
Tons(short)	907.2	Kilograms
"	2000	Pounds(avdp.)
Watts	3.4144	Btu./hr.
"	0.05691	Btu./min.
"	14.34	Calories/min.
"	0.001341	Horsepower
"	1	Joule/sec.
Watts/sq. cm.	3172	Btu./sq. foot/hr.
Watt-hours	3.4144	Btu.
"	860.4	Calories
"	0.001341	Horsepower-hours
Yards	3	Feet
"	0.9144	Meters

INDEX

For additional information, see the listings of manufacturers and products and the Bibliographies following individual chapters.